Ready to Return?

The Need for a Fundamental Shift in
Church Culture to Save a Generation

Ken Ham with Jeff Kinley
research by Britt Beemer

First printing: August 2015
Second printing: November 2015

Master Books®, P.O. Box 726, Green Forest, AR 72638
Master Books® is a division of the New Leaf Publishing Group, Inc.

ISBN: 978-0-89051-836-6
Library of Congress Number: 2015947460
Cover by Diana Bogardus

Please consider requesting that a copy of this volume be purchased by your local library system.

Printed in the United States of America

Please visit our website for other great titles:
www.masterbooks.com

For information regarding author interviews,
please contact the publicity department at (870) 438-5288.

Master
Books®
A Division of New Leaf Publishing Group
www.masterbooks.com

Dedication

As this book is about younger generations who will be the leaders in the culture in the future, I dedicate this book to our 14 grandchildren:

Malachi, Kathryn, Noah, Kylie, Caleb, Lacey, Madelyn, Nicole, Emma, Josiah, Lexie, Kendra, Amelia, Olivia. May God mightily use godly offspring as these to call Church and culture back to the authority of the Word of God.

— Ken Ham, President of Answers in Genesis

Parent Dedication

Having great parents is worth more than all the gold at Ft. Knox!

My parents, Elvin and Margaret Beemer gave me freedom to experience the world at a young age by allowing me to work on Capitol Hill through my high school, college and graduate school days. My father taught "he would rather see a sermon than hear one." My mother lovingly pushed me to do mighty things such as starting ARG with little capital.

My wife's parents, Tom and Catie Cook, represent the most perfect, loving couple who are so gentle to one another that their undying love for each other oozes out of them for all the world to see.

These two couples come from different backgrounds, but help me to better understand love.

— Britt Beemer, America's Research Group

Contents

Chapter 1

A Call to Reformation

On October 31, 1517, a German priest nailed a sheet of paper to a Catholic Church door in Wittenburg, Germany. Little did he know in doing so that his protest would change the world. But it wasn't so much his act of defiance that got people's attention as what was written on that particular piece of paper. Long concerned and dissatisfied with the state of Christianity in his day, Martin Luther's now immortal "95 Theses" itemized serious grievances he had against the Church he loved and served. He had originally intended his objections to be used as points of discussion, calling the corporate church institution back toward more biblical understanding beliefs and practices.

Instead, what it got him was excommunicated.

And with that, Protestantism was born.

As with many other organizations, the Church tends to drift and fade over time, losing her original simplicity, passion, and purpose. Without strong leadership and a constant calibration back to her primary calling, the Bride that Jesus courted is in danger of losing her very identity.

But it's not so much that we need another Martin Luther. No, instead we need an entire generation of Luthers! We are in desperate need of Christians who are not content to allow the church to drift, disconnected

from the anchor of God's truth. Tossed back and forth by every wind
and wave of doctrine, and without a clear course to guide her, she is in
peril, susceptible to imminent shipwreck or sinking. And those on board
are destined to drown in a sea of ignorance, impotence, uncertainty, and
ineffectiveness.

And nothing would grieve God's heart more than this.

From a human perspective, the Western Church appears to be in
big trouble. Any astute observer can see that the culture of the Church
is becoming more secularized with each passing day. And in this book,
we are detailing new research on the Church that will reveal distress-
ing trends — and particularly with millennials. In many ways, even the
leadership of the Church has adopted many of the world's beliefs and
teachings. As a result, Jesus' Bride does not influence the culture as it
once did. On the contrary, this book will demonstrate how the culture is
influencing the Church in critical areas. But what often goes unnoticed
is the damage that has been done in the hearts and minds of coming
generations. The latest research conducted by America's Research Group
reveals shocking realities concerning the state of the evangelical Church
in America — a picture of what is happening through the Western
world. And the looming question is, "Where will the Church be in
the next generation?" The research is very eye opening, and provides a
grave warning for the Church and its leaders. The results of our research
should also alert every parent, as it reveals where their children and the
next generation already are, spiritually speaking. This generation of millennials will fundamentally change the culture, unless they return to a
truly biblical foundation. But this is also a call to action for Christians in
this millennial demographic.

The Bible makes it clear that the true Church is made up of the body
of believers throughout the world. Even so, we continue to struggle and
drift because of our inherent bent toward sin. As Paul wrote,

> . . . but I see in my members another law waging war against
> the law of my mind and making me captive to the law of sin
> that dwells in my members. Wretched man that I am! Who will
> deliver me from this body of death? Thanks be to God through
> Jesus Christ our Lord! So then, I myself serve the law of God

with my mind, but with my flesh I serve the law of sin (Rom. 7:23–25).

And yet, even as believers struggle, the Lord Jesus Christ nevertheless declared,

> I will build my church, and the gates of hell shall not prevail against it (Matt. 16:18).

Paul's words to the Philippians echo this truth for the Church:

> And I am sure of this, that he who began a good work in you will bring it to completion at the day of Jesus Christ (Phil. 1:6).

These two oppositional truths — our struggle with sin and Jesus' commitment to build His Church and to bring believers to maturity — both co-exist, though admittedly with great tension at times. So while Christians contend with sin, the Church itself is still being built by Jesus, moving forward by His sovereign decree.

In the book *Already Gone*, we discussed why there's an exodus of coming generations from the church.[1] We featured photographs of church buildings in England that were no longer being used for Christians to gather in to worship and hear the teaching of the Word of God. Instead, these buildings have been transformed into music stores, nightclubs, museums, etc. But the buildings themselves are not the issue. What's even more tragic is that the exodus from the church's facilities is but a physical picture of the spiritual departure across the United Kingdom, and actually across all of Europe. Today, only a small percentage of Europeans attend any type of church, with most identifying as having no religious affiliation at all. Such a phenomenon is on the rise here in the USA as well. What is happening in Europe is a picture of where the USA will be in the future if the spiritual state of coming generations is not changed.

Of course, God's Word does not promise that a particular local church will necessarily continue in existence. However, the Church universal *will* continue as long as the church age endures. God will preserve

---

1. Ken Ham and Britt Beemer, *Already Gone* (Green Forest, AR: Master Books, 2009).

His Church (those who are redeemed by the blood of the lamb) and its work in this world (the preaching of the gospel). This, despite the fact that "we wrestle not against flesh and blood, but against principalities, against powers, against the rulers of the darkness of this world, against spiritual wickedness in high places" (Eph. 6:12; KJV).

Yes, God will preserve His Church. No principality or power will ever be able to stop His work, halt the preaching of the gospel, demolish His Church in general, or ruin any particular soul that is built upon the rock that is Christ.

At the same time, this does not mean there will not be great failings within the Church, just as we saw great failings with God's people in the Old Testament and in the Middle Ages.

Uncompromising Faith

Our latest research reminds me of the ministry of two great men in the Old Testament. The first is the prophet Jeremiah, who warned people about God's judgment because of rampant compromise. The second is King Hezekiah, who was prepared to bring very needed reforms.

Many failings of God's people are recorded in the Old Testament, but there are three in particular I want to bring to your attention. They're summarized through the Word of the Lord given to Jeremiah and what happened in Hezekiah's day:

1. God's people had not been influencing the world for the Lord God as they were instructed to do by His Word, but instead were learning the ways of the pagan world. As Jeremiah reminded the people: "Learn not the way of the nations . . ." (Jer. 10:2).

2. Having been influenced by pagan gods and the rampant idolatry of the time, Israel had not stood uncompromisingly for their Creator-God. Instead, she ignored His Word while pursuing contemporary pagan practices. Jeremiah's words then became a scathing rebuke: "But the Lord is the true God; he is the living God and the everlasting King. At his wrath the earth quakes, and the nations cannot endure his indignation. Thus shall you say to them: 'The gods who did not make the heavens

and the earth shall perish from the earth and from under the heavens' " (Jer. 10:10–11).

The third way that Israel had failed was that,

> 3. The shepherds (the religious leaders) were leading people astray: "For the shepherds are stupid and do not inquire of the LORD; therefore they have not prospered, and all their flock is scattered" (Jer. 10:21).

As I read Jeremiah 10, I couldn't help but apply this to the Western Church today as I thought about the results of this latest research. Please read it and decide for yourself:

> Hear the word which the LORD speaks to you, O house of Israel. Thus says the LORD:
> "Do not learn the way of the Gentiles; do not be dismayed at the signs of heaven, for the Gentiles are dismayed at them. For the customs of the peoples are futile; for one cuts a tree from the forest, the work of the hands of the workman, with the ax. They decorate it with silver and gold; they fasten it with nails and hammers so that it will not topple. They are upright, like a palm tree, and they cannot speak; they must be carried, because they cannot go by themselves. Do not be afraid of them, for they cannot do evil, nor can they do any good."
> Inasmuch as there is none like You, O LORD (You are great, and Your name is great in might), who would not fear You, O King of the nations? For this is Your rightful due. For among all the wise men of the nations, and in all their kingdoms, there is none like You. But they are altogether dull-hearted and fool-ish; a wooden idol is a worthless doctrine. Silver is beaten into plates; it is brought from Tarshish, and gold from Uphaz, the work of the craftsman and of the hands of the metalsmith; blue and purple are their clothing; they are all the work of skillful men. But the LORD is the true God; He is the living God and the everlasting King. At His wrath the earth will tremble, and the nations will not be able to endure His indignation.

Thus you shall say to them: "The gods that have not made the heavens and the earth shall perish from the earth and from under these heavens." He has made the earth by His power, He has established the world by His wisdom, and has stretched out the heavens at His discretion. When He utters His voice, there is a multitude of waters in the heavens: "And He causes the vapors to ascend from the ends of the earth. He makes lightning for the rain, He brings the wind out of His treasuries." Everyone is dull-hearted, without knowledge; every metalsmith is put to shame by an image; for his molded image is falsehood, and there is no breath in them. They are futile, a work of errors; in the time of their punishment they shall perish. The Portion of Jacob is not like them, for He is the Maker of all things, and Israel is the tribe of His inheritance; the LORD of hosts is His name. Gather up your wares from the land, O inhabitant of the fortress!

For thus says the LORD: "Behold, I will throw out at this time the inhabitants of the land, and will distress them, that they may find it so." Woe is me for my hurt! My wound is severe. But I say, "Truly this is an infirmity, and I must bear it." My tent is plundered, and all my cords are broken; my children have gone from me, and they are no more. There is no one to pitch my tent anymore, or set up my curtains. For the shepherds have become dull-hearted, and have not sought the LORD; therefore they shall not prosper, and all their flocks shall be scattered. Behold, the noise of the report has come, and a great commotion out of the north country, to make the cities of Judah desolate, a den of jackals. O LORD, I know the way of man is not in himself; it is not in man who walks to direct his own steps. O LORD, correct me, but with justice; not in Your anger, lest You bring me to nothing. Pour out Your fury on the Gentiles, who do not know You, and on the families who do not call on Your name; for they have eaten up Jacob, devoured him and consumed him, and made his dwelling place desolate (Jer. 10:1–25; NKJV).

As you look at the culture we're in, can you see how we too have forgotten God and replaced Him with our own idols? Jeremiah laments the desolation of his people while at the same time warning them of God's impending judgment. In her brief history, America was once a nation heavily influenced by the Church and biblical principles. However, the latest research on the Church we are detailing in this book shows that, across the denominations, the modern Church,

> 1. Is not influencing the culture as it once did, because many aspects of secular culture have infiltrated the Church.
> 2. So much of the Church has adopted the pagan religion of the day and compromised God's Word.
> 3. The majority of Church leaders have been leading the people astray by not teaching God's Word as they should, and by not preparing the Church to be equipped to defend the faith.

At the same time, it's important to understand that there is a remnant among God's people and among Church leaders. Like Elijah, they're fully standing on God's Word against the "prophets of Baal." This remnant reminds us that God's work can never be thwarted (Job 42:2).

I pray these findings will be a wakeup call to the Church. After considering this research in detail, my heart is burdened because of the sad state of Christianity today. But I am also encouraged because I know that with God's enablement, Bible-believing Christians can turn things around. The task seems so impossibly great, and the challenges overwhelming. But our God is greater!

Being "On Mission"

As I was recently rereading our ministry's mission statement, the Lord brought something to my mind that should encourage every believer who is burdened to reach this world with the gospel.

Our ministry's official goal at Answers in Genesis is "to support the church in fulfilling its commission." To accomplish this goal, our "vision statement" reads, "Answers in Genesis is a catalyst to bring reformation by reclaiming the foundations of our faith which are found in the Bible, from the very first verse."

This comprehensive vision includes our,

Mission

- We proclaim the absolute truth and authority of the Bible with boldness.

- We relate the relevance of a literal Genesis to the Church and the world today with creativity.

- We obey God's call to deliver the message of the gospel, individually and collectively.

Core Values

- We resourcefully equip believers to defend their faith with excellence.

- We willingly engage society's challenges with uncompromising integrity.

- We sacrificially serve the AiG family and others.

- We generously give Christian love.

Note that our vision involves "to bring reformation."[2] When we think of the word *reformation*, Christians usually think of the great reformer Martin Luther whom I spoke of at the beginning of this chapter. However, long before Martin Luther, Scripture gives examples of other key reformers from whom we can learn many lessons. One of the most valuable examples is that of King Hezekiah. God made sure details about his life and reforms would be written down in His holy Word, so we could learn from his actions and be challenged in our own walk of faith.

Concerning the magnitude of Hezekiah's amazing reforms, the Bible says, "So there was great joy in Jerusalem, for since the time of Solomon the son of David, king of Israel, there had been nothing like this in Jerusalem" (2 Chron. 30:26).

---

2. You can read our full Vision/Mission/Core Beliefs Statement online. It tells more about what drives this ministry, but for our purpose here let me focus on the "Vision" portion.

Hezekiah reformed God's people by destroying idol worship and restoring temple worship. He reinstituted the Passover, and did whatever he could and needed to do to get people back to obeying His Word.

We need a "Hezekiah-style happening" in our own culture today. As our research shows, so many believers in our generation have compromised God's Word, beginning in Genesis! We are also seeing the sad consequences (abortion on demand, gay "marriage," increasing violence, etc.) of a Western world that is becoming increasingly more anti-Christian, and attempting to remove any vestiges of Christian influence and heritage from these nations.

So what are the lessons we can learn from Hezekiah?

1. Reformation begins with us

What was different about Hezekiah compared to so many of the other kings of Israel and Judah who came before him? At the beginning of 2 Chronicles' account of Hezekiah we read: "And he did what was right in the eyes of the LORD, according to all that David his father had done" (2 Chron. 29:2).

In addition to his reforms, Hezekiah was also a man of godly character:

> Thus Hezekiah did throughout all Judah, and he did what was good and right and true before the LORD his God. And every work that he undertook in the service of the house of God and in accordance with the law and the commandments, seeking his God, he did with all his heart, and prospered" (2 Chron. 31:20–21).

So what's the lesson? In order to impact the world around them, God's people first need to seek God and be obedient to His Word. Sadly, so many Christians and Christian leaders today exalt *man's* word (like swallowing the lie of evolutionary biology, geology, astronomy, anthropology, etc., which is an attempt to explain life *without* God) and by twisting God's infallible Word to fit that false narrative (theistic evolution). This is no different from the efforts by the people of Judah and Israel to adopt the pagan religion of their age and mix it with what God had instructed.

Reformation begins with a return to the authority of the Word of God and obeying God's revelation to man. By returning to God's Word, beginning in Genesis, and by repenting of the rampant compromise that has spread throughout the Church and Christian institutions, we can reform the failing Church.

2. We should expect resistance and opposition

We read about some of Hezekiah's specific initiatives in 2 Chronicles 30:1 and 30:5:

> Hezekiah sent to all Israel and Judah, and wrote letters also to Ephraim and Manasseh, that they should come to the house of the LORD at Jerusalem, to keep the Passover to the LORD, the God of Israel. . . . So they decreed to make a proclamation throughout all Israel, from Beersheba to Dan, that the people should come and keep the Passover to the LORD, the God of Israel, at Jerusalem, for they had not kept it as often as prescribed.

However, this return to obedience was not enthusiastically received by everyone.

> So the couriers went from city to city through the country of Ephraim and Manasseh, and as far as Zebulun, but they laughed them to scorn and mocked them (2 Chron. 30:10).

As Hezekiah was calling on people to "return to the Lord" (2 Chronicles 30:9), many scoffed. The same is true today, reminding anyone who shares the Word faithfully that there will be those who oppose and ridicule such faithfulness. In fact, we should *expect* scoffers. However, we also read, "However, some men of Asher, of Manasseh, and of Zebulun humbled themselves and came to Jerusalem" (2 Chron. 30:11). God had a remnant that were committed to do what was right before the Lord. And there is a remnant today in our Western cultures. As I travel across the USA and meet people visiting the Creation Museum, I am encouraged at the remnant who are faithful to the Lord and His Word, and who are training up generations to boldly and uncompromisingly stand on the authority of the Word. They are a remnant (and I see them as a growing remnant in the USA), amidst a world of scoffers.

Presumably, nearly everyone scoffed at Noah for preaching God's Word before the Flood came. In 2 Peter 3, we are warned that the most basic teachings of God's Word will be mocked and ridiculed, including the truth about creation, the Flood, and Christ's Second Coming and judgment by fire.

Peter, writing under the inspiration of the Holy Spirit, records,

> Knowing this first, that there shall come in the last days scoffers, walking after their own lusts, and saying, Where is the promise of His coming? For since the fathers fell asleep, all things continue as they were from the beginning of the creation. For this they willfully are ignorant of, that by the word of God the heavens were of old, and the earth standing out of the water and in the water: whereby the world that then was, being overflowed with water, perished (2 Pet. 3:3–6; KJV).

Clearly, many in our world today ridicule and repudiate those who stand on God's Word in Genesis and reject man's beliefs concerning the supposed big bang, billions of years, and other evolutionary ideas. As Answers in Genesis moved forward with the construction of a life-size ark, we experienced this same type of scoffing, and it has only increased with time. So if we are staying true to God's Word and we "contend for the faith" (Jude 1:3), we will be mocked, ridiculed, and even persecuted, as Jesus predicted in John 15:18–21.

3. Religious leaders often compromise

There's an interesting contrast in 2 Chronicles 29:34 between the priests (the religious leaders) and the common Levites (those who assisted them).

> But the priests were too few and could not flay all the burnt offerings, so until other priests had consecrated themselves, their brothers the Levites helped them, until the work was finished — for the Levites were more upright in heart than the priests in consecrating themselves.

Throughout the Old and New Testaments, we're warned of shepherds (religious leaders) who lead the people astray. This is certainly not true of all leaders — but even in our world today, we find a large number of Church leaders compromise God's Word as it relates to Genesis or other areas of morality (e.g., homosexuality). Some prefer not to preach tough topics (like sin, repentance, and hell) for fear of upsetting people, especially those who make significant financial contributions.

In 2006, Answers in Genesis contracted with America's Research Group to conduct research on the state of Christian colleges in the USA. The results were published in our book *Already Compromised*.[3] One of the surprising results of that research showed that, by and large, the *science* departments at Christian colleges were more likely to believe in a young earth and reject other evolutionary ideas than the *Bible* (or theology) departments!

It confirmed one of the observations I've made over the past 30-plus years in creation apologetics: even in the more conservative Christian colleges, the professors in the science departments tend to be much more vocal and diligent than Bible departments in dealing with the issue of origins and taking a stand on a literal interpretation of Genesis!

So today, we experience the same problems with our religious leaders that Israel did thousands of years ago. It's true that the heart of the human problem is that of the human heart. It remains deceitful and diseased (Jer. 17:9).

4. Pride threatens us all

Now here is a very serious warning for all of us! The problem of pride. Even as great a man of God as Hezekiah was, his pride nevertheless got the best of him. At first, he was humble and God greatly blessed his faith. After the many reforms Hezekiah performed, God allowed the king of Assyria to come against Judah and intended on war against Jerusalem. Hezekiah fortified the city, made weapons, and prepared for the battle. But most importantly, he encouraged the people to trust in God, who was on their side:

---

3. Ken Ham and Greg Hall, *Already Compromised* (Green Forest, AR: Master Books, 2011).

"Be strong and courageous. Do not be afraid or dismayed before the king of Assyria and all the horde that is with him, for there are more with us than with him. With him is an arm of flesh, but with us is the LORD our God, to help us and to fight our battles." And the people took confidence from the words of Hezekiah king of Judah (2 Chron. 32:7–8).

When the king of Assyria sent people to taunt the Jews and mock their God, Hezekiah did what we should all do for every challenge, every day: "And for this cause Hezekiah the king, and the prophet Isaiah the son of Amoz, *prayed and cried to heaven*" (2 Chron. 32:20; KJV, emphasis added).

Because of this, God gave Hezekiah great victory, and I find it thrilling every time I read it:

> And the LORD sent an angel, who cut off all the mighty warriors and commanders and officers in the camp of the king of Assyria. So he returned with shame of face to his own land. And when he came into the house of his god, some of his own sons struck him down there with the sword. So the LORD saved Hezekiah and the inhabitants of Jerusalem from the hand of Sennacherib king of Assyria and from the hand of all his enemies, and he provided for them on every side (2 Chron. 32:21–22).

What a great victory for the Lord!

But now comes the lesson every one of us must learn. Scripture warns us about pride. Because of our sin nature, this is a problem we all have. After the great victory God gave Hezekiah, we read these sad words:

> In those days Hezekiah became sick and was at the point of death, and he prayed to the LORD, and he answered him and gave him a sign. But Hezekiah did not make return according to the benefit done to him, for his heart was proud. Therefore wrath came upon him and Judah and Jerusalem (2 Chron. 32:24–25).

Because of the wonderful defeat of the Assyrian army, Hezekiah became proud! When we are involved in serving the Lord, no matter how great or small, we must always remember to give God the glory and honor. We must recognize how easy it is to be lifted up in pride and thus set the wrong example for those looking at us.

This episode could have been his downfall, but then "Hezekiah humbled himself for the pride of his heart, both he and the inhabitants of Jerusalem, so that the wrath of the LORD did not come upon them in the days of Hezekiah" (2 Chron. 32:26).

We can never forget that Satan's greatest temptations often come immediately on the heels of a great victory. It is typically then that our guard is down and we are most vulnerable to attack and to the deceptive nature of human pride. Solomon reminds us,

> One's pride will bring him low, but he who is lowly in spirit will obtain honor (Prov. 29:23).

5. A lasting legacy requires vigilance

There is one final lesson I want to highlight in Hezekiah's reformation story. When Hezekiah died, we read that his son Manasseh became king in his place. But then "[Manassah] did what was evil in the sight of the LORD, according to the abominations of the nations whom the LORD drove out before the people of Israel" (2 Chron. 33:2).

It is hard to fathom how such a godly king as Hezekiah could end up with such an evil son as Manasseh to take his place. We don't know the circumstances of why Manasseh ended up the way he did. But it underscores the fact that every generation must choose for itself to follow the Lord. It's also a warning to us that we must always be vigilant and do the very best we can to raise up offspring who will carry on the spiritual legacy to the next generation and then the next and so on.

It's sad to observe that as compromise has crept in, many Christian institutions (colleges, etc.) in our Western world have forsaken the biblical stand of our nation's founders. Ironically, many such institutions, established on biblical principles, have now become leaders in indoctrinating generations *against* the authority of the Word of God. This is tragic and unacceptable.

Charles Spurgeon, the great Baptist preacher who brought revival to his native Britain, proclaimed,

We want again Luthers, Calvins, Bunyans, Whitefields, men fit to mark eras, whose names breathe terror in our foemen's ears. We have dire need of such. Whence will they come to us? They are the gifts of Jesus Christ to the Church, and will come in due time. He has power to give us back again a golden age of preachers, and when the good old truth is once more preached by men whose lips are touched as with a live coal from off the altar, this shall be the instrument in the hand of the Spirit for bringing about a great and thorough revival of religion in the land. . . . I do not look for any other means of converting men beyond the simple preaching of the gospel and the opening of men's ears to hear it. The moment the Church of God shall despise the pulpit, God will despise her. It has been through the ministry that the Lord has always been pleased to revive and bless His Churches.[4]

Yes, we need Luthers and Hezekiah-type reformers today. But we must understand and embrace the sober lessons from the life of Jeremiah (in warning the people) and Hezekiah's (in bringing needed reforms), which God put in His Word for our good. We must return to God's infallible Word, and pursue the true reform that rests in Him alone.

---

4. Charles Spurgeon, *Autobiography Vol. 1: The Early Years* (Edinburth, UK: Banner of Truth, 1973).

Chapter 2

The State of the Modern Church

Christendom in Decline

Few Americans are aware of the spiritual epidemic that devastated the land of our Christian forefathers. Even fewer are aware that the same epidemic has reached our own shores, spreading like a virus.

In 2009, I attended Sunday services at an impressive 19th-century church in London. In a building with seating for 3,000 in ornate pews, a handful of elderly people sat inside . . . in chairs set up in the foyer.

The service, held in a vibrant city full of millions of people, reminded me of a funeral — not the funeral of a person, but the funeral of a once-great institution. In the past 40+ years, 1,600 churches in England, with hundreds of years of ministry behind them, have shut their doors, according to an architectural preservation group called the Victorian Society.

American Christianity could in a sense become almost extinct in less than two generations — if Christians in this country don't act quickly and decisively. Respected pollster George Barna was one of the first to put numbers to this epidemic, finding that six out of ten 20-somethings who were involved in a church during their teen years are already gone. Since that research was published in 2000, survey after survey has confirmed the same basic trend. Many of the 20s generation are leaving the Church in droves with few returning.

Young people see through the hypocrisy of those who claim to believe the Bible — just not as it's written. And when they do, they leave both the Church *and* their trust in God's Word behind. Hear what we have to say in the revealing book *Already Gone*.

In 2009, the book *Already Gone* (co-authored by myself and researcher Britt Beemer) was published, detailing the results of what we believe to be the first scientific study of its kind on the 20s generation, which was conducted by respected Americas Research Group led by CEO Britt Beemer. The "Beemer Report" reveals startling facts discovered through 20,000 phone calls and detailed surveys of a thousand 20–29-year-olds who used to attend evangelical churches on a regular basis, but have since left it behind.

The results were shocking:

- Those who faithfully attend Sunday school are more likely to leave the Church than those who do not.

- Those who regularly attended Sunday school are more likely to believe that the Bible is less true.

- Those who regularly attended Sunday school are actually more likely to defend that abortion and gay marriage should be legal.

- Those who regularly attended Sunday school are actually more likely to defend premarital sex.

The authors challenged the Church to deal with this issue before we lose coming generations!

The problem, in both the United Kingdom and America, began when the Church basically disconnected the Bible from the real world. Churches in America are not places where people typically talk about dinosaurs, fossils, or the age of the earth — that is left up to the secular schools and colleges. Effectively, the Church concentrates on the spiritual and moral aspects of Christianity.

But the Bible is not some "pie in the sky" theoretical book. It's a real book of history connected to the real world. It has everything to do with history, geology, biology, anthropology, and sociology. It provides the true history of the world, as opposed to evolution, whose narrative claims millions of years and naturalism.

The "disconnect" between faith and fact is an illusion created by an overwhelming misinterpretation of the difference between what one can observe versus one's interpretation of the facts in regard to the past. Observational science (based on direct observation, the repeatable test etc.), confirms the Bible's history and, thus, also the Christian doctrines (like the gospel) that are based in that history.

As I travel around the world teaching how to defend biblical principles and history, I find that whether my audience is secular or Christian, they ask the same questions, such as,

- How do you know the Bible is true?[1]

- Hasn't science disproved the Bible?[2]

- Isn't the world millions of years old?[3]

- How did Noah get all the animals on the ark?[4]

- But don't we observe evolution because we see animals change — bacteria become resistant to antibiotics?[5]

- How can you believe in a loving God with so much death and suffering in the world?

- Don't dinosaurs disprove the Bible's account of creation in Genesis?

- How can you believe there were only two people to begin with when we have so many different races of people?

1. https://answersingenesis.org/bible/.
2. https://answersingenesis.org/science/.
3. https://answersingenesis.org/age-of-the-earth/.
4. https://answersingenesis.org/noahs-ark/.
5. https://answersingenesis.org/evolution/.

Fortunately, there are answers to these and the many other questions people ask today. But sadly, in most churches and homes, those answers have not been taught to coming generations that have become so secularized (much like a "Greek" pagan culture).

Typical churches use resources more geared for what could be called the "Jew in Jerusalem" — someone who has developed a religious background and who lives in a religiously friendly community of faith and understands the terms used.

A Disturbing Trend

But we are now in the era of the "Greeks" — like the secular philosophers the Apostle Paul encountered on Mars Hill. Yet our churches and Sunday schools are still teaching us like Jews.

With our society immersed in secularism, it's essential that we learn how to defend the Bible and the Christian faith in that arena, and to do it for our sake and our children's — for unless we do, the empty and obsolete churches of England will foreshadow the future of Christianity in America.

The Victorian Society's magazine in 2007 carried a headline that read, "Redundant Churches: Who Cares?"[6] Churches in the United Kingdom have been turned into theaters, restaurants, museums — even mosques and temples. I have a whole series of photographs that I have taken of such buildings that were formerly churches.

Where England is today, America will be tomorrow — unless we act now and pray for God's favor.

As stated in the previous chapter, it is time for a new Reformation in the Church — to call the Body of Christ back to the authority of the Word of God, beginning with His first words in Genesis.

As a follow-up to the research detailed in the 2009 publication *Already Gone*, in 2014, Answers in Genesis contracted with America's Research Group (ARG) once again, to understand more about the state of the modern Church and particularly the younger generations. The data obtained in this study was by telephone interviews of a qualified sample in the United States. This sample was selected by random digit

---

6. http://www.victoriansociety.org.uk/publications/redundant-churches-who-cares/.

procedure insuring construction of a probability sample. The survey began on July 23, 2014, and concluded on August 1, 2014.

ARG conducted this research to provide Answers in Genesis a completed study of people in their 20s and 40s who attend church. One of AiG's goals was to determine what exactly has happened to their faith and their church attendance. Specifically, this study investigated the following areas of concern:

- Denomination

- Current church attendance

- Sunday school teaching

- Personal beliefs in biblical accounts

- Church relevance

- Evolution/creation

In this book we will provide and explain various aspects of this research in detail. My hope in doing this is that,

- An alarm bell will be sounded concerning problems with the beliefs of a significant number of people currently attending church — and in particular the 20s generation.

- The meaning of words and terms will be carefully defined and explained in the Church because of the influence of post-modernism. One cannot assume younger generations have the same definitions of terms as previous generations.

- People will gain an understanding of why increasing numbers in the Church are doubting the Scriptures and no longer believing God's Word.

- What should be done in our churches and homes to deal with those in the coming generations that are leaving the Church and those who have adopted a very secularized worldview.

- Help wake up Christian leaders and others to see the problems that need to be addressed in the Church and the home, or else the Church's influence will continue to wane in our Western world.

- See clearly that certain Church people will hold biblically contradictory positions and yet not even understand they are doing so.

- People in the Church will develop consistency in how they apply Scripture to their daily lives.

The Research Doesn't Lie

The following is a summary of just some of the highlights of this cutting-edge research to urge you to carefully consider what ARG found.

For instance, of those in their 20s and 40s who attend church,

1. Twenty percent (20.6%) said they don't believe the Bible is true and historically accurate.

2. Twenty-two percent (22.1%) of the people who do not believe the Bible is true and accurate said "the Bible has errors," and that is what made them begin to doubt the Bible.

3. Eighteen percent said their pastor said something to make them believe the Book of Genesis contained many myths and legends.

4. Eighty-three percent said their science teachers taught them that the earth was millions or billions of years old. In addition, 65.2% said their teachers taught them that humans definitely evolved from lower forms of life to become what they are today.

5. Among the 20.6% who do not believe that the Bible is true and historically accurate, 22.1% said the "Bible has errors," while 20.6% said "science shows that the earth is very old," and 20.4% said the "Bible was written by men," stating that this was what made them begin to doubt the Bible. In addition, 13.8% said "the Bible contradicts itself" and 13.4% said their belief that "it hasn't been translated correctly" was that made them begin to doubt the Bible.

6. Only fifty-nine percent said they consider themselves born-again.

7. Forty-two percent who attended Sunday school said their Sunday school teachers did not teach them how to defend their Christian beliefs by reading certain verses in their Bible.

8. Sixty-two percent said they believe if you are a good person on earth, you will go to heaven upon your death.

9. Twenty-three percent (22.9%) said they left high school believing that the Bible is less true. In addition, 28.0% said they feel people with a college education are less likely to attend church.

10. Over seven in ten (72.0%) said they believe the Bible is true and historically accurate. However, 27.0% said they don't believe homosexual behavior is a sin and 30.6% said abortions should continue to be legal in most instances. Thirty-eight percent said they think premarital sex is okay. Two in five said gay couples should be allowed to marry and have all the legal rights of heterosexual couples. Five in nine said homosexual behavior is a sin.

11. Over seven in ten (70+%) said they have not read the Bible from cover to cover.

12. Twenty-two percent (22.4%) said the Bible is a book that many men wrote years ago and it is simply a collection of writings by wise men.

13. Eighty-two percent (82.8%) believe Adam and Eve were real people in the Garden of Eden and 83.6% believe Adam and Eve sinned and were expelled from the Garden. In addition, 73.7% believe in the account of Sodom and Gomorrah and that Lot's wife was turned to salt when she looked back at the city. Further, 89.5% believe in Noah's ark and the global flood and 82.5% believe in the birth of Isaac when Abraham was about 100 years old.

14. Over one in five said they believe other holy books like the Qur'an (Koran) are inspired by God.

15. Of those who do not believe the Bible is true and historically accurate, one in two (50%) said they first had doubts in middle school.

16. Five in nine said they believe that dinosaurs died out before people were on the planet.

17. Two in three said they believe the Bible, which teaches the world was created in six 24-hour days.

18. Less than 50% said someone taught them how to defend their Christian faith if they were challenged.

19. Of those who said no one taught them how to defend their Christian faith, nearly 50% said they would have liked someone to have prepared them better when they were younger on how to defend their faith and Christian principles.

20. Over 20% (one in five) said their pastor taught that Christians could believe in an earth that is millions or billions of years old.

21. One in six said their pastor said something to make them believe that the Book of Genesis contained myths and legends that we now know are untrue.

22. One in three said they currently attend church most Sundays. Nearly one in four said they currently attend church every week. Six in seven said that in elementary school, they primarily attended a public school. Seven in eight said that in high school, they primarily attended a public school.

23. Over one in five said that by the time they graduated from high school, they believed that the Bible was less true. Of those who said that by the time they graduated from high school, they believed that the Bible was less true, five in nine said their high school teacher was the person who convinced them the most that the Bible was less true. Over one in four said the Bible contains errors.

24. Of those who said the Bible contains errors, over one in three said that "human writers of the Bible made mistakes".

25. Fewer than three in five said they believe only those who have received Christ as their Lord and Savior will go to heaven.

26. Seven in eight said science teachers should be allowed to teach the problems with evolution.

27. Six in seven said prayer should be allowed in public schools.

Again, this research was conducted on those who are *attending church*. One in five said they primarily attend a Baptist church (this was the biggest denomination represented). One in nine said they primarily attend a Catholic church. However, when the Catholic denomination was taken out of the groups, the statistics in regard to the answers did not change.

The above summary of the results should in itself generate concern about the state of those attending church today. But it also reveals areas where the Church can (and needs to) address issues to help alleviate these problems. Of course there were some very positive aspects found from the research as well.

As we continue in this book, we will not only provide additional details of this research, but also more importantly give teaching and discuss ways that can be used to address the problems revealed.

As we begin to do this, I believe the first topic we need to address relates to how people in the Church view Scripture itself.

Chapter 3

The Blind and the Bland

The Tragedy of Biblical Devaluation

As we delve into the alarming findings of the latest research on the state of the modern Church, we first need to address the issue of how we view and approach the Bible — the Word of God.

In the ARG survey (of those in their 20s and 40s), we discovered an alarming result indicating that many attending church do not understand what it means to say the Scriptures are the "inspired Word of God."

When asked, "Do you believe all the books of the Bible are inspired by God?" 95 percent answer yes. Now this sounds very encouraging. But the very next question revealed a serious problem. When asked, "Do you believe other holy books are inspired by God?" 22 percent answered yes, and 10 percent didn't know if they were. So to 32 percent of those attending church, God's Word is not just the Bible, but includes or probably includes other books.

The problem in regard to how people in the Church view God's Word is further illustrated when asked "Do you believe the Bible is true and historically accurate?" and 21 percent answered with a no and an additional 7 percent didn't know! We did ask what caused them to answer this way and will deal with that later in the book, but it does relate to a major area of compromise within the church.

When they were asked, "Do you believe God truly inspired each of the authors of books of the Bible?" an encouraging 90 percent answered yes. But when asked, "Does the Bible contain errors?" then 26 percent answered yes, an additional 11 percent didn't know, and 63 percent said no! This means there is a problem in the Church in regard to people understanding what the word "inspired" means. There are obviously different definitions! It's also important to find out then when given the opportunity to express what those errors supposedly are, the largest percentage (37 percent) stated it was that the Bible was wrong about the age of the earth! We will discuss this further on, but there is no doubt the teaching of evolution and "millions of years" has had a dramatic effect on how a significant number of churchgoers view the Bible (let alone those who have already left the Church).

Another glaring problem in regard to how people view Scripture showed up when these churchgoers were asked, "Do you believe if you are good person you will go to heaven?" An alarming 62 percent answered yes! So even a significant number of those who believe the Bible is the inspired Word of God and don't believe it has errors, believe if you are a good person you will go to heaven! Something is seriously wrong here with their understanding of Scripture! But then, an inconsistency shows up which means there is much confusion. Many people are not thinking through the positions they hold. When asked, "Do you believe only those who have received Christ will go to heaven," 61 percent say yes. Before we go any further into this research, the results certainly show that there is confusion in the Church with the 20s and 40s generations in regard to what it means to say the Bible is the Word of God, specifically the need to interpret it consistently.

One of the major crises in the Church today is that Christian leaders (and Christians in general) have begun to treat God's Holy Word as a fallible *human* work. In other words, they choose to either not take it literally (meaning naturally — the grammatical historical interpretative method), or in some way amend it in order to accommodate a newer, more "enlightened" understanding of the universe, mankind, and truth. Relativism, pluralism, and unorthodox teaching have seeped into many churches, with the most immediate effect being a pandemic biblical illiteracy among church members. This doesn't mean the average churchgoer can't recognize the major accounts from the Bible, but rather that he/she has no basic understanding of the Bible as a whole or the theology it teaches. This sort of theological bankruptcy naturally leads to an outbreak of spiritual anemia. And from there, the Church begins to decay and die. Solomon understood this principle, and thus penned,

> Where there is no prophetic vision the people cast off restraint, but blessed is he who keeps the law (Prov. 29:18).

The idea is that without a clear word from God, the spiritual and moral quality of our lives is directly and severely impacted — thus, "spiritual anemia" and weakness. The result is a vulnerability to attack from our enemies (the world, the flesh, and the devil).

Inevitably, without a high view of Scripture, Christians have no framework of theology or truth about God. Because of our sin nature, left to our own ideas, desires, and the propaganda of culture for our guidance, we end up at the wrong destination.

Why the Bible Is Such a Big Deal

I think it's worth asking, "Why is it so critical that the Bible be the foundation of our thoughts, beliefs, and behavior?" Why not secular society? Government? Philosophy or personal feelings? The first and foremost reason is that the Bible is the only divine book ever written in all of history. Many religions, religious leaders, and philosophers have documented their musings and mandates on paper. But *not one* of them has ever supernaturally *validated* those claims as undeniable truth. Jesus Christ is the only person in history who has certified and substantiated his own claims as well as those of the Old Testament. And He did it in the most unmistakable way, by rising from the dead. Because of this, everything we read in Scripture is not only valid and dependable, but also becomes the ultimate source of truth itself. Paul wanted there to be no doubt as to the divine nature of Scripture and its subsequent effect on us, writing,

> All Scripture is breathed out by God and profitable for teaching, for reproof, for correction, and for training in righteousness, that the man of God may be complete, equipped for every good work (2 Tim. 3:16–17).

So often today, many in the Church treat the Bible as written by mere men —but as we read in 1 Thessalonians 2:13, "For this reason we also constantly thank God that when you received the word of God which you heard from us, you accepted it not as the word of men, but for what it really is, the word of God, which also performs its work in you who believe" (NASB).

The word "inspired" comes from a Greek word meaning "God-breathed." That's how connected Scripture is to God. It's like the very breath of God. His Word, spoken and faithfully recorded on paper for us, reveals His thoughts and the desires of His heart. As such, by its very nature it is perfect, infallible, and most of all, authoritative!

So, given this fact, that authority obviously extends all the way back to the first words in the Bible. Unfortunately, not everyone understands this relationship between God and His Word. Objecting to my strong stand on the six literal days of creation, a pastor once wrote,

> Ham uses deductive reasoning, with only the Bible text as his referent, to make a case for the literal historicity of everything in Scripture. Without such authentication, he claims, the truth of the resurrection is jeopardized. I'm unable to make that jump with him, because to do so would be to make my faith totally dependent on something, i.e., the Bible text historicity, which is, ultimately, a human work.[1]

How tragic that a man who has been tasked by God to declare authoritatively, "Thus says the Lord," treats the Scripture, practically speaking, as a work of *man* (with some divine bits occasionally thrown in).

---

1. Personal letter from a Georgia (USA) pastor on file at AiG-USA.

To be clear, there are conservative Christian scholars who admit that Genesis chapter one, taken on its own, teaches six literal days. However, many of these same Christian leaders, by their own words, were shown to reject the six literal days, because they accepted the billions of years for the age of the earth and universe.[2] This is not only self-contradictory, but is a betrayal of Scripture's very nature and character. It really doesn't require a post-graduate degree in biblical exposition or theology to comprehend that Moses chose the word for "day" (*yom*) in Genesis 1, which when taken in context in accord with the Hebrew language, means a *literal 24-hour day* for each of the days of creation. It follows then that when pastors and teachers cower to evolutionary thought and fallible man-made dating methods used to "reinterpret" what this word means, they end up making God's Word fallible and man's dating methods *in*fallible.[3]

This obviously sets a very dangerous precedent. You can see how, if a typical biblical historical narrative (such as the creation account) doesn't mean what it plainly says and means — then virtually *any* passage in the Bible is up for reinterpretation.[4] Thus, the New Testament would be open to massive reinterpretation and new meanings as well. It makes reading the Bible the same as reading tea leaves at the bottom of a cup — with anyone's interpretation being as valid as anyone else's.

---

2. Ken Ham, "Evolution or Millions of Years — Which Is the Greater Threat?" *Answers Magazine*, July–September 2012; https://answersingenesis.org/theory-of-evolution/millions-of-years/evolution-or-millions-of-years/.

3. Simon Turpin, "Evangelical Commentaries on the Days of Creation in Genesis One," *Answers Research Journal*, 6 (2013): 79–98, https://answersingenesis.org/days-of-creation/evangelical-commentaries-on-the-days-of-creation-in-genesis-one/; also Terry Mortenson, "Six Literal Days," *Answers Magazine*, April–June, 2010, https://answersingenesis.org/days-of-creation/six-literal-days/

4. Some scholars have attempted to reject Genesis as a literal historical account by claiming it was written as poetry. However, this claim is easily refuted: "The Genre of Genesis 1:1–2:3: What Means This Text?" Steven W. Boyd, in *Coming to Grips with Genesis*, Terry Mortenson and Thane Ury, eds. (Green Forest, AR: Master Books, 2008), and https://legacy-cdn-assets.answersingenesis.org/assets/pdf/am/v8/n2/coming-to-grips-with-genesis-ch6.pdf, "Parallelism in Hebrew Poetry Demonstrates a Major Error in the Hermeneutic of Many Old-Earth Creationists," Tim Chaffey, *Answers Research Journal*, 5 (2012): 115–123, https://answersingenesis.org/hermeneutics/parallelism-in-hebrew-poetry-reveals-major-hermaneutic-error/. E.J. Young, in his book *In the Beginning* (Edinburgh: Banner of Truth Trust Publishers, 1976), p. 18, stated: "Hebrew poetry had certain characteristics, and they are not found in the first chapter of Genesis."

Now it is true that Christians can have differing interpretations in regard to issues like eschatology, modes of baptism, and so on. But such differences do not alter the very foundation of history, humanity, or the Christian faith. At least those who disagree about certain non-essential doctrines are still looking at the Bible, interpreting Scripture with Scripture. But the reason so many Christians have differing views of Genesis is because they are starting *outside* of Scripture with man's fallible ideas, and using them to reinterpret the plain meaning of God's Word. In doing so, they force an outside interpretation on God's Word.

Man's Word or God's?

Fortunately, despite man's misinterpretation, God has not left us in the dark when it comes to understanding His Word. For example, in many cases we can understand Old Testament passages through New Testament explanations of them. In other words, very often the Bible interprets itself! Comparing Scripture with Scripture is what is referred to as the "Analogy of Faith."[5]

Paul effectually does this by citing Genesis as actual history in many passages, including Romans 5, 1 Corinthians 15, and Acts 17:26. However, let me show you what happens if you take what God wrote through Paul, reject a literal interpretation of Genesis, and accept a faulty teaching concerning the age of the earth.[6]

The United Kingdom was once a country deeply influenced by Christian thought. However, now it has few vestiges of Christianity left. One of that country's most influential Christian organizations publishes a magazine that includes Sunday school lessons that are used by many

---

5. www.theopedia.com/Analogy_of_faith.
6. The following papers expose the fallibility of radioactive dating methods: "Radiometric Dating: Problems with Assumptions," Andrew Snelling, *Answers Magazine*, October–December, 2009, https://answersingenesis.org/geology/radiometric-dating/radiometric-dating-problems-with-the-assumptions/; Andrew Snelling, "Radioactive 'Dating' Failure," December 1, 1999, https://answersingenesis.org/geology/carbon-14/radioactive-dating-failure/; Andrew Snelling, "U-Th-Pb 'Dating': An Example of False 'Isochrons,'" *Answers in Depth*, December 9, 2009, https://answersingenesis.org/geology/radiometric-dating/u-th-pb-dating-an-example-of-false-isochrons/; A. Snelling, "The Cause of Anomalous Potassium-Argon Ages for Recent Andesite Flows at Mt. Ngauruhoe, New Zealand, and the Implications for Potassium-Argon Dating," *Proceedings of the Fourth International Conference on Creationism*, 1998, p. 503–525.

churches (including many of the more conservative ones) to teach children and adults.[7]

In the March 1998 edition for all ages, we read,

> The study of paleontology has rendered it virtually impossible for a serious scientist to make a case for a six day creation about six thousand years ago, as Christians would once have believed without question.[8]

Of course, the reason most Christians would have "once believed" in a six-day creation "without question" is that this is the obvious and straightforward reading, in context, of Genesis 1, and the understanding of almost 2,000 years of church history and theology.

This prominent Christian magazine was plainly stating that man's study of the fossil record (and his interpretations of it) must now be the standard used to interpret Genesis and the biblical account.

So what then would the person who wrote this Sunday school lesson do with what Paul wrote in the New Testament concerning Genesis?

Further down the same page, the author of this same lesson states:

> Paul clearly believed, as one would expect of a thinker of that era, in a humanity which was descended from a single male — Adam (v. 26). Because at the end of the twentieth century we have access to scientific and literary scholarship that he never had, many would now see that using the Bible as a geological textbook requires it to answer questions in a way that was never intended.

Are you believing this?

There is no doubt that the implication is that because Paul didn't have the fossil and dating research we have today, his writings would

---

7. *Salt: all ages* magazine. The leadership of this organization told us that they do not agree with denigrating those who hold to literal Genesis, (and have taken steps to avoid a repetition). However, they made it clear that in doing so, they are not supporting literal Genesis, and would allow for such views as long ages and theistic evolution. They told us that a correction in *Salt: all ages*, was considered, but decided against. Many historically sound organizations, though many within their ranks are still solid Bible believers, are subject to pressure to "drift" away from the inerrancy of Scripture; this usually starts in Genesis, because of "science."

8. Milton Keynes, *Salt Magazine*, Scripture Union, UK, Jan/Mar 1998 p. 29.

therefore reflect this lack of knowledge and understanding. As a result, we can't really trust what Paul stated concerning origins. After all, he was at a great disadvantage in this area, not being a scientist or enlightened like we are. Poor Paul, all he had was *direct revelation* from Almighty God, the Creator and source of all knowledge!

This cuts to the heart of the Church's problem. It seems most Christians have a gross misunderstanding concerning the nature of divine revelation and the authority of biblical truth. And this can be traced back to a dereliction of duty in the pulpit where pastors propagate such misinterpretations.

But herein lies the core issue: Are the words of Paul (and other authors in the Bible) just human words, reflecting human thoughts and knowledge? If some of the words of Scripture cannot be trusted as accurate, how can we be certain that other parts of Scripture are true? Are only *some* parts of the Bible inspired? Or are some simply "more inspired" than others? And how can we know for sure?

First, let's consider just some of the claims the Bible makes for itself. Over 3,000 times the Bible claims that it is God's Word. As we've already seen from 2 Timothy 3:16, *every word* of Scripture is literally God-breathed. By definition then, they are infallible. Then there are passages such as Psalm 119:160 (KJV), "Thy word is true from the beginning," and verse 89, "Forever, O Lord, thy word is settled in heaven."

Jesus Christ often settled arguments by citing Scripture, which He said "cannot be broken" (John 10:35). Countering Satan's temptations, Jesus repeatedly answered, "It is written" followed by direct quotes from Old Testament Scripture (Matthew 4). Using human logic, if Paul, who lived in a more educated and advanced first century, was misinformed and ignorant concerning truth, how much more misinformed and misguided would the Old Testament writers be? And yet Jesus quoted Moses as His authoritative basis for resisting Satan. How can this be . . . *unless* he believed that *all* Scripture was historically accurate and spiritually trustworthy? You see, if we simply pick and choose which Scriptures are valid and which are not, there remains no ultimate, unchanging standard by which to make such a distinction. Again, interpreting Scripture becomes a "personal thing," a roll of the dice depending on the person. And *we* become the judges of the Bible to see which parts of the book are "believable" to us, based on what secular reasoning dictates. And we also need to remember that concerning Jesus, we read, "In the beginning was the Word, and the Word was with God, and the Word was God" (John 1:1). Jesus is the Word, so every word from Genesis to Revelation is the word of Jesus — not just those in red in the red letter editions of the Bible!

To be clear, some of Scripture's truths and commands were applied to a specific time period, such as Old Testament Temple sacrifices, ceremonial cleansings, etc. Even so, there are still timeless *principles* we were meant to learn from those truths. Paul does not discount the truth of the Law of Moses, even though that Law was no longer in effect and applicable because of Jesus' New Covenant (Testament). However, he did point out many contemporary lessons we can still learn from the Law (Rom. 3:19–31; Gal. 2:15–21, 3:10–4:6). But other truths transcend time, flowing seamlessly from age to age and culture to culture. Among these are those truths that speak to the nature of God, man, and the universe. To amend God's truth concerning creation because of new "scientific" discoveries or methods is like declaring mankind to be inherently "good" because of an overwhelming consensus in the modern psychiatric community. This is absurd. When man's opinion contradicts God's clear revelation, we have to stand with God's Word every time. As Paul told the Romans,

> Let God be true though every one were a liar, as it is written, "That you may be justified in your words, and prevail when you are judged" (Rom. 3:4).

The Authority of the Written Word

Even if the entire world's population were to disagree with Scripture, our allegiance remains with God's Word. Noah sure understood this principle. So did Elijah, Daniel, Peter, and John.

The reality is that many in the world and the Church don't like the implications of Scripture's raw theological or historical truths. So they alter and reinterpret them to "fit" a post-modern understanding of the world, life, and themselves. Currently, this is also being done to those Scriptures that claim truth about marriage, sexuality, and morality. But our latest research illustrates how rampant a problem this is in the modern Church — even among those who call themselves "born again."

For Jesus Christ, when Scripture speaks, the Creator speaks (Matt. 19:5). In Matthew 22:23–34, Christ based an argument on resurrection on the tense of a single Old Testament verb. He endorsed the Genesis record of creation (Matt. 19:3–6), as well as Noah's Flood and the ark (Luke 17:26–27). There are hundreds and hundreds of other Scriptures that demonstrate how every word (in the original autographs) is the exact word God wanted there for all people and for all time. And even though God used human authors, He superintended them, so that they recorded without error what He wanted written down (2 Pet. 1:20–21). Throw out this fundamental fact, and we are left with nothing more than another religious book.

Keep in mind, God is infinite in knowledge. *Infinite.* Limitless. No boundaries. That means He has never been hampered by a lack of understanding in geology or astronomy! In fact, He is the reason geology, astronomy, and all science exists. True science always agrees with Scripture. It's man's presuppositions and interpretations of the facts that cause confusion and disagreement. God is not in heaven saying "Okay, I admit it. Paul got it wrong. I sure wish I could have prevented him from writing what more enlightened men will later contradict." Yet that is how an increasing number of people in the Church really view Scripture!

In reality, God actually spoke through Scripture's writers, and He did not stutter, skip a beat, or miss a word. However, because evangelical Christianity is currently suffering from a really low view of Scripture (and particularly in much of the leadership), we see the outworkings of this in publications like the Sunday school literature I quoted earlier. We also see it in Christian college newspapers such as the following.

Referring to the Bible, one writer states:

> Perhaps it would be better to read it as it was intended to be read, as a variety of texts intended to reveal God's unchanging truth to ancient cultures. Because the Bible was not directly

addressed to our culture, it is important that we read it in its proper context instead of deifying it by reading it literally.[9]

"Deifying it?" Since when does seeing the Bible as relevant across all time and cultures make it an object of worship? Yes, the Bible *was* written in the context of past cultures, and the key to interpreting and understanding Scripture is to consider it in its historical, grammatical, cultural, and literal context. That resulting *interpretation* is the meaning of the biblical text, though it may have varying *applications* from culture to culture and person to person.

One meaning. Many applications.

The Purity of Simplicity

This underscores the fact that the Word of God is for *all* people for *all* time — and it will stand forever. "The grass withers, the flower fades, but the word of our God will stand forever" (Isa. 40:8).

To illustrate this philosophy of using conclusions from outside the Bible to depart from its plain teaching, consider the following. Today, some in the Church claim Paul didn't understand that certain people were supposedly born pre-programmed by their genes to be homosexual.[10] Therefore, they say, Paul's statements condemning homosexual behavior (e.g., in Romans 1) cannot be accepted or meant for today. Paul is accused of a lack of knowledge in this area, so he wrote down "incorrect information" in the Bible. However, remember — the Creator God, who inspired Paul to write the exact words He wanted, has *all* information. With that approach to understanding Scripture (specifically homosexuality), Moses would also be wrong. So would the two angels who visited Sodom and Gomorrah. And so would God Himself, who historically and consistently condemns such a lifestyle.

---

9. "Settling for Second Best: A Search for Truth," *The Crusader*, May 20, 1998, Student Newspaper, Northwest Nazarene College, Nampa, Idaho.

10. Contrary to popular press reports, it has not been established that genes program people to be homosexual. It is true, however, that in this fallen world, we can be predisposed (genetically or otherwise) to certain sins — homosexual behavior may turn out to be one of them. However, as God through Paul said in 1 Corinthians 10:13 (KJV): "There hath no temptation taken you but such as is common to man: but God is faithful, who will not suffer you to be tempted above that ye are able; but will with the temptation also make a way to escape, that ye may be able to bear it."

Even though the customs of people from various cultures in the Bible (e.g., in the Book of Genesis), may well differ from ours, we must treat each custom according to the immediate context of the Scripture passage, *before* attempting to use sources *outside* the Bible to explain it. Because it is God's Word (and not merely a human work), Scripture by definition must be self-authenticating and self-attesting. Therefore, as a first step, Scripture must interpret Scripture. This is not circular reasoning, but rather is supported by Christ's belief in every word of Scripture, and validated to be true by His glorious Resurrection.[11]

Certainly, extra-biblical sources can be used to aid us in understanding the background against which a particular passage was written — but these sources must be secondary to the specific and general context of the words themselves.

Ever since the Fall of man, when Adam chose to "interpret" God's plain words using his own finite understanding, humans have been doubting, and ultimately shaking their fist at Him and His Holy Word.

So it comes as no surprise that those who *do* let God's Word speak plainly to them (particularly in Genesis) are looked down upon with disdain by most of today's scholars, making statements such as,

> Christians are often inclined to take the young-earth position simply because it appears to be the plainest reading of the Bible.[12]

My response is, "Yes! That's right!"

My challenge to the Church and her pastors is simply this: Let us repent of our low view of Scripture, humble ourselves, and learn the lesson God taught the Israelites in Deuteronomy 8:3:

> And he humbled you and let you hunger and fed you with manna, which you did not know, nor did your fathers know, that he might make you know that man does not live by bread alone, but man lives by every word that comes from the mouth of the LORD.

---

11. Matthew 5:18; 1 Corinthians 15:15–22.
12. D. Stoner, *A New Look at an Old Earth* (Eugene, OR: Harvest House Publishers, 1997), p. 37.

Let us also remember Psalm 138:2, "I bow down toward your holy temple and give thanks to your name for your steadfast love and your faithfulness, for you have exalted above all things your name and your *word*" (emphasis added).

If the Church is going to grow, mature, and spread the gospel effectively — if she is ever going to defend the faith and reestablish her presence in the marketplace again, then she *must* return to a high view of the Word of God and a deep reverence for the God of that Word. And this can never happen unless we receive that Word plainly and humbly, as it was meant to be understood. As Christ warned the church at Laodicea, only this kind of repentance will enable us to truly see again (Rev. 3:15–19). This, therefore, is the cure for our blindness and the blandness so prevalent in the Church today.

Chapter 4

Under the Influence

How to Lose a Generation

Something is happening to the 20s generation!

In 2015, Answers in Genesis contracted with America's Research Group (ARG) to conduct research to provide AiG with an idea of America's interest in seeing the life-size ark (under construction in 2015, set to open in 2016). We also sought updated projections from a previous 2008 study.

After considering the results of the 2014 research conducted on those in the Church as is being detailed in this book, we asked ARG to include questions to help us understand what was happening in the culture generationally, specifically with regards to church attendance and people's attitudes towards Christianity. As this was a general population research project (with a 3.8 percent margin of error), we wanted this research to supplement the 2014 research conducted on those who attended church. Specifically, this study investigated the following areas of concern:

- The building of the ark

- The ark location

- Denomination

- Current church attendance

From this 2015 study, we found the following about those in the general population, in regard to church attendance.

Of the 60s age group, 35 percent are disengaged from the Church.[1] The rest attend church regularly or fairly regularly. But of the 20s age group, 64 percent are disengaged from the Church. That is a dramatic generational drop in church attendance! In fact, this is similar to the statistic from the Barna research we quoted in the book *Already Gone* where we state,

> Respected pollster George Barna was one of the first to put numbers to the epidemic. Based on interviews with 22,000 adults and over 2,000 teenagers in 25 separate surveys, Barna unquestionably quantified the seriousness of the situation: *six out of ten 20-somethings who were involved* in a church during their teen years are already gone.[2]

Another statistic from the 2015 research that illustrates the 20s generation has a major problem from a Christian perspective is seen in the answer to the question, "Do you believe people of Christian faith are under attack today?" While 60 percent of the 60s generation answered yes to this question, only 34 percent of the 20s generation answered yes. I do believe (as we will show later on) this reflects the increasing secularization of the 20s generation, and is a sad reflection on the overall state of the Church.

We also see this decline concerning a Christian worldview in the 2014 research conducted on those who *do* attend church.

Comparing the 40s and 20s generations of churchgoers, (the two groups specifically targeted for this research) we found the following.

When asked, "Is homosexual behavior a sin?" 67 percent of the 40s generation answered yes, but 56 percent of the 20s generation gave the yes answer. When asked, "Should abortions continue to be legal in most instances?" 58 percent of the 40s group said no, but 49 percent of the 20s group gave the no answer. When asked, "Is premarital sex okay?" 34

---

1. This number (64%) includes those in their 20s who attend church once a month or less, only on holidays, and never, and thus are considered disengaged from the church.
2. https://answersingenesis.org/christianity/church/already-gone/.

percent of the 40s generation said yes, but 42 percent of the 20s generation gave the yes answer. Questions about gay marriage and legalizing smoking marijuana revealed similar trends.

Now for the research for the book *Already Gone* (published in 2009), America's Research Group selected those between 20 and 30 who once attended conservative and "evangelical" churches as children. We deliberately skewed the research toward conservatives so that we could all understand that whatever problems showed up would be much worse for the church population in general.

The results? Of these thousand 20 to 29-year-old evangelicals who attended church regularly but no longer do so,

- 95% of them attended church regularly during their elementary and middle school years.

- 55% attended church regularly during high school.

- Of the thousand, only 11% were still going to church during their early college years.

This was one of the most revealing and yet challenging statistics in the entire survey — and something we didn't expect. Most people assume that students are lost in college. We've always been trying to prepare our kids for college (and I still think that's a critical thing to do, of course), but it turns out that only 11 percent of those who have left the Church were still attending during the college years. Almost 90 percent of them were lost in middle school and high school. By the time they got to college, they were already gone! We discovered that about 40 percent are leaving the Church during elementary and middle school years!

This leaves no doubt that there is a downward trend in Christian influence generationally in the culture as a whole, and in the Church.

Brainwashed from Birth

Which leads us to rethink the crucial questions: What does it take to influence a generation? How do you change the way an entire demographic looks at life? How do you alter their sense of what is real and true? If you could fundamentally transform history going forward, how would you go about doing that? How would you ensure that what you drop in humanity's pond will produce concentric rippling effects that continue on for decades. Want to know? I'll tell you.

You target the minds of young people — beginning from when they are born! Many parents have the idea that once their kids are old enough to go to college, they need some instruction to help them cope with whatever attacks may occur on their Christian beliefs. But by then it's way too late. Those attacks start basically when a child is born — and as our research shows, most of those who leave the Church do so because of doubts they succumb to through elementary, middle school, and high school. We should be reminded that many places in Scripture remind parents to be diligent in training their children.

> Train up a child in the way he should go; even when he is old he will not depart from it (Prov. 22:6).

> You shall teach them diligently to your children, and shall talk of them when you sit in your house, and when you walk by the way, and when you lie down, and when you rise. You shall bind them as a sign on your hand, and they shall be as frontlets between your eyes. You shall write them on the doorposts of your house and on your gates (Deut. 6:7–9).

While their minds are still open and impressionable, you create a comprehensive campaign of indoctrination, both covert and overt in nature. And then you repeatedly pound it into them in the most palatable and persuasive ways possible until there is no room left for dissenting views. Unfortunately, this has already happened to most children from the secular world! And if the Church continues sleeping in regard to this tragic trend, then coming generations will become more and more disengaged from the Church — which is exactly what the research is showing.

During the past 30 years of traveling the world and speaking in churches, I have been deeply burdened by distraught parents pleading for advice on how to reach their children who were brought up in the Church but who no longer attend. "How can I reach them?" they ask. "How can we get them back to God and church?"

I've often thought how I'd like to get into the heads of these young adults who have left Church to understand what (and how) they are thinking. What caused them to walk away from the Church (and the truth) they were brought up in?

After teaching thousands of children and adults in churches, I've developed a big picture understanding concerning a number of issues — some of which thrill me (such as the hunger many young people have for answers), while others greatly trouble me.

For example, I've met many young people who no longer see the Church as relevant, nor do they consider the Bible a real book of history that can be trusted. Further, most parents have delegated the spiritual training of their children to the Sunday school, youth group, or some other Christian organization. Additionally, whenever I speak, I typically find that church audiences usually ask the same questions, regardless of what country or church (conservative or liberal) I visit. Among the most frequently asked questions are,

- How can we know the Bible is true and is God's Word?

- Where did God come from?

- Where did Cain get his wife?

- Can't Christians believe in the earth being millions of years old, the big bang, and evolution, as long as they say God was involved?

- Are the "days of creation" regular 24-hour days or millions of years, and does it *really* matter?

- How could Noah fit all the animals on the ark?

- And many more.

As I observed such identical patterns across America, Australia, Europe, and the United Kingdom, I became convinced there must be a connection. I wondered if the lack of teaching biblical apologetics in our churches, youth groups, Sunday schools, and Bible studies could be a major reason why young people leave the Church. As I spoke with parents, I discovered that an overwhelming number of them admitted they didn't know how to answer their children's questions — whether they were about dinosaurs, the age of the earth, or the origin and nature of the Bible. And most churches certainly were not teaching people how to answer such questions. In fact, most church leaders saw such questions as irrelevant, or even taught people that they could believe in evolution, millions of years, etc., as long as they trusted in Jesus (whatever that meant for the people).

The Fruit of Failure

What our research has shown is that the skepticism, doubt, and denial of Scripture's truths so prevalent among college-age students actually begins as young as elementary and *middle school.*

Further, and perhaps more shocking, the research for the *Already Gone* book revealed something many in the Church did not expect — though from my extensive traveling and speaking ministry it did not surprise me. In our survey of 1,000 20-somethings who regularly attended church as children and teens, we asked the question, "Did you often attend Sunday school?" In reply, 61 percent said yes; 39 percent said no! Then our research uncovered something very disturbing. We found Sunday school was actually more likely to be detrimental to the spiritual and moral health of our children.

Of the 20-somethings surveyed, those who went to Sunday school were more likely to be antichurch, defend gay marriage and abortion, and believe in evolution/millions of years than those who didn't go to Sunday school. But we found that the basic cause comes down to being taught the Bible in Sunday school as a book of *stories* (most today regard a "story" to basically mean a fairy tale), rather than real history that can be defended in this scientific age. Also, those who went to Sunday school were more likely to have heard a Christian leader (pastors, Sunday school teacher, etc.) subvert the Bible's authority and accuracy by endorsing evolution/millions of years.

Discussing this in radio interviews, I'm typically asked, "But why the disconnect — after all, surely the churches are teaching the gospel to these children." To which I respond that while that's true, consider where it is we actually get that gospel message. How do we know Jesus rose from the dead? We were not there to see the Resurrection, and we do not have a movie of it, so how do we know it really happened? We know primarily because we trust the authority of the book from which we get the Resurrection account — the Bible. We accept the words of that book as God-breathed, letting them speak to us as coming directly from God.

But these young people we're talking about have been brought up in a culture (and in many cases, churches) where the historical accuracy of Genesis, in particular, has been attacked or greatly undermined. So many have been taught evolutionary ideas and that the world was formed over millions of years. And sadly, most Christian leaders (Sunday school teachers and others) have essentially told these kids that Genesis doesn't matter by telling them they can trust in a secularist's version of mankind evolving over millions of years, just as long as they also trust in Jesus. What they do not realize is that this embeds a seed of doubt in these young people's minds — a seed that will take root and later bear much negative fruit. Around 90 percent of churched kids attend a public school where God, the Bible, and prayer have been thrown out. Thus, they are being systematically educated in a secular philosophy of naturalism — which is in reality, atheism.

At school, these children have been effectively taught that the Bible cannot be trusted. Meanwhile, over at the church, these same children are not being taught how to take a stand for the Bible's authority, beginning with the very first verse. They are not trained and equipped to answer skeptical attacks on the Bible. So ultimately, even when the message of Jesus is taught to them, they don't really believe it because their belief in the book from which it comes has already been severely eroded.

Satanic Deception and Human Doubt

Of course, no man or human organization could have the foresight to sit down and plan such a comprehensive strategy of indoctrinating children at school while watering down their faith in Scripture at church. The mere thought of such a strategy smacks of conspiracy theories and paranoid subversive plots. Those who subscribe to ideas like these are often categorized as part of the "lunatic fringe." And yet, believe it or not, according to the Bible, such a strategy *is* being implemented all across the world. Beginning with the first man and woman, Satan planted a seed of doubt and skepticism concerning the character of God and the trustworthiness of His Word. You remember the event. Having been provided with a perfect spouse and a paradise environment, Adam and Eve were in need of nothing. They enjoyed a pristine creation environment and an unimaginable relationship with God. They were fulfilled and satisfied. That is, until the serpent suggested otherwise.

The serpent begins his brainwashing regime by posing a question that, in reality, questions the very word God had just spoken: "Did God actually say, 'You shall not eat of any tree in the garden'?"

Satan launches his strategy by suggesting the possibility Adam and Eve could have misheard, misinterpreted, or misunderstood God's clear command to them. "Are you sure that's what He said? 100 percent positive that's what He meant? Really?" he asked.

From Eve's response, it appears as if the serpent's suggestion has no effect on her, as she recounts almost verbatim what God had commanded them regarding the tree.[3] But here is where Satan's sinks his fangs into Eve's mind. Having successfully slithered up next to her by proposing the possibility of reinterpreting God's truth, he now injects his poisonous venom of lies.

> But the serpent said to the woman, "You will not surely die.
> For God knows that when you eat of it your eyes will be opened,
> and you will be like God, knowing good and evil" (Gen. 3:4–5).

Notice the relationship between the serpent's two statements here. First, he flatly contradicts God's revealed truth, in essence calling God a liar. This was new information to Eve, as she had never distrusted God's Word prior to this. But Satan doesn't stop there. He follows up his claim about God by giving Eve his own apologetic to back up his claim. He convinces her God has knowledge that He is withholding from her and her husband.

Once Eve sees the fruit's beauty and its potential to enhance their lives, she shares with Adam and they eat, and in doing so were bitten themselves. Sin's curse then took root in them. All because they doubted God's Word. And humanity has been doubting and questioning ever since.

It's not news to you that most people today do not see the Bible as having the absolute authority it once did. Pollster George Barna found that in the United States, "A minority of born-again adults (44 percent) and an even smaller proportion of born-again teenagers (9 percent) are

---

3. Concerning God's command regarding the fruit, Eve does add "or touch it." This may be an added prohibition, since in the original command, God only told Adam not to eat from the tree (Gen. 2:17).

certain of the existence of absolute moral truth."[4] Similar surveys in the United Kingdom reveal even lower percentages.

So what has happened? Why the dramatic change? Why is the moral position of previous generations being outlawed more and more? What has driven this moral collapse? Why is this war going on?

Whereas Judeo-Christian thinking once permeated the public education system, today the Christian God, prayer, Bible study, and biblical creation have been virtually erased from the system. Now, generations (including the majority of students from church homes) are being trained in a secular (anti-God) religion. They are being indoctrinated to believe that the universe — and all that exists within it — can be explained (and lived) *without* God by natural processes. And naturalism is just another word for atheism. What these secularists are doing is imposing their religion on the culture. Sadly, many Christians think that when Christian symbols like nativity scenes, crosses, or the Ten Commandments are removed from public places, then it makes the situation neutral. But this is not so. "Whoever is not with me is against me, and whoever does not gather with me scatters" (Matt. 12:30). There is no neutral position.

Sadly, generations today are taught, with increasing intensity, a cosmology, geology, biology, and anthropology that are *all* evolutionary. In essence, these students are being educated *against* the truth of the Bible's history in Genesis, and thus, against its message of salvation and absolute moral standards. This is yet another way Christians and their values are being marginalized in our culture.

But not only are our schools indoctrinating our children this way, but so is the media. Television shows, movies, comic books, video games, advertisements, and so on are all laced with evolutionary thought, subtly (and not so subtly) reinforcing the idea that we are nothing but evolved pond scum, the result of billions of years of natural processes.[5] Molecules in motion and nothing more.

---

4. Barna Research Online, "The Year's Most Intriguing Findings," from Barna Research Studies, December 12, 2000.

5. For example, the more highly evolved "X-Men" and the "millions of years" taught in *Jurassic Park* and *Dinosaurs*. Magazines like *Time*, *Nature*, and *National Geographic* often feature cover stories touting evolution as fact. And who can ignore the many cable channels, such as Discovery Channel, The History Channel, and Animal Planet, which regularly broadcast shows on animal and human evolution?

Consider that children ages 2 to 17 spend an average of 19.4 hours watching TV each week (Nielsen Media Research, 2000). And this doesn't include the time spent going to movies, playing computer games, surfing the Internet, or reading comic books and magazines. Our children are inundated with messages from the media, which by and large have an evolutionary, anti-Christian foundation.

In the United States, there are approximately 400,000 churches and 6,000 first-run theaters. Which do you think affects our culture more? Unfortunately, the Hollywood writers and producers have more influence on our youth today than our pastors and spiritual leaders.

Sadly, many Christian leaders in the Church have aided the enemy by compromising with evolutionary ideas (either wittingly or unwittingly) through adding millions of years to the Bible, and teaching that evolution and Christianity are somehow compatible. These leaders have, in effect, helped this takeover by reinforcing culture's values and philosophy. The unintended result is that recent generations have begun to reject or reinterpret the Bible's history in Genesis, thus opening a door to undermine biblical authority in general for the other 65 books of the Bible.

But "Theistic Evolutionists" (those who believe in both God and evolution) represent neither theism nor evolution very well, as the two are biblically impossible and mutually exclusive. It should come as no surprise that as generations are trained to disbelieve the Bible's account of origins, the more they doubt the rest of the Bible, as all biblical doctrines (including marriage) are founded (directly or indirectly) in the history found in Genesis 1–11. We see the direct result of this doubt and compromise reflected in the increasing number of moral battles (even in the Church) concerning gay marriage, abortion, and so on. Again, the more people believe evolution and reject Genesis 1–11 as history, the more they will reject the rest of the Bible — including the morality that is based in that history. That's a part of the greater Satanic strategy that had its origin in the Garden.

To practically illustrate this, let's consider some of the results from the ARG research on churchgoers. These are the cumulative results of the 20s and 40s groups surveyed.

When asked, "Did science teachers teach the earth was millions/ billions of years old?" 83 percent answered yes. When asked "Did any teachers teach that humans evolved from lower life forms?" 65 percent answered yes. Then when asked, "By the time you graduated high school, did you believe the Bible was less true?" 23 percent said yes! Now think about this with the answer to the question, "Have you ever had anyone teach you how to defend the Christian faith?" and 45 percent said no! Now for those churchgoers who do not believe the Bible is historically accurate, when asked, "What is it that made you begin to doubt the Bible?" 21 percent stated that science showing the earth is old was the reason! There is no doubt the teaching of evolutionary ideas (such as millions of years) has been used to cause many in the coming generations to doubt God's Word — and that doubt easily puts one on a slippery slide of unbelief. And here is a warning for parents and the Church. For the 23 percent who believed the Bible was less true by the time they graduated from high school, 56 percent of them said it was their high school teacher who convinced them the Bible was less true! Not only is this a warning to parents about where they send their children for education, but a warning to Church leaders and parents about the importance of training the coming generations to be able to defend the Christian faith and strengthen their belief in the Word of God.

Conflicting Worldviews

There's an intense battle for the hearts and minds of emerging generations, and churches and homes, by and large, are not preparing people for that battle.

Secularism, with its moral relativism, is in direct opposition to Christianity and its claims of absolute morality. The battle lines are drawn between these two worldviews — one that stands on God's Word and one that accepts man's opinions.

So what will be the outcome of this epic conflict? Can the West return to a Christian worldview that will once again permeate the culture? Yes, it can, but only if there is a return to the authority of the Word of God in churches . . . beginning in Genesis.

Some may wonder why can't we just tell people, "Jesus loves you and has a wonderful plan for your life"? Because as true as that statement is, there are many roadblocks that often prevent non-believers from receiving that love. Scripture tells us that Satan "has blinded the minds of the unbelievers, to keep them from seeing the light of the gospel of the glory of Christ, who is the image of God" (2 Cor. 4:4)

One way this blindness manifests itself is through the pervasive skepticism of our world concerning the Bible. Specifically, people now demand answers concerning how the Bible relates to the real world — like, "Does the Bible deserve credible respect when it speaks about matters of the sciences of biology and astronomy, and also history and anthropology?"

Christians who are fighting for a return to biblical morality cannot hope to win this "war of the worldviews" unless they understand that the real foundational nature of the battle is *biblical authority*, beginning with God's Word in Genesis. This is a primary line of defense that must be upheld without compromise.

The secular world itself already understands this battle — but the Church mostly does not. Therefore, Christian leaders must be awakened by a battle cry. We need to systematically dismantle the false foundation of autonomous human reasoning that leads to an evolutionary mindset by effectively unmasking its folly. And in the Church, we must equip believers concerning how and why God's Word is authoritative and its history of the world foundational to Christian morality and the gospel of Jesus Christ.

So then, practically speaking, what (and who) does Satan's strategy involve? We've already mentioned the role of the classroom and the media, but let's address this a bit more specifically in the context of our enemy's attempt to influence this generation. What does Satan's "Garden Deception" look like today? What questions is he posing to Adam and Eve's descendants? What are some of his modern-day venomous lies?

Defending against Satan's Lies

1. Did God really make you? Is He really the Creator?

We've heard so many times from secular groups like the Freedom from Religion Foundation (FFRF) or the Americans United for Separation of Church and State (AU) that students in science classrooms in public schools can't be taught about creation, as that would be teaching "religion" in government-funded schools. And yet, such secular groups clearly contradict themselves by teaching their own brand of religion (naturalism — atheism) in the public schools. And the government uses our tax dollars to do it.

Imagine for a moment if public school science classes were encouraged to worship the sun. Sound ridiculous? Unfortunately, this is actually happening! But how, and more importantly, how do they get away with it? Well, they just simply call worshiping the sun, "science," and then proceed to teach this "science" in the public schools!

Consider the following quote:

> Our ancestors worshiped the sun. They were far from foolish. It makes good sense to revere the sun and stars because we are their children. The silicon in the rocks, the oxygen in the air, the carbon in our DNA, the iron in our skyscrapers, the silver in our jewelry — were all made in stars, billions of years ago. Our planet, our society, and we ourselves are stardust.[6]

Sounds more like bad science fiction than science, right? And yet, this statement was made by well-known celebrity astrophysicist Neil deGrasse Tyson in the new *Cosmos* series, and teachers are being encouraged to use this series in public school classrooms. Another self-proclaimed evolution expert states the following:

> The Fox television series *Cosmos: A Spacetime Odyssey* hosted by Neil deGrasse Tyson is an excellent way for students at the high school, and even the middle school, level to supplement their learning on various science topics. With episodes that cover almost all of the major disciplines in science, teachers are able to use these shows along with their curriculum to make the topics more accessible and even exciting for learners of all levels.[7]

6. Neil deGrasse Tyson in *Cosmos: A SpaceTime Odyssey* (National Geographic Channel, Cosmos Studios, and Fuzzy Door Productions, 2014). Cosmos is a 13-part American science documentary television series that is further marketed for use in classrooms. The show is a follow-up to the 1980 television series *Cosmos: A Personal Voyage*, which was presented by Carl Sagan.

7. Heather Scoville, "Cosmos Episode 4 Viewing Worksheet," About.com, accessed January 26, 2015, http://evolution.about.com/od/Cosmos-Teaching-Tools/fl/Cosmos-Episode-4-Viewing-Worksheet.htm.

Incidentally, Neil deGrasse Tyson is not the first disciple of naturalism in recent times to suggest a distinctly religious message derived from stardust. Tyson's statement echoes one made by prominent atheist Lawrence Krauss (professor at Arizona State University), author of *A Universe from Nothing: Why There Is Something Rather Than Nothing* (2012). In it he casts stardust in the religious role of both "creator" *and* "savior."

Krauss said the following during a lecture:

> You are all stardust. You couldn't be here if stars hadn't exploded, because the elements — the carbon, nitrogen, oxygen, iron, all the things that matter for evolution — weren't created at the beginning of time. They were created in the nuclear furnaces of stars, and the only way they could get into your body is if those stars were kind enough to explode. So, forget Jesus. The stars died so that you could be here today.[8]

So now stars (hydrogen and helium) are "kind" and "sacrificial," while Jesus is obsolete. I get it.

Krauss' own words reveal he is clearly a religious zealot as he proclaims his atheistic, pagan religion. And by doing so blasphemes the true Savior.

Krauss, Tyson, and the producers of the new *Cosmos* series openly draw the battle lines between biblical Christianity and their own substitute religion of evolution. They not only wrongly claim that biblical Christianity is anti-science but also claim that evolutionary science satisfies humanity's spiritual need. Evolution is all you need. But by doing this, they effectively become mouthpieces, pawns of Satan, smugly suggesting, "You don't really still believe God is the Creator, do you?"

Tyson speaks in the series not just about observational science overlaid heavily with his evolutionary claims, but also extols the spiritual satisfaction he derives from his evolutionary beliefs. For instance, in the same episode ("Sisters of the Sun") Tyson says, "Accepting our kinship with all life on earth is not only solid science; it's, in my view, also a soaring spiritual experience." Or in other words, *worship*.

Yet even before the series premiered, the producers made its religious position clear by defining scientific literacy as belief in evolution and

---

8. Lawrence M. Krauss, *A Universe from Nothing*; http://www.goodreads.com/author/quotes/1410.Lawrence_M_Krauss

blaming the exposure of students to creationism for rampant so-called "scientific illiteracy."

On March 11, 2014, AiG writer/researcher Dr. Elizabeth Mitchell wrote this at the beginning of a series of reviews on the new *Cosmos* program she did for the Answers in Genesis website:

> Rebooting the 1980 Carl Sagan series, *Cosmos: A Personal Voyage*, the new 13-part series has a similar goal: to encourage science literacy. Executive producer Seth MacFarlane says, "I think that there is a hunger for science and knowing about science and understanding of science that hasn't really been fed in the past two decades. We've had a resurgence of creationism and 'intelligent design' theory. There's been a real vacuum when it comes to science education. The nice thing about this show is that I think that it does what the original 'Cosmos' did and presents it in such a flashy, entertaining way that, as Carl Sagan put it in 1980, even people who have no interest in science will watch just because it's a spectacle."
>
> MacFarlane blames scientific illiteracy on the "rise of schools questioning evolution" and hopes the series will put an end to the sort of thinking that would question evolution so that scientific literacy can march forward. Ironically, despite the claim that this series is designed to advance science literacy, by adopting Sagan's theme — "The cosmos is all that is, or ever was, or ever will be" — the producers have hoisted a most unscientific flag above this "ship of the imagination."[9]

So it's okay to teach children they really should be worshiping the sun, as Neil deGrasse Tyson states, but it's not okay to teach them the observational science that confirms the account of the history of the universe and earth as given in the Bible.

Which belief is really "imagination"?

Are Christians aware that this activity exists? And if so, why aren't they up in arms about it?

---

9. Elizabeth Mitchell, "Cosmos Review: 'Standing Up in the Milky Way,' " Answers in Genesis, March 11, 2014, https://answersingenesis.org/reviews/tv/cosmos-review-standing-up-in-the-milky-way/.

Do Christians really understand the anti-God agenda of atheists like Tyson and Krauss? For instance, Professor Krauss also gave a speech in Australia in 2014, proposing how children should be taught about faith in schools, claiming that religious systems shouldn't be treated "as if they're all sacred." He is quoted as stating,

> "Change is always one generation away," the scientist said. "So if we can plant the seeds of doubt in our children, religion [by religion he basically means Christianity] will go away in a generation, or at least largely go away — and that's what I think we have an obligation to do."[10]

That sounds exactly like the method Satan used in Genesis 3 — to create doubt to lead to unbelief. These skeptics are becoming more blatant in aggressively going after the coming generations to indoctrinate them in an atheistic worldview. And sadly, much of the Church and many Christian parents are letting it happen.

2. Isn't Christianity just a "faith-based fairy tale?"

Another way Satan calls into question God and His Word is by questioning the very existence of God Himself. As we've seen, the natural conclusion of evolutionary secularism is that God is no longer considered "necessary." Governments and individuals alike have become *self*-dependent, *exactly* as Satan urged our first parents to become way back in the Garden.

Think of it. If Christianity is not the product of a loving Creator God whose Word is unchanging, infallible, and completely reliable, then what is it?

I'll tell you: *It's simply an illusion. A mind trick. A book of fables, dramatic tales, happy thoughts, and wishes concerning a non-existent afterlife. Nothing more than a man-made story meant to keep bad people in check and make good people feel good about themselves.* This is exactly the conclusion to which atheistic, evolutionary thought and secularism leads. And the more prevalent the belief in evolution becomes, those who embrace it

---

10. http://www.theblaze.com/stories/2014/11/06/prominent-atheist-scientist-cites-slavery-and-gay-marriage-in-this-dire-prediction-religion-will-go-away-in-a-generation/.

become more arrogant and condescending toward God and those who believe in Him and His Word.

By labeling those who believe in biblical creation as "anti-science," they (by direct intention or indirect inference) attempt to discredit Christianity and the Bible from being historically and scientifically accurate and trustworthy. By default, our faith to them is relegated to the same category of those who believe in Greek gods or Santa Claus. To them, God simply *isn't*. Satan would love nothing more than to devalue belief in the existence of God, discredit the person of Christ, and demean His people and His cause in an effort to further his own deceptive, damning agenda.

A "Building Program" Worth Joining

Clearly then, this highlights the urgent need for apologetics. But what kind of apologetics? The biblical issues non-believers question today go beyond traditional presentation of evidence for the Resurrection or the deity of Christ. Therefore, since Satan's strategy is comprehensive, so must ours be, especially as it relates to apologetics. To accurately interpret our culture, we must understand that culture in light of Scripture. Jude wrote that we must "contend for the faith that was once for all delivered to the saints" (Jude 1:3).

Think of what is at stake here. From a human perspective, Christianity as we know it is always just a generation from extinction at any given time. Of course we know from Matthew 16:18 that Christ has pledged to "build His church," ensuring its perpetual existence. But that in no way lessens *our* responsibility in defending and contending for the faith. Like with Timothy, God is counting on us to guard, defend, and share that body of truth we know as the Christian faith (1 Tim. 1:11, 6:20). We have been commanded to "fight the good fight," and we cannot let our Lord down (1 Tim. 1:18, 6:12).

We must help the Church become strong, spiritually and intellectually as we contend for the faith in the marketplace. That is one of the primary missions of the pastor — to "equip the saints for the work of ministry" (Eph. 4:11–12). A healthy and effective church is one that does more than simply dispense messages on "How to Communicate with Your Spouse" or "Steps to Overcoming Stress." We find ourselves in these last days in a wartime scenario. Along with occasional need-based sermons, God's people fundamentally need training on how to confidently engage unbiblical ideas and worldviews. We must be armed with Scripture's truth, God-inspired logic, and the power of the Holy Spirit.

One of AiG's goals is to provide continued training to pastors and Christians through speaking, print, and media resources. But the Church cannot (and was never meant to) shoulder this burden alone. God ordained that the *home* is where this training and equipping begins.

Peter wrote in 1 Peter 3:15, "but in your hearts honor Christ the Lord as holy, always being prepared to make a defense to anyone who asks you for a reason for the hope that is in you; yet do it with gentleness and respect."

Since that is God's command to every believer, shouldn't we begin training toward this at home? I've spoken to scores of parents who feel inadequate to train their children in apologetics. I suspect that one reason for this is that they themselves have never been trained. Many times after I've given a creation apologetics presentation in a church, the pastor will ask where I learned to do this. The pastor then bemoans that he was never taught practical apologetics and really feels ill equipped to answer the skeptical questions of our day that haunt the coming generations. That's why many pastors resort to just teaching spiritual and moral things — but sadly, the coming generations are leaving the Church in droves. However, none of us should feel intimidated by this. All believers can understand and communicate a rational and biblical defense of their faith. There is no good reason why every Christian can't "give an answer" for his/her faith. It is not beyond any of us. But since you cannot share what you don't possess, you must first decide to learn for yourself.

The fact that churched young people are so disconnected from faith and God's Word speaks to the crying need for churches and parents to take on this challenge of equipping the next generation. Still, some may wonder, "Why is all this such a big deal? What's the relationship between destroying a fundamental (and really elemental) belief in a Creator God and the current spiritual/moral state of this generation?"

1. If we are not created by a personal, loving God, then we are, by definition nothing more than random accidents of the universe

(never mind the intellectual suicide required to embrace such an idea/proposition).

2. Without a divine, moral lawgiver, the ultimate (and only) authority for morality and civilization is man himself. On a macro scale, this means we are subject to the changing morality attached to however the winds of culture and government may blow. On a personal level, we are left to our own thoughts and desires, which at best is civil, and at worst is depraved and ungodly.

3. The logical end of such an atheistic philosophy/belief system is existentialism, or the proposition that there is no inherent meaning to life and that nothing actually matters. No afterlife. No judgment or reckoning. And certainly no God before whom you will one day bow.

The natural path of this belief system logically leads us to an undeniable, inevitable conclusion: Do whatever you want to do, because you're nothing more than an evolved animal. You are your own god and self-contained authority. Life is truly meaningless, and when you die you won't know you ever existed. Become an atheist and live an empty life, and then die and never know you were even alive!

This is really the message of much of the public education system today where students are taught as *fact* that life (and the universe) evolved by natural processes (naturalism is atheism). Are we so surprised that kids turn to drugs, sex, suicide, and so on? If evolution is true, why shouldn't they? What difference does it make?

But the message of Christianity is so radically different from the hopelessness atheism promotes. God's Word teaches that man was created with purpose. The life, death, and Resurrection of Jesus Christ has made possible the free gift of eternal life with God for those who receive it, by faith alone, in Christ alone.

Turning the Tables

But Christians don't always have to be on the defensive in these arguments. In fact, it's the *atheist* who should be asked to defend his beliefs and to justify his non-belief in God. With that in mind, try asking the atheist the following questions.

If someone stabs you in the back, treats you like nothing, steals from you, or lies to you, does that ultimately matter in an atheistic worldview where everything and everyone are just chemical reactions doing what chemicals do? Can you really assign blame to them for their actions?

Knowing that you are essentially/ultimately no different from a cockroach in an atheistic worldview (since people are just animals) isn't that disheartening and depressing? That you literally possess no real, intrinsic value.

Doesn't it bother you that atheism (which is based in materialism) has no foundation for logic and reasoning?

Is it tough getting up every day believing that truth, which is immaterial, really has no foundation?

Are you bothered by the fact that atheism cannot account for uniformity in nature (the basis by which we can do real science)?

Why would everything explode from nothing and, by pure chance, form beautiful laws like $E=MC^2$ or $F=MA$?

For professing atheists, these questions can be overwhelming to try to answer within their worldview. Further, within an atheistic framework, atheists are forced to view themselves as God. Instead of saying there *may not* be a God, they say there is *no* God. To make such a statement, they, by default, are claiming to be omniscient (an essential attribute of the God of the Bible). So, by saying there is no God, the atheist refutes his own position by addressing the question as though he or she were God!

Here are more questions for the atheists to defend.

Are you weary of looking for evidence that contradicts the Bible's account of creation and finding none? Do the assumptions and inconsistencies of dating methods weigh on your conscience when they are misrepresented and portrayed as fact?

Where do you suppose all those millions of missing links you base your religion on are hiding?

Doesn't belief in them require more faith (in essence a blind faith) than belief in a God who actually *has* revealed Himself?

If you consider yourself a skeptic, are you ever skeptical of your own skepticism, or of atheism itself?

Don't you feel insecure not being able to explain how everything came from nothing?

Why do you care to live one moment longer in a broken universe where one is merely rearranged pond scum and all you have to look forward to is . . . death, which can be around any corner?

In 467 trillion years, will anyone care one iota about what you did or who you were or how and when you died, because in an atheistic, evolutionary worldview, death is the ultimate "hero"?

Aren't you ready to consider the possibility that you actually aren't "God?" That you could be wrong? Lost? Blind? Mistaken? Ignorant? Sick. Already dead, spiritually? Perhaps in need of answers beyond yourself?

If any self-proclaimed atheist dares to explore that kind of honesty, transparency, and search for truth, then I invite them to reconsider the false religion of atheism. The truth is that atheism is a lie (Rom. 1:25). As a Christian, I understand that truth exists because God exists, who is the Truth (John 14:6). Unlike an atheist, whose worldview doesn't allow him to believe in a foundation for truth or lies, the Bible-believer has a foundation that enables him to speak about that which is true and that which is untrustworthy. This is because those who believe in God have in Him an ultimate authority, the ultimate authority upon which to base such statements.

And here is that truth. There is a God, and you are made in His image (Gen. 1:26, 9:6). This means you (and every other person) have intrinsic value and worth. Whereas consistent atheists teach that you have no value, I see you differently. I see you as a relative (Acts 17:26) and one who — unlike animals, plants, and fallen angels — has the possibility of salvation (a free gift) from eternal death and suffering, which is the result of sin (i.e., disobedience to God; see Rom. 6:23). We have all fallen short of God's holy standard of perfect obedience thanks to our mutual grandfather, Adam (Rom. 5:12). And God sees you differently, too (John 3:16). While you were *still* a sinner, God stepped into history to become a man to die in your place (Rom. 5:8) and offer the free gift of salvation (Rom. 5:15; Eph 2:8–9).

Atheists have no consistent reason to proselytize their faith, but Christians do have a reason — Jesus Christ, who is the Truth, commands us to (Matt. 28:19). We want to see people repent of their evil deeds and be saved from death (Acts 8:22, 17:30). Could there be a greater joy? (Luke 15:10).

Where atheists have no basis for logic and reason (or even for truth, since truth is immaterial), Bible believers can understand that mankind is made in the image of a logical and reasoning God who is the truth. Hence, Christians can make sense of things because in Christ are "hidden all the treasures of wisdom and knowledge" (Col. 2:3). Christians also have a basis to explain why people sometimes don't think logically, due to the Fall of mankind in Genesis 3. The most logical response then is to give up atheism and receive Jesus Christ as Lord and Savior to rescue you from sin and death (Rom. 10:13). Instead of death, God promises believers eternal life (1 John 2:25; John 10:28) and in 467 trillion years, you will *still* have value in contrast to the secular view of nothingness.

The day is coming when we all will give an account before God for our actions and thoughts (Rom. 14:12). Will you repent and receive Christ as your Lord and Savior today so that you will join Christ in the resurrection from the dead (John 11:25; Rom. 6:5)? I challenge you to become an *ex*-atheist, to join the ranks of the forgiven through Jesus Christ, and become a new creation (2 Cor. 5:17).

God is calling Christians at home and in the Church to raise up generations who know what they believe, know why they believe what they do, can defend the Christian faith, can answer skeptical questions, and can preach the salvation message with authority because they believe the authority (the Word of God) from which it comes. Such would change the world!

It's all about influence.

To change a generation, we must begin by training and changing individuals, families, churches, schools and communities. And that begins with *you*.

Chapter 5

The Great Disconnect

Focusing on the Next Generation

We've seen how the Church has already lost much of the 20s generation, and how slow erosion of confidence in both God and His Word typically begins in middle school. We lose them due to the secularized teaching of the public schools, the propaganda through media influence and subtle brainwashing, and through homes and churches that fail to equip and engage their young people in biblical apologetics.

Every generation has the same decision to make: Will I serve the God of the Bible or a false god?

The "god of this world" may shift his seductions slightly from generation to generation, but the basic challenge is always the same. So Christians must be ever vigilant. Every newborn must be taught the truth from scratch or else that soul could be completely lost. While statistics indicate that churches and Christian homes are failing to reach kids, God has given us all the resources we need to turn the tide!

How long does it take to lose a culture, from a Christian perspective?

Actually, it takes only one generation. The devil knows this, and of course God warns us about it. Adolf Hitler understood this when he said, "He alone, who owns the youth, gains the future!"[1]

Over and over again in Scripture, God instructs His people to make sure they train up the next generation.

For instance, when God miraculously enabled Joshua to lead the people through the Jordan River, the first thing He told Joshua to do was to take 12 stones from the riverbed to build a memorial. But what was the memorial for?

Joshua explained, "When your children ask their fathers in time to come, 'What do these stones mean?' then you shall let your children know. . . . the LORD your God dried up the waters of the Jordan for you until you passed over . . . that all the peoples of the earth may know that the hand of the LORD is mighty, that you may fear the LORD your God forever" (Josh. 4:21–24).

The stones were to remind the parents to make sure they taught the next generation about the true God. They were instructed to pass on the knowledge and fear of God to their children.

I think one of the saddest pages in the Bible is in Judges 2:10–12, "And all that generation also were gathered to their fathers. And there arose another generation after them who did not know the LORD or the work that he had done for Israel. And the people of Israel . . . abandoned the LORD, the God of their fathers, who had brought them out of the land of Egypt. They went after other gods, from among the gods of the peoples who were around them."

After Joshua and all the first generation of parents who entered the Promised Land died, the next generation served false gods! It took only one generation to lose the spiritual legacy that should have been passed on.

What happened? In Deuteronomy 6:6–7, God had given clear instructions to the fathers: "These words that I command you today shall be in your heart. You shall teach them diligently to your children, and shall talk of them when you sit in your house, and when you walk by the way, and when you lie down, and when you rise."

---

1. http://www.nizkor.org/hweb/imt/nca/nca-01/nca-01-07-means-46.html.

Obviously, the parents in Joshua's day did not teach their children as they should have — and in one generation, the devil had those kids! While it's ultimately a matter of God's grace that anyone is saved, God has given parents an immense responsibility to do their part. Over and over again, the Jewish fathers were told about their crucial role but they shirked it (see Ps. 78).

Sadly, this same situation already has occurred or is happening now in Western nations once influenced by Christianity. Many fathers today are not carrying out their God-given, God-commanded role to be the spiritual head of their house and to take the responsibility for training their children in spiritual matters.

This generational loss of the spiritual legacy that should be passed on to the coming generations can be seen in ARG's 2014 research on churchgoers. Let's just consider the 20s generation in our churches and what they believe. I trust this is eye-opening and shocking enough to cause parents and Christian leaders to diligently consider how they can address this situation.

Of those in the 20s group who attend church today,

1. 43% do not consider themselves born again

2. 22% believe there are other holy books (other than the Bible) inspired by God

3. Only 21% have read the Bible from cover to cover

4. 22% say the Bible is not true and historically accurate

5. 18% do not believe in the account of Sodom and Gomorrah and Lot's wife becoming a pillar of salt

6. 50% do not believe in a young earth

7. 23% believe God used evolution to change one kind of animal to another kind

8. 19% believe humans evolved from ape-like ancestors

9. 27% believe the Bible has errors

10. 30% believe people don't need to go to church

11. 65% believe if you are a good person you will go to heaven

12. 26% believe the Bible is just a collection of writings

13. Only 45% knew David wrote most of the Psalms

14. 21% didn't know who baptized Jesus

There were many other interesting statistics, but the above is meant to illustrate that there is considerable biblical illiteracy and compromise in the 20s generation in our churches.

Faith, Not Feelings

We live in a culture that teaches us to rely on *subjective experience* rather than *objective truth*. Our studies have shown that "millennials" (those identified as having been born anywhere between the early 1980s to the early 2000s) are not as interested in Christ or Christianity as the previous generation. Further, those who are in the Church have major biblical literacy issues. With the cultural surge of pluralism and an obsession with serving self, even many churches have slid into providing "worship-tainment" for its members instead of equipping them with the Word of God. Thus, there is a whole lot more of entertaining the goats than tending the sheep.

The result is that these millennials in the Church end up with only a thin veneer of biblical understanding (they are familiar with the "stories" in the Bible). However, some appear to be content with this level of knowledge. They cry, "What difference does it make? As long as millennials understand the gospel, who cares if they believe in a literal Adam and Eve or a six-day creation? God's not going to base entrance into heaven based on someone's view of Genesis creation."

True. I would wholeheartedly agree with that statement. Believing in a literal Genesis account is *not* a salvation issue. The Bible is crystal clear that "everyone who calls on the name of the Lord will be saved" (Rom. 10:13), and that "For by grace you have been saved through faith. And this is not your own doing; it is the gift of God, not a result of works, so that no one may boast" (Eph. 2:8–9). Therefore, there is no religious work, good deed, or additional belief attached to saving faith that God requires. It's faith alone. Grace alone. Christ alone.

Period.

However, having settled the issue of salvation, it does not logically follow that nothing else matters from that point on. As critical as they are to Christian doctrine, understanding the complexity of the Trinity or believing in the Second Coming is also not essential in order to be saved — but no respectable believer would deny their fundamental importance to Christian doctrine. Additionally, just because a person is saved doesn't give them the option of now believing whatever they choose about other biblical doctrines and theology which don't speak directly to the issue of salvation. It certainly doesn't give them the freedom to reinterpret a fundamental Christian belief or to suggest an abstract understanding about key passages in Scripture.

Growth Follows Birth

By saying that saving faith in Christ is not ALL that matters, we are saying that there are other important things God would also have us believe and do. Granted, they have nothing to do with salvation, but by definition, Christianity is more than just "becoming a Christian." To say otherwise would be equivalent to saying that being born is all that matters. Food, growth, development, and everything else that follows birth is now optional. What an absurd approach to life!

But this is effectively what some say when they downplay the importance of Scriptures that are fundamental to our understanding of God, His work, creation, the Fall, and the nature of man. It cuts at the very heart of God's ability to accurately reveal and record His own history! And the previously cited research certainly reveals that many in our churches have a problem when it comes to how they view the Word of God.

Of course, all genuine Christians would agree that *obedience to God* is the important thing, that how we live *after* receiving the gospel actually matters.

But let's examine this a bit further. Exactly why is our "Ticket to Heaven" not the only thing we should care about as believers?

First of all, God never says that.

Second, He is clear about many, many other very important truths He wants us to believe and embrace. Otherwise the Bible would contain just one verse about believing in Jesus instead of *66 books* of doctrine and truth!

Third, embedded in true, saving faith is the guarantee of spiritual fruit, particularly the fruit of ongoing faith, obedience, and growth (Matt. 7:15–20, 21–29; Rom. 1:17; Col. 1:20–23; James 2:14–26; Phil. 1:6).

Fourth, it's the *whole* of Scripture that gives us hope, perseverance, and encouragement *after* we come to faith in Christ (Rom. 15:4).

Fifth, ALL of the Bible is inspired and is meant to fuel our faith with nourishment (2 Tim. 3:16–17; 1 Pet. 2:2).

Sixth, God saves individuals so that they might fulfill a greater purpose here on earth. Part of that purpose involves "always being prepared to make a defense to anyone who asks you for a reason for the hope that is in you" (1 Pet. 3:15).

Seventh, there are many important Scriptures that support the truth about Christ and the gospel. To ignore, discount, or demean them is to undercut the foundation of the gospel message itself.

Eighth, you cannot deny one biblical truth without effectually denying many others. For example, you cannot deny the deity of Christ and then believe in Him as Savior. You cannot deny the Resurrection and then still believe in the Cross and its accomplishments. These truths are inseparably linked. Mutually *in*clusive, and bonded with the glue of God's unbroken revelation.

Of course, I know some people say that we should simply avoid controversy and conflict in the world and within certain Christian circles by only focusing on the gospel message itself, and like Paul, "decided to know nothing among you except Jesus Christ and him crucified" (1 Cor. 2:2).

But there are several fatal flaws in this oversimplification of Paul's words. First, no one denies that the gospel message of Christ is what leads sinners to salvation. However, not even Paul limited his evangelistic approach to "Jesus saves," but rather utilized the rest of the Word of God as foundational evidence for his apologetic regarding Jesus. In Acts 17:1–4, Paul reasoned with the Jews using the Old Testament Scriptures. By doing so, he built a solid apologetic case for Jesus being the

Messiah. It was the Apostle's "custom" to reason with both religious leaders and pagans, using the truth of God contained in the Old Testament Scripture (Acts 17:2). He also took the opportunity when encountering secular, pagan religious sites to demonstrate to unbelievers that God was *Creator*, Judge and Savior (Acts 17:16–34). He even quoted pagan poets to support his argument (Acts 17:28–29).[2] For Paul, establishing God as common Creator of all mankind was foundational to his argument and gospel presentation. Therefore, if God is not Creator, Jesus cannot be Savior. But you've probably never heard a preacher say that.

All Scripture Matters

This of course is not to say that every time we share the gospel we must survey the entire redemption story from Genesis to Revelation. It is, however, to say that the *whole of Scripture* is true and has *direct bearing* on the truth about Jesus Christ and what He accomplished on the Cross. Therefore, to focus only on the gospel as our sole beginning *and* ending point in evangelism is not only without support in Scripture, but also isn't smart missionary work. And make no mistake about it — we are *all* missionaries to the pagan culture in which we live.

So in short, yes, it really does matter what you believe *after* you become a Christian. Theology matters. Sound doctrine matters. All biblical truth — from Genesis 1:1 to Revelation 22:21 is inseparably linked, connected from truth to truth. You can't merely cut out a particular portion of Scripture or deny 4,000 years of belief and interpretation and then replace it with a pagan understanding of that portion of Scripture. We don't have that option with God's Word. Otherwise we become judges of the Word, exalting ourselves above it. And by doing this, we are consumed with arrogance, and fall into the same condemnation incurred by the devil (1 Tim. 3:6).

When reading David's masterpiece of Psalm 119, we encounter 176 stanzas, of which all but 3 expound upon the value, reliability, and personal benefit of God's Word. It's as if David can't stop himself from highlighting the importance and benefits of Scripture. This becomes

---

2. Here Paul quotes Epimenides, a Cretan poet from 600 B.C. and Aretas, a poet from Paul's home region of Cicilia (300 B.C.). As Paul spoke without notes, it is impressive that he had such a recall of secular literature and keen understanding of culture.

even more amazing when you consider that David's "Bible" was basically limited to the first five books of Moses (Genesis through Deuteronomy)!

Being of infinite intelligence, God is totally logical and rational — much more so than man. And throughout Scripture, He clearly indicates when accounts are meant to be understood as illustrations, parables, or metaphors, such as those found in Luke 15:1–32 and John 10:1–7.

Consequently, there is nothing in all of Scripture that gives the slightest hint of the creation or Flood accounts found in Genesis as being anything other than literal, actual, and historical events.

You might be thinking, "I see what you're saying, but practically speaking, what real difference does it make in my daily life whether or not I take those accounts literally? As long as I follow Jesus and obey the truth of His Word, is it really *that* big of a deal?"

That's a good question. So let's answer it by considering the belief in a literal Adam and Eve as an example of how God's "chain of truth" is linked. This exercise will help you connect the dots and see the "domino effect" that truths in Scripture have on one another. Suppose someone claims Adam and Eve were fictional characters created by Moses to illustrate certain truths about God as Creator and mankind as being sinners. Their story, they claim, didn't actually happen as the Bible describes, but rather is more of a parable pointing us to our need for a Savior. So the bottom line is that we see our need for God and come to faith in Christ. How can you say that's a bad thing? As long as the applicable truth is understood, what difference does it make whether Adam was literal or figurative?

To begin with, if God didn't create Adam as a specific individual, then this suggests a massive reinterpretation concerning the origin of man, one that for some Christians lends itself to (theistic) evolution. In that case, at what point in the evolutionary development of man did God impart His image *(imago dei)* into His human creation? Was it when he was still a primate or was there some definitive point over the millions of years evolution requires that God decided one day He was "finished" with man's ascent to full human status? At what point then did sin enter the picture? When, in this evolutionary scenario, did "Adam" become morally responsible for his actions?

Six Days and Salvation

Because Answers in Genesis and other biblical creationists take an authoritative stand on six literal (approximately 24-hour) days of creation and a young (approximately 6,000-year-old) age for the earth and universe, some have mistakenly taken our unwavering stand to mean these beliefs are salvation issues. However, nowhere does the Bible even imply salvation in Christ is conditional upon one's belief concerning the days of creation or the age of the earth or universe.

For instance, Romans 10:9 states, "If you confess with your mouth that Jesus is Lord and believe in your heart that God raised Him from the dead, you will be saved." It does not state, "If you confess with your mouth the Lord Jesus and believe in your heart that God has raised Him from the dead, and believe in six literal days of creation and a young earth and universe, you will be saved."

Salvation is conditional upon faith in Christ — not belief about the six days of creation or the earth's age. So these are not salvation issues per se. But it is a salvation issue in an indirect sense. Let me explain.

Many Christians, including Christian leaders, believe fossils, the earth, and the universe are millions or billions of years old. I contend that when they accept this timeframe and try to fit millions of years into the Bible, they are violating *three* vital issues.

1. You cannot get the idea of millions of years from the Bible. This idea comes from *outside* of Scripture. When a Christian adds millions of years to the Bible and reinterprets the days of creation or tries to fit this extra time into the first verse in Genesis or a supposed gap between the first and second verses, he is allowing fallible man to be in authority over God's Word. I assert that such compromise (which I believe it really is) is setting an example for others that fallible man can take ideas outside of Scripture and reinterpret God's Word to fit these in.

Ultimately, accepting this view means God's Word is not the final authority and is not without error. It also opens the door to others doing this with other historical claims of Scripture — such as the Resurrection and virgin birth. So it's an authority issue.

But it's also a gospel issue. First, Genesis 1:29–30 teaches that man and animals were originally vegetarian (before Adam's sin). How do we know this for sure? Humans weren't told they could eat meat until after the Flood in Genesis 9:3. This later verse makes it clear that mankind was originally vegetarian, but this changed after the Flood. Verse 30 of Genesis 1 (about animals' diet) is worded in the same way as verse 29 (man's diet), so it makes sense that originally the animals were vegetarian, too.

2. At the end of the creation week, God described everything He had made as "very good" (Gen. 1:31).

3. Genesis 3 makes it clear that the animals (v. 14) and the ground (v. 17) were cursed. And verse 18 makes it clear that thorns came into existence *after* sin and the Curse: ". . . thorns and thistles [the ground] shall bring forth for you."

Now the idea that things have been around for millions of years came from the belief that the fossil record was laid down slowly over millions of years, long before man's existence. So again, when Christians accept millions of years, they must also accept that the fossil layers were laid down before Adam — before the first human sin. Yet the fossil record contains fossil thorns — claimed by evolutionists to be hundreds of millions of years old. How could that be if thorns came after Adam's sin? The fossil record also contains lots of examples of animals that ate other animals — bones in their stomachs, teeth marks on bones, and so on. But according to the Bible, animals were vegetarian before sin.

Also, the fossil record contains examples of diseases, such as brain tumors, cancer, and arthritis. But if these existed before man, then God called such diseases "very good."

Taking all this into consideration, it seems obvious that bloodshed, death of animals and man, disease, suffering, and thorns came *after* sin. So the fossil record had to be laid down after sin as well. Noah's Flood would easily account for most fossils.

But what does this have to do with a gospel issue? The Bible calls death an "enemy" (1 Cor. 15:26). When God clothed Adam and Eve with coats of skins (Gen. 3:21), a good case can be made that this was the first death — the death and bloodshed of an animal. Elsewhere in Scripture we learn that without the shedding of blood there is no remission of sins (Heb. 9:22), and the life of the flesh is in the blood (Lev.

17:11). Because Adam sinned, a payment for sin was needed. Because sin's penalty was death, then death and bloodshed were needed to atone for sin. So Genesis 3:21 would describe the first blood sacrifice as a penalty for sin — looking forward to the one who would die "once for all" (Heb. 10:10–14).

The Israelites sacrificed animals over and over again, as a ceremonial covering for sin. But Hebrews 10:4 tells us that the blood of bulls and goats can't take away our sin — we are not physically related to animals or ascended from them. We needed a perfect human sacrifice. So all this animal sacrifice was looking forward to the one called the Messiah (Jesus Christ).

Now if there was death and bloodshed of animals before sin, then this undermines the atonement. Also, if there were death, disease, bloodshed, and suffering before sin, then such would be God's fault — not our fault! Why would God require death as a sacrifice for sin if He were the one responsible for death and bloodshed, having created the world with these bad things in place?

One of today's most-asked questions is how Christians can believe in a loving God with so much death and suffering in the world. In fact, in the 2014 ARG research on the Church, nearly 20 percent of the 20s generation said their faith had been challenged by someone asking why bad things happen. The correct answer is that God's just Curse because of Adam's sin resulted in this death and suffering. We are to blame. God is not an unloving or incompetent Creator of a "very bad" world. He had a loving plan from eternity to rescue people from sin and its consequence of eternal separation from God in hell.

So to believe in millions of years is a gospel issue. This belief ultimately impugns the character of the Creator and Savior and undermines the foundation of the soul-saving gospel. It's an authority issue — is God's Word the ultimate authority on all matters of life and practice?

So, if evolution were true, then this evidence of sin (disease and death) entering the world occurred *before* the first homo sapien (man) appeared. This notion is a clear contradiction of the entire biblical narrative regarding creation, mankind, and sin. In reality, man (Adam) first sinned, *then* disease and death appeared, not before. Therefore, to claim to be a Christian and believe in evolution is to, in the strictest sense of the word, be *ignorant* of the Bible as well as the logical and theological flow of truth recorded in it.

A Real Adam and a Real Jesus

Another problem with interpreting Adam as figurative is that all those who subsequently understood Moses' written account of Adam as a literal, created man would then be mistaken, including: the Jewish people, the author of Chronicles (1:1), Job (31:33), Dr. Luke, who traces Jesus human genealogy back to Adam (Luke 3:38), Jesus Himself[3] (Matt. 19:4) Paul (Rom. 5:14; 1 Cor. 15:22, 45; 1 Tim. 2:13–14) and Jude (1:14). All these held a literal interpretation of the first man, Adam. In fact, Paul goes so far as to make a direct parallel between Jesus' historicity, deeds, and impact on humanity with Adam's. In Romans, he writes,

> Therefore, just as sin came into the world through *one man*, and death through sin, and so death spread to all men because all sinned — for sin indeed was in the world before the law was given, but sin is not counted where there is no law. Yet death reigned from *Adam* to Moses, even over those whose sinning was not like the transgression of *Adam, who was a type of the one who was to come.*
>
> But the free gift is not like the trespass. For if many died through one man's trespass, much more have the grace of God and the free gift by the grace of that one man Jesus Christ abounded for many. And the free gift is not like the result of that one man's sin. For the judgment following one trespass brought condemnation, but the free gift following many trespasses brought justification. For if, because of one man's trespass, death reigned through that one man, much more will those who receive the abundance of grace and the free gift of righteousness reign in life through the one man Jesus Christ.
>
> Therefore, as one trespass led to condemnation for all men, so one act of righteousness leads to justification and life for all men. For as by the one man's disobedience the many were made

---

3. But we must also understand that because Jesus is the Word, then every Word in Scripture is the Word of Jesus.

sinners, so by the one man's obedience the many will be made righteous. Now the law came in to increase the trespass, but where sin increased, grace abounded all the more, so that, as sin reigned in death, grace also might reign through righteousness leading to eternal life through Jesus Christ our Lord (Rom. 5:12–21, emphasis added).

Here Paul compares and contrasts Jesus' historicity and gift of salvation to mankind to the historicity and sin of Adam. It's a direct, intentional, one-to-one association. In an effort to argue for the gospel's essence and power, Paul links the factual reality of Adam's existence and deeds compared to those of Jesus. If the one (Adam) didn't actually do what he did (sin), then the other (Jesus) didn't do what He did (bring salvation). He does this again in 1 Corinthians 15:45. You cannot have a savior without an original sinner. Take away God's example of original sin and His argument for the efficacy of Jesus' sacrificial death is made void.

Moses was pretty confident when it came to the facts about Adam. He knew so much about this man Adam that he even tells us how old he was when he died! (Gen. 5:5). If evolution were true and the Genesis account were symbolism or allegory, it would have also taken God millions of years to create Eve from Adam's rib!

The bottom line is that all of Scripture is in agreement that Adam was a literal, historical man, formed in a single act of creation, not the result of millions of transitionary, human-like species. So can you see how removing just one literal truth from a few thousand years ago affects the rest of the Bible, theology, and eternal salvation?

So if the Bible cannot be trusted historically, then it is flawed and cannot be trusted in areas of greater significance, such as heaven, hell, marriage, sexual identity, family, etc. If Moses got it wrong (along with Jesus, Paul, and others), then how can we say, "*All* Scripture is inspired?" More importantly, how can we say Jesus is God if He didn't even know the difference between history and mere *story*? But in fact, He *does* know the difference, as He consistently used illustrations and parables to teach the multitudes. But at no time did He ever come close to mistaking one for the other. He also accepted the Old Testament as a literal and reliable account.

By contrast, the interpretative methods used in Genesis by many Christians who believe in millions of years are not interpretative decisions that most biblical scholars would apply to any other place in Scripture! So why do they pick on Genesis? Well, because these Christians tell us that "science" (practiced by fallible scientists) has shown us that we need to believe in millions of years, and thus we must fit these long ages into the Bible — even though they do not fit!

A religion professor once accused me (and by association all Christians who take God at His Word) of weaving a "web of lies" concerning the Genesis account. Of course, the saddest part of that accusation is that he ultimately is calling God a liar. But the Scripture itself states, "God is not man, that he should lie" (Num. 23:19).

100% True from the Beginning

Genesis is clear. The account of biblical creation we hold to comes straight out of God's Word, so to claim that it's a lie is to accuse God of being a liar. And if God lied in Genesis, then where did He stop lying? And what does that say about our Holy God's character?

I remember a young lady once telling me that her pastor was preaching from Genesis and telling the congregation that what was stated was just a myth used to explain religious truth. This pastor insisted people had to believe evolution and millions of years and thus couldn't take the account in Genesis literally. This lady was a young Christian, so she went to the pastor and asked, "So when does God start telling the truth in His Word?"

Good question — and God's Word has the answer:

> Thy word is true from the *beginning* (Ps. 119:160; KJV, emphasis added).

Some have claimed that biblical creation is simply my "own dubious understanding of Christianity," but it just so happens that biblical creation has been by far the dominant view of creation for most of Christian history as well as for the Jews *before* Christ. It is those compromising positions like theistic evolution, the gap theory, the day-age theory, the framework hypothesis, or progressive creation (or the many others that pervade the modern Church) that are newcomers to the scene. Those views developed only after geologists abandoned Scripture and began assigning old dates to the rock layers! The reason most scholars and people of the past two hundred years believe those compromising positions has nothing to do with what the Bible says in Genesis. Rather, it's because they've been influenced by secular beliefs about man's past — particularly the belief in millions of years. Beliefs that were birthed and nourished due to a calculated rejection of God's Word!

Now, it is true that some people who have been taught to trust the Bible from the very first verse still abandon Christianity. Satan continues to be very clever at drawing people away from God. Remember, having faith is not simply a matter of being exposed to enough evidence. Even some of those who saw Jesus raise the dead didn't believe (Luke 16:31)! People walk away from the faith for many different reasons, and they are not always intellectual ones. That being said, studies we've done in partnership with America's Research Group show that the vast majority of young people are walking away from the faith because they *doubt God's Word*. So while having good, solid answers does not always guarantee faith, it certainly does help, and we receive hundreds of testimonies from people who have been strengthened in their faith or brought back to the faith because of our ministry.

This is why we published the book *Already Gone* in 2009. If you haven't read this, I encourage you to do so and find out what real scientific research has found in regard to young people leaving the Church.

Others, in an attempt to discredit the belief in biblical creation, have referred to it as an "idol." But idolatry is placing something or someone above God Himself. Simply believing what God's Word says and defending it can hardly be considered idolatry. On the contrary, it is honoring God even more when you take Him at His Word and respect it. And those who do so are only upholding and proclaiming God's Word as Christians have done for centuries. The Word of God is "living and powerful" and certainly an impenetrable rampart because it is "flawless" (Prov. 30:5; NIV) "truth" (John 17:17) that "endures forever" (Isa. 40:8) and will "never pass away" (Luke 21:33).

So can you see how God's Word is bound together by its own character? To contain an error, particularly one that relates to creation, sin, Christ, and salvation would cast a dark shadow of doubt over the entire Bible, and rightfully so. When Paul says "all Scripture" (Greek: *pasa graphe* or "every individual portion of Scripture") is "inspired by God" (2 Tim. 3:16; NLT), he means exactly what he says. Jesus affirmed this belief in the totality of God's written revelation when He said (referring to the "Law and the Prophets," i.e., Moses' first five books and the rest of the Old Testament),

> For truly, I say to you, until heaven and earth pass away, not an *iota*, not a *dot*, will pass from the Law until all is accomplished" (Matt. 5:18, emphasis added).

Christ was so specific that He goes beyond merely affirming the accuracy of the Bible's general themes, historical accounts, or its individual truths. No, He goes even further by saying that God's commitment to the integrity and reliability of His Word goes all the way down to the very letters (iota) and punctuation (dot) of Scripture!

Therefore, all of God's truth in Scripture fits and works together, seamlessly and without flaw. What we are facing today, however, is a generation that cannot link theological "cause and effect" together. Instead, they approach God's Word "buffet style," picking and choosing what truths and beliefs are most attractive to them, while rejecting those truths that are less likely to be mocked in the marketplace. And this will continue as long as they remain untrained and unequipped in biblical truth and apologetics.

A low view of Scripture also has a "domino effect," leading not only to biblical illiteracy, but also to theological bankruptcy, doctrinal error, and spiritual anemia. This trend in the Church must be reversed. And it *can* be. But in order to do so, we must help this generation begin taking ownership of their faith (more about that in the next chapter).

As a final section for this chapter, and to ensure that people do not misunderstand what is being said, let me specifically deal with our stand on a young earth in relation to the topic of biblical authority.

Many Christians believe in millions of years and are truly born again. Their belief in millions of years doesn't affect their salvation. But what does it do? It affects how other people, such as their children or others they teach, view Scripture. Their example can be a stumbling block to others. For instance, telling young people they can reinterpret Genesis to fit in millions of years sets a deadly example: they can start outside Scripture and add ideas into Scripture.

Ultimately, this approach eventually suggests that the Bible is not God's infallible Word. This creates doubt concerning God's Word — and doubt often leads to unbelief. Eventually, they may reject Scripture altogether. And since the gospel comes from a book they don't trust or believe is true, there's nothing to prevent them from rejecting the gospel itself.

So the age of the earth and universe is not a salvation issue per se — somebody can be saved even without believing what the Bible says on this issue. But it is a salvation issue indirectly in that all Scripture is inseparably linked, particularly regarding core doctrine. Pull out one of these foundational stones and the entire structure of Scripture is affected.

Today, there is a crying need to teach the coming generations to stand uncompromisingly, boldly, and unashamedly on the whole Word of God, beginning in Genesis.

Chapter 6

Owning Up — Embracing a Faith of Your Own

The Ultimate Handoff

In any relay race, the passing of the baton is critical. The transfer of that nearly weightless hollow metal tube determines who goes home with gold, and who simply *goes home*. Runners do not show up the day of the race and simply "wing it." Instead, there are countless hours spent on the track practicing their exchange, with the eventual race itself becoming the result of hundreds of similar previous transfers.

If the one possessing the baton performs his/her job effectively, the baton is passed and the race goes on. Of course, the one receiving the baton also has a responsibility. Unless he is open to accepting it, and grips it firmly, the baton may be dropped and the race lost.

I believe the Christian faith is very much like a relay race. One generation carries the responsibility to pass on the faith to the next. When that generation dies, the generation that remains becomes responsible to carry on the gospel to their world, and to faithfully place it in the hands and hearts of their physical and spiritual children. Since A.D. 33, the baton of faith has been passed — and sometimes dropped. And to the degree that those who pass on the faith and those who receive it do their job, Christianity will continue. But as we have seen from the new research ARG conducted, the Church is currently failing at this critical task in many areas in the West.

In England, two-thirds of young people now say they don't believe in God — in a culture where most people once went to church.

In America, about two-thirds of young people will leave the Church once they live on their own. As I have stated before, Answers in Genesis commissioned America's Research Group to find out why this is happening and published the results in the book *Already Gone* in 2009. It revealed that these kids began doubting and disbelieving the Bible at a very young age.

We also established that around 90 percent of those who leave Church attended public schools, where, by and large, God, creation, the Bible, and prayer (in other words, Christianity) were thrown out long ago. Atheistic evolution, however, is taught as fact. The vast majority of these students represented in our research were not taught apologetics (how to give a reasoned defense of the Christian faith) in their homes or churches, so they don't believe it themselves and certainly can't defend it to others.

The public schools have been teaching their own brand of apologetics: how to defend the idea of evolution and history over millions of years, thus causing multitudes of U.S. students from Christian homes to doubt the history in Genesis. Doubts about Genesis place young people on a slippery slide of unbelief that eventually destroys their confidence in the rest of Scripture. Their trust in the soul-saving gospel itself, which is grounded on the Bible's historical claims, is also undermined.

Even when parents pull their kids out of public school, the anti-God message is so prevalent in the media, museums, and colleges — and even among friends, neighbors, and workmates — that young people are woefully unprepared to understand and defend their beliefs. Let's face it. We live in a pagan, post-Christian society, not a Christian nation. We should therefore not be surprised when most people and institutions are godless, anti-Christian, and anti-Bible. But tragically, even many leaders in Christian education have compromised with evolution and earth history over millions of years. Many groups are now even producing homeschool curricula that promote evolution and millions of years!

The Secularization of America

Joseph Stalin certainly knew the power of education as a propaganda tool. In just one generation, he converted hordes of the deeply religious Russian people into followers of atheistic Marxism. He said, "Education is a weapon, the effect of which is determined by the hands which wield it."[1]

Sadly, most of the people who control the West's publishing and video industries today reject the God of the Bible, and they are winning over the next generation, indoctrinating them in evolutionary humanism. Day after day, our children are bombarded with their message.

The consequences in America were again confirmed in October 2012, when the Pew Forum on Religion and Public Life released new survey results. The CNN website reported, "The fastest growing 'religious' group in America is made up of people with no religion at all, according to a Pew survey showing that one in five Americans is not affiliated with any religion. . . . The survey found that the ranks of the unaffiliated are growing even faster among younger Americans. Thirty-three million Americans now have no religious affiliation, with 13 million in that group identifying as either atheist or agnostic, according to the new survey."[2]

For years, I have been warning churchgoers about this danger in my presentations. Despite the fact America has many megachurches and more Christian resources than any other country in history, as a culture we are becoming more secular every day. America is heading down the same path as Europe and England.

The CNN item reported that atheist and secular leaders were elated by the Pew poll. Jesse Galef, communications director for the Secular Student Alliance, expected the growth to translate into greater political

---

1. Amy R. Caldwell, John Beeler, Charles Clark, *Sources of Western Society Since 1300,* "Joseph Stalin: An Interview with H.G. Wells" (Boston, MA: Bedford/St. Martin's, 2011), p. 516.
2. Dan Merica, CNN, "Survey: One in Five Americans Has No Religion," October 9, 2012, http://religion.blogs.cnn.com/2012/10/09/survey-one-in-five-americans-is-religiously-unaffiliated/.

power for secular interests: "As more of the voters are unaffiliated and identifying as atheist and agnostics, I think the politicians will follow that for votes. We won't be dismissed or ignored anymore."[3]

Just before the poll was released, Bill Nye the "Science Guy" (from a popular 1990s TV program) expressed the agenda of today's elite in public education and the media. In a video entitled *Creationism Is Not Appropriate for Children*, Nye basically says if children aren't taught evolution as fact, America will lose its edge in science, and no longer have engineers and other innovators. Bill Nye, incidentally, was voted humanist of the year in 2010. His words reflect the growing, deliberate agenda of the media elite to capture the next generation for the secular humanists.

In an article by a staffer from the National Center for Science Education (an organization begun in 1983 for the explicit purpose of attacking the influence of biblical creationism and now headed by ardent evolutionist Brian Alters), it is very clear that the atheists today are out to indoctrinate our kids.

The last paragraph of the article reads, "What we can do is work toward the day when American school children are taught evolution in the same way as any other well-established scientific idea, without caveats or apologies. With evolution at the center of biology, and thus important to the success of medicine, biotechnology, and agriculture, we can't afford to keep it bottled up or to kick the can."[4]

Plainly stated, atheists don't want Christians teaching kids about God — they want to teach your kids there is no God! They really are out to get your kids, and they are using the public schools, secular media, museums, and other outlets to do this. The public schools (despite a minority of Christian teachers who are trying to be missionaries in the system) have mostly become churches of secular humanism.

Yes, the atheists, like Hitler and Stalin, know that if they can capture the next generation (through the education system, media, etc.), they will have the culture.

---

3. Ibid.
4. Steven Newton, "Creationism, Mr. Nye, and Dr. Pepper," Huffington Post Blog, http://www.huffingtonpost.com/steven-newton/creationism-mr-nye-and-dr-pepper_b_1934407.html.

Beyond Bible Facts

Christians need to take heed of God's Word and ensure they are capturing the next generation for the Lord — passing that spiritual legacy along to the children, so they will not be captured by the world!

Yes, it takes only one generation to lose a culture, and America is on the brink of such a change right now! God's people need to wake up and understand a battle for their kids is raging around them — a battle that is being won, at the present time, by those who seek to destroy the next generation spiritually.

In view of such relentless indoctrination that bombards our young people every day, giving a couple of 30-minute lessons at church or home isn't enough. While many parents have already opted to put their kids in Christian schools, weekly church programs, and homeschools, few appear to be doing a very good job filling in the gaps. More is needed.

Teaching young people how God's Word — rather than the atheistic worldview — makes sense of our world requires intense study, commitment, and fervent prayer. The Church and parents must reevaluate their old assumptions about the way we should be teaching our kids in a hostile culture, and work together to build the next generation by following the directives from God's Word.

Our research published in 2009 demonstrated that the majority of our churched kids drop out of church by college age. Sadly, many never return — although the research also showed great potential for many to do so.[5] And though we've already shown several reasons for this falling away, one stands out pretty clear. So why do they lose the grip on the baton?

One of the key reasons why kids don't embrace their parent's/church's faith in adulthood is because they never learned how to "own" their own faith. They never asked tough questions about their faith in a safe environment. Perhaps they were raised in a church or home where questions and doubts were discouraged. Whatever the case, they never worked through some of these difficult issues while they were young; therefore never being challenged with *what* they believe or *why* they believe it.

---

5. Ken Ham and Britt Beemer, *Already Gone* (Green Forest, AR: Master Books, 2009).

The ARG research on the 20s and 40s groups that class themselves as churchgoers, showed that when asked, "Has anyone ever challenged you and your Christian faith?" only 23 percent said yes. When those who were challenged were asked, "At what time in your life were you challenged?" the answers were middle school 13 percent, high school 24 percent, college 24 percent, after college 40 percent.

When a believer's faith is challenged by the world, friends, the classroom, or even self-doubt, we must pause to address those answers from Scripture. This is how ownership of one's faith is made strong. Before we can give an answer to others concerning our faith, we must first develop a *personal apologetic*. After being born again and growing spiritually, the next season of your spiritual life is to embrace personal responsibility for your own faith. Doing this births confidence and breeds courage in the heart of those who follow Jesus Christ in a world filled with skeptics and scoffers.

Here are some questions to ask regarding the next generation in our homes and churches:

- Do they really know what they believe? Do they understand the basic doctrines of the Christian faith?

- How do we prevent them from simply "parroting" back what they've heard others say, like parents or youth leaders?

- How can we create an environment of honesty and transparency so that they don't merely accept God's truth as a way to please (or appease) parents and other adults?

- What are the questions they are going to be confronted with so we can make sure they are equipped with answers?

For instance, the ARG research on churchgoers dealt with what those who were challenged about their Christian faith had to say. Without giving any suggestions, the people surveyed provided the topics that were brought up. Here are the results in order beginning with the biggest: 24 percent age of the earth; 18 percent why only Christians go to heaven; 16 percent why bad things happen to people; 15 percent how one can believe the Bible.

Sadly, many church leaders (see the research from the book *Already Compromised*[6]) will tell Christians they can believe in millions of years — and yet this is one of the main issues used to challenge people's Christian faith. And, as discussed in the previous chapter, this is an issue that undermines Bible authority and the gospel.

We would all agree that our kids have a crucial need to take ownership of their faith, for unless they do, they will likely cast off their Christian beliefs like an old sweater as soon as they are no longer relevant or perceived as necessary, or when they can't answer questions that undermine the Christian message. Like a rocket booster that has burned out its fuel, our kid's Christianity may also burn out as soon as they hit the city limits. They may put on a Christian facade when they're home, but in reality their faith is practically useless.

The Journey from Doubt to Confidence

Picture in your mind a bridge. This metaphorical bridge represents the passageway from ignorance and doubt to confidence and taking ownership of your faith. It pictures your journey of embracing and maturing in a personal faith in God. This bridge spans a deep chasm, a huge abyss, below which are the jagged rocks and roaring rapids of spiritual disaster. Many young Christians never make it all the way across this bridge. Some tumble over the side when the strong winds of doubt and hard times blow against them. Their beliefs fall with them and are crushed to bits on the rocks below. Others grow afraid as they cross this bridge, becoming paralyzed at the prospect of going forward by faith. They freeze as they look down, dwelling on their doubts. Meanwhile, others pass them by. Still more turn back for fear they will stand alone in the world upon their arrival on the other side. The time comes in every Christian's journey of faith when he/she must journey across this "bridge."

Crossing this bridge means gaining a firm grasp of Scripture. It means understanding how the Bible's truths are tightly woven together, inseparably linked with one another. Walking across this bridge means embracing Jesus Christ and what He has done for you. It means learning to process and apply the truths of Scripture to everyday life and to be

---

6. Ken Ham and Greg Hall, *Already Compromised* (Green Forest, AR: Master Books, 2011).

able to "give an answer" that you can "contend for the faith that was once for all delivered to the saints" (Jude 1:3). It signifies that you stand for all that Christ stands for. It means forming a personal apologetic based on Scripture.

The word *apologetic* comes from the Greek word *apologia*. It is usually translated "answer" or "defense" in 1 Peter 3:15: "But sanctify Christ as Lord in your hearts, always being ready to make a defense to everyone who asks you to give an account for the hope that is in you, yet with gentleness and reverence" (NASB).

If Christianity is true, and the Bible is the infallible, inspired Word of God, Christians should be able to defend their faith when asked skeptical questions. This doesn't mean that we automatically know all the answers — but from a big-picture perspective, we should be able to give a reasoned argument to counter attacks on the Christian faith. Unfortunately, most Christians have not been taught practical, basic apologetics (and from our research, they don't even recognize they haven't been taught). Consequently, they don't know how to adequately defend the Christian faith when it is challenged. This new research on churchgoers illustrates that many in our churches really have problems with the very basics of Christianity. For example, our research yielded the following results:

- 39% say they attend church but are not born again.

- 95% say that all the books of the bible are inspired, but 22% believe there are other holy books inspired by God — and 21% say the Bible is not true and historically accurate! So what do many of these people mean when they say the Bible is "inspired." I suggest many have never been taught what "inspired" means, therefore they don't understand it.

Now here is a very telling statistic:

- 45% say no one ever taught them to defend the Christian faith! No wonder we have problems with the coming generations! In the book *Already Gone* we emphasized, based on research (and on what happened to those who attended Sunday school) that most churches and Christian homes are not teaching apologetics.

Now, crossing the bridge of ownership I mentioned earlier also requires much time, and though you reach certain milestones of growth and understanding along the way, it actually involves a *lifetime* of discovery, dedication, and faith. There is no time or room to stand still on this bridge. Every believer must decide whether or not he or she will move on toward the other side. Behind you, back on the mountainside, are those who are merely "renting" someone else's faith and beliefs (their parent's, youth leader's, pastor's). They are either too afraid or too preoccupied with other things to take a step of faith onto this bridge. From where they stand, they're still not sure this bridge will hold their full weight. These people will never move forward in their faith. Their fear, unbelief, and unwillingness to walk with God disqualifies them from truly possessing a faith of their own.

But others have crossed this bridge before. They have proven its worth, strength, and reliability. Ahead, on the other side, are those who have owned their own faith. They have assumed the responsibility of examining the Scripture and interacting with their God. They have tested the faith and tasted the goodness of the Lord, and He has not let them down (Ps. 34:8; Rom. 1:16–17, 10:11). Since the book *Already Gone* was published, I have heard numerous testimonies of how parents and churches had begun teaching apologetics to equip people to defend the Christian faith. Thousands of churches decided to use the Answers in Genesis evangelistic Bible Curriculum (Answers Bible Curriculum: A for Apologetics; B for Biblical authority; C for Chronological), and the Answers in Genesis VBS programs (that have an emphasis on biblical authority and apologetics and are very evangelistic). The feedback has been exciting — so many saying this has revolutionized the younger generations and even made the older generations realize what has been missing from much of the Church in recent times.

So which way are you heading today? Which way are your children headed? What about the young people in your church?

A Faith That Doesn't Fizzle

Every Christian receives his or her faith from someone else. As we've seen, like a baton in a relay race, faith is handed over from one person to another. It's the passing on of a spiritual legacy. Thinking back over your life, who has helped pass the faith on to you? What attitudes/ perspectives did you learn or catch from them? I praise the Lord for Christian parents who passed a wonderful spiritual legacy on to me. They taught me not only to stand boldly and unashamedly on God's Word, but also how to answer skeptical questions and to never knowingly compromise God's Word! How I pray that this would be so for every parent as they train their children. As I've said so many times, the ministries of Answers in Genesis, the Creation Museum, and the Ark Encounter involve a legacy of parents who passed on a spiritual legacy to their children.

So how do we do our best to pass on a faith that won't fizzle over time? First, we must give them *reasons* to believe. That's the meaning implicit in Peter's admonition to "give an answer" and is the very essence of apologetics. Having reasons behind their beliefs puts "steel" in their faith. And perhaps at no other time in history has such strength been needed. In an age of pluralism, atheism, and skepticism, a "Sunday school" faith built on stories alone won't cut it out there in the real world. Instead, our children's faith will be easily and quickly devoured by worldly philosophy, demonic deception, and unbelief. And from the ARG research, it's very obvious there needs to be teaching in apologetics in two main areas:

1. General Bible apologetics (how do we know the Bible is true; what does it mean that it's inspired; how do we know Jesus is God, etc.)

2. Creation apologetics (one of the challenges most often posed to Christians is the attack on biblical authority, beginning in Genesis, e.g., how did Noah fit the animals on the ark; doesn't carbon dating disprove the Bible; where did Cain get his wife; how could all the people today come from Adam and Eve; what about evolution, dinosaurs, the age of the earth, the big bang, etc.)

So what's involved in taking ownership? Here are some practical suggestions on how to foster personal ownership of faith for the next generation:

- Help them discover the foundations of their faith and why they believe, not only through teaching, but also through personal interaction and small group discussion.

- Never avoid the hard questions. God is not threatened by our confusion or questions. He can handle them. And His Word can give us direction and insight when faced with mystery and apparent contradictions in Scripture.

- Never judge a young person for asking what may be considered a "taboo" question in some Christian circles, such as, "How do we know the Bible is really God's Word?" or "Why is Jesus so different from the angry God of the Old Testament?" or "If God is so real, why don't more people believe in Him?" or "Why are we the only ones who believe in a literal account of Genesis? Why does it seem like its 'us against the world'?"

  It is critical that young people feel free to voice their thoughts, doubts, and struggles without fear of ridicule or condemnation. Unless this generation is allowed to do this, they will likely either become hardened and bitter, walk away from the faith, or politely suppress negative feelings and thoughts about God in order to appear compliant and obedient.

- Let *them* come up with the reasons why God, the Bible, and the Christian life seem so hard to understand at times. Young people are in touch with where their generation is. They aren't concerned with reaching adults, but are living in the "now" with their own age group. By addressing the questions their generation is asking, we help them face contemporary apologetic difficulties head on.

- Challenge their answers. Ask "Why?" and "What do you mean by that?" Force them to think through what they're saying/ believing as well as why.

- Don't be afraid to create a little tension. Play the role of "devil's advocate." Don't provide all the answers. Don't hesitate to end your discussions with unanswered questions.

- Pick the top ten issues your kids are facing in their world and use them as a way to help them understand what they believe (evolution, sex, abortion, moral relativism, sexual identity, etc.).

- It's our job to create an environment where hard questions and doubting are encouraged.

- Praise them for their honesty, insights, and thoughtful questions.

- Give them individual assignments in which to study and research on their own regarding some of the hard questions you discuss.

- Provide resources (books, articles, websites, videos) for them to use. This is why we do what we do at AiG. We are here to serve you! We are a resourcing ministry raised up to help provide answers to the challenging questions of our day.

As I mentioned before, many churched young people today are simply carrying around someone else's faith — their parent's, or their church's, or their friend's. They're "borrowing" Christianity for a while, perhaps because it meets a particular social or emotional need in their life at the moment, though they may not even realize it. It's like borrowing money or clothes from a friend, only to give it back when you're done with it or when it no longer serves its purpose anymore. They're "renters" and not yet full-fledged "owners." Maybe you've known someone who at one time was very committed to God while in junior or senior high only to jettison their faith and fall away later in high school or college! It is very likely that they never had a "faith of their own" to begin with. They may have been at church because their friends were there or came because their mom and dad brought them. But when their friends changed or when mom and dad were no longer around, their faith was cast aside. And this reveals the fact that they had never really owned that faith in the first place. It *could* indicate that they have never truly come into a saving relationship with Jesus. Only God really knows.

So how can someone know if they have come to "own their faith"? How can a person know the difference between "renting" someone else's faith and having a faith of their own?

The following is a checklist — a sort of personal inventory — to see just how much of your faith is really yours. Go through and check the ones that apply to you and your spiritual life.

"RENTERS" vs. "OWNERS"	
Apathetic/indifferent about spiritual things.	Eager to grow and learn. Wants to know more.
Enjoys the "shallow end" of Bible study.	Desires depth and more insight.
Externally motivated from the outside. Needs to have a "jump-start." Has to be "enticed" w/fun spiritual activities at church.	Motivated from the heart. Doesn't need to be "begged" to partici-pate in things.
Inconsistent. Sporadic. Casual commitment.	Faithful. Consistent. Can be counted on.
Has a "two-faced faith." One person at church and another at work / school / weekends.	Is genuine and real. Same person at all times.
Only interested in the benefits of Christianity. Asks, "What's in it for me?"	Interested in serving others. Asks, "How can I help someone else?"
Doesn't last. His/her faith fizzles out. Loses interest in spiritual things.	Keeps on going. Perseveres. Crosses over to the other side of the bridge.
Can't defend the faith.	Is trained to defend the faith.

Those are some of the differences between renting and owning your own faith. Of course, still being in the *process* of fully owning your faith doesn't mean you're a second-class Christian. To varying degrees, we are all continuing to grow, learn, and embrace God's Word at different levels.

What about you? Where are you on the "bridge"? This isn't just a journey confined to young people, as most Christian adults struggle in this area as well. Are you closer to the "renting" side or the "owning" side? Are you currently progressing forward spiritually, moving backward, or standing still?

Pause for a moment before reading further and pray about those areas of faith you have yet to fully "own."

- Are there doctrines, truths, or passages in the Bible of which you remain skeptical? If so, then seek out answers.

- Is there a belief you are struggling with?

- An area of your life you're unwilling to give over to Christ?

- Do you fear walking across that bridge, afraid you won't do a good job "giving an answer" for your faith to the world?

- Do you feel like you're still "renting"?

- Are you secretly fearful unbelievers or your children will ask questions you can't answer?

- Do you have doubts because of your questions and you need those answers?

Talk to God about those areas and give them over to Him. Ask Him for His strength to deal with them. Ask, "Lord, what do I need to do in these areas of my life in order to move on toward maturity? What decisions do I need to make? What practical steps do I need to take? Who do I need to talk to? What resource should I consult?"

From the Inside Out

Jesus and Paul knew something that many pastors in America need to re-discover — that we cannot do something *for* God until God first does something *in* us. God desires to work in this generation before He works through them. And that's exactly what happens when we invest the Word of God into our young people. You can change a person's behavior through gimmicks, but you can only change a heart through the Holy Spirit and the Word of God.

Paul spent years establishing individuals and churches in their faith. He himself spent three years being privately grounded in truth by the

Holy Spirit (Gal. 1:11–17). Jesus spent three years helping His disciples own their faith. Though He spoke often to large crowds, the majority of His time and teaching was spent with just 12 men. To large crowds, He spoke primarily about salvation. But to His small group, the topic was discipleship — how to know God intimately and follow Him passionately. The Bible says Jesus chose these men that "they might be with him" (Mark 3:14). That's the heart of ministry — time together sharing our lives *and* God's Word with one another. Here then, in Paul's own words, is the biblical balance of discipleship:

> But we were gentle among you, like a nursing mother taking care of her own children. So, being affectionately desirous of you, we were *ready to share with you* not only the gospel of God but also our own selves, because you had become very dear to us (1 Thess. 2:7–8, emphasis added).

The "gospel of God" is the Word of God, the body of truth we know as the "faith," beginning in Genesis and ending in Revelation. That's the *content* of our apologetic. We do not redefine that truth, but rather teach it plainly and passionately. But it doesn't stop there. "Our own selves" refers to us imparting our lives in service to those whose spiritual care God has entrusted to us. That's the *character* of our apologetic.

Both are necessary for an effective transfer of faith. Content without character only makes people smarter. Character without content only gives a good example. To teach the Word outside the context of relationship often produces cold doctrine, lifeless truth, and a pharisaical sort of pride. But when life is shared *without* the Word, it produces superficiality, ignorance, and experientialism. We need both, producing a much needed balance. While *sharing* the truth, we at the same time *incarnate* it.

Aren't you glad God gave us this balance in our life and ministry? And the result?

Paul wrote to the Corinthians,

> You yourselves are our letter of recommendation, written on our hearts, to be known and read by all (2 Cor. 3:2).

In other words, those to whom we pass the baton become the *valida-tion* of our lives and ministries. *Disciple making is a generational affair.* The glory of God in the next generation is *why* we do what we do. To see them grip the baton of faith and run with it is our highest reward. It makes everything we do worth all the toil and sacrifice. Therefore, we must make it a top priority to train, equip, mentor, and model an effective apologetic for this generation of young believers living in a post-modern world.

Jesus chose this approach to ministry because He knew it would make the greatest impact in their lives. And apparently it worked, because you and I are the glorious result of His men owning their faith!

Chapter 7

Jesus and the Ark

In the year this book is being written, Answers in Genesis is in the midst of constructing a life-size Noah's ark. As part of the due diligence in regard to this undertaking, ARG contracted a general population study to project attendance to "Ark Encounter." As a result of this study, ARG predicts a minimum of 1.4 million visitors to the structure in the first year.

In this study (of which 55 percent indicated they were regular church attendees), participants were asked, "Do you believe Noah's Ark was actually built or only a legend?" and 77 percent said it was actually built.

Concerning the building of a replica ark, ARG also discovered that only 11 percent said it was *not* a worthy idea; 68 percent said they would personally like to see the ark built; and 63 percent (that's approximately 200 million people in the USA alone) indicated they would likely visit the ark.

Obviously, there's a lot of interest in the topic of Noah's ark. However, in this same study, we discovered that the 20s generation is less sympathetic to the Christian worldview. For instance, when asked "Do you believe Noah's ark was actually built or only a legend?" the results for those who said yes were as follows:

60s — 86%
50s — 74%
40s — 81%
30s — 81%
20s — 52%

It's clear that the 20s generation is drifting away from believing the biblical account of the ark and the Flood. Of the people who regularly attend church, 89 percent of the 20s generation said they believe in Noah's ark and the Flood. But the 20s group in the general population, as discussed earlier, has continued drifting away from the Church, with a significant increase in the number who reject the biblical account of the ark and Flood. Though alarming, this comes as no surprise to those who are familiar with Scripture.

A Ship with No Anchor

One of the Apostle Paul's passions was preserving the purity of the Bride of Christ, the Church. In fact, most of his epistles were written to counteract false teaching and those who would threaten the integrity of the Word of God and the gospel of grace. Of particular importance is his prophetic warnings concerning the Church in the last days. Writing to Timothy, Paul predicted,

> Now the Spirit expressly says that in later times some will depart from the faith by devoting themselves to deceitful spirits and teachings of demons, through the insincerity of liars whose consciences are seared (1 Tim. 4:1–2).

And again, in his final letter to the young pastor,

> But understand this, that in the last days there will come times of difficulty. . . . having the appearance of godliness, but denying its power. Avoid such people (2 Tim. 3:1–5).

> But as for you, continue in what you have learned and have firmly believed, knowing from whom you learned it and how from childhood you have been acquainted with the sacred

writings, which are able to make you wise for salvation through faith in Christ Jesus. All Scripture is breathed out by God and profitable for teaching, for reproof, for correction, and for training in righteousness, that the man of God may be complete, equipped for every good work (2 Tim. 3:14–17).

But where today do we see this "departing from the faith"? Are we currently living in the "times of difficulty" Paul wrote about? I believe we certainly are in a particular time of difficulty. At no time since before the Protestant Reformation has the integrity and teaching of God's Word been so questioned, misinterpreted, and maligned as it is today, particularly in regard to the Book of Genesis. When an arsonist burns a house down, he doesn't throw a match on the roof. Rather, he pours gasoline in the basement so the fire burns from the bottom up. The Book of Genesis is like a foundation to biblical structure.[1] Many core doctrines (directly or indirectly), including the gospel of Jesus Christ, are founded in Genesis 1–11. We also find the doctrine of marriage between a man and woman in Genesis 1 and 2 (later quoted by Jesus in Matthew 19:4–7). Therefore, to undermine Genesis, we subvert marriage itself, as well as the gospel, as the historical account of original sin and the resulting need for a Savior are outlined there.

Now in order to effectively discredit the historical veracity of the Bible, you would have to definitively disprove Scripture's record with undeniable facts, which of course, no one has been able to do in over 2,000 years. On the contrary, with every turn of the archeologist's spade, and the more we understand biology, geology, astronomy, and anthropology, the Bible is proven trustworthy over and over again — right from the very beginning. However, this certainly hasn't discouraged those ignorant of Scripture's impeccable track record from continually casting doubt on its account of humankind's history. One of the targeted areas secular evolutionary scientists attack vehemently is the testimony of the ark and the Great Flood. However, secularists have to denigrate the account of the Flood in order to do this, because if there really was a global Flood as the Bible describes, then the whole timeline

---

1. This is discussed in detail in the book *The Lie: Evolution* by Ken Ham (Green Forest, AR: Master Books, 1987).

of evolutionary geology collapses, imploding under its own weight. If Genesis is true, evolutionary thought is decimated.

Biblical creationist Dr. Terry Mortenson has conclusively documented how the idea of millions of years of time grew out of naturalism (atheism) in the late 18th and early 19th centuries.[2] They claim most of the fossil record was laid down over millions of years and was not the result of a catastrophic, global Flood. Only through millions of years can Darwin propose that changes were made in biology (e.g., adaptation/speciation etc.), enabling one kind of animal to change into a completely different kind of animal. This is their "molecules to man" evolutionary proposal.

Even though we know sin is the ultimate "disease problem" in this world, I liken the teaching of millions of years to a disease, with the teaching of evolution as a mere symptom of that disease.

The Real Reason Secularists Reject Noah

Most of the questions I get from the secular media concern the age of the earth or why we believe dinosaurs lived with people — not so much about evolution itself. I've found that if a Christian doesn't believe in evolution, secularists will scoff a bit. But if a Christian rejects millions of years, then they really go ballistic. They will call you anti-academic, anti-science, anti-intellectual, etc. This happens because millions of years is really the religion of this age used to justify explaining life without God.

You see, without millions of years, the secularists can't propose a molecules-to-man evolution. As one Nobel prize-winner, George Wald, said,

> Time is in fact the hero of the plot. . . . What we regard as impossible on the basis of human experience is meaningless here. Given so much time, the "impossible" becomes possible,

---

2. See his article, "Philosophical Naturalism and the Age of the Earth: Are They Related?" https://answersingenesis.org/age-of-the-earth/are-philosophical-naturalism-and-age-of-the-earth-related/, as well as his article "The Historical Development of the Old-Earth Geological Time-Scale," https://answersingenesis.org/age-of-the-earth/the-historical-development-of-the-old-earth-geological-time-scale/, his chapter 3 in Terry Mortenson and Thane H. Ury, eds., *Coming to Grips with Genesis* (Green Forest, AR: Master Books, 2008), and his book (a shortened version of his PhD thesis), *The Great Turning Point* (Green Forest, AR: Master Books, 2004).

the possible probable, and the probable virtually certain. One has only to wait: time itself performs the miracles.[3]

He also stated, ". . . the origin of life . . . However improbable we regard this event, or any of the steps which it involves, given enough time it will almost certainly happen at least once."[4]

If the earth is only *thousands* of years old (as calculated using the six days of creation and the genealogies in Scripture), then molecules-to-man evolution as Darwin discussed is logically and biologically impossible. Further, one cannot observe evolution, in the molecules-to-man sense, happening. Yes, we see changes in animals and plants, but those changes do not involve the addition of brand new genetic information as required by such an evolutionary process. Secularists have to have an incomprehensible amount of time (millions of years), to propose an incomprehensible process (molecules-to-man evolution).

Sadly, because secularism intimidates people to believe in millions of years, many Christians have adopted this pagan thinking and thus compromise God's Word, undermining its authority.

We have previously discussed that a fossil record involving millions of years would place death, bloodshed, disease, and thorns *before* man's sin — which is contrary to what the Bible teaches. But if the global Flood of Noah's day really did occur (about 4,300 years ago), then this would explain most of the fossil record, thus "washing away" the idea of millions of years! Therefore, the secularists *have* to oppose the idea that there was a global Flood, otherwise they cannot propose biological evolution! They also cannot allow each animal kind to be represented on an ark, as they insist the various species within these kinds evolved over millions of years.

For these reasons, I believe an apologetic for the ark and Global Flood narrative is not only necessary, but also increasingly relevant for this generation.

Think about it. You rarely hear of secularists attacking the account of Samson killing 300 Philistines? Or Elijah and the prophets of Baal?

---

3. George Wald, "The Origin of Life," *Scientific American* 191, no. 48 (August 1954).
4. George Wald, "The Origin of Life," *A Treasury of Science*, 4th Rev. Ed., Harlow Shapley et al., eds. (New York: Harper and Brothers Publishers, 1958), p. 311.

Or Jesus walking on water? I believe this is because atheistic secularists and scientists do not see these biblical accounts as a threat to their belief system. In other words, whether there really was a "Samson" is not as big of a concern because, in their view, his account has little to do with mankind and world history. However, a catastrophic worldwide flood that altered continents, the topography of the planet, and destroyed every land animal (except those on the ark) . . . well *that* kind of account gets their attention! The Flood messes with not only their "official" version of earth's historical record, but also threatens their very worldview!

If the Flood really happened as Scripture claims it did, then everything secular and evolutionary scientists, geologists, and anthropologists have believed for over 100 years is suddenly transformed into a glorified fairy tale for adults. And that would make both them and an entire body of thought irrelevant, meaningless, and worthless. In other words, they would be considered fools.

And they can't have that, now, can they?

Therefore, they continue in their relentless attack on the credibility and claims of Scripture as it relates to the Flood.

But even for those who profess belief in Scripture, the story of the ark and the Flood raises many questions, which when left unanswered, tend to also raise the *Christian's* doubt level. To be clear, the credibility of the Flood event has a huge impact on how people view the rest of Scripture. So let's address some of the most-often asked questions concerning the ark and the Flood that I have been asked from inside and outside the Church. If such questions remain unanswered, this can be a major contributing factor to why so many in the 20s generation have left (and are leaving) the Church. Answering them is part of equipping believers with a reasonable apologetic concerning the ark and Flood. So here are some of those questions:

- How large was Noah's ark?

- Could Noah have built the ark, and if so, how?

- How could Noah have rounded up so many animals?

- Were dinosaurs on the ark?

- Could all those animals fit on one boat?

- How did he care for the animals for over a year?

- Could the ark really survive such a violent flood?

- Where did all the water come from? And where did it go afterward?

- Was the Flood really global, or merely regional?

- Where is the evidence for such a Flood?

- Where is Noah's ark today?

- Why is the ark so important to Christians?

- What are the theological problems with denying the ark account?

- How did Jesus and the New Testament authors understand the Flood account?

- Is there credible extra-biblical evidence for the Flood?

- What are the spiritual implications of dismissing the Flood as myth?

How Large Was Noah's Ark?

Unlike many whimsical drawings that depict the ark as some kind of overgrown houseboat (with giraffes sticking out the top), the ark described in the Bible was a huge seaworthy vessel. In fact, not until the late 1800s was a ship built that exceeded the capacity of Noah's ark.

The dimensions of the ark are convincing for two reasons: the proportions are like that of a modern cargo ship, and it is about as large as a wooden ship can be built. The cubit gives us a good indication of size.[5]

After much research, Answers in Genesis is using a 20.4-inch cubit. There are several articles about cubits on the worldwideflood.com website.

---

5. The cubit was defined as the length of the forearm from elbow to fingertip. Ancient cubits vary anywhere from 17.5 inches (45 cm) to 22 inches (56 cm), the longer sizes dominating the major ancient constructions. Despite this, even a conservative 18-inch (46 cm) cubit describes a sizeable vessel.

Our main researcher on this topic argues for using a royal cubit.[6] His rationale is based on the following reasons.

Royal cubits were often used in monumental structures throughout the Ancient Near East, indicating that the people may have been a little taller than evolutionists usually assert.[7]

The smaller cubits (17.5–18 inches) are often chosen to simply give a worst-case scenario for the size of the ark to hold the animals rather than a careful study of ancient cubits.

So assuming that a 20.4-inch cubit was actually Noah's cubit, then Noah was roughly 6'3" tall. This would mean that for the Ark Encounter project, the life-size ark will be 510 feet long, 85 feet wide, and 51 feet high.

In the Western world, wooden sailing ships never got much longer than about 330 feet (100 m), yet the ancient Greeks built vessels at least this size 2,000 years earlier. China built huge wooden ships in the 1400s that may have been as large as the ark. Thus, the biblical ark is one of the largest wooden ships of all time. Our life-size ark project in Kentucky shows the feasibility of such a wooden ship. For more information go to www.arkencounter.com.

How Could Noah Build the Ark?

Scripture doesn't specifically tell us Noah and his sons built the ark by themselves. Noah could have hired skilled laborers or had relatives help build the vessel. However, nothing indicates that they could not — or that they did not — build the ark themselves in the time allotted. The physical strength and mental processes of men in Noah's day was at least as great (quite likely, even much superior) to our own.[8] The genius of ancient man certainly would have had efficient means for harvesting and cutting timber, as well as for shaping, transporting, and erecting the massive beams and boards required.

---

6. http://worldwideflood.org/ark/noahs_cubit/cubit_paper.htm.

7. The cubit described in Ezekiel 40:5 is a cubit and a handbreadth, perhaps indicating that the original cubit was longer than the cubit that would be popular at the time Ezekiel described. Our researcher cites a reference that puts this cubit at 20.4 inches.

8. For the evidence, see Dr. Donald Chittick, *The Puzzle of Ancient Man* (Newberg, OR: Creation Compass, 1998). This book details evidence of man's intelligence in early post-Flood civilizations.

Today, one or two men can erect a large house in just 12 weeks. How much more could three or four men do in a few years? Noah's generation was making complex musical instruments, forging metal, and building cities, so their tools, machines, and techniques were not as primitive as many might imagine. History has also shown that technology can be lost. In Egypt, China, and the Americas, earlier dynasties built impressive buildings and were skilled in fine art and science. Many so-called modern inventions, like concrete, turn out to be re-inventions that were used by the Romans. Even early post-Flood civilizations display all the engineering know-how necessary for a project like Noah's ark. People sawing and drilling wood in Noah's day, only a few centuries before the Egyptians were sawing and drilling granite, is very reasonable! The idea that early civilizations were primitive and unskilled is an evolutionary concept. And sadly, even many Christians tend to think in an "evolutionary" way about the past — that humans weren't as intelligent or didn't have advanced technology at the time of Noah.

In reality, when God created Adam, he was perfect. Today, the individual human intellect has suffered from 6,000 years of sin and decay. The sudden rise in technology in the last few centuries has nothing to do with increasing intelligence; it is a combination of publishing and sharing ideas, and the spread of key inventions that became tools for investigation and manufacturing. One of the most recent tools is the computer, which in reality compensates a great deal for our natural decline in mental performance and discipline, while also permitting us to gather and store information as perhaps never before.

How Could Noah Round Up So Many Animals?

Genesis 6:20 tells us that Noah didn't have to search or travel to far away places to bring the animals on board. Consider that the world map was completely different before the Flood, and on the basis of Genesis 1, there might have been only one continent. The animals simply arrived at the ark as if called by a "homing instinct" (a behavior implanted in the animals by their Creator). However He did it, according to Scripture it was God who brought the animals to Noah.

Though this was no doubt a supernatural event (one that cannot be explained by our understanding of nature), compare it to the impressive migratory behavior we see in some animals today. We are still far from understanding all the marvelous animal behaviors exhibited in God's creation: the migration of Canadian geese and other birds, the amazing flights of monarch butterflies, the annual travels of whales and fish, hibernation instincts, earthquake sensitivity, and countless other fascinating capabilities of God's animal kingdom. So to claim that so many could not have come to the ark is a faulty conclusion.

Were Dinosaurs on Noah's Ark?

This is one of the questions most often asked of me. The history of God's creation (told in Genesis 1 and 2) tells us that all the land-dwelling creatures were made on day 6 of creation week — the same day God made Adam and Eve. Therefore, dinosaurs (being land animals) were clearly made with man. Keep in mind the word "dinosaur" was only invented in 1841 as a name for a particular group of land animals.

Also, two of every kind (seven of some) of land animal (which must have included the dinosaur kinds) boarded the ark. The description of "behemoth" in chapter 40 of the Book of Job (Job lived after the Flood) seems to fit with something like a sauropod dinosaur. The ancestor of "behemoth" must have been on board the ark.[9]

Additionally, we also find many dinosaurs that were trapped and fossilized in Flood sediment. And just as the numerous Flood legends point back to the real Flood of Noah's day, creationists believe the many dragon legends could be the result of encounters with real creatures, perhaps even what we today call dinosaurs. The only way this could happen is if dinosaurs were on the ark.

Juveniles of even the largest land animals do not present a size problem, and, being young, they have their full breeding life ahead of them. Yet most dinosaurs were not very large at all — some were the size of a chicken (although absolutely no relation to birds, as many evolutionists

---

9. For some remarkable evidence that dinosaurs have lived until relatively recent times, see chapter 12, "What Really Happened to the Dinosaurs?" Also read *The Great Dinosaur Mystery Solved* (Green Forest, AR: New Leaf Press, 2000). Also visit www.answersingenesis.org/go/dinosaurs.

claim). Most scientists agree that the average size of a dinosaur is actually the size of a bison. So God most likely brought Noah two young adult sauropods (e.g., apatosaurs), rather than two full-grown sauropods. The same goes for elephants, giraffes, and other animals that grow to be very large, even though there was adequate room for most fully-grown adult animals anyway.

It should also be noted that, although there are hundreds of names for different varieties (species) of dinosaurs that have been discovered, there are probably only about 50 different kinds, because there are only around 50 families of dinosaurs.

How Could Noah Fit All the Animals on the Ark?

First of all, the ark did not need to carry every kind of animal — nor did God command it. It carried only air-breathing, land-dwelling creatures. Aquatic life (fish, whales, etc.) survived outside the ark (although the variety we observe today makes it obvious that many did not survive the Flood). This cuts down significantly the total number of animals that needed to be on board.

Another factor greatly reducing the space requirements is the fact that the tremendous variety in species we see today did not exist in the days of Noah. Our researchers (in preparation for the life-size ark project), on the basis of which animals have been documented to breed together, believe that the Hebrew word for "kind," in most instances, is equivalent to the "family" level in mans' classification system. So only the parent "kinds" of the various species of land creatures were required to be on board in order to repopulate the earth.[10] For example, only two dogs (there is one dog family), were needed to give rise to all the dog species that exist today. Our researchers believe the number of actual

---

10. For example: more than 200 different breeds of dogs exist today, from the miniature poodle to the St. Bernard — all of which have descended from one original dog "kind" (as have the wolf, dingo, etc.). Many other types of animals — cat kind, horse kind, cow kind, etc. — have similarly been naturally and selectively bred to achieve the wonderful variation in species that we have today. God "programmed" variety into the genetic code of all animal kinds — even humankind! God also made it impossible for the basic "kinds" of animals to breed and reproduce with each other. For example, cats and dogs cannot breed to make a new type of creature. This is by God's design, and it is one fact that makes evolution impossible.

kinds needed on the ark could be as low as 1,000, but up to 1,500 (using fossil evidence that is very fragmentary). Also, there is debate as to whether those that went on the ark in sevens means seven pairs or seven individuals. So the number of land animals needed on the ark could be as low as 3,000 (or even less) or as high as 7,000 (which is probably way too high an estimation). Most land animals are not that large. The point is, when considering the size of the ark there was plenty of room for all the land animal kinds.

We would conclude that much less than half of the cumulative area of the ark's three decks were needed for the animals. This meant there was plenty of storage room for fresh food, water, and lodging for Noah and his family.

How Did Noah Care for All the Animals?

Just as God brought the animals to Noah by some form of supernatural means, He surely also prepared them for this amazing event. Creation scientists suggest that God gave the animals the ability to hibernate, as we see in many species today. Most animals react to natural disasters in ways that were designed to help them survive, so it's very possible many animals did hibernate, perhaps even supernaturally intensified by God.

There could also have simply been a normal response to the darkness and confinement of a rocking ship, as the fact that God told Noah to build rooms ("*qen*" — literally, in Hebrew, "nests") in Genesis 6:14 implies that the animals were subdued or nesting. God also told Noah to take food for them (Genesis 6:21), which tells us that they were not in a year-long coma.

If we could walk through the ark as it was being built, we would undoubtedly be amazed at the ingenious systems on board for water and food storage and distribution. As Woodmorappe explains in *Noah's Ark: A Feasibility Study*,[11] a small group of farmers today can raise thousands of cattle and other animals in a very small space. One can easily imagine all kinds of devices on the ark that would have enabled a small number of people to feed and care for the animals, from watering to waste removal.

---

11. John Woodmorappe, *Noah's Ark: A Feasibility Study* (Santee, CA: Institute for Creation Research, 1996).

It's entirely possible for Noah to have constructed a plumbing system for gravity-fed drinking water, a ventilation system driven by wind or wave motion, or hoppers that dispense grain as the animals eat it. *None* of these require higher technology than what we know existed in ancient cultures.

How Could a Flood Destroy Every Living Thing?

Scripture claims that every thing that breathed on land was killed in the Flood (Genesis 7:21–22). Noah's Flood was much more destructive than a massive rainstorm ever could be, as the "fountains of the great deep" also broke open, as well as rain. In other words, earthquakes, volcanoes, and geysers of molten lava and scalding water were squeezed out of the earth's crust in a violent, explosive upheaval. These fountains were not stopped until 150 days into the Flood — so the earth was literally churning underneath the waters for about five months! (Gen. 7:24). Then the Floodwaters ran off the earth into the oceans. Psalm 104 possibly indicates how God ended the Flood, by raising the mountains and lowering the ocean basis. This produced more catastrophic events that shaped the earth's surface. The Flood's duration was extensive, and Noah and his family were aboard the ark for approximately a year (Gen. 7:11, 8:14–16).

Relatively recent local floods, volcanoes, and earthquakes — though clearly devastating to life and land — are tiny in comparison to the worldwide catastrophe that destroyed "the world that then existed" (2 Peter 3:6). All land animals and people not on board the ark were destroyed in the floodwaters, with billions of creatures preserved in the great fossil record we see today.

Could the Ark Really Survive Such a Violent Flood?

For many years, biblical creationists have simply depicted the ark as a rectangular box, helping to accentuate its size. It also explained its capacity, illustrating how easily the ark could have handled the payload. With the rectangular shape, the ark's stability against rolling could be demonstrated by simple calculations.

However, the Bible does not say the ark was a rectangular box. In fact, Scripture does not elaborate about the shape of Noah's ark beyond those superb, overall proportions — length, breadth, and depth. Ships have long been described like this without implying a block-shaped hull.

Noah's ark was the focus of a major 1993 scientific study headed by Dr. Seon Hong at the world-class ship research center KRISO, based in Daejeon, South Korea.[12] Dr. Hong's team compared 12 hulls of different proportions to discover which design was most practical. No hull shape was found to significantly outperform the 4,300-year-old biblical design. In fact, the ark's careful balance is easily lost if the proportions are modified, rendering the vessel either unstable, prone to fracture, or dangerously uncomfortable.

The research team found that the proportions of Noah's ark carefully balanced the conflicting demands of stability (resistance to capsizing), comfort ("seakeeping"), and strength. In fact, the ark has the same proportions as a modern cargo ship.

The study also confirmed that the ark could handle waves as high as 100 feet (30 m). Dr. Hong is now director general of KRISO and claims "life came from the sea," obviously not the words of a creationist on a mission to promote the worldwide Flood. Endorsing the seaworthiness of Noah's ark obviously did not damage Dr. Hong's credibility.[13]

In Hebrew, "Ark" is the obscure term *tebah*, a word that appears only one other time in the Bible, describing the basket that carried the infant Moses (Exodus 2:3). One was a huge, wooden ship and the other a tiny, wicker basket. Both floated, both preserved life, and both were covered; but the similarity ends there. If the word implied anything about shape, it would be "an Egyptian basket-like shape," typically rounded. More likely, however, *tebah* means something else, like "lifeboat."

The Bible leaves the details regarding the shape of the ark wide open — anything from a rectangular box with hard right angles and no curvature at all, to a ship-like form. Box-like has the largest carrying capacity, but a ship-like design would be safer and more comfortable in heavy

12. Dr. Seon Won Hong was principal research scientist when he headed up the Noah's ark investigation. In May 2005 Dr. Hong was appointed director general of MOERI (formerly KRISO). Dr. Hong earned a B.S. degree in naval architecture from Seoul National University and a Ph.D. degree in applied mechanics from the University of Michigan, Ann Arbor.

13. worldwideflood.com/ark/hull_form/hull_optimization.htm.

seas. Such discussion is irrelevant if God intended to sustain the ark no matter how well designed and executed.[14]

Was Noah's Flood Global?

> And the waters prevailed so mightily on the earth that all the high mountains under the whole heaven were covered. The waters prevailed above the mountains, covering them fifteen cubits deep (Gen. 7:19–20).

Many Christians today claim that Noah's Flood was only a local phenomenon. They generally believe this because they've accepted the evolutionary history of the earth, which interprets fossil layers as the history of the sequential appearance of life over millions of years.[15] At one time, scientists understood the fossils, which are buried in water-carried sediments of mud and sand, to be mostly the result of the Great Flood. Those who now accept millions of years of gradual accumulation of fossils think they have explained away the evidence for the global Flood. However, the evidence says otherwise.

First, if the Flood only affected the area of Mesopotamia, as some claim, why did Noah have to build an ark? He could have simply walked to the other side of the mountains and escaped. Additionally, if the Flood were local, people not living in the vicinity of the Flood would not have been affected by it, and thus escaped God's judgment on sin.

In 2 Peter 3, the coming global judgment by fire is likened to the former judgment by water in Noah's Flood. A partial judgment in Noah's day, therefore, would mean a partial judgment in the future.

Second, if the Flood were only local, how could the waters rise to 20 feet (6 m) above the mountains (Gen. 7:20)? Water seeks its own level; it could not have risen to cover the local mountains while leaving the rest of the world untouched.

---

14. Based on additional research, Answers in Genesis has designed aspects of the life-size ark as part of the Ark Encounter project, including a bow and a wooden "sail" as seen on ancient ships. Such structures help with stability for such a vessel.

15. For compelling evidence that the earth is not billions of years old, read *The Young Earth* by Dr. John Morris (Green Forest, AR: Master Books, 1994), and *Thousands . . . not Billions* by Dr. Don DeYoung (Green Forest, AR: Master Books, 2005); also see www.answersingenesis.org/go/young.

Even what is now Mt. Everest was once covered with water and then uplifted afterward.[16] Again, if we even out the ocean basins and flatten out the mountains, there's enough water to cover the entire earth by about 1.7 miles (2.7 km).[17] The ark would not have been riding at the current height of Mt. Everest, thus no lack of oxygen at high altitudes for Noah.

Third, if the Flood were local, God would have repeatedly broken His promise never to send such a flood again. God put a rainbow in the sky as a covenant between God and man and the animals that He would never repeat such an event. But there have been huge local floods in recent times (e.g., in Bangladesh).

Obviously, if the Flood of Noah were only local in extent and because we have seen lots of local floods since Noah's day that have destroyed both man and animals, God has broken His promise many times over! To the contrary, this rainbow covenant God made with Noah and his descendants could only have been kept by God if the Flood were global in extent, because never since in human history has a global flood been experienced.

Fourth, if the Flood were only local in extent, why did Noah have to take birds on board the ark (Gen. 7:8), when the birds in that local flooded area could simply have flown away to safe unflooded areas? Similarly, why would Noah need to take animals on board the ark from his local area, when other representatives of those same animal kinds would surely have survived in other, unflooded areas?

Fifth, if it was only a local flood, why would Noah have had to build the ark on such a large scale as previously described. Obviously, an ark of such dimensions would only be required if the Flood were global in extent, designed by God to destroy all land animals around the world, except for those preserved on that ark. Indeed, God could have simply

---

16. Mount Everest is more than 5 miles (8 km) high. How, then, could the Flood have covered "all the mountains under the whole heaven"? Before the Flood, the mountains were not so high. The mountains today were formed only toward the end of, and after, the Flood by collision of the tectonic plates and the associated up-thrusting. In support of this, the layers that form the uppermost parts of Mt. Everest are themselves composed of fossil-bearing, water-deposited layers.

17. A.R. Wallace, *Man's Place in the Universe* (New York: McClure, Phillips & Co, 1903), p. 225–226; www.wku.edu/~smithch/wallace/S728-3.htm.

told Noah and his family to migrate with any required animals and birds out of the area that was going to be flooded.

Where Is the Evidence for Such a Flood?

> For they deliberately overlook this fact, that the heavens existed long ago, and the earth was formed out of water and through water by the word of God, and that by means of these the world that then existed was deluged with water and perished (2 Pet. 3:5–6).

Evidence of Noah's Flood can be seen all over the earth, from seabeds to mountaintops. Wherever you go, the physical features of the earth's terrain clearly indicate a catastrophic past, from canyons and craters to coal beds and caverns. Some layers of strata extend across continents, revealing the effects of a huge catastrophe. The earth's crust has massive amounts of layered sedimentary rock, sometimes miles deep! These layers of sand, soil, and material — mostly laid down by water — were once soft like mud, but they are now hard stone. Encased in these sedimentary layers are billions of dead things (fossils of plants and animals) buried *very quickly*. The evidence all over the earth is staring everyone in the face.

Where Is Noah's Ark Today?

Scripture says Noah's ark rested "on the mountains of Ararat" (Gen. 8:4). The location of these mountains could refer to several areas in the Middle East, such as Mt. Ararat in Turkey or other mountain ranges in neighboring countries. Mt. Ararat has attracted the most attention because it has permanent ice, and there have been reports of supposed past sightings of the ark there. But though many expeditions have searched for the ark, there remains no conclusive evidence of the ark's location or survival. Considering it landed about 4,300 years ago, the ark could easily have deteriorated, been destroyed, or been used as lumber by Noah and his descendants.

Some Christians believe the ark could indeed be preserved — perhaps to be providentially revealed at a future time as a reminder of the past judgment and the judgment to come. However, this is not prophesied in Scripture, and such discoveries may not be as convincing as one may think. Jesus said, "If they do not hear Moses and the Prophets, neither will they be convinced if someone rise from the dead" (Luke 16:31).

Why Is the Ark So Important to Christians?

As God's Son, the Lord Jesus Christ is like Noah's ark. Jesus came to seek and to save the lost (Luke 19:10). Just as Noah and his family were saved by the ark and rescued by God from the floodwaters, so anyone who believes in Jesus as Lord and Savior will be spared from the coming final judgment of mankind, rescued by God from the fire that will destroy the earth after the last days (2 Pet. 3:7). Noah and his family had to go through a doorway into the ark to be saved, and the Lord shut the door behind them (Gen. 7:16). So we too have to go through a "doorway" to be saved so that we won't be eternally separated from God. The Son of God, Jesus, stepped into history to pay the penalty for our sin of rebellion. Jesus said, "I am the door. If anyone enters by me, he will be saved and will go in and out and find pasture" (John 10:9).

What Are the Theological Problems with Denying the Ark Account?

Those Christians who accept an evolutionary timeframe, with its fossil accumulation, also rob the Fall of Adam of its serious consequences. Chronologically, they put fossils (which testify of disease, suffering, and death) *before* Adam and Eve sinned and brought death and suffering into the world. By doing this, they also unknowingly undermine the meaning of the death and Resurrection of Christ. Such a scenario also robs all meaning from God's description of His finished creation as "very good."

For the evolutionist, fossil-bearing sedimentary layers were laid down over millions of years *preceding* the appearance of man on earth, including Adam. So for a Christian to accept the millions of years scenario means that animals were living, dying, suffering disease, eating each other, and being buried and fossilized *prior* to Adam's appearance in the Garden of Eden. In the geologic record we find the fossilized remains of fish eating other fish, animals eating other animals, animals with diseases like cancer, and much more, which indicates that these fossils are a record of disease, violence, carnivory, and death.

This presents a huge theological problem. In Genesis 1:30–31 we are told that when God created all the animals they all were vegetarians, and that God was pleased with everything that He had created because it was "very good." This means all of creation was perfect.

But according to the Bible, it is not until *after* God pronounced the Curse on all of creation because of Adam and Eve's disobedience that we are told the ground would bring forth thorns and thistles (Gen. 3:17–18). Evolutionary geologists claim there are fossilized thorns in Canadian sedimentary layers that are supposedly 400 million years old.[18] Those who believe the Bible cannot accept this age-claim however.

If God's Word is true, then these fossilized thorns could only have grown *after* the Curse, *after* Adam was created by God. So the geologic record in which these fossilized thorns are found could *only* have been deposited after the Curse. However, the only event after the Curse that could have been responsible for burying and fossilizing these thorns, and most of the billions of other plants and animals we see in the vast rock layers of the earth, is the yearlong Genesis Flood. This effectively rules out millions of years claimed by evolution.

How Did Jesus and the New Testament Authors Understand the Flood Account?

Jesus made special reference to Noah and the Flood in Luke 17:26–30, where He said that, "the flood came and destroyed them all." Further, Jesus describes the Flood and all the ungodly being destroyed by it, comparing it to a parallel future judgment. Again, if the coming judgment is global, then so was the former judgment. In addition, there is nothing to indicate Jesus understood God's Flood judgment to be anything other than global.

Paul believed in the accuracy and historicity of the Old Testament record. He even compares the literal existence of Jesus to the literal existence of the one man, Adam (Rom. 5:12–21). This scenario is impossible under evolutionary thought.

Similarly, the Apostle Peter in 2 Peter 3:3–7 warned of last-days scoffers who would willfully forget that after the earth was created by God, once flooded with water, and that the present earth is "stored up

18. W.N. Stewart and G.W. Rothwell, *Paleobotany and the Evolution of Plants* (Cambridge, UK: Cambridge University Press, 1993), p. 172–176.

for fire . . . until the day of judgment." There are three events he is thus referring to: the creation of the world (Greek *kosmos*), the destruction of that world (Greek *kosmos*) by a watery cataclysm (the Flood), and the coming destruction of the heavens and the earth by fire in the future.

In context, it's clear Peter is teaching a literal, global Flood. Indeed, the use of the Greek term *kosmos* for both the world that was created and the world that was flooded leave no doubt as to his intended meaning.

Is There Credible Extra-biblical Evidence for the Flood?

The world teaches that the vast majority of the rock layers were laid down slowly over millions of years; but in light of a global Flood in Genesis 6–9, it makes more sense that the bulk of the rock layers that contain fossils were laid down during this catastrophe only thousands of years ago.

On the other hand, the description of the Flood in Genesis 6–8 is not hard to understand. We are told that the "fountains of the great deep" burst open and poured water out onto the earth's surface for 150 days (five months). Simultaneously, and for the same length of time, the "floodgates of heaven" were open, producing torrential global rainfall.[19]

The combined result was that the waters destructively rose across the face of the earth to eventually cover "*all* the high hills under the *whole* heaven." The mountains also were eventually covered, so that every creature "in whose nostrils is the breath of life" perished. If the Flood occurred, we should expect to find evidence today of billions of dead animals and plants buried in rock layers composed of water-deposited sand, lime, and mud all around the earth. And indeed, that's exactly what we do find — billions of fossils of animals and plants buried in sedimentary rock layers stretching across every continent all around the globe.[20] So the evidence is consistent with the biblical record. Millions of years are

---

19. The reference to 40 days and 40 nights (Gen. 7:12, 17) appears to be telling us how long it was before the ark started to float, for the windows of heaven were closed on the same day (150th) as the fountains of the deep were (Gen. 7:24–8:3). For a detailed argument based on the Hebrew text, see William Barrick, "Noah's Flood and Its Geological Implications," in Terry Mortenson and Thane H. Ury, eds., *Coming to Grips with Genesis* (Green Forest, AR: Master Books, 2008), p. 251–282.

20. See Ken Ham, ed., *The New Answers Book 3* (Green Forest, AR: Master Books, 2010), ch 29, Andrew A. Snelling, "What Are Some of the Best Flood Evidences?"

not necessary to form fossil-bearing sedimentary rock layers, as seen in the walls of the Grand Canyon and elsewhere, and could have formed rapidly during the year long catastrophic Flood of Noah.[21]

It should immediately be obvious that these two interpretations of the fossil evidence are mutually exclusive! Most of these rock layers are either the sobering testimony to Noah's Flood or the record of millions of years of history on this earth. One must be true and the other must be false. We can't consistently or logically believe in both, because the millions of years can't be fitted into the approximately year-long global cataclysmic Flood of Noah described in Genesis 6–8.

What Are the Spiritual Implications of Dismissing the Flood as Myth?

How do we establish beyond a doubt the details of an event that supposedly happened in the past? One way is to find witnesses who were there, or look for records written by witnesses. The Bible claims that God moved men through His Spirit to write down His words, and that they are not just the words of men but the Word of God (1 Thess. 2:13; 2 Pet. 1:20–21). The Book of Genesis claims to be the records from God telling us of the events of creation and of other events in this world's early history that have great bearing upon our present circumstances. Thus, the present is *not* the key to the past, as evolutionists claim. Rather, *revelation* is the key to the past.

The revelation in Genesis tells us about such events as creation, Noah's Flood, and the Tower of Babel. These are events that have made the earth's geology, geography, biology, etc., what they are today. Therefore, it's also true that what happened in the past is the key to the present. The entrance of sin into the world explains why we have death and mistakes occurring in our genes. The global devastation caused by Noah's Flood helps to explain the fossil record. The events at the Tower of Babel help us to come to an understanding of the origin of the different nations and cultures around the world.

---

21. Some localized fossil-bearing deposits may have formed after the Fall of Adam and Eve in sin and before Noah's Flood, and some of the localized fossiliferous rock layers at the top of the geological record were formed in post-Flood events. But creationist geologists are in general agreement that most of the fossil-bearing sedimentary rock record is a result of Noah's Flood.

Today, evolutionists deny that the biblical record can be taken seriously. They put their faith in their belief that "all things continue as they have done from the beginning," fulfilling the prophecy in 2 Peter 3.

Peter's prophecy tells us that men will deliberately reject three things:

1. That God created the world, which at first was covered with water (which means its surface was *cool* at the beginning, not a molten blob, as evolutionists teach).

2. That God once judged this world with a global, cataclysmic flood in Noah's time.

3. That God is going to judge this world again, only this time with fire.

People often make the statement, "If there is so much evidence that God created the world and sent a global cataclysmic flood, then surely all scientists would believe this." But Peter explains that it's not simply a matter of providing evidence to convince people, because people do not *want* to be convinced (2 Pet. 3:5). Romans 1:20 says there's enough evidence to convince everyone that God is Creator, so much so that we are condemned if we do not believe. Furthermore, Romans 1:18 tells us that men "by their unrighteousness suppress the truth." So it's not a matter of lack of evidence to convince people that the Bible is true; the problem is that they do not *want* to believe the Bible, and thus have closed their minds to truth. The reason for this is obvious. If people believed in the God of the Bible, they would have to acknowledge His authority and submit to Him. However, every human being suffers from the same problem — the sin which Adam committed in the Garden of Eden — a "disease" which we all inherit. Adam's sin was rebellion against God's authority. Likewise, people everywhere today are in rebellion against God, so to admit that the Bible is true would be an admission of their own sinful and rebellious nature and of their need to be born again through Christ.

It is easy to see this "willing ignorance" in action when watching debates over the creation/evolution issue. In most cases, the evolutionists are not interested in the wealth of data, evidence, and information the creationists put forward. Instead, they typically try to attack creationists by attempting to destroy their credibility. They're not interested in data, logical reasoning, or any evidence pointing to creation or refuting evolution, because they are totally committed to their religious faith in evolution.

For evolutionists to accept the facts presented by creationists would mean admitting the Bible is right, and thus the whole of their evolutionary philosophy would have to be rejected. *That's* what being "willingly ignorant" means.

Further, if they conceded that the Bible was true, they would have to agree with Jesus Christ, who uses the event of Noah's Flood as a warning that God has judged the earth, and will judge it again (Matt. 24:37–39). They would have to agree that God is going to come back as judge. The next time He will use fire as the method of judgment rather than water. Sinful man in rebellion against God does not want to admit that he must stand before the God of creation one day and account for his life. Thus, in rejecting creation and Noah's Flood, and claiming "scientific" evidence that supposedly supports his own belief, he becomes comfortable in not thinking about the coming judgment.

The late Isaac Asimov, an active anti-creationist, gave warnings about creationists. He was quoted as saying (in regard to creationists getting equal time for presenting the creation model in school), it is "today equal time, tomorrow the world."[22] Isaac Asimov was right! We are out to convince the world that Jesus Christ is Creator. Isaac Asimov was one who signed the Humanist Manifesto — he was out to convince the world that Jesus Christ is *not* the Creator.

We are out to convince people like Isaac Asimov that Jesus Christ is Creator. Why? Because we want a good fight? Because we like controversy? No, because we know that those who do not trust the Lord will spend eternity separated from Him.

And that is the ultimate purpose of any good apologetic (defense) — to convince someone of the truth and reasonable nature of the gospel. For all these reasons we've discussed, every believer should be acquainted with the overwhelming evidence concerning the ark and the Flood.

22. Isaac Asimov, *The Roving Mind* (Buffalo, NY: Prometheus Books, 1983), p. 19.

Failing to do so represents a departure from historic faith, and is an insult to the very God who claims His Word *is* "truth" (John 17:17).

So why all this information regarding the ark? The reason is that once belief in the ark and Genesis has eroded or been compromised, people are less likely to trust the rest of Scripture. These are foundational issues, not peripheral ones. I strongly believe that if general Bible and creation apologetics had been taught consistently in churches and Christian homes, we would likely not be seeing the 20s generation drift and depart from God as they have. So is there anything we can do to help undo what has happened?

Chapter 8

Already Too Late?

Lightning Strikes and Lava Flows

Some things in life happen in an instant — a car accident, a heart attack, or a lightning strike. They are sudden, immediate, and can change life as we know it. But other things in life happen gradually. Their impact is not glaring or obvious, but they nevertheless change things — sometimes dramatically. They move, not with giant steps, but rather incrementally. Like a slow-moving lava flow, they creep by the inch, bringing radical change to the landscape.

When it comes to a nation's spirituality and morality, change is typically more like a lava flow than a lightning strike. To the average citizen, these changes largely go unnoticed as they are small and seemingly insignificant. But then this change reaches a critical juncture, and catastrophic change ensues. I believe we are at that point in America — even in the whole Western world. And when it comes to morality, change is a critical component of Satan's evil agenda. And in the absence of moral leadership, there is virtually no way to impede the infringing flow of godlessness.

In the Book of Judges, twice we read what happens when there is no human authority to enforce what is right and wrong according to God's Word. In what is one of the saddest verses in all of Scripture, Joshua writes,

> In those days there was no king in Israel. Everyone did what was right in his own eyes (Judg. 17:6, 21:25).

This verse aptly spells out what we see happening in our own American culture. As I've said many times before, when a culture no longer builds its worldview on the foundation of the absolute authority of the Word of God, then increasingly people will want to do what is "right" in their own eyes. Eventually we reach a tipping point, a twisted perspective where, like Israel, we "call evil good and good evil," becoming those who "put darkness for light and light for darkness" (Isa. 5:20). Sadly, this is not just occurring outside the Church, but inside also.

Perhaps in no other area of society and morality are we seeing this happening than in the acceptance and legalization of same sex marriage. As gay "marriage" has been condoned and progressively legalized across this nation — from the U.S. president to individual states — there has been an increase in people justifying any relationship they desire, and defining marriage however they please. Since the Supreme Court of the United States has ruled in favor of gay "marriage," as I have said many times, we will also see polygamists clamoring to demand the legalization of polygamy as well.

To that point, the *New York Times* reported on a recent case in Utah with this headline:

A Utah Law Prohibiting Polygamy Is Weakened

The article begins this way:

> A federal judge has struck down parts of Utah's anti-polygamy law as unconstitutional in a case brought by a polygamous star of a reality television series. Months after the Supreme Court bolstered rights of same-sex couples, the Utah case could open a new frontier in the nation's recognition of once-prohibited relationships.[1]

Similarly, Jillian Keenan is an independent journalist who has contributed to *The New York Times* and the *Washington Post*. Earlier this year she wrote an article that contained the following:

---

1. www.nytimes.com/2013/12/15/us/a-utah-law-prohibiting-polygamy-is-weakened. html?_r=0.

While the Supreme Court and the rest of us are all focused on the human right of marriage equality, let's not forget that the fight doesn't end with same-sex marriage. We need to legalize polygamy, too. Legalized polygamy in the United States is the constitutional, feminist, and sex-positive choice. More importantly, it would actually help protect, empower, and strengthen women, children, and families. . . ."

That's just another way of calling evil "good."

As one article accurately summarizes, "The definition of marriage today has become fluid and open to debate regarding its very definition. As a result, heterosexual marriage is now no better or worse than homosexual "marriage," and marriage between two consenting adults is not inherently more or less "correct" than marriage among three (or four, or six) consenting adults. Though polygamists are a minority — a tiny minority, in fact — freedom has no value unless it extends to even the smallest and most marginalized groups among us."[2]

So a growing contingency is fighting for "marriage equality" until it extends to every same-sex couple in the United States. But they're not stopping there. The erosion of America's moral foundation clearly personifies Solomon's words,

> Where there is no prophetic vision the people cast off restraint; but blessed is he who keeps the law (Prov. 29:18).

Clarke's commentary states: "Where Divine revelation, and the faithful preaching of the sacred testimonies, are neither reverenced nor attended, the ruin of that land is at no great distance."[3]

Once a culture abandon's God's law (the absolute authority of the Word of God), then ruin is sure to follow. As America continues rejecting a worldview based on God's Word, the floodgates will be opened — and anything goes. Be warned — those activists who have been successful in opening the door to gay "marriage" across the country know this is only the start.

---

2. http://www.slate.com/articles/double_x/doublex/2013/04/legalize_polygamy_marriage_equality_for_all.html.

3. www.pinknews.co.uk/2013/01/25/comment-the-same-sex-marriage-bill-isnt-the-end-of-the-journey-towards-gay-rights/.

In an article in the UK *Pink News* entitled "The same-sex marriage bill isn't the end of the journey towards gay rights," Chris Ashford, Reader in Law and Society at the University of Sunderland argues at the end of his article:

> Legislative victory should not mean identity erasure. There remain numerous sexual freedoms to campaign on — yes sexual — that's what gay rights is about, not merely a civil rights campaign — and there are battles still to be won. Battles relating to pornography, the continued criminalization of consensual sexual acts, re-constructing our ideas of relationships in relation to sex, monogamy and the illusion that only "couples" might want to enter into a state-sanctioned partnership, are just a handful which spring to mind.

From a Christian perspective, I actually agree with him. For when people believe there are no absolute restraints, when there is no respect for God's law — *anything* goes — ruin is on the way. As went Rome, so goes the United Kingdom, Australia, and the United States of America.

Moral relativism is flooding the USA — and it's going to get much worse. The more this culture has built its worldview on man's word instead of God's Word, the more we will see our once-Christianized worldview collapsing. Increasingly, moral relativism will permeate the culture. And the more this happens, the more Christians will be seen as the enemy. Even now, Christian persecution — socially, legally — is already happening in this nation — but it's only the start!

How Firm a Foundation

Part of what makes this so tragic is that America began on such a good foundation. She had a good start. In this nation's past, there have been many reminders of a Christianized heritage in the culture, such as nativity scenes in public places, Ten Commandments displays, crosses and Christian symbols out in the open, school prayer, the teaching of creation, and even Bible reading in government schools. There was a time when abortion and gay "marriage" were illegal. All these things remind us of America's predominantly Christian roots.

But sadly, many of these foundation stones have been (and are continuing to be) removed. And with them go our national conscious and moral compass.

- 1962 — school prayer was ruled unconstitutional

- 1963 — Bible reading in school was ruled unconstitutional

- 1973 — abortion was legalized in the Roe v. Wade case

- 1985 — nativity scenes on public land were deemed to violate the so-called "separation of church and state"

- 2015 — U.S. Supreme Court legalizes gay "marriage"

Even the president himself, a man who twice placed his hand on the Word of God under oath, has publicly, enthusiastically, and unashamedly supported abortion and gay "marriage," even proclaiming June 2009 as "Lesbian, Gay, Bisexual, and Transgender Pride Month."[4]

He has also proclaimed,

> My expectation is that when you look back on these years. . . . You will see a time in which we as a nation finally recognize relationships between two men and two women as just as real and admirable as relationships between a man and a woman.[5]

This current president (President Obama) has indeed championed change in this nation from the Christianized worldview (and the Christian morality that once permeated the culture), to one of moral relativism.

In the past, those previously mentioned practices (Christian symbols in public places, the Bible in public schools, etc.) were reminders to the coming generations of the Christian heritage and foundation of this nation. They were also a witness to other nations concerning the true God and the truth of His Word. America was once a great Christian light in a dark world, a witness to the nations. But this has changed markedly

4. Barack Obama, "Lesbian, Gay, Bisexual, and Transgender Pride Month, 2009," The White House, http://www.gpo.gov/fdsys/pkg/FR-2009-06-04/pdf/E9-13281.pdf.
5. Barack Obama, "Remarks by the President at Human Rights Campaign Dinner," October 11, 2009, The White House, https://www.whitehouse.gov/the-press-office/remarks-president-human-rights-campaign-dinner.

in just the past few decades. That's all it took, though the seeds of change were sown many years earlier. America has become a secularized country. Moral relativism has permeated the culture. And it only takes one generation to ultimately lose a culture.

In short, this nation has changed its foundation: from God's Word to man's word. From God's unchanging ways to man's ever-changing justification for sin and immorality. We have systematically and progressively pushed God out of the picture: out of the government, out of the educational system, out of the marketplace, and even out of many churches.

And God has given us exactly what we have asked for. Like those He describes in Romans 1, we have exchanged the worship of Him to worshiping man-made religions and philosophies (like evolutionary biology, geology, astronomy, anthropology). In an ultimate sense, it is really a change of religion from God's values to man's. And as we've chosen to indulge in our own darkened desires over His ways, He has given us over to those desires and the consequences — both natural and divine — that result from them (Rom. 1:18–32).

We are fast becoming an unholy hybrid of Rome and Sodom — two cultures who rejected God and subsequently suffered His judgment. They now both lay on the figurative (and literal) ash heap of history.

This transformation has weakened us to the eventual point of collapse. But while discerning believers point out these cracks in our foundation, offering real solutions, those who promote such evil consider these changes to be "unnecessary" as they consider godliness and decency to be part of an outdated, archaic biblical moral code.

Sadly, many churches and Bible colleges/seminaries have also compromised God's Word by accepting the pagan, evolutionary religion of the age that attempts to explain life without God. The book *Already Compromised*, published in 2011, details the research conducted on such institutions. When the question, "Would you consider yourself to be a young-earth or old-earth Christian?" was asked, 78 percent of the heads of the religion departments answered "old earth."

An Internal Issue

Surprisingly, the Church has actually contributed to the undermining of biblical authority in America. In so doing, Christians have actually paved the way for the nation's change, helping (unwittingly in most cases) to build a worldview foundation that is becoming more man-centered and less Bible-centered.

Also, many in the Church and culture have been duped into thinking that the so-called "separation of church and state" issue (a perversion of what the First Amendment actually states concerning freedom of religion) means that the Bible and Christian symbols should be eliminated from the public sector, and thus bring in a neutral situation. But there is no such position as neutrality. Think about it. One is either for Christ or against Him! What has happened is that the religion of naturalism (atheism) has been imposed on the public education system (and on the culture as a whole), effectively making it a state-sponsored religion.

Therefore, the only way for the Christian reminders that have been removed to be restored is for Christians and the culture to return to the authoritative Word of God as the foundation for all thinking. After all, "Blessed is the nation whose God is the LORD" (Ps. 33:12).

This, then, is the face of relativism — or the idea that there is no absolute standard for right and wrong.

The rapidly declining moral state of America was the subject of a recent *New York Times* opinion piece.[6] In it, the author bemoaned the deplorable state of many of today's families and nationwide moral problems, writing,

> We now have multiple generations of people caught in recurring feedback loops of economic stress and family breakdown, often leading to something approaching an anarchy of the intimate life.

Titled "The Cost of Relativism," this opinion piece certainly shows what moral relativism is costing this nation. The author, David Brooks, states,

> It's increasingly clear that sympathy is not enough. It's not only money and better policy that are missing in these circles; it's norms. The health of society is primarily determined by the habits and virtues of its citizens. In many parts of America there

---

6. http://www.nytimes.com/2015/03/10/opinion/david-brooks-the-cost-of-relativism. html?_r=0.

are no minimally agreed upon standards for what it means to be
a father. There are no basic codes and rules woven into daily life,
which people can absorb unconsciously and follow automatically.

Brooks hits the proverbial nail on the head by correctly stating that
moral relativism has created a morally sick generation because there is
no agreed upon standard to follow. And yet this is something Answers in
Genesis has been warning about for years. As we continued rejecting the
absolute authority of the Creator God and His Word in the culture, ruin
and destruction are guaranteed to follow.

Brooks' solution to this pervasive problem is first "reintroducing . . .
a moral vocabulary" and then "holding people responsible" and "holding everybody responsible." But herein lies the problem, for how will
this relativistic culture ever decide on what values and morals to promote
or prescribe? And who gets to decide? Our culture has, by and large,
replaced God's absolute foundation for morality — His Word — with
the idea that man now decides what truth, decency, and morality are. As
soon as man decides truth, we're right back to "everyone did what was
right in his own eyes" (Judg. 21:25) and you end up with a society like
ours! We see this pattern repeated over and over in Scripture, and now
we are seeing it in our own generation. And the pattern still repeats itself
today. I predicted in the 1980s in my book *The Lie: Evolution* that the
turn of our culture from basing its thinking on God's Word to man's
ideas in the issue of origins would result in a steady loss of biblical morality and values across the nation. And unfortunately, that's exactly what
has happened.

What people need to see is that moral relativism simply doesn't work.
In any community or culture, there must be an unchanging standard for
morality and ethics, and the only absolute standard that transcends culture, society, and generation is God's unchanging Word.

We've built a few buildings at Answers in Genesis, and any contrac-
tor will tell you that when pouring a foundation upon which a building
will rest, that foundation must be solid, not shifting.

Jesus grew up in a carpenter's home. And he knew something about
building things that last. What He later said concerning individuals
equally applies to societies.

Everyone then who hears these words of mine and does them will be like a wise man who built his house on the rock. And the rain fell, and the floods came, and the winds blew and beat on that house, but it did not fall, because it had been founded on the rock. And everyone who hears these words of mine and does not do them will be like a foolish man who built his house on the sand. And the rain fell, and the floods came, and the winds blew and beat against that house, and it fell, and great was the fall of it (Matt. 7:24–27).

Unless we reverse course and return to the bedrock, foundational Judeo-Christian beliefs in the Creator and His unchanging morality, we too will fall. And the experiment that was once America will have failed, having lasted only a few centuries. The cracks in our foundation are openly visible, though some try to deny it. The truth is that we are rapidly crumbling and soon to collapse unless Christians take action.

Time to Return and Stand

Sadly, our culture and even much of the Church has rejected what God's Word says about these foundational truths. This is what may have prompted one of the wisest men who ever lived to write,

Righteousness exalts a nation, but sin is a reproach to any people (Prov. 14:34).

While some may point out the need for common values and morality, and accountability to these values, they do not point out the only true solution to moral relativism and moral decline. Jesus Christ and His gospel message are the only answer to our society's problems and tremendous moral landslide. As Christians, we must be bold and unwavering in sharing the good news of the gospel to our dying culture. Jesus Christ is *still* the answer! However, increasingly we have generations who don't understand the gospel and won't listen because they have been led to believe the Book (God's Word) the gospel comes from is flawed in this "scientific age." In many ways, the 20s generation is speaking a different language and doesn't understand the gospel when it's communicated to them in the same way the older generations have done. For instance, generations ago, when someone said the word "God" in the public schools in America, most students and teachers would think of one God — the Creator God of the Bible. But when you say the word "God" in the public (government) schools today, most students and teachers will ask, "Which god?" — as there are many gods — the Muslim god, Hindu gods, the Buddhist concept of god, and so on. Unless one begins by defining the terms (such as God, sin, etc.) and giving the foundational history to understand the gospel, the coming generations don't "hear" the message!

I believe God has raised up the evangelistic ministries of Answers in Genesis, the Creation Museum, and the coming Ark Encounter in our day to call both Church and culture to return to a firm stand on the authority of the Word of God. We are here to do our part! And understanding the culture and how the coming generations think and interpret words is key to knowing how to present the gospel in this era of history. At Answers in Genesis, the Creation Museum, and Ark Encounter, we have a unique way of presenting the gospel — by starting at the beginning. This is the same way God does it in the Bible! And we define the words we use (God, sin, etc.) so those listening understand the message. We also present the answers to the skeptical questions people have today because they have been so brainwashed in evolutionary humanistic ideas. Such brainwashing (which intensely occurs in much of the public education system that most kids from the Church attend) has resulted in the coming generations doubting God's Word from the very beginning. We use creation and general Bible apologetics to deal with this doubt and unbelief, so they will listen as we explain the terms and give them the foundational history to then understand the saving gospel message.

In May 2015, news headlines appeared across America and around the world similar to this one from CNN: "America's Changing Religious Landscape," which clearly shows Christianity declining in America. Headlines appeared in secular news sources stating: "Millennials leaving church in droves, study finds."[7]

The actual survey (conducted by the Pew Research Center) stated:

---

7. http://www.cnn.com/2015/05/12/living/pew-religion-study/.

But the major new survey of more than 35,000 Americans by the Pew Research Center finds that the percentage of adults (ages 18 and older) who describe themselves as Christians has dropped by nearly eight percentage points in just seven years, from 78.4% in an equally massive Pew Research survey in 2007 to 70.6% in 2014. Over the same period, the percentage of Americans who are religiously unaffiliated — describing themselves as atheist, agnostic or "nothing in particular" — has jumped more than six points, from 16.1% to 22.8%. And the share of Americans who identify with non-Christian faiths also has inched up, rising 1.2 percentage points, from 4.7% in 2007 to 5.9% in 2014.

This just verifies the alarm Answers in Genesis has been sounding for years, and the dire need to proclaim the truth of God's Word and the gospel as we are doing at AiG, through the Creation Museum and through the life-size ark (the Ark Encounter).

As we ponder the cultural changes that seem to be escalating before our eyes, my wife often says to me:

My heart aches as I think about the culture our grandchildren are growing up in — what are they going to be dealing with? It's so important we help train them to stand solidly on God's Word, knowing how to defend the faith. They are going to have so many pressures to deal with if the anti-Christian sentiment keeps growing as it is — I pray God will protect them and help them to be strong in their faith!

Imagine if you could open a window and look into the future to see where America will be spiritually in coming generations. What would you see?

Actually, Answers in Genesis has opened that window, in fact *two* windows — and what we see burdens us even more to ramp up the spread of God's Word and the gospel as we "contend for the faith."

Window 1: Our 2014 research analyzing the state of the 20s (and 40s) age groups in our churches by America's Research Group (ARG).

Window 2: In the first half of 2015, we contracted with ARG to conduct a general population study to determine how many people will come to the life-size ark when it's eventually opened.

As part of that research, we asked them to also find out the spiritual state of the general population.

As we specifically consider the 20-somethings (ages 20–29), we can get a glimpse of what the "new America" will be if this culture continues on the same downward spiraling path it is on spiritually.

What a critical time it is to publicly, boldly, and unashamedly "contend for the faith" and to call both Church and culture back to the authority of the Word of God.

I've already shared some of these results, but let's consider the research in more detail, taking a look into these windows and into the future.

Window 1 — looking into the 20s age group in churches today. The 20s group (often the group called "the Millennials"), will be the leaders of the culture in the near future.

Of those in their 20s who attend church regularly:

(a) 42.5% state they are not born again.

(b) 85.1% attended a public elementary school; 87.9% attended public high school.

(c) 22.8% left high school believing the Bible was less true.

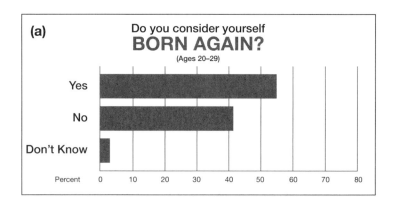

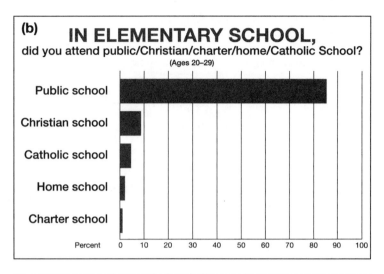

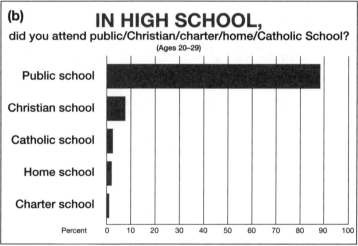

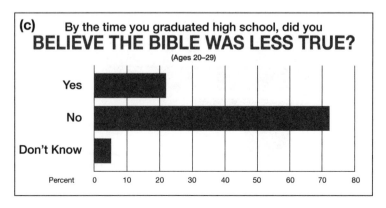

(d) 45.7% said they were not taught to defend their faith at Sunday school.

(e) 29.2% say homosexual behavior is not a sin and 14.5% don't know if it is a sin.

(f) 41.4% believe gay couples should be allowed to "marry" and have legal rights; an additional 11.5% say they don't know if they should or not.

(g) 21.8% believe there are other books (other than the Bible) that are inspired by God and an additional 10.9% don't know if there are.

(h) 64.9% believe if you are a good person you will go to heaven.

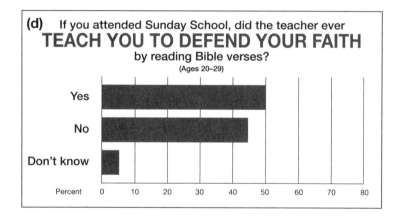

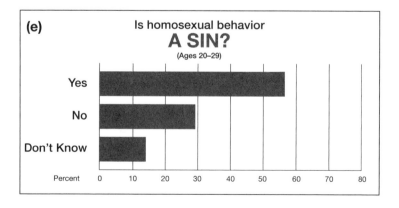

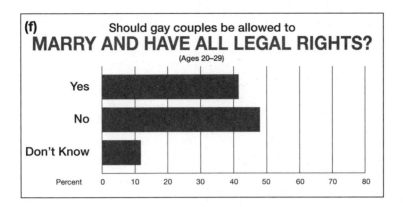

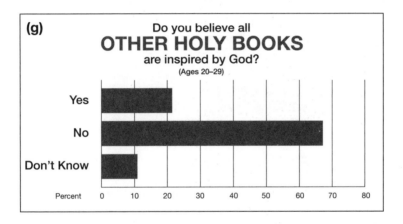

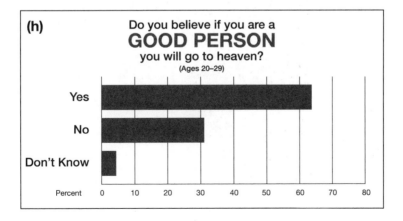

Our research also showed conclusively that the issue of the age of the earth/universe was one of the major factors causing this generation to doubt the Bible can be trusted as the inerrant Word of God.

> (i) 26.6% believe the Bible contains errors (and an additional 12.3% don't know if it has errors).

For those who say the Bible has errors, when asked to identify one of those errors, the age of the earth was one of the biggest issues. Also note that problems with the Book of Genesis and specifically the Flood of Noah's day also rated highly. In other words, the origins issue is a major issue with those who believe the Bible has errors.

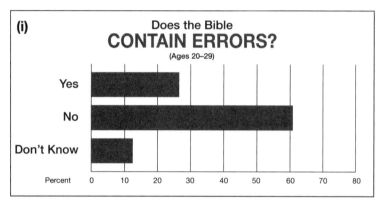

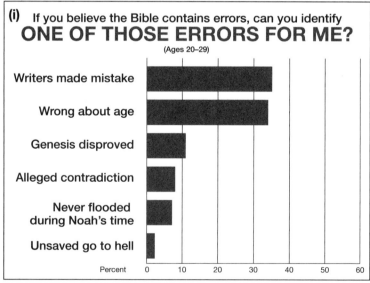

When the researchers then gave the options listed in the graph and asked the question, "Which of these makes you question the Bible the most?"

(j) the majority picked the age of the earth as the major issue.

(k) 23.2% said someone had challenged their Christian faith.

When asked which Christian principle they were challenged on, the age of the earth remained the predominant one.

Our previous research and 40 years of ministry experience clearly shows that the majority of Christian leaders either compromise with millions of years or say the age of the earth/universe doesn't matter. Yet, our

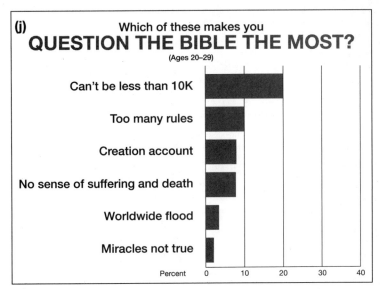

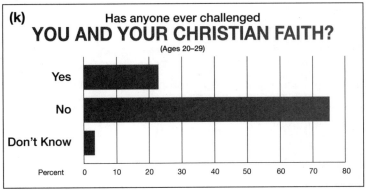

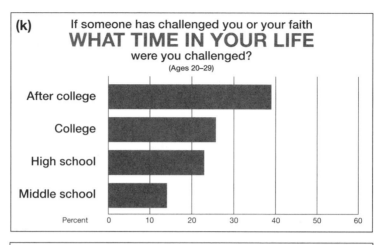

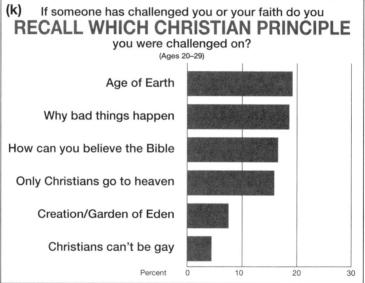

2009 *Already Gone* published research showed the age of the earth was a significant problem among the two-thirds of the 20s age group that was leaving the church by college age. This new research confirms this is an issue. In a way it's a "big elephant" in the room in our churches that most Christian leaders either refuse to acknowledge or endorse the compromise with millions of years.

Don't you sigh when you read the previous statistics? Aren't you troubled and burdened when you realize that these are the 20s group *that attend church!* There's something dreadfully wrong here.

The Reshaping of a Nation

Now let's look at Window 2.

In the general population study for the ark research, our researchers also found the following:

a. Of those who regularly attended church as children, 22% of the 60s age group had stopped attending, but 53% of the 20s age group had stopped attending.

b. 86% of the 60s age group believe Noah's ark was actually built, but only 52% of the 20s age group believe this.

c. 60% of the 60s age group believe the Christian faith is under attack today, but only 34% of the 20s group believe this.

There is much more revealing detail in the sad results of this research, but there is no doubt that the 20s group in the churches and in the world is much more secular than previous generations.

Remember, it only takes one generation to lose a culture. And we are certainly seeing the loss of the once predominantly Christianized worldview in our culture.

This generation — the 20s age group — if it doesn't change, will clearly represent a fundamentally new America.

Back in 2009, Answers in Genesis published the book *Already Gone*. This book detailed research by ARG into the 20s age group that once attended church regularly but had left the Church. Nearly two-thirds of the 20-somethings are in this group.

We found out then, and have found out again in our new 2014 research on the Church, that the acceptance of millions of years (old earth) by the majority of church leaders, the lack of teaching of apologetics in churches and Christian homes, and the effect of public school education are hands down the major reasons the 20-somethings are leaving the Church.

This 20s age group within and without the Church increasingly have a very secular worldview. And most of the ones who still attend church regularly don't really understand Christianity.

Back in 2011, I co-authored the book *Already Compromised*. In it, we dealt with research ARG conducted on the state of primarily conservative Christian universities, Bible colleges, and seminaries.

In this study, the beliefs/teachings of their presidents, vice-presidents, and heads of the science and religion (Bible) departments were researched. Sadly, as stated previously, we found that the majority of them believe in millions of years. We also found many other shocking and revealing statistics regarding the sad state of the majority of these institutions. Parents need to carefully research Christian colleges before sending their students off to an institution that could sadly undermine the foundation of their Christian faith.

So that's the bad news! In reality, it's much worse than the summary I've just given you, as there were so many other areas that show that so many of the 20s group in the Church do not have a Christian worldview.

You may wonder, "But what can we do? It seems so overwhelming." Many have said to me they just get depressed and feel like giving up and waiting for Jesus to come. But we need to listen to how God's Word instructs us. In Luke 19 we read a parable by Jesus:

> A nobleman went into a far country to receive for himself a kingdom and then return. Calling ten of his servants, he gave them ten minas, and said to them, *"Engage in business until I come"* (Luke 19:12–14, emphasis added).

One translation states, "occupy till I come."

Jesus gives Christians (His servants), talents and gifts that they are to use until He comes. The point is, we need to be faithful in being about the Master's work — *regardless* of what we see happening around us. We don't know where we are in the time-line of the last days — if anything, we need to be more fired up, more passionate, show more "righteous anger" (like Nehemiah), and be more urgent in proclaiming the truth of God's Word and the gospel so people will hear and listen.

Too Late for a U-Turn?

Perhaps you've heard the fictional account of radio transmission between American and Canadian authorities off the coast of Newfoundland during a heavy fog. This radio conversation reads,

U.S. Naval Vessel: "Please divert your course 15 degrees to the north to avoid a collision."

Canadians: "Negative. Recommend you divert YOUR course 15 degrees to the South to avoid a collision."

U.S. Naval Vessel: "This is the captain of a U.S. Navy ship. I say again, divert YOUR course."

Canadians: "No, I say again, you divert YOUR course."

U.S. Naval Vessel: "THIS IS THE AIRCRAFT CARRIER *USS ABRAHAM LINCOLN*, THE SECOND LARGEST SHIP IN THE UNITED STATES' ATLANTIC FLEET. WE ARE ACCOMPANIED BY THREE DESTROYERS, THREE CRUISERS, AND NUMEROUS SUPPORT VESSELS. I DEMAND THAT YOU CHANGE YOUR COURSE 15 DEGREES NORTH. THAT'S ONE-FIVE DEGREES NORTH, OR COUNTER MEASURES WILL BE UNDERTAKEN TO ENSURE THE SAFETY OF THIS SHIP."

Canadians: "This is a lighthouse. Your call."

While humorous, this apocryphal story nonetheless illustrates a sobering truth. We are a country very much like that ship's captain — blind, misguided, trusting his instincts instead of the facts, and way too stubborn to admit he is wrong. What we need is national course correction that begins with repentance. Though originally made in the context of God's relationship to His covenant people, Israel, the principle of repentance and blessing applies to us today as well.

> If my people who are called by my name humble themselves, and pray and seek my face and turn from their wicked ways, then I will hear from heaven and will forgive their sin and heal their land (2 Chron. 7:14).

Notice God's word to King Solomon begins with a call to humility. If we are to ever turn back the tide of relativism, we must first humble ourselves before God. This means admitting that man and his foolish ideas and ways have failed. So can we do this? Is it possible? Can we bow our stiff necks before Almighty God, or will we continue in the charade of pretending we know better than Him?

Humility, however, is only the beginning. God also requires that we pray, seek His face, and turn from our wicked ways. We have to repent of the cancerous evils we've allowed to plague our nation. Homosexuality, gay "marriage," abortion, and the pagan religion of evolutionary thought — those are the altars we've built to the gods of pluralism, relativism, atheism, and immorality. And like ancient Israel, we must tear down those altars and return to the godly values and pursuits that once made this country great. It is *only then* that God will hear from heaven, forgive our sin, and heal our land.

However, this healing will not magically happen on its own. We cannot continue depending on political leaders to right the wrongs in our country. Rather, it's the Holy Spirit, working through you and the Church that must be the initial and primary catalyst causing such radical, sweeping change. According to 2 Thessalonians 2:6–7, God's Spirit working in the Church is the current restraining influence in the world today preventing evil from completely flooding our land. And though there is no promised last days' revival in Scripture prior to the Rapture, that doesn't mean there will not be one. Even so, if we are to begin turning things around in the right direction, we must be willfully intentional and spiritually strategic. And such a "turning things around" must begin in the home and church!

No White Flag

There is no doubt that we are in a war. It's a cultural conflict and a moral battle. It's a fight for the minds of a generation. Our ultimate enemy is not people, but rather an entity whose mission is to destroy those whom God loves. Paul wrote to the Ephesian believers,

> For we do not wrestle against flesh and blood, but against the rulers, against the authorities, against the cosmic powers over this present darkness, against the spiritual forces of evil in the heavenly places. Therefore take up the whole armor of God, that you may be able to withstand in the evil day, and having done all, to stand firm (Eph. 6:12–13).

Our adversary, the devil, roams about like a roaring lion, seeking someone to devour (1 Pet. 5:8). And though these words are directed at believers,

Satan also seeks to destroy humanity itself. Like a thief, he comes only to "steal and kill and destroy" (John 10:10). His greatest desire is to blind people to the gospel and keep them from experiencing the forgiveness, freedom, and salvation found in Jesus Christ (2 Cor. 4:4).

Because we have such a formidable enemy, this is precisely why believers must be educated, trained, equipped, and armed with the will to do battle, even if it comes down to the last man.

This courageous spirit is modeled throughout the Bible, and is what separated men and women of faith from the vast compromising crowd. It's a ferocious faith that refuses to give up.

We see it in Moses, leading two million Hebrews out of Egypt and across the Red Sea in the midst of impossible odds.

We see it in Joshua, taking the next generation of Jews into the conquest of the Promised Land, and just before his death, challenging an entire nation, "Choose this day whom you will serve, whether the gods your fathers served in the region beyond the River, or the gods of the Amorites in whose land you dwell. But as for me and my house, we will serve the LORD" (Josh. 24:15).

We see it in young David, who refused to stand by and let a pagan giant taunt the armies of the living God.

We see it in Paul who could not tolerate seeing so many idols in Athens. Something moved him to speak. Paul wasn't merely "street preaching." He was engaging his culture by reaching them where they were and demonstrating the evidence for the true God (Acts 17).

We see it on display through the lives of faith's heroes in Hebrews 11 — men and women who fought valiantly in the fields of faith, casting aside comfort for something better that awaited them.

But nowhere do we see this spirit of courage, faith, and perseverance displayed more than with the Lord Jesus Christ. If ever there was a time to give up the fight, it was when He was arrested in the Garden of Gethsemane. If ever there was a time to turn back, it was when He was being whipped and beaten beyond belief. If ever there was a time to surrender and raise a white flag, it was at the Cross when God the Father unleashed the full fury of eternal wrath on Him.

And yet He persevered. But why?

Hebrews 12:1–2 tells us why:

Therefore, since we are surrounded by so great a cloud of witnesses, let us also lay aside every weight, and sin which clings so closely, and let us run with endurance the race that is set before us, looking to Jesus, the founder and perfecter of our faith, *who for the joy that was set before him endured the cross, despising the shame,* and is seated at the right hand of the throne of God (emphasis added).

Jesus, the fountainhead of faith itself, is the One who perfectly modeled it for us. He endured the horror of the Cross, disregarding the shame associated with such a death because of the "*joy* that was set before Him." But what kind of joy is this referring to? I believe there are three possibilities:

1. The joy of having pleased His Father, and to have fulfilled the mission/work God sent Him to do (John 17:4)

2. The joy of being reinstated at the right hand of the Father following His Resurrection (John 17:5; Heb. 1:3, 12:2)

3. The joy of accomplishing salvation for sinners like you and me (Heb. 2:10)

Perhaps His joy encompassed all three of these honorable goals, seeing as how they were all realized once the suffering of the Cross had run its course.

It is His enduring faith, forged through a life of obedience and tested through suffering that we seek to emulate. And it is exactly His example we look to when encountering opposition in our walk of faith. So many Christians cringe at the slightest sign of hostility, challenge, or backlash regarding their beliefs. But the author of Hebrews reminds us that we have not "resisted to the point of shedding . . . blood" like our Lord did (Heb. 12:4). And even then, He did not surrender the fight. His example is the reason we "may not grow weary or fainthearted" (Heb. 12:3).

Jesus fought and endured to the end because He had a passion to honor the Father. He fought because He longed to return to His rightful place of authority at the Father's side. And He persevered because He knew there was something worth fighting for.

You.

You and I are alive in God today because He stayed the course. Jesus did not allow the Pharisees and religious teachers of His day to misinterpret and compromise the Word of God. He corrected them, showing God's people a better way (Matt. 5–7, 23).

When Christ ascended back to heaven following His Resurrection, He left His disciples in charge of carrying on the task of "making disciples" (Matt. 28:18–20). Deputizing them with the power of the Holy Spirit (Acts 1:8), they were to take His life-changing gospel to the nations, even to the "uttermost part of the earth" (KJV). Anything that undermines that message by subverting the truth of God's Word must be fought. Our war is not waged out of hatred *against* people, but rather due to love *for* them. It is a war to redeem, rescue, and deliver them from lies which blind them to the truth and saving grace of Jesus Christ.

There is a time for tolerance, a time to turn the other cheek, and a time to be silent. But there is also a time to fight. But it's not just fighting for fighting's sake. Or even just to be "right" or win an argument. It's doing battle for the sake of humanity, the Christian faith, and the glory of God. Unlike other religions that wage "holy wars," spilling the blood of their enemies and the innocent, being a "soldier of the cross" means fighting on your knees before moving forward into the workplace, the marketplace, the high school and university classroom. But as we've seen, the battle must also be fought in our own churches. We must lovingly challenge our church's leadership to go before us into battle through equipping an army of Christ-followers.

The best way to change a society or culture is not to enact laws but to redeem hearts. After all, God's Word teaches us, "For as he thinketh in his heart, so is he"(Prov. 23:7; KJV). It seems the secularists understand this principle more than many Christians! Secularists have captured the minds of generations of kids from the Church, and now they are capturing their hearts also. In many ways, so many Christians handed their children over to the secularists (such as in the public education system) to be trained, and now we wonder why we are losing them from the Church. And we wonder why even many of those young people in the Church have such a secularized worldview! Christians need to be active in training their children as the Bible instructs us — from birth.

And what happens should we remain mediocre and silent, hiding behind the walls of our homes and churches? Should this be our strategy, we as a nation will certainly become Rome. It is foolish naiveté and ignorance to think otherwise. We will become Sodom and Gomorrah. And the floodwaters of evil will continue to rise, drowning out the voice of righteousness.

As Christians though, we do not quit. The word "surrender" is not in our vocabulary. We do not give up. It is not in our spiritual DNA, as we are by nature overcomers. "Greater is he that is in you, than he that is in the world" (1 John 4:4; KJV). Among the most admirable characteristics followers of Christ possess is the ability to persevere.

So take down your white flag of surrender. Burn it if you need to. And in its place raise the banner of the Cross. Lift high the standard of truth in your heart, home, and church. Let the light of God's truth in your words and deeds shine before all men, so that they may see and glorify your Father who is in heaven.

Chapter 9

A Game Plan

Start at Home

So where do we go from here? How should these truths we've discussed impact us going forward? What should be our strategy and what are some practical ways to implement it?

To begin with, it's no secret that there is a crisis of leadership today in the Christian home. And unfortunately, men are often the most difficult group to motivate toward spirituality. You could attempt to blame this on the pressure and preoccupation men have with making a living and providing for their families. But Scripture tells a different story. This spiritual passivity in Christian men traces its roots all the way back to Genesis, to the very beginning of mankind itself.

In Genesis 2 we see God creating Adam, giving him responsibility to cultivate and keep the garden He's provided (Gen. 2:15). God then created woman from Adam's rib, appointing him as head, leader, and protector over her (Gen. 2:21–23; Eph. 5:22–27). But when we read the account of the serpent's temptation in Genesis 3, we find the man strangely absent in his leadership role. Instead of protecting and shielding his wife from the serpent's influence, he stood idly by while she was tempted into sin. Though not explicitly mentioned, when Eve gave the fruit to her husband in Genesis 3:6, it is assumed that he was nearby. Following God's declaration that it was "not good that the man should be alone" (Gen. 2:18), and Adam, having felt the void of not having a "helper suitable" for him in 2:20, it makes sense that the man and woman were virtually inseparable as newlyweds. The "cleaving" (bonding commitment) of the man to the woman goes far beyond a mere sexual purpose, but extends to the emotional, relational, and spiritual aspects of their union. They were *together*.

Thus, Adam exhibited passivity in his leadership when he allowed his wife to be deceived by the devil. Today, we see man's sin demonstrated either in blatant passivity or in dominating his wife, "lording" his influence over her. Both are unscriptural. Further, as part of the post-sin curse upon humanity, Eve would capitalize on the man's failure to lead, and desire to "rule" over her husband (Gen. 3:16). We see this today in Christian homes where the wife is the primary spiritual influence in the children's lives. Of course she should be a powerful presence spiritually in her children's lives, but when husbands and fathers fail to initiate that leadership and influence, a void is created, and women typically fill it.

However, this is not God's design.

We need to be diligent and realize that every child conceived in a mother's womb is a being who will live forever either in heaven or hell. What a reminder of the awesome responsibility parents have to do their best to teach their children to worship the Son and to put their faith in the Lord Jesus Christ as their Creator Redeemer.

According to Scripture, the home, above everywhere else, is the epicenter of spiritual development. As God commanded Moses,

> You shall love the LORD your God with all your heart and with all your soul and with all your might. And these words that I command you today shall be on your heart. You shall *teach* them diligently to your children, and shall *talk* of them when you sit in your house, and when you *walk* by the way, and when you lie down, and when you rise. You shall bind them as a sign on your hand, and they shall be as frontlets between your eyes. You shall write them on the doorposts of your house and on your gates (Deut. 6:5–9, emphasis added).

Moses' words speak to the practical, daily nature of imparting faith to our children. It begins by loving "the Lord your God with all your heart." A dynamic relationship with God is a dad's greatest asset. It is from this vertical relationship that wisdom, patience, and endurance flows horizontally to the family. And these are three indispensable qualities in parenting. Further, having God's Word "on the heart" of the father makes it an inward reality and not just an outward expression. Though as parents we have in inherent authority over our children, our *position* as fathers is not enough to effectively raise children. Mere external pressure from parent to child may curb some behavior, but it cannot make a disciple. Our authority as parents is enhanced by our spirituality, and that begins in the heart, from the inside out. Fathers must be changed supernaturally by being born again from above. But it doesn't stop there. An effective Christian father is one who continues to progress in his faith. And nowhere is this more important than in his interaction with God's Word. Hearing from God on a regular basis is what keeps a dad strong, centered, and tethered to the anchor of faith. This spiritual transformation is essential to male leadership in the home.

Next, Moses outlines practical ways to impart wisdom and faith to our children, using three memorable words.

Teach — "You shall teach them diligently to your children." This speaks of a commitment to faithfulness on the part of fathers to consistently communicate God's character and truth to their children. Remember the account of Mary and Martha of Bethany? Dr. Luke writes of one particular scene in chapter 10, verses 38–42 of his gospel. Martha is busy serving the Lord, preparing a meal for Him. A worthy task? Yes. An honorable offering? Absolutely. But meanwhile, Mary is "doing nothing," just sitting at the feet of Jesus, soaking in His words. So Martha tells Jesus to rebuke Mary for not serving. Jesus responds by politely but firmly telling Martha to back off, because Mary had chosen a higher and more important activity. Mary would later serve Jesus in a way the whole world would remember (John 12:1–8; Mark 14:3–9). Martha could have taken some lessons on spirituality from her sister.

So Jesus also elevated the importance of teaching the Word of God in His ministry. For us to do this in the home, I believe we must be

diligent to communicate the Scriptures in a way that is both accurate
and relevant. And this includes teaching them to defend the Christian
faith against the attacks of our day.

Again, Jesus is our model, as He spent times of *formal teaching* with
His disciples (Matt. 5:1–2). These are the "official" times set aside to
impart truth to our children, both at home and when the church gath-
ers. These times are planned and scheduled. They take place at prear-
ranged times and often require some advance preparation.

The second word Moses uses to describe imparting the faith in the
home is *talk.* — This refers to the informal discussions about God, His
Word, life, and spirituality. It naturally happens when you "sit in the
house," or times when your family is together. It doesn't mean every conversation has to be a spiritual one, but just that your home has a "godly
ambience" about it. It means talking about the Lord is a natural thing
for your family, and not something that's forced or awkward.

The third way Moses counsels us to lead our family spiritually is
to *walk* — ". . . when you *walk* by the way, and when you lie down,
and when you rise." This type of communication is *spontaneous* and
unplanned. Jesus would use these "life moments" to teach spiritual truth
to his disciples (Mark 8:14–21). Someone has wisely noted that truth
is more often "caught" than "taught." And certainly the Master Teacher
demonstrated this truth as He regularly took advantage of "teachable
moments" to impart knowledge and wisdom from God. It's a way for
a family leader to look for God in life, and pass that knowledge and
wisdom on to his kids.

Moses concludes by commanding Israel to "bind them [God's words]
as a sign on your hand, and they shall be as frontlets between your eyes.
You shall write them on the doorposts of your house and on your gates."
Though the Jews literally did this, the idea here is that your home and
family are permeated with truth from Scripture. Again, it's a heart issue.
A Scripture verse written on a plaque in a home is simply decoration
unless it is also written on the hearts of those who live in that home.

While we cannot downplay the role of a wife and mother in spiritual
influence and "training up a child," the initial and primary responsibility
lies with the man. Like Adam in the Garden, he is ultimately responsible

for the spiritual well-being of his wife and children, and he will answer to God for that stewardship (Gen. 3:9).

The Role of the Local Church

A second critical area of influence is, of course, in the church. America is joining the trend among Western nations to slide into secularism and unbelief. This downward spiral has impacted churches and Christian homes, as well. Two-thirds of children will leave the Church after they leave home, and very few return. So what's missing in their lives? What can we do to stop the exodus and these times of great difficulty in the Church?

Through what Paul called a "falling away from the faith," many churches and even denominations have abandoned the faith Jesus commanded them to pass on (1 Tim. 4:1). I believe this is part of the "times of difficulty" the Apostle spoke of in 2 Timothy 3:1–5:

> But understand this, that in the last days there will come times of difficulty. For people will be lovers of self, lovers of money, proud, arrogant, abusive, disobedient to their parents, ungrateful, unholy, heartless, unappeasable, slanderous, without self-control, brutal, not loving good, treacherous, reckless, swollen with conceit, lovers of pleasure rather than lovers of God, having the appearance of godliness, but denying its power. Avoid such people.

And what was Paul's remedy for this coming epidemic of apostasy? "Stay true to the Word of God!" (2 Tim. 3:14–17).

Two words stand out in Paul's admonition to pastor Timothy. The first is "learned." Timothy had been taught the Scripture "from childhood," faithfully passed down to him from his grandmother to his mother, and then finally to Timothy (2 Tim. 2:1–5). That's *three generations of faith*, preserved and passed down. And now Timothy was doing the same thing with "faithful men," who in turn were to "teach others also." It was important for Paul that Timothy "continue" in the truths he had learned and come to embrace by faith. Many churches today are focused on using their church services and ministries for evangelistic purposes, often to the neglect of equipping believers.

But the primary job of the organized church is to train followers of Christ, *not* reach the world (Eph. 4:11ff). Believers themselves are to be salt and light, reaching the lost with the gospel as they go into the world (Matt. 28:18–20). We have reversed this mandate, removing the stewardship of the individual Christian for evangelism and instead abdicating it to the corporate church. But the church's job is "to equip the saints for the work of ministry, for building up of the body of Christ" (Eph. 4:12). We gather for edification and equipping and scatter into the world for evangelism. But when "doing church" for the purpose of attracting the unsaved is what drives Sunday morning services, the church has lost her way.

This kind of Pauline "discipleship learning" is part of what's missing in Christian churches and homes today. We have the appearance of godliness (what Paul refers to as a "form of godliness" in 2 Tim. 3:5), but the supernatural power of this godliness is being denied because of a preoccupation with pleasing and entertaining self (2 Tim. 3:1–4). In a church culture obsessed with consumerism and "customer satisfaction," there is little room to think of others or giving your life away for the sake of another, perhaps younger, disciple. Many churches focus their energy on elaborate Sunday morning productions to attract people — instead of emphasizing the teaching of the Word and equipping God's people to answer the skeptical questions of our day. There is nothing wrong with music, drama, or technology, of course, but I'm talking about the main emphasis within the church. Sadly, many churches think entertainment is what the 20s generation wants, instead of giving them the answers they need to know so they can trust God's Word from the beginning. Personally, I've found the 20s generation to be hungry for answers! But the Church also needs to be involved in training men to be husbands and fathers, and women to be wives and mothers.

It has been wisely stated, "You cannot impart what you do not possess." If you haven't been taught, trained, discipled, and equipped, there's no chance you will do the same things for someone else.

Consequently, most fathers haven't been taught to be the spiritual head by their church. Nevertheless, part of the church's role should be to teach and help fathers to be the spiritual heads of their homes. And how is this to be done? Why not do it like Jesus and Paul did? Find faithful men who are hungry to be the men God wants them to be and "entrust" the truth of God to them. In the Church, we often obsess over planning, packaging, programming, and ministries. For Jesus and Paul, what mattered was spending time with men in order to invest the Word into them. What that looks like in a particular church is not as important as the fact that it gets done. We cannot let *form* trump *substance*. Every church should be committed to discipling men. And this training and equipping must be *comprehensive*. Remember, Jesus had a relatively short amount of time to impart a very large amount of truth to His disciples, and yet He had resolved in His heart to give them a wide variety of content. But it wasn't just content for content's sake. Jesus gave His closest followers a well-rounded theological education. He wanted their knowledge of God to be comprehensive, and that necessitated much time teaching them. In John 17:4–8, Jesus gives us a private look into His innermost thoughts and feelings as He prays His great high priestly prayer. In it, He tells the Father He has completed the work He was given to do (4), having faithfully "manifested your name to the people whom you gave me out of the world" (6). This took place, Jesus prays, because he had given them "the words that you gave me," and they accepted them (8).

Paul followed Jesus' example, motivating him to declare the "whole counsel of God" to the believers at Ephesus during his three-year stay there. (Acts 20:27–31).

What this says to us is that pastors should teach the whole Bible to the church. Not that they have to cover every detail in Scripture's 66 books, but the idea is that they are given a solid working understanding of the Bible as a whole, along with an ability to understand and articulate a defense of God's Word and the person and work of Christ. This helps to ensure churches produce a generation of well-rounded and fully equipped disciples.

Specifically, this means teaching through books of the Bible, overviews of Scripture, Bible study books, Bible-based Christian books, topical studies, the attributes of God, the fundamentals of the faith, basic Christian doctrines, character studies and modern-day issues and how Scripture speaks to them, and in-depth general Bible and creation apologetics. At times of national crisis or newsworthy items regarding theology or morality, it is necessary to "capture the moment" by taking a break from what you're studying to address or discuss a certain issue (e.g., school shootings, war, moral issues, terrorism, attack on the family, death and suffering and a loving God, etc.). Doing this mirrors in the Church what Moses commanded Israel to do in the home — demonstrating that Scripture is "living and active" and applies to any and all life situations.

I am reminded of 1 Chronicles 12:32 and the sons of Issachar, "who had understanding of the times. . . ." These men interpreted the times in which they lived and applied wisdom regarding what needed to be done. Christian parents today need to understand the times we live in and what needs to be taught to their children — how to pass the spiritual legacy on to the coming generations and influence the world for Christ.

No one would ever say that "training up a child" was an easy task. It involves time, energy, preparation, and hard work over much time. It requires the Church and family to cooperate and work together for the common good of our young people and for the greater glory of our God.

It's all about *investment*, which is the heart of discipleship. It's what Jesus did, what Paul practiced, and what got the Church this far in history. Though challenging and often risky, I firmly believe it pays off and comes back to bless you in the long run.

Additionally, the ripple effects of this discipleship from pastor to congregation extends beyond the home to the community as well. As Christians, we need bold, brave, and equipped brothers and sisters who will become active in their communities, school boards, and other organizations in order to promote godly change from the bottom up. Isn't that what being "salt and light" is all about? In these settings, Christians can ask challenging questions about the exclusion of sound Christian values from schools, the acceptance of the religion of humanism, and the absence of critical thinking when it comes to teaching evolution, etc. Based on the U.S. Constitution, no single religion should be endorsed in a government-run school. Unless we stand up to challenge these ideas, the schools will continue to indoctrinate students with the religious beliefs of humanists.[1] At the present time, the government in America is using tax dollars to fund indoctrinating students in public schools in a religion — the religion of naturalism (which is atheism).

The first step is for dads and moms (God's leaders in the home) to take this cultural and spiritual crisis seriously and then to become equipped in defending their faith. Talk to your pastor. Mobilize and organize a group of parents, other adults, and teenagers for a series in basic apologetics. Contact us at AiG and we can connect you to the appropriate resources. If Christian parents truly understood the intensity of the warfare in which we are engaged, they would not hesitate to pursue such a course of action.

The time is now!

Public School, Private Decision

In the last chapter, I stated that an "elephant in the room" was the fact that so many Christian leaders have compromised with millions of years or ignore this issue that our research has shown has had a significant influence on the 20s generation in regard to doubting and disbelieving Scripture.

But there's another "elephant in the room" that also needs to be dealt with. It's one many parents and Christian leaders won't address, or don't know how to, or don't have the courage to. But we need to face it head on!

Nearly 90 percent of kids from church homes attend public (government) schools in America. Now consider all that's been shown about the state of the 20s generation in the Church — and in the culture as a

---

1. Answers in Genesis is often misrepresented as trying to get creationist teaching into the public schools. AiG does not lobby any government agencies to include the teaching of biblical creation in the public schools. We do not believe that teaching biblical creation should be mandated in public school science classrooms. If it were mandated, it would likely be taught poorly (and possibly mockingly) by a teacher who does not understand what the Bible teaches and who believes in evolution. At the same time, it is not right that the tenets of secular humanism can be taught at the exclusion of Christian ideas. This type of exclusivity does not promote the critical thinking skills of students demanded by most science education standards. Teachers should be allowed, at the very least, the academic freedom to present various models of the history of life on earth and teach the strengths and weaknesses of those models. Recognizing that in the current political climate we can only expect to see evolution taught, it is only reasonable to include teaching the shortcomings of evolutionary ideas.

whole. I will go on record as stating that public education has had a devastating effect on children — including those from church homes. Most students do not ultimately survive the public school system spiritually, and those that do have been negatively influenced in many ways that most don't realize.

We have many of the science textbooks used in public schools in America in our library at Answers in Genesis. Over and over again these textbooks teach students that science does not involve the supernatural, and science can only allow explanations involving natural processes. Naturalism is nothing but atheism! Most public schools have, by and large, thrown out God, the Bible, prayer, and creation teaching. They now claim they are neutral, and not religious. But that is simply not true. Now such schools are imposing the religion of naturalism or atheism on generations of students.

From a biblical perspective, we are taught, "He who is not with Me is against Me; and he who does not gather with Me scatters" (Matt. 12:30; NASB). There is no neutral position here. Many Christians even think that public education is neutral in regard to religion, but this is simply not true. If the system is not for Christ, then it is against Him. If the textbooks do not harmonize with God's truth, they will naturally teach the opposite of that truth.

Do you think it would make a difference in how we view our children's training, how much time we've spent with them, who we entrust their education to if we were prepared to say, "Well, Johnny, it's Monday. I'm sending you to the church of atheism today for six hours. And then I will send you to the church of atheism for four more days this week. I do hope the hour you spend at church on Sunday will counter any wrong things you are taught."

Now I realize this is a very emotional topic for people. Many pastors know if they were to speak against the public education system, they would receive negative reactions from many, especially those who teach in government schools. But I ask you to consider this topic from a biblical perspective. How should parents view public schools?

I often hear Christian parents say something like this: "Your kids should be in the public school to witness to the other kids; you need to throw your children out into the world so they will learn to survive; they need to be mixing with non-Christian kids so they can be an example to them," and many other similar arguments. But when asked for biblical references for such a position, I often get an answer that goes something like this: "The Bible says we are to be the salt of the earth. Our children therefore need to be in the public schools so they can be salt and light to the other students." Now, it is true that Matthew 5:13 says, "You are the salt of the earth," but let's look at this passage in full context:

> *You are the salt of the earth. But if the salt loses its saltiness, how can it be made salty again? It is no longer good for anything, except to be thrown out and trampled underfoot* (NIV, emphasis added).

Mark 9:50 states something else about salt that is very important and must be taken into consideration:

> Salt is good, but if it loses its saltiness, how can you make it salty again? *Have salt among yourselves*, and be at peace with each other (NIV, emphasis added).

The point is this: *A person can't be the salt of the earth until they have salt, and it needs to be uncontaminated salt that retains its saltiness.*

Let's face it: Children are being contaminated as a result of their secular education, television, the books they read, and their friends. In a world of no absolutes, evolution, sex outside marriage, gay "marriage," attacks on gender distinction, humanism, and false religions — children will be tossed to and fro. How do they know which way to go? How do they know what to choose? They *don't*, unless they've been trained in truth and can recognize the difference between good and evil in the world. I do feel very strongly that this training is best done in the sanctifying environment of a home-based education, or diligent training at home in conjunction with a Christian school that does not compromise the Word of God, beginning in Genesis. Sadly, I have concluded from 40 years of experience in active ministry that the majority of Christian schools do compromise God's Word and really just add God to a secular worldview.

Because so many children from church homes have been trained by the government education system (which has become more and more anti-Christian over the years — to the point of eliminating Christianity totally), and because most fathers haven't really trained their children with a biblical foundation as they should, there are now generations of adults who attend church, but are so contaminated by the world that they think like the world — as we have seen in our latest research project. They lack salt, and the salt they have has lost its saltiness by contamination. These people then contaminate those around them and their own children. These children are often given no salt at all, or the little they have becomes even more contaminated than the parents' salt.

I believe that in many instances (not all, of course), what people call "teenage rebellious years" is due to a lack of being trained to acquire a taste for the things of the Lord in the early years. Once children become teenagers (and we all know that there are hormonal changes and certain behavior patterns related to puberty and adolescence), it is very difficult to change their behavior.

Contamination comes in many forms, but perhaps the saddest aspect is that much of institutional Christianity has compromised the Word of God, particularly concerning the doctrine of creation. Genesis (especially the first 11 chapters) is foundational to all Christian doctrine. Let me state my warning again: if generations are trained to disbelieve the Book of Genesis as literal history, and to embrace man's fallible ideas concerning evolution and an earth that is millions of years old, they are put on a slippery slide of unbelief through the rest of the Bible. If the Bible's *history* is not accurate, then why should the Bible's *morality* be accepted? After all, the morality is based in the history.

The literal understanding of the events in the Book of Genesis is necessary to an understanding of what Christian doctrine is all about. Sadly, some children from Christian homes are being contaminated by what are called "Christian" schools. More and more schools are being established on secular humanism and a secular curriculum to which God is added, but you can't Christianize a secular philosophy! You can't have both!

If you are going to opt for a private Christian education for your kids, don't assume *anything* when it comes to the content of the courses or the convictions of the faculty. Don't assume that the students there are going to be a positive influence on your children. Do your research on the school; monitor everything carefully, and never *shirk* your responsibility to be the one who trains your kid.

No matter what education you choose, know that you must be pouring the "salt" into your children — and this salt should be as uncontaminated as possible. Children need to be taught to acquire a taste for biblical teaching as early and as repeatedly as possible.

This process is most assured in a home-based education where the parents can take hour-by-hour responsibility for the task. A private Christian education can also be a good option, as long as a parent doesn't forget their responsibility to monitor the environment and content of the education.

Yes, we are all called to be "salt" to the world. Our children are to be this as well, but they must first be filled with pure salt from God's Word — leading to spiritual maturity and stability, so that they can be missionaries to the world without being contaminated themselves and made useless for the gospel.

Some Christian parents justify their choice of public education by saying, "Yes, but I've got *good* kids." Many child psychologists teach that children are basically "good" too, but the Bible teaches otherwise. Psalm 51:5 states, "Surely I was sinful at birth, sinful from the time my mother conceived me" (NIV). Scripture tells us that children are a precious "heritage from the LORD" (Ps. 127:3; NIV), and that they are a great blessing in a Christian home. Nevertheless, children, like adults, must be viewed first of all as sinful creatures, "For all have sinned and fall short of the glory of God" (Rom. 3:23).

I remember visiting the hospital in Australia where my sister had just had a baby. I looked at this beautiful infant and said, "What a beautiful looking sinful creature you have there!" (I was thinking of Jeremiah 17:9 that says, "The heart is deceitful above all things, and desperately sick; who can understand it?" I was nearly thrown out of the hospital, as you might imagine, but when they took this baby home, it didn't take the parents long to find out I was right!

Because of the sin nature inherent in all mankind, and the natural desires of our flesh to do evil, none of us should ever think that we are "good" enough to be able to resist temptation.

When placed in a compromising situation, we are more likely to be influenced by the bad than by the good. It's a challenge to get children to do what is right, but it is easy to let children do that which is wrong — just leave them to themselves, and they will express their true sinful tendencies.

Maturity comes with training, discipline, renewing the mind according to Scripture, and learning to walk in the power of the Holy Spirit rather than in the power of the flesh. That doesn't come naturally! It comes with maturity, and maturity takes time. Children are not miniature adults. They are unable to discriminate between good and evil. They don't have the discipline to choose between the truth and the cleverly crafted evolutionary philosophies.

Ephesians 4:14 states,

> Then we will no longer be infants, tossed back and forth by the waves, and blown here and there by every wind of teaching and by the cunning and craftiness of people in their deceitful scheming (NIV).

Paul also says in 1 Corinthians 13:11,

> When I was a child, I talked like a child, I thought like a child, I reasoned like a child. When I became a man, I put the ways of childhood behind me (NIV).

The Bible makes it clear that children are easily led astray, easily tossed to and fro, easily deceived, and so on. Because of the sin nature and the flesh, a child in a pagan environment is likely to lose saltiness faster that gaining it, even if the parent is trying hard to fill the child with uncontaminated salt at home. (Consider how much time your children spend being trained in the pagan secular system compared to how much time they receive authoritative biblical input!)

When the child becomes a man or woman, exhibiting spiritual discernment and biblical maturity, then they can maintain their salt and be salt and light to the world. Let's face it, when we as adults are given choices, our sinful tendencies draw us in the wrong direction. Would you rather read the Bible or a secular magazine? Are you more inclined to spend time praying or watching television? Would you rather go to a missions program at church or a football game at the stadium? If you have some extra money, would you prefer to buy Christian books or a new piece of furniture or new car?

I'm sure we all get the point. It's not that we shouldn't read magazines or buy a new car, but we need to consider our priorities according to what the Bible says is important, and children who still have much maturing in the Christian faith are very unlikely to do this.

So, in a sense, what I'm saying is that the salt is more likely to pour out of the children rather than to be retained by them. And if we've allowed a lot of contamination to fill up these "vessels," it is going to be very hard to "decontaminate" them. That's why parents need to work so hard to avoid as much contamination as possible, and that's why dads and moms have to work with much prayer, patience, and perseverance to ensure as much salt as possible stays in the "vessel." There also needs to be much remedial work that reminds children over and over again of biblical truths that continually instill in them a Christian worldview (and the more that happens, the more the culture as a whole will be influenced for good). And as I've stated so many times, we need to be teaching children to defend the Christian faith. An emphasis on creation apologetics and general Bible apologetics is so needed today — and it's so absent from most Christian homes and churches.

But these things are very difficult to do when the child is spending all day in an anti-God, Bible-denying, secular humanist enforcing environment.

Because of the fallen world we live in and the desires of our flesh and sinful nature, it is impossible to avoid all contamination. There are no perfect parents on this earth. We need to be aware of this and do our best to limit the contamination as best we are able, because our kids, as much as we might love them and adore them, are not "good."

Others object to my education recommendations by saying, "Wait a minute! Don't homeschooling and Christian schools force Christianity down their throats?" Sadly, I have had people tell me from time to time that their parents harshly imposed Christianity on them, causing them to reject it. "I'm not going to force religion on my kids," they assert.

In every instance where I've talked to people who have been hurt like that, Christianity was imposed legalistically from the "top down," through pressure (and sometimes power trips) where the parent tried to make themselves the ultimate authority, rather than the Bible. When parents humbly start with the Word of God and build "from the foundation up," starting with the logical foundations of all the doctrine in Genesis, not trying to prove the Bible with science, but using the Bible to understand science, and teaching children how to defend the faith by giving them answers to skeptical questions of the age — then it makes a world of difference.

Christianity then is presented as a logical and defensible faith that makes sense of the world and is confirmed by real observational science, instead of what seems to be just a collection of opinions.

This is how we need to teach our children — from the time they are born until the time they leave home.

Parents are to train children in the truth of Scripture, giving no options. For a Christian, it is not that truth is the *best* policy (as if it were one of several acceptable alternatives). No, truth is the *only* policy. Children who are merely *taught* can hear other teaching and easily depart from the truth because of their sinful flesh and their bias against God as expressed in their fallen nature. Thus, to cause children to be influenced for good, much work must be done. We must diligently *train* them in truth, exposing and condemning error for what it is. In Paul's letter to the Ephesians, he brings up another element that reduces the risk of legalism. Consider verse 4:15:

> Rather, speaking the truth in love, we are to grow up in every way into him, who is the head, into Christ.

In 1 Corinthians 13:4–7, Paul describes this "love" in detail:

> Love is patient, love is kind . . . is not arrogant, does not act unbecomingly . . . is not provoked . . . bears all things, believes all things, hopes all things, endures all things (NASB).

I would propose to anyone who has legalistic concerns about homeschooling, that when the truth is taught in an environment of this kind of love, kids will never feel like Christianity is being forced upon them. In fact, I believe the home is the *best* environment for children to experience this kind of love from the parent, even as they learn to fulfill the greatest commandment in all of Scripture:

> You shall love the LORD your God with all your heart and
> with all your soul and with all your might (Deut. 6:5).

That love becomes the basis for the "teaching . . . talking . . . and walking" we saw earlier in this passage.

Even when homeschooling or a private Christian education seem like the best options, however, circumstances can make it impossible. Allocating the time and finances for homeschooling can be difficult for single-parent families. Many families depend on a dual income, and still don't have enough for tuition at a private Christian school. In other situations, there might be disagreement between parents when either the father or mother is not a Christian. It's also possible that a solid Christian school doesn't exist in your area, or maybe you live in a country where homeschooling resources are very, very limited (or you live in a country where homeschooling is illegal). These are all serious struggles, and reflect the fact that we certainly live in a fallen world where difficulty is a part of life.

If you are one of the people in this category, the fundamentals still apply. You may have to work harder than others and you may have to access more help, but you have the same responsibility to provide foundational scriptural instruction to your children. You have the responsibility to belong to a strong Bible-believing and teaching church, and you have the responsibility to manage the circles of influence that your children are exposed to. If you have no option but for your children to be educated in the secular system, then you must acknowledge that the responsibility of the position you hold has just been magnified, and therefore checking homework and monitoring your children's friendships will be of the utmost importance.

Always remember that it is your responsibility, within your means, to see that your child is trained and educated according to biblical principles.

God is a gracious God and forgives, but the consequences of your actions will still be part of the legacy you leave . . . and you only have one opportunity to leave it, so you better be sure you're doing it as you should. If God's people do not produce godly offspring, then the application of the truth of God's Word will be severely and negatively impacted for generations to come or to the world around. Who then will be our evangelists, pastors, missionaries, Christian teachers, and Sunday school teachers?

Remember, as said earlier, every child conceived in a mother's womb is a being who will live forever in heaven or hell! And each child is a gift from God entrusted to parents to train! As parents, we will be held accountable by our Creator God. How will each of us stand up to this accountability?

Our whole Western world is changing. But really, it's the failure of so many Christian homes and churches who have not understood the times, have not stood uncompromisingly on the authority of the Word of God, and have not trained coming generations in a Christian world-view. Yes, it only takes one generation to lose a culture. That is happening right now in America and across the Western world. In many countries it has already happened.

Who has the courage to stand up and challenge homes and churches concerning the reality of what has been happening to generations of children and now the dramatic changes in the 20s generation?

As one person in his 20s said to me, "The loss of the 20s generation is really in many ways a failure of the previous generations in our homes and churches."

I agree!

So, are you ready to return? Will you help this generation return to God? If so, let's join together and fight for their souls. Much is at stake, and the time is right now!

Afterword

Over the years, I've had many parents/grandparents approach me after I have given a presentation dealing with the issues detailed in this book. Their comments typically are as follows. "We recognize the problems and admit we didn't train our children like we should have. We tried to teach them to defend their faith but in reality allowed the public education system and their peers to train and influence them. Now what can we do?" Some of them tell me their kids no longer go to church, or the grandkids have nothing to do with church. A number of these people are quite distraught as they talk to me — some even sobbing.

So what *can* we do? Here's my counsel to those struggling with this issue:

1. We have to admit that we can't go back to redo the training of our children. And if there's been a lack of training on our part as parents, there will be consequences, not only in the children, but also in generations to come — negative consequences. So we have to be willing to acknowledge that. Scripture is clear that children are not punished nor do they bear the guilt of their parents' sins.

Moses wrote,

> Fathers shall not be put to death because of their children, nor shall children be put to death because of their fathers. Each one shall be put to death for his own sin (Deut. 24:16).

The Prophet Ezekiel records,

> Yet you say, "Why should not the son suffer for the iniquity of the father?" When the son has done what is just and right, and has been careful to observe all my statutes, he shall surely live. The soul who sins shall die. The son shall not suffer for the iniquity of the father, nor the father suffer for the iniquity of the son. The righteousness of the righteous shall be upon himself, and the wickedness of the wicked shall be upon himself.
>
> But if a wicked person turns away from all his sins that he has committed and keeps all my statutes and does what is just and right, he shall surely live; he shall not die. None of the transgressions that he has committed shall be remembered against him; for the righteousness that he has done he shall live. Have I any pleasure in the death of the wicked, declares the Lord God, and not rather that he should turn from his way and live? But when a righteous person turns away from his righteousness and does injustice and does the same abominations that the wicked person does, shall he live? None of the righteous deeds that he has done shall be remembered; for the treachery of which he is guilty and the sin he has committed, for them he shall die (Ezek. 18:19–24).

However, this does not mean there aren't natural and spiritual ripple effects resulting from negligent or faulty parenting. As the Lord told Israel,

> You shall not bow down to them or serve [idols], for I the Lord your God am a jealous God, visiting the iniquity of the fathers on the children to the third and the fourth generation of those who hate me, but showing steadfast love to thousands of those who love me and keep my commandments (Exod. 20:5–6).

The undeniable truth is that every child is a product of a home and the parenting practiced in that home. Each day, we as parents impact our children, for good or for bad. This is not to say that our children will automatically become godly adults, as each person must make their own spiritual choices. But it is to say that the influence a parent exerts on a child, whether good or bad, is felt for a lifetime — or *even for generations.*

2. I believe it's important to acknowledge this problem before the Lord and seek forgiveness from Him. And He is a God who forgives. However, even with forgiveness, we may still experience the hurt of seeing the negative consequences of our previous actions before our eyes. Nonetheless, we need to know God has forgiven when there is true repentance and then work to rectify the situation as best as we are able. For the believer in Jesus, failure is never final. And Scripture's heroes are living proof that it is never too late to get right before God.

3. In many instances, I believe the fathers will have to admit to their families that they did not carry out their God-commanded responsibilities to be the spiritual head of the house. The father should ask forgiveness from his family and pray that through this example of reconciliation his adult children will be pointed to Christ. After all, God honors a "broken and contrite heart."

> The sacrifices of God are a broken spirit; a broken and contrite heart, O God, you will not despise (Ps. 51:17).

Depending on many circumstances, a dad could sit down with each child and explain how he now sees things and admit he should have done things very differently in regard to their upbringing. He should let them know he has confessed this to the Lord and then ask them to forgive him too (even if they don't even understand what this means right now). Sometimes the prodigal is not the son, but rather the father.

4. Determine going forward that you will be an example to them of what a good father (or mother) can be. The best way to do this is through practical illustrations of love for them in the circumstances they are in. It may be through being a great grandparent or by relating to your children as adults, being an encouragement to them in tangible ways.

5. In meekness and gentleness, begin offering apologetics resources (books, DVDs) for them and their children for birthdays, Christmas, or just for no reason at all. Sponsor a trip to the Creation Museum and Ark Encounter (and other biblically based facilities like Sight and Sound). Go with them on the zip lines at the Creation Museum. I've met many grandparents who paid to bring their grandkids (and kids) to the Creation Museum, giving them a great vacation as well as visiting other places (e.g., theme parks, zoos, aquariums, etc.). This can be a great time for bonding, and with the Creation Museum mixed in with other places, also a time for sharing the truth of God's Word without preaching to them. This is a practical way those with adult children can still "make a defense to anyone who asks you for a reason for the hope that is in you; yet do it with gentleness and respect" (1 Pet. 3:15).

6. Spend much time in prayer with your spouse for your children, grandchildren, and the generations to come. Prayer is the source of our power, and according to James is effective when offered by the one who has confessed his sins.

Therefore, confess your sins to one another and pray for one another, that you may be healed. The prayer of a righteous person has great power as it is working (James 5:16).

The Survey

Denomination Comparative

As part of the research America's Research Group conducted on the state of the church, those responding were asked to give what denomination they belonged to. These statistics are very revealing in a number of ways:

> 1. When those who indicated they were Catholic were removed, the overall results for the other denominations remained essentially the same!
>
> 2. The largest Protestant denomination in the USA is the Baptist group. The results showed that overall, the 20's group in the Baptists was not as bad as other denominations, but the same inherent problems are present nonetheless.

The following includes many of the detailed questions and responses that contain a wealth of information that would take another book to discuss. As you study this denominational comparative, no doubt it will provoke much discussion and more questions. The bottom line is that there is a problem throughout church denominations that needs to be addressed. There is no doubt many even in the most conservative churches need in-depth Bible and apologetics teaching.

An Important Note About the Data

To properly understand this set of comparative aggregates — you are looking at 6 columns of data for 20-year-olds based upon which church they currently attend.

We used question 2 to create these 6 sets of results.

When reviewing these findings, you need to examine the answers vertically.

For example: look at question #8, you will see 68.7% of Baptists consider themselves born again while only 35.8% of Catholics describe themselves that way. And on Question #26, 33% of Methodists believe other books like the Koran are inspired by God, while only 11.5% of non-denominationals feel that way.

Q1: Age?

	Baptist	Catholic	Non-denominational	Methodist	Church of Christ	Presbyt. USA
25–29	49.7	62.5	60.6	53.0	60.0	51.0
20–24	50.3	37.5	39.4	47.0	40.0	49.0

Q2: Which church denomination do you primarily attend?

	Baptist	Catholic	Non-den.	Methodist	Ch. of Christ	Presbyt. USA
Baptist Church	100.0	0.0	0.0	0.0	0.0	0.0
Catholic	0.0	100.0	0.0	0.0	0.0	0.0
Non-denominational	0.0	0.0	100.0	0.0	0.0	0.0
Methodist	0.0	0.0	0.0	100.0	0.0	0.0
Presbyterian USA	0.0	0.0	0.0	0.0	0.0	100.0
Church of Christ	0.0	0.0	0.0	0.0	100.0	0.0

Q3: How often did you attend church when you were growing up?

	Baptist	Catholic	Non-den.	Methodist	Ch. of Christ	Presbyt. USA
Most Sundays	46.9	22.5	39.4	40.0	20.0	33.3
Every week	24.6	51.7	19.2	19.0	28.6	19.6
Twice a month	11.7	10.0	14.4	19.0	31.4	17.6
Less than lx month	7.8	2.5	15.4	16.0	5.7	17.6
Never	3.9	7.5	9.6	4.0	2.9	3.9
Once a month	5.0	5.8	1.9	2.0	11.4	7.8

Q6: When you lived at home with your parents, how often did you pray together as a family?

	Baptist	Catholic	Non-den.	Methodist	Ch. of Christ	Presbyt. USA
Only at mealtime	43.6	25.0	36.5	44.0	40.0	51.0
Few times a week	16.2	30.8	15.4	20.0	8.6	25.5
Every day	17.9	31.7	16.3	9.0	25.7	7.8
Christian holidays	17.3	8.3	26.9	22.0	17.1	13.7
Once a week	5.0	4.2	4.8	5.0	8.6	2.0

Q8: Do you consider yourself born-again?

	Baptist	Catholic	Non-denom.	Methodist	Ch. of Christ	Presbyt.
Yes	68.7	35.8	69.2	47.0	48.6	37.3
No	30.2	60.0	27.9	46.0	51.4	62.7
Don't know	1.1	4.2	2.9	7.0	0.0	0.0

Q11: While living at home, to which church denomination did you belong?

	Baptist	Catholic	Non-denom.	Methodist	Church of Christ	Presbyt. USA
Baptist	85.5	0.8	12.5	0.0	17.1	7.8
Catholic	2.2	90.0	0.0	0.0	0.0	0.0
Methodist	1.7	0.0	3.8	87.0	0.0	3.9
Non-denom.	1.1	6.7	61.5	2.0	0.0	0.0
Presbyt.	0.6	0.0	1.0	0.0	0.0	76.4
Church of Christ	0.0	0.0	0.0	0.0	65.7	2.0
None	3.4	1.7	1.9	4.0	0.0	3.9
Church of God	0.6	0.0	1.0	0.0	8.6	3.9
Christian Ch.	0.0	0.0	4.8	2.0	0.0	0.0
United Church of Christ	0.6	0.8	0.0	0.0	5.7	0.0

Q12: Did you attend church regularly during your elementary and middle school years?

	Baptist	Catholic	Non-denom.	Methodist	Church of Christ	Presbyt. USA
Yes	84.4	90.0	76.6	75.0	85.7	72.5
No	15.6	10.0	24.0	25.0	14.3	27.5

Q16: Has anyone, like a friend, school teacher, or college professor, ever challenged you and your Christian faith?

	Baptist	Catholic	Non-denom.	Methodist	Church of Christ	Presbyt. USA
No	67.6	79.2	63.5	86.0	85.7	90.2
Yes	29.1	20.0	36.5	14.0	11.4	7.8
Don't know	3.4	0.8	0.0	0.0	2.9	2.0

Q17: If yes, at what time in your life were you challenged?

	Baptist	Catholic	Non-denom.	Methodist	Church of Christ	Presbyt. USA
After college	55.8	50.0	50.0	50.0	0.0	0.0
College	26.9	25.0	28.9	28.6	25.0	0.0
High school	7.7	12.5	10.5	21.4	0.0	100.0
Middle school	9.6	12.5	10.5	0.0	75.0	0.0

Q18: If yes, can you recall which specific Christian principle you were challenged on?

	Baptist	Catholic	Non-denom.	Methodist	Church of Christ	Presbyt. USA
Why bad things happen	13.5	33.3	15.8	14.3	75.0	50.0
How can believe Bible?	25.0	16.7	15.8	21.4	25.0	0.0
Age of earth	17.3	8.3	26.3	21.4	0.0	0.0
Only Christians to heaven	19.2	4.2	21.1	14.3	0.0	25.0
Can Christians be gay?	5.8	8.3	2.6	7.1	0.0	0.0
No	13.5	0.0	0.0	0.0	0.0	0.0
Creation/Garden of Eden	0.0	8.3	7.9	7.1	0.0	0.0
Why is there hell?	3.8	8.3	0.0	14.3	0.0	0.0
Virgin birth	1.9	4.2	7.9	0.0	0.0	0.0
Abortion	0.0	8.3	2.6	0.0	0.0	25.0

Q25: Do you believe all the books of the Bible are inspired by God?

	Baptist	Catholic	Non-denom.	Methodist	Church of Christ	Presbyt. USA
Yes	95.0	96.7	86.5	99.0	94.3	86.3
Don't know	3.4	1.7	8.7	0.0	0.0	7.8
No	1.7	1.7	4.8	1.0	5.7	5.9

Q26: Do you believe other holy books like the Qur'an (Koran) are inspired by God?

	Baptist	Catholic	Non-denom.	Methodist	Church of Christ	Presbyt. USA
No	72.1	68.3	82.7	51.0	71.4	62.7
Yes	16.2	26.7	11.5	33.0	28.6	11.8
Don't know	11.7	5.0	5.8	16.0	0.0	25.5

Q27: Have you ever read the Bible from cover to cover?

	Baptist	Catholic	Non-denom.	Methodist	Church of Christ	Presbyt. USA
No	78.8	74.2	76.9	80.0	82.9	84.3
Yes	20.7	23.3	23.1	19.0	17.1	15.7

Q28: If not, have you read much of the Old Testament?

	Baptist	Catholic	Non-denom.	Methodist	Church of Christ	Presbyt. USA
No	65.2	71.9	77.5	76.3	79.3	67.4
Yes	34.8	28.1	22.5	23.8	20.7	32.6

Q29: If not, have you read much of the New Testament?

	Baptist	Catholic	Non-denom.	Methodist	Church of Christ	Presbyt. USA
Yes	60.3	52.8	60.0	43.8	62.1	53.5
No	39.7	47.2	40.0	56.3	37.9	46.5

Q30: Do you believe more in creation as stated in the Bible or more in evolution?

	Baptist	Catholic	Non-denom.	Methodist	Church of Christ	Presbyt. USA
Biblical creation	88.3	91.7	76.9	71.0	82.9	58.8
Evolution	11.7	8.3	23.1	29.0	17.1	41.2

Q31: Do you feel the church is relevant today to your needs?

	Baptist	Catholic	Non-denom.	Methodist	Church of Christ	Presbyt. USA
Yes	75.4	80.8	86.5	72.0	77.1	72.5
No	20.7	13.3	12.5	25.0	20.0	25.5
Don't know	3.9	5.8	1.0	3.0	2.9	2.0

Q32: If no, in what way do you feel the church is not fulfilling your needs?

	Baptist	Catholic	Non-denom.	Methodist	Church of Christ	Presbyt. USA
Not feel closer to God	78.4	6.3	30.8	88.0	57.1	84.6
Not learn about God	2.7	62.5	23.1	0.0	14.3	7.7
Not meet emotion	0.0	31.3	15.4	4.0	0.0	7.7
Bible not practical	2.7	0.0	7.7	8.0	28.6	0.0
Don't know	16.2	0.0	0.0	0.0	0.0	0.0
Music is poor	0.0	0.0	23.1	0.0	0.0	0.0

Q33: Do you believe the bible is true and historically accurate?

	Baptist	Catholic	Non-denom.	Methodist	Church of Christ	Presbyt. USA
Yes	76.5	82.5	68.3	69.0	82.9	56.9
No	13.4	11.7	15.4	20.0	17.1	41. 2
Don't know	10.1	5.8	16.3	11.0	0 . 0	2.0

Q34: If no, what is it that made you begin to doubt the Bible?

	Baptist	Catholic	Non-denom.	Methodist	Church of Christ	Presbyt. USA
Written by men	41.7	14.3	62.5	5.0	16.7	47.6
Science shows earth is old	16.7	21.4	18.8	10.0	16.7	19.0
Not translated correctly	12.5	7.1	0.0	45.0	0.0	9.5
Bible contradicts	25.0	14.3	12.5	10.0	0.0	4.8
Bible has errors	0.0	35.7	0.0	5.0	66.7	9.5
Evolution	0.0	0.0	6.3	20.0	0.0	0.0
Christians don't live by it	4.2	0.0	0.0	5.0	0.0	9.5
Suffering and death	0.0	7.1	0.0	0.0	0.0	0.0

Q35: If no, when did you first have doubts?

	Baptist	Catholic	Non-denom.	Methodist	Church of Christ	Presbyt. USA
Middle school	58.3	28.6	6.3	70.0	83.3	81.0
High school	29.2	35.7	50.0	10.0	0.0	9.5
Elementary school	4.2	7.1	37.5	10.0	0.0	0.0
College	4.2	28.6	6.3	5.0	16.7	4.8
Don't know	4.2	0.0	0.0	0.0	0.0	4.8
Misc	0.0	0.0	0.0	5.0	0.0	0.0

Q36: Do you believe Adam and Eve were real people in the Garden of Eden or were they fictional characters?

	Baptist	Catholic	Non-denom.	Methodist	Church of Christ	Presbyt. USA
Real	86.6	96.7	84.6	70.0	77.1	72.5
Fictional	12.8	3.3	14.4	19.0	14.3	27.5
Don't know	0.6	0.0	1.0	11.0	8.6	0.0

Q37: Do you believe Adam and Eve sinned and were expelled from the Garden?

	Baptist	Catholic	Non-denom.	Methodist	Church of Christ	Presbyt. USA
Yes	87.2	96.7	84.6	74.0	80.0	72.5
No	12.8	3.3	9.6	19.0	17.1	27.5
Don't know	0.0	0.0	5.8	7.0	2.9	0.0

Q38: Do you believe in the account of Sodom and Gomorrah and that Lot's wife was turned to salt when she looked back at the city?

	Baptist	Catholic	Non-denom.	Methodist	Church of Christ	Presbyt. USA
Yes	79.3	70.8	75.0	68.0	74.3	56.9
No	11.7	5.8	12.5	23.0	20.0	33.3
Don't know	8.9	23.3	12.5	9.0	5.7	9.8

Q39: Do you believe in Noah's ark and the global Flood?

	Baptist	Catholic	Non-denom.	Methodist	Church of Christ	Presbyt. USA
Yes	88.3	97.5	81.7	89.0	91.4	86.3
No	10.6	1.7	18.3	9.0	5.7	11.8

Q40: Do you believe in the birth of Isaac when Abraham was about 100 years old?

	Baptist	Catholic	Non-denom.	Methodist	Church of Christ	Presbyt. USA
Yes	79.3	71.7	76.9	86.0	77.1	66.7
Don't know	14.0	23.3	7.7	3.0	2.9	21.6
No	6.7	5.0	15.4	11.0	20.0	11.8

Q41: Some biblical scholars estimate the earth to be 6,000 years old, and other biblical scholars estimate the earth to be 10,000 years old. Which one do you believe?

	Baptist	Catholic	Non-denom.	Methodist	Church of Christ	Presbyt. USA
Neither	38.0	50.0	56.7	59.0	42.9	56.9
IOK years old	43.0	36.7	30.8	35.0	57.1	29.4
6K years old	19.0	13.3	12.5	6.0	0.0	13.7

Q42: Do you believe God created universe, the heavens, and earth in 24-hour days or do you believe those days were much longer than 24 hours?

	Baptist	Catholic	Non-denom.	Methodist	Church of Christ	Presbyt. USA
Actual 24 hours	71.5	66.7	53.8	59.0	80.0	58.8
Longer than 24 hours	27.9	33.3	45.2	41.0	20.0	41.2

Q43: Do you believe God is truly almighty, holy, and full of love?

	Baptist	Catholic	Non-denom.	Methodist	Church of Christ	Presbyt. USA
Yes	99.4	100.0	99.0	99.0	100.0	100.0

Q44: Do you believe God truly inspired each of the authors of the various books of the Bible?

	Baptist	Catholic	Non-denom.	Methodist	Church of Christ	Presbyt. USA
Yes	91.1	96.7	81.7	89.0	91.4	92.2
No	3.9	3.3	18.3	10.0	5.7	5.9
Don't know	5.0	0.0	0.0	1.0	2.9	2.0

Q45: Do you believe that dinosaurs died out before people were on the planet?

	Baptist	Catholic	Non-denom.	Methodist	Church of Christ	Presbyt. USA
Yes	53.1	47.5	55.8	47.0	68.6	60.8
Don't know	29.6	24.2	25.0	23.0	14.3	17.6
No	17.3	28.3	19.2	30.0	17.1	21.6

Q46: Which do you believe — secular science which has dated the earth at billions of years old, or the Bible which teaches the world was created in six 24-hour days?

	Baptist	Catholic	Non-denom.	Methodist	Church of Christ	Presbyt. USA
Six 24-hr days	75.4	69.2	60.6	62.0	77.1	47.1
Billions of years	24.6	30.8	39.4	38.0	22.9	52.9

Q47: Do you believe that God used evolution to change one kind of animal into another kind (e.g., the evolutionary belief that dinosaurs evolved into birds)?

	Baptist	Catholic	Non-denom.	Methodist	Church of Christ	Presbyt. USA
No	76.0	80.8	63.5	60.0	68.6	45.1
Yes	16.8	15.8	32.7	33.0	17.1	43.1
Don't know	7.3	3.3	3.8	7.0	14.3	11.8

Q48: Do you believe that humans evolved from ape- like ancestors?

	Baptist	Catholic	Non-denom.	Methodist	Church of Christ	Presbyt. USA
No	78.8	83.3	76.0	68.0	71.4	54.9
Yes	14.5	10.0	22.1	24.0	22.9	27.5
Don't know	6.7	6.7	1.9	8.0	5.7	17.6

Q49: When you were younger, did your pastor ever preach on Darwinism and why it is not true and should not be believed?

	Baptist	Catholic	Non-denom.	Methodist	Church of Christ	Presbyt. USA
No	61.5	74.2	65.4	64.0	68.6	56.9
Yes	29.1	17.5	11.5	21.0	22.9	27.5
Don't know	9.5	8.3	23.1	15.0	8.6	15.7

Q50: When you were younger and listening to your minister's sermon, do you recall him preaching about Adam and Eve, evolution, or the number of days in which God created the heaven and earth?

	Baptist	Catholic	Non-denom.	Methodist	Church of Christ	Presbyt. USA
Yes	77.7	88.3	71.2	78.0	77.1	70.6
No	15.1	8.3	25.0	21.0	17.1	17.6
Don't know	7.3	3.3	3.8	1.0	5.7	11.8

Q51: Have you ever had anyone, your minister, your Sunday school teacher, your youth pastor, or your youth leader teach you how to defend your Christian faith if ever challenged in the future?

	Baptist	Catholic	Non-denom.	Methodist	Church of Christ	Presbyt. USA
Yes	49.2	70.0	44.2	44.0	42.9	27.5
No	47.5	25.0	53.8	50.0	54.3	72.5
Don't know	3.4	5.0	1.9	6.0	2.9	0.0

Q53: Did your pastor ever teach that Christians could believe in an earth that is millions or billions of years old?

	Baptist	Catholic	Non-denom.	Methodist	Church of Christ	Presbyt. USA
No	69.8	65.0	56.7	71.0	54.3	47.1
Yes	14.0	20.0	31.7	20.0	20.0	33.3
Don't know	16.2	15.0	11.5	9.0	25.7	19.6

Q54: Did your pastor teach that God created the earth in six days, each 24 hours in length?

	Baptist	Catholic	Non-denom.	Methodist	Church of Christ	Presbyt. USA
Yes	76.5	82.5	71.2	73.0	80.0	70.6
No	13.4	16.7	24.0	14.0	14.3	7.8
Don't know	10 . 1	0.8	4.8	13.0	5.7	21. 6

Q55: Did your pastor ever say anything to make you believe the Book of Genesis contained many myths and legends that we now know are untrue?

	Baptist	Catholic	Non-denom.	Methodist	Church of Christ	Presbyt. USA
No	82.7	89.2	86.5	76.0	88.6	56.9
Yes	11.2	9.2	12.5	23.0	5.7	39.2
Don't know	6.1	1.7	1.0	1.0	5.7	3.9

Q56: Do you believe in Joseph being sold into slavery and later becoming the pharaoh's closest advisor and eventually seeing his brothers?

	Baptist	Catholic	Non-denom.	Methodist	Church of Christ	Presbyt. USA.
Yes	76.5	76.7	76.0	76.0	65.7	68.6
Don't know	21.2	17.5	16.3	22.0	31.4	29.4
No	2.2	5.8	7.7	2.0	2.9	2.0

Q60: Do you have children or plan to have children in the future?

	Baptist	Catholic	Non-denom.	Methodist	Church of Christ	Presbyt. USA
Have	60.9	46.7	50.0	42.0	60.0	25.5
Plan to	25.1	42.5	25.0	48.0	34.3	56.9
No	11.7	7.5	22.1	6.0	2.9	15.7
Don't know	2.2	3.3	2.9	4.0	2.9	2.0

Q61: If you have children, are you taking them or encouraging them to go to church?

	Baptist	Catholic	Non-denom.	Methodist	Church of Christ	Presbyt. USA
Yes	88.1	98.2	96.2	88.1	100.0	92.3
No	10.1	0.0	3.8	9.5	0.0	7.7

Q62: If you plan to have children, do you plan to take them to church?

	Baptist	Catholic	Non-denom.	Methodist	Church of Christ	Presbyt. USA
Yes	68.9	74.5	96.2	68.8	50.0	79.3
Don't know	31.1	25.5	3.8	31.3	16.7	20.7
No	0.0	0.0	0.0	0.0	33.3	0.0

Q63: If you have children or plan to, how important is it to you to attend church regularly as a family?

	Baptist	Catholic	Non-denom.	Methodist	Church of Christ	Presbyt. USA
Very important	28.6	40.2	33.3	34.4	27.3	21.4
Important	20.8	37.4	41.0	32.2	21.2	19.0
Extremely important	36.4	20.6	21.8	12.2	33.3	38.1
Somewhat important	12.3	1.9	3.8	14.4	6.1	21.4
Little/no importance	1.9	0.0	0.0	6.7	12.1	0.0

Q64: Do you attend any church services at Easter or Christmas?

	Baptist	Catholic	Non-denom.	Methodist	Church of Christ	Presbyt. USA
Both	65.4	65.0	75.0	56.0	62.9	72.5
Christmas	16.2	15.0	12.5	24.0	8.6	7.8
No	12.8	14.2	4.8	17.0	20.0	17.6
Easter	5.6	5.8	7.7	3.0	8.6	2.0

Q65: In elementary school, did you primarily attend public school, Christian school, charter school, home school, or Catholic/parochial school?

	Baptist	Catholic	Non-denom.	Methodist	Church of Christ	Presbyt. USA
Public school	86.6	60.0	89.4	97.0	100.0	94.1
Christian school	10.1	7.5	6.7	3.0	0.0	3.9
Catholic-parochial	0.0	31.7	0.0	0.0	0.0	0.0
Charter school	0.6	0.0	3.8	0.0	0.0	0.0

Q66: In high school, did you primarily attend public school, Christian school, charter school, home school, or Catholic/parochial school?

	Baptist	Catholic	Non-denom.	Methodist	Church of Christ	Presbyt. USA
Public school	87.7	78.3	90.4	97.0	100.0	94.1
Christian school	9.5	5.8	4.8	3.0	0.0	3.9
Catholic-parochial	0.0	15.8	0.0	0.0	0.0	0.0
Charter school	0.6	0.0	4.8	0.0	0.0	0.0

Q67: Did your science teachers teach you the earth was millions or billions of years old?

	Baptist	Catholic	Non-denom.	Methodist	Church of Christ	Presbyt. USA
Yes	85.5	83.3	86.5	88.0	91.4	74.5
No	11.2	14.2	12.5	10.0	5.7	23.5
Don't know	3.4	2.5	1.0	2.0	2.9	2.0

Q68: Did any of your schoolteachers teach you that humans definitely evolved from lower forms of life to become what they are today?

	Baptist	Catholic	Non-denom.	Methodist	Church of Christ	Presbyt. USA
Yes	73.2	55.0	71.2	65.0	62.9	62.7
No	24.6	40.0	25.0	32.0	17.1	37.3
Don't know	2.2	5.0	3.8	3.0	20.0	0.0

Q69: By the time you graduated from high school, did you believe that the Bible was less true?

	Baptist	Catholic	Non-denom.	Methodist	Church of Christ	Presbyt. USA
No	76.0	87.5	80.8	67.0	71.4	66.7
Yes	18.4	10.8	14.4	29.0	25.7	27.5
Don't know	5.6	1.7	4.8	4.0	2.9	5.9

Q70: If yes, which person or persons convinced you the most that the Bible was less true?

	Baptist	Catholic	Non-denom.	Methodist	Church of Christ	Presbyt. USA
Hgh school teacher	57.6	69.2	73.3	24.1	33.3	92.9
Teenage friends	30.3	23.1	13.3	48.3	66.7	7.1
Adult friends	12.1	7.7	13.3	27.6	0.0	0.0

Q71: Does the Bible contain errors?

	Baptist	Catholic	Non-denom.	Methodist	Church of Christ	Presbyt. USA
No	73.2	82.5	45.2	62.0	65.7	33.3
Yes	14.0	12.5	30.8	32.0	17.1	56.9
Don't know	12.8	5.0	24.0	6.0	17.1	9.8

Q72: If yes, can you identify one of those errors for me?

	Baptist	Catholic	Non-denom.	Methodist	Church of Christ	Presbyt. USA
Wrong about age	52.0	20.0	43.8	46.9	33.3	27.6
Writers made mistakes	40.0	26.7	21.9	37.5	66.7	55.2
Alleged contradiction	0.0	26.7	25.0	3.1	0.0	0.0
Genesis disproved	4.0	6.7	6.3	3.1	0.0	13.8
No flood in Noah's tme	4.0	6.7	3.1	6.3	0.0	0.0
Unsaved go to hell	0.0	13.3	0.0	0.0	0.0	0.0
Miracles didn't occur	0.0	0.0	0.0	3.1	0.0	0.0
No	0.0	0.0	0.0	0.0	0.0	3.4

Q77: Do you feel good people don't need to go to church?

	Baptist	Catholic	Non-denom.	Methodist	Church of Christ	Presbyt. USA
No	69.8	60.8	81.7	58.0	71.4	60.8
Yes	26.8	35.8	11.5	34.0	25.7	35.3
Don't know	3.4	3.3	6.7	8.0	2.9	3.9

Q78: Do you feel people with a college education are less likely to attend church because they have been greatly influenced by professors who taught them the Bible was not reliable and was not the Word of God?

	Baptist	Catholic	Non-denom.	Methodist	Church of Christ	Presbyt. USA
No	45.8	71.7	42.3	52.0	65.7	58.8
Yes	38.0	15.0	29.8	28.0	28.6	27.5
Don't know	16.2	13.3	27.9	20.0	5.7	13.7

Q79: Do you believe if you are a good person you will go to heaven upon your death?

	Baptist	Catholic	Non-denom.	Methodist	Church of Christ	Presbyt. USA
Yes	49.2	70.8	64.4	63.0	65.7	76.5
No	48.0	20.0	34.6	32.0	28.6	21.6
Don't know	2.8	9.2	1.0	5.0	5.7	2.0

Q81: Do you believe only those who have received Christ as their Lord and Savior will go to heaven?

	Baptist	Catholic	Non-denom.	Methodist	Church of Christ	Presbyt. USA
Yes	71.5	53.3	52.9	49.0	51.4	47.1
No	25.7	44.2	23.1	28.0	25.7	31.4
Don't know	2.8	2.5	24.0	23.0	22.9	21.6

Q82: Do you believe you have become anti-church through the years?

	Baptist	Catholic	Non-denom.	Methodist	Church of Christ	Presbyt. USA
No	81.6	80.0	85.6	77.0	74.3	96.1
Yes	15.6	17.5	12.5	11.0	25.7	2.0
Don't know	2.8	2.5	1.9	12.0	0.0	2.0

Q83: Of these choices, which one makes you question the Bible the most?

	Baptist	Catholic	Non-denom.	Methodist	Church of Christ	Presbyt. USA
None	63.1	60.0	42.3	47.0	48.6	31.4
Age of earth can't be less than 10K	12.8	19.2	26.9	26.0	8.6	43.1
Too many rules	8.9	5.0	9.6	10.0	22.9	5.9
No sense in suffering/death	6.1	5.0	11.5	10.0	14.3	2.0
Creation account	6.1	5.0	2.9	4.0	5.7	17.6
Worldwide flood	1.1	4.2	3.8	2.0	0.0	0.0

Q84: Which of these best describes your belief — the Bible is the Word of God written down by men who God inspired, or the Bible is a book that many men wrote years ago and it is simply a collection of writings by wise men?

	Baptist	Catholic	Non-denom.	Methodist	Church of Christ	Presbyt. USA
Bible is the Word of God	78.8	91.7	77.9	69.0	74.3	64.7
Bible is a collection of writings	21.2	7.5	22.1	31.0	25.7	35.3

Q85: Should gay couples be allowed to marry and have all the legal rights of heterosexual couples?

	Baptist	Catholic	Non-denom.	Methodist	Church of Christ	Presbyt. USA
No	64.8	42.5	44.2	30.0	40.0	33.3
Yes	23.5	48.3	51.0	58.0	31.4	47.1
Don't know	11.7	9.2	4.8	11.0	28.6	19.6

Q86: Is homosexual behavior a sin?

	Baptist	Catholic	Non-denom.	Methodist	Church of Christ	Presbyt. USA
Yes	67.6	60.0	53.8	39.0	74.3	35.3
No	21.2	25.0	31.7	44.0	14.3	41.2
Don't know	11.2	15.0	14.4	16.0	11.4	23.5

Q87: Should abortions continue to be legal in most instances?

	Baptist	Catholic	Non-denom.	Methodist	Church of Christ	Presbyt. USA.
No	60.9	45.8	44.2	38.0	62.9	39.2
Yes	27.4	29.2	46.2	47.0	28.6	23.5
Don't know	11.7	25.0	9.6	14.0	8.6	37.3

Q88: Should marijuana be allowed for persons with certain medical conditions?

	Baptist	Catholic	Non-denom.	Methodist	Church of Christ	Presbyt. USA
Yes	64.2	72.5	72.1	77.0	77.1	68.6
No	22.3	18.3	12.5	16.0	11.4	5.9
Don't know	13.4	9.2	15.4	7.0	11.4	25.5

Q89: Should marijuana be made legal all across America?

	Baptist	Catholic	Non-denom.	Methodist	Church of Christ	Presbyt. USA
No	68.2	51.7	52.9	40.0	48.6	60.8
Yes	27.9	45.0	43.3	51.0	45.7	25.5
Don't know	3.9	3.3	3.8	9.0	5.7	13.7

Q90: Should science instructors be allowed to teach the problems with evolution or strictly teach about evolution?

	Baptist	Catholic	Non-denom.	Methodist	Church of Christ	Presbyt. USA
Allow to teach problems	92.7	88.3	80.8	90.0	97.1	92.2
Strictly teach	7.3	9.2	19.2	10.0	2.9	7.8

Q91: Should prayer be allowed in public schools?

	Baptist	Catholic	Non-denom.	Methodist	Church of Christ	Presbyt. USA
Yes	91.1	77.5	82.7	88.0	91.4	88.2
No	7.3	8.3	13.5	9.0	5.7	5.9
Don't know	1.7	14.2	3.8	3.0	2.9	5.9

Q92: Do you believe many of the problems facing public schools are a result of taking God out of the classroom and out of the school?

	Baptist	Catholic	Non-denom.	Methodist	Church of Christ	Presbyt. USA
Yes	72.6	60.0	67.3	48.0	71.4	54.9
No	23.5	37.5	24.0	31.0	25.7	31.4
Don't know	3.9	2.5	8.7	21.0	2.9	13.7

Q93: Is premarital sex okay?

	Baptist	Catholic	Non-denom.	Methodist	Church of Christ	Presbyt. USA
No	62.0	60.0	43.3	33.0	60.0	35.3
Yes	33.5	25.0	55.8	52.0	31.4	47.1
Don't know	4.5	15.0	1.0	14.0	8.6	17.6

Q94: Should smoking marijuana be made legal?

	Baptist	Catholic	Non-denom.	Methodist	Church of Christ	Presbyt. USA
No	68.2	50.8	53.8	34.0	40.0	43.1
Yes	27.9	35.0	44.2	53.0	48.6	27.5
Don't know	3.9	14.2	1.9	13.0	11.4	29.4

Q95: Do you believe the Church is too judgmental and discriminates against those who don't attend?

	Baptist	Catholic	Non-denom.	Methodist	Church of Christ	Presbyt. USA
No	54.7	51.7	50.0	42.0	42.9	31.4
Yes	29.1	41.7	33.7	39.0	25.7	39.2
Don't know	16.2	6.7	16.3	19.0	31.4	29.4

Q96: Who smashed the tablets on which God had written the 10 Commandments?

	Baptist	Catholic	Non-denom.	Methodist	Church of Christ	Presbyt. USA
Moses	74.9	74.2	61.5	70.0	57.1	62.7
Don't know	21. 2	23.3	31.7	20.0	28.6	35.3
David	2.8	0.0	4.8	6.0	14.3	0.0

Q97: What is the first book in the New Testament?

	Baptist	Catholic	Non-denom.	Methodist	Church of Christ	Presbyt. USA
Matthew	71.5	83.3	69.2	66.0	62.9	66.7
Don't know	24.6	10.0	27.9	29.0	34.3	33.3
Genesis	3.9	3.3	2.9	5.0	2.9	0.0

Q98: Who baptized Jesus?

	Baptist	Catholic	Non-denom.	Methodist	Church of Christ	Presbyt. USA
John the Baptist	82.1	76.7	75.0	71.0	68.6	70.6
Don't know	15.1	19.2	14.4	28. 0	31.4	27.5
John	1.1	2.5	4.8	1.0	0.0	2.0
Moses	0.6	0.0	5.8	0.0	0.0	0.0

Q99: Who built the ship known as the ark?

	Baptist	Catholic	Non-denom.	Methodist	Church of Christ	Presbyt. USA
Noah	91.6	88.3	90.4	94.0	85.7	94.1
Don't know	7.8	9.2	8.7	6.0	5.7	3.9
Moses	0.6	2.5	1.0	0.0	5.7	2.0

Q100: What king wrote most of the Psalms?

	Baptist	Catholic	Non-denom.	Methodist	Church of Christ	Presbyt. USA.
Don't know	43.0	35.8	52.9	57.0	57.1	49.0
David	49.2	52.5	32.7	35.0	31.4	37.3
Solomon	2.8	5.8	3.8	4.0	2.9	2.0
Luke	2.8	2.5	1.0	1.0	5.7	7.8
Jacob	0.0	0.8	8.7	0.0	2.9	0.0
John	0.0	0.0	0.0	3.0	0.0	3.9

Q101: In what town was Jesus born?

	Baptist	Catholic	Non-denom.	Methodist	Church of Christ	Presbyt. USA
Bethlehem	94.4	97.5	81.7	95.0	88.6	98.0
Jerusalem	2.2	1.7	8.7	3.0	8.6	0.0
Don't know	2.8	0.8	6.7	2.0	2.9	2.0

Q102: Did you ever memorize the names of the books of Bible in order?

	Baptist	Catholic	Non-denom.	Methodist	Church of Christ	Presbyt. USA
No	52.0	75.0	63.5	61.0	54.3	76.5
Yes	47.5	24.2	36.5	39.0	45.7	23.5

Q103: Did you memorize many verses of the Bible?

	Baptist	Catholic	Non-denom.	Methodist	Church of Christ	Presbyt. USA
Yes	68.7	52.5	70.2	63.0	65.7	68.6
No	30.2	45.8	29.8	36.0	34.3	31.4

Q104: What is your family status?

	Baptist	Catholic	Non-denom.	Methodist	Church of Christ	Presbyt. USA
Married/children	48.0	45.0	38.5	38.0	51.4	21.6
Single	27.4	28.3	35.6	35.0	31.4	35.3
Married	16.2	22.5	16.3	23.0	8.6	35.3
Single/children	6.7	1.7	7.7	3.0	8.6	3.9
Married/children away	1.7	2.5	1.9	1.0	0.0	3.9

Q106: What is the last grade of school you have completed?

	Baptist	Catholic	Non-denom.	Methodist	Church of Christ	Presbyt. USA
Some college	45.8	29.2	31.7	43.0	31.4	43.1
HS graduate	33.0	38.3	35.6	27.0	37.1	15.7
College graduate	19.0	32.5	26.9	23.0	31.4	35.3
Graduate school	1.1	0.0	4.8	7.0	0.0	5.9

Q109: Your sex?

	Baptist	Catholic	Non-denom.	Methodist	Church of Christ	Presbyt. USA
Female	74.9	65.0	65.4	76.0	68.6	60.8
Male	25.1	35.0	34.6	24.0	31.4	39.2

Gay Marriage and the 21st Century

A Fundamental Change in the Western World

Most people have heard of the story of Pandora's box. (Apparently the original myth was about Pandora's jar, but it's commonly known as Pandora's box.) Just as there are Flood legends around the world, there are also other legends with elements similar to Genesis. One of those is the legend of Pandora's box. The story claims the pagan god Zeus gave man the first woman along with a box that had a warning not to open it. But Pandora chose to open it, and by doing so unleashed all the evils known to man. Sounds like a spinoff account of the Fall as recorded in Genesis 3.

I believe the decision of the Supreme Court of the United States (SCOTUS) to legalize gay "marriage" has, in a sense, opened Pandora's box. Consider just a few of the headlines that appeared shortly after their decision to give you an idea what has now been unleashed on our culture:

- Polygamy Attorney On Gay Marriage Decision: SCOTUS Opinion "Resonates With Our Arguments"[1]

- Next frontier for gays is employment and housing discrimination[2]

- How Will the U.S. Supreme Court's Same-Sex-Marriage Decision Affect Religious Liberty?[3]

- Now's the Time to End Tax Exemptions for Religious Institutions[4]

- It's Time to Legalize Polygamy[5]

Pandora's Box indeed. Of course, it remains to be seen how and to what degree these agendas will be pursued. And though no gay "marriage" has the ability to naturally procreate, the above examples prove it has already birthed an odious offspring.

Mike Johnson is chief counsel of Freedom Guard, a nonprofit, constitutional law organization that has assisted Answers in Genesis with its Ark Encounter project. He says of the SCOTUS decision:

> Millions of Americans are also rightly concerned about what might happen if these critical boundaries on marriage are erased. The federal district court judge in our successful case last year asked some important questions of our opposing counsel that they could not answer. He asked the plaintiffs' attorneys: if they are correct — that the State has no authority to regulate marriage — then where could we then draw the line? Would first cousins have the right to marry? A father and his daughter? An uncle and his nephew? A 20-year-old man and a

---

1. http://dailycaller.com/2015/06/26/polygamy-attorney-on-gay-marriage-decision-scotus-opinion-resonates-with-our-arguments/

2. http://www.latimes.com/nation/la-na-gays-employment-20150626-story.html#page=1

3. http://www.theatlantic.com/politics/archive/2015/06/how-will-the-us-supreme-courts-same-sex-marriage-decision-affect-religious-liberty/396986/

4. http://time.com/3939143/nows-the-time-to-end-tax-exemptions-for-religious-institutions/

5. http://www.politico.com/magazine/story/2015/06/gay-marriage-decision-polygamy-119469.html?ml=po#.VbIq6HjbDRo

13-year-old girl? If the "right to marry" is determined to have no rational boundary, chaos is certain to follow. And all of those other "interest groups" will present equally fervent arguments as to why THEIR particular preferences and behaviors should be honored with equal protection under the law.[6]

This is certainly true. If marriage can be redefined on the basis of "love has no boundaries," as many people say to argue for same-sex "marriage," then where do we stop redefining marriage? Why not two men and three women? Why not a man and an animal? Where do you stop redefining marriage? It is only in God's Word that we get a standard for marriage given to us by the Creator. Marriage is for one man and one woman because God created it that way (Gen. 1:27, 2:24; Matt. 19:4-5). Since God created marriage, God — and only God — has the right to define what marriage is and is not.

As I've said many times over the years, once a worldview is built on man's opinions (man's word) and not God's Word, then, ultimately, anything goes! The best way to sum it up is from this verse of Scripture:

> In those days there was no king in Israel. Everyone did what was right in his own eyes (Judg. 21:25).

That verse is the "Pandora's box" that SCOTUS opened. In reality, this box was gradually being pried open over the years — but this latest declaration on gay "marriage" opened it widely. In an article titled, "Ending Tax Exemption means Ending Churches," one writer stated,

> Legal gay marriage is not the endgame for the gay-rights movement. It never was. Moral approval is the endgame. The agenda is not tolerance for different beliefs and lifestyles. The agenda is a demand that everyone get on board with the moral revolution or be punished. That means if you or your church won't get with the program, then the revolutionaries will endeavor to close you down.[7]

I totally agree. This is what their agenda is all about.

---

6. https://answersingenesis.org/family/marriage/supreme-court-affirms-gay-marriage/
7. http://thefederalist.com/2015/06/29/ending-tax-exemptions-means-ending-churches/.

Typically in Greek mythology, after the bad things come out, then something good also comes out. In the Bible, after the account of the Fall of man, God provides a solution in Jesus. And I'm confident God will use this SCOTUS ruling for good. Historically, persecution has been known to awaken God's people to increased fervor to serve Him and spread the gospel.

Even so, the Supreme Court ruling in favor of gay "marriage" will fundamentally change the culture in America and, apart from a miracle of God, it will prove to be an irreversible situation. To understand what is happening to America now, simply read Romans 1. Though profoundly true for Paul's day, it has proved to be prophetic for ours. I believe we're going to see increased persecution against Christians and increased antagonism specifically toward Christianity. We're going to see the restriction of the free exercise of religion, freedom of religion, and free speech in this nation, particularly with regard to our faith. Don't be surprised when you see the government move against Christian churches, colleges, institutions, and organizations that take a stand on biblical marriage as God commands in the Bible, going all the way back to the Book of Genesis.

As Jesus stated in Matthew,

> Have you not read that He who made them at the beginning "made them male and female," and said, "For this reason a man shall leave his father and mother and be joined to his wife, and the two shall become one flesh"? So then, they are no longer two but one flesh. Therefore what God has joined together, let not man separate (Matt. 19:4–6; NKJV).

Misinformation and Confusion

I must admit I have been amazed (and saddened) by the number of Christians who either completely ignore these words from Jesus or who twist and reinterpret them to fit their preferences. They also claim that because we call gay "marriage" a sin, we are being judgmental, because the Bible "tells us not to judge." Of course, many non-Christians also inconsistently quote the Bible in an attempt to prove that Christians shouldn't judge those who believe in gay "marriage."

Ironically, many of these people become judgmental themselves by making this (false) accusation. But it's not just gay "marriage" we call sin, but rather *all* sexual immorality (like adultery and fornication), along with lying, murder, and thieving, among other sins. And how dare we judge these actions as being "sin"? Because we have an absolute authority by which *all* our actions must be judged — the authority of the Word of God. God obviously is the ultimate Judge, but He has given us His Word with which to understand, discern, and judge actions. Without Scripture, we are literally left to the moral whims of the individual or the collective beliefs of a fallen society.

People regularly take Matthew 7:1 ("Judge not, that you be not judged") out of context, claiming we are not to judge. And yet that very statement becomes a judgment against those who use Scripture as a standard for morality and behavior. This is part of the inconsistent logic of unbelievers. However, when you read the whole passage carefully and in its context, Christ is actually warning believers against making judgments in a hypocritical or condemning manner. Jesus also stated in John 7:24, "Do not judge by appearances, but judge with right judgment." Notice the Lord's *command* to judge, but when doing so, we must make sure we are judging righteously from God's Word and not relying on our own human prejudice or personal opinion.

I've observed a pattern with those who disagree with the biblical stand against gay "marriage." They claim the gay "marriage" issue is all about "love" — and yet the irony escapes those who post very hateful comments against Christians and those who simply disagree with them. It appears that many who accept gay "marriage" interpret our scriptural view of not accepting their behavior as unloving and hateful. But their real goal is for everyone to accept their sinful position! However, Christians can, and do, love people with whom we disagree. And not agreeing with them and judging their position as sin based on Scripture is not being hateful or unloving! On the contrary, it's the most loving thing we can possibly do, as it helps them realize their genuine need for salvation and a Savior!

Of course, another great concern right now is that those in authority are beginning to claim that speaking against homosexual behavior or gay "marriage" is "hate speech." The president has already claimed it's a civil rights issue, even though it's clearly not. While we cannot change the shape of a person's eyes or skin shade (which are genetically determined), people can change their moral behavior. Homosexual behavior and gay "marriage" are moral issues, not genetic or civil rights issues. Still, Pandora's Box has been opened, with secularists now claiming the Bible itself is full of hate speech. How long before we are told we can't use certain passages in the Bible or we will be judged, fined, or even imprisoned for using "hate speech?" How long will we be able to have the free exercise of Christianity in this nation, as guaranteed by the U.S. Constitution?

For further information on this topic, I encourage you to read a short article I coauthored on our website titled "Does the Bible Tell Christians to Judge Not?"[8]

The Reality Behind the Reality

If you think all this sounds like war, you're right. We are currently in a battle of good versus evil, a conflict between righteousness and ungodliness — and its roots are found in the spiritual realm. Paul wrote to the Ephesians,

> For we do not wrestle against flesh and blood, but against the rulers, against the authorities, against the cosmic powers over this present darkness, against the spiritual forces of evil in the heavenly places (Eph. 6:12).

That being reality, we must primarily do battle with *spiritual* weapons. That same Apostle wisely wrote,

> For the weapons of our warfare are not of the flesh but have divine power to destroy strongholds. We destroy arguments and every lofty opinion raised against the knowledge of God, and take every thought captive to obey Christ (2 Cor. 10:4–5).

We're not fighting surface issues or physical enemies, but rather the spiritual forces behind them. Unless we keep this perspective, we can easily slip into hatred and animosity for the very people for whom Christ

8. https://answersingenesis.org/bible-questions/does-the-bible-tell-christians-to-judge-not/.

died. Moral and biblical conviction must always partner with compassion and the free offer of salvation to anyone who desires to call on the name of the Lord.

Gay "Marriage" Doesn't Work

Many gay "marriage" activists argue that "married" gay couples are just as suitable parents as married heterosexual couples, that there is no difference between the two. However, the president of the American College of Pediatricians, "a nonprofit organization of pediatricians and health care professionals dedicated to the health and well-being of children," said the following in a statement on their website about the SCOTUS decision to legalize gay "marriage":

> This is a tragic day for America's children. The SCOTUS has just undermined the single greatest pro-child institution in the history of mankind: the natural family. Just as it did in the joint Roe v. Wade and Doe v. Bolton decisions, the SCOTUS has elevated and enshrined the wants of adults over the needs of children.[9]

Despite what many gay "marriage" activists say, having two mommies or two daddies does not replace God's design of one mom and one dad. God — not man or government — designed marriage for one man and one woman. From the very beginning He blessed this union, commanding, "Be fruitful and multiply" (Gen. 1:28). Homosexual couples are incapable of this as they cannot procreate like the rest of humanity usually does naturally. This, even from an evolutionary standpoint, makes the sin of homosexuality aberrant and unnatural.

Since God is the all-wise, all-knowing Creator, what He designed is obviously the only biologically feasible way for humanity to exist. It's also the only true way for us, not what sinful, fallible human beings try to make. Of course, no family is perfect. We live in a fallen world that is groaning from sin — but the creation is not at liberty to change the Creator's design for marriage and family. When we do, we are fastly approaching a head-on collision with a cultural collapse and disaster.

---

9. http://www.acpeds.org/tragic-day-for-americas-children.

I encourage you to be bold in standing on God's Word and refusing to compromise with man's ideas about what a marriage or a family should look like. Christians must unashamedly uphold the design given to us by our Creator.

My message to the president and the Supreme Court regarding gay "marriage" is this: Mr. President and members of the Supreme Court, you did not invent marriage — God did! The *Supreme Court*, ruled by the *Judge* who has ultimate and absolute authority, has already decided what marriage is:

> And He answered and said to them, "Have you not read that He who made them at the beginning 'made them male and female,' and said, 'For this reason a man shall leave his father and mother and be joined to his wife, and the two shall become one flesh'? So then, they are no longer two but one flesh" (Matt. 19:4–6).

AiG stands with others who embrace the clear and historic truth of Scripture regarding this critically important issue.

As churches, pastors, and even entire denominations cave in to compromise on homosexuality and gay "marriage," we stand resolute and unmoved, firmly rooted in God's Word which affirms,

> Forever, O Lord, Your word is settled in heaven (Ps. 119:89; NKJV).

Men and their beliefs may change, but God's Word never does. Envisioning this type of future departure from Scripture, Paul admonished pastor Timothy,

> I charge you therefore before God and the Lord Jesus Christ, who will judge the living and the dead at His appearing and His kingdom: Preach the word! Be ready in season and out of season. Convince, rebuke, exhort, with all longsuffering and teaching. For the time will come when they will not endure sound doctrine, but according to their own desires, because they have itching ears, they will heap up for themselves teachers; and they will turn their ears away from the truth, and be turned

aside to fables. But you be watchful in all things, endure afflictions, do the work of an evangelist, fulfill your ministry (2 Tim. 4:1–5; NKJV).

Peter reminds us, "They will give account to him who is ready to judge the living and the dead (1 Pet. 4:5).

Hope for the Remnant

Now, especially after this decision by the Supreme Court, many people are comparing and will compare America with Sodom and Gomorrah, two cities notorious for homosexuality that were eventually destroyed by God because of their wickedness (Gen. 19). But unlike in Sodom and Gomorrah, where God could not even find ten righteous people (Gen. 18:16–33), there is a remnant of Christians here in America who *do* base their thinking, beliefs, and behavior on God's Word. And it's a larger remnant than you may think. We meet these faithful followers of Christ every day at the Creation Museum and at conferences and other ministry events. We praise God for these faithful followers who remain true to His Word and who have not compromised themselves with man's ideas about morality.

We certainly hope that it won't reach the point where Christians and pastors are going to prison for their religious beliefs, but, realistically, with the way things are going, our precious religious freedom might just vanish in the wake of this decision by a bare majority of five justices who apparently deem themselves more knowledgeable and righteous than God on the subject of marriage. But this will only get worse if the Church doesn't wake up and return to its firm foundation of God's Word.

Despite this disappointing decision from SCOTUS that is sure to cause more challenges and redefinitions of marriage down the road, true Christians (the Remnant) need to be bold in doing our part to share the gospel — in love and without compromise — with those who desperately need it. God can use each and every one of us to reach someone with the gospel of Jesus Christ. And it's only through the gospel that we will see hearts and lives changed for eternity and eventually see change in this nation.

Sometimes I fear that even many Christians think that the solution to America's moral problems (including the legalization of gay "marriage," abortion, and so on) is a political one — to work at mainly changing the culture through legislation and sometimes litigation. I suggest that these social problems are spiritual ones — heart issues. The Bible doesn't say to go into all the world and change the culture; we are told:

> Go into all the world and proclaim the gospel to the whole creation (Mark 16:15).

> Go therefore and make disciples of all nations (Matt. 28:19).

Now as we follow this command, we are also told to

> . . . contend for the faith that was once for all delivered to the saints (Jude 3).

> . . . in your hearts honor Christ the Lord as holy, always being prepared to make a defense to anyone who asks you for a reason for the hope that is in you; yet do it with gentleness and respect (1 Pet. 3:15).

The point is, if you just try to change the culture in the sense of just working for political change, what will happen when the next generation comes through who may reject God even more, and then just change the laws back to what they want? Ultimately, any legal document, such as the U.S. Constitution, is only as good as the worldview of those interpreting it. Because of man's sinful heart, people will interpret such a document to say whatever they want it to say — which we have seen already happen in regard to abortion, the so-called "separation of church and state," and the gay "marriage" issues.

We need to be reminded that God's Word states, "For as he thinks in his heart, so is he" (Prov. 23:7; NKJV).

Hearts and minds change a culture. That's why the Scripture informs us that we are "the salt of the earth" (Matt. 5:13), but it goes on to warn us that if the salt is contaminated, it is not good for anything. We are also instructed in Mark 9:50 to "have salt in yourselves." You can't be the salt until you have salt (and you need to have uncontaminated salt).

I am not saying Christians should therefore not get involved polit-ically — quite the opposite. What I'm saying is that Christians need to understand that we need to be raising generations who are filled with as much uncontaminated salt as possible. They need to be taught what they believe and know how to defend the Christian faith. We need to raise generations of godly people committed to the Lord Jesus Christ, who will have a consistent Christian worldview, so when they get into posi-tions of authority in the government, education, business, and so on, their Christian worldview will enable them to view the legal documents in the correct way — and then be real salt in influencing the culture.

Christians should vote in elections. By doing so, they can help be salt and light to influence the culture for good by voting for those people who have a consistent Christian worldview. But if we just think that all we need to do is vote for some so-called "conservatives" (whatever that word means these days) and it will change the culture, then the effort will fail! We need to be concentrating on raising up hearts and minds who will stand on God's Word so they can be the ones to influence the culture.

Sadly, most children from our church homes have been trained by the world, and so they have adopted a very secular worldview. Because they've been trained by the world and therefore think like the world, many are voting in a very anti-Christian way. Many so-called "conserv-atives," for instance, are voting for gay "marriage." We need people who have an absolute basis for their worldview — based on the absolute authority of the Word of God.

As Jeremiah warned God's people, "Thus says the LORD: 'Do not learn the way of the Gentiles' " (Jer. 10:2; NKJV). He was telling them they were to influence the world, not the other way round. Sadly, just as in the times of Jeremiah, Christians have, by and large, let the world influence generations in the Church, and now much of the Church thinks like the world.

You cannot ultimately change a culture from the top down, when it has changed from the foundation up. Sadly, the secular world has understood that by capturing the hearts and minds of generations of young people, they could change the culture from the foundation up.

Many Christians look at the consequences of this change and try to effect change from the top down! Instead, our change has happened to the foundation, so now it will be a hard, long, slow process to reverse this massive change in the culture. But again, the way to do this is for Christians to be diligent in helping change one heart at a time, little by little (starting in their homes and churches), and continue to be salt and light as best they can in a culture that has increasingly been overtaken by darkness.

We urge you to pray that God will use us — this generation of His Church — to bring revival to the United States and a return to God's Word as the foundation for our nation's thinking. And though originally written in the context of Israel and the Temple, the principle of this well-known verse still rings true:

> If my people who are called by my name humble them-selves, and pray and seek my face and turn from their wicked ways, then I will hear from heaven and will forgive their sin and heal their land (2 Chron. 7:14).

Ken Ham

Ken Ham is president and founder of Answers in Genesis and one of the most in-demand speakers in the world today. He is the author of numerous books, including co-authoring *Already Gone* and *Already Compromised*, addressing the issues of young people leaving the Church and the impact of secular concepts at Christian colleges. *Ready to Return?* is the final book in this landmark series and reveals a biblically relevant path to church leaders and pastors to bring those lost back to the faith.

Ken is part of the visionary team behind the Creation Museum and now the Ark Encounter, an all-wood full-size Noah's ark being built to the historic dimensions stated in Genesis 6 (using the long cubit) in Kentucky. It will be both one of the largest "green" construction projects and timber-frame structures in the United States.

Ken is heard daily on the radio feature *Answers with Ken Ham*, broadcast on more than 850 stations, and is a frequent guest on national TV talk shows. He has appeared on Fox's *The O'Reilly Factor* and *Fox and Friends in the Morning*, CNN's *The Situation Room* with Wolf Blitzer, ABC's *Good Morning America*, the BBC, *CBS News Sunday Morning*, *NBC Nightly News*, the PBS *NewsHour* with Jim Lehrer, and many others.

Ken's emphasis is on the relevance and authority of the Book of Genesis to the life of the average Christian, and how compromise on Genesis has opened a dangerous door regarding how the culture and church view biblical authority. His 2014 creation/evolution debate with Bill Nye "The Science Guy," has been watched by an estimated 15 million people.

Britt Beemer

In 1979, Beemer founded America's Research Group, a full-service consumer behavior research and strategic marketing firm. Recognized nationally as a premier marketing strategist, he has gained wide acclaim for his work on how, when, and why consumers select their products and services. His client list represents America's top retailers, leading brands, and smaller entrepreneurial companies. His knowledge of consumer preferences increases monthly as ARG conducts thousands of new interviews.

Britt Beemer's expertise covers each phase of survey research, including questionnaire design, sample construction, and data analysis, but especially interpretation. He serves as the senior director of research at America's Research Group, where he personally reviews all research and prepares and presents each strategic marketing plan.

He holds a BA from Northwest Missouri State University and has an MA from Indiana State University. His work has been cited in the media, including the *Wall Street Journal, the New York Times, Investor's Business Daily,* CNN, Fox News, Fox Business News, and many others. He is the author of *Predatory Marketing, It Takes a Prophet to Make a Profit,* and *The Customer Rules.*

Jeff Kinley

Author and speaker Jeff Kinley has spent over three decades empowering people with vintage truth. He has written over 20 books, including the bestselling *As It Was in the Days of Noah.* Jeff holds a ThM. from Dallas Theological Seminary and speaks across the country. He and his wife live in Arkansas and have three grown sons. See jeffkinley.com for more information about his ministry.

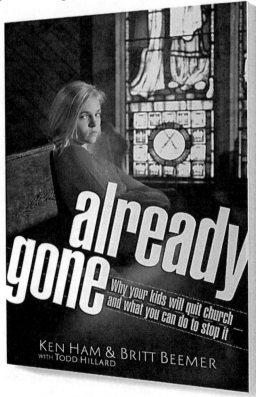

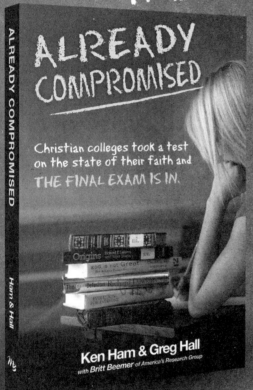

ALREADY COMPROMISED

Christian colleges took a test
on the state of their faith and
THE FINAL EXAM IS IN.

Ken Ham & Greg Hall

with *Britt Beemer* of America's Research Group

First printing: May 2011
Fourth printing: October 2012

Master Books®, P.O. Box 726, Green Forest, AR 72638
Master Books® is a division of the New Leaf Publishing Group, Inc.

ISBN: 978-0-89051-607-2
Library of Congress Number: 2011926096

Cover design: Joseph David Advertising, jdausa.com
Photo credit, pages 8, 10, and 11: Shutterstock.com

Unless otherwise noted, Scripture quotations are from the New American Standard Bible.

Please consider requesting that a copy of this volume be purchased by your local library system.

Printed in the United States of America

Please visit our website for other great titles:
www.masterbooks.net

For information regarding author interviews,
please contact the publicity department at (870) 438-5288

Master
Books®
A Division of New Leaf Publishing Group
www.masterbooks.net

Endorsement

I have no doubt that the average church member would be shocked and outraged to discover how many supposedly evangelical colleges and universities have more or less given up their commitment to biblical inerrancy and the authority of Scripture—especially when dealing with the early chapters of Genesis. I'm grateful for this important work by Ken Ham and Greg Hall, documenting the many compromises that have ravaged the Christian academy. *Already Compromised* is a much needed wake-up call and a summons to arms for faithful, courageous Bible believers. We need to stand up, declare our faith, and defend the truth of Scripture courageously. The stakes are high and the battle may be more fierce than ever, but God will bless those who honor His Word. May He bless us with clear, unwavering voices.

—John MacArthur
Pastor of Grace Community Church
President of The Master's College and Seminary
President, Grace to You ministry

Dedications

This book is dedicated to our young people in the Church. Be bold and uncompromising regarding the authority of the Word of God!
—Ken Ham

For my family:
My love, admiration, and appreciation for you
knows no limit.
— Greg Hall

Acknowledgments

- Britt Beemer and America's Research Group. Thanks for your amazing work. By putting statistics to our concerns, you prove what we see and sense.

- AiG . . . Steve Ham and Terry Mortenson.

- Roger Patterson and Bodie Hodge for reviewing this book.

- Alane Richardville, for help with research.

- Tim Dudley, Laura Welch, and the team at Master Books. Thanks for your personal dedication to the cause and your professional devotion to excellence in publishing.

- Todd Hillard, our editor/writer, who ds and our thoughts and crafted them into a cohesive message.

Contents

Introduction

The Rise and Fall of Higher Education

Ken Ham

founder and president of Answers in Genesis

E arly every fall, one of the great American traditions takes place from coast to coast. Planes take off, trains depart, and compact cars stuffed full of bikes and clothes and computers pull out of driveways. At the end of the journey, teary-eyed parents hug their children in the parking lots of dormitories, say one last goodbye, and then turn around, leaving their child on the threshold of one of the most important milestones of life: college.

Higher education, of course, has done much good for our society. It is the reason we enjoy many life-enhancing blessings. Through education we have learned to prosper in so many ways. Our lives have been transformed by medical advances and technology. We have learned to build the economy of the world. We feed the hungry and heal the sick. We build buildings and cities and nations. We explore the universe. The advances now realized by humankind have been made possible by education.

The American higher education system used to be the envy of nations around the world, but in several profound ways, it is not making the grade. Many Christian parents are concerned about the secular forces at work in public schools and concerned about the worldly environment that festers without restraint on most campuses. So early every fall Christian parents engage in another great American tradition: they shell out hundreds of thousands of dollars to send their children to a Christian university, Bible college, or seminary. In good faith they entrust their "heritage from the LORD" (Ps. 127:3; NKJV) to the professors and administrators they believe will protect their children and train them in the truths of the Scriptures and nurture them in their young adult faith.

The students themselves enter eagerly, committed and excited to begin their training — often with a view of being involved in missionary work, becoming a pastor, or in some way use their educational training to be a more effective witness for the Lord Jesus Christ. Both parents and students enter the whole experience with high expectations. What they don't know is that, like the secular schools they wish to avoid, and like the majority of the great Christian institutions of higher learning of the past, a growing number of the Christian schools they attend are . . . *Already Compromised.*

The Ivy League Legacy

Seniors of secular and Christian universities graduate as different people; much different than the wide-eyed, impressionable freshmen who entered. But sadly, in many instances, the changes are not all positive. The reasons are many, but the trends are now well documented. It's almost as if there is an

entropy taking place on campus — a moral and theological slippery slope that seems to take institutions in the wrong direction — usually taking the hearts and minds of naïve students with them. Like the proverbial frog boiled to death in a pot of slowly warming water, universities often end up far, far from their intended purpose.

Harvard

Harvard University was established in 1636 and is the oldest institution of higher learning in the United States. Would you be surprised to find out that it had its roots in a strong Puritan philosophy? It was never affiliated with any denomination, but many of its early graduates went on to be clergyman throughout New England.

Conflict arose, however, between Harvard's sixth president, Increase Mather, and the rest of the clergymen. Mather was deeply concerned that Harvard was becoming increasingly liberal, lax in its theology, and vague in its church policy. But his warnings went unheeded. Harvard's curriculum became increasingly secular through the end of the 1700s and was taken over by the Unitarians in 1805, resulting in the secularization of the university. By 1850, it was known as the "Unitarian Vatican." Charles W. Eliot, who was president between 1869 and 1909, eliminated Christianity as the dominant foundation of the curriculum in order to accommodate Transcendentalist Unitarian beliefs. Currently, Harvard Divinity School embraces a wide spectrum of religious belief. From meditations in the Buddhist tradition to the "Seasons of Light" — a multi-religious festival held each December — Harvard Divinity School strategically encourages an atmosphere of religious pluralism where almost any belief is encouraged, not just tolerated.

Yale

Yale, founded in 1701 in Connecticut, is the third oldest university in the United States. Its original purpose? To establish a training center for clergy and political leaders of the colony. A group of ten Congregationalist ministers, called "the founders," met in the study of Rev. Samuel Russell and donated their books for the school's first library. Like many universities and educational institutions, Yale came into its own during the Great Awakening and the Enlightenment. Presidents Thomas Clapp and Ezra Stiles pursued both religious and scientific interests as they studied Hebrew, Greek, and Latin — languages that were essential for the study of the Scriptures.

In 1872, however, a professor of economics and sociology named Graham Sumner began to use a textbook by Herbert Spencer that supported a naturalistic, agnostic view of the world. President Noah Porter objected, concerned that it would cause religious and moral harm to his students, but Sumner continued to teach until 1909. The compromise had begun.

A few decades later, President James R. Engel and psycho-biologist Robert M. Dierks were creating research programs testing the outer boundaries of naturalistic, humanistic theory. In one study, they analyzed the sexual behavior of chimpanzees, hoping to discover the evolutionary roots of human development. Today, little residue can be found of the school's former foundation of faith.

Princeton

Princeton University was founded in 1746 to train ministers for the Presbyterian denomination. For several decades, the college was the religious capital of Scottish and Irish Americans, helping build the spiritual foundation for the emerging nation of immigrants.

John Witherspoon became the sixth president of Princeton in 1768 and led the transformation of the college into a school that would equip the "revolutionary generation." At the same time, significant changes were taking place in the school's philosophy of morality as well as the school's devotion to what they called "natural philosophy." Witherspoon's view of morality was

more influenced by the Enlightenment and the ethics of philosophers than the Christian virtues espoused by Jonathan Edwards. He still supported "public religion" on a social level, but he did not believe that it was the only source of virtue. He believed that all human beings could be virtuous independent of God. There was opposition at first, but the momentum was strong and the school began to fragment.

Princeton Theological Seminary was established in 1811 — officially separating the secular and religious focuses of the school. In the late 1860s and 1870s, debates between the president of the college, James McCosh, and the head of the seminary, Charles Hodge, focused on the rising conflict between "science" and religion and Darwin's evolutionary model. Significantly, President McCosh became one of the first religious leaders to publicly endorse evolution.

In the next decade, President Francis Landey Patton came under fire for his traditional views and administrative methods. He insisted on a structured Christian education program, but many felt that approach limited academic freedom. In 1902 Patton was forced out of the presidency.

Liberal Christians dominated Princeton in the early 20th century. Evangelist Billy Sunday was not allowed to preach on campus, but liberal theologians had an open door to influence the university as it became a "modern" institution. Soon even the liberal Christian leaders lost their influence as it was eroded by secularization. By the 1920s, Princeton had ceased to be a Presbyterian institution. Evangelist Charles Templeton, a founder of Youth for Christ International, and crusade partner of Billy Graham, abandoned his faith during his years at Princeton Seminary starting in 1948.

Dartmouth

Dartmouth College was established in 1769 by Puritan Congregational minister Eliezer Wheelock. Dartmouth was the last university to be established in America under colonial rule and is the nation's ninth oldest college. Wheelock was inspired by Mohegan Indian Samson Occom. Occom had become an ordained minister after studying under Wheelock. He later went to preach to the Montauk Indians on Long Island. Wheelock's desire was to see a training school for Native Americans so that other Mohegans could be trained to reach their own people with the gospel. For this new school, he chose the motto *Vox Clamantis in Deserto*, a Latin phrase that appears five times in the Bible and is translated "the voice of one crying in the wilderness."

He chose a seal that strongly resembled the seal of the Society for the Propagation of the Gospel — a missionary society started in 1701 in London. Among its most famous alumni is Daniel Webster, who was purported to be able to recite the entire Bible, chapter and verse.

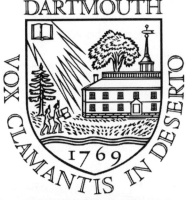

But that was then. Now, 240 years later, Dartmouth has established itself as a

premier in the university of the Ivy League but shows little or no expressions of its spiritual legacy.

History Repeating Itself?

This is the legacy of the Ivy League, and many of us have become concerned that the same trends are taking place today among Christian institutions that were founded on the same values and principles as these historic schools. The blatant disregard for the Bible and God is obvious on the secular campus, but even more disconcerting is the significant level of compromise we sense taking place among "Christian" institutions — most of which started with intentions as strong as the Ivy League but now show clear signs of the same decline.

How bad is it? We wanted to find out for certain, so we turned again to Britt Beemer, founder and president of America's Research Group (ARG), a nationally recognized surveying and marketing firm (americasresearch-group.com). When we were considering building the Creation Museum, we asked Britt for his advice. He took down all the pertinent information and went to work with his surveys and number crunching. What he came back with astounded us: ARG thought that 400,000 people would be willing to visit a museum like this in the first 365 days. The actual number turned out to be 404,000! He has done exceptional work for us in the past, including the survey for the book *Already Gone: Why Your Kids Will Quit Church and What You Can Do to Stop It.*

That study dealt with the two-thirds of the young people who grew up in the Church who are leaving when they reach college age. But this research indicates a far greater failure — a failure in regard to those who train the trainers who influence the minds of the coming generations — a failure at the level of the "shepherds" in many of our Christian academic institutions.

Over and over again, the Israelites were warned not to contaminate the purity of God's Word with the pagan religious ideas of the day. Jeremiah warned, "Do not learn the way of the Gentiles" (Jer. 10:2; NKJV). The Israelites were to be a nation to shine the light of God's truth to all the other nations. However, they contaminated their culture by adopting the pagan religion of the age into their thinking. This contamination basically destroyed them.

We contend (and scientifically conducted research will back this up) that many of the professors at many of our Christian institutions today have exhibited a behavior no different than those of the compromising Israelites. They have, by and large, adopted the pagan religion of this age and contaminated God's Word, thus contaminating the thinking of those to whom they impart their teaching. And we also contend, as the research will clearly show, that there is almost what one could call "deceptiveness" in the way some of these shepherds use language. Subtle twists in semantics clearly show up in their attempts to allay the fears of the unsuspecting parents in regard to what their children are really being indoctrinated in.

In Part 1, I will walk you through the research conducted by Britt Beemer and America's Research Group. After interviewing more than 300 presidents, vice presidents, religion department chairs, and science department chairs from 200 different colleges, we discovered great cause for concern in the curriculum, conflict between departments, and confusion among the leaders on many levels.

As the numbers came in, our concerns were not only confirmed, they were intensified. As I share the results of the survey, President Greg Hall gives a heart-piercing account of "the battle for the mind" that is raging on college campuses today — both secular and Christian. Greg is the president of Warner University. Not only does he know the ins and outs of both secular and Christian higher education, he also knows the heartache and the joy that comes with maintaining an institution of higher education that upholds the authority of Scripture. Greg has a tremendous heart and a tremendous passion for students. His love for God and his commitment to the Word is obvious in his life and in his career. His insights will lead us through the war of the worldviews between naturalism and Scripture and why the outcome of these battles is so important for our children and our society.

Our research shows that an "uncertain sound" is emanating from many of our Christian colleges. The authority of Scripture is being undermined at many levels, and the voices of naturalism, agnosticism, and even atheism are permeating the eardrums of generations of young people who become the leaders of tomorrow. And as they step into those leadership roles, most do not have the certain sound of the trumpet of truth to advance the battle as it should be fought. What do we do about it?

In Part 2, Greg and I will leave you with a personal challenge and an action plan that can help protect your children and begin to initiate changes in the system as a whole. You'll find guidelines for choosing the best schools for your children and questions to ask to verify what they are really teaching. Finally, we will offer students a "Spiritual Survival Kit" that will equip them to thrive, and not just survive, during the college years.

I believe that this book will prove to be even more controversial than the study we did for the book *Already Gone*. It's factual, but it's also personal. As fathers, both Greg and I have had to decide which colleges are best for our kids. Knowing that compromise (to one degree or another) awaits our kids, we had to contend with where to send them and try to prepare them for battle and encourage them to keep their guard up. All we can hope and pray is that if one person is saved or has his or her life changed, or parents can be equipped to help protect their kids from blatant faith-destroying compromise because of the research in this book, we believe that's enough. All we ask is that this book might be a guide and a defense for the truth as our children leave our homes and begin to walk through a world and an educational system that is *Already Compromised*.

Want to know which colleges were contacted as part of the ARG study? Visit www.creationcolleges.org and also find a growing list of Christian colleges we recommend you search out.

PART I

An Uncertain Sound

For if the bugle produces an indistinct sound, who will prepare himself for battle?

— 1 Corinthians 14:8

Chapter 1

Concern for the Curriculum

Ken Ham

> Let not many of you become teachers, my brethren, knowing
> that as such we will incur a stricter judgment (James 3:1).

This book really began with a hunch — one of those hunches that comes from repeated observation over 30 years — but nothing that you can objectively put your finger on. As part of my ministry through Answers in Genesis, I travel extensively, meeting with families, churches, and educators.

When the topic of parents' and students' experiences in colleges and universities comes up, I hear a lot of good; and I also hear a lot of bad. I hear far too many stories of well-meaning parents who have sent their children off to college with the highest of hopes, only to have them return skeptical, disillusioned, and uncertain about their former faith. Many of them leave the faith of their family altogether. I have also met with students at Christian institutions where I have spoken, and I hear from their own mouths what certain professors teach them and which books they are encouraged to study.

At one Christian college, I met with the chaplain before I was to speak at chapel. The chaplain told me, "We aren't narrow-minded like you young earth creationists at this college — we allow all views here."

I said to him, "Oh, I consider the view of taking a strong stand on six literal days and a young earth as the correct biblical view, and the other views are incorrect. Do you allow that view?"

The man replied, "No, because we allow all views." Of course, he didn't realize he was actually saying they do not allow all views, as they didn't allow mine. He thought they were being neutral, but as we will discuss, there is no neutral position.

Before speaking at another well-known conservative college, a person high up in the administration spoke to the students — basically giving them a disclaimer in regard to what I was going to teach them. I found out later from the students that, to their knowledge, I was the first person ever to be given a disclaimer in chapel — even though there had been speakers who would be considered somewhat liberal in their theology!

At another (what is considered to be) conservative Christian college, I was ushered into the president's office, where he began to "dress me down" in regard to our stand on six literal days and a young earth. He wanted me to know he did not approve of what I believed and was upset with my being at the college. (There were other reasons why I was actually invited to speak.)

At a conservative Bible college in Australia, the president asked me into his office, where he proceeded to admonish me because I had spoken against the gap theory and millions of years.

Yes, I knew that something was happening out there. Over the years I've been engaging in an increasingly heated debate not only with secularists, but also with Christian brothers and sisters involved in Christian higher education. . . . those were the administrators and professors at respected and trusted Christian colleges and universities. My concerns continued to grow, but before I spoke too "loudly" I wanted to make sure that I could prove it. When we produced the book *Already Gone*, we were simply verifying what everyone was already experiencing: Christian students, who grew up in evangelical churches, are leaving the church at an astounding rate. We had some ideas from experience as to why this was happening, but we set out to use statistically valid, professionally conducted research to determine what was happening. Our findings were very controversial.

I expect that this study will be far more shocking because people don't know that in most cases, their child's education at Christian institutions is "already compromised." Sometimes parents aren't even aware of this until their student's junior or senior year — when the discussion around the dinner table during the holidays reveals that there have been problems from the very beginning. What is the core of that problem?

A blind man cannot guide a blind man, can he? Will they not both fall into a pit? A pupil is not above his teacher; but everyone, after he has been fully trained, will be like his teacher (Luke 6:39–40).

When parents and students willingly submit themselves to a teacher, accepting him or her as authoritative, accepting what he or she says as truth, they *will* become like that teacher. Because of that, we felt strongly compelled to find out what is really being taught in colleges and universities today. Our primary focus of study, however, was not secular institutions. For the most part, secular institutions are rather upfront and honest about what they teach. As you will see, their goals and objectives have been clearly stated.

But this is not often the case in the Christian institutions. Because parents and students make assumptions about the beliefs of their Christian teachers that may or may not be true, we wanted to get an objective, quantifiable picture of what is really being taught in the classrooms. And, as we will show, we can't accept that the terminology being used by administrators and professors at such institutions means the same to us as it does to them! That is scary!

Review of the Survey

The goal of the survey conducted by America's Research Group and Britt Beemer was to survey 200 different Christian institutions of higher learning through interviews with people in four different positions:

- the president of the university
- the academic dean/vice president
- the head of the science department
- the head of the theology/religion department

Not every school used the same titles to describe these positions;[1] however, we are able to easily categorize them appropriately by their function. In a perfect world, we would have interviewed 800 people. Virtually everyone that we could reach wanted to answer the questions. The problem was getting to them — some were on sabbatical and some of their staffers filtered us. But once we actually got through to them, we had less than 40 people turn down the opportunity to be interviewed.

In the end, we were able to interview 312 people. Of these, 223 were from schools associated with the Council for Christian Colleges and Universities (CCCU), a group of over 90 colleges that require all of their professors to sign a personal statement of faith. The other 89 respondents were from schools that were "religiously affiliated" through an association with a religious denomination.[2] (These two groups responded in very similar ways to survey questions, by the way.) The only real difference in their demographics is that Catholics labeled themselves as being religiously affiliated and Baptist colleges tended to be members of the CCCU. Other than that, these two distinctions simply confirm that we have a good cross section here of a number of different denominations from different backgrounds — more than plenty to make generalized considerations according to the data.

So out of a potential of 800 people, we had a sample size right at 40 percent. That was much higher than anyone expected we would be able to get. This response rate gives us an error factor of about +/- 2.5 percent. (Statistically, that means that if we say "50 percent," the actual number across the whole country is somewhere between 47.5 percent and 52.5 percent. Because of this small error factor, we will be rounding all of our results to a 10th of a percent.)

Many of our questions required simple yes or no responses. Others were more open-ended and each person was allowed to give one response to the question, their number-one answer. So the data you see on the open-ended questions is not word-for-word, but rather grouped together with other similar responses.

The survey went very well. We were allowed to get not only a big picture view of what's happening on the Christian college campus, but also insights into specific issues that should be of concern for everyone involved. Let's take a quick look at the big picture responses. In upcoming chapters, we will dissect them in much more detail.

New Testament Agreement / Old Testament Dividing Lines

We were pleased to find nearly 100 percent agreement on some important New Testament issues:

- Do you believe in the virgin birth of Christ? Yes: 99.0%
- Do you believe in Christ's substitutionary death on the Cross? Yes: 99.0%
- Do you believe in a literal heaven and hell? Yes: 96.5%
- Do you believe in Christ's Second Coming? Yes: 99.0%
- Do you believe in the bodily Resurrection of Christ? Yes: 99.0%

But the minute we stepped into the Old Testament, division began to arise. The more detailed the question, the clearer it became that there were serious problems.

Immediately we see a rift forming over the historical account of Noah and the Flood, but that was just the tip of the iceberg. When we started to look at issues regarding creation and evolution, the issues became more pronounced. Once more, the more detailed our questions became, the deeper the division became.

Q13: Do you believe the Genesis 1–2 account of creation is literally true?

- Yes: 83.0%   • No: 14.7%   • Don't know: 2.2%

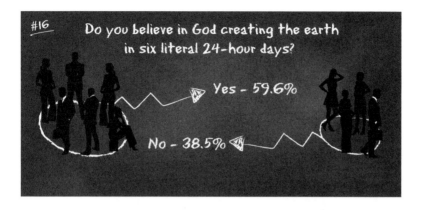

It's clear that we have some confusion here. We are beginning to see a trend that concerned us throughout the entire survey: *people didn't always mean what they said.* For example, 83 percent said that they believe Genesis 1 and 2 are literally true. But when we asked whether they believe God created in six literal days, only 59.6 percent answered yes. That means about 23 percent are either confused, wrong, or just haven't thought this through. Or it could also be how people in a postmodern culture determine the meaning of words. I have realized over the years that many professors will sound like they believe in a literal Genesis, but what they mean by the words is not what I (and many others) understand them to mean. This is a major issue we will deal with in this study.

Questions 16 and 17 are virtually the opposites of each other (with 16 being positive and 17 being negative), but almost 10 percent of the people answered yes to both questions, indicating that they believe in six literal days of creation and they don't believe in six literal days of creation! These concerns continued to grow as we gathered data about what they teach about evolution.

#6 What does your institution teach about evolution?

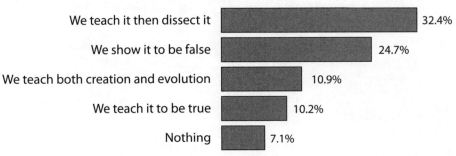

We teach it then dissect it	32.4%
We show it to be false	24.7%
We teach both creation and evolution	10.9%
We teach it to be true	10.2%
Nothing	7.1%

This was an open-ended question. These five answers accounted for 95 percent of all the respondents, with more saying that they "teach and dissect" evolution. That word "dissect" is interesting and requires some further investigation (9 percent of them used the same word when describing how they teach the Bible!). I would like to give them the benefit of the doubt. We hope they mean that they (1) explain the idea, (2) give an accurate critique of the idea's strengths and weaknesses, and (3) show how it is absolutely contrary to the authoritative account in God's Word. At least I hope so — but the further we look into the answers to the questions, the more I have my doubts.

I don't think there's anything wrong at all with "teaching evolution" as long as it is put under the same scientific and biblical scrutiny that any idea would be. On the other hand, "dissect" might mean "we teach and let them decide." That is a big concern. Are they presenting the issues loosely and just letting students decide what is true? Or are they explaining all the facts and pointing to the definitive conclusion that evolution is false and creation is true? That's a big question, and the answer hinges on the fundamental difference between relativism (no absolute truth, i.e., people decide their own truth) and the biblical worldview: *is there absolute truth or is there not*?

Twenty-four percent said that they teach evolution to be false. Not a lot. In the next two responses, we see that at *least* 20 percent of Christian colleges are teaching evolution as a viable option and another 11 percent admit to teaching evolution as truth. That's more than 30 percent. If we add to that a portion of those who are in the "we dissect it" category (who probably aren't taking any sort of stand in favor of creation), this number could be much, much higher. The answer "nothing" is a concern as well. To teach nothing about evolution, when it is the dominant worldview theme in our culture that is in opposition to biblical creation, leaves students vulnerable and ignorant.

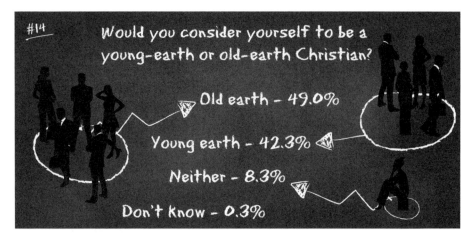

This number turned out to be quite a bit bigger than we had expected — 42 percent say that the earth is young. I'm actually fairly encouraged by that because it doesn't seem like that many people are taking a stand on the issue publicly. My guess is that many of them feel intimidated because of academic peer pressure and are "closet" young-earth creationists. If the system is already compromised, individuals within the system will feel pressure to compromise or hide their position in order to keep their jobs and advance their careers. One continually risks rejection when taking a stand on this issue (as has been documented by others).

They also need to be published in academic journals to have respect in the community. By taking a stand on the age of the earth (and evolution) one can "slit his or her own throat" when it comes to advancement. Tragically, in both secular and Christian institutions, people will be more dedicated to their academic discipline in order to get published in the journals than they are to the institution and its beliefs. They have to look good within their field of study, even if it doesn't reflect the values of the school.

At one seminary where I spoke, I asked the head of the seminary (who invited me as he had the same view of Genesis as I do) why so many professors in such institutions would not take a stand on six literal days (no death before sin, young earth, etc.). He told me that a lot of it had to do with peer pressure and being published in the academic journals. He said if someone is labeled as a literal six-day, young-earth creationist, they basically could not get published in such journals.

Still, we were encouraged by the number of people who said they believed in a young earth.[3] But as we evaluated the survey as a whole, another "hunch" was clearly confirmed . . . and when it comes to Christian colleges, this clearly has become one of our greatest concerns.

"Newspeak" and the Old Testament

In his stunning book *1984*, George Orwell introduced a concept called "newspeak," in which characters in positions of power began using terms and phrases that sounded right to the masses — when in fact, they meant something very, very different. I've been concerned that the same sort of thing is happening in Christianity, so we began comparing what teachers claimed they believe about the Bible, and tried to determine what they actually mean by what they teach.

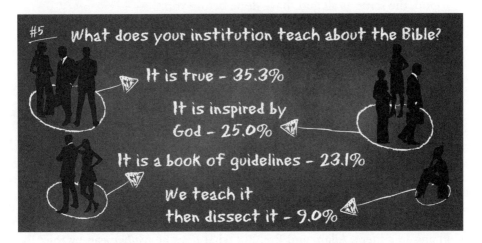

#5   What does your institution teach about the Bible?

It is true – 35.3%

It is inspired by God – 25.0%

It is a book of guidelines – 23.1%

We teach it then dissect it – 9.0%

These first four responses accounted for 92.3 percent of all the answers. What was the fifth most popular answer? Five people, or 1.6 percent, made it clear that they teach the Bible to be false. At least they are honest about it! And further, this is supposed to be a Christian college!

Our question is this: what do they mean when they say "true"? Because when you correlate these answers with the answers they gave on other questions, you quickly find out that people don't necessarily believe the Bible is "literally" true.

There's a postmodern influence here about what "true" means. Unfortunately, many people believe something is "true if it works for you." This allows the speaker to put a spin on his or her words, making them sound acceptable even though they really mean something totally different. Politicians do this all the time. When forced to explain what they really mean, they will dodge the truth by saying things like "it depends on what your definition of 'is' is."

The cults do this as well. The Mormons, for example, have become masters at using words that *sound* like Christian terminology, even though they *mean* something *entirely* different. And the masses (most Christians included) think their usage of these words means the same thing the Bible does. For example, Joseph Smith, the founder of the Mormon church, said:

> God himself was once as we are now, and is an exalted man. . . . We have imagined and supposed that God was God from all eternity. I will refute that idea. . . . He was once a man like us. . . . ere, then, is eternal life — to know the only wise and true God; and you have got to learn how to be gods yourselves and to be kings and priests to God, the same as all gods have done before you.[4]

So when a Mormon says "God," he is really talking about one of thousands of gods that were once men and earned their way to be gods just as you or I can! Their definitions of "Jesus," "grace," "atonement," and "heaven" are equally different from the biblical view. This "newspeak" has allowed them entrance into mainline evangelical Christian circles, even though what they mean by what they say is absolute heresy according to the Bible.

Similar word-twisting, truth-skewing "newspeak" is going on in the debate over the creation account in Genesis. Dr. William Dembski is a research professor in philosophy at Southwestern Baptist Theological Seminary in Fort Worth, Texas, and a senior fellow with the Discovery Institute's Center for Science and Culture in Seattle. He *says* that he believes in the inspired, inerrant Word of God and in a literal Adam and Eve. But what does he *really* mean by this? By scrutinizing his own words from one of his latest books (*The End of Christianity*) we quickly discover that he believes in billions of years, evolution, *and* Adam and Eve. The mental gymnastics used are dizzying. Consider this one quote: "For the theodicy I am proposing to be compatible with evolution, God must not merely introduce existing human-like beings from outside the Garden. In addition, when they enter the Garden, God must transform their consciousness so that they become rational moral agents made in God's image."[5]

I go into much, much more detail on Dr. Dembski and others in appendix A: "Speaking of Newspeak." Please take the time to read it. There are many other inconsistencies in Dr. Dembski's beliefs, but what they show are the outrageous lengths some Christian academics will go to in order to try to reconcile billions of years and evolutionary ideas with the Scriptures, all the while trying to keep their belief in a literal Adam and Eve and the original sin while telling unsuspecting parents and prospective students that they believe in inerrancy.

Another example is Professor Bruce Waltke, acknowledged to be a world-renowned Old Testament scholar and considered to be a "conservative evangelical." But even this label, "conservative evangelical," is an example of "newspeak," for it just doesn't mean what it used to. He resigned his position at a "conservative evangelical" seminary (Reformed Theological Seminary in Orlando) in 2010 over the issue of his public endorsement of evolution.

Dr. Waltke made statements that became very public, especially through a video that had appeared on a theologically liberal website: The BioLogos Foundation. He subsequently asked for the video to be removed from the site, but not before his pro-evolution statement had become widely known. It helped lead to his resignation from the seminary. So what did Dr. Waltke say in that video? Well, here is one quote:

> I think that if the data is overwhelming in favor, favor, of evolution, [then] to deny that reality will make us a cult, some odd group that's not really interacting with the real world, and rightly so.[6]

As of the writing of this book, Dr. Waltke had a teaching position at what is considered to be a conservative evangelical seminary — *Knox Theological Seminary* in Florida.

So, what does "conservative evangelical" really mean?

In the end, we discovered from the research that it really doesn't matter what people *say*, it's what they *mean* by what they say that needs to be discerned.

Defining Terms Practically

In order to determine what people really mean by what they say, we used open-ended and closed-ended questions so we could compare answers.

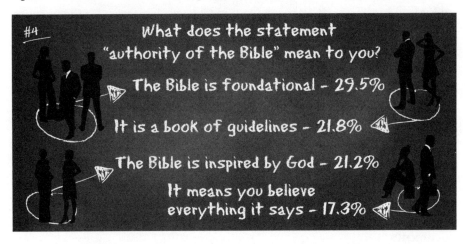

#4 What does the statement "authority of the Bible" mean to you?

The Bible is foundational - 29.5%

It is a book of guidelines - 21.8%

The Bible is inspired by God - 21.2%

It means you believe everything it says - 17.3%

The remaining 10 percent used words like "priority," "inerrant," or "expertise." Most of the answers sounded good, but very few, if any, of the

312 respondents had a clear definition of what they meant by "authority of the Bible."

Do you see why this is so important? I mean, these phrases sound right, but what do people mean when they use words like "foundational"? When they say the Bible is a book of "guidelines" are they really saying that it's just a general list of suggestions? When they say that the Bible is "inspired," do they mean it in the same way that Rembrandt or Michelangelo were inspired? Do they simply mean God's Word is "inspirational"?

Our definitions of the key biblical terms must be both clear and practical. When I speak of the authority of the Bible, what I mean is this:

> The Bible is the absolute standard for life and practice and every-thing it touches upon. It is the foundation for all of my thinking in every area.

A definition like that helps to rule out liberal interpretations that mean something different. It's important to have clear definitions like that for all of the important words we use in Christianity. However, as careful as we can be, this research has found that even the very best of words and definitions can't necessarily be trusted to mean the same things to good Christian people. One will have to go far beyond the words and definitions and delve deeply with very specific and detailed questions to really discern what someone believes and teaches.

Let me give an example to help further explain.

On October 26–28, 1978, the first summit of the International Council on Biblical Inerrancy (ICBI) took place in Chicago. This was "for the purpose of affirming afresh the doctrine of the inerrancy of Scripture, making clear the understanding of it and warning against its denial."

If you have never read this document,[7] I urge you to do so. It covers in detail definitions of inspiration, infallibility, and inerrancy. There were around 300 signers of this document, including Dr. Henry Morris (president and founder of the Institute for Creation Research, and co-author of famed book *The Genesis Flood*), Dr. John Whitcomb (theologian and co-author of *The Genesis Flood*), and Dr. Duane Gish (who was vice president of the *Institute for Creation* Research when Dr. Henry Morris was president). There is no doubt the authors of this current book could sign this document.

However, I want to bring your attention to Article XII from the 1978 document:

> We affirm that Scripture in its entirety is inerrant, being free from all falsehood, fraud, or deceit.

We deny that Biblical infallibility and inerrancy are limited to spiritual, religious, or redemptive themes, exclusive of assertions in the fields of history and science. We further deny that scientific hypotheses about earth history may properly be used to overturn the teaching of Scripture on creation and the flood.

And I would say AMEN to that. Nonetheless, Dr. Henry Morris said this of the document and the ICBI:

The leadership of this group includes many who accept theistic evolution or progressive creation, as well as many who prefer to ignore the creation issue altogether. Consequently, unless the ICBI can somehow become convinced of the foundational importance of strict creationism for maintaining a consistent belief in inerrancy, its efforts will likely prove of only ephemeral effectiveness. The writer and others were able to persuade the ICBI to incorporate a brief article on creation and the flood into its "Chicago Statement on Inerrancy," but the Council leadership felt it could not stand on literal-day creationism and a worldwide flood, so the article was mostly innocuous.[8]

Note that although Dr. Morris (and myself) agree with the definitions of inerrancy, inspiration, and infallibility in this document, Dr. Morris understood that did not stop many who believed in millions of years and even evolution from signing it. Obviously, what a number of these scholars understood by these terms was not how Dr. Morris understood the same terms! This is a major problem in modern Christianity.

Interestingly, the ICBI conducted a second summit in 1982. Dr. Henry Morris, in writing about this summit and the papers presented concerning how to interpret the Genesis record of creation, stated: "Dr. Bradley presented the only full-length paper. The presentations by Dr. Archer and myself were merely discussions of Bradley's paper. The 'stacking' of the ICBI program was evident in that both Dr. Bradley and Dr. Archer were known to be opposed to the literal-day record of Genesis. The statement finally adopted by the council was so innocuous on the subject of origins that it would not even exclude evolution as an acceptable interpretation. *That* was the reason I could not sign their statement on biblical hermeneutics."[9]

Dr. Henry Morris would not sign this second ICBI document called "The Chicago Statement on Biblical Hermeneutics" because he understood it really did not stand on an inerrant, infallible Scripture — even though those signing it would all say they believed such.

Keeping all this in mind, now consider these questions asked as part of our research project:

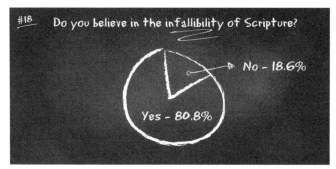

The percentage of no answers is in itself a great concern, but what do those who answered yes really mean? That is one of the major problems our research has once again brought to light.

Clearing Things Up

I began looking at various statements of faith from churches, Christian colleges, etc., on the Internet. I found that most statements of faith had a very general statement (if any) on creation. They were so general, in fact, that they could certainly allow for billions of years and evolution. Such general statements can sadly lead to the door of compromise being opened and eventually lead a college, church, etc., down the liberal path.

One can't just accept what one is told from a college as it may not mean what we think it means (infallible and inerrant mean something different to some of these professors than it would to you). We need to understand that many colleges are actually destructive because of their compromise/liberalism/belief in millions of years.

It was thrilling to read this creation statement from *Appalachian Bible College* (located in Beckley, West Virginia, in the beautiful Appalachian mountains):

> We believe that the first eleven chapters of Genesis are the literal history of the early Earth (Matthew 19:4, 24:37).
>
> We believe that this material universe is the result of a sequence of unique creative acts of God the Son, accomplished with the aid of God the Holy Spirit and directed by God the Father (Genesis 1:1, 2; Colossians 1:16). We believe these creative acts were *ex nihilo*, completed by the mere spoken commands of God (2 Peter 3:5). We further believe that these creative acts were accomplished in six literal twenty-four hour days (Exodus 20:11). Therefore we hold to a young earth view supported by the genealogies and other time information provided in the Word of God. We also believe that the material universe was created in total perfection (Genesis 1:31) but subsequently was sentenced to a slow decay and eventual destruction by the Curse (binding), which was part of the penalty for the disobedience of the parents of all mankind, Adam and Eve, whom we view as real, literal people, created on the sixth day of Creation (Genesis 1:27, 2:7–3:19). We reject all concepts of a pre-Adamic race. We believe that the biblical Noahic Flood (Genesis 6–8) was a real, year-long global event, the result of the judgment of God on the hopelessly rebellious descendants of Adam and Eve (Genesis 6:5, 1 Peter 3:6), and resulted in much of the present geology of the Earth, including most of the fossil graveyards of myriads of plants and animals then living. We believe that only eight human souls, Noah and his family, survived the Flood (Genesis 7:13 and 8:18) and that all mankind now living are descended from this family, dispersed over the face of the Earth by the confusion of tongues described in Genesis 11.

Now that's the type of strong statement we need to have in our Christian institutions. How refreshing to find a Christian college that is prepared to make such a statement with such detail to do their best to not allow the secular religion of this age (humanism, which encompasses millions of years/evolution) to in any way infiltrate the college and undermine the authority of God's Word — and lead young people down the path of doubt to unbelief! I challenge Christian colleges, churches, etc., to begin to reconsider their statements of faith to see how they can be strengthened in this area that has involved so much compromise in today's world.

Just as an encouragement, here is the text of a letter I received from the president of Northland International University (one of the few Christian universities that stands on a literal Genesis):

> Dear Friends at Answers in Genesis,
>
> Thank you for the incredible support you have been to Northland International University. As we prepare this next generation of leaders, we do it in a postmodern era where God has been left out, the idea of absolute truth has been jettisoned, and society has been thrown into a moral free fall.
>
> You have rightly identified this battle as a battle for the authority of the Word of God. If we cannot believe what God has clearly stated in Genesis 1–11, how can we trust the rest of the Bible? We fully concur with your doctrinal statement and in this foundation: God's Word is inspired, infallible, inerrant, and sufficient. It is trustworthy in every way. We also believe that true science confirms what God has said.
>
> Thank you for the investment you have made in our undergraduate and graduate programs, for the exceptional teaching, and abundant resources. We hope to build stronger ties with AIG and give our full support.
>
> Your friend,
> Matt Olson, President, Northland International University,
>   http://www.ni.edu

There are very few well-known Christian leaders who are willing to take a vocal stand on taking the Book of Genesis as literal history. Thankfully, there are some leaders who have the boldness to make such an uncompromising stand, such as Pastor Johnny Hunt, Reverend Brian Edwards (UK), Dr. John MacArthur, and Dr. Albert Mohler, as well as a number of others.

Dr. Mohler is president of The Southern Baptist Theological Seminary in Louisville, Kentucky. At the 2010 Ligonier Ministries/Christianity.com conference "Tough Questions Christians Face," Dr. Mohler gave a presentation entitled "Why Does the Universe Look So Old?" In his conclusion, he declared:

> I would suggest to you that in our effort to be most faithful to the Scriptures and most accountable to the grand narrative of the gospel, an understanding of creation in terms of 24-hour calendar days and a young earth entails far fewer complications, far fewer theological problems, and actually is the most straightforward and uncomplicated reading of the text as we come to understand God telling us how the universe came to be and what it means and why it matters."[10]

"Truth"

President Greg Hall was recently teaching a class at Warner University on the topic of the authority of Scripture. During the discussion, he posed the question, "Do you believe the Bible is true?" Almost everyone in the class agreed that it is true but not everyone. A few found the question impossible to deal with. One student said, "It depends what you mean by 'truth.'"

Greg said, "Truth is that which corresponds to reality."

The students brought up the so-called errors and contradictions in the Bible — and the need to be able to interpret the text given the cultural setting, etc. They said the Scripture is "true in what it affirms" (a statement that is, in and of itself, almost completely meaningless). Greg publicly defended the Scripture in front of the whole class, affirming that the Bible does correspond to objective reality, that it is a book that accurately describes life as we experience it, that it tells the truth about historical events, and is reliable in every issue that it speaks to.

Then Greg pulled the students aside privately into his office for deeper discussion. He took a stand, being concerned not only for the students' well-being but for the possible compromise that their influence would have on the class and the school. The compromise that we're seeing in Christian colleges always centers on this: what we believe about the inspiration, inerrancy, and infallibility of Scripture. *This is the issue.* The authority of Scripture is a central point of faith. If you don't get the first two chapters of the sacred text right, you cannot get the rest right either.

Unfortunately, the survey revealed little consistency in these issues, showing the great number of people in Christian institutions who are conflicted about what they truly mean by what they say.

What is the truth? That depends on who you ask and their particular viewpoint or interpretation of the Scripture. In the above table, note virtually all young-earth believers, 93.9%, believe the Bible is literally true. It is surprising this number is not higher. Also, nearly four in five who adhere to an old-earth theory believe the Bible is literally true. Keep in mind these two concepts are polar opposites. These findings quickly reveal the large number of Christian leaders who are mistaken and hold a biblical position contrary to the literal interpretation of God's Holy Word. This is extremely important to understand because once a Christian accepts a non-biblical view, they must then accept other non-biblical ideas to fulfill the logic of their error.

The so-called gap theory is a great example of this. Many great Christian leaders of the past 200 years have been gap theorists. They thought fitting the millions of years into a supposed gap in Genesis 1 was a way of dealing with the issue. In that sense, I have a much greater respect for such people than I do for those proposing theistic evolution or other old-earth views that reinterpret much of the Bible to mean something other than what it says. Theistic evolutionists, day-agers, advocates of the framework hypothesis, etc., are reinterpreting the clear teaching of Scripture to fit millions of years, and often Darwinian-type evolution, into the Bible (be it geological, astronomical, or biological evolution).

I say that the gap theory does (in spite of contrary intentions of godly men) "unlock a door" to allow a "crack" to undermine Scripture, and thus even great men (who were head and shoulders above people like me theologically) were inconsistent in this area. If one allows a crack in the door (as we would see the gap theory doing), then the next generation will open it further. It usually doesn't get shut by the next generation.

In chapters 3 and 5, we will look more closely at the results of this survey. The news does not get better. As we look into the issues more deeply, you'll see reasons to become more and more concerned about what is happening — and it's not just about secular campuses but about the infiltration that is taking place in Christian institutions. We have nearly 100 percent agreement on New Testament issues, but when we get back to Genesis, we can clearly see that changes. They don't typically discuss different "theories" about the virgin birth or the Resurrection, but they definitely discuss different "theories" about how things came into being in Genesis!

Overall, we found that only 24 percent of the 312 people surveyed answered every question correctly . . . and these are the "good guys"! These are the institutions that require testimonies of faith from their professors or have strong religious affiliations. Please understand this: if you send your students to a Christian college or institution, three out of four times they will stand in front of teachers who have a degraded view and interpretation of Scripture.

We do understand the "world" is the enemy and what those in the world say doesn't surprise us. But we should be dismayed and shocked at what is happening in the Church. A trumpet is making an uncertain sound — and our children are increasingly becoming the casualties.

Like it or not, we are at war — "a war of worldviews," as Greg Hall will describe in the next chapter. We've been fairly aware of our fight with the secularists who deny God and adhere to humanism where man's thinking rules. What most families are not aware of, however, is the depths to which these influences have infiltrated Christian institutions.

And most parents aren't finding out until it's too late.

Endnotes
1. For a full list of the colleges that took part in the survey, go to creationcolleges.org.
2. For a full list of the colleges that took part in the survey, go to creationcolleges.org.
3. A young earth is a corollary for trusting the Bible as the authority — having six normal days of Genesis 1 (which are almost negligible), about 2,000 years from Adam to Abraham (Genesis 5 and 11), about 2,000 years from Abraham to Christ (genealogies and scholars generally agree on this), and about 2,000 years from Christ until today.
4. Larry E. Dahl and Donald Q. Cannon, editors, *The Teachings of Joseph Smith* (Salt Lake City, UT: Bookcraft, 1997), p. 345–347.
5. William Dembski, *The End of Christianity: Finding a Good God in an Evil World* (Nashville, TN: Broadman & Holman Academic, 2009), p. 159.
6. Bruce Waltke, "Why Must the Church Come to Accept Evolution?" http://biologos.org/blog/why-must-the-church-come-to-accept-evolution/, posted March 24, 2010; accessed and downloaded March 29, 2010; pulled from the website on about April 2, 2010.

7. *The Chicago Statement on Biblical Inerrancy,* International Council of Biblical Inerrancy, Dallas Theological Seminary Archives, 1978.
8. Henry M. Morris, *King of Creation* (San Diego, CA: Creation Life Publishers, 1980), p. 45–46.
9. Henry M. Morris, "The Days Do Matter," *Back to Genesis*, No. 190 (October 2004).
10. http://www.christianity.com/ligonier/?speaker=mohler2.

Chapter 2

Welcome to the War

Greg Hall
President of Warner University

The fool has said in his heart, "There is no God" (Ps. 14:1).

We are at war. We are at war with weapons far greater than any bomb, missile, or gun. And these weapons are aimed at targets far more strategic than any building, land mass, or army, because "our struggle is not against flesh and blood, but against the rulers, against the authorities, against the powers of this dark world" (Eph. 6:12; NIV). We are at war against thoughts, thoughts raised up *against* the knowledge of God. And these thoughts are aimed at the minds of our children.

In the secular arena, the battle is often blatant, where the best the Christian can hope for are the condescending glances of those in power. In the Christian arena, however, the battle is often much more subtle. If the survey taught us anything, it's that the battle has now come home again, where many — if not almost all — of our Christian institutions of higher learning are turning out to be "already compromised" to one degree or another.

It is spiritual warfare. There is a great deal at stake: our culture, our well-being, our way of life . . . but most importantly, the hearts and minds of our youth. It has been said that (from a human perspective) the Church is always only one generation away from extinction. Here in the 21st century, we have come face to face with that reality. We live in a time when we must "demolish arguments and every pretension that sets itself up against the knowledge of God, and we take captive every thought to make it obedient to Christ" (2 Cor. 10:5; NIV).

One national publication recently proclaimed that the United States is no longer a Christian nation.[1] This has been a long time coming, but it has not come by accident. Yet we also know that the gates of hell themselves cannot stand against the Church as she takes the light of truth into enemy territory (Matt. 16:18). The anti-Christian, atheistic segment of our culture has become very militant.[2] What were once skirmishes between the two sides is now open warfare. The prominent players in this anti-Christian movement and the books they have written include Dr. Richard Dawkins, *The God Delusion*; Dr. Sam Harris, *The End of Faith*; Dr. Victor Stenger, *God: The Failed Hypothesis*; Christopher Hitchens, *God Is Not Great*; and Dr. Michael Onfray, *The Atheist Manifesto*. They all talk about the final battle being against Christianity.

Nobel laureate Dr. Steven Weinberg writes: "Anything that we scientists can do to weaken the hold of religion should be done and may in the end be our greatest contribution to civilization."[3] At the core of all these so-called scientists and educators is the commitment to Darwinism (with its tenets of evolution and millions of years) — and unless you think I am talking about a few militant educators/writers, consider that a recent poll of the National Academy of Science shows only 7 percent of this group consider themselves believers.

Virtually every student in America who goes through public education is required to read text books written by this group. Thank God that a remnant of committed Christian educators exists in grade school, high schools, and colleges and universities. They are among those who understand the deception that can happen at all levels of education — those who take a daily stand for truth, who believe and teach that the best explanation for the existence of the universe is stated in the Bible beginning with "In the beginning God created the heavens and the earth" (Gen. 1:1).

This creation versus evolution/millions of years debate is as current as this morning's newspaper. All over this land, school boards now debate with teachers and townspeople whether their schools should teach only evolution and keep creation only in the realm of what they define as religion. It is such a hot topic that during the presidential campaign season, candidates from both parties were asked their position on the topic.

The following militant atheists are the people our secular college and university students and faculty are paying attention to. What are they saying? Listen to a brief compendium of thoughts directly from their literature and you will get an idea of what we are up against:

- Dr. Francisco Ayala: "Life is the result of a natural process, without any need to resort to a Creator."[4]
- Dr. William Provine: "Modern science directly implies that there are no inherent moral or ethical laws and, when we die, we die."[5]
- Dr. Steven Pinker: "Religion taught men to believe in an immortal soul, modern science has destroyed that belief."[6]
- Christopher Hitchens writes "of the moral superiority of atheism."[7]
- Dr. Douglas Futuyma: "By coupling undirected, purposeless variation to the blind, uncaring process of natural selection, Darwin made theological or spiritual explanations of the life processes superfluous."[8]
- The National Association of Biology Teachers (NABT) asserted that all life is the outcome of "an unsupervised, impersonal, unpredictable, and natural process."[9]

These people consider themselves brave pioneers, teaching the *truth* about man's origin and facing death and extinction with valor. They worship at the altar of Darwinian evolution. They are, I am convinced, more interested in promoting their philosophic anti-Christian agenda than a scientific one. Their agenda is very simple: get the biblical God out of the picture and replace it with a humanistic worldview (i.e., man is the ultimate authority to determine truth apart from God; Darwinism is arguably the most popular form of humanism). And they have figured out exactly how to do it. This was stated nearly 30 years ago in a magazine called *The Humanist*:

> I am convinced that the battle for humankind's future must be waged and won in the public school classroom by teachers who correctly perceive their role as the proselytizers of a new faith: a religion of humanity that recognizes and respects the spark of what theologians call divinity in every human being. These teachers must embody the same selfless dedication as the most rabid fundamentalist preachers, for they will be ministers of another sort, utilizing a classroom instead of a pulpit to convey humanist values in whatever subject they teach, regardless of the educational level — preschool day care or large state university. The classroom must and will become an arena of conflict between the old and the new — the rotting corpse of Christianity, together with all its adjacent evils and misery, and the new faith of humanism.[10]

They have made the battleground public education where they have a captive audience. They represent the ideas of a secular culture that is determined to eliminate any reference to the God of the Bible as the sovereign

Creator of the universe. They know they can easily change these concepts in the culture by implanting them daily into the minds of impressionable youth — our children. And they have sadly, in large measure, succeeded.

The Body Count

Steve Henderson, president of *Christian Consulting for Colleges*, has researched the faith commitments of college students at evangelical and secular colleges. Read what he says:

> A few years ago, George Fox University professor Gary Railsback, a fellow researcher, prepared an interesting study. Using his data, I determined that more than 52 percent of incoming freshmen who identify themselves as born-again upon entering a public university will either no longer identify themselves as born-again four years later or, even if they do still claim that identification, will not have attended any religious service in over a year. This means over half of our kids are reporting a rejection of family religious values if they attend a public university.[11]

A recent press release on the ongoing *National Study of College Students' Search for Meaning and Purpose* offered some interesting information on students who are beginning their college years. While 79 percent of all freshmen believe in God, 69 percent pray, and 81 percent attend religious services at least occasionally, 57 percent question their religious beliefs, 52 percent disagree with their parents about religious matters, and 65 percent feel distant from God.[12]

In a revealing study, UCLA Higher Education Research Institute tracked 16,000 high school seniors from freshman days to graduation, demonstrating the impact of college choice on spiritual commitment. The 16,000 kids identified themselves as "born-again" in high school. Upon graduation, 52 percent no longer considered themselves Christian.[13]

College students are asking deep questions about their faith. Unless they are at a solidly biblical Christian college, they may find themselves in an environment that is not conducive to providing supportive answers. Even if they are at a Christian college, our research has proven that they may be getting hit with "friendly fire," as professors they consider to be allies attack the foundations of their faith with liberal, compromising ideas that undermine biblical authority, create doubt, and can lead to unbelief.

A March 29, 2005, *Washington Post* article by Howard Kurtz titled "Study Finds College Faculties a Most Liberal Lot" reports that most faculty at non-Christian colleges disdain Christianity, with 72 percent indicating they are liberal, 84 percent favoring abortion, and 67 percent indicating homosexuality is acceptable. In most cases, students reflect the values of college faculty they encounter in their upper division coursework. These faculty members are typically the advisors and mentors of students. Certainly the above findings indicate that the answers and directions students receive from most faculty at these institutions will not be supportive of traditional morality and religious values.

After sharing this study in a message in an evangelical church, I had a woman call me the following morning. She was very polite and asked if she could comment on my Sunday sermon. I had shared this study and attempted a strong advocacy for Christian higher education.

She politely suggested I might want to change my sermon. She explained I had offended her daughter by my remarks, home from a semester at a major public university. She felt I had been too hard and unreasonable in my comments about secular public education. I apologized for creating this offense but told her I honestly believed in what I said. She still suggested I moderate my comments but added as we ended our conversation, "In all honesty, I must tell you, my daughter was in church yesterday for the first time in a year."

According to the research, this woman's daughter is not alone. Scores of parents are spending a significant amount of their savings to pay for an education that is undercutting the foundations of Christian faith! Scores of parents are unwittingly paying the way for educators to destroy the beliefs of their children (Prov. 22:6). You have to admit, that's pretty clever on secularists' part — and pretty foolish on the parents' part.

Infiltration in the Ranks

I do find, however, that students have little problem understanding that the enemies of God will stop at nothing to discredit the Scripture. What they don't understand, though, are the numbers of Christian institutions, ministries, churches, pastors, and Christian educators who are doing the same. But in many ways, these influences are more dangerous: they are a lurking and growing enemy within our own camp. In the worst of cases, these people are wolves in sheep's clothing, many times very intentionally leading students away from the authority of the Scriptures while posing as our friends (Matt. 7:15).

My point is this: I cannot take the position I have on secular education and not be honest about the issues related to Christian education, too. I find folks want simple explanations of what is really taught at Christian schools, and they have a right to know. I believe in the significance, importance, and eternal value of a Christ-centered education. Yet it is only honest to say that it is very, very important to be discerning when choosing Christian schools, too.

My life in Christian higher education has been amazingly fulfilling. I have met some wonderful and committed believers. I have had association with numerous outstanding Christian institutions making a difference in countless lives in expanding the kingdom. I will remain an outspoken advocate for Christian education as a tool God uses to raise up new generations of competent and caring individuals.

There is, however, an issue that persists — one that needs to be addressed or some Christian institutions will find their influence diminished or, in the future, nonexistent. The issue is this: the spiritual well-being for many students is hindered and not enhanced while attending Christian schools. The church knows this and is miffed by it. Some people find it unacceptable and will encourage some of their youth to attend secular institutions as a result. Over the course of 35 years in ministry (nearly 20 as a college/university president), I have heard this issue raised over and over again, sometimes with deep contempt.

I am sure the loss of spiritual vitality of some students is a matter of personal discontent that is no fault of any institution. But some of the stories deal directly with who we are and what we do. In those cases, we must own the problem and deal with it. The Church wants and needs to be strong. It does not want to hear stories about young people whose lives are hurt by our schools instead of helped. They do not want to hear their faith was disassembled in the classroom by those who discredit the Scripture or have a view of the Christian faith that is far afield from orthodox Christian belief.

However, I do acknowledge there are still a number of faithful people, terrific scholars among them, who believe the Bible to be true in every way (these people should be encouraged and prayed for; we need more of them). I have heard other scholars say that "the Bible is true in all it affirms" (whatever that means), but they go on to say that it was never intended to be an academic text and should be trusted only in matters of faith, not matters of science. That equivocation is heresy to me, considering that *all* the treasures of wisdom and knowledge are hidden in Christ (Col. 2:3, and "*all* Scripture is given by inspiration of God, and is profitable for doctrine, for reproof, for correction, for instruction in righteousness" (2 Tim. 3:16; NKJV, emphasis added).

Based on research, we find that many of today's young people are being contaminated by the very people parents trust with their children's spiritual training. In most cases, the students are not being prepared for the spiritual battle we observe daily in our culture.[14] Sadly, they are becoming casualties of this battle — but casualties caused from those supposedly on their side of the battle. If this was a matter of a few select personal instances that would be one thing — yet still a cause for concern. However, there are far too many instances and far too many testimonies of what went spiritually wrong. This is a matter of spiritual concern for Christian institutions everywhere. The *Grand Rapids Press* ran a survey of colleges in Michigan recently and stated:

> In a recent survey of area colleges and universities, *The Press* found all of the institutions that teach biology teach Darwinian evolution. Only one, Cornerstone University, questions the theory's validity and spends significant time teaching alternative explanations. Even most of the Christian schools — Calvin, Hope, and Aquinas colleges — base their curricula on Darwin's theory.
>
> "Evolution is the paradigm out of which we teach biology," said David Warners, a biology professor at Calvin. "We're not trying to hide things; it's just that we're not looking for a fight."

Notice that they say they are "not looking for a fight"; this helps reveal that they realize that what they are teaching *is in opposition* to the Church's teachings! Even at the one university where evolution is questioned, some professors base their teaching on Darwin. The article continues:

> Bultman notices many students enter Hope with a "creationist/ intelligent design" worldview, he said, and are frustrated by the biology curriculum. Warners said there is a similar trend at Calvin, as many students begin college as strong opponents of evolutionary theory.
>
> "It's a challenge," Warners said of teaching evolution, "and it needs to be done very sensitively."[15]

In other words, these Christian colleges strategically take students who believe the Bible and systematically destroy that belief and teach them to believe in evolution. This is the sad state of the Church in America. No wonder we are losing the coming generations! Dr. R.C. Sproul recently sent out this warning:

> The classroom is not a place where open debate is usually encouraged. To the contrary, on the campuses of many universities and even seminaries, open season has been declared on Christian students. For some reason, it seems that professors in such settings take delight in trying to undermine the faith of their students. . . . In most cases, it is easy for a man or woman with a doctorate in years of experience in higher education to humiliate a student, no matter how strong the student's faith is or how articulate the student may be.

If you're looking to send your children to an institution that has a Christian history or a Christian relationship, do not assume that the current faculty is fully persuaded of the truth claims of Christianity. You may indeed be throwing your children into the fire of crucible they are not expecting and are not really prepared to withstand. I am not for educating people in a sheltered environment where there is no interaction with the secular mindset and with pagan worldviews, but we need to be fully prepared to understand when and where those worldviews come into collision with Christianity and how to avoid collisions that may be disastrous.[16]

Is my institution free from this problem and do we exhibit perfect fidelity to all matters of Christian teaching? Frankly, no; we've had our issues. As with all schools, some of the criticism is fair and some of it is not. But no matter what, it's time for all of us to do some self-evaluation, even as we do our best to discern the content and intent of others (Luke 6:41–42).

There are probably still a good number of people who think that the time-honored foundation of the Christian tradition is at the core of our educational system today. Not so. To believe this system is undergirded by biblical principles is entirely false. Not only is our educational system not based on Christian principles, but there is a growing hostility in educational circles, especially in higher education, toward all things Christian. And it all has to do with worldview. If you are not familiar with this raging battle for the minds of humanity, please turn to appendix B. It is simply imperative that you understand what is happening and how it affects our education system at all levels. For example, biologist Dr. Richard Lewontin says of science education:

The objective . . . is not to provide the public with knowledge of how far it is to the nearest star, and what genes are made of. The problem is to get them to reject irrational and supernatural explanations of the world.[17]

The anti-God perspective has obviously gained a foothold in our public education system. That comes as no surprise when you consider who is behind this and how militant they have become toward Christianity. Christopher Hitchens writes:

How can we ever know how many children had their psychological and physical lives irreparably maimed by the compulsory inculcation of faith? If religious instruction were not allowed until the child had attained the age of reason, we would be living in a quite different world.[18]

Again, Dr. Lewontin writes:

> The objective . . . is to get them to reject irrational and supernatural explanations of the world, the demons that exist only in their imaginations, and to accept a social and intellectual apparatus, science as the only begetter of truth.[19]

Or, how about this quote from Dr. Richard Dawkins:

> How much do we regard children as being the property of their parents? It's one thing to say people should be free to believe whatever they like, but should they be free to impose their beliefs on their children? Is there something to be said for society stepping in? What about bringing up children to believe manifest falsehoods? Isn't it always a form of child abuse to label children as possessors of beliefs that they are too young to have thought out?[20]

These ideas and philosophies are the foundation of the curriculum of public education and *have infiltrated* Christian education at almost all levels. Your children may be captive in a system intent on discrediting Christianity. It is not surprising that this is the intent of the secularist educators. What is surprising is that so many Christian parents seem to not care.

The central issue is this: as Christian leaders it is time to face the issue of just how committed we will be to the authority of Scripture. It is also time to answer to the Church for this problem. It is time to realize that it is possible to hurt young minds. With vigilance we must work to put our young people in classes taught by professors who are committed believers, who even though they might require students to think and develop their own faith, will not compromise Christian truth and exchange it for a liberalism or unbelief that breaks faith instead of building it.

I pray that the tone of this book will, if needed, castigate and challenge, but also build unity and nurture the Body of Christ. I am absolutely for "hammering" both secular and Christian institutions — but doing so in a way that asks the Church to "wake up" and be the "jury" in this matter of taking responsibility for the education of our youth. We must teach both parents and students to discriminate and do so in a way that builds the Kingdom of God, not breaks it.

Where England is today spiritually (it is all but dead), the USA will be tomorrow if we keep heading in this direction. In the research we saw that our kids were *already gone* from the Church. Now we see it in the Christian colleges and the universities that are following in the footsteps of the Ivy

League — those that are *already compromised*. In order to protect ourselves and our children, we must be prepared to fight in the battle of the world-views. But in order to do that, we must be aware of where the attacks are coming from. And as you will see in the next chapter, the source of compromise is coming from a very unexpected place.

Endnotes

1. *Newsweek,* February 2009
2. Interestingly, this is without warrant by their worldview. In an atheistic worldview, nothing matters, so why care enough to oppose Christianity? The fact that they oppose Christianity reveals they really don't believe what they profess to believe.
3. Remarks by Steven Weinberg at the Freedom from Religion Foundation, San Antonio, November 1999.
4. Francisco Ayala, "Darwin's Revolution," in John Campbell and J. W. Schoff, eds., *Creative Evolution* (New York: James & Bartlett Publishers, 1994), p. 4–5.
5. Cited by Kenneth R. Miller, *Finding Darwin's God: A Scientist's Search for Common Ground Between God and Evolution* (New York: Harper Perennial, 1999), p. 171.
6. Steven Pinker, "Is Science Killing the Soul?" A dialogue with Richard Dawkins and Steven Pinker (London, February 10, 1999).
7. Christopher Hitchens, "The Future of an Illusion," in *Love, Poverty and War: Journeys and Essays* (New York: Nation Books, 2004), p. 334.
8. Douglas Futuyma, *Evolutionary Biology* (Sunderland, MA: Sinauer, 1986).
9. "NABT Unveils New Statement on Teaching Evolution," *The American Biology Teacher* 68, no. 1 (January 1996): 61. The NABT statement created such an uproar that the organization subsequently dropped the words "unsupervised" and "impersonal." The change was largely cosmetic, however, since the remaining words "unpredictable" and "natural" were understood to mean essentially the same thing.
10. J. Dunphy, "A Religion for a New Age," *The Humanist* (Jan.–Feb. 1983): p. 23, 26.
11. "A Question of Price Versus Cost," *Christianity Today,* March 2006.
12. *Christianity Today,* March 2006, p. 86.
13. *Christianity Today,* March 2006, p. 87.
14. One way to start getting prepared is by reading the New Answers Book Series, by Master Books, that answers around 95 of the top questions surrounding the creation/evolution and biblical authority debate.
15. "150th Birthday of 'On the Origin of Species' Prompts Area Colleges to Assess Darwin's Impact," *Grand Rapids, Michigan, Press* (September 26, 2009).
16. R.C. Sproul, "Be Prepared," *Tabletalk Magazine* (November 1, 2010).
17. Richard Lewontin, "Billions and Billions of Demons," *New York Review of Books,* January 9, 1997.
18. Christopher Hitchens, *God Is Not Great: How Religion Poisons Everything* (New York: Twelve Books, 2007), p. 217, 220.
19. Richard Lewontin, "Billions and Billions of Demons," *New York Review of Books,* January 9, 1997.
20. Cited by Gary Wolf, "The Church of the Non-Believers," *Wired,* November 2006; Richard Dawkins, *The God Delusion* (Boston, MA: Houghton-Mifflin, 2006, 2008), p. 315.

Chapter 3

Conflict between the Classrooms

Ken Ham

> But now there are many members, but one body. And the eye cannot say to the hand, "I have no need of you"; or again the head to the feet, "I have no need of you" (1 Cor. 12:20–21).

was having lunch with a highly educated man some time ago when he turned and asked with a slight air of cynicism, "Do you take a religious view of Genesis or the scientific view?"

I responded this way, "Let me ask you a question. Can you define for me in the context of this conversation what you mean by the term 'scientific'?"

There was a long silence. "Hmmm, I don't really know. I haven't really thought about that," he admitted.

Part of the problem we see in Christian colleges that are already compromised is that *most* people haven't thought about that! Most people think that the battle over creation and evolution is being fought between "science" and "religion." But there are two problems with this thinking:

1. Most people can't define the word "science," and thus they end up misunderstanding how the word is used in our modern world.
2. Most people have an incorrect understanding of the word "religion" and, as a result, falsely think in terms of neutrality and nonreligion versus religion.

The primary dictionary definition of the word *science* is basically "knowledge." We need to understand that one can have knowledge concerning what happened in the past (e.g., the origins issue). This is called "historical science." However, this knowledge is based on certain assumptions about the past. If the assumptions are wrong, the conclusions reached will likely be wrong and we will misunderstand history. Understanding the assumptions used to build historical knowledge is extremely important.

But knowledge gained by observation (five senses) and based on the repeatable test (empiricism) is called "observational" or "operational science." This is the knowledge that enables us to build our technology, understand how a cell works, and develop medicines.

When most people use the word science today, they are usually thinking in terms of "operational science." This becomes very confusing when secularists use the word science when talking about aspects of genetics that can be examined in a lab, and then turn around and use the word science when discussing the topic of nonobservable aspects of evolutionary ideas (e.g., life from nonlife, reptiles evolving into birds, etc.). Knowing that mutations in DNA can occur and be measured is not the same as asserting that we know how those mutations occurred in various populations over millions of years.

Because most people (including most students — and most professors) do not understand the distinction between historical (origins) and operational science, they wrongly think that the battle of origins is one of science versus the Bible. That is simply not true. It is a battle between two totally different accounts of the past — a battle between people holding to different accounts of the past based on the conclusions of historical science.

The role of operational (or observational/repeatable) science is that it can be used to confirm which historical science best explains the evidence. Operational science can be used to help confirm or deny which account of historical science is true. Historical science uses certain assumptions to arrive at conclusions about the past. If these assumptions are incorrect, they will lead to a false knowledge of the past.

Actually, creationists and evolutionists both have the same operational science but different accounts of origins based on the assumptions in their methods of historical science. This needs to be clearly understood so people don't incorrectly believe that creationists are against science! Creationists love science; we praise God for making a universe where operational science is possible and for the benefits it has brought to mankind through technology and understanding.[1] We also love historical science, but only when the assumptions used to understand the past are firmly rooted in what God has revealed to us in the Bible.

We wanted to detail the above for you so that as we continue this discussion aimed at understanding what is happening in our Christian colleges, we will be using the same definition of the word science. Unless otherwise stated, when we speak of *science* from this point on, we will be referring to observational or operational science — not historical science.

Also, when we use the word *religion* in our discussion, it will be used mostly in the context of Christianity. People need to understand that there is no nonreligious position. A religion is basically a system of belief held to with ardor and faith. Atheism is a religion, Islam is a religion, Secular Humanism is a religion, and so on. Although scientists will use operational science when discussing evolutionary ideas, there are also many aspects of belief (or religion) in embracing evolution as the explanation for the life we see on this planet (such as the belief that life arose by only natural processes from matter over time). This can be called a naturalistic worldview since it rejects supernatural explanations of the origin of the universe and the life that we find on this planet.

The same can be said for biblical creationists. We use operational science to help us understand the past. However, there is a major difference: we accept the supernatural account of origins revealed in Genesis as a core belief and use operational science to confirm those ideas. What anyone believes about origins is ultimately based in a faith about the past.

Most people falsely assume that the "facts of science" *support* evolution and millions of years, while biblical creation is supposedly a matter of "religious faith." We hear this type of rhetoric in the media all the time when both the secularists and the theists draw distinctions between the supposed scientific "fact of evolution" and an old earth, and the religious "faith of creation" and a young earth.

In other words, people, even in our churches, have been led to believe that real scientists will adhere to evolution while it is religious people who believe in creation. In fact, the numbers from the survey of Christian colleges prove the exact opposite: in many cases, it tends to be the scientists who believe in the Bible's account of origins and accordingly a young earth, while the majority of those in the religion departments embrace evolution and undermine the authority of Scripture!

When we look at the history of science, we see a remarkable list of amazing achievements (because of operational science) that have made life better in our world. Man's ability to think, critically analyze, experiment, and imagine have resulted in these remarkable achievements. Space shuttles, instant worldwide communications, satellites . . . operational science is propelling us forward at light speed. It's been a long time since Copernicus, Kepler, Galileo, and Einstein, but our knowledge in physics still continues to grow. Scholars research relativity to quantum physics to string theory in pursuit of an increasing knowledge of how our universe works.

Or consider the astounding advances in medical technologies and practices made possible by science. Greg was attending the University of Pittsburgh during the days the School of Medicine was developing transplantation technology. What was once almost science fiction is now commonplace surgery. Many lives have been saved as a result of this science. And this is just one example of how medical science has amazingly advanced. The growth in medical science has made it possible to understand the intricate workings of the human body. It has made it possible to diagnose an illness and develop cures for diseases once thought impossible to deal with. Formerly high-risk procedures such as heart surgery or organ transplantation have become routine.

Consider the science behind computer technology. Some of us can remember the days before the computer. Some can remember the first computers as massive instruments that could only do simple computations. Today, the average cell phone has far more computational power than the computer that sent the first man to the moon.

Yes, mankind has accomplished incredible things using science. But does a proper understanding of science really support the beliefs of the evolutionist? That was the assumption of the man I was having lunch with when he asked, "Do you take a religious view of Genesis or the scientific view?" His question opened up a really good discussion about historical science, operational science, and so forth. He had never even heard of it before. He (like most professors at these colleges) did not understand the distinction between beliefs about the past (historical science) and knowledge gained by repeatability and observation (operational science) that is used to build our technology. He was actually mixing a naturalistic view of origins (i.e., no supernatural/no God) with operational science.

Many a scientist has become a creationist when he is willing to look beyond the closed-minded presuppositions of the naturalistic worldview and when he opens his mind to using the historical science rooted in the Bible to build his way of thinking about the evidence. Then he can often clearly see that what he observes confirms the Bible's account of history.

We also have a growing number of people from the naturalist community who are looking at current evolutionary belief and saying, "We have some real problems here!" Many secularists don't want to discuss the problems, as they don't want people given even a hint that there could be problems with evolution and millions of years. They want naturalistic evolutionary explanations presented as fact, regardless.

Of course, those who already believe in the authority of Scripture are not surprised to find the scientific evidences confirm what they already know to be true from God's infallible Word.

Now, surprisingly, when it comes to Christian colleges, the creation/evolution/age-of-the-earth debate takes an interesting twist. The one department that you might think would be the most conservative in their beliefs, the religion department, turns out to be the most liberal — having dismissed what the Bible clearly teaches concerning certain events in Genesis in favor of the interpretation of evidence emanating from the naturalistic worldview.

The Science Department Versus the Religion Department

As was noted in earlier chapters, our survey was taken by 312 people at 200 Christian colleges and universities. The 312 were categorized into four different groups: college presidents, vice presidents, members of the religion department, and members of the science department. We will talk about the presidents and vice presidents in chapter 5, but for now, let's take a look at the responses of those who are actually in charge of teaching your kids in the classrooms of the religion and science departments.

First off, the heads of the science (teaching biology, physics, geology, etc.) and religion (teaching theology, Bible, etc.) departments showed unanimous agreement with important issues about Christ. With very little fluctuation, both the religion and science departments believe in the truthfulness of the New Testament. Both groups strongly affirmed the virgin birth of Christ, His substitutionary death on the Cross, heaven and hell, Christ's Second Coming, and the bodily Resurrection of Jesus Christ.

Second, their responses (even though we will later show serious issues with how these professors use language to suit their own ideas) to views about the nature of Scripture did not vary with glaring significance either.

Inspiration
Q19: Do you believe in the inspiration of Scripture?

	Religion Department	Science Department
Yes	100.0%	93.0%

Q18: Do you believe in the infallibility of Scripture?

	Religion Department	Science Department
Yes	92.6%	88.9%
No	6.2%	11.1%

As you can see, the responses are fairly close, with the religion departments claiming a slightly higher view of Scripture than the science departments. But are the rest of their answers consistent with this claim of a high view of the Bible, or is this just more "newspeak"? Answers to more probing questions show the fuller picture:

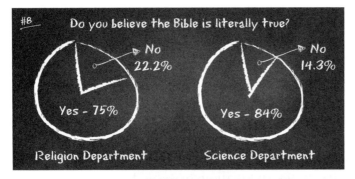

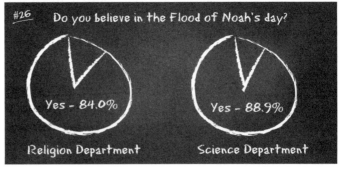

Q27: Do you believe the Flood was worldwide, local, or nonliteral?

	Religion Department	Science Department
Worldwide	56.8%	55.6%
Local	30.9%	41.3%
Nonliteral	12.3%	3.2%

Notice that while 75 percent and 84 percent said they believe the Bible is literally true, only slightly more than half of people from each department believe in a literal worldwide flood! Approximately 25 percent are being inconsistent in their answers. If they really believed the Bible is literally true, they would also believe in a literal interpretation of Genesis that clearly says the Flood was worldwide. But they don't.

How did they answer when we asked questions about creation and evolution?

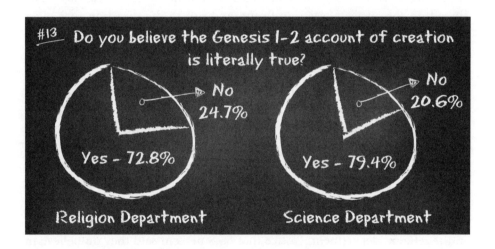

Q15: Do you believe in the Genesis account of creation as written?

	Religion Department	Science Department
Yes	90.1%	84.1%
No	7.4 %	15.9%

Again, we see relatively high numbers regarding what they say they believe about creation, though the no answers by a significant percentage should greatly concern us in regard to what some professors at these Christian colleges are teaching our kids. But when we ask more specific questions, we begin to see stunning differences.

Q16: *Do you believe in God creating the earth in six literal 24-hour days?*

	Religion Department	Science Department
Yes	56.8%	71.4%
No	42.0%	27.0%

Q17: *Do you believe in God creating the earth, but not in six literal days?*

	Religion Department	Science Department
Yes	55.6%	27.0%
No	44.4%	71.4%

This question was so important that we asked it both ways. We first asked if they believed that the earth was created in six 24-hour days. Then we asked if they believed that the earth was created, but *not* in six literal days. The spread on the answers was significant, and not in the direction that most people would think. *It turns out that the science department is much more biblical in their beliefs than the religion department!* Notice in question 17 that only 27 percent of people in the science department believe in nonliteral creation days. Yet 55.6 percent of the people in the religion department believe in nonliteral creation days.

This question also revealed one of the more graphic examples of the "newspeak" that concerns us in regard to Christian colleges today. In the religion department, 72 percent said they do believe in a literal interpretation of Genesis 1–2, but then 55.6 percent turn around and say, "I do not believe in six literal days"!

Since we asked this question both ways, it also revealed further confusion in the religion department. Notice that 56.8 percent said they do believe in six literal days, and 55.6 percent do not believe in six literal days. Several people say they both believe and don't believe!

The survey confirmed what I have been seeing on Christian campuses for years. In general, the science department is more likely to hold to the more conservative point of view. The scientists are the ones that I think understand the difference between operational and historical science. Oftentimes the science department is trying to tell the religion department that they are in error. But the Bible professors often point to secular scientists (whose starting point is usually naturalism) to justify their beliefs.

The religion chairs and the Bible departments are choosing to be influenced by worldly philosophy rather than what the Bible clearly teaches concerning historical science and the facts of observational science that confirm the biblical record. This isn't surprising, considering most of them attended seminaries that adhere to compromise views such as the "documentary hypothesis," a theory that denies that Moses wrote a cohesive historical account of history in the first five books of the Bible. This theory became popular in the late 1800s and claims that the first five chapters of the Bible came from a variety of sources, that the compilers of the Bible borrowed from pagan creation accounts, and that Genesis was written using Babylonian myths and legends. Virtually every seminary, with very few exceptions, liberal or conservative, will teach this "documentary hypothesis" as truth, and nearly everyone teaching in religion departments today came out of that system. They are the ones who are discrediting the Scriptures, they are the ones who capitulate to naturalistic science textbooks, and they are the ones trying to compromise with the world rather than standing to defend the Word of God. Even some of the most historically conservative universities in the country struggle with this issue.

The division between the science and religion departments was most obvious in the question about the age of the earth.

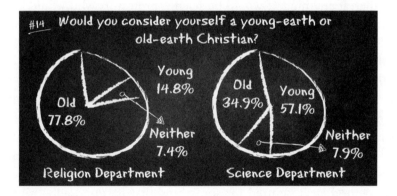

I find this result intriguing and very disturbing. Those who understand how things work on an operational scientific level are some of the strongest advocates for a biblical worldview. In our opinion, based on years of experience, even in the real conservative Christian colleges in America, the science professors, by and large, are the ones who often aggressively support and defend the biblical worldview . . . much more so than those in the religion (or Bible) departments!

Beyond that, the survey also showed that the science department is more aware of these differences than the religion department is. The religion department thinks everyone has the same view, but the science department tends to know better.

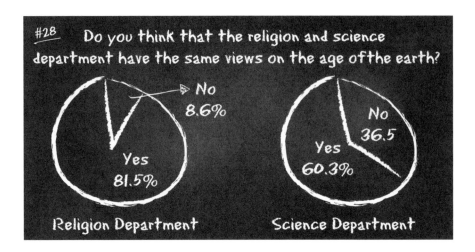

#28   Do you think that the religion and science department have the same views on the age of the earth?

No 8.6%

Yes 81.5%

Religion Department

No 36.5

Yes 60.3%

Science Department

Because I have talked to so many professors at so many schools over the years, I wasn't surprised by this result. But what I am finding is that most Christian parents and students are stunned by this discrepancy. They still expect that, if anything, it would be science professors who would be more likely to lean toward evolution/millions of years and that religion professors would be more likely to lean toward a literal creation. But that's not the case — as the survey clearly shows.

When I engage liberals from the religion departments on these issues, most of them repeat the familiar mantra: "Science has proven that evolution/millions of years is true." But when I ask them for specifics, they often don't have much of a clue, as they are depending on some other authority. If I ask them why they believe in an old earth, they invariably answer, "Because of radiocarbon dating." But any scientist should know that the radiocarbon dating method can't be used for something that is supposedly millions of years old. It can only be used to go back 100,000 years at the most. And the presence of radiocarbon in fossils/deposits/diamonds claimed to be millions of years old contradicts such an old age, as after 100,000 years there would be no detectable radiocarbon.[2]

Can the religion department explain the existence of coal deposits and how they were formed? Can they explain the actual structure of the fossil record? Can they explain the assumptions behind radiometric dating methods? No, they can't. They just say, "Because science has proven . . ." when in reality, science has done no such thing. What they are really accepting is not operational science; they have simply given in to the worldly pressures from those in power who boldly and blindly hold to a naturalistic worldview.

I was recently at a campus where the leaders of the science department wanted me to get together with the religion department so that I could explain this to them. It can be very frustrating for the scientists because the Bible and religion departments of their own schools often won't listen to them. Instead, they listen to scholars who believe in ideas such as the documentary hypothesis and hold to a naturalistic worldview. This unwillingness to listen to creation scientists who trust the Bible can cause considerable consternation between the departments, leading to conflict for the students in regard to what they hear in the various classrooms.

It is surely worse than an eye saying to a hand, "I have no need of you." What is really happening is that many religion professors are, in reality, saying to their science colleagues, "I disagree with you!" It's worse because of the consequences of such compromise with the world: they are causing division that is impacting the souls of the students by undermining biblical authority and creating a doubt of God's Word that can lead to unbelief (Rom. 16:17).

There's no question that this problem is bigger than just colleges and universities. It's a problem at all levels of Christianity. Recently, even the Assemblies of God denomination has rewritten their theological belief statements in order to accommodate evolution and millions of years because they believe "science has shown" it to be true. Again, nothing could be further from the truth.

Science in Perspective

While we celebrate the mind-boggling advances in numerous fields of study made possible through scientific inquiry, it is important for students today to put science in proper perspective. To explain that perspective, let me ask you a question. Choose either comment A or B based on your understanding of science:

A. Science gives us objective knowledge of an independently existing reality.

B. Scientific knowledge is always provisional and tells us nothing that is universal, necessary, or completely certain about the world.

The reason this is an important question is that science education in our schools is solidly based on proposition A. This is exactly what you would expect from the science being driven by naturalistic philosophy. Many scientists have become very dogmatic, almost religiously so, about living up to proposition A. Most people believe that the knowledge scientists provide is objective and exists as an independent reality. The scientific method does work and it provides a knowledge of sorts. It is just not the absolute knowledge that secular scientists have claimed it to be.

Some, like Dr. Thomas Kuhn in *The Structure of Scientific Revolutions*,[3] have shown how scientific knowledge is developed. First, the scientist begins with a set of beliefs. These assumptions form the scientific educational process. At the center of the science education literature promoted in the majority of this nation's schools is the Darwinian concept of evolution. Naturalism, the philosophy at the center of most historical science, promotes the idea (in fact, works hard to sell it as truth) that the general laws and forces of nature are enough to explain the existence of the universe and everything in it. The naturalists have no use for a Creator; that concept is unnecessary for them.

This naturalistic science has a tendency to be less than honorable. It has a tendency to be less than academic. Students need to know these flaws and be able to explore them and discuss them and should be able to offer the explanation of the origin of life from Scripture free from the typical scorn and ridicule they receive from naturalistic scientists.

Why is it that scientists are so fearful of the debate with believers about the origin of life? Why cannot both beliefs of origin — creation and evolution — be discussed with students? Why do evolutionists attempt to control this conversation; is there something to hide? What is the real problem?

Astronomer and physicist Dr. Lee Smolin gives us the needed insight. He admits that if science concedes that the universe began at a point in time (some call it the big bang; I call it the moment of creation) then, he says, "It leaves the door open for a return of religion."[4] And that is a problem of biblical proposition for the naturalistic scientist, who, first and foremost, must get God out of the picture.

At the very heart of the science our students have been raised on is the assumption that there is absolutely no room for the supernatural or miracles in the explanation of the origin of life. The point must be made that this is a religious belief — the religious belief of naturalism or atheism. It is all about worldview. There was a time when the Christian faith promoted study and exploration because it was an "act of worship." Science began as the religious pursuit of knowing the mind of God, of learning to "think our thoughts after Him." In other words, the worldview used to understand the evidence in the present was built on God's Word.

Then came the presupposition that the Bible should be left out of the discussion. With this came the suggestion of an earth that had aged millions of years (geological evolution), followed by Darwin and his speculations (biological evolution). A scientific revolution followed that presented a natural explanation for all that exists with no further need for what was called religion as an explanation for anything (such as astronomical evolution like steady state or big bang and chemical evolution for the origin of life). As the famous evolutionary scientist Ernst Mayr writes, "The Darwinism revolution was not merely the replacement of one scientific theory by another, but rather the replacement of a worldview in which the supernatural was accepted as a normal and relevant explanatory principle by a new worldview in which there was no room for supernatural forces."[5]

This is how science became dishonest. How can anyone who claims to be a scientist turn aside categorically from anything that may be a useful or truthful understanding of the world around us? Yet, when it comes to investigating or promoting — even as a possibility — the creation of our universe and life by a sovereign Creator, they cast it aside. This is intellectual suicide and these scientists should know it . . . and so should the teachers in religion departments at Christian colleges that support and propagate such closed-mindedness.

The extreme some scientists and philosophers have gone to in order to maintain their naturalistic philosophy and keep God out of the picture is astounding. Dr. Francis Crick, in his book *Life Itself*,[6] seems to at least recognize that the origin of life has miraculous features and offers this theory: space aliens brought life to earth from some other planet. Dr. Crick is on the one hand a very serious scientist — the co-discoverer of DNA! On the other hand, perhaps he hopes this theory of his will be picked up by the *National Enquirer*.

Thankfully, there are many scholarly and intellectual scientists who are believers (such as those at organizations like Answers in Genesis and the Institute for Creation Research — and there are many who do leading research in the secular world). Today's student needs to turn to them for perspective and help.

Our survey clearly showed that some scientists and many professors of religion at Christian colleges seem closed to any way of inquiry other than science based in a naturalistic, materialistic philosophy — even though they would claim they believe God's Word as written. If there is a discrepancy between what the atheists say and what God's Word says about the natural world, they tend to defer to those who do not believe in God at all.

The Conflict in Perspective

Another open-ended question shed a great deal of light on these issues.

Q7: *What does your institution teach about science and faith?*

- We compare and contrast: 43.0%
- We teach science and God are one: 20.5%
- We teach science is valid: 17.6%
- We teach that there is no real conflict: 7.7%

In light of all the things we have discussed in this chapter, these answers are difficult to interpret because we have to ask, What do they mean by science? What is the worldview behind the "science" they are talking about? In *general*, science is usually defined as a worldview and philosophy that includes millions of years of evolution and anything that secular scientists say is true. It is built upon man's fallible ideas. If your science is based on assumptions that have already ruled out the possibility of God, then attempting to add God or the Bible to this requires one to change God's Word to fit with man's word. But if you approach the evidence from the starting point of God's Word, then the facts will have a very different interpretation: observational science will be shown to overwhelmingly confirm the interpretation as God's world agrees with what is recorded in God's Word.

What do these people mean when they say that they "compare and contrast science and faith"? Does that mean that they are teaching secular science alongside of the Bible and trying to get them to fit together? How about those who say that "science and God are one"? A scientist who believes in God could make this statement in good conscience, knowing that the results of operational science reflect the truth about the Creator who designed and brought everything into being. Others might say that "God and science are one" in an attempt to make the creation account in the Bible conform to the ideas of secular scientists who have a godless worldview. See the problem here?

When they say "science and God are one," do they really mean that evolution/millions of years and the Bible are one? When they say that science is valid, are they claiming that secular dating methods for the age of the earth are valid? We can't say so for sure, but this all has to do with how you define the word *science*.

If you define it in the way that it is commonly used today (that science cannot allow the supernatural, only explaining things from a perspective of naturalism), then this is a real mess. As we have stated, the word *science* means knowledge. Are they gaining knowledge by starting their thinking from God's Word or man's word? As the Bible teaches in several places, "The fear of the Lord is the beginning of knowledge" (and wisdom).

Certainly the other parts of the survey showed that the mess indeed exists. There is a strong movement in evangelicalism that is trying to make the facts of the Bible conform to the naturalistic worldview. But we must remember: the starting point determines your worldview, and therefore your interpretation. If you start with man's ideas (humanism) to develop your worldview, there's no question about where your conclusions will end up.

In the end, it's actually very difficult to determine what these people mean by what they say. Therefore, it is absolutely imperative that you ask clarifying and probing questions when you're evaluating a school, listening to a lecture, or even reading a written statement of faith. As we discovered in this survey, compromise can come at you from every direction. And in many cases, it will come from those who you might expect it the least — the religion and Bible teachers in Christian colleges and universities.

Let me again make an important distinction here: the battle is not between religion and science but between a biblical and a naturalistic worldview. Please understand this: the scientific method is an absolutely brilliant research paradigm (developed by a creationist, no less). The things that have been discovered and confirmed by using the scientific method have been an indispensable part of advancement in the modern world. The scientific method is perhaps the most beneficial tool, next to the Bible, for investigating the physical world in the history of mankind. Science is not the enemy. The enemy is a naturalistic worldview that is closed off to the possibility of the existence of God and that His Word is true and the only starting point to understand the universe that He created. It's not a matter of "science" versus "faith." The problem is that the naturalistic worldview has hijacked science in a way that has supposedly disproved the existence of God (because they started with that assumption, which is self-refuting anyway). Nothing could be further from the truth.

Christian leaders representing the Church need to stand up in this nation and condemn the compromise with the pagan religion of the age (millions of years/evolution — the pagan religion of the age to explain life without God) and stand for God's authoritative Word. Only then will we see God's blessing on the Church and the resulting change in the culture that is so needed.

I don't question whether such scholars are Christians, but we still need to point out their compromise of accepting man's opinions over God's Word. The problem with many Christian colleges is they will believe the science text written from a naturalistic worldview *first*, and the sacred text *later*. My heart is also taken by those, like many of my friends and colleagues, who love the Word, love God, love the Church, and, even if in some ways they may need to be "trained" in the truth, serve God out of sincere, heartfelt devotion.

Let there be no mistake: as believers committed to the authority of God's Word, we are facing an epic battle — a "collision of worldviews" in our churches, in the marketplace, and in the secular and Christian colleges and universities. And as you will see in the next chapter, the stakes could not be higher. At stake are our kids and how they will respond to the life-transforming truths of the gospel of Jesus Christ, who is the Way and the Truth and the Life.

Endnotes

1. In fact, few realize that committed Christians were often the ones who developed most fields of operational science (Mendel, Pasteur, Faraday, Newton, Galileo, and others).
2. L. Vardiman, A.A. Snelling, and E.F. Chaffin, editors, *Radioisotopes and the Age of the Earth: Results of a Young-Earth Creationist Research Initiative* (Santee, CA: Institute for Creation Research and Chino Valley, AZ: Creation Research Society, 2005).
3. Thomas S. Kuhn, *The Structure of Scientific Revolution,* Third Edition (Chicago, IL: University of Chicago Press, 1996).
4. Lee Smolin, *The Life of the Cosmos* (New York: Oxford University Press, 1997), p. 183, 264.
5. Ernst Mayr, "Evolution and God," *Nature* (March 1974): 285.
6. Francis Crick, *Life Itself* (New York: Simon & Schuster, 1981).

Want to know which colleges were contacted as part of the ARG study? Visit www.creationcolleges.org and also find a growing list of Christian colleges we recommend you search out.

Chapter 4

Worth Fighting For

Greg Hall

For what do righteousness and wickedness have in common?
Or what fellowship can light have with darkness? (2 Cor. 6:14; NIV).

When I was a student studying German, I was given an assignment to read an essay by the title *"Welche Religion ist die wehre?"* The translation: "Which Religion Is the True Religion?" The message of the essay was simply this: they are all true. Every person has their own religion and it is as true as the next person's religion.

This essay would fit well into our culture today. The spirit of our time is tolerance. There is no such thing as "truth." What is true for you may or may not be true for the next person . . . and who is to judge? Consequently, with tolerance and relativism as the prevailing way of thinking, Christianity is not in any sense unique. It is like all other religions of the world, and Jesus is one among many gods.

This is why the issue of the authority of Scripture is so paramount. When we see the compromise of the religion departments and (to a lesser degree) the science departments and the conflict that arises because they don't adhere to a unified worldview, we see the potential for relativism to find its way into the institution — just as it has time and time again in the

Ivy League and other schools that started strong and then lost the focus on the authority of Scripture.

And that's tragic, because the Bible carries the most precious and important of all messages.

The Uniqueness of Christianity

In some ways the religions of the world *seem* similar. All *seem* to advocate various ways to reach "god" or some form of greater "truth." Each religion generally has a commanding personality as a leader. The religions of the world each teach a system of belief that serves as some sort of moral basis for humankind. Most religions have ways of helping human beings relate to each other. If men and women seek peace and harmony and understanding of the world around them, each of the religions has something to say.

However, eventually each of the religions makes certain claims about things like the nature and character of God, how exactly man reaches this God, the prospects of life after death, etc. There we find the subtle and sometimes not-so-subtle distinctions among the religions. And then we must remember the concept of the law of noncontradiction and admit, as it suggests, that two contradictory ideas cannot both be true.

If you are interested in any religion for the express purpose of reaching God (which is religion's main purpose) I would like to point you to the main distinction between Christianity and other religions (and remember — ultimately there are only two religions: God's Word or man's word) because the significance of this distinction is eternal . . . and it's worth fighting for.

> 1. *Christianity does not teach you how to reach for God. It teaches you how God has reached for us.*

This concept changes everything. It puts into perspective how religions function with considerations of a moral code and patterns of required behaviors and beliefs. This is how Christianity is unique. The emphasis is not on how or what you do but what's been done for you. What's been done is that God the Father, in His Son, Jesus, reconciled the world to Himself by the work of atonement (Col. 1:20), Jesus dying on the Cross for the sins of all who believe in His name (1 John 2:2; Rom. 10:9). It is not what we have done but what He did (Eph. 2:8). This points us in the direction of the most amazingly unique thing about Christianity when compared to all other religions — *the person of Jesus Christ*. Anyone seeking religious truth will be blown away by Jesus. He is so unique that Christians know Him to be both fully man and fully God. Christians call this the incarnation "God with us," Immanuel. Jesus has no rival in any aspect of His life:

- No one ever loved like He did.
- No one ever treated a person with dignity or respect like He could.
- No one ever taught what He taught or modeled a way of life like He did.
- No one ever was a better mentor.
- No one ever spoke like He did or commanded respect like He did.
- There is not one person in history who could approximate His wisdom or virtue.
- There has never been a healer like Him.
- No one ever prayed like He prayed.
- No man or woman has ever had a better friend.
- There is no scholar with His intelligence.
- No scientist has ever understood the physics of the universe like Him.
- There has been no other human who had His power — over the created order or over the human heart.
- No psychologist has ever understood the human mind like Him.
- No sociologist ever understood how cultures and societies function with the exception of Him.

He is not an icon representing a deity we do not know, understand, or relate to. No, He remains actively involved with His subjects, offering on a moment's notice help, support, guidance, wisdom, power, mercy, and love. He literally wrote the book on human existence and the history of the universe. As the author of life, He holds the keys for unlocking the mysteries of this life and the life to come.

He is Jesus, our Lord and God, and there is no other. "Salvation is found in no one else, for there is no other name under heaven given to mankind by which we must be saved" (Acts 4:12; NIV). There is no one as glorious as He.

The really glorious part of the uniqueness of the Christ of Christianity is that He solves a problem that, in our very honest moments, we all recognize we share in common.

2. Christianity teaches that mankind is born with a sinful nature since the Fall that wreaks havoc with virtually everything about life in this world.

This human nature is responsible for the vast evil and innumerable problems we face in every facet of life. As a group, humanity is broken. There is unimaginable empirical evidence that helps verify this, so we all know it. In our inner being, we know this problem requires a cure. No one has ever been able to cure themselves.

And so, while the other religions try to reach for God, Christianity teaches it is the other way around: He, through Jesus, reaches for us, a notion unique among all of the religions. In our hearts, we know it's true because God puts the evidence of the rightness of the cure of Christ deep in the human spirit. And "since the creation of the world God's invisible qualities — his eternal power and divine nature — have been clearly seen, being understood from what has been made, so that people are without excuse" (Rom. 1:20; NIV). The unchanging truth of the living, written Word of God attests to this. That is the primary and final testament to Jesus. That is why when people ask for evidence that Christianity is true, I say, "Look in your own heart and find the answer; it is there. There is a place in every human heart that only God can fill."

Who can you possibly compare to Jesus? He has no equal and no rival. When we are honest in our innermost being, we know that who He is and what He does is the truth for all humankind.

3. Christianity proclaims a unique urgency to believe.

In the other religions of the world, there is not the sense of urgency to believe the message of the religion like there is in Christianity. In most religions, man operates in his own strength, making every effort at self-improvement. Hinduism and Buddhism use techniques of meditation to deal with problematic issues of the "self." Judaism and Islam use rituals. They use these rituals to cope with the expectations of the law.

The God of Christianity does not ask for endless efforts of self-improvement. When it comes to measuring the condition of the human nature, He demands perfection. That is right. The standard for Christians is perfection; He settles for nothing less. *The Christian only receives this perfection by believing in the only real perfect man who ever lived, Jesus.* It is only by believing in the atoning, sacrificial death of Jesus upon the Cross as the payment for our sinful condition that the righteousness (perfection) of Jesus is imputed to everyone who believes. This is a response never conceived by any other religion. It is unique in every way.

Do you need evidence of the truthfulness of this message? Consider again your own heart. I really do believe most people in the inner sanctum of their own spirit know and comprehend the reality of this message (Romans 1 makes it clear there are no atheists — people suppress the truth in unrighteousness): we are sinners, unable to save ourselves, facing a holy God to whom we will give an account of our lives, a God who settles for nothing less than perfection. We also know in this inner place that it is Jesus — uniquely demonstrated to be God's Son and the only sacrifice He accepts that makes for peace with Him. The Creator has created the human heart with the capacity to know this truth.

And here, Christianity differs from other religions in the most profound way imaginable:

> 4. *When it comes to the claims of Christ, you can reject them but you cannot ignore them.*

With the truth about Christianity as revealed in Scripture, you cannot pick and choose what you will accept (that is humanism, having yourself as the ultimate authority over God). You take it all or not at all. Many have attempted this, trying to select certain aspects of the truth while ignoring others. A good example of this strategy of trying to eliminate Scriptures that do not seem to apply to our case is Thomas Jefferson. He seemed drawn to Christ but did not buy His claim to be divine, to perform miracles, and to serve as the only way to reach heaven. So Jefferson devised his own version of the Scripture, *The Jefferson Bible*, where he literally cut out the parts of Scripture he did not want included. Don't be too hard on Mr. Jefferson; this is an oft-repeated phenomenon. People may not go to the extreme of actually dismantling the book, the Bible; they just do so in the confines of their hearts and minds. The problem is, we do not get to experience Christianity on our own terms, only His.

If Jesus is not one among many gods, and the message of Christianity is uniquely true, it would stand to reason that there is a sense of urgency about believing this truth. In a culture so relativistic, where tolerance is key and all ideas considered equally valid, it is a challenge to get even earnest believers to catch a vision of how urgent it is to get this message out. At the very least, it is so clear to see that the worldview of naturalism and the worldview of the Bible are absolutely at odds — oil and water that truly cannot be mixed.

How Christianity Got Marginalized

America has become an increasingly diverse nation, and that includes religious diversity. We are growing, and as a nation full of people from different faiths it stands to reason that their influences are going to be felt. If America has become a non-Christian nation due to this trend, it is a demographic issue. It also becomes a wonderful opportunity for those of us who are Christian to enter the marketplace of ideas and engage this diversity with a message we believe to be for all people, cultures, and religious backgrounds.

But, there is another reason we are not a Christian nation (or really "Christianized nation," as no nation has ever been truly a "Christian" one) any longer. Unfortunately, this reason doesn't have much to do with demographics. While there is reason to celebrate the changing diversity of America, there is reason to fear what is really happening. It is not that our Christian message suffers from diversity, it is suffering because, in the marketplace of ideas, it has been marginalized. It has been moved to the edges of society.

Through the ages, Christians have been among the greatest thinkers and influencers of life in this world. How many scientific innovations and inventions have been forged in the minds of godly men and women? How many great works of literature have been written by devoted followers of Christ? How many of the world's greatest institutions of service and learning were developed by Christian leaders and servants? How many humanitarians, public servants, community activists, and inspiring religious leaders are Christ followers? The list is amazingly impressive.

So what happened? Why are Christians not the major shapers and influencers of our culture like they once were? Why has the Christian faith been marginalized in recent times?

1. We Christians have abdicated our positions in the battle for the mind.

We lack talent, critical thinking skills, and a willingness to engage with intellectual vigor and rigor the ideas that compete for attention. Where is it today that Christians go to prepare themselves intellectually? Does the mind have a chance to grow in Sunday school? If you think Sunday school is intellectual and spiritual training for Christian youth, read *Already Gone*[1] and you will find out it is clearly not there. How about in our church worship services? Is this where we gain enough knowledge and wisdom to stand against the intellectual tide raging against us? It is not likely in a typical, consumer-driven church where worship is driven by personal preference and followed by the mind-numbing therapeutic pulpit. How about in our colleges, universities, and seminaries? Is this where Christian intellectual virtues are developed? Unfortunately, the answer to these questions is too often no. Where did we go? Answer: we went to the world. We sent ourselves to be among the liberal bastions of our culture that break faith instead of building it.

The current disposition of Christians seems to be anti-intellectualism. Faith, in many circles, has been trivialized or marginalized because we have lost the desire for critical thinking and sound scholarship. Dr. Os Guinness, in his book *Fit Bodies, Fat Minds*, says:

> Anti-intellectualism is a disposition to discount the importance of truth and the life of the mind. Living in a sensuous culture and an increasingly emotional democracy, American evangelicals in the last generation have simultaneously toned up their bodies and dumbed down their minds. . . . Evangelical anti-intellectualism is both a scandal and a sin. It is a scandal in the sense of being an offense and a stumbling block that needlessly hinders serious people from considering the Christian faith and coming to Christ. It is a sin because it is a refusal, contrary to the first of Jesus' two great commandments, to love the Lord our God with our minds.[2]

Feelings seem to be the dominant concern in the Church today. These concerns for the issues of the heart are completely legitimate. But it is only half the story. Christianity is a heartfelt experience, but it is an experience of the head as well. We are similar to the Tin Woodman in L. Frank Baum's *The Wonderful Wizard of Oz*, who chooses a heart rather than a head:

> "Why didn't you walk around the hole?" asked the Tin Woodman.
> "I don't know enough," replied the Scarecrow cheerfully. "My head is stuffed with straw, you know, and that is why I am going to Oz to ask him for some brains."
> "Oh, I see," said the Tin Woodman. "But, after all, brains are not the best thing in the world."
> "Have you any?" enquired the Scarecrow.
> "No, my head is quite empty," answered the Woodman; "but once I had brains, and a heart also; so having tried them both, I should much rather have a heart. . . ."
> "All the same," said the Scarecrow, "I shall ask for brains instead of a heart; for a fool would not know what to do with a heart if he had one."
> "I shall take the heart," returned the Tin Woodman; "for brains do not make one happy, and happiness is the best thing in the world."[3]

Too many Christians today have gone missing in action in the battle for the mind. Many have opted for the therapeutic happiness of the Christian subculture instead. Again, to quote Dr. Guinness:

Never mind that "heart" in the Bible is more a matter of under-standing than sentiment — so "heart" versus "head" is a false choice. . . . Ever since the mid-eighteenth century we evangelicals have had a natural bias toward the Tin Woodman's choice — empty brains and happy hearts.[4]

2. Christians have twisted the message of the gospel of Christ to the point that we repel men and women who are "unchristian," instead of attract them.

In his book *Unchristian*, David Kinnaman surveyed the new generation to find out what they really think about Christianity. The negative percep-tions of Christians are striking. The secular world thinks Christians are hypocritical, too focused on getting converts, anti-homosexual, sheltered, too political, and judgmental.[5]

There are exceptions, of course. We all know genuine, authentic Christians who live much like Jesus before us; we are compelled by the overwhelming evidence of Christ in their lives. They are probably, in large measure, the rea-son many of us are Christians. But even if this research angers you or makes you cry "foul," can't you see its truthfulness, too?

The research of *Unchristian* rings true, and we have to admit that as Christians, we need to take responsibility for this dilemma. We can change this perception, one attitude at a time. We do so by presenting our faith win-somely, as a proposal of truth, not in the ways of putting others down or combativeness.

Recently I listened to a debate that happened several years ago on the subject of the origins of life between creationist Dr. Phillip Johnson of Berkeley and Dr. Will Provine of Cornell. These two great intellects really went at it. The intellectual interchange was magnificent. They pulled no punches and gave each other no slack. They were straightforward in their criticism and analysis of the other's argumentation.

This Stanford University debate, however, was not characterized by acri-mony; quite the contrary. At one point in the proceedings, Dr. Will Provine explained to the students that even though they debate sharply, they have the utmost respect for each other as men; in fact, they will have dinner together when the debate is over. Our relationship with the world, as Christians, should be the same. We should be able to tell the opposition the truth, but do so in a way that's winsome and seen as a proposal to be considered for what we know to be true. We should be connected to and sincerely engaging with those who may vehemently disagree.

There is one final reason I feel that Christianity has been marginalized:

3. As we bought into our anti-intellectual Christianity geared toward personal preference and happiness, and as we have failed to produce a winsome intellectual approach to belief, the opposition seized the moment and monopolized the debate.

In the Stanford University debate between Dr. Phillip Johnson and Dr. Will Provine, a student asked a very perceptive question. She asked evolutionist Dr. Provine why in the debate of creation versus evolution it's so one-sided. Why is it so, she wanted to know, that across America only evolution is taught in public schools? Why is there such an uproar when a group of Christians here or there have tried to get creation science in schools and it is categorically denied? Dr. Provine said, "The answer is simple: evolutionists monopolize the debate."

They monopolize the debate and control the information. They teach in the colleges and universities of our nation. They write the textbooks our students read. These schools graduate the political leaders and school board members who make policy decisions on curriculum. We have eliminated ourselves from serious intellectual debate on this and other prominent social, political, or philosophical issues and have forfeited our right of influence.

A Call to Christian Soldiers

So what do we do about all this? We are in a war where subtle and militant attacks on the Bible continually bombard us. We have been marginalized and our voice has been largely muted in the marketplace and in the classroom. What do we do? How do we find our voice again and begin to speak the truth in love once more?

First, we clearly need to be continually developing our own biblically based worldview. If we understand the authentic truth, we will be unlikely to be fooled by the counterfeits. The biblical worldview, like Jesus Himself, is unique in its explanation of life and existence. The biblical worldview remains the only authentic explanation of the origin of life. The Scripture teaches humankind what we need to know about life's beginning and ending. It is a credible historical document with a perfect understanding of human nature and our place in the grand scheme of creation.

We need to understand that as Christians, all our thinking should begin with the revelation of God's Word. We need to know what it means to build a consistent Christian worldview and be able to correctly understand and interpret the facts of the present. We need to know what we believe and why we believe as we do.

We also need to understand that those who don't start with the Bible start with the fallible ideas of man. On this they build their worldview. Both Christians and non-Christians have starting points. The reason they interpret the same evidence in regard to origins differently is because of those different starting points. I highly recommend the book *The Ultimate Proof of Creation*, by Dr. Jason Lisle, to further understand how a person can learn to think logically and understand how to argue consistently in these matters.

Second, I think we need to become experts in evolution and the "millions of years" mindset. That's right. There is nothing to be afraid of. In fact, once students become familiar with what Darwinism is, how the age of the earth is interpreted from data, how these ideas gained notoriety, and an understanding of the numerous flaws in the thinking, it becomes clear that even many scientists know that evolution is an idea in serious trouble and millions of years is not proven fact. If students will research the issue, they will find many problems with the interpretations crucial to the foundation of evolution, the big bang, and the various dating methods. There is the myth of absolute dates from radiometric dating; the myth of strict uniformitarian geology; the myth of a gradualistic fossil record; the myth of beneficial information-adding mutations; the myth of natural selection as a mechanism for molecules-to-man evolution; the myth of evolution not contradicting the bio-genetic law; the myth of homology supposedly supporting evolution; the myth of the so-called missing links.

It is the case that biblical creation cannot be taught in the public schools today — something that clearly reflects a one-sided, closed-minded approach to education (closed-minded to any supernatural aspects). As believers, we should not want it said of us that we do not want our students to be exposed to such ideas. The Bible doesn't hide error from us, but it clearly speaks to us concerning the nature of the error and teaches us what we should believe. All of us need to know how to defend our faith, and as part of that, we need to understand how secularists think and how to combat their false religious ideas, including evolution and millions of years.

Third, we need to understand the basic tenets of naturalism. Most people are totally unaware that they live under the control of this worldview. It is up to us to explain it to them, show its consequences, and offer the biblical worldview as an alternative. (Again, I recommend the book *Ultimate Proof of Creation*.)

We consider the concept of a sovereign, all-powerful God who created the universe *ex nihilo* (out of nothing) to be the only logical position to take as an explanation for the origin of life. After all, why would there be laws of logic, the uniformity of nature, and the laws of nature if there were no God? These only make logical sense in the context of the infinite Creator God of the Bible. There is nothing philosophically or intellectually invalid about such a position. Unless, that is, someone comes into the discussion with a mind closed off to the possibility of God altogether (and they would no longer have a basis for uniformity, morality, or logic either!). If someone starts off closed-minded, "suppressing the truth" as Romans 1:20 states, they will not believe, no matter what evidence is presented to them. They first need to change their starting point. And only the Holy Spirit in a person's heart and mind can start that process.

A sovereign, all-powerful God can create what He desires out of nothing and, as our Scripture says, hold it all together. He can also decide to reveal Himself in meaningful ways to those who will believe, be it in nature around us, in the Word (Scripture) He gave, in the Son (Jesus) He sent us as His exact representation, or in the Spirit He left to live in His children.

Christian students need to be confident and assured that these Christian worldview tenets are philosophically, intellectually, and spiritually valid if by no other reason than that of the definition of God, let alone by the personal experience of believers. Your personal experience of God matters in this discussion!

But this will require a new kind of thinking for a new generation of Christians. Romans 12:2 is an often-cited Scripture on this subject: "Don't copy the behavior and customs of this world, but let God transform you into a new person by changing the way you think" (NLT).

David Kinnaman puts it like this:

> We are learning that one of the primary reasons that ministry to teenagers fails to produce a lasting faith is because they are not being taught to think. This gets to the core of the get-saved perception: young people experience a one-size-fits-all message that fails to connect with their unique sensibilities, personality, or intellectual capabilities. Young people desperately need to be taught to process the rich complexities of life, to probe and test and stretch their faith from the perspective of a Christ follower.[6]

And this new kind of thinking needs to begin *now*. There is no time to waste. Today is the day of action for soldiers of truth to take up the Bible, the sword of truth, and run toward the battle. As our research has clearly illustrated, we have generations of our youth going to Christian colleges where God's written revelation (which is foundational to a proper Christian worldview) is being undermined. As generations of students begin to doubt God's Word as written (particularly in Genesis), and as they are encouraged to accept many of the fallible ideas of man (e.g., millions of years and evolution), they are being conformed to the world's thinking instead of thinking as a Christian needs to (Rom. 12:2).

Many in the Christian academic community point the finger at those who take a literal interpretation of Genesis and accuse them of being the cause of the anti-intellectualism discussed earlier. These same professors who compromise Genesis are the ones who themselves have actually helped bring on this seeming anti-intellectualism.

Because so much of the Church has been confused on the issues of origins and because so many Christian leaders have taught people to accept millions of years and even evolution, many Christians basically ignored the whole issue and concentrated on spiritual, relationship, and doctrinal matters. They avoided the historical science of Genesis, and gradually their "faith" shifted toward more emotionalism and experientialism in the Church, along with watered-down teaching. Yes, one can see what seems to be anti-intellectualism, but it is because the Church has not taken a stand on God's Word from the very beginning! What hope is there for the right sort of Christian leadership when so many of those training our leaders have already embraced the world's philosophies in many areas?

A story is told about Satan calling his emissaries of hell together because he wanted to send them to earth to aid men and women in the ruination of their souls. He asked, "Who would go first, and what would be the strategy?" One said, "I will go." "And what will you tell them?" Satan asked. "I will tell them there is no heaven." And Satan said, "They will not believe you, for there is a bit of heaven in every human heart. In the end everyone knows that good will triumph over evil. You may not go."

Then another came forward, darker and fouler than the first. "If I send you," Satan said, "what will you tell them?" "I will tell them there is no hell." Satan looked at him and said, "No, they will not believe you, for in every human heart there is a thing called conscience, an inner voice which testifies to the truth that not only will good triumph but evil will be defeated. You are not to go."

The last creature that came forward was more diabolical than them all. Satan said to him, "If I send you what will you say to men and women that will lead to the destruction of their souls?" And he said, "I will tell them there is no hurry." Satan said, "GO. You are the one."

And that seems to be the place we are today; the strategy seems to be working. As Christians we are certainly in no hurry; there is no sense of urgency. But there is urgency. The Church has been marginalized. What is at stake is the very heart and soul of our faith, particularly of our youth. It is essential that this generation of young people be confronted with this astounding truth, again from the pen of C.S. Lewis in his essay "A Slip of the Tongue": "In the end, if you have not chosen the Kingdom of God, it will not matter what you have chosen instead."[7]

The survey confirmed our hunch that compromise *is* taking place in Christian higher education. We know that the natural tendency of fallen man gravitates toward naturalism, liberalism, and an eroding of the authority of the Bible. We have grave concerns that this great compromise is marginalizing the central, life-giving message about Jesus Christ.

Christianity is in desperate need of leadership right now. Gone are the strong voices of the past that spoke out with confidence about the authority of Scripture. Parents and students would like to believe that the leadership of Christian colleges is focused, unified, and standing on God's Word. But as you will see in the next chapter, the survey suggests otherwise. Floundering leaders are part of the widespread confusion we see in all levels of campus life and learning. While the leaders stumble, the battle rages. At stake is the truth about Jesus Christ and the gospel of His grace — and that is worth fighting for.

Endnotes

1. Ken Ham, *Already Gone* (Green Forest, AR: Master Books, May 2009).
2. Os Guinness, *Fit Bodies, Fat Minds* (Grand Rapids, MI: Baker Books, 1994), p. 9–11.
3. Ibid., p. 30.
4. Ibid., p. 31.
5. David Kinnaman, *Unchristian* (Grand Rapids, MI: Baker Books, 2007), p. 29–30.
6. Ibid., p. 81.
7. C.S. Lewis, "A Slip of the Tongue," *The Weight of Glory* (San Francisco, CA: Harper-SanFrancisco, a division of HarperCollins, 2001), p. 190–191.

Want to know which colleges were contacted as part of the ARG study? Visit www.creationcolleges.org and also find a growing list of Christian colleges we recommend you search out.

Chapter 5

Confusion across the Campus

Ken Ham

God is not a God of confusion but of peace (1 Cor. 14:33).

The uniqueness of Christianity, as Greg Hall shared with us in the last chapter, must always be at the forefront of our minds. Yes, a war over worldviews is being waged across the globe. The battles are intensely fierce on the campuses of both secular and Christian colleges and universities. Sometimes it is so easy to get wrapped up in the fight that we forget the cause. We are not fighting for some obscure ideology, for some sort of social morality, or even for political integrity. What we're fighting for is truth.

Jesus said, "You shall know the truth and the truth shall make you free" (John 8:32; NKJV). Why do we fight for the authority of Scripture? Because the message Scripture proclaims has the power to set captives free and to liberate those who are living in the shackles of lies that bind them to the world system. When Jesus said, "I am the way and the truth and the life" in John 14:6, He claimed to be the one and only way to the Father, to a life of liberty, peace, grace, mercy, and forgiveness. Truly the Bible contains the most valuable and precious message on earth and for all eternity. God has placed it in our care to share it, protect it, defend it, and live it. Jude 1:3 boldly calls us to this stance:

I felt compelled to write and urge you to contend for the faith that was once for all entrusted to the God's holy people (NIV).

The words that Peter wrote nearly 2,000 years ago are as true today as they ever have been:

Who is there to harm you if you prove zealous for what is good? But even if you should suffer for the sake of righteousness, you are blessed AND DO NOT FEAR THEIR INTIMIDATION, AND DO NOT BE TROUBLED, but sanctify Christ as Lord in your hearts, always being ready to make a defense to everyone who asks you to give an account for the hope that is in you, yet with gentleness and reverence (1 Pet. 3:13–15).

Are Christian colleges and universities living up to this verse today? Are we?

Confusion in the Cockpit

When someone buys an expensive airline ticket and steps onto an airplane, they do so trusting that the pilot and the copilot are working together to ensure the direction and the safety of the aircraft and everyone on board. Recently we've seen heroic cooperation in the midst of life-threatening emergencies, where the leadership of the aircraft works together, saving all onboard.

When Christian parents begin writing substantial checks and send their children into the care of Christian colleges, it is usually accompanied with similar expectations. They believe that they are putting their children into a safe spiritual environment where their faith will be nurtured and where they will learn to defend and stand strong in their faith as they enter into adulthood. Parents do this in good faith, believing that those who are in leadership over the institution share their values and concerns, and are working together with the parents to provide the best environment possible for their children to grow mentally and spiritually.

Are these expectations reasonable? Or are they simply hope in an illusion? When we looked at how presidents and vice presidents of Christian colleges and universities answered our survey, the answers became profoundly clear.

Q11: What makes education different at Christian compared to secular schools?

The number-one answers given were grouped as follows:

#11   ## What makes education different at Christian compared to secular schools?

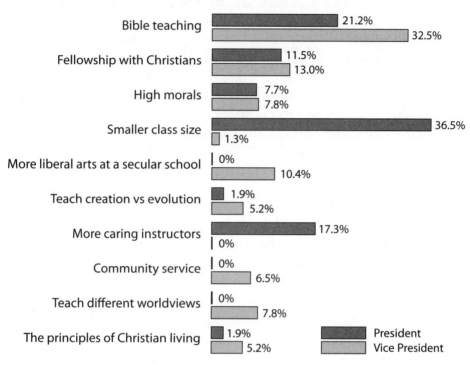

Bible teaching — 21.2% / 32.5%
Fellowship with Christians — 11.5% / 13.0%
High morals — 7.7% / 7.8%
Smaller class size — 36.5% / 1.3%
More liberal arts at a secular school — 0% / 10.4%
Teach creation vs evolution — 1.9% / 5.2%
More caring instructors — 17.3% / 0%
Community service — 0% / 6.5%
Teach different worldviews — 0% / 7.8%
The principles of Christian living — 1.9% / 5.2%

President
Vice President

Important observations can be made here, about both what the presidents and vice presidents said and what they didn't say. One of our immediate concerns is that no one mentioned apologetics and defending their faith! In fact, throughout the whole survey of 312 people, only one person mentioned the importance of apologetics and defending the Bible. I am wondering if one of the most blaring issues here is that none of them mention "the gospel" as a differentiating factor. I think this too would floor people in considering that "Christian" colleges don't even differentiate themselves in terms of gospel when compared to the world. And there's nothing about teaching them to have a comprehensive Christian worldview and little about preparing them for interacting in the secular world.

We have found from our own personal experiences that most Bible colleges, Christian colleges, and seminaries do not teach apologetics. Apologetics is basically missing from our churches and Sunday schools, youth ministries included. (Which is not surprising, given that most pastors were not trained in apologetics at their colleges/seminaries!)

Second, 25 percent of the answers had nothing to do with Christianity at all! Smaller class sizes, fewer liberal arts classes, and caring instructors? Are those the most important things that distinguish a Christian school from a secular school? We would hope for something different than that! Yet these responses are consistent with other things we see in the study. Christian schools are reluctant to differentiate themselves from the world. There are plenty of liberal arts schools that would distinguish themselves by class size, the care of their professors, etc. The most critical analysis of the situation might lead someone to conclude the Christian schools are really just like secular schools, except with some stricter rules, a few Bible classes added in, and a chapel service that may or may not be mandatory to attend. We hear story after story from students who go to Christian colleges hoping for a refreshing and distinctive Christian environment, only to be confronted with behavior and activities such as drunkenness and promiscuity, which they were hoping to avoid. Are some Christian colleges basically secular institutions in disguise?

The third concern we gather from the data shows a drastic lack of agreement between the president and the vice president on important issues. (As we will show, this lack of agreement extends to other areas.) There should have been one answer that stood out for each school — a rallying cause, belief, or vision that distinguishes them from the world. But other than saying they "teach the Bible" in some of their classes, we couldn't find any clear vision among these leaders of Christian education. In some circumstances it seems like they may be upholding a handful of Christian "traditions" rather than equipping the next generation of believers. Now it may be that the school has some sort of mission statement, but regardless, the survey shows clearly what was on the minds of the leaders of these institutions.

Skim the numbers in the following graphs once again, and you'll find great disagreement between the president and the vice president. If the pilot and copilot of an airliner functioned in the same way, we know that the flight would be headed for disaster. This "confusion in the cockpit" appears to be the reality at most Christian colleges and universities. No wonder so many students' experiences end in disaster.

We were encouraged, however, to find that presidents and vice presidents, like those in the religion and science departments, have a strong belief in issues regarding the New Testament. But as usual, once we started asking questions about Old Testament — particularly detailed questions — the answers became much more concerning. In many cases, the division between the president and the vice president was striking.

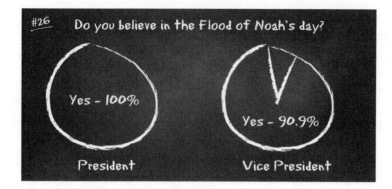

#26 Do you believe in the Flood of Noah's day?

Yes - 100%

President

Yes - 90.9%

Vice President

Both of these percentages were higher than were the religion and science departments (84.0 percent and 88.9 percent, respectively), so we're pleased to see at least a general belief in this historic event.

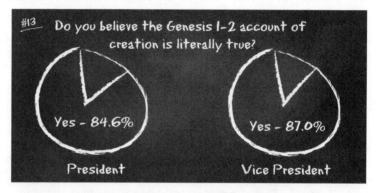

#13 Do you believe the Genesis 1-2 account of creation is literally true?

Yes - 84.6%

President

Yes - 87.0%

Vice President

Again, the president and the vice president showed slightly higher levels of belief than the religion and science departments, and we see only a minimal amount of discrepancy between these two offices. They gave similar responses and compatible numbers when asked if they believed the Genesis account "as written."

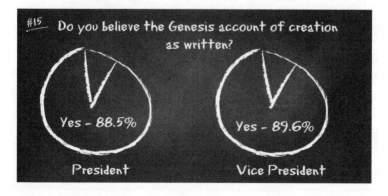

#15 Do you believe the Genesis account of creation as written?

Yes - 88.5%

President

Yes - 89.6%

Vice President

So in the general questions everything appears (and as you will understand as we go on, we have to emphasize "appears") to be fairly solid and headed in the right direction. But then again, we haven't gotten to any of the details yet. When we asked specific questions that show what they mean by what they say, the numbers are quite different.

Q14: Would you consider yourself to be a young-earth or old-earth Christian?

	President	Vice President
Old earth	48.1%	37.7%
Young earth	51.9%	50.6%
Neither	0.0%	10.4%

There is some indecision on the parts of the vice presidents; other than that there's a fair amount of unity here, even though the leaders, like the rest of the faculty, are almost evenly split in their beliefs about a young and old earth. This issue draws the line in the sand time and time again and helps us to discern between what people say and what they actually mean. As we have seen, it's much easier to agree on general statements than on the specifics. As the questions become more detailed, a very unusual "disconnect" begins to appear between the presidents and the VPs of the schools.

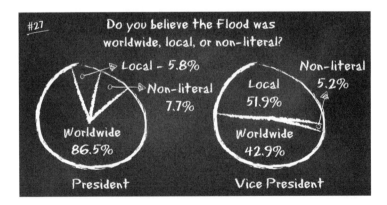

The presidents' responses are somewhat encouraging, but it is disheartening to see that well over half of the vice presidents of Christian universities believe in a local or nonliteral flood. And we are really giving them the benefit of the doubt about what they mean by "worldwide." This is yet another area where "newspeak" shows up. Many times when someone says "worldwide" what they really mean is "the whole world as it was known to exist then." Many people think that Noah's Flood covered only the known world at that time

— meaning that it was simply a regional flood. Hugh Ross (from the biblically compromising ministry *Reasons to Believe*), for example, says he believes in a "universal" flood, but it's only part of the world that was covered. Some people say they believe in a global flood, but they only believe it was on part of the globe. So even those words don't necessarily mean to these academics what they mean to us. I'm not saying that they're necessarily being deceptive; they're just not being descriptive. If you want to find out what they really mean, you have to ask very specific questions. In fact, the more we considered the results of this research, the more this problem became apparent. It is really an epidemic. You can't really assume that what these professors and presidents are saying to you is equivalent to your plain understanding of the words and phrases.

Several years ago I got a supporter to write to a number of colleges to get in writing what they believed about the Flood. The responses were mind-boggling. Most colleges won't even give you a statement anymore. They don't want to be held accountable in black and white, and even if they did, what would they say? When the president and vice president believe such radically different things, what could they write that would represent the school? They couldn't write anything specific, because there is no consensus on the details.

Q16: Do you believe in God creating the earth in six literal 24-hour days?

	President	Vice President
Yes	78.8%	40.3%

Again, notice that nearly twice as many presidents say that they believe in a six-day creation compared to vice presidents. Not only is this result telling, but it also calls for the question, "Why is that?!" Why in the world would there be such a huge difference in belief between these two positions?

Q17: Do you believe in God creating the earth, but not in six literal days?

	President	Vice President
Yes	42.3%	58.4%

The vice presidents answered this follow-up question consistently, though the majority did so incorrectly. But the presidents? Notice that 78 percent said they do believe in six literal days, but 42 percent said they do NOT believe in six literal days. If you add that up, it means that 20 percent of the presidents answer yes to both questions!

So much of this hinges on their views of the authority of Scripture. Notice how they answered these key yes/no questions:

Q19: Do you believe in the inspiration of Scripture?

	President	Vice President
Yes	98.1%	98.7%

Q20: Do you believe in the inerrancy of Scripture?

	President	Vice President
Yes	21.2%	77.9%
No	78.8%	5.6%
Don't know	0.0%	6.5%

Q18: Do you believe in the infallibility of Scripture?

	President	Vice President
Yes	17.3%	94.8%
No	82.7%	3.9%

Take a look at that again. Both offices strongly believe in the "inspiration" of Scripture (98%+). But when asked about inerrancy and infallibility, the presidents answered with an apparently low level of belief. Only 21 percent believe in inerrancy and only 17.3 percent believe in infallibility! And let me remind you that these are the presidents of religiously affiliated colleges and universities that are members of the CCCU (Council for Christian Colleges and Universities). These are the men and women in the big office, with the big desks, who are charting the direction of the school. They are the representatives, the guardians, and the voice of the school. These are the *leaders*. And this is their level of belief in the authority of Scripture? Does that concern you as one possibly entrusting your children to them?

Interestingly, the vice presidents seem to have a much higher view of Scripture than the presidents do, though this doesn't really line up with their answers to questions about the days of creation and the Flood as outlined above. The vice presidents are the ones who are usually approving the hiring of faculty. They are the ones that are in the middle of the division between the science and religion departments, and they appear to show a relatively higher view of Scripture.

One huge part of the concern, however, is this huge gap of belief that exists between the president and the vice president. You look at these kinds of numbers (21.2%–77.9%, 17.3%–94.8%) on central issues regarding the authority of Scripture, and you have to wonder what is going on.

We can only speculate on why these huge gaps exist between presidents and vice presidents. Do they *really* believe this differently? If not, why would they skew their answers? How could they ever really work together in a unified way for the institution?

Unfortunately, other questions only lead to more head scratching.

The differences between the president and the vice president are less pronounced on this issue, but we should still be concerned about the 25 percent of the presidents who do not believe the Bible is literally true. Yet again, when we correlate this question with one that we already looked at, the results are not consistent:

The vice presidents say they believe the Bible is literally true, but far less than half believe in six literal 24-hour days. More presidents believe in six literal 24-hour days than claim that the Bible is literally true. It is tempting to try to get inside their heads and figure out where these discrepancies and inconsistencies come from. For example, the vice presidents said that they have a higher view of Scripture than the presidents, yet on important issues such as the Flood, they show a much lower belief level in historical biblical events.

In all honesty, it's tough to interpret such inconsistent data. Perhaps the only logical conclusion is that their belief systems/worldviews are highly inconsistent as well. What we can conclude from this data, however, is that some presidents of Christian colleges answered regrettably on key issues regarding the authority of Scripture, and we find very, very little unity between the presidents and the vice presidents who are in the cockpit of these institutions.

Detached from the Classroom

The interesting finding about this question is that there is virtually *no* agreement between the leadership about the educational background of their faculty. In most institutions the president does not hire the faculty. Generally, the chairs of the individual departments recommend faculty to

#3 Do you know if your faculty and administrators received their degree from a Christian institution?

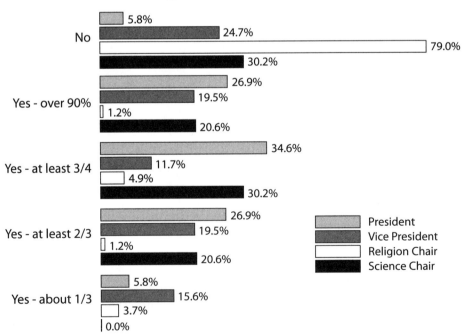

the vice president, who makes the decision. But even so, 24.7 percent of vice presidents didn't know.

One of the big reasons you have evolution/millions of years (and other compromises in regard to Genesis/Old Testament) being taught in Christian colleges is because so many of the faculty come from secular institutions. They don't know any other way of thinking than what they heard in their own personal education. Yet if the educational background of the faculty is an important issue for you when you start choosing schools, we don't know who to tell you to ask. Unless you actually see a piece of paper listing the faculty's educational background, it will be very difficult to determine how many people actually did get their degree from Christian institutions (and it depends on which Christian institutions anyway, because some are no different than the secular ones!). The mixed data did reveal one thing, however: for the leaders, unbelievably, this does not seem to be an important question at all . . . but even if it is, nobody really knows the answer.

A further concern is that presidents seem to be very detached and unaware of what is actually being taught in their classrooms on key issues regarding the evolution/creation debate.

#6 What does your institution teach about evolution?

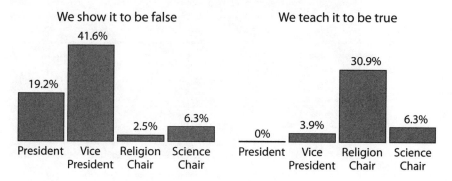

You can see problems all through this data, but the most obvious one is this: 0.0 percent of college presidents think that their institution is teaching evolution to be true. Yet 30.9 percent of the religion departments are clearly doing so. (If you remember our analysis of this data in an earlier chapter, you will recall that this number might be significantly higher depending on what the "teach and dissect" category means.) Only slightly more of the vice presidents (3.9 percent) are aware that the religion department is teaching evolution to be true.

There is a huge disconnect going on here. And on issues as critical as this one, the disconnect is scary.

Unaware of the Conflict

Not only are some of these presidents apparently unaware of what is being taught in the classrooms, but because of this they are also unaware of the conflict that exists between the departments they oversee.

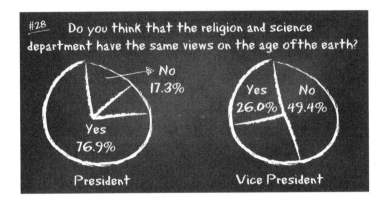

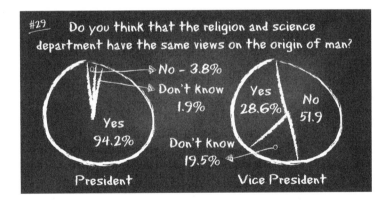

Note that the presidents have significantly higher impressions on unity of curriculum across the campus than the vice presidents do. We already know from the data whose perception is more accurate. The vice president knows about the conflict. While the president is out shaking hands at luncheons, raising money, and promoting the school to potential students and their parents, the vice president is getting all the calls from the parents and is in the crossfire of the squabbles between the departments.

This lack of perception is not exclusive to Christian colleges and universities, however. America's Research Group recently did a survey for a mattress company where the same questions were asked to the president, to the head of merchandising, to the mattress buyer, and to the salespeople. What the owners thought and what the salesperson did coincided only 6 percent of the time. What the merchandising manager thought and what the buyer said coincided only 45 percent of the time. But the buyer and the salespeople were fifty-fifty, so they had four different people in four different positions all believing four different things about what was going on in the organization. Christian colleges are no exception — but they should be!

The leadership at most of the Christian colleges doesn't know what is being taught in the classroom, and it's very difficult for them to find out. The leaders have dozens or hundreds of professors in the classrooms for many hours every week . . . and the president is supposed to monitor that? Sure, maybe a few professors will sign off on a doctrinal statement that they maybe don't fully believe in — or even disagree with — to get the job. And, as we have already shown and discussed, they can agree to words and phrases in the statement that may mean something different to them than what it meant to those who formulated the statement for the institution. Some might just skim it and sign it without serious consideration — and when they get to the classroom they can teach whatever they want. We hate to say that, but it's true. There is a strong emphasis on "academic freedom," as they have been taught and have experienced in the secular world. Many professors consider it an insult to be told what they should be teaching.

Indifferent to Consequences

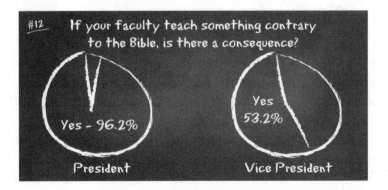

#12 If your faculty teach something contrary to the Bible, is there a consequence?

Yes - 96.2%
President

Yes 53.2%
Vice President

Again, we see a significant difference here between what the president thinks is happening and what the vice president thinks is happening. The presidents think that there are definite consequences when someone teaches contrary to the Bible; only about half of the vice presidents believe that this is taking place. That's a huge spread again.

Several factors could be contributing to this. As we saw above, the presidents are largely unaware of what is being taught in their classrooms, and they probably think that everyone is teaching in accordance with the Bible. The vice presidents know that this isn't true, yet only half of them are aware of any consequences to unbiblical teaching. From the survey, we know that there are a lot of things being taught contrary to the Bible, and nobody seems to be doing anything about it.

As usual, the questions we asked brought up even more questions. What did most of the people we interviewed think when they heard the phrase "contrary to the Bible"? My guess is that they may have only thought about blatant issues, such as teaching that Hinduism and or Islam is true and Christianity is false. When they heard this phrase, did they even think evolution? Did they think millions of years? Did they think of a historical Adam? Those are things that some of them don't consider to be contrary to the Bible anyway!

And what did they think of when we said "consequences"? Did they think we're talking about social consequences? Professional censorship? Perhaps we should have asked the question this way: if someone teaches something contrary to the Bible, do you have the will to fire them or publicly correct them?

We have seen very few instances where faculty were fired for compromise teachings. In those cases it usually has to be something really outlandish. But worrying about the details of "inerrancy," "infallibility," or even evolution/creation/millions of years? There's no consequence for that — and many times it is even encouraged.

In many situations, there is really only a "consequence" if the word gets out to the public and parents become involved. Once it becomes public and the parents become concerned, then there is action. The action is not necessarily because of what is being taught (because others are probably teaching the same things and haven't been highlighted) but because of public relations damage and possible loss of donors and support.

A Disconcerting Conclusion

The analysis of this data unfortunately confirmed the hunches that we had about what was happening and what is happening at the highest levels of leadership at many Christian colleges and universities. These numbers show such Christian institutions and those that are "religiously affiliated" may have a disconnect from the reason the college should exist. There is great disunity among the leadership, and compromise teachings have infiltrated the classrooms. Many schools struggle to differentiate themselves from secular institutions, and clear conflict exists between departments.

Equally concerning are the inconsistencies that we find in people's answers. As a group, these respondents are highly educated and amazingly confused. Many of us have *felt* this was true, but now we have the statistics, drawn from their own words, to show it. President Greg Hall summarized the situation this way:

> There is no idea or concept that more accurately describes my 20 years of experience in "Christian" higher education than the periodic, but continual, evidence of equivocation, capitulation, and compromise among those of us who lead and teach in these institutions when it comes to whether or not we will stand on the truth of biblical authority. In the equivocation we cause massive confusion among students, who are far more discerning than we realize at times, and see it for what it is. I have observed this phenomenon among other Christian colleges and my own. If we are not willing to stand upon the truth and veracity of Scripture, we have no choice but to capitulate and compromise in the classroom. In more than just the disciplines related to science we will find secular philosophies and ideologies in direct conflict with the clear instruction of the Word of God. In most cases there are some very strange intellectual "gymnastics" going on to try to reconcile these worldly philosophies with the eternal truth of God's Word. It is a fool's errand in the worst sense of the word. To cause confusion among students because we can't decide on the place to stand as our first priority, that being the Word of God, is to render ourselves incompetent as Christian educators.

Professing to be institutions of truth, many schools have become the propagators of confusion. They are the authors of confusion. "If the trumpet does not sound a clear call, who will get ready for battle?" (1 Cor. 14:8; NIV). The reason young Christians are not prepared for the battle is that they don't take a firm stand on the authority of the Bible. This generation does not know there is a battle, does not care if there is a battle, does not know the enemy, does not know what is at stake, and does not care. You would hope that the Christian colleges would have been preparing "warriors" for the ensuing conflict. But they have not. They have bought into the enemy's strategy to divide and conquer. As President Hall notes, "While we should have been equipping students, we have been confusing them." And of course all this flows over into the pulpit, Christian schools, other Christian institutions, and so on down the line to the Christian public.

The Leadership Vacuum

Let's take another look at the question that asks about what differentiates a Christian school from a secular one. As we probe deeper to find explanations for the division and difficulties we see emerging from Christian schools, two of the answers might offer us some helpful insight.

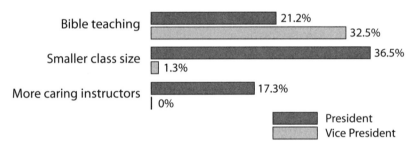

#11   **What makes education different at Christian compared to secular schools?**

Bible teaching — President 21.2% — Vice President 32.5%
Smaller class size — President 36.5% — Vice President 1.3%
More caring instructors — President 17.3% — Vice President 0%

Again, notice that there is striking contrast between what the president and vice president prioritize. Is it possible that these responses reflect the different priorities of their specific positions? As we broke up these answers, an interesting profile of the presidency emerged. It appears that the presidents, rather than being the defenders and leaders of a spiritual institution, give answers that make them sound more like salesmen. But these responses certainly reflect financial and social realities facing many college presidents and would be consistent with what are otherwise unexplainable responses.

Let's take the most obvious one: when asked what makes a Christian school different from a secular school, the presidents' number-one answer was "smaller class size." At 36.5 percent, no other category of answers was close. Is this what should distinguish a Christian school from a secular school? This is a typical mantra for *any* private school — one of their big marketing angles that helps them justify higher tuition (because most people believe that smaller classes equate with a better education). But what does that have to do with being Christian?

The same can be asked of the high response "caring instructors" the presidents gave. None of the other three positions of leadership gave this any sort of statistical significance. Not only is the president's view on this completely different than the rest of his faculty, but we must also question why.

In many situations, it appears that the president is giving answers that put their schools in the best light for Christian parents. They gave the highest numbers when asked how many in their faculty were trained in Christian institutions. But is this number objective? Do they really know? Or is this another situation where the president is trying to sell the institution to Christian parents? In all honesty, we simply couldn't tell.

Presidents believe in the highest levels of unity between their departments, they don't see conflict in the curriculum, and none of them believe that evolution is being taught as truth in their school. Smaller class sizes and caring instructors could be just another pitch for enrollment.

If this is the situation, it's not unique to Christian colleges and universities. In bigger churches, the lead pastor is often more detached. It's the associate pastor who is in the trenches, aware of the division between the committees, and more concerned about what is being taught in the Sunday school classrooms. The senior pastors tend to be more concerned about how they are coming across to the congregation, how the church is being branded, and how the church's image affects the offering plate. I think it's the same in these colleges. The president tends to be more political and the vice president and the chairs tend to be more personal.

Particularly in the wake of the recession, many of these schools are struggling financially. Many institutions are sitting on a time bomb of debt. In this economy, the temptation certainly exists to tell the parents what they want to hear in order to keep the classrooms filled. The pressure to meet enrollment could also be driving these fuzzy answers. We know that's a horrible accusation to make, but it's at least one possibility that must be considered and addressed.

Dr. John Maxwell said, "Everything rises and falls on leadership."[1] The survey found that leadership is in a questionable and chaotic state on Christian colleges and campuses. The tone and precedents set at the highest levels of leadership will, and are, having an effect on the rest of the campus and ultimately the Church in general.

Someone must take ownership and responsibility for the situation and step out with clear leadership in the midst of this crisis. So far, it seems like we just don't see the type of leadership we have known in the past: the men and women who held the authority of Scripture in highest regard, above all things, and then taught and lived and learned accordingly. Where are those leaders today? It's only a matter of time before an institution falls to the level of its leadership. We saw this time and time again with the Ivy League schools, which started with such high and bold principles and eventually descended into compromise with the world.

Somehow, someway, we must regain the certain sound of our trumpet so that the next generation will take up their weapons of faith and join us in the battle for life-changing truth.

Endnotes
1. John C. Maxwell, *The 21 Indispensable Qualities of a Leader* (Nashville, TN: Thomas Nelson, Inc., 2007).

PART 2

The Battle for the Mind

For our struggle is not against
flesh and blood, but against the
rulers, against the powers, against
the world forces of this darkness,
against the spiritual forces of
wickedness in the heavenly places.

– Ephesians 6:12

Chapter 6

The High Call of Taking Action

Greg Hall

All that is necessary for evil to triumph is for good men to do nothing. — Edmund Burke

December 7, 1941, Pearl Harbor. It is yet another stunningly beautiful morning in "paradise." As the sun rises over the Pacific Ocean and spreads its golden rays across the small community, the island slowly comes to life — oblivious to the "day of infamy" that lies ahead. There is an interesting book on the history of what happened that day entitled *At Dawn We Slept*. While the attack that morning was a "surprise" to those who were stationed on this beautiful little piece of volcanic rock in the middle of a vast ocean, the reader learns that in reality there were plenty of "signals." In fact, there were several who had a very good inkling that such an attack was imminent, but they either said nothing, or their warnings fell on deaf ears. The majority of Americans and most of America's leadership were in fact taken by surprise.[1]

This is an interesting comparison to the current battle raging for the hearts and minds of our youth who face daily the onslaught of anti-Christian, atheistic philosophy. When I talk about this in messages around the country, I find Christian parents surprised and shocked at what has happened to public education and particularly how militant the fight against Christianity has become.

And now we find out that as we have slept, compromise has infiltrated Christian institutions as well, creating possibly an even more dangerous situation in colleges and universities that appeared to be our allies. They are, in fact, minimizing the authority of Scripture. It is as though the title of the book *At Dawn We Slept* describes those of us who have just not been paying enough attention to this collapse within the Church.

Yet in the midst of the raging battle, there is something that is happening that gives great hope. The open militancy of those opposed to Christianity will awaken a sleeping giant. It is possible to envision a generation of believers who will rise up and say, "No more!" It is time to join the battle for the hearts and minds of generations to come. I am hoping and praying for a day of renewed influence upon our public educators by Christians who understand this battle and will equip themselves for the fight. I am hoping and praying for the day when compromising Christian colleges and universities humbly confess and repent. I look forward to the day when we will see a strengthening and expanding of a biblical worldview across the Western world. Specifically I pray for:

- The Church to capture a vision of the importance of starting Christian schools.
- The Church to capture a vision for connecting with students in secular schools.
- A strengthening of the home school movement.
- Support for Christian teachers in the public schools. They are strategic in influencing students in a biblical worldview.
- The support of Christian colleges and universities that are committed to a biblical worldview. They are the alternative to secular education.
- The support of committed believers who work on secular college and university campuses making the biblical worldview known to students who may never otherwise hear the message.

Mostly, I pray for the resurgence of commitment to the Word of God as the authentic explanation of all issues of human existence. In the end, the entire discussion of which worldview will gain prominence in our culture is one of *authority*. We believe God's Word to be the authority upon which we are expected to build our lives, and we are fighting back to regain recognition of that authority in our churches, our schools, and our families. Yes, it is time to recapture a generation. We may have lost some important battles; but the war we can still win (Matt. 28:18–20).

The attack of December 7, 1941, catapulted a nation into war — a war we ultimately won. Maybe God is calling us to spiritual warfare, too. It is the war being waged to determine what ideas will gain prominence in the coming generations. It is a war that ultimately we win, too (Isa. 11:9). But we get the clear message now that it is time for believers to stand, fight, and advance. It is time to be honest and forthright about what is at stake — the minds and souls of our youth. It is time for a clear "call to battle." We must not forget the admonition of Scripture. If the trumpet gives an uncertain sound, who will prepare for the battle? It is time for a clear call to arms; a time to join the battle. From the bottom of my heart, I'd like to make that call to the local church, educators at all levels, and parents.

Action for the Church

Frankly, a portion of the local church has abandoned one of its first priorities: to educate its youth in the truth of God's Word as the first order of business in any educational pursuit. Furthermore, we need to convince the Body of Christ that our youth should be highly encouraged to education in a biblical worldview as the foundation of all life-long learning. The education of the churches' youth is a situation that needs to be redeemed.

The Church must get involved early in educating our youth in Christian biblical worldview and apologetics. This is a foreign topic in many congregations, but its implications are profound. Our worldview is the way we look at life. A Christian biblical worldview is learning to look at all aspects of life through the eyes of God. The problem is that Christians have developed a worldview that includes influences from a variety of sources, many expressly unchristian, and this destroys the ability to do good apologetics.

Consequently, it becomes possible to raise kids in church and subsequently turn them over to secular institutions for education without having thought through the potential outcomes of them losing faith in the process. The issue for us is this: if we are going to be Christian, then it requires surrender in every area of life. It makes a claim on every area of our lives and is very important in how we educate our young. If we are going to reclaim the ground lost in this battle, we are going to have to develop strategies for the Church to move *forward* and not into further retreat.

We must be willing to sound the trumpet and let the Church know just how serious the problem is. The enemies of Christian faith learned a long time ago where to wage the war — in the education of our youth. They understood the influence they could gain by this daily captive audience. We Christians played right into their hands by leaving the battle behind and simply joining in. We have lost the concept of what is at stake, *the hearts and minds of our youth.*

Second, the Church needs to support and encourage the Christian teachers whose calling has led them into the center of this battle in the public school setting. These individuals are God's instruments of influence in enemy territory. Thankfully, there are still good numbers of them, and they *are* making a difference day by day, child by child, school by school. The Church and Christian colleges and universities should continue to educate those who will continue to enter the public schools and be sure they are adequately prepared to represent the Christian worldview in a hostile environment. It can and is being done. It happens only intentionally, not by default.

The teachers at the private Christian schools of our nation need encouragement, too. They do their work at a fraction of the pay of public education and do it well. Even at that, due to economic hard times, Christian schools all over the nation are closing — precisely the opposite of what needs to be done in these times. Christians who are committed to the authority of Scripture in all areas of life need to be affirmed and recognized, because as we have seen, many times they are in the minority, even on a "Christian" campus.

Finally, instead of looking at the world and lamenting how corrupt it has become, we need to focus our attention on the Church — on God's people — especially on those to whom the sheep look for leadership. Attention needs to be given to the shepherds of our day who lead us congregation by congregation, and also to the presidents, vice presidents, and professors at our Christian institutions who influence and train the sheep in a campus environment. The nurture and care of souls and minds of the youth of our nation is our duty and opportunity. It is time for the Church to rise to this occasion.

Action for Parents

As we survey the landscape of education in America, do we really realize the philosophy being promoted by these atheistic educators as it relates to child rearing? Dr. Richard Dawkins asks:

> How much do we regard children as being property of their parents? It's one thing to say people should be free to believe whatever they like, but should they be free to impose their beliefs on their children? Is there something to be said for society stepping in?[2]

It's interesting that Dr. Dawkins wants his views imposed on children, all the while arguing that those of parents shouldn't be! And further, society has, in fact, stepped in. These atheist educators are plenty clever enough to know where and how to enjoin the battle for whose ideas shall have mastery and control. They know to make the battleground education — especially the higher education classroom. And so, it should come as no surprise when someone like evolutionary biologist Kenneth Miller admits:

> A presumption of atheism or agnosticism is universal in academic life. . . . The conventions of academic life, almost universally, revolve around the assumption that religious belief is something that people grow out of as they become educated.[3]

If you think this is over-stating the case, you have not spent time enough on a secular campus, listened to a lecture from a secular professor, or read from his or her books. For the most part, well-intentioned Christian parents have directed their children to secular public institutions with big football stadiums and housing with all the expected amenities, and have considered it a great bargain compared to the cost of private Christian higher education. Yet others write checks to compromising colleges and then "check out," unaware (or unconcerned) about liberal, secular influences that are driving curriculum in the classroom.

Parents, it is time to engage again. The battle is raging. Don't give over authority. Don't assume. You need to get educated on this matter. You need to understand the nature of our current education system. When you are choosing a college for your student, whether it is grade school, high school, or college/university, we know that you are making many of these decisions based on cost. But when you consider the spiritual cost, as we have tried to show throughout this book, the cost is too high.

For those who are concerned about the loss of Christian values in our culture, we must face the fact that, in large measure, we have been party to our own undoing almost without a fight. We have turned over generation after generation of young men and women to be fully inculcated with the thoughts, ideas, and precepts that are absolutely contrary to our Christian faith. And we wonder why this nation is in the shape it is in? The Church systematically, seemingly without guilt, turns one generation after another of children over to a pagan, godless, secular education system that turns them from the faith. We do it in public elementary and high schools and colleges and universities. And we pay the enemy to steal their souls. It is time to wake up.

I wish I could tell you all of the stories of how, when I have preached on this subject, parents have come to me in tears. One parent said, "I sent my lovely Christian daughter to the state university, and she came home an atheist." Story after story. *But*, does that mean all will? No, it does not. Parents, I encourage you to redeem the situation. Particularly in the vacuum of leadership from the Church on this issue, your efforts must be intelligent, proactive, and pastoral.

Then, in all honesty, we must address the situation at "Christian" schools. It is possible to go to a Christian school and have the same result — a broken, devastated faith — as with secular schools. This is true. The research shows it to be true, and we must hit it hard. As the research discussed in this book illustrates clearly, one has to be extremely discerning when considering a Christian institution. Just because it is said to be "Christian" does not mean it will teach a Christian worldview as it should. And just because the professors claim they believe in the "infallible" Word of God and in "inerrancy," that does not necessarily mean they are using those terms in the same way as you. If the intent of higher education is to place your students in a godly environment, you need to get as far away as possible from the secular and compromising institutions. Ken uses a biblical analogy to make this point:

> When Moses went before Pharaoh in Exodus chapter 8, one of his responses was to allow the Israelites to go and sacrifice to their God, but they were told, "only you shall not go very far away" (Exod. 8:28). Pharaoh didn't want them to go too far from Egypt. As we know, Egypt can be used as symbolic of the world and its pagan philosophies. Pharaoh wanted to keep them close — not too far from the world.
>
> As you begin to consider the results of the research conducted by America's Research Group (headed up by renowned researcher Britt Beemer) into what the Christian colleges of our age teach, you will find that many of them have tried to stay close to "Egypt." Sadly, so many have not wanted to go very far from what the world teaches in certain areas, and this can (and has) lead to generations being put on a slippery slide of unbelief — the opposite of what their parents were hoping (and paying) for.
>
> Yes, we are advocating that Christian parents need to go far from "Egypt." We should not entrust our children to the Philistines to be trained. But at the same time, this research will awaken us to understand the great need to deeply research, using the right terminology and asking the right questions of the right people (as we will outline for you later on), when considering a Christian institution for the education of our children.
>
> We do need to be far away from those of "Egypt" and those who have stayed close to "Egypt." We so need generations of young people

who are not defeated before they even begin to make their place in this world.

We need to be reminded of what God said to the Israelites in 2 Chronicles 7:13–14: "If . . . My people who are called by My name humble themselves, and pray and seek My face and turn from their wicked ways, then I will hear from heaven, will forgive their sin and will heal their land." Just as the Israelites needed to repent of their compromise with the world's teaching (the pagan religions of the day), we, God's people today, beginning with many of the leaders in our academic Institutions, need to repent of compromise and humble ourselves before the Lord and his Word.

For Educators

I say this again to those of you who are believers and work in the public/state schools: You are God's chosen instruments to do something about this. At the very least, remain faithful and do not fear making your Christian ideas known.[4] You have rights, too! There is no reason to cower or fear. You are able to stand up to this attack. Just like the Christian students intermixed with your unbelieving students, you are the salt and light to the public education world. You are a remnant of truth and grace and mercy in the midst of a compromised culture that desperately needs your influence and your love.

If you don't go to them, who will? How will they experience and know the truth if there's no one there to share it with them and to show it to them? You are that light. You are the salt. By the power of God's Spirit working through you, may Jesus use you as vessels of hope, of forgiveness, and of mercy in the midst of this needy generation. May He use you as a beacon of courage and dedication to the other Christian students in your classes and on your campus. And may God bless and protect you and your families as you execute this vitally important mission. We salute you and affirm you. Godspeed!

Responding to the Attack

December 7, 1941, was not the end. It was just the beginning. The brash and blatant attack of the enemy was a wake-up call to a sleeping nation that rose to the challenge. In this book, we have shared with you many sets of statistics and painted one of the first objective pictures of what is really happening on both secular and Christian campuses. Does this in any way discourage you? Not me. I see the greatest opportunity the Church has ever had to change the coming generations. Many people feel like there is nothing we can do about the decline of our culture. They have become not only inconsolable, but inactive.

On the one hand it is understandable. People, even if once engaged in the cultural struggle, look around and see only defeat and despair. There is probably no one who cannot recite a litany of disaster in our nation: a decline in morals, violence in our streets and schools, corruption at high levels of leadership, loss of integrity in our greatest institutions — the list is endless. And so on that one hand, the despair we sense about the future is understandable. But on the other hand, if we really do believe in a sovereign Creator who is all about the business of reclaiming His lost creation, then not only is this despair not justified, it is inexcusable! It is absolutely time to wake up.

It will take recognition of the issues we face in education. It will take parents making a commitment to send their children to committed Christian educational institutions. It will take a new generation of qualified Christian educators who know worldview matters — and who believe that the war of the worldviews can be won. We may be currently losing, but God is still in control. It will take a new dedication in the local church to make sure its own teaching mission is solid. In general, believers have failed to bring Christian truth to bear in society. As a result, we have a culture that has moved far away from God. We have a culture that does not consult the Word of God. We as Christians are not salt and light to our world and we have lost our influence — for the time being.

It is not time for despair; it is time for hope. It is time to reclaim this generation for Christ. But we have all the resources needed to once again influence our culture for Christ. It is time for the situation to be transformed. God's Word tells us clearly how this transformation takes place, "By the renewing of your mind" (Rom. 12:2). Our day of infamy has arrived. Now we must learn to contend for the authority of Scripture, as a Church, as parents, as educators, and as never before. Are you ready to be equipped to contend for the biblical worldview and the authority of Scripture from Genesis to Revelation?

Endnotes
1. Gordon William Prange, *At Dawn We Slept,* various publishers.
2. Richard Dawkins, *The God Delusion* (Boston, MA: Houghton Mifflin), p. 315, cited by Gary Wolf, "The Church of the Non-Believers," *Wired* (November 2006).
3. Kenneth R. Miller, *Finding Darwin's God: A Scientist's Search for Common Ground Between God and Evolution* (New York: Harper Perennial, 1999), p. 19, 184.
4. Some options are to offer a free class after school hours once or twice a month to refute an evolutionary worldview and build good apologetic teachings, so the school is not liable. Other options are to be available to students after school or point out that certain things come from a Christian worldview and they are often borrowed (wearing clothes, good and bad exist, morality, a basis for logic, uniformity in nature, etc.).

Chapter 7

Ready to Give an Answer

Greg Hall

Sanctify Christ as Lord in your hearts, always being ready to make a defense to everyone who asks you to give an account for the hope that is in you, yet with gentleness and reverence (1 Pet. 3:15).

When I was a graduate student at the University of Pittsburgh, I attended classes with a number of Islamic students, most of whom were from the nation of Saudi Arabia. They were very good students, highly motivated, very devoted to one another, and especially zealous for their Islamic beliefs. At the graduate level, students are continually making presentations of one kind or another. It was always striking to me that along with the presentation, the Islamic students invariably talked about their religion.

For instance, if a student was giving a presentation on some kind of educational policy in his country, he would likely begin like this: "Before I speak of the educational policies of my nation, it is first important for me to talk about the tenets of Islam with you. The reason is, you cannot understand the educational policy of my country without understanding Islam. They go together." And so the student had a captive audience, and they always, courageously and forthrightly, told us first about the basic tenets of Islamic religion.

I can remember being impressed with their zeal and their sincerity. One night I said a prayer during the break of a class, asking God to give me the courage and opportunity to share openly about my faith in Christ. At the end of class one of the students from Saudi Arabia came to me and said, "Mr. Greg, do I understand correctly that you are a Christian minister?"

"Yes," I said, "I am."

He then asked me if I had time to spend with him and teach him about the Christian Scriptures.

We made plans to meet a few days later in one of the empty classrooms before class so I could teach him about the Christian Scriptures. Prior to that scheduled meeting, I thought he probably did not even have a copy of the Bible. When I gave him one the next day, I could tell that I had done something very, very wrong. He quickly took the Bible, shoved it into a book bag and took off very abruptly. I honestly thought I would never see him again.

But he did show up for our appointed meeting, and he explained what happened when I gave him the Bible. "Mr. Greg, it is a capital offense for me to have a copy of the Christian Bible. I could be killed for this. We must not let my colleagues know what we are doing. We must meet in secret." And meet in secret we did, for many weeks as I taught him about the Scriptures.

I began by having a discussion with him about our common ancestor in the faith, Father Abraham. The connections between Abraham, Sarah, Hagar, Ishmael, and Isaac were fascinating to him and he would take copious notes on everything I said. I will never forget the lessons we had on the Gospel of John. One night he opened that Gospel and read these words to me: "And the Word became flesh, and dwelt among us, and we saw His glory, glory of the only begotten from the Father, full of grace and truth" (John 1:14).

"What, Mr. Greg, is the meaning of this?" I can honestly say, even after 20 years, that when I recall the enthusiasm he had for learning and his desire for truth, a feeling comes over me that I cannot explain. When I realize that God has put the desire to know His truth in every human heart no matter what our background or faith, I am awed at how God works to make His truth known.

"What you are reading about is the 'incarnation,'" I told him. "Christians believe that Jesus is God incarnate. God in human flesh. We believe He is fully God and fully man. Jesus is Immanuel, 'God with us.'"

Then he questioned me about the phrase "the glory of the One and Only," and I talked to him about the Christian conviction of the uniqueness of Jesus, that we believe that He is the only way any of us ever get to God. He alone is the payment God accepts for sin. He alone has the plan for the salvation of all who believe in Him.

At that, my friend got angry. *Very* angry. And he said to me, raising his voice, "Do you mean to tell me that Jesus is the only way we can get to God?" I said that was exactly what I meant. And I tell you honestly, I was scared. But then, all of a sudden a calm and peace came over him and he said to me, "Thanks, for telling me the truth."

Over the course of many weeks we continued to meet. I would talk and he would take notes. I would write on the board and he would take more notes. He asked question after question. I thought, *I have never encountered anyone with more enthusiasm and energy for God's Word*. He could not get enough. I had in fact, never had a student like him. And have not since.

Then one day, he asked "the" question. He began with these remarks. "I thank you for spending time with me. I have enjoyed our discussions. And I am impressed with your command of the topic and especially your knowledge of your Bible, *but* . . . do you have any evidence that it is the truth?"

The Question

"Do you have any evidence that it is the truth?" That is a fair question. In the marketplace of philosophies, ideologies, or worldviews, it is a question anyone must answer before putting their faith in any one particular system or pattern of thought. Now, I understood that we all have the same evidence and that how one interprets it depends on one's starting point. However, from his perspective he obviously wanted me to defend the Christian faith. As Christians we are commanded to give a reason for the faith that is within us. As a matter of intellectual honesty and practicality, what possible good is a worldview for which you cannot give a defense? If we cannot give a defense, we probably don't know enough about our alleged worldview for it to be of much value to us either!

Having an answer to this question is far more important than most people realize. The main issue is this: ideas have consequences. Truth is at the heart of what has become nothing less than warfare in the marketplace of competing worldviews as to which ideas will get your attention and gain prominence in your mind. Once those ideas are firmly embedded in your thinking, your mind will devise the ways for you to act in accordance with what you "know."

What we believe about the world around us and developing a framework for thinking and acting starting with the Bible is the single most important thing we do as humans. When we see that these "ideas" have serious personal consequences, we will naturally want to see the evidence that confirms they are true. I have been in the ministry of the Church for over 30 years as a pastor and university president and there has never been a time in those years when Christians have not had to learn to contend for the truth of God's Word, the Bible.

It has always been the case that the enemies of God have tried to dishonor and discredit the Scripture. In fact, the original sin of humankind was a moment of an attempt to pervert the very Word of God. From Genesis 3 we read:

> The serpent . . . . said to the woman, "Did God really say, 'You must not eat from any tree in the garden'?" The woman said to the serpent, "We may eat fruit from the trees in the garden, but God did say, 'You must not eat fruit from the tree that is in the middle of the garden, and you must not touch it, or you will die.'"

Then, in an attempt to pervert the truth again, the serpent responded:

> "You will not certainly die. . . . For God knows that when you eat from it your eyes will be opened, and you will be like God, knowing good and evil" (Gen. 3:1–4; NIV).

Note that the very first attack was on the Word of God. Eve believed the tantalizing lie of the deceiver rather than the truth of God's Word. This encounter brought sin into a perfect world — it was an "act of cosmic treason"[1] as Dr. R.C. Sproul put it — and it was a result of a successful attempt to discredit God and His Word. That has always been the case, and it always will be. Today, both secular and Christian colleges are filled and infiltrated with people who seek to discredit God's Word in the same way. Thankfully, there are a number of highly skilled, highly credentialed scholars and pastor/teachers who have a very high view of Scripture and teach it as the truth.

- They understand the Bible to be God's written revelation to man and that the 66 books of the Bible have been given to us by the Holy Spirit as the plenary (inspired equally in all parts) Word of God.
- They believe the Bible to be an objective propositional revelation, verbally inspired in every word, absolutely inerrant in the original documents. As such, it is "God breathed" and infallible as a rule of faith and practice and on everything it touches upon (biology, geology, etc.).
- They teach that God spoke in this Word through the Holy Spirit, who superintended the human authors so that by using their own personalities and varying styles of writing still composed and recorded God's words to man without error.

- They show that while there are many applications of Scripture to the issues of life, there is one true interpretation. Through the Holy Spirit who guides us into truth, it is possible for believers to ascertain the absolute intent and meaning of Scripture.

But it must be recognized at all times and in all ways, the truth of the Bible stands in judgment of man, and not the other way around. As Dr. R.C. Sproul says in the introduction to the *New Geneva Study Bible*:

It is a sacred book because it transcends and stands apart from, above, every other book. It is holy because its ultimate author is holy. It is holy because its message is holy. . . . The Bible is an inspired book that is "breathed out" by God . . . it offers more than brilliant insight, more than human sagacity. It is called "inspired" not because of its supernatural mode of transmission via human authors, but because of its origin. It is not merely a book about God; it is a book from God. Therefore, the church confesses its trust and confidence that the Bible is Vox Dei, the veritable "voice of God."[2]

At stake in the battle for the Bible is the very nature and character of God. And at stake in the greatest issues, questions, and debates about the meaning and purpose of life around us is the authority of Scripture. You must remember and be willing to be discriminating and discerning, because there are plenty of persons who think what I have just described for you is crazy and they will do anything possible to discredit this position and the Scripture itself.

The Bible is true in all it says, equally inspired in all parts. When it describes the origin of life in the Book of Genesis there are actually those of us who believe it actually happened just that way — just as the writers of the New Testament believed. And contrary to what naturalistic philosophers try to teach our students, operational science has in no way proved this to be false — it is the other way around. Observational science today has strengthened the case for understanding the creation account in Genesis 1, not undermined it.

You *must* "get it right" when it comes to Scripture. That is of utmost importance, because the debate of the origin of life is not Darwinism versus creationism, the debate is really over the very authority of Scripture itself. It is an issue of authority. Where do you stand and what do you believe? And do you realize how your thinking will likely be affected by the educational environment you place yourself in? Are you prepared to answer "the question" of "evidence" when you are confronted with personal doubts and attacks from militant naturalists and compromising Christian institutions? Your life and mind are literally at stake in this whole discussion.

Some will agree with me that this book, the Bible, is glorious. Some detest it. Some ignore it. Some professing to be believers will argue with me, preferring that I would eliminate words like "inerrant" and "infallible" when describing it. They will consider me a fool. And all I can say is, "Guilty as charged. I would be honored to be a fool for Christ's sake" (see Matt. 5:11).

But I have a question for believers who undermine the authority of Scripture. Why, if you are a believer, do you spend so much effort on teaching a different position? Some think it is a matter of intellectual honesty. I just have a hard time understanding the energy I see expended on making the Bible look like any other religious text rather than the supernatural work of God that it claims itself to be. In other words, why call yourself a believer if you do not trust the Bible, which is the source of why you claim to believe?

In an age where "tolerance" is the spirit of the day, people (non-Christians and Christians alike) do not want anyone telling them what is truth and what is not. People want to decide for themselves (i.e., elevate themselves to level of God); picking and choosing from the options according to their momentary desires. Some say, "What is true for you may not be true for me." And so they say, "We discover truth by deciding what it means to us." Fewer and fewer people today believe in objective truth. It's all "relative." So why can't we handle the truth?

Suppose two men were standing at the top of a very high building. One man says to the other, "I am going to jump."

The other man says, "You cannot jump; you will die in the process because of the law of gravity. It is a fact you will die if you jump."

So the man replies, "I do not believe the law of gravity is true. I do not think it will happen like you say. The law of gravity might be true for you, but it is not true for me."

Will such a belief change reality? Of course not. However, we accept the jumper's rationale every day in the spiritual dimensions of life. We do so every time we deny objective truth and think truth is only personal preference. We readily agree that physical laws remain true no matter what we may think about them. But sadly, we, as a whole, believe spiritual laws and moral laws are anything we want to make them.

What is at stake in that silly illustration? Authority. And it is why each of us must draw the battle line for what spiritual authority will dominate our lives. I implore you to trust the Bible and the God who gave it. At the center of the believability of Christianity is the question of the reliability and validity of the sacred text — our Scripture, the Bible. And sadly, it is doubt with regard to this sacred text that is being promulgated by many of those entrusted to teach our children — as our survey sadly shows.

Evidences of Truth: Historical and Prophetic Tests

At the same time I was meeting with my Muslim friend, I had been studying Paul's sermon from 1 Corinthians 15. When he asked if I had evidence for the truth, part of the answer to his question was in those verses.[3]

First, we talked about *historical* evidence for faith. In verse 3, Paul said, "For what I received I passed on to you as of first importance: that Christ died for our sins according to the Scriptures, that he was buried, that he was raised the third day according to the Scriptures" (NIV). And we talked about the historical reliability of the Bible. This is evidence that is important in seeking the truth of Christian faith.

As he came from an Islamic background, I understood that he already believed in a creator — in one god. So I didn't in essence have to deal with that issue at that time. The Koran, though, does not give a history as Genesis does. So he did not understand the origin of sin and death and his need for a Savior. I asked a question: Would you believe in Jesus if it was determined some or all of Scripture could not be considered to have actually happened in history? The fact is, if you put the Bible to the test any other document must be put to, through the academic discipline of historiography, you will find out the New Testament alone is one of the most, if not the most, historically reliable documents in human history.

Next, we talked about the *prophetic* evidence for the truthfulness of the Christian message. I asked him if the Koran had prophecy and his answer was no. The Bible however, in the Old Testament, foretold events that came true in the New Testament with phenomenal accuracy. I can remember telling him about the dozens of prophecies of Jesus that were made hundreds of years before they were fulfilled in His life.

We talked about Josh McDowell's book, *Evidence That Demands a Verdict*. The prophetic evidence presented in this book includes a mathematical calculation of the odds of prophecy coming true — overwhelming odds! As a scholar, my Muslim friend identified with the historic and prophetic evidence. We already had some "common ground," if you like. Thank God that many, many volumes of material are readily available to anyone who wishes to strengthen their faith by being able to explain the evidence and use the correct interpretation of that evidence (based on

God's Word) to give a gentle, reverent answer to others who are asking the question.

The final evidence I want to share with you is far more powerful than the first two combined, they actually pale in comparison. First Corinthians 15:10 reads, "But by the grace of God I am what I am, and His grace to me was not without effect" (NIV). *The dynamic evidence for the truth of the Christian message is the power of Christ to change and transform the human heart and experience, now and forever.*

But further, the Bible is true because only it satisfies the preconditions of intelligibility. Only the Bible has the basis for knowledge, logic, uniformity, morality, and so on. In other words, if the Bible is not true, nothing would make sense. Other worldviews, including Islam, must borrow from the Bible to make sense of reality. For example, why we wear clothes comes from Genesis 3; why does logic exist and why can we use it, because God is logical and we are made in the image of a logical God. (Logic, which is not material but abstract, has always been a problem for a naturalistic/materialistic world-view where only material things are said to exist.)

Evidences of Truth: The Personal Test

We need to know if the Bible is true. We need to know if it can be trusted. We need to determine if the Scripture should in fact be considered as any kind of authority for the issues of our lives. Does Scripture make claims or demands upon the human family with which we must contend?

The Bible has for all time been a source of contention for those inclined not to believe it and for those who gladly base their lives upon it. The most powerful thing about the Bible is that it is not neutral — in fact, there is no such position as a "neutral" one. One way or another, we must all contend with its claims. To not make a decision about whether or not it will serve as the authority for your life is, in fact, to decide against it.

There is no way out of this dilemma. And so you can see why its message can be so contentious for so many. Is there any other literature in human history that has caused such a situation? The Bible stands alone in its claim to be a written revelation of the sovereign God, its author. Its authority carries the weight of its author — authority and author share a common root word for an especially good reason when it comes to Scripture.

Now, when you consider the Scripture's claims upon your own life, you can do so in different ways. One, you can approach it like a scholar might. You can contend with the historicity of the document, or its several literary styles and genres. You may want to approach it in a more scientific way, trying to determine if the scientific evidence related to such physical events as the origin of life in the creation account or the events of the Flood are consistent with operational science. Today, doubts in regards to these accounts are where the slippery slide of unbelief has really begun for many.

But I suggest at some time in your life you explore it simply by reading it (starting at the beginning — Genesis) in its context and believing that the God who gave it has a message to give to His creation. It's a message that can be understood. It's not a secret; it does not take special talent. It is a message laser-focused for understanding to any human heart trying to comprehend it. You must realize this book was not given to the theologians and scholars in the first place. It was given to common folk who, I believe, were created with a place in their soul to seek the knowledge and apply the wisdom to life in this world and the one to come. Romans 1:20 states that an awareness of God comes from the evidence of creation. I also know that the Scripture itself teaches that "faith comes from hearing, and hearing by the word of Christ" (Rom. 10:17).

You can be sure the scholars and theologians who believe in the Bible as God's Word have clearly helped in our appreciation and understanding of this book. They have verified the historicity of the Bible many times over. In fact, it is not a stretch to say that the Bible is the most historically reliable book in human history. Sadly though, our survey confirms that many scholars today are dismantling belief in the Bible — and it is creating havoc in our churches and culture.

But the real power of the Bible is that those who read it find it to be the most plausible and authentic explanation of human existence. The Bible claims for itself a kind of spiritual power that many are looking for. If you want a glimpse of what is available for you in the Bible, consider the words of Psalm 19:7–9. This is the Scriptures' own testimony of itself. Here is what it says:

The law of the Lord is perfect, restoring the soul. It perfectly tells the truth about every subject included in the sacred text. It is truth that transforms our souls. Do you ever feel empty inside? Are you looking for more out of life? Do you ever wonder what is true in this life? The Bible is for you; it is God's perfect law of life and it will restore your soul.

The testimony of the Lord is sure, making wise the simple. Do you have all the answers you need for life or is there anything you would benefit from knowing? Do you need clarity of mind as you face the pressures and struggles of life? Do you need to face destructive patterns in your life? The Bible is "sure." That means you can believe it and trust it. You find wisdom for life in its pages. The accounts given there are the stories of all of life's questions and the answers given are your answers, too. The Bible is God's guarantee to you of wisdom enough to live a good life — and yet it is so much more.

The precepts of the Lord are right, rejoicing the heart. The Bible sets the right path for you and it is a path of joy. Do you need direction in your life? Are you confused or scared about the track you are currently on? Do you realize you will end up in the direction you are headed right now? Is it really the way you want to go? Have you seen the alternative route? Just because you don't see it yet does not mean it's not there. God delights in showing you the way to go. Jesus said in the Bible, "I am the way" (John 14:6). He is your direction and destination. He gives the direction for your journey in the Bible. It is the path of joy to follow Him.

The commandment of the Lord is pure, enlightening your eyes. Are you able to face the dark, calamitous days of life? Disease, devastation, and death — they are all part of the human experience. You cannot make believe they are not, and all of us must one day face the darkness of this life. In these times the Bible enlightens our eyes. This is so powerful because in the dark world we need light. In dark times, the Bible gives us vision we otherwise would not have. The vision God gives in His Word is the ability to see the tragic side of life through the eyes of God. Once your eyes are enlightened by Scripture you will see a picture of the glorious life God has for you that makes all the darkness go away forever.

The fear of the Lord is clean, enduring forever. The Scripture remains the only thing in our world untouched by the evil of sin. It is pure and clean, devoid of error. Its truth endures forever. The truth of God's Word is timeless and endures for all generations.

The judgments of the Lord are true; they are righteous altogether. God's Word says of itself it is true. We all want to know what is true in life. People do not follow what is fake or purposefully untrue. There is a desire in every human heart to be right and know what is true. All the evidence supports what the Bible itself claims: it is a trustworthy and true description of a sovereign God who created all that exists and who desires to walk with us in a personal relationship full of grace, joy, and forgiveness.

Decision Time

Every time we are confronted with propositional statements (statements that claim to be true) we have a decision we must make: is it true or not? And there is a follow-up: if it is true do I need to do anything about it (1 Thess. 5:21)?

In our relativistic, postmodern culture there is a paucity of those committed to any kind of objective truth. The postmodern mind says language is the only way we construct meaning and any reference to truth is forever hidden. And so we tell our stories and truth becomes what you can get others to agree to.

But above that wasteland of belief and meaninglessness stands a worldview that claims there is, in fact, objective truth with which to contend in this universe. This truth is that which corresponds to reality. It is truth that is non-contradicting, it does not violate laws of logic, it is absolute, it does not depend on time, place, or conditions. This truth is discovered, for it exists independently of our minds. We do not create it. It is inescapable. To deny its existence is to affirm we are bound by it. It is unchanging. It is the only standard upon which any other claim is measured.

This is the kind of truth we find in the sovereign God revealed in nature and in His Word, the Bible. This is the reality of the One who made these claims:

> I am the way, and the truth, and the life (John 14:6).

> No one comes to the Father but through Me. If you had known me, you would have known My Father (John 14:6–7).

> Jesus said to the people who believed in him, "You are truly my disciples if you remain faithful to my teachings. And you will know the truth, and the truth will set you free (John 8:31–32; NLT).

Answers in Genesis and Warner University seek to give glory and honor to God as Creator, and to affirm the truth of the biblical record of the real origin and history of the world and mankind. Part of this real history is the bad news that the rebellion of the first man, Adam, against God's command brought death, suffering, and separation from God into this world. We see the results all around us. All of Adam's descendants are sinful from conception (Ps. 51:5) and have themselves entered into this rebellion (sin). They therefore cannot live with a holy God, but are condemned to separation from God.

The Bible says that "all have sinned and fall short of the glory of God" (Rom. 3:23) and that all are therefore subject to "eternal destruction, away from the presence of the Lord and from the glory of His power" (2 Thess. 1:9). But the good news is that God has done something about it. "For God so loved the world, that He gave his only begotten Son, that whoever believes in Him should not perish, but have eternal life" (John 3:16). Jesus Christ the

Creator, though totally sinless, suffered on behalf of mankind, the penalty of mankind's sin, which is death and separation from God. He did this to satisfy the righteous demands of the holiness and justice of God, His Father.

Jesus was the perfect sacrifice; He died on a Cross, but on the third day He rose again, conquering death, so that all who truly believe in Him, repent of their sin and trust in Him (rather than their own merit) are able to come back to God and live for eternity with their Creator. Therefore, "He who believes in Him is not condemned; but he who does not believe is condemned already, because he has not believed in the name of the only begotten Son of God" (John 3:18; NKJV). What a wonderful Savior and what a wonderful salvation in Christ our Creator!

My friends, this type of thinking is not an option — it is essential both for our salvation, our survival, and for the integrity of our witness in the world. We need to be thinking about what our children are being taught in regard to such matters, and as our survey makes clear, as we consider the college we are entrusting their education to. If we as a Church, parents, and educators are going to have a credible response to the attacks that we have suffered from secular forces, we must understand how high the stakes are in this war, and then learn to think strategically and accurately about God's Word and the world that He created.

And, oh yes, you may be wondering what happened to my friend from Saudi Arabia. Our time together abruptly came to an end the day the first Gulf War started. I never saw him after that. I think he may have been called back home. But I will always remember him as the most intensely interested person in the Scripture I have ever known. And I will always consider it a privilege to have shared with him the Book that is the truth for life and hope for his salvation in Jesus Christ.

Endnotes

1. R.C. Sproul, *The Holiness of God* (Wheaton, IL: Tyndale Publishing, 1998), p. 116.
2. R.C. Sproul, general editor, *New Geneva Study Bible* (Nashville, TN: T. Nelson, 1995).
3. All evidence is God's (Ps. 24:1 and Col. 1:16). What really matters is the proper interpretation of that evidence.

Chapter 8

The High Stakes of Good Thinking:
The Age of the Earth

Greg Hall and Ken Ham

Love the Lord your God with all your heart and with all your soul and with all your strength and with all your mind (Luke 10:27; NIV).

Greg Hall

When the Psalmist declared, "I am fearfully and wonderfully made," it was never more true than as it relates to the functioning of the human mind. Our cognitive abilities are an endowment from our Creator. Over the course of a lifetime, these abilities are squandered or developed. In fact, the greatest change and development in your life comes from your personal attention to your ability to grow in your power to think and reason. The Apostle Paul put it like this in Romans 12:2:

> Do not be conformed to this world, but be transformed by the renewing of your mind.

Here again is the importance of worldview. It will be the framework for human thinking. Worldview is all about making decisions about what ideas you will think about, embrace, and apply to your life. Christian worldview is about discovering the ideas, thoughts, values, and perspectives of Jesus Christ. It is applying these concepts to our lives in such a way that Christ can be woven into the fabric of our lives.

If we are going to bear the marks of a Christian mind, it is time to engage with the person and work of Jesus Himself in ways yet unrealized. To "have the mind of Christ" is what the Scripture promises us. But you cannot know it from a distance. You do not see it from a long way off — you must get up close. And you certainly don't see it vicariously, through someone else's experiences. Stop blindly reading and listening to what others say about Christ. Go to Scripture, read, meditate, pray, and find out what He says to you. Others' experiences may bring clarity to understanding the mind of Christ, but it will never bring reality.

We might think we desire the mind of Christ, but every time we seek information, understanding, or wisdom from other sources or other teachers, we betray our so-called belief in the greatest teacher who ever lived. It is time to understand that the reason we have any inclination to have the mind of Christ or think Christianly in the first place is because Jesus is the smartest man who ever lived. His comprehension about every topic of interest in the human condition is impeccable. We should want to know what Jesus "thinks" about any topic first and foremost. The words attributed to Him in Scripture and about Him in Scripture present everything every person who ever lived needs to know to live a meaningful life in this world and in the world to come. It is time to "think Christianly."

To "think Christianly" is to consider ourselves as His students in every moment of time, in every circumstance of our lives. It is in moments like this that we have the potential to be transformed. The transformation comes as a result of being connected to the One whose thoughts are right about everything. This is the environment in which God wants us to function.

Thinking Christianly means we face the reality and amazing possibilities for life when we say it is God in whom, "we live and move and exist" (Acts 17:28). Jesus knew this connection to the Father. He knew it would be our very sustenance to keep our lives going. He knew it would be for us too — it is the design by which the Creator established how we exist. This kind of connectedness has the very power for living. It meets every need of the human being for meaningful existence. It means God is very much at work and available for help and support in every area of life, and it is impossible to miss Him when we first connect to Him in this way. In Him we live and move and have our being. What a way to live — with the Sovereign God of the universe interactively involved in our daily experience.

To think Christianly is to imitate how God Himself thinks. Jesus undoubtedly made this the focus of attention in His earthly life. Even at the most crucial point of Jesus' move toward the Cross, as He prayed in the Garden of

Gethsemane, He labored over the plan of redemption now reaching its crisis moments. He actually prayed that "this cup would pass," that this particular event of crucifixion could somehow be averted;[1] however, He ultimately sought the mind of God on the matter. Nevertheless, He said, "not My will, but Yours be done" (Luke 22:42). In Christ's humbled state (Phil. 2:8), He submitted to the mind of God the Father (see also John 14:28) in the most significant crisis in human history since the Fall of mankind.

The philosophies and ideologies of the world have seemed to eclipse the face of God; we should not be fooled along with the world — this is still His world, His creation, His life. To seek Him as the great mind behind the design of the universe and all living things is the most intelligent work we could ever do. That we seek any number of worldly resources for wisdom, and solutions to dilemmas of our lives is not only an indictment on our faith but our intellect, too.

To think Christianly is to have a relationship with Jesus that is not commonplace. You can't be a typical church member or believer and have Christ involved in your life the way He and the Father intended. It goes way beyond the experience of the "consumer Christianity" of today. Perhaps people don't interact with Him in the way defined by Scripture because:

1. They don't know Scripture — how could they, given the failure of the pulpit to teach God's Word from the beginning without doubt or compromise with the world's teaching, and produce life-changing doctrine.
2. They don't think He's available — how could He be available given the sorry state of our prayer ability?
3. They really don't think it's Jesus' place to do anything about their lives in a personal way or He just won't, it's not how it works today. Or it may be that today's believer suffers from all the above.

To think Christianly is to firmly believe there is not a question being asked in our culture, or any other culture, for which Jesus does not have the answer. Is your Jesus competent enough to do anything about the issues of your life? And does He have the interest to join with you in the struggles of your life? Does what He thinks matter to you or even cross your mind?

We should be thinking like Paul, who proclaimed in Colossians 2:3 that Jesus holds "all the treasures of wisdom and knowledge." But today we do not think Christianly because we do not consider Him competent in the intellectual or academic pursuits of our lives. And we do not have the mind of Christ because we neither desire it nor seek it. And we live like this to our peril.

To think Christianly is to have this steadfast preoccupation of the pursuit of the mind of Christ and His willingness and ability to be intimately involved in the thinking of His followers. It is also about the continued efforts we must make in our minds toward reformation. In our human brokenness and frailty, our minds need constant attention. There is always a need for reformation. This is why the Apostle wants us to be transformed, and knew the way to do it was by the renewal or reformation of our minds. Furthermore, when Jesus asks us to "repent," as His message clearly was, what else can it mean but to change and reform our thinking about the issues of life? We must learn to think differently about every area of life.

This takes a massive effort of humility. There is nothing more contrary to our human condition than to be responsible enough for our thinking to change it. This change does not come easily, but it is not impossible. The change does not come easily because at the center of our sinful humanity is *hubris* — pride. And it is pride that keeps us attempting to be in control of all aspects of our lives, especially our thinking.

The prideful mind does not respond well to the concept that there is an intellectual force that is greater than our self. The prideful mind cannot fathom that this Jesus is a master intellect whom we must turn to for reformation or reclamation. But this is the very essence of conversion, that in our thinking we understand the need to repent and follow the One who alone is the wisdom of all creation.

And here is precisely the place where thinking Christianly is at play in our culture and where the stakes could not be higher. Here is the place where Christians need to stand most firm. Here is the place where the battle of ideas and/or worldview needs to be won; otherwise, the rest of the discussion is fruitless.

The ultimate goal of thinking Christianly is to present God as Creator and Father of everything that He has made and build our entire worldview on the foundation of His written revelation. He is the maker and owner of everything that is made. Here is where humankind is made to realize we owe our very existence to something (someone) other than ourselves. Here is where *hubris* is put in its place. Here is the beginning of knowledge and wisdom. In the beginning God created the heavens and the earth . . . and that is the only foundation for clear thinking ever made available.

When we study Romans 1, we see the significance of God making Himself known in creation. "God's invisible qualities — his eternal power and divine nature — have been clearly seen, being understood from what has been made" (Rom. 1:20; NIV). In our secular, naturalistic culture, people have rejected what God has clearly presented to them. This is precisely why they want to fight and believe they can win the war at this battlefront — the origin of life. In the naturalistic scheme of things, it is impossible to conceive of anything transcendent or supernatural. The study of origins, of creation, is where they want to eliminate God once and for all.

But it will not happen. This is remarkably poor thinking on their part. Evidence for God as Creator abounds for the thinking person. The naturalistic way of thinking of the world is flawed and prejudiced by promotion of a vain philosophy not founded in Christ (Col. 2:8–9), and not based on good science. The truth of life is that the ultimate questions of life — where we come from and where we are going — have not changed since the beginning of time. We can, and should, seek the mind of Jesus on these matters. Jesus, our master teacher and Creator of the universe, has been the one and only to ever know every answer. And He's revealed what we need to know in His written Word to us.

Second only to surrendering to Jesus Christ as your Lord and Savior, I believe that thinking Christianly is the most important thing you will ever do. But please understand, this does not happen by default. As Romans 12 says, by default we are conformed to this world. Transformation comes through commitment to moment by moment intimacy with Jesus, a very practical relationship with His living Word, and a daily walk of obedience that allows the Holy Spirit to move in our lives so that we naturally live according to the truth as He lives through us.

In the next section, Ken will discuss a very important aspect of thinking Christianly, but before you read on, please stop right here and spend some time talking with Jesus. Ask Him to move in your life. Ask Him to be the Lord of your mind. Ask Him to set aside your pride so that you can willingly and joyfully submit to His compassionate authority, and be set free by the truth of His life and the words of the Bible. My friends, this is not a place where you need God's "help." This is something that only He can do (1 Cor. 12:3). Ask that He would begin the supernatural transformation that only comes through the renewing of our minds according to the truth and authority of the Scriptures.

Thinking Christianly about the Age of the Earth

Ken Ham

As Greg mentioned earlier, *the ultimate goal of thinking Christianly is to present God as Creator and Father of everything that He has made.* Certainly, that includes each and every one of us. He is our Creator, and He is our father. He is the provider of everything that we have. He is responsible for everything we are and He is the source of strength for everything that we are going to become.

The pressure to conform to the world is everywhere we turn. It's in the media, in books, in museums, and in zoos. And as we've seen, it's not only in public schools and secular universities, but even Christian colleges have given in to the pressure to conform to the naturalistic worldview. Many are engaging in "newspeak" in order to justify their compromise so they can stand on both sides of the issue. The problem is that this double-mindedness is neither necessary nor consistent with good thought. It is certainly not "thinking Christianly."

The professors and leaders in the education world are highly educated . . . but have they learned the skills of consistent, biblical thinking? When we look at how the presidents, vice presidents, and professors of Christian universities responded to several of the questions regarding the age of the earth in the survey, the answer is obvious.

Q14: Would you consider yourself a young-earth or old-earth Christian?

Old earth	49.0%
Young earth	42.3%
Neither	8.3%

Because this issue is so hotly debated, we are not surprised about this nearly even split in belief. What is revealing, however, is the inconsistency between this belief and the other things that they claim about their belief in Scripture.

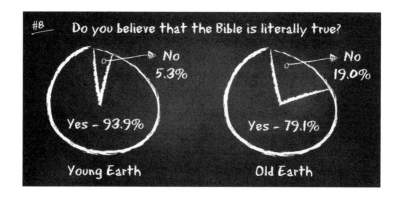

Of those who believe that the earth is young, 93.9 percent believe that the Bible is literally true; and the consistency in these two beliefs is clear. But notice that 79.1 percent of those who believe the earth is old also believe that the Bible is literally true. The word "literally true" apparently means nothing to them. Some may actually believe that the Bible literally teaches that the word "day," as used in Genesis 1, is a long period of time that allows for millions of years. But in order to allow for this interpretation, they must twist the established rules of biblical interpretation to the extreme *and* reinterpret massive numbers of Scriptures throughout the rest of the Bible such as Mark 10:6 and Exodus 20:11. This certainly isn't the intent of "thinking Christianly," and we must ask the question, "Why would they force such an interpretation when it is not the clear and simple reading from Scripture?" It's clear that something besides the truth of God's Word is influencing their thinking here. Obviously, it's the influence of the naturalistic worldview and probably the pressure from their peers who believe in an old earth who may also believe in evolution over millions of years.

Since the 1800s, we've had many scholars say, "We take the Bible as literally written; it says six days." But then they add the word "but." And this is where they begin to become conformed to this world, rather than being transformed by the renewing of their minds according to the truth of Scripture. It usually sounds like this: "Yes, the Bible says six days, *but* because 'science' has proven the earth to be billions and billions of years old, these must not be six literal days." (Remember, "science" has done no such thing. Evidence from operational science does not confirm an old earth. But that's not the main thing I'm trying to emphasize here.)

The point I'm making is that these people are ultimately reinterpreting Scripture through the lens of the secular, godless, naturalistic worldview. It is an *authority* issue. What they are really doing is taking outside ideas from the world and trying to force Scripture to fit with them. They are conforming to the world, rather than being transformed by the renewing of their minds according to the truth of God's Word. Of course, with God's Word as the source of truth, this doesn't work at all, and their explanations come across as weak and inconsistent.

Some will argue that this is really just a matter of different interpretations, similar to the debates that we have about end-times scenarios and eschatology. But I say, "Wait a minute. People who argue different views on eschatology by and large argue *from* Scripture. People who argue against Genesis argue because of secular influences (i.e., from a different religious viewpoint: that of secular humanism)." That is a big difference. Unquestionably, figurative language is used throughout Scripture to make analogies or metaphors (for example: God is our rock and our fortress) but in these passages the figure of speech is obvious. One still interprets it literally, for to do so is to consider the genre. Understanding the symbolic or figurative language enables one to literally interpret what is intended. In Genesis 1, there is no indication for any reason that the Hebrew word for "day" doesn't mean "day" in its ordinary (approximately 24-hour) meaning. Scripture makes this clear as the six days of creation are qualified by a number, evening and morning. This is a matter of authority, and it is a matter of truth — of correct interpretation. Even leading Hebrew lexicons do not leave open Genesis days as long ages:

> *Yom*: "Day of twenty-four hours: Genesis 1:5"[2]
> *Yom*: "Day as defined by evening and morning: Genesis 1:5"[3]

Seriously, those people who leave open long ages are either misinformed or they are consciously engaged in "newspeak." Observe the inconsistencies in the answers to the following questions:

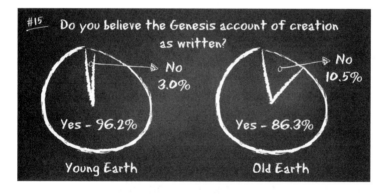

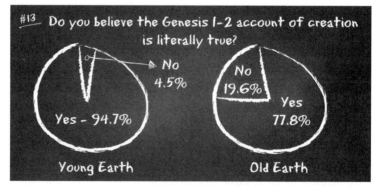

Again, the more specific the question, the more clear the inconsistencies become. We're not just asking if they believe the Bible is literally true in general, we specifically asked if they believe that the *Genesis 1–2 account of creation* is literally true. Of the people who believe in an old earth, 77.8 percent say yes! It's possible that some of these people believe in what is known as the "gap theory" (which teaches that God did create in six literal days, but that each of these days were preceded by millions of years), but I really doubt it. Very few people in the Christian world give much credence to this idea anymore.

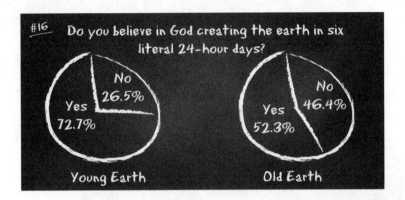

Do you see the inconsistency of belief? And a failure to "think Christianly"? Let's not even argue about who's right or who's wrong here. On both sides of the issue, people are talking out of both sides of their mouth. Of people who believe in an old earth, 77.8 percent say that they believe the Genesis 1–2 account of creation is literally true, yet only 52.3 percent of them believe in God creating the earth in six literal 24-hour days?

Clearly, more than 25 percent of them either don't understand that Genesis teaches six literal days, or they just never simply thought this through! More astoundingly, 52.3 percent of people who believe in an old earth believe that God created it in six literal 24-hour days! How can someone be an old earther and say they believe in a six-day creation (unless they do adhere to the gap theory)? I don't know. Believers in a young earth, however, also show inconsistencies: 26 percent of them do not believe that God created in six literal 24-hour days. So if somebody believes in a young earth, but does not believe in six 24-hour days, what do they believe?

Q17: Do you believe in God creating the earth but not in six 24-hour days?

	Young earth	Old earth
Yes	31.1%	59.5%
No	68.2%	37.9%

Again, we see great inconsistencies in these responses. Are there some "hybrids" of belief here that we can't categorize? Do these leaders and professors not understand the issues? Or are they talking out of both sides of their mouth? We saw earlier how Dr. William Dembski says he actually believes in six literal 24-hour days of creation, and yet he believes that the world is billions of years old. His explanation for this is outlandish — that Adam and Eve were made from human-like animals that God gave souls as well as amnesia regarding their former, pre-human existence. But we at least have to give him credit for trying and recognizing there is a problem! I'm concerned that the majority of these people are not only not thinking Christianly, but they're just not thinking at all! Clearly, what they say they believe is not consistent with what they say they also believe. This is again illuminated when we look at their views of Scripture:

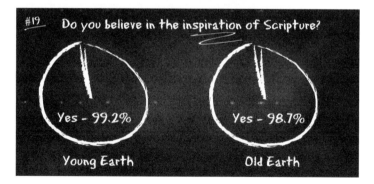

This is an interesting claim as well! Wouldn't you think that the young-earth group would have a higher view of Scripture when it comes to infallibility and inspiration than the old-earth group? Basically this is about even, with those believing in an old earth having just a slightly higher view of Scripture than those who believe in a young earth (backward from what we would expect). What can we conclude? There is no correlation between their purported view of Scripture and whether or not they believe in young or old earth at all.

What we appear to have is a basic biblical illiteracy among some of the leaders and professors of Christian colleges. Not only are their responses contradictory to the clear teachings of Scripture, but they are also inconsistent with themselves. This is far, far from "thinking Christianly." Perhaps this is because most of them have never been trained in it, and are therefore stuck in a quagmire of belief, where they claim to believe in Scripture but are really being influenced by the secular worldview. This confusion becomes clear in their responses to questions about the Flood:

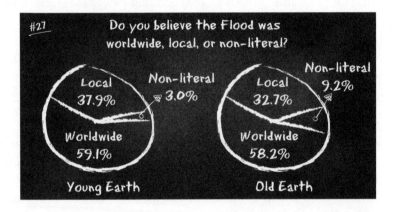

People who believe in an old earth are statistically more likely to believe that the Flood was not a real event at all, but other than that there's not much distinction between whether or not they believe the Flood was worldwide or local. It's intriguing to see that 58.2 percent of those who believe that the earth is old actually believe that the Flood was worldwide. At least they believe the Bible on this point — but it shows another inconsistency: if you believe in an old earth, you really shouldn't believe in a global Flood.

The idea that the earth is millions of years old, in our modern era, first arose in the early 19th century. The supposed evidence for millions of years was considered to be the fossil record, said by secularists to have been laid down gradually over millions of years. But if there had been a worldwide Flood, this would have destroyed this record and re-deposited it, thus destroying the supposed evidence for millions of years! There are so many problems one could consider. If you're going to believe in an old earth and believe in a global Flood, you must either do some amazing mental gymnastics to accommodate the conflicting ideas or allow for inconsistency in your thinking.

Those who believe in a young earth show similar inconsistencies. Of the people who believe in a young earth, 37.9 percent also believe that the Flood was local. That's inconsistent as well. How do they believe that the massive sedimentary strata containing billions of fossils formed if it neither happened during a worldwide Flood nor took place over millions of years? That stance doesn't even make sense. Their understanding of history in light of Scripture is not consistent. I have found that many academics in the Christian world do not have a big picture understanding in geology, biology, astronomy, theology, etc. — and they don't realize the massive inconsistencies and dilemmas they are living with.

Another problem is the issue of death — physical death. The Bible makes it clear that humans and animals were vegetarian before sin (Gen. 1:29–30). Also, the original creation was "very good" (no diseases like cancer, no thorns). Man wasn't told to eat animal flesh until after the Flood (Gen. 9).

However, in the fossil record, said to pre-date humans by millions of years, we find:

1. Thorns said to be millions of years old (but thorns came AFTER sin — after the Curse — Gen. 3:17–19)
2. Animals with evidence they were eating each other — bones in their stomachs/teeth marks on bones (but animals were vegetarian before man sinned)
3. Animal bones with evidence of diseases like cancer, brain tumors, arthritis, etc. (but everything was "very good" before sin)

There is great concern here that people are not thinking Christianly, even though they say they are. If you walked up to the president or vice president or a professor on a Christian campus, and asked them if they believe that the Bible is literally true, almost all of them will give you the same answer. When you ask them specific questions related to the truth of Scripture, however, we again find out that many of them don't believe that at all. So words really don't matter, and many of them have concocted convoluted explanations for their compromised beliefs. They have turned to the secular scientists to tell them about history while still trying to cling to parts of the Bible.

I believe that some of it is just ignorance in the context of Scripture and a consciously thought-out biblical worldview. But I have to be honest. I meet with a lot of these leaders and professors, and many times their attitudes are laced with an arrogance and a condescending attitude that looks down on other Christians in a voice that says, "Don't worry about it, you wouldn't understand anyway. Of course what we teach is true. You don't know what we mean by that, but we do — and that's all that matters." What we're seeing is 1 Corinthians 8:1–3 being lived out:

> We know that we all have knowledge. Knowledge makes arrogant, but love edifies. If anyone supposes that he knows anything, he has not yet known as he ought to know; but if anyone loves God, he is known by Him.

I am sometimes belittled and cut down by professors at "respected" Christian universities because I don't have the academic credentials that some of these people do. They think that because they have the credentials, they have the truth. They say, "How dare Ken Ham question us, because he is not trained in biblical languages; he didn't go to Bible college; he didn't go to seminary; etc." In some ways I'm glad that I don't have those credentials, because I might have ended up like some of them: compromising the truth clearly laid forth by Scripture in the midst of a bunch of academic mumble jumble created to accommodate secular scientific ideas.

Or worse than that, they might actually believe that since *they* teach it, that *makes* it true — that they are the ones who actually determine truth. You might as well not argue with men and women like that. Not only do they think that what they teach is right, but they feel like they *are* right because of their position of authority and their level of education. Once again, it's a matter of authority. Do these people submit to the authority of the Word of God? Or have they submitted themselves to the authority of fallen men, and their own personal knowledge of what they think is truth? Certainly, they have become like the Chaldeans that the minor prophet Habakkuk spoke of in Habakkuk 1:7:

> They are dreaded and feared; their justice and authority originate with themselves.

Unquestionably, we have been "fearfully and wonderfully made." God has given us a mind, and our lives can be transformed by the renewing of that mind. Will we be conformed to the world? Or will the transforming power of God's living word become our final authority?

May God, by His infinite grace and mercy, give us the willingness to bend the knee to the authority of His Word. By the power of His Spirit may we be empowered and willing to "think Christianly" in every aspect of our lives, that we may be willing to receive His love and His forgiveness for our own arrogance and our own personal compromise, so that we can speak the truth in love through our words and through our lives in the midst of this world that so desperately, desperately needs to see Christ in us and being lived through us.

Endnotes

1. And rightly so, for God was about to punish the sinless Christ for the sins of the world. The anguish of this was being torn between punishing Christ who did not deserve it to save mankind, or not doing it that would result in no salvation.
2. Ludwig Koehler and Walter Baumgartner, *Hebrew and Aramaic Lexicon of the Old Testament,* Volume 1 (Leidin; Boston, MA: Brill, 2001), p. 399.
3. Francis Brown, S.R. Driver, and Charles A. Briggs, *Hebrew and English Lexicon of the Old Testament,* 9th printing (Peabody, MA: Hendrickson Publishers, 1906), p. 398.

Want to know which colleges were contacted as part of the ARG study? Visit www.creationcolleges.org and also find a growing list of Christian colleges we recommend you search out.

Chapter 9

Decisions, Decisions, Decisions:
Choosing the University That's Right for You

Greg Hall

I am afraid that schools will prove to be the great gates of Hell unless they diligently labor in explaining the Holy Scriptures, engraving them in the hearts of youth. I advise no one to place his child where the Scriptures do not reign paramount. Every institution in which men are not increasingly occupied with the Word of God must become corrupt. — Martin Luther

I was on my way to speak at a church in the Midwest. One of the alumni of our university picked me up at the airport. Accompanying him was a sharp young man from his youth group who was thinking about enrolling in our school. So we talked about the usual: majors, campus life, financial aid, job prospects, etc. Then the young man asked me a question that I had not been asked before, or since, in my 20 years serving as a university president. He asked, "So, if I come to your school, will my faith be built or broken?"

I asked him what he meant by that question, but I already knew exactly what he meant. He clarified the question in exactly the way I thought he would. He told me a number of the young men and women from his youth group had gone to "Christian" colleges. He said he noticed something about several of them that bothered him. In his words, "They were once 'on fire' for God" but having gone to these schools it appeared their faith had been broken. Some of them seemed no longer Christian at all. They did not go to church, or if they did it no longer seemed to occupy the place of importance in their lives it once did. And so, he asked the question again, "If I come to your school, will my faith be built or broken? Will I end up like some of them?"

The young man's question surprised me, but his reason for asking it did not. His question surprised me because for a high school junior it is very astute. He knew his observations of the lives of some who have attended Christian schools were real. At a place where it seemed obvious that Christian faith should be developed, grow, and thrive, for some, it had done just the opposite.

The reason the question didn't surprise me is because I have heard similar stories over and over again. In all honesty, it is not reasonable to criticize the way secular education has tried to eclipse the face of God. But we should be evaluating the experience of some who attend Christian schools whose faith was diminished or even destroyed as a result.

Perhaps you have heard some of the rationalizations. Some say the teaching is misunderstood by these students. It is claimed, "We are simply asking the tough questions, helping students struggle with faith in real and meaningful ways." Sometimes it is claimed these students have been too sheltered and need to be exposed to the deeper questions of life. I have heard some say, "We may break down faith but it is only so we can build it back in a sophisticated and intellectual way."

All this rationalization may have elements of truth, but by and large it is less than compelling. The fact is there are those who teach in Christian schools whose faith is not worth emulating. They teach what they themselves have been taught — much of it at the hands of liberal professors from secular institutions or seminaries well known for naturalism and faithlessness.

A recent press release on the ongoing *National Study of College Students' Search for Meaning and Purpose* offered some interesting information on students who are beginning their college years. While 79 percent of all freshmen believe in God, 69 percent pray, and 81 percent attend religious services at least occasionally, 57 percent question their religious beliefs, 52 percent disagree with their parents about religious matters, and 65 percent feel distant from God. College students are asking deep questions about their faith.

Unquestionably, the college years are a very critical time of life. Older adults look back at those years and can clearly recall how the course of their life was shaped by their time on campus. Parents and students who are looking ahead to college should be humbled by the magnitude of the decision and the implications that it will have on the rest of their life. This is not a time to make a blind decision. We must choose wisely and go in with our eyes wide open, aware of the educational environment that has been chosen. What do we feel are the most important criteria? Dr. R.C. Sproul nailed the issue on the head when he wrote:

> One of the problems we have here is the criteria we use when choosing colleges or university to attend in the first place. So often parents are impressed by the beauty of the campus of the particular institution or by their own remembrance of the commitment of the institution a generation ago, overlooking the reality that the approach to Christianity changes in various institutions as the faculty changes. The most significant barometer for choosing any kind of institution of higher learning is not the beauty of its campus. It is its faculty.[1]

Yes, the type of education you choose is ultimately dependent on who is in front of the classroom teaching your student. When you boil down all the options, first of all you'll have to decide between three general forms:

1. You can choose a secular institution.
2. You can choose a compromising Christian institution.
3. You can do your best to find an institution that is thoroughly committed to the authority of Scripture — understanding that none are perfect! As someone once said, if you find the perfect church, don't join it or you will destroy it!

A Secular Institution

To gain some insight into the decision, we asked the presidents, vice presidents, and professors of Christian universities what *they* thought Christian parents used as criteria when deciding to send their children to secular schools.

#10   **Why do you think Christian parents send children to secular institutions?**

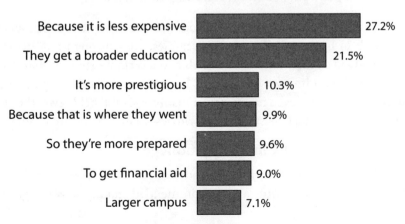

Because it is less expensive	27.2%
They get a broader education	21.5%
It's more prestigious	10.3%
Because that is where they went	9.9%
So they're more prepared	9.6%
To get financial aid	9.0%
Larger campus	7.1%

When we add up some of these categories, it's revealed that the staff of Christian colleges believes that at least 36.5 percent of Christian parents are sending their kids to a secular university for financial reasons. In my opinion, that number is too low. The vast majority of the Christian parents I talk to confess that financial concerns rule out the "possibility" of sending their children to a private Christian institution. They're making decisions because of money, sending kids to a non-private school, leaving them to navigate their way through the debauchery. Along with financial considerations, most parents offer other justifications for this decision:

- Kids need to learn to be in the world. They know that they're going into enemy territory, but we have raised them well. They are young adults now. We believe that they are solid in their faith, able to defend the truth, and will be able to survive.

- As young adults, it is time for them to be in the world, but not of it. Sooner or later they are going to have to learn to navigate through the world on their own. Now is that time.

- There needs to be Christian witness on the campus. Our child is going into this setting as a student and missionary. They are the light of the world. We don't want to put that light under a bushel. It's time to let that light shine to the benefit of those on campus who need to hear and see the truth about Jesus Christ.

- In other cases though, the parents simply do not realize the gravity of the situation. Many years ago, even most secular institutions were still rather Christian in their beliefs. So grandparents and parents may not know what the secular institutions are like in today's culture (even 50 years ago, public high schools still had prayer!).

To be fair, both Ken and I are living proof that surviving secular schools is possible. Both of us attended secular universities, grew through that experience, and, by God's grace, were used as lights to a certain extent in that dark world. However, we admit we had lots of "baggage" to discard along the way — and we grew up when even many secular institutions still held (even though inconsistently) more of a Christianized worldview to one degree or another.

Community College

One prominent Christian financial advisor not only recommends less expensive state schools, but also recommended taking advantage of community colleges near home. There are several advantages to this option. First of all, community colleges create a sort of "buffer zone" where students experience the realities of the secular world while still living at home. It can be something of a transition period, where a student gets their general studies done at a fraction of the price while still being under the guidance, protection, and watchful eye of their parents. Then, after a year or two, they transfer to a different institution that specializes in their area of interest. As finances become more and more of an issue, several families are going this direction.

But let there be no doubt, if you choose the option of a secular public school, know that students are systematically bombarded with the messages of the philosophy of naturalism — the philosophy that is the driving force behind the dominant worldview of public education. The entire premise that your education is being built on is contrary to the truths of Scripture:

- Naturalism assumes that the world you are in today is the only reality — there is nothing beyond this life.

- Naturalism assumes that the origin of life is due to random forces of nature — there is no Creator, no God.

- Naturalism teaches that ethics is a human-based concept — there is no objective truth or reality, only subjective feelings, each with as much merit as the other. All ideas are equally valid and we must be tolerant of all ideas (with the exception of Christianity it seems).

If you choose the secular option, you must go in prepared and with your eyes wide open. You must take with you the weapons you need to defend your faith and take a stand for the authority of Scripture. This can be a faith-building experience — and clearly, there is a need for this type of witness on any campus. But in order to survive, you have to realize that you are going as a defender and a proclaimer, not as a learner and a student. You really have to go in prepared for battle, because the academic atmosphere on a secular university is enemy territory in the battle for your soul and these professors often affect grades if you hold to biblical position (and they are aware of it), especially in science fields like biology and geology. We suggest there are some students more able to cope in a situation than others — and the parents need to be discerning in regard to this matter and understanding where their own children are spiritually.

A March 29, 2005, *Washington Post* article by Howard Kurtz, titled "Study Finds College Faculties a Most Liberal Lot," reports that most faculty at non-Christian colleges disdain Christianity, with 72 percent indicating they are liberal, 84 percent favoring abortion, and 67 percent indicating homosexuality is acceptable. In most cases, students reflect the values of college faculty they encounter in their upper-division coursework. These faculty members are typically the advisors and mentors of students. Certainly the above findings indicate that the answers and directions students receive from most faculty members at these institutions will not be supportive of traditional morality and religious values.

I did my undergraduate degree in philosophy at the State University of New York. I had planned to go to a Christian college to study for the ministry, but for a variety of reasons that did not happen. I know I got a good education as it relates to math, English, social science, etc., at the university — the kind of education that is supposed to prepare you for a life of gainful employment. But there was absolutely *no* evidence of anything Christian or spiritual on that campus. I do not even remember there being any kind of Christian ministry on campus. In classes it was not unusual to hear Christianity mocked.

I stayed spiritually strong during those days because I was very well connected to my home church where my father was the pastor. This is a big key for students who go to secular schools. You must stay connected to a Bible-believing fellowship and, if available, be connected to a Bible-believing campus ministry. This strategy has protected many a student who otherwise would not have withstood the pagan culture of a secular campus.

I had a very negative, fearful experience on that campus when I was a senior preparing to graduate. One day in class, one of my philosophy professors asked me what I was going to do upon graduation. He said he was hopeful I would continue in philosophy and go to graduate school. I told him I was planning to go to seminary and train to become a minister. His reaction is etched in my memory. He was incredulous: "You're going to do *what*?" he said. "You are going to seminary and become a minister?" The ridicule in his voice I still recall. Then he said, "I will do anything I have to do to stop you from such foolishness!"

And what followed was the scariest thought I have ever had. I can remember thinking, *Maybe he is right, maybe seminary and ministry is foolishness and my future should be in philosophy. Maybe I should become like my professor. . . .*

The thoughts did not stick, but in that moment I certainly entertained the possibility — thoughts that would have set my life on a course where I might very well have missed God's calling for me. That story is quite mild compared to many others who have lost their way in the pagan culture of secular education. Some of the most destructive, ungodly, unholy ideas known to mankind have come out of the secular institutions of our nation. That is why I say the secular classroom has the potential of being one of the most dangerous places for Christians in America.

It was tough on a secular campus back then, but I believe it is far more intense today than when I was an undergraduate. And that's just the ideology. There is also the issue of morality. I know what goes on at a lot of secular schools. To be honest, I wouldn't be the least bit comfortable sending my kids into that environment. The reality is that many young persons, once committed Christian young men and women, have gone to secular schools where an anti-Christian, atheistic philosophy has devastated their lives.

At the same time, there are so many exceptions that we can't draw an absolute black-and-white line. I've seen plenty of students flourish spiritually on a secular campus. We've seen many who lose their faith while attending conservative Christian universities. Can we say that this is the one factor that makes a difference in a student's life? We cannot. There is no formula that will guarantee the spiritual safety of the student, but still, the decision must be approached with prayerful wisdom. And a lot of it does come down to how they were trained in the home by their parents.

A Christian College

The vast majority of American young people go through the public schools. Even the vast majority of young people from Christian families also go to public grade schools, high schools, and public institutions of higher education. Only a minority go to private Christian schools and on to Christian institutions of higher learning. In my church, I would estimate that no more than 10 percent of college-bound young men and women go to our church-related institutions. There are undoubtedly more who go to other Christian colleges or universities, but the fact is the numbers are low. When we asked the presidents, vice presidents, and professors of Christian institutions why they felt parents chose a Christian institution, their answers were revealing:

#9 **Why do you think Christian parents send children to Christian institutions?**

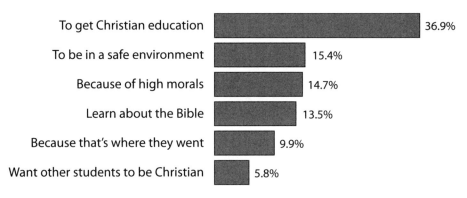

To get Christian education	36.9%
To be in a safe environment	15.4%
Because of high morals	14.7%
Learn about the Bible	13.5%
Because that's where they went	9.9%
Want other students to be Christian	5.8%

There were other answers, but these accounted for 96.2 percent of all responses. The administration and faculty feel that a safe campus and high morals account for 30 percent of the decisions. We believe that most parents would agree with this, and we also believe that these are very important factors! All you have to do is check out a tailgate party at any college football game and you will understand what we are talking about — tens of thousands of students doing the most unbelievable stuff. There's a reason that parents want a safe campus and high morals for their student. College campuses are notorious for drug use, sexual promiscuity, and alcoholism. Hey, Ken and I saw it firsthand while we were studying at secular colleges. Many other parents have been there as well, and have little desire to see their children submerged in that environment.

For those who feel the college years are still a time of preparation before going out into the "real world," the option of Christian education looks very good indeed. It looks more advantageous, safer, and more morally nurturing. In some cases, that's true. But as we've seen, in far too many cases it's not.

A Compromised Christian College

Both Ken and I feel that perhaps the worst option for a student is going blindly into a so-called "Christian" college that is compromising the authority of the Word of God. As the research has shown, this is far too prevalent. There's a massive amount of confusion across the board. It needs to be called out. We need to deal with it. There *are* good Christian schools out there and we feel they are better than the secular alternatives by far. But these issues of compromise have to be addressed.

Parents are sending their students into the schools assuming that they are going to be faith-nurturing and truth-affirming institutions. In reality, many of them discredit faith, discredit the Bible, and break kids down rather than build them up. That's why both of us are strong advocates for home-schooling, Christian schools, and carefully selected Christian higher education, because kids are dying out there and the Church doesn't seem to care enough to do anything about it. When it comes to colleges and universities, the problem is that the majority of Christian schools seem to be just like the secular — disguised with a few Christian elements.

I have had many parents say to me that they would rather send their kid to a secular school, knowing how blatantly pagan it is, than send them into a Christian school where they are told that they believe in the Bible and its authority, when in fact they really don't. It seems that Christian schools naturally progress from focused conservative faith into compromised secular ideologies.[2] If we learn nothing else from the Ivy League, it should be this: if the salt is contaminated, it's no longer good for anything. If the schools are already compromised, what good are they? Many well-known Christian schools are becoming conformed to the world, rather than to Christ. Jesus says that He would rather we be hot or cold rather than lukewarm. But lukewarmness seems to be the natural trend. Who is the worst enemy? Certainly, the enemy is the world. But doesn't the enemy also include the compromising leaders who lead people astray?

In Jesus' day, He didn't call out the world and the Romans. Jesus called out the Pharisees and the scribes who were hiding behind their religiosity. It was the religious leaders that He called the snakes and the vipers. We should not be surprised at the attacks we get from the world. We should call out those who claim the name "Christian" and yet subtly compromise the authority of Scripture in so many different ways.

Why was Stephen killed? It was because he confronted the religious leaders, calling them stiff necked and pointing out their false teaching. Ken is sometimes rebuked by Christians who don't like the way that he calls out compromising Christian leaders. They say that the real enemy is the world, and we shouldn't be attacking our own brothers and sisters in Christ. But I don't think so. I think the real enemy is the compromise within the Church, and, as we have seen too clearly, in the Christian colleges and universities that are already compromised. We should not be surprised at how the world acts — but we should be appalled at God's people when they compromise God's Word. And for those who are teachers influencing the coming generations — the Scripture has a warning: "Let not many of you become teachers, my brethren, knowing that as such we will incur a stricter judgment" (James 3:1).

So how do we help you decide where to go? I don't want my kids going to a secular institution. But I'd rather have them go to a state institution than send them to the wolves who are dressed in sheep's clothing. Thankfully, there is a third option.

A Committed Christian College

My kids attended the Christian college where I serve. It was a decision of their own choosing. Sure, I gave advice and direction — including telling them my experience in going to a secular undergraduate school. While they could have gone anywhere, they chose a Christian college. I sometimes ask them about their experience at a Christian college and ask what sticks out in their minds as being the most important outcomes of that choice. The answers always center on the same three things:

1. First, they talk about their wonderful friends that they met during college days — friends that they cherish and still are very close to this day, Christian friends.

2. They also talk about the faculty that made a difference in their lives. They will talk about their mentoring, about their kindness, even recalling lectures that meant something to them.

3. Then, they always talk about the importance of the chapel worship services. They describe these as the most important thing about going to a Christian school.

On top of that, they often recall the importance of serving others and being part of a local church. They see the value of finding a Christian mate who shares similar values and similar desires to raise a Christian family. When I added it all up, I realized that this Christian education has helped them to write a biblical Christian worldview with the alphabet of their souls. And I rejoice.

Ken didn't send any of his kids to secular schools, nor did he send them to compromising schools. He and his wife Mally sent them to a couple of the best conservative schools that they could find. Are they perfect? No. On several occasions Ken had to intervene and square off with professors and administrators who were compromising the Word of God. But at least the schools had a clear commitment to the authority of Scripture, rather than a subtle or blatant denial of absolute biblical truth.

So if you want to see what we really recommend, I guess you don't have to look any further than what we did with our children. What we are really saying is that your kids probably shouldn't go to a secular college. Send them to a Christian college, but be very discerning, because there are only a few that are on track in all areas — and even then you have to be careful as they all have "warts."

If your intent is to send your child into a spiritually nurturing environment you must ask the question, "What is the best opportunity for my kid to go and hear the proclamation of true Scripture?" But to get the right answers to that question, you have to ask a lot of other questions.

Asking Questions

Certainly, one of the biggest lessons we learned from this survey is that people don't always say what they mean, and many times even what they mean is in conflict with what they actually believe. So how do you find out what an institution actually believes and teaches? How do you find out what each individual professor believes and teaches? You can look at the official brochures, or you can even ask the president, but does that guarantee that's what the institution and professors believe and teach? Sometimes, but certainly not always.

The survey showed that some presidents seem to be disconnected with what is really happening on campus. Not only that, but we've seen that there is confusion between the departments as well. At the same school, there may be great disagreement on important issues between the religion and the science departments. And within those departments, there can be professors who teach whatever they want without consequence. Even if the school has pinpointed a particular faculty member who is compromising the Word of God, it's very difficult to remove them, particularly if they have tenure. Unfortunately, very few schools have clear doctrinal statements, and even those that do often don't have consequences for those who teach things contrary to the Bible. So it's clear that if you want to find out what a school is really all about, you not only have to ask questions, but you have to know the *right* questions to ask.

Asking the Right Questions

The naturalistic worldview has gained a very powerful foothold on many Christian campuses. This worldview can make it very difficult to get clear answers. Sure, the answers might sound clear at first, but often the answers are coming from a relativistic view of truth that says, "What's true for you may not be true for me." And as we've seen, "newspeak" allows people to say contradictory things as if both are true. People also define words differently, so key concepts might mean something totally different to someone else. So not only do you have to ask questions, but you have to ask the right questions. How do you do this?

First, we would suggest starting with the same kinds of questions that we asked in this survey. These questions are important because they are the questions the average person in the Church is asking Christian colleges to answer. When we were designing this survey, we asked the questions carefully and from several different angles so that we could compare the results. You'll need to do the same thing. They are not the typical "academic" questions. They are the simple, down-to-earth questions that the people ask, and those who ask them have every right to a clear simple answer. They are not "trick" questions. These are the questions the Church wants answers to.

Second, we would suggest asking questions that are both hypothetical and actual. For example, question 12 asks if there are consequences for anti-biblical teaching. The answers you get to this may be vague. You can help clarify that by asking questions like these:

- If someone on your faculty began to teach that literal truths from Scripture were actually figurative, how would their department head respond?

- Do you know of anyone who has recently been disciplined for teaching something contrary to the Bible? Can you tell me more about that?

Figuring out what people mean by what they say is also a challenge. People use words that we are familiar with even though they may mean something different to them. When you are sorting through their catalogs and sitting down to talk to someone, you'll need to ask them what they mean when they say something like "We believe in a literal interpretation of Genesis." But then you'll need to double-check these answers with specific questions that reveal what they really believe, such as, "How much time do you teach it took God to create the world and everything in it?" or "Were Adam and Eve real people that God specially created?" or "Do you teach that the Flood described in Genesis covered the entire surface of the globe?" Hopefully this way you will be able to learn what people really mean when they say things like "infallible" or "worldwide."

Without being deceptive, you might also want to ask questions that play to the liberal mindset, and see if the leaders or professors are willing to take a stand for the truth. For example, you might ask something like this: "If a student presented a speech in class where she professed her sincere belief in evolution and why she thinks it's true, how would you respond?" Or something like this: "If one of your students was struggling with his sexual identity and was truly contemplating whether or not God had created them for same-sex relationships, how would you counsel them?"

From our own experience we have found conservative Christian colleges that have certain professors that teach a compromising message — yet other faculty are either unaware of it or they turn a blind eye to it. Sometimes the administration will say that because of tenure, they can't do anything about a certain professor who is obviously teaching material that undermines the authority of Scripture. And sometimes a conservative Christian college will employ someone who doesn't strictly adhere to the statement of faith — but they are supposedly "okay" in a certain area of expertise the college needs. More and more such professors are employed — and the slippery slide is underway.

You're going to have a challenge finding out from a few individuals what is actually taught across the whole campus. Remember that the survey discovered wide discrepancies between individuals, departments, and positions. So whom do you ask?

Asking the Right Questions of the Right People

You're going to want to talk to as many people in as many different positions as possible. At larger schools it's going to take effort just to get past the admissions department and the students who give you a campus tour. But be persistent. Try to meet with the president or the dean of students. Find out the office hours of professors in various departments and drop in to meet them. The more that parents begin to do this, the more these people will realize they are being held accountable. Eventually, this will cause many colleges to think about these issues — particularly if parents stop supporting them and stop sending their children to them.

Some of the best people to ask are going to be former students or the parents of those students. Experience is a good teacher, and what other people have experienced at a college you're considering can teach you a lot about what things are really like there. Former students will generally be able to tell you the good and the bad about what's really happening on campus and in the classroom. Ken said that he has been on Christian campuses and spent time at lunch with some of the students. He then asks them what they are taught in certain areas — he has been quite shocked at what he heard from students at what he thought were really conservative colleges. This is another way to find out what is being taught — spend time with those who know what their professors are teaching them. These students also hear from their friends about other professors.

At the center of the whole issue is what the teacher teaches, particularly about the Word of God, the Bible. Because of that, we think it's worth it to investigate the educational background of the faculty. Smaller universities should have a complete list of their staff available that lists their experience and educational background. At larger schools, you might have to go to the specific departments to find this information. Oftentimes this is all posted online, and with a few clicks of the mouse you can get a good feel for where the professors were trained. Sometimes it is very tough to stay faithful to a high view of Scripture as God's Word to us when you are part of the secular academy. Many have done so, but it takes strength and discernment to remain faithful. While educational background alone does not determine what someone's worldview actually is, knowing this information will give you a feel for the worldview under which the faculty were formally trained.

Making the Best Choice for Your Family

Unfortunately, choosing a college or university is no longer a clear, black-and-white decision. If we have accomplished nothing else in this book, I pray that we have brought to light important variables that you may have never even considered when selecting a school for yourself or your children. The variables are many, and at the end of your search there will still be a certain number of unknowns. We do believe that by being aware of the issues and asking the right questions of the right people, you can make a much more informed decision than you would have by blindly choosing a college based on more superficial criteria . . . and then naïvely walking into that situation unaware of adversaries that await you. In the next chapter Ken and I are going to share from our hearts a final challenge to students. We believe that by being aware and informed, and by prayerfully trusting in the Lord for wisdom as well as financial provision, you will now be able to make the best choice possible.

Endnotes
1. R.C. Sproul, "Be Prepared," *Tabletalk Magazine* (November 1, 2010).
2. Bodie Hodge, "Harvard, Yale, Princeton, Oxford — Once Christian?" *Answers* magazine, volume 2, number 3 (July–September, 2007).

Chapter 10

For Students Only:
Keys for Surviving and Thriving in College

Ken Ham and Greg Hall

Blessed is the man who finds wisdom, the man who gains understanding, for she is more profitable than silver and yields better returns than gold (Prov. 3:13–15; NIV).

As we wrap up our discussion and analysis of the survey that we did of 200 different Christian colleges, as we put the final comments on our analysis of higher education today, both of us, Ken and Greg, want to share our hearts with you, the students and future leaders of the Church in the world.

In this book we have dissected a lot of numbers, pointed a lot of fingers, and come to some pretty scary conclusions about what's happening on campuses today. But truly, this book isn't about college presidents and professors; this book is really all about you, the college student.

Whether you're headed to college in the next couple of years or are currently enrolled, we want you to know that the reason we have taken up this issue at all is because we believe that you are worth it. Your hearts and minds are worth defending. But in all honesty, we can only do that to a certain extent, and now, even your parents will be limited in their ability and availability for keeping watch over your souls. During the college years, the responsibility for your spiritual well-being rests increasingly with you, not with anyone else.

The college years are tremendously exciting. It's really hard to overestimate the impact that they will have on the rest of your life. During college you are likely to solidify your core beliefs and worldview. It's possible that you will meet and choose a lifelong spouse. And although God will direct you throughout the course of your whole life, it's quite likely that during college you'll also discover your purpose and mission — God's obvious leading in your life for your future. And on top of that, you're probably going to have a blast doing it!

At the same time, as parents and leaders, we need to confess that we are leaving you with a world and a Church that has been seriously compromised. A frightening percentage of your peers are leaving their traditional church. Many are leaving their faith. Many will walk away from Christian devotion no matter what kind of school they go to. The truth is this: you are walking into a spiritual battle. It may not seem like it, but it's true. Satan is strategically using subtle compromise as one of his most powerful weapons to degrade the authority of Scripture and undermine the faith of the next generation.

In other parts of the world, the battle is much more graphic. In China, for example, claiming to be Christian is a life or death decision. The book *The Heavenly Man: The Remarkable True Story of Chinese Christian Brother Yun* shares the remarkable story of Christians in China who have developed home churches and in their devotion and commitment to Christ have watched the power of God explode and thousands become Christian.[1] He and his fellow believers have suffered greatly but remained enthusiastic and faithful in spite of it. They are part of a movement called "Back to Jerusalem." It is a missionary movement, and they are winning thousands to Christ as they retrace the Silk Road from China back to Jerusalem, sharing the gospel as they go. As he says in his book, they are an army of brokenhearted Chinese men and women who have already been through years of hardship and deprivation for the sake of the gospel. In worldly terms, they have nothing and appear unimpressive. But in the spiritual realm they are mighty warriors for Jesus Christ.

They have also started a college where they receive training in the following subjects:

- How to suffer and die for the Lord. We examine what the Bible says about suffering and look at how the Lord's people have laid down their lives throughout history for the advance of the gospel.

- How to witness for the Lord. We teach how to witness under any circumstances . . . on the bus or trains, in the back of a police van or on our way to be executed.

- How to escape for the Lord. Sometimes we need to be in prison to witness and sometimes we know the devil sends us to prison to try to stop our message and it becomes our job to set ourselves free.

This is not exactly the curriculum of a normal or average college or seminary! But then again, there is nothing average or normal about pursuing a life of devotion to God at this level. The point is this: God is calling from our midst a group of students who in days ahead will pursue such a life of uncommon commitment and it will only be by wisdom that the Lord will allow any of us into such a life of significance.

The way we see our Western culture moving away from a Christian perspective before our very eyes (and we believe increasing compromise in churches, colleges, etc., has contributed greatly to this), we may even be in for a time of persecution in countries where there has been much freedom in regard to the proclamation of the gospel. Maybe such persecution will cleanse and strengthen the Church?

No matter where you go to school, we want to finish up this book by sharing with you a handful of principles that we firmly believe will help you to not only survive your college experience, but thrive through it all and maximize this opportunity for all it's worth, that you might become some of those who share such an "uncommon commitment" and experience "such a life of significance."

1. Treasure Christ above all things

If you're going into a Christian college, it's important that you are aware of one of the responses that we *didn't* get to, Q2: "What does it mean to be a Christian institution?" This was an open-ended question; the presidents, vice presidents, and professors said whatever came to their minds first, so this list reflects their priorities:

The Bible guides us:	36.9%
We teach the Bible as literally true:	27.6%
We require Christian behavior:	16.0%
We don't allow secular teaching:	10.6%

Think about this for a minute — 91 percent of the answers were about the Bible and behavior and the teaching — and we are all for that. These are all good answers, but what's missing? Jesus. Hardly anybody mentioned Christ or even the gospel! It seems obvious to us that the most important thing that should distinguish a Christian institution is Jesus Christ Himself — that a college or university that claims the name of Christ should prioritize, above all things, Him and what He has done.

This is just to say that even though you may be going to a Christian college, it's really still just an institution with a Christian name attached. It will be up to you and you alone to prioritize Jesus Christ in your life and in your education and in your future ministry. No one else can do that for you. In order to survive and thrive through the college years, the first and most important thing that we can encourage you to do is to have the same attitude that the Apostle Paul showed in Philippians 3:8–9:

> I count all things to be loss in view of the surpassing value of knowing Christ Jesus my Lord, for whom I have suffered the loss of all things, and count them but rubbish so that I may gain Christ, and may be found in Him, not having a righteousness of my own derived from the Law, but that which is through faith in Christ.

No one can lead you into this level of intimacy with God. The hand-holding is over. It's your choice now. When you make Christ the priority, understanding He *is* the Word, you will then make sure you take His Word as it should be taken — as the revealed Word of the Creator God, who knows everything (Col. 2:3), who never tells a lie (Heb. 6:18), and who has always been there (Rev. 22:13). This will help you to not take the words of fallible man and reinterpret the clear teaching of the Word of God.

The compromising of God's Word at Christian colleges is really an attack on Christ.

Let us explain. When church leaders reinterpret Genesis for instance, we insist this is an undermining of the authority of the Word, in spite of some scholars' sincere intentions to the contrary. It is what we call "The Genesis 3" attack (i.e., creating doubt in regard to God's Word and asking "Did God really say?") and it ultimately undermines the authority of the Scripture. Although such beliefs as those above don't affect the scholars' salvation as such, they do have a great influence on the students and other Christians these professors influence.

Many young people in our churches are already doubting and disbelieving God's Word. The result? At least two-thirds of children raised in theologically conservative churches now walk away from the church (or even the Christian faith altogether).

Do you realize how serious such compromise really is? Consider the following truths:

1. We can only know the Father through the Son (Matt. 11:27).
2. We know the Son (Jesus Christ) through the Word (Rom. 10:14–17).
3. Jesus is the Word (John 1:1–3).

Then consider these verses:

> Jesus said to him, "Have I been so long with you, and yet you have not come to know Me, Philip? He who has seen Me has seen the Father; how can you say, 'Show us the Father'?" (John 14:9).

> He is the image of the invisible God, the firstborn of all creation (Col. 1:15).

Here are two more verses that help show the connection between the Word and the Son of God:

> God, who at various times and in various ways spoke in time past to the fathers by the prophets, has in these last days spoken to us by His Son, whom He has appointed heir of all things, through whom also He made the worlds (Heb. 1:1–2; NKJV).

> In the beginning was the Word, and the Word was with God, and the Word was God. He was in the beginning with God. All things were made through Him, and without Him nothing was made that was made (John 1:1–3; NKJV).

Since Jesus is God, then God's Word (the Old and New Testaments of the Bible) is Jesus Christ's Word. Christ said, "Heaven and earth will pass away, but My words will not pass away" (Matt. 24:35). He also declared, "If you abide in My word, you are My disciples indeed" (John 8:31; *NKJV*; see also John 5:24, 8:37, and Rev. 3:8). And Jesus clearly demonstrated that He accepted Genesis 1–11 as true literal history.

What's the bottom line?

When Christian leaders deliberately reinterpret God's Word on the basis of man's fallible ideas (taken from outside the Bible), not only are they undermining the Word of God, they are actually (though unwittingly) conducting an attack on the Son of God! This is very serious. Yes, when you compromise the Word of God, it is also an attack on the Son of God whose Word it is.

May God help each of us to cling to — and tremble before — His Word (Josh. 1:6–9; Isa. 66:1–2). And may He help us not to follow the teachings that compromise His Word and thereby (even unknowingly) attack His Son.

And this should be a reminder to all of us. We all fall short somewhere (Rom. 3:23) and when we are confronted with the Word of God, we need to humble ourselves, and trust what the Bible teaches in context and correct ourselves (2 Tim. 3:16–17). We need to let go of any pride and be still and know God is God. We need to lay our trust in Him in *every* area — all of us.

For those compromising professors, they have no excuse not to trust the Word of God regarding creation, so the rebuke of this book should be met with wisdom that comes from God:

> Rebuke a wise man, and he will love you (Prov. 9:8; NKJV).

2. Experience the living Word

No matter where you go to school, it is vitally important to have a steady intake of truth from God's Word. Not only this, but it is vital to understand that God's Word is to be the foundation for all of your thinking in every area. Ken's father reminded him of this in many ways — here are a couple of examples he taught:

1. Study Bibles: Always remember when reading a study Bible (or a commentary), that the notes are not inspired like the text (Scripture), but the text (Scripture) is the commentary on the notes!
2. When something in God's Word seems to contradict what fallible man is saying (maybe a scientist or theologian, etc.), then you do two things:

   a. You first of all go to the text and make sure you are taking it according to the genre and context — if you are sure that you are taking it as it is meant to be taken and there is still a conflict, then:

   b. You don't change (reinterpret) God's Word to fit with what fallible man is saying — you stand upon God's Word and continue to research and seek answers. Remember, only God knows everything — always put God's Word first.

But please understand that you must have an intimate personal relationship with God's living Word, and not just take it second hand through other people's teaching, or through daily chapel services. We are all called as students of His Word and way. Proverbs 3:13–15 says:

> Blessed is the man who finds wisdom, the man who gains understanding, for she is more profitable than silver and yields better returns than gold. She is more precious than rubies; nothing you desire can compare with her (NIV).

Of this you can be sure. If you do not want to do your own thinking, there are plenty of people who will do it for you. In fact, that characterizes more people than not who are so undiscriminating about what they allow into their minds. Thinking Christianly is hard work. The easy way out is to let others inform you about how you should think. That's when it could really be said, "A mind is a terrible thing to waste." We have found over the years that so many students will just believe what the professor says because he or she is such a nice person. This should not be the case. As the Scripture states in 2 Timothy 2:15, you should "Be diligent to present yourself approved to God as a workman who does not need to be ashamed, accurately handling the word of truth."

The very meaning and quality of your life is at stake when it comes to what worldview you will use to consider the truth claims you will be exposed to. The only way to be a consistent Christian and build a consistent Christian worldview is to build all your thinking on God's Word — beginning in Genesis. Never take man's fallible ideas and add them to God's Word — never reinterpret the clear teaching of God's Word to fit with man's fallible word.

The purpose and meaning of Christian higher education has never been any better described than in these verses from Proverbs 1:1–7:

> The proverbs of Solomon son of David, king of Israel: for attaining wisdom and discipline; for understanding words of insight; for acquiring a disciplined and prudent life, doing what is right and just and fair; for giving prudence to the simple, knowledge and discretion to the young — let the wise listen and add to their learning, and let the discerning get guidance — for understanding proverbs and parables, the sayings and riddles of the wise. The fear of the LORD is the beginning of knowledge, but fools despise wisdom and discipline (NIV).

And, Proverbs 9:10: "The fear of the LORD is the beginning of wisdom."

That is an important perspective because it is biblical, but important, too, for living in what is called the information age. Knowledge is increasing and we are being offered more and more information. You would think people would be getting smarter. In fact, if knowledge is doubling every three years, as some say, you would think it would not be too long before we, as very smart human beings, would be able to possess the virtues and qualities that would make our world a much better place. You would think by now there would be fewer wars than in the past, and that humankind would, at the very least, be able to see the futility of wars waged. You would think there would be less crime, less hunger, less suffering, stronger families, more integrity, responsible governments, more peace and tranquility, and less disease. Yet, on the contrary, the opposite is clearly the case and it seems to be going from bad to worse — at least here in the United States.

Don't be surprised when this happens — we need to learn the lesson God teaches in His Word. Romans 1:18 says that "the wrath of God is revealed from heaven against all ungodliness and unrighteousness of men who suppress the truth in unrighteousness." The reason so many atheist bloggers and secular media reporters react so negatively and write so furiously against Bible-upholding ministries like Answers in Genesis is because they know in their hearts that there is a God — and they actively suppress that. What we are observing is the outworking of this active suppression. God's Word is being illustrated before our eyes on this matter.

Also, remember that "The heart is deceitful above all things, and desperately wicked" (Jer. 17:9; NKJV). There is "none who understands; none who seeks after God" (Rom. 3:11; NKJV). Proverbs 1:29 reminds us that these people "hated knowledge."

And don't be surprised when certain religious leaders oppose those who stand for the truth of God's Word. The prophets of old spoke about this — when Jesus walked on earth as the "God-man," He had to deal with the religious leaders of the day.

> Beware of the false prophets, who come to you in sheep's clothing, but inwardly are ravenous wolves (Matt. 7:15).

> Their shepherds have led them astray (Jer. 50:6).

So be advised that listening to lectures, reading text books, writing papers, exploring research, completing assignments, attending class, and all the things that are virtues of the collegiate academic experience are no guarantee that you will become smarter. The increase in knowledge must go hand in hand with the pursuit of wisdom — placing God's Word first! Wisdom is knowledge being applied. It is seeing life through God's eyes, through God's perspective. Wisdom means thinking God's thoughts after Him. It is the ability to have insight and discretion. It is having a discerning spirit.

Wisdom leads us to do what is right, being righteous, which is simply that — doing right in the eyes of God. It is being just and fair. Wisdom means we value the life God has given us and value the lives of others. Wisdom guides us in our plans for the future and places confidence in our hearts that everything is in control of the One who is greater than ourselves and that He wants the absolute best for us in every way. It is wisdom that teaches us to "fear" the Lord in the sense, not that we are afraid of Him, but that we revere Him and honor Him and live *Coram Deo* — which means before the face of God and under His authority. Instructing students in the pursuit of wisdom is in fact the moral imperative of a Christian college. It is the moral imperative for this institution.

We tell you on the basis of the truth of the Word of God that seeking after wisdom, putting God and His Word first, is the greatest blessing known to man, and ignoring it will lead to your ultimate destruction. But you must first know that your Father in heaven wishes to bless you today and give victory in the face of any issue of life. Listen to these words from Proverbs 2:1–11:

> My son, if you accept my words and store up my commands within you, turning your ear to wisdom and applying your heart to understanding — indeed, if you call out for insight and cry aloud for understanding, and if you look for it as for silver and search for it as for hidden treasure, then you will understand the fear of the Lord and find the knowledge of God. For the Lord gives wisdom; from his mouth come knowledge and understanding. He holds success in store for the upright, he is a shield to those whose walk is blameless, for he guards the course of the just and protects the way of his faithful ones. Then you will understand what is right and just and fair — every good path. For wisdom will enter your heart, and knowledge will be pleasant to your soul. Discretion will protect you, and understanding will guard you (NIV).

Proverbs 3:1–8 reads:

> My son, do not forget my teaching, but keep my commands in your heart, for they will prolong your life many years and bring you prosperity. Let love and faithfulness never leave you; bind them around your neck, write them on the tablet of your heart. Then you will win favor and a good name in the sight of God and man. Trust in the Lord with all your heart and lean not on your own understanding; in all your ways acknowledge him, and he will make your paths straight. Do not be wise in your own eyes; fear the Lord and shun evil. This will bring health to your body and nourishment to your bones (NIV).

Think of it: You are promised victory when you honor God's Word. You will be protected, for God Himself will become a shield for you. He guards you and guides you and protects you. You will find a long, productive, and prosperous life. You will be full of love and faithfulness. You will find favor and have a good name and reputation with both God and men and you will enjoy good health, being nourished by the very hand of God. Who could possibly promise so much and make good on all that is promised besides God? No one! What a blessing these words are. They are life and light, they are sustenance and prosperity. They are promised by God the Father, delivered in Jesus Christ His Son, and reserved for all who believe in the Holy Spirit.

Will you, to your own peril, reject the promises of God? Consider these words from Proverbs 1:20–33:

Wisdom calls aloud in the street, she raises her voice in the public squares; at the head of the noisy streets she cries out, in the gateways of the city she makes her speech: "How long will you simple ones love your simple ways? How long will mockers delight in mockery and fools hate knowledge? If you had responded to my rebuke, I would have poured out my heart to you and made my thoughts known to you. But since you rejected me when I called and no one gave heed when I stretched out my hand, since you ignored all my advice and would not accept my rebuke, I in turn will laugh at your disaster; I will mock when calamity overtakes you — when calamity overtakes you like a storm, when disaster sweeps over you like a whirlwind, when distress and trouble overwhelm you. Then they will call to me but I will not answer; they will look for me but will not find me. Since they hated knowledge and did not choose to fear the LORD, since they would not accept my advice and spurned my rebuke, they will eat the fruit of their ways and be filled with the fruits of their schemes. For the waywardness of the simple will kill them, and the complacency of fools will destroy them; but whoever listens to me will live in safety and be at ease, without fear of harm" (NIV).

If you are in Christ, God is for you today and willing and more than able to bless you beyond your wildest imagination. He alone is able to heal all your hurts, to forgive all your sin. He alone has written a personal plan for your life. He knows you and calls you by name. You can belong to Him. You can seek Him and find Him, for He is as near as your very breath. One of the greatest blessings of wisdom is that it alone will open the door for you to a life of significance — something that God puts in the hearts of the creatures He loves. We are destined for a life of purpose — a life that will glorify our Creator. It is a life of joy and enthusiasm.

But it is a life different from what many typically expect. It is not necessarily a life full of the trappings of our culture. It may or may not include vast resources of financial or physical assets; it is rather a life of significance available to those who through wisdom seek what only God can give.

But it all starts when you jump in and pursue the living Word of God on your own. Again, this is something that no one else can do for you. You may or may not sit under gifted spiritual teachers during college, but nothing, *nothing*, can be a substitute for the time that you will spend in the Word of God yourself, experiencing its wisdom and power as the truth sets you free to be all that God created you to be.

3. Church and para-church involvement

The Christian life was not designed to be lived alone. Repeatedly, God describes us as a body that works together and encourages each other for His purposes. No matter where you go, we feel that it is imperative to surviving and thriving in the college years to find committed fellowship under the guidance of spiritual leaders who both know and apply the authority of God.

Many students will find this in a local church where the Body of Christ is alive and well, and where the truth of the Word is lived out naturally. It is vital that you find a local church where the Word of God is preached and the members live in light of that teaching as the body of Christ. You may also find support on campus in a para-church ministry (but beware — many of them compromise in the same way we have seen from the research we have detailed in this book). On both Christian and secular campuses, these para-church organizations can be spiritual lifesavers, and often times they are the training and equipping stations that can ignite you for a lifelong strategic mission. Sadly, there are those that do more harm than good because they do not stand on God's Word as they should — you will need to be discerning and judge what they believe and teach against the authority of God's Word. No matter where you go to school, supplement your academic education with dynamic fellowship, teaching, and worship experiences. We all need that. That's how God created us! It is simply an essential.

4. Prepare for battle

The surveys that were conducted by America's Research Group for this book clearly showed that the biblical worldview is under attack by secular influences within the Christian colleges. These enemies of faith have, to a certain degree, succeeded in infiltrating and influencing Christian institutions. We are in a battle with the world's system. You must prepare yourself, no matter where you go. Listen again to what's at stake. These kinds of quotes should awaken us and call us to action:

> Dr. Richard Dawkins: "Faith is one of the world's great evils . . . it is capable of driving people to such dangerous folly . . . it seems to me to qualify as a kind of mental illness."[2]

> Dr. Steven Weinberg: "If scientists can destroy the influence of religion on young people, then I think it may be the most important contribution we can make."[3]

Richard Rorty: Secular professors should "arrange things so that students who enter as bigoted, homophobic religious fundamentalists will leave college with views more like our own."[4]

5. Keep your guard up wherever you go

Students, even if you think you're going into a conservative Christian educational institution, our research has proven that you need to be wary and enter with a healthy skepticism of what will be taught. Your commitment to the Bible as your authority means that you must check *everything* that you are taught by *anyone* by comparing it to the truth of Scripture.

Don't let your guard down by letting anything except the Bible become your final authority. Hopefully you'll meet many committed and caring professors along the way, but they are not your source of truth. Just because your parents endorsed you going to this school does not mean that your teachers know best. In many situations liberal professors are more personable than staunch conservatives who come across as closed-minded and impersonal. (That's not always the case, just a generalization here.) If you allow their position and personality to justify their theology (which may be seriously compromised), you're setting yourself up for problems. Truth is determined by the Word, not by someone's social skills. Keep your guard up, and protect your soul by the truth of Scripture.

6. Have a mission

The last message that we have from the Apostle Paul is 2 Timothy, written as final advice to his close friend and young disciple. Consider this challenge from 2 Timothy 2:22:

Now flee from youthful lusts and pursue righteousness, faith, love and peace, with those who call on the Lord from a pure heart.

If you want to survive and thrive, having a clear mission is not an option. It's imperative. The account of David and Bathsheba in 2 Samuel is a clear warning: Anyone who is not engaging in the battle as they should becomes an easy target for sin and compromise. God has designed you to go for it! During college you have an unprecedented opportunity to allow the Lord to work through you to minister somewhere in some specific way. Pursue this with brothers and sisters in the Lord who share your passion. It's the best way to flee from the lusts and the lies of the world that seek to bring you down.

7. Plan on victory

A few years ago, Warner University experienced the fury and devastation of four killer hurricanes. The school had damages of $3 million. In Florida, losses totaled $42 billion. But what was experienced in Florida in the summer of 2004 is overshadowed by overwhelming power and destruction of the events of December 26, 2004, when a 9.0 magnitude earthquake struck 100 miles from the western coast of Sumatra Island. It was the strongest quake in the world since 1964. It was the fourth-strongest quake since recording began in 1899. This slippage of the tectonic plates caused a tsunami that traveled 500 miles an hour and made landfall in several locations with catastrophic devastation. The earthquake that caused the tsunami was calculated as having the power of 23 atomic bombs, the like of which destroyed Hiroshima and Nagasaki. It was a power so great that seismologists detected the earth literally shaking on its axis. These natural disasters revealed just how fragile the world really is, and is an illustration of how the kingdom of this world is shaking at its very foundations. This earthly kingdom will pass away and it will be far more dramatic than the most recent earthquake and tsunami. According to 2 Peter 3:10:

> The heavens will pass away with a roar and the elements will be destroyed with intense heat, and the earth and its works will be burned up.

We understand why Jesus said we should not love the kingdom of this world. It is passing away in the physical sense and in the spiritual sense too. If we are feeling any consolation or any confidence in being part of this world we are missing the point of the message of the gospel.

Jesus explained to us that the kingdom of this world promotes and encourages everything that God is against. The earthly kingdom is full of pride, jealousy, hatred, malice, murder, and deceit. It promotes everything that is unwholesome and ungodly. Those who oppose God and everything He stands for lead it. And so as it says in 1 John 2:15–17:

> Do not love the world or anything in the world. If anyone loves the world, the love of the Father is not in him. For everything in the world — the cravings of sinful man, the lust of his eyes and the boasting of what he has and does — comes not from the Father but from the world. The world and its desires pass away, but the man who does the will of God lives forever (NIV).

God will eventually judge the kingdom of this world and expose its darkness by turning on His light. And this light is Jesus. And He is shining on the world to expose our evil deeds. Everything about the ways of the earthly kingdom God will destroy. And not just the earth, but all the spiritual wickedness and unrighteousness that goes with it. It is one thing to honestly struggle with our persistent sin . . . God is *for* that person, not against him or her . . . but He is dead set against us when we sin, acting like we do so with impunity and never understanding the need we have for the Savior.

God plays no games on this account. He has offered full forgiveness and mercy by the sacrifice for sin, taking the responsibility for our salvation on Himself alone. He requires us only to repent of our sin and believe in His name to enter the eternal kingdom. He is justified in destroying those who sin against Him and reject this offer of salvation. We must realize God is under no obligation to save anyone. He does so only as He exhibits His own nature and character. Consider the sobering words of Hebrews 2:1–3:

> We must pay more careful attention, therefore, to what we have heard, so that we do not drift away. For if the message spoken by angels was binding, and every violation and disobedience received its just punishment, how shall we escape if we ignore such great salvation? (NIV).

The signs are all around us that the shaking of the kingdom of this world is imminent. As college students, you must choose for yourselves whether you will become a servant to this worldly kingdom or choose the Kingdom of God. Staying connected to this world means living in fear instead of knowing peace. It is remaining as a slave to sin instead of being set free. It is being lost instead of rescued.

To refuse Him is to wallow in that tormenting guilt instead of knowing forgiveness and grace. Instead, God is offering you right now the choice to be part of a Kingdom that cannot be shaken. It is the eternal Kingdom of God and Jesus said it is with you and shall be in you. It is the kingdom of peace and righteousness and holiness. It is the kingdom of victory and power. It is the kingdom of deliverance. It is the kingdom of life and light. And it cannot be shaken. And of His Kingdom there shall be no end. Hebrews 12:25–29 reads:

> See that you do not refuse Him who speaks. For if they did not escape who refused Him who spoke on earth, much more shall we not escape if we turn away from Him who speaks from heaven, whose voice then shook the earth; but now He has promised, saying, "Yet once more I shake not only the earth, but also heaven." Now this, "Yet once more," indicates the removal of those things that are being shaken, as of things that are made, that the things which

cannot be shaken may remain. Therefore, since we are receiving a kingdom which cannot be shaken, let us have grace, by which we may serve God acceptably with reverence and godly fear. For our God is a consuming fire (NKJV).

Consider this quote from Malcolm Muggeridge.

We look back upon history and what do we see, empires rising and falling, revolutions and counter-revolutions, wealth accumulated and wealth disbursed. Shakespeare has spoken of the rise and fall of the great ones. I look back upon my own fellow countrymen, once upon a time dominating a quarter of the world, most of them convinced of the words of what is still a popular song, that the God who made the mighty shall make them mightier yet. I heard a crazed Austrian announce to the world the establishment of a Reich that would last a thousand years. I've seen an Italian clown saying he was going to stop and restart the calendar with his own ascension to power. I met a murderous Georgian Brigand in the Kremlin acclaimed by the intellectual elite of the world as wiser than Solomon, more humane than Marcus Aralias, more enlightened than Ashoka, all in one lifetime, all gone. Gone with the wind. England, part of a tiny island off the coast of Europe, threatened with dismemberment and even bankruptcy, Hitler and Mussolini dead, remembered only in infamy. Stalin a forbidden name in the regime he helped found and dominate for some three decades, all in one lifetime, all in one lifetime, gone. Still behind the debris of these self-styled Solomon supermen and imperial diplomatist, stands the gigantic figure of one person because of whom, by whom, in whom, and through whom mankind might still have hope, the person of Jesus Christ. And He has given a kingdom that cannot be shaken, and of this kingdom there shall be no end.[5]

Our charge to you as students, therefore, is to not be afraid. Be strong and courageous for the Lord your God is with you wherever you go. Consider these words from Haggai 2:6–7:

For thus says the LORD of hosts, "Once more (it is a little while) I will shake heaven and earth, the sea and dry land; and I will shake all nations, and they shall come to the Desire of All Nations, and I will fill this temple with glory" (NKJV).

There is no way we will lose the war. The heavens and earth shake, but we are receiving a kingdom that will not be shaken. We are the ultimate survivors and victors. We need not be discouraged or be in despair. We may falter and exhibit our frailties, but Jesus said, "I will build My church, and the gates of Hades will not overpower it" (Matt. 16:18).

And so, with all that has been said and done in this book, we have little left to say, and nothing left to do but to release you, as students and future leaders and servants of the Church, into the hands of God. You're entering institutions of higher learning that to one degree or another are already compromised. You're stepping across the threshold into a fallen world, and this is where God calls you to be — to be in this world, yet not of it. The battles will be many, but we believe that you can do more than just survive; we believe that you can thrive as you grow in intimacy with God in Christ like you have never, never experienced before. And we firmly believe that you are part of the Kingdom that cannot be shaken, even as the fallen world around you proceeds from bad to worse.

Would you allow us to leave you with this one final blessing?

> *May the Lord bless you, and keep you and cause his face to shine upon you. May his peace, which surpasses all comprehension, guard your hearts and your minds in the knowledge of Christ Jesus, always. In any and every circumstance may you know the secret of contentment: You can do all things through Christ who strengthens you, yet apart from Him, you can do nothing. May the truth of His living Word, and the reality of His Spirit within you, be your ultimate authority in all things. As you learn and grow in knowledge, may your hearts and minds be receptive to the life-giving truths of Scripture, which is living and active and sharper than any two-edged sword. By God's grace and mercy, may you know the truth. And may the truth set you free.*
> *Amen.*

Endnotes

1. Brother Yun with Paul Hattaway, *The Heavenly Man: The Remarkable True Story of Chinese Christian Brother Yun* (Peabody, MA: Hendrickson Publishers, 2009).
2. Richard Dawkins, *The selfish Gene* (New York: Oxford University Press, 1989), p. 330–31; Richard Dawkins, "Is Science a Religion?" *The Humanist* (January–February 1997); Richard Dawkins, "The Improbability of God," *Free Inquiry*, vol. 18, no. 3.
3. Remarks by Steven Weinberg at the Freedom from Religion Foundation, San Antonio, November 1999.
4. Cited by Jason Boffetti, "How Richard Rorty Found Religion," *First Things* (May 2004).
5. Quoted by Ravi Zacharias in a sermon, "Jesus Christ Among Other Gods," 1993; www.urbana.org/articles/jesus-christ-among-other-gods-1993.

Chapter 11

Final Thoughts: A Plea for Unity

Ken Ham and Greg Hall

My prayer is not for them alone. I pray also for those who will believe in me through their message, that all of them may be one, Father, just as you are in me and I am in you. May they also be in us so that the world may believe that you have sent me (Jesus, in John 17:20–22; NIV).

We have taken a look at the state of Christian higher education in this book. The survey gave us dependable statistics to form logical conclusions. As a result, we have dared to question the very core and foundation of colleges functioning in the name of Christ. Reputation and pride is at stake. As often is the case, the first responses are accusations that we are being divisive, causing unnecessary conflict, and stirring waters that should be left alone. We are often told we should be concentrating on our unity in Christ alone. The accusations usually sound like this: "Only Christ should matter and those elements of the gospel message essential for salvation — and differing interpretations in Genesis should be acceptable and tolerated."

But this view ignores a larger question — can we separate the centrality of Christ from the authority of His Word? Surely we would all agree that our unity should be centered in Christ. After all, it is only through faith in

Jesus Christ that one can be saved. The question, however, is not whether we are saved, but what Christians should hold as being essential for Christian unity. The Christian Church can only know about Jesus Christ through His Word. If the Word of God is not an authoritative document, then how can we know that the message of Jesus and the gospel is reliable? It's easy to say wonderful statements about how Jesus is all we need for unity and quickly forget that Christ is not only the Christ of the Cross but also the giver of His Word. Shouldn't this then mean that we need to be united in the authority of the document He has given as His message?

What about the history that provides the foundational understanding for His gospel? Is it possible to de-unify the God of creation from the God of redemption by being willing to accept only one truth in the gospel while accepting the world's views in origins? The Bible tells us that the God of creation IS the God of redemption, so surely this means that unity in Jesus has much wider ramifications than many are realizing. Sadly, the modern Church has been very selective about what aspects of Jesus we are willing to be unified in. If the Church continues to go down a path that restricts Jesus simply to what we are willing to be unified in, we will end up with an undefined Christ.

Since the Apostles, the Church has increased in number and divided in doctrines and established denominational boundaries. America has over 20 Baptist denominations alone; each one is distinctive in its own emphases. Even within each of the evangelical denominations, we have numerous factions according to the persuasions of pastors, pew sitters, denominational leaders, and college faculties. Before any finger is pointed in the area of division, perhaps we should first admit to the distinctive characteristics we allow to divide us every day.

Many of those denominational differences disappear at Answers in Genesis (AiG) conferences. AiG staff routinely sees great cross-denominational unity as people are taught to defend their faith. People become excited when they can have increased confidence in His revealed Word, and greater understanding for His redemptive history recorded in His Word from the very first verse.

Answers in Genesis is a para-church ministry that has a specific calling to support the local church in defending the authority of the Word of God from the very first verse against the attacks of the world. Even when teaching people apologetics, AiG does so with the ultimate view of pointing to the person and work of Jesus Christ, and He can never be disjoined from the authority of His Word. Why teach people to defend the Bible simply for defense sake?

After all, our only assurance and hope of salvation is in Jesus Christ. AiG's ultimate purpose and unifying factor is always Jesus, and He can never be disjoined from the authority of His Word.[1]

It is Christ and His Word that uncovers the ugliness and consequences of our sin. Nobody likes to be exposed — because of the sinful nature within us. We desire to cling to our own foolishness rather than accept the truth that Christ has revealed to us in His Word. Every human struggles in this area and it really does expose the war we have with sin. It is this sin that we should struggle against as Paul does in Romans 7 and that we should be dead to as explained in Romans 6. Human pride often causes us to be greatly offended in the light of God's truth. This is why Christ Himself divided one against another (Luke 12:51). Nobody likes to be exposed.

One major and foundational area where God's Word is exposing the compromising positions of many Christian leaders today is in the area of biblical history in Genesis that relates to geology, astronomy, anthropology, biology, etc. This is also the area where the world's attack against the gospel of Jesus Christ is most heavily pointed.

A proper biblical defense of this attack will support and strengthen the Church to preach Christ and Him crucified. Our hearts should desire that the Church would preach the centrality of Christ with the strongest possible foundations, and not with a history that contradicts or causes someone to question the validity of the gospel message:

> How do we know man is a sinner?
> How do we know we are all sinners?
> How do we know that death is the penalty for sin?
> How do we know that God's Son became a man — the God/man, Jesus Christ?
> How do we know Jesus died and rose again physically?
> How do we know Jesus paid the penalty for sin on the Cross?

We know because the Bible tells us so. Scripture is an accurate account of the redemptive history between God and His people. We know because we believe the *authority* in which this is revealed — the Bible. Biblical authority is therefore essential for Christian unity and foundational faith.

Jesus Himself teaches that He is the way, the truth, and the life (John 14:6). Evangelical Christians should know this and rejoice in it. It wouldn't be difficult to get a room full of evangelical Christian leaders agreeing to and preaching the centrality of Jesus Christ in the message of Scripture. When it comes to accepting and preaching Jesus as the revealer and Creator, and everything that it means, unity starts to fray. Certainly the Bible testifies to Jesus being the revealer of truth. In John 1 we read that Jesus is the Word, is God, is light and life who created all things and became flesh. John 1 teaches us that Jesus is the revealer, the Creator, and the central point of redemption.

If Jesus is the pre-eminent, supreme revealer of truth, then the search for truth must start with His pre-eminence over man's philosophies. Our unity must come through Scriptures given to us by Jesus shedding light on this world, and not on man's interpretations of this world supposedly telling us what Jesus is saying. To do otherwise is essentially shifting the power of supremacy from Jesus to man. And this is something those committed to the centrality of Jesus cannot tolerate.

This begs a very important question: Is the Church today trying to find unity in Christ as the center of truth, without recognizing Him as the revealer of truth in the entirety of the biblical account — from Genesis 1:1 to Revelation 22:21?

Christ taught that truth is important. Today, however, one of the most common definitions of "Christian unity" revolves around a consensus of fallible man's opinion rather than the truth of God's infallible Word. Depending on which circles you are in, you will find varying levels of pressure to accept the consensus of opinion as truth. Particularly in today's academic circles, immense pressure is placed upon students to accept this consensus-centered view.

Every word of man must be viewed and scrutinized in the light of the revealed Word of God. While great respect should be given to our teachers, we must be careful that we are not placed in a situation similar to the time before the Reformation where it was proposed only "clergy" could understand the Bible. We must not allow the ideas of professors to become the final word. Nowhere in Scripture are we taught that unity comes through consensus of opinion. The truth of God trumps consensus every time.

It is in the biblical Book of John that we get the first key points of insight in answering these crucial issues. In John 17 Christ prays for the unity of the Church:

> I will remain in the world no longer, but they are still in the world, and I am coming to you. Holy Father, protect them by the power of your name, the name you gave me, so that they may be one as we are one. While I was with them, I protected them and kept them safe by that name you gave me. None has been lost except the one doomed to destruction so that Scripture would be fulfilled.

I am coming to you now, but I say these things while I am still in the world, so that they may have the full measure of my joy within them. I have given them your word and the world has hated them, for they are not of the world any more than I am of the world. My prayer is not that you take them out of the world but that you protect them from the evil one. They are not of the world, even as I am not of it. Sanctify them by the truth; your word is truth. As you sent me into the world, I have sent them into the world. For them I sanctify myself, that they too may be truly sanctified (John 17:11–19; NIV).

In verse 11, Jesus prays unity may be kept with the Apostles, as it is in the Trinity. The unity Jesus was looking for did not come from consensus. Jesus is talking about a unity that is already perfectly present in Christ; it is the *supremacy* of Christ.

In verses 17–19, He prays that we may be kept in the *truth* — *His* truth. Unity for the believer is full in Christ rather than something to be obtained by consensus of opinion. This unity is to be kept, not established. It is unity that is separate from this world, and maintained in the truth of Christ and His Word.

Is the division over the interpretation of Genesis a result of an earnest desire to be unified around the Word of God, or a desire to be unified around the words of sinful fallible human beings (regardless of whether they are highly qualified scientists or theologians)? Richard Baxter said:

> Indeed, no truth is inconsistent with any other truth: but yet when two dark or doubtful points are compared together, it is hard to know which of them to reject. But here it is easy; nothing that contradicteth the true nature of God or man or any principle, must be held.[2]

Logic tells us that something cannot be both true and false at the same time, and truth is always consistent with itself. For the sake of unity, this logic particularly applies to the nature of God and man. God is holy, pure, and perfect. Man however has a heart that is "deceitful above all things, and desperately wicked" (Jer. 17:9; NKJV).

The only truth consistent with the nature of both God and man is the literal interpretation of the historical narrative in Genesis. Genesis tells us of a perfect and unblemished creation free of death, disease, or suffering. Scripture tells us that man is a creation of God. It tells us God's creations were good. Therefore, evil and death cannot be a part of man's beginning (or of any part of the creation for that matter), as it would contradict the truth of who God is.

Death, thorns, carnivorous diet, a cursed ground, groaning physical creation, and eternal judgment are the consequences of sin. Such things were not in existence before the Fall. It is only this understanding that is consistent with the truth that Jesus came to physically die and then rise again to conquer the consequences of man's sin. Later Scripture also tells us that man is essentially evil, destined to die, and then face judgment for sin.

Back in chapter 1 we mentioned the theodicy of Dr. William Dembski (which is further elaborated on in the appendix). He comes up with what we consider to be a bizarre scenario to try to maintain "unity" on what God's Word teaches and "unity" on what fallible man teaches. In doing so, he creates division and undermines biblical authority. The question that must be answered is: Can that which contradicts God's Word really be considered truth?

Truth is important in unity; this is echoed and emphasized throughout Scripture. Consider Ephesians 4:11–13:

> And He Himself gave some to be apostles, some prophets, some evangelists, and some pastors and teachers, for the equipping of the saints for the work of ministry, for the edifying of the body of Christ, till we all come to the unity of the faith and of the knowledge of the Son of God, to a perfect man, to the measure of the stature of the fullness of Christ (NKJV).

It is the job of the officers in the Church to utilize the unity we have in the foundation of truth and lead us toward the fullness of Christ. This foundation is essential for Christian growth and Church leadership. We don't see that kind of unity today. Our survey certainly illustrates there is division, and sometimes division is actually necessary. But is it the right sort of division? Is it division for the sake of unity on God's Word? Or is it division for the sake of unity on man's word? Therein lies the issue. Sadly, the division we see in regard to Genesis really comes down to a unity many Christian academics want to have in regard to fallible man's word. This is the problem with the Church — and really has been the problem with man since Genesis 3 when the temptation was one of getting man to question God's Word, but decide truth for one's self (trusting man's word).

It is in Ephesians 4:14 that we find a very strong warning. We are to grow in the knowledge of Christ and His fullness "that we should no longer be children, tossed to and fro and carried about with every wind of doctrine, by the trickery of men, in the cunning craftiness of deceitful plotting" (NKJV).

Unity is not only in Christ and His truth, but is maintained by committing to *that* truth and not being persuaded otherwise by men. In Colossians, a similar warning is given by Paul to a newly established church as he desires to keep a strong unity within:

> Beware lest anyone cheat you through philosophy and empty deceit, according to the tradition of men, according to the basic principles of the world, and not according to Christ (Col. 2:8; NKJV).

You will not find millions of years or evolution anywhere in the text of Scripture. Nor can such teachings fit consistently into the text of Scripture. Yet those who have not allowed the intrusion of man's ideas of millions of years into the first chapter of Genesis are often accused of causing division. These beliefs are philosophies and "empty deceit" according to the "traditions of men." The Church is warned to be on the lookout for this and to shut the door to the compromise of human philosophies. Paul wrote to encourage them to keep the truth and maintain the unity.

To others, Paul wrote to rebuke them for divisions that were already among them. In 1 Corinthians we find a church that was full of contentions. Some were following Paul, others Apollos or Peter. There was in-fighting and factions and a general rebellion against God's truth. Paul spends considerable time discussing the difference between men and God when it comes to wisdom:

> Where is the wise? Where is the scribe? Where is the disputer of this age? Has not God made foolish the wisdom of this world? For since, in the wisdom of God, the world through wisdom did not know God, it pleased God through the foolishness of the message preached to save those who believe. For Jews request a sign, and Greeks seek after wisdom; but we preach Christ crucified, to the Jews a stumbling block and to the Greeks foolishness, but to those who are called, both Jews and Greeks, Christ the power of God and the wisdom of God. Because the foolishness of God is wiser than men, and the weakness of God is stronger than men (1 Cor. 1:20–25; NKJV).

Paul exhorts the Corinthians to come back to the essential truth of Christ and to unity within *that* truth, emphasizing that the true teaching of Christ was not compatible with the signs required by the Jews, or the man-centered philosophies of the Greeks.

To bring the unity of Christ to the Jews, Peter preached to them the gospel of Christ. We see a great example of this in the account of Pentecost in Acts 2. They already believed in one God and the history concerning Adam and Eve, the entrance of sin, and thus the need for a Savior and Messiah. The

Jews, however, did not believe that Jesus was the Messiah (there was division over this), but they had unity on all of the history that lead up to Jesus from creation (sin, the law, and the prophets foretelling the coming Messiah). The history was understood and the message of Jesus was consistent with the history. As a result of Peter's preaching, many were saved.

In Acts 17, Paul had a much more difficult challenge. Paul was preaching to the Greeks, with particular mention given to his encounter with the Epicureans and the Stoics. Neither group had any real understanding of the history as understood by the Jews. To offer unity in Christ, Paul first had to ground them in a new history (the same history the Jews understood). This was a new foundation of truth to enable them to understand who Jesus was and what He had done for them on the Cross.

The Epicureans must have found this to be a new revelation since they held to atheistic evolutionary philosophies. The Epicureans believed that all life came from the basic component of all matter and formed over long ages of time. Without a rewrite of their history, the Epicureans were lost to understand the truth of Christ. The message of Jesus made no sense to them without an understanding of what sin is and what it did to God's perfect creation — and thus their standing before a Holy Creator God as judge. As a result of Paul's foundational teaching on the true God and the true history of humanity as a lead up to the message of the Cross, some were saved.

How would Paul feel to see many in the Church today embracing a new version of Epicurean (Greek) philosophy and rewriting a history that undermines and contradicts the biblical truth of history within Genesis that points to Christ? Many Christian leaders and scholars are leading people in the Church back to the type of evolutionary philosophies of the Epicureans and compromising this with God's Word — a compromise with the very philosophies that were causing these Greeks to see the message of the Cross as mere foolishness.

In today's Church, the compromise with millions of years and evolution has undeniably increased the problem of division within the Church. It is time for the Church to again review the prayer of Christ in John 17 and commit to return to the keeping of the unity that is only in Christ. It is time to take heed of the warning in Colossians 2:8 and beware of the philosophies of men that keep us from the truth *that is in Christ*.

People have been persuaded into thinking that if they don't adhere to the consensus of the scientific and or theological establishment, they have checked their brains at the door. The many PhD scientists who do start with the truth of Scripture and use all of the principles of logic in operational science to confirm biblical history might have something to say about that.

In Christian academic settings today, there is a great appeal to experts as the authority. They say we need to follow Professor X, or Dr. Y on this point or that, seeking a unity around the words of an academic, instead of one based on the clear teaching of the Word of God. No matter the stature of a leader, the number of the consensus, or the multitude of letters in a title, our unity is not in man or his philosophies but in Christ and His truth. This is why Paul warned the Corinthians not to follow men even though he was one of them being mentioned with Cephas and Apollos.

This phenomenon of people following the teachings of so-called great men rather than Christ is not new. In studying the Puritan pastors of the 1600s, Dr. Martyn Lloyd-Jones commented on the voluminous writings on Christian unity by John Owen. In relation to schisms in the Church, Dr. Lloyd-Jones offers the following in reference to Owen:

> The trouble, as he points out repeatedly, over the whole question of schism is that people will defend the position that they are in. They shut their minds; they are not ready to listen, to be instructed, and to change.[3]

What Dr. Lloyd-Jones understood was that Owen in his day found that rather than being conformed to the truth that is in Christ and His Word, men were more likely to hold strong to their own belief. This is called pride.

The great divide in the Church today has its roots in this pride. Few people are able to admit error, even when it comes to biblical truth. Yet all want to rejoice and find unity in Christ. The Church is in need of those who will unite uncompromisingly on God's Word, because of the division caused by those who use man's fallible word to reinterpret Scripture. In doing such, we are really calling for a new reformation as it happened in the 16th century. Yes, we call for a new reformation in our churches and Christian academic institutions!

Our closing prayer echoes that of Christ. Throughout this book we have shown the division within the Body of Christ caused by the compromise of scriptural authority starting with the first verse. We see the division between the leadership of Christian colleges. We see it between the departments of respected Christian universities. And we see this division causing the same compromise that brought down once-strong institutions like Dartmouth and Princeton. Yes, we pray and strive not for division, but for unity, that we might all be one, in truth, as Jesus prayed we would be.

God's grace to you all,

Ken Ham (with thanks to Steve Ham for his assistance in putting this chapter together)

Greg Hall

> I have given them the glory that you gave me, that they may be one as we are one — I in them and you in me — so that they may be brought to complete unity. Then the world will know that you sent me and have loved them even as you have loved me (Jesus, in John 17:22–23; NIV).

Endnotes

1. It should be noted that Scripture, such as Romans 10:9, makes it clear that salvation is conditioned upon faith in Christ, not what a person believes about the age of the earth or evolution. Many born-again Christians do believe in millions of years and many also believe in evolution. AiG would not question their salvation when they testify to being born again as the Scripture defines, but challenge these people to understand that such acceptance of fallible man's ideas and reinterpreting parts of Scripture is an undermining of the authority of the Word of God. The consequences of this particularly show up in the next generation, who tend to open the door of undermining God's Word even further — until eventually generations arise who, by and large, reject biblical authority. This is what we observe across our Western world today.
2. Richard Baxter (1615–1691) *Christian Directory* (Morgan, PA: Soli Deo Gloria Publications, 2008).
3. Martyn Lloyd-Jones discussing John Owen and his teaching on schisms, *Diversity in Unity* (London: A.G. Hasler and Co.), The Puritan and Reformed Studies Conference December 1963, p. 63.

Want to know which colleges were contacted as part of the ARG study? Visit www.creationcolleges.org and also find a growing list of Christian colleges we recommend you search out.

Appendix A

Speaking of Newspeak

Ken Ham

In the late 1700s and early 1800s, the idea of a long age (millions of years) for the earth was being popularized by deists, atheists, and other non-Christians.[1] They were attempting to use a so-called "scientific investigation of the world" to justify their rejection of God and His Word. At the time, their primary target was to undermine the plain reading of the Bible concerning the Flood of Noah (and its consequence of rock layers and worldwide fossil deposits) and a young age for the earth. It was really their attempt to undermine the authority of the entire Bible.

At that time, there were church leaders who adopted these ideas (millions of years) into Scripture (e.g., Thomas Chalmers with gap theory, Hugh Miller with day-age ideas, etc.). This was no different than today, and really no different than what happened with the religious leaders in the Apostle Paul's day, and also no different to what was happening with the priests and false prophets in ancient Israel.

Fallible, sinful man, ever since Genesis 3, has had the propensity to believe the fallible words of humans rather than the infallible Word of God. That is really our nature. At heart, because of sin, we are against God and what He teaches. People will go out of their way to trust in man rather than trust what God has clearly revealed.

In the early 1800s, there were church leaders in England who began to reinterpret the days of creation and the Flood account in Genesis to fit in the millions of years. Some advocated the idea of a gap between Genesis 1:1 and 1:2, like Chalmers. Others said that Christians could interpret the creation days as long ages, like Hugh Miller. Others realized that if one interpreted the fossil layers as representing millions of years, then how could one believe in the global Flood of Noah's day? Such a flood would destroy those layers and deposit more layers with fossils. Thus, it was postulated that Noah's Flood was only a local (regional) flood in the Mesopotamian Valley (modern-day Iraq).

As the 19th century progressed, Darwin popularized his ideas of biological evolution, which built on the ideas of geological evolution. There were church leaders who then reinterpreted Genesis to fit into evolution, even human evolution. When the idea of the big bang (astronomical evolution) was popularized in the early 20th century, in the same manner many church leaders then adopted this into God's Word.

Over the past two hundred years, many different positions regarding the creation account of Genesis have arisen in the Church, such as the following:

- Day-age idea
- Gap theory
- Local flood
- Theistic evolution
- Progressive creation
- Framework hypothesis

There are other positions or variations on those listed above, but they all have one thing in common: trying to fit man's ideas of millions of years into the Bible.

A number of Christian scientists actually opposed these compromise positions. Various books and articles were written to challenge the Church to stand on God's Word and not compromise with the fallible ideas of man that, intentionally or unintentionally, seriously undermined the authority of the Bible.

Biblical-creation scientists and theologians have been able to conduct tremendous research and have provided many answers in geology, biology, astronomy, anthropology, archaeology, and theology, which have equipped Christians to stand uncompromisingly on Genesis. The several thousand articles on the Answers in Genesis website[2] are a good example of providing such answers, as well as the hundreds of books, DVDs, and other resources now available there.

The modern biblical-creation movement has been highly successful at informing Christians of the numerous inconsistencies that try to add millions of years and evolution into the Bible. Many articles on the AiG website (or in the *Answers* magazine) deal with this issue.

Even with this wonderful research and its dissemination, the spiritual battle is intensifying. We don't fight against flesh and blood but "principalities and powers" (Eph. 6:12). As more and more answers have been given and inconsistencies pointed out, the arguments against God's Word in Genesis move on to different topics. This is why we continually need to be on our guard as we "contend for the faith" (Jude 3).

Word-twisting, truth-skewing newspeak is happening in the debate over the creation account in Genesis. Dr. William Dembski *says* that he believes in the inspired inerrant Word of God and in a literal Adam and Eve. But what does he *really* mean by this?

Dr. William Dembski (Southern Baptist)

Because he believes in billions of years and evolution (which means death, disease, and suffering before sin), consider what he does in an attempt to convince people he believes in a literal Adam and Eve, with death, disease, and suffering coming after sin. Here are some quotes from one of his latest books:

> For the theodicy I am proposing to be compatible with evolution, God must not merely introduce existing human-like beings from outside the Garden. In addition, when they enter the Garden, God must transform their consciousness so that they become rational moral agents made in God's image.[3]
>
> Any evils humans experience outside the Garden before God breathes into them the breath of life would be experienced as natural evils in the same way that other animals experience them. The pain would be real, but it would not be experienced as divine justice in response to willful rebellion. Moreover, once God breathes the breath of life into them, we may assume that the first humans experienced an amnesia of their former animal life: Operating on a higher plane of consciousness once infused with the breath of life, they would transcend the lower plane of animal consciousness on which they had previously operated — though,

after the Fall, they might be tempted to resort to that lower consciousness.[4]

Now when a Christian reads the above quotes, the average believer responds with, "What? This is bizarre!" But it is more than bizarre — it undermines the authority of the Word of God. But please keep in mind as I make these statements that I am not questioning anyone's Christian faith. We are encouraged to know that many Southern Baptist leaders (e.g., the late Dr. Adrian Rogers, Dr. Paige Patterson, and others) have been standing up for biblical inerrancy, but we are greatly concerned that there are some professors in Southern Baptist schools (as well as many other schools) who are actually undermining biblical authority — contrary to what they claim.

So why does Dr. Dembski propose ideas such as those above? Let's hear from his own words:

> The young-earth solution to reconciling the order of creation with natural history makes good exegetical and theological sense. Indeed, the overwhelming consensus of theologians up through the Reformation held to this view. I myself would adopt it in a heartbeat except that nature seems to present such a strong evidence against it. I'm hardly alone in my reluctance to accept young-earth.[5]

Notice his admission that if one takes God's Word as authoritative ("makes good exegetical and theological sense"), then it is obvious the earth is young. However, note the "except" word when he states that "*except* that nature seems to present such a strong evidence against it" (emphasis added).

So what does Dr. Dembski mean by stating that "nature seems to present such a strong evidence against it"?

He further states:

> A young earth seems to be required to maintain a traditional understanding of the Fall. And yet a young earth clashes sharply with mainstream science.[6]

In an article, he wrote:

> Dating methods, in my view, provide strong evidence for rejecting this face-value chronological reading of Genesis 4–11.[7]

It really comes down to the fact that Dr. Dembski accepts the fallible secular dating methods (based on numerous fallible assumptions[8]) and uses their results to trump the Word of God! That is the problem with many in the

Church — accepting man's words over God's Word. And yet, he claims to believe in inerrancy.

But without even dealing with the age of the earth issue (there are numerous articles on the www.answersingenesis.org website dealing with this topic), let us compare parts of his "theodicy" with Scripture — and you can be the judge.

Consider these statements concerning his above quotes:

> God must not merely introduce existing human-like beings from outside the Garden. In addition, when they enter the Garden, God must transform their consciousness so that they become rational moral agents made in God's image. . . . We may assume that the first humans experienced an amnesia of their former animal life: Operating on a higher plane of consciousness once infused with the breath of life, they would transcend the lower plane of animal consciousness on which they had previously operated.

Could God have introduced "human-like beings" into the Garden? Dr. Dembski is saying the Garden was perfect, but because of his belief in billions of years, death and suffering existed in the world with animals eating each other, etc. What I understand him to be saying is that because God is infinite and knew man would fall, He created a world in which there would be billions of years of death and suffering — so that when God gave Adam and Eve souls and they were then made in the image of God, they would fall (sin) in a perfect Garden and then see the effects of their sin in the death and suffering outside the Garden (which chronologically existed before sin but is actually a result of their sin, as God knew they would fall)!

Let's consider this passage of Scripture:

> Then the LORD God formed man of dust from the ground, and breathed into his nostrils the breath of life; and man became a living being (Gen. 2:7).

Note the order here: God made man from dust, added the divine breath, and this caused Adam to become a living being. The Hebrew words translated "living being" are the same Hebrew words used to describe sea creatures, birds, and land animals in Genesis 1:21, 24, 30, and 9:10. So the Bible is absolutely clear: God did *not* make some human-like living being and then add the divine breath that became man. The Scriptures teach man plus divine breath equals living being, *not* living being plus divine breath equals man. Paul affirms the literal truth of Genesis 2:7 when he says (in 1 Cor. 15:45) that "the first man Adam was made a living soul" (KJV). This is further confirmed by the judgment of God in Genesis 3:19. Adam was made from dust, and when he died, he returned to dust — he did not return to a human-like or ape-like being! Also, consider these passages of Scripture:

> Then the Lord God took the man and put him into the garden of Eden to cultivate it and keep it (Gen. 2:15).

> Then the Lord God said, "It is not good for the man to be alone; I will make him a helper suitable for him" (Gen. 2:18).

> The man said, "This is now bone of my bones, and flesh of my flesh; she shall be called Woman, because she was taken out of Man" (Gen. 2:23).

Note that Eve was made *from* Adam (by supernatural surgery, not by any natural process) after Adam was *in* the Garden. Eve did not come into the Garden as some "human-like" being and then get transformed by God into a full human being.

Note also what the Apostle Paul wrote as part of the infallible Scriptures:

> For as woman came from man . . . (1 Cor. 11:12; NIV).

> For man did not come from woman, but woman from man (1 Cor. 11:8; NIV).

> For Adam was formed first, then Eve (1 Tim. 2:13; NIV).

These passages all quote from Genesis 2:23 and Genesis 2:24 as literal history — so the literal history from Genesis is that the woman was made *from* Adam after he was already *in* the Garden.

Also, while in the Garden, God had made the animals and brought certain land animals to Adam for him to name and to show that he was alone. Obviously these animals weren't aggressive, so God had to have non-aggressive animals in the Garden, but outside the Garden, according to Dr. Dembski, there was a world that was "red in tooth and claw," as the poet Tennyson stated. (Actually, Gen. 1:30 states that all the animals were plant eaters originally — not sure how Dr. Dembski handles this, but maybe he would suggest this was just for the animals in the Garden.)

Another fatal flaw in Dr. Dembski's theodicy (i.e., the question of evil) is that he proposes that God judged the world with millions of years of animal death, disease, and extinction and other natural evil — and this judgment was because of man's sin, which occurred *after* all this natural evil had been occurring for billions of years. What kind of judge would punish a man with prison resulting in great suffering for his family *before* he committed a crime? Dr. Dembski's theodicy turns God into a grossly unjust Judge. But as Genesis 18:25 says, "Shall not the Judge of all the earth deal justly?"

There are many other inconsistencies in Dr. Dembski's beliefs. But what they show are the outrageous lengths some Christian academics will go in order to blend billions of years with the Scriptures. Yet they try to keep their belief in a literal Adam and Eve and the original sin, telling unsuspecting parents and prospective students that they believe in inerrancy.

Now many might believe we are just being divisive, or splitting hairs. Why does it really matter anyway? Let me explain by once again considering the writings of Dr. William Dembski quoted earlier. I have had interaction with a Christian leader concerning why we see the writings of Dr. Dembski as a major problem for the Church. This leader said that the world is the enemy and we shouldn't critique someone who believes in the inerrancy of Scripture. In my response I stated:

> I believe there is a misunderstanding in regard to the emphasis of our Answers in Genesis ministry and why our presenters (including myself), at appropriate times, quote scholars like Dembski, Sailhamer, Grudem, Waltke, Kline, Archer, Young, Falk, Giberson, Bohlin, Harlow, Craig, Hodge, Warfield, and others. We have never called into question these men's salvation. And we are not attacking them personally. But we are convinced that they are making a serious and significant mistake regarding the age of the earth (and in some cases evolution, too), and thereby (no doubt unintentionally) undermining the gospel and the authority of Scripture, which seriously hurts the church and her witness.

I went on to state:

> Over the years, we have written many articles (most are available on our website) to help people understand that we are first and foremost a ministry standing on the authority of the Word of God and proclaiming the saving gospel of Jesus Christ. We do not just want to see people converted to believe in creation, or an intelligent designer, but to believe in and trust the Creator, the Lord Jesus Christ, for salvation. Many people have the erroneous idea that our main emphasis is that of arguing against evolution and teaching a young earth. However, like you I am sure, the reason we believe in a young earth/

universe and reject evolution is because of our stand on the authority of God's Word. In other words, our belief in a young earth/universe is part of the greater belief that the Bible is true and should be taken as written (e.g., 2 Cor. 4:2; Prov. 8:8–9). An abundance of biblical evidence in the Old and New Testament shows that Genesis is written as literal history and therefore our stand is that it should be interpreted as such. I believe you wholeheartedly agree.

I have included with this letter one of our latest publications (*Already Gone*) in which we detail the results of research conducted by renowned researcher Britt Beemer from America's Research Group. This research deals with why the majority of our young people are leaving their theologically conservative churches after they graduate from high school. Actually, this research also showed that the belief in millions of years was a significant contributing factor to creating doubt in these young people about the Bible's accuracy. We all know that churches have problems with the younger generation and their commitment to church and the Christian faith. We also observe the massive decline of Christianity throughout Europe and the United Kingdom — and we know that the USA is also moving rapidly down the same path.

This research and other studies (and our own experiences) have convinced us that a major contributing factor in the youth exodus has been the undermining of biblical authority. Of course, we all know that God's Word has come under attack since Genesis 3, and the Apostle Paul warns us in 2 Corinthians 11:3 that Satan is going to use the same method on us as he did on Eve. That method has been used to lead people to doubt God's Word and put them on a slippery slide of unbelief. In this era of history (beginning in the late 18th and early 19th centuries), there has been a very specific attack on the history of the first eleven chapters of the Bible.

We insist that what Dr. Dembski proposes in his book *The End of Christianity* is undermining the clear teaching of Scripture and thereby also undercutting biblical authority. God's people need to be warned concerning this serious slide.

And I further stated:

If there is truly an undermining of the authority of God's Word in a publication that is now very public, then I believe we should firmly and graciously confront this issue. Did not Paul set an example for us in Galatians 2:11–14, when he "withstood him [Peter] to the face" for compromising the gospel by his eating habits, which on the surface seemed so insignificant?

Dr. Karl Giberson and Dr. Darrel Falk (Nazarene)

We could obtain examples of "newspeak" and compromise from a variety of denominations. Here is an example from the Nazarene denomination. As you read below, keep in mind this quote about one of the founders and the first president (Phineas Bresee) of Point Loma Nazarene University in San Diego:

> There is a Bible on campus, encased in protective glass. This Bible belonged to Phineas Bresee. It's opened to Isaiah 62, the chapter Bresee claimed for the school. Permanently marked with his fingerprints, it displays a double message: God's words in Isaiah 62 and Bresee's love for those words. It's a message of being grounded in Scripture, of pursuing a well-rounded education and serving the poor out of a first and intense love for God and His Word. Bresee died in 1915, but his message still resonates. In fact, it defines Point Loma Nazarene University.[9]

Now consider the following in regard to that college and another Nazarene college. Students at Eastern Nazarene College (Boston), and Point Loma Nazarene University (San Diego) who came under the teaching of ardent evolutionists Dr. Karl Giberson and Dr. Darrel Falk respectively, would not only have been taught evolution as fact, but sadly, probably came under such teaching described below and endorsed by these same professors in the roles of vice-president and president of the BioLogos Foundation:

> Belief in a supernatural creator always leaves open the possibility that human beings are a fully-intended part of creation. If the Creator chooses to interact with creation, he could very well influence the evolutionary process to ensure the arrival of his intended result. . . . Furthermore, an omniscient creator could easily create the universe in such a way that physical and natural laws would result in human evolution. . . .
>
> God planned for humans to evolve to the point of attaining these characteristics. . . . For example, in order to reflect God's Image by engaging in meaningful relationships, the human brain had to

evolve to the point where an understanding of love and relationship could be grasped and lived out. God's intention for humans to have relationships is illustrated in the opening chapters of Genesis, where many fundamental truths about God and humankind are communicated through the imagery of a creation story. After placing Adam in the Garden of Eden, Genesis 2 describes God's decision to provide Adam with a partner. . . . The Image of God also includes moral consciousness and responsibility. Humans did not have a fully formed moral consciousness prior to the time of Adam and Eve. . . . However, general consciousness must have already evolved so that a moral consciousness and the associated responsibility were possible. . . . When Adam and Eve received God's image, they had evolved to where they could understand the difference between right and wrong. It seems that Adam and Eve first demonstrated their new moral prowess when, using their free will, they chose wrong by eating from the forbidden tree of knowledge of good and evil. Adam and Eve then knew the difference between right and wrong in a more personal way than before, having experienced the guilt and shame that accompanied their decision (see Genesis 3:1–13). . . . When Did Humans Receive the Image of God?

We cannot know the exact time that humans attained God's image. In fact, it may be that the image of God emerged gradually over a period of time. Estimates of the historical time of Adam and Eve are varied. . . . While some literalist interpreters of Genesis argue that God created Adam and Eve in their present form, the evidence of DNA and the fossil record establishes that humans were also participants in the long evolutionary continuum, and God used this process as his means of creation. . . .

We also do not know if humanity received the image of God by the immediate onset of a relationship with God or by a slower evolutionary process. In either case, this development occurred before the fall of Adam and Eve, since moral responsibility and a broken relationship with God are both involved in the story of the fall. Perhaps God used the evolutionary process to equip humankind with language, free will and culture, and then revealed God's will to individuals or a community so that they might then enter into meaningful relationship with God through obedience, prayer, and worship. In this scenario, the evolutionary process is necessary but not sufficient to encompass the biblical teaching on the image of God.[10]

This is just a small amount of the teaching these Nazarene professors endorse — certainly not consistent with orthodox Christianity.

Dr. Giberson was also the co-author of an opinion column that appeared on the *USA Today* website and in the print edition.[11] The piece began:

> We believe in evolution — and God. Nearly half of Americans still dispute the indisputable: that humans evolved to our current form over millions of years. We're scientists and Christians. Our message to the faithful: Fear not. . . . The "science" undergirding this "young earth creationism" comes from a narrow, literalistic and relatively recent interpretation of Genesis, the first book in the Bible.[12]

What many parents don't realize is these two Nazarene professors (like certain other Christian college professors) don't just teach students evolution — it is much worse than that. The section above from the BioLogos website is just a tiny sample of the incredible attack on the authority of Scripture such teachers are imparting to students while the unsuspecting parents think they are doing a great thing in paying thousands of dollars for the children to be educated in a Christian school — but educated against the Bible!

In the *USA Today* article,[13] Dr. Giberson (and Dr. Falk) state: "We have launched a website to spread this good news (www.biologos.org) and — we hope — to answer the many questions those of faith might have. . . . The project aims to counter the voices coming from places such as the website Answers in Genesis. . . ."

By the way, the "good news" includes the statements above from the BioLogos website,[14] as well as such things as:

> The Everyman Reading of the creation story provides a very different metaphorical take on the text. This view understands the Fall as an allegorical story representing every human's individual rejection of God. In this light, the Fall was not a historical event but an illustration of the common human condition that virtually everyone agrees is deeply flawed and sinful. In this view, it does not matter if Adam and Eve were historical figures. Their deeds simply represent the actions of all humans and remind us of this troubling part of our natures.
>
> . . . where did the wife of Cain, Adam's son, come from? The only possibility is that she was Cain's sister, but this conflicts with later Biblical commands against incest. Even more problematic are

the people whom Cain fears when he is banished from his home-land for killing his brother Abel. It is highly implausible that the people Cain fears are also offspring of Adam and Eve; the text certainly does not suggest this. The people trying to kill Cain would have to be his extended family — siblings, nieces, nephews and so on — all united in trying to kill him. Along the same lines, Genesis mentions the city that Cain built and named after his son (Genesis 4:17). Who would populate this city or help to build it? The scientific evidence suggests a dramatically larger population at this point in history. Recently acquired genetic evidence also points to a population of several thousand people from whom all humans have descended, not just two.

So, no literal Fall, no literal Adam and Eve — so much for Christianity! And all people have descended from several thousand people, not just two — which means the Apostle Paul in Romans 5 and 1 Corinthians 15 is wrong concerning the gospel! And if that's the case, then Jesus didn't even tell the truth in Matthew 19 when he quoted Genesis and built the doctrine of marriage on the literal history in this account.

It seems the atheists understand theology better than these compromised Christians. They realize that if a literal Fall and a literal Adam and Eve are indeed false, then there is no use being a Christian because it undermines the very basis for the Gospel. One leading atheist claims:

> Christianity has fought, still fights, and will fight science to the desperate end over evolution, because evolution destroys utterly and finally the very reason Jesus' earthly life was supposedly made necessary. Destroy Adam and Eve and the original sin, and in the rubble you will find the sorry remains of the son of god. Take away the meaning of his death. If Jesus was not the redeemer that died for our sins, and this is what evolution means, then Christianity is nothing.[15]

For Christmas 2010, the American Atheists sponsored a billboard for people to see as they exited the Lincoln Tunnel. The billboard read: "You KNOW it's a Myth — This Season, Celebrate REASON!" It then directed people to their website. A statement on this website illustrates clearly that atheists do understand the importance of a literal Adam and Eve and a literal Fall to Christianity. They stated:

> Chances are, if you're reading this, you don't believe in the fable of Adam and Eve and the talking snake. You probably think it's a

story, created out of ignorance, to explain the origin of life. You probably don't believe that Adam literally ate a fruit, resulting in God expelling him and Eve out of the idyllic Garden of Eden.

In other words, you know that's a myth.

Right so far? So if Adam and Eve and the Talking Snake are myths, then Original Sin is also a myth, right? Well, think about it. . . .

Jesus' major purpose was to save mankind from Original Sin.

Original Sin makes believers unworthy of salvation, but you get it anyway, so you should be *grateful* for being saved (from that which does not exist).

Without Original Sin, the marketing that all people are sinners and therefore need to accept Jesus falls moot.

All we are asking is that you take what **you know** into serious consideration, even if it means taking a hard look at all you've been taught for your whole life. No Adam and Eve means no need for a savior. It also means that the Bible cannot be trusted as a source of unambiguous, literal truth. It is completely unreliable, because it all begins with a myth, and builds on that as a basis. No Fall of Man means no need for atonement and no need for a redeemer. You know it.[16]

But atheists aside, there is so much more on the BioLogos website — I actually encourage you to read all their questions and answers. If you stand on God's infallible Word, you will be shocked at some of the things you read. The trouble is most people in our churches do not know the reality of what is being taught at these colleges and through the books and websites! "Giberson has been on the faculty at Eastern Nazarene College in Quincy, Massachusetts, since 1984, where he teaches interdisciplinary honors seminars and the history of science. He is also the director of the Forum on Faith and Science at Gordon College in Wenham, Massachusetts, codirector of the Venice Summer School on Science & Religion and a fellow of the American Scientific Affiliation."[17]

May God have mercy on us when one considers this is the shocking state of a growing number of seminaries and Christian colleges in this nation.

Dr. William Lane Craig (Talbot School of Theology)

Some of you may have heard of Dr. William Lane Craig, research professor of philosophy at Talbot School of Theology in La Mirada, California. He says he believes in biblical inerrancy.[18] However, listen to the podcast referenced to understand what he means by inerrancy. And then of course it is not surprising to hear him in this television interview as he discusses the question of the age of the earth and Genesis:[19]

> Coren: How old is the world?
>
> Dr. Craig: The best estimates today are around 13.7 billion years.
>
> Coren: Now this is good, you see. This is a position I can embrace. Because there are people who will sit here and say, "No, it's six and a half thousand years old." That is not a tenable position?
>
> Dr. Craig: I don't think it's plausible. The arguments that I give are right in line with mainstream science. I'm not bucking up against mainstream science in presenting these arguments. Rather I'm going with the flow of what contemporary cosmology and astrophysics supports.
>
> Coren: Is there a contradiction or an inconsistency between the biblical account of the age of the earth and your statement?
>
> Dr. Craig: That's interesting because there isn't any biblical account of the age of the earth. There's nothing in Genesis or elsewhere in the Bible that says how old the universe is, so no, I don't think it is incompatible.
>
> Coren: We often hear the rather caricatured argument that Christians believe that man and dinosaur coexisted.
>
> Dr. Craig: There are some creationists — they typically style themselves "young earth creationists" — who believe that. I've even seen children's books where Noah takes dinosaur eggs on the ark with him. Well, all of this is reading between the lines. There's nothing like that in the book of Genesis.

What does inerrancy really mean? This is a major problem within Christianity. The point we make over and over again is that when we teach the next generation to reinterpret God's Word this way (i.e., by using the majority view in secular science), it unlocks a door that undermines all of biblical authority. Subsequent generations will continue to push that door open wider, which has already happened all across our Western world. After all, the majority of secular scientists also insist that virgins don't have babies and dead men don't rise from the dead. So should we also reinterpret Matthew 1 and Matthew 28 accordingly and just go with the flow of mainstream science?

Now I have observed an interesting phenomenon that is permeating Christian colleges and seminaries, which influences future church leaders and what they take to the pulpit, mission field, etc.

I believe many Christian academics recognize the inconsistency in trying to add millions of years and evolution to Genesis. The compromise is obvious. Many of them recognize that one has to totally change the meaning of the words in Genesis to allow such compromise. For example, creating Adam out of dust and Eve from a rib have to be changed to mean that ape-men and ape-women changed into Adam and Eve. But this ignores many details in the biblical text and ends up playing language games. Various articles on the Answers in Genesis website point out the numerous problems with such compromise.

Ultimately, of course, the result of this compromise undermines the authority of God's Word. And in the Church today, we see two-thirds of young people leaving the Church by the time they reach college age, and it's largely because the reliability and authority of God's Word has been undermined (as our research for the book *Already Gone* has shown).

Today, the same battle rages, but we see a change in what is being foisted on the Church as the enemy continues to attack God's Word. Remember, the attack has always been on God's Word, as it started with the questioning of what God said to Adam and Eve in Genesis 3 and has never let up.

That attack just manifests itself in different ways in different eras. I have observed that more and more Christian academics, in their attempt to adopt man's ideas of evolution and millions of years, are continuing this attack in a different sort of way. The following is a specific example from a professor at Wheaton College, Illinois.

Dr. John Walton (Wheaton College, Illinois)

Dr. John Walton is professor of Old Testament at Wheaton College in Illinois and is author of *The Lost World of Genesis One*.[20]

A summary of what Dr. Walton teaches is that Genesis 1 is not history in regard to the material world; it has to do with what he calls God's "Cosmic Temple." He basically insists that one can only understand Genesis if one has an understanding of ancient Near Eastern thinking — and surprise, surprise — this has been lost for thousands of years. Now a few academics like Dr. Walton have unearthed this thinking so now they can tell us what the writer of Genesis 1 really meant! It is an academic elitism.

Dr. Walton tries (unsuccessfully) to insist that he is not coming up with this new idea of his because of the influence of evolution/millions of years — but the clear fact is that he is doing just that! He knows that young people today have a conflict between the secular view of origins and the Bible — so his solution is to relegate Genesis 1 as having nothing to do with material origins and thus people are free to believe whatever they want — though he is obviously convinced that evolution and millions of years should be believed.

The bottom line is, it is just another way of trying to come up with a "solution" to fitting millions of years and evolution into the Bible. Because Dr. Walton knows (and admits) that the days of creation are ordinary days in Genesis 1, according to the Hebrew language, he had to come up with a way to allow for millions of years and evolution and yet agree that the days of creation are ordinary days. So his solution? Relegate Genesis 1 to mean it is the creation of God's Cosmic Temple, and not allow it to have anything to do with material origins. Then he can say that students will have no conflict — they can believe in millions of years/evolution/or whatever — and it doesn't matter!

And of course, the reason the Church greats of the past (whether Luther, Calvin, Gill, or whomever) never thought of this is because they did not discover how ancient Near Eastern cultures were thinking! This has now been discovered by an elite few who can now tell us for the first time in thousands of years what Genesis 1 really means. Sound bizarre? I encourage you to read the book for yourself! Following are just a few quotes from the book.

Were Adam and Eve two real people? Dr. Walton states:

> This archetypal understanding applies also to Genesis 2. An individual named Adam is not the only human being made of the dust of the earth, for as Genesis 3:19 indicates, "Dust you are and to dust you will return." This is true of all humans, men and women. It is an archetypal feature that describes us all. It is not a statement of chemical composition nor is it describing a material process by which each and every human being is made. The dust is an archetypal feature and therefore cannot be viewed as a material ingredient. It is indicative of human destiny and mortality, and therefore is a functional comment, not a material one.[21]

Is Genesis 1 an account of material origins? Dr. Walton states:

> When we thought of Genesis 1 as an account of material origins, creation became an action in the past that is over and done with. God made objects and now the cosmos exists (materially). Viewing Genesis 1 as an account of functional origins offers more opportunity for understanding that God's creative work continues.[22]

> Genesis 1 would be viewed as a temple text — we gain a different perspective on the nature of the Genesis creation account. Genesis 1

can now be seen as a creation account focusing on the cosmos as a temple. It is describing the creation of the cosmic temple with all of its functions and with God dwelling in its midst.[23]

Was the Garden of Eden a real garden? Dr. Walton states:

> The garden of Eden is not viewed by the author of Genesis simply as a piece of Mesopotamian farmland, but as an archetypal sanctuary, that is a place where God dwells and where man should worship him. Many of the features of the garden may also be found in later sanctuaries particularly the tabernacle or Jerusalem temple. These parallels suggest that the garden itself is understood as a sort of sanctuary.[24]

Does Dr. John Walton believe in millions of years?

> The day-age theory and others that attempt to mitigate the force of the seven days do so because they see no way to reconcile seven twenty-four-hour days of material creation with the evidence from science that the earth and the universe are very old. They seek a solution in trying to stretch the meaning of yôm, whereas we propose that once we understand the nature of the creation account, there is no longer any need to stretch yôm.[25]
>
> Some variation exists as to whether the cosmic origins go back 10,000–20,000 years as some would allow, or only go back about 6,000 years from the present (as promoted at the Creation Museum in Petersburg, Kentucky). The challenge they face is to account for all of the evidences of great age of the earth and of the universe.[26]

Of course he believes in millions of years, and despite his insistence to the contrary, this is part of his ultimate motivation to relegate Genesis 1 to something other than material history.

So what does Dr. Walton say Genesis 1 means?

> In summary, we have suggested that the seven days are not given as the period of time over which the material cosmos came into existence, but the period of time devoted to the inauguration of the functions of the cosmic temple, and perhaps also its annual reenactment. It is not the material phase of temple construction that represents the creation of the temple; it is the inauguration of the functions and the entrance of the presence of God to take up his rest that creates the temple. Genesis 1 focuses on the creation of the

(cosmic) temple, not the material phase of preparation. In the next chapter we will track the implications of the idea that the seven days are not related to the material phase of creation.[27]

There is so much more. He does not believe in a global Flood and believes there was death of animals (and disease and thorns because he allows for millions of years) millions of years before man (however man came into existence.)

There is a very telling statement from his book:

> This is not a conclusion designed to accommodate science — it was drawn from an analysis and interpretation of the biblical text of Genesis in its ancient environment. The point is *not* that the biblical text therefore supports an old earth, but simply that there is not biblical position on the age of the earth. If it were to turn out that the earth is young, so be it. But most people who seek to defend a young-earth view do so because they believe that the Bible obligates them to such a defense. I admire the fact that believers are willing to take unpopular positions and investigate all sorts of alternatives in an attempt to defend the reputation of the biblical text. But if the biblical text does not demand a young earth there would be little impetus or evidence to offer such a suggestion.[28]

Well he is correct here in one sentence — biblical creationists do insist on a young earth because we "believe the Bible obligates" us "to such a defense." Of course! But notice he is trying to see his conclusion is not "designed to accommodate science" — yet as one reads the book, one finds that is *exactly* what it is all about.

What does Dr. John Walton teach in regard to the Flood of Noah's day?

I will use the almost one-thousand-page *Dictionary of the Old Testament Pentateuch* edited by T. Desmond Alexander and David W. Baker[29] to document Dr. Walton's teaching on the Genesis Flood. Starting on page 315, there is 12-page section on the Genesis Flood account written by Dr. John Walton, professor of Old Testament at Wheaton College in Illinois.

In the section above, I outlined Dr. Walton's approach to Genesis, pointing out that he believes Genesis 1 is not an account of material origins, but an account of God's "Cosmic Temple." Dr. Walton believes that a person needs to understand ancient Near Eastern thinking and culture in order to understand Scripture. He argues that such an understanding has been lost for ages, but that academics, like himself, have been able to regain an understanding of this ancient Near Eastern thinking so the rest of us in the Church can finally (after thousands of years) understand what Genesis 1 means.

Dr. Walton certainly has a different view of inspiration to that of Drs. Whitcomb and Morris who authored the famous *The Genesis Flood* publication, our AiG staff, and millions of other Christians around the world. Dr. Walton, though, looks at the person(s) who wrote Genesis and the pagan cultures of the day as authoritative. Drs. Morris and Whitcomb (and Answers in Genesis and the Institute for Creation Research — two of the leading creation apologetics organizations), however, understand that it is the *words* of Scripture that are inspired.

I think of this passage of Scripture: "All Scripture is inspired by God, and profitable for teaching, for reproof, for correction, for training in righteousness" (2 Tim. 3:16).

In the original Greek language, "inspiration of God" is one word and it means literally "God-breathed." This verse clearly states that the words of Scripture are God-breathed! Every one of them came from Him as the Spirit of God worked through the prophets and Apostles. We are also told that God's Word will stand forever. If the infinite God, who created language, cannot move people to write His "God-breathed" words so all people (regardless of culture) can understand them, then there is something dreadfully wrong. If it is only now, after thousands of years, that we can finally understand what Genesis means because of what a few academics claim about ancient Near Eastern thinking, how can we be sure we know anything? How do we know those academics like Dr. Walton have it right? No wonder Scripture cautions us that "knowledge puffs up" (1 Cor. 8:1; NIV). We are seeing academia in the Christian world going mad as "Protestant popes" are popping up all over the Christian world.

Regarding the Flood, Dr. Walton applies the same misguided approach as he does in Genesis 1. He states the following:

> The theological message of the Bible was communicated to people who lived in the ancient Near Eastern world. If we desire to understand the theological message of the text, we will benefit by positioning it within the worldview of the ancient cultures rather than simply applying our own cultural perspectives.[30]

Dr. Walton then discusses ancient Near Eastern mythology and relates it to Scripture and its Book of Genesis. In essence, he is using pagan, idolatrous mythology to supposedly help enable us to understand what God and Moses really meant!

But really, the whole underlying reason for what he is doing (as I noted previously) relates to the ideas of millions of years and evolution. Dr. Walton recognizes that you can't fit millions of years and evolution into Genesis, so he is hoping to popularize an idea that Genesis is not revealing an account of material origins. Genesis chapter 1, for instance, is supposed to be about God's Cosmic Temple and the function of the different creatures in that temple (which came into existence who knows when)!

So what does the Flood account mean then? Dr. Walton declares the following:

> It has already been suggested that the boat in Mesopotamian accounts may have served as a floating shrine. In its dimensions, the Genesis ark is much more realistic for a boat, though conceptually it may also represent a sanctuary where order is maintained floating on a sea of resurgent chaos. In this sense the Mesopotamian ark appears as a physical representation of a sanctuary, while the Genesis ark appears as a functional representation of a sanctuary. Creation both in the Bible and in the ancient Near East entailed deity bringing order while pushing back chaos. . . . The forces of chaos were most consistently represented in the cosmic waters. In this sense, the flood represents a reversal of creation. This is more the case in the biblical account than in the ancient Near Eastern accounts, for in the latter there is no textual representation of re-creation.[31]

Now that makes sense to the average person, doesn't it? Why didn't any Jews or Christians before the 20th century ever think of this? Obviously, the answer to this is that they trusted the Bible as the authority, whereas today many trust man's ideas as being *greater* than God's and therefore demote God's Word to be lesser than their own ideas (Ps. 118:8).

While Dr. Walton insists that he does not propose his views as a response to millions of years and evolution, that is exactly what his underlying motive is. It is obvious when you read his writings carefully. For instance, Dr. Walton objects to a global Flood by bringing up the same old arguments that Drs. Morris and Whitcomb were confronted with and answered in their book!

For instance, Dr. Walton makes the following claims:

1. It would be impossible to cover Mt. Ararat with the waters of the Flood. Answer: this assumes Mt. Ararat existed before the Flood! This mountain is one that has undergone massive volcanism and uplift. If you were to smooth out the earth's surface and oceans basins, there is enough water on the earth's surface right now to cover the earth to a

depth of about two miles. The oceans were not as deep and the mountains not as high before the Flood. There has been a lot of uplift — particularly associated with the ending of the Flood (as Ps. 104:6–9 tells us — and the promise in verse 9, which reflects God's rainbow promise in Genesis 9, shows that this passage is not referring to day 3 of Genesis 1). That is why marine fossils are found near the top of Mt. Everest (and other high mountains); the mountains were not covered by the Flood but the once-horizontal sediments were tilted and raised up at the end of the Flood. One also can see evidence of this uplift at the Grand Canyon, where layers supposedly millions of years old were uplifted while they were still soft.

2. Dr. Walton brings up the old accusation that there are too many species of animals to fit on the ark. Answer: First of all, God brought the animals to Noah; Noah didn't have to locate them. Second, God sent two (seven of some) of every *kind*, not species. There are good biblical and scientific reasons to conclude that many species or even genera are descended genetically from each original created kind. For example, only one male and one female of the dog kind (not two wolves, two jackals, two dingoes, two poodles, two Great Danes, etc.) were needed. Far fewer animals were required than what Dr. Walton is imagining and claiming.

3. Dr. Walton states, "one must also explain how the animals today found only in Australia could have gotten to that continent."[32] He needs only to purchase our *New Answers Book 1* — or just go to the Answers in Genesis website — for a very plausible answer of land bridges during the Ice Age that followed the Genesis Flood. Frankly, this academic has not done his homework.

4. Dr. Walton states, "How could Noah and his family and animals such as elephants and hippopotami make the trek down the mountain (Mt. Ararat)."[33] First, the Bible does not say the ark landed on Mt. Ararat; it landed on the "mountains of Ararat," which this Hebrew expert should have known. So the Bible doesn't tell us what particular mountain it was. The Mt. Ararat Dr. Walton refers to has undergone massive changes since the Flood: volcanism, earthquakes, and uplift. Answers in Genesis's geologist, Andrew Snelling, Ph.D., has stated that based on technical data that has been publicly available in maps and scientific papers for more than a decade, he is convinced that modern Mt. Ararat is almost certainly a post-Flood volcano, with most of its lavas having erupted during the post-Flood Ice Age. Therefore, the ark most

likely landed on some other mountain in that range. And unless Dr. Walton is going to say the Flood account is a myth, then it is obvious that Noah's family and all the animals could safely descend the mountain they landed on so that they could repopulate the earth.

There are many more problems with what Dr. Walton states. But the bottom line is that he does not believe in a global Flood, and he does believe in an earth that is millions of years old. In this section of the book, he certainly speaks positively about a possible regional event millions of years ago. He states, "If the reader finds it difficult to put the flood 5.5million years ago, the Black Sea theory may be more palatable."[34] He really sums it up when he states, "There is presently no convincing archaeological evidence of the biblical flood." So does he believe it was a myth? That belief would be contrary to the teaching of Jesus (Matt. 24:37–39) and the Apostle Peter (2 Pet. 2:4–6 and 3:3–7).

So the battle rages. It is the same battle Drs. Morris and Whitcomb were dealing with in their classic *The Genesis Flood*. These great scholars were passionate for the Word of God. In the 50 years since their book's publication, the biblical creation movement is more passionate than ever for the Word of God. At the same time, we now see Christian academics like Dr. Walton using the argument that Genesis is not an account of material origins and that a Christian has to understand ancient Near Eastern thinking to know what Genesis really means.

Dr. Walton's own arguments can be summed up this way; he states the following:

> Some feel they are protecting theories that account of the details of the traditional interpretation of the text. Too often, however, these theories prove to be implausible and are easily discredited by the scientific thinkers whom they intend to win over.[35]

Let me reword this for you (my words are interspersed in Dr. Waltons' and are in brackets to help explain what I believe Dr. Walton is saying):

> Some [those like Drs. Whitcomb and Morris] feel they are protecting theories [protecting the clear teaching of the text] that account for details of the traditional interpretation of the text [the interpretation that greats like Luther, Calvin, Wesley, Gill, and others held because of what the text clearly states]. Too often, however, these theories [their views based clearly on the text — Scripture alone] prove to be implausible [to unbelievers, but not

to Bible-believers] and are easily discredited by scientific thinkers [fallible, sinful humans whose hearts are "deceitful above all things and desperately wicked," and who arrogantly claim that "science" has disproved the Bible's account because they insist millions of years are a fact] whom they intend to win over [who need to listen to God's Word, but instead "suppress the truth in unrighteousness" (Rom. 1:18)].

Today, let's praise God for the faithfulness of scholars like Drs. Whitcomb and Morris and for the publication of their book *The Genesis Flood*. In some ways, this was the beginning of a new "reformation" in the modern church, which continues to this day as organizations like Answers in Genesis, Institute for Creation Research, Creation Research Society, etc., continue to challenge the Church and culture to return to the authority of the Word of God.

Why are we seeing more and more bizarre and elitist ideas (like those of Dr. Dembski and Dr. Walton) coming out of Christian academia? I believe it is an academic pride, from academic peer pressure, because ultimately some of these people love "human praise more than praise from God" (John 12:43; NIV).

Why should we bother bringing such matters to the attention of the Church? I believe we need to be watchmen as described in Ezekiel, warning people about the teaching that is in the public arena that attacks biblical authority. We must be willing to defend God's Word and warn God's people of the damage some of these teachers are doing. Also, some of them must be called to return to God's sovereign authority, and we invite any and all educators to privately dialogue with us on these fundamentally important and essential matters.

Son of man, speak to the children of your people, and say to them: "When I bring the sword upon a land, and the people of the land take a man from their territory and make him their watchman, when he sees the sword coming upon the land, if he blows the trumpet and warns the people, then whoever hears the sound of the trumpet and does not take warning, if the sword comes and takes him away, his blood shall be on his own head. He heard the sound of the trumpet, but did not take warning; his blood shall be upon himself. But he who takes warning will save his life. But if the watchman sees the sword coming and does not blow the trumpet, and the people are not warned, and the sword comes and takes any person from among them, he is taken away in his iniquity; but his blood I will require at the watchman's hand."

So you, son of man: I have made you a watchman for the house of Israel; therefore you shall hear a word from My mouth and warn them for Me (Ezek. 33:2–7; NKJV).

I have included more quotes below from professors associated with well-known Christian colleges to help people understand the extent of such compromise in these institutions. (Of course, this is just scratching the surface of this problem ingrained in most such academic institutions across the nation.)

Calvin College, Michigan

1. Dr. Davis A. Young, emeritus professor of geology, Calvin College

The Bible has traditionally been read to imply that the universe is young; astronomy concludes that the universe is billions of years old. The Bible has been widely interpreted as saying that the Earth was created in six days; geology concludes that the Earth has undergone a long and complex history spanning 4.5 billion years. The Bible has been interpreted as implying fixity of animal and plant species; paleontology and biology conclude that organisms have developed from one another through time, that they have evolved. Some believe that the Bible teaches that all death entered the world only after human beings appeared and fell into sin; paleontology concludes that animals and plants died, and in some cases died violently by being devoured by other animals, before human beings were even on the Earth. Many Christians have a very difficult time accepting such conclusions since they cannot see how the Bible can possibly be in accord with them.[36]

Contrary to the view held by many Christians, we believe that historical reconstructions by modern astronomy and geology are neither uncontrolled speculations nor founded upon unbiblical presuppositions. We hold that these reconstructions are firmly grounded in a wealth of carefully gathered data and have been repeatedly tested by the respected canons of science.[37]

If rocks are historical documents, we are driven to the related conclusion that the available evidence is overwhelmingly opposed to the notion that the Noahic flood deposited rocks of the Colorado Plateau only a few thousand years ago or that the rocks were formed from a diminishing ocean.[38]

2. Dr. Howard J. Van Till, emeritus professor of physics, Calvin College

According to contemporary cosmological models, which incorporate evidence drawn from a variety of phenomena, the beginning of the universe took place about fifteen billion years ago, the exact figure depending on the evaluation of certain model parameters. We call this fifteen billion years the "age" of the universe, and we call the first episode of cosmic history the "big bang."[39]

I have often suggested that the historic Judeo-Christian doctrine of creation is better summarized by saying that *the universe is God's creation* than by saying *that the universe was created by God.*[40]

3. Dr. Deborah B. Haarsma, chair, Department of Physics and Astronomy, Calvin College

Because of this kind of evidence, by about 1840 virtually all practicing geologists, including Christian geologists, believed that the earth must be at least millions of years old. Moreover, if a flood had occurred, it must have been local, not global. The data from many locations indicated that the world's stratified rocks and fossils could not have been deposited in a single global flood. While local floods certainly did take place here and there, a longer time period and more gradual processes are required to explain the entire picture. Scientific study indicated that the earth had long geological history *before* humans arrived on the scene.[41]

The careful structure of this passage [Genesis 1] shows that the author selected the sequence of events and number of days with symbolism and thematic order in mind rather than our modern scientific concept of historical sequence. The organization and structure of the text support non-concordist interpretations of Genesis 1, since it appears that historical sequence was not the top priority for the original author.[42]

Thus, if Christians today wish to interpret Genesis 1 completely literally, they must believe that:

• The earth is flat rather than spherical.
• The earth rests on pillars rather than orbiting the sun.
• The sky is a solid dome rather than a transparent atmosphere.
• An ocean of water is above the sky.

Any other so-called *literal* interpretation of Genesis 1 is, at best, a semi-literal interpretation in which the reader picks and chooses some pieces to view literally and others to view figuratively.[43]

4. Dr. Loren Haarsma, associate professor of physics, Calvin College

The Bible teaches that God can precisely select the outcome of events that appear random to us. It is also possible that God gives his creation some freedom, through random processes, to explore the wide range of potentials he has given it. Either way, randomness within natural processes is not the absence of God. Rather, it is another vehicle for God's creativity and governance.[44]

5. Dr. Daniel C. Harlow, associate professor of religion, Calvin College

Roberts accuses Calvin of propounding "dangerous beliefs" that foster "misguided views" among our students on such topics as homosexuality. He then charges the Religion faculty with feeding a generation of Calvin students "the lie that what they are learning is Christian orthodoxy rather than 20th century modernism." Our "lie" is that we deny that the Bible is inerrant. In defending my department, I am speaking only for myself and not for the rest of my colleagues, who would doubtless want to word things differently.

To begin with, the Bible itself nowhere claims that it is inerrant (free of factual errors of any sort). . . .

Mr. Roberts is also mistaken when he asserts that the doctrine of inerrancy represents "the historic position of the Church on Scripture." The fact of the matter is that no ancient Church council ever debated the issue of inerrancy, let alone pronounced favor of it. No ecumenical creed even addresses the issue — not the Apostle's Creed, not the Nicene Creed, not the Athanasian Creed. None of the Reformed confessions that Calvin College adheres to asserts Scripture's inerrancy, but rather its "sufficiency." As the Belgic Confession states, "We believe that this Holy Scripture contains the will of God completely and that everything one must believe to be saved is sufficiently taught in it" (Article 7). The great theologians of the Church, including Protestant Reformers like Luther and Calvin, had the highest regard for Scripture's inspiration, authority and truthfulness, and at times they used words like "infallible" and even "unerring" when affirming its truth claims. But they also acknowledged factual discrepancies and other problems in the Bible and recognized the cultural limitations of its human authors. So if inerrancy is supposedly the "historic position of the Church," as Roberts asserts, how is it that the Church's great councils, creeds, confessions and theologians missed the boat? . . .

When thoughtful Christians turn to the historical narratives in the Bible, they see ancient authors who wrote according to the methods and standards of their own day. By those ancient standards, which involved the use of a variety of sometimes conflicting oral and written traditions, they were very good historians. But they made occasional errors of fact in areas like geography, chronology and political history. To acknowledge this is not to demean Scripture but to accept it as it is. It's rather like noticing one day that your beloved has a small mole or other blemish; instead of considering the feature a defect, you come to regard it as an endearment.[45]

Dr. Dan Harlow as professor of biblical and early Jewish studies in the Department of Religion at *Calvin College* stated the following in a recent paper:

Recent research in molecular biology, primatology, sociobiology, and phylogenetics indicates that the species *Homo sapiens* cannot be traced back to a single pair of individuals, and that the earliest human beings did not come on the scene in anything like paradisal physical or moral conditions. It is therefore difficult to read Genesis 1–3 as a factual account of human origins. In current Christian thinking about Adam and Eve, several scenarios are on offer. The most compelling one regards Adam and Eve as strictly literary figures — characters in a divinely inspired story about the imagined past that intends to teach theological, not historical, truths about God, creation, and humanity.

Taking a nonconcordist approach, this article examines Adam and Eve as symbolic-literary figures from the perspective of mainstream biblical scholarship, with attention both to the text of Genesis and ancient Near Eastern parallels. Along the way, it explains why most interpreters do not find the doctrines of the Fall and original sin in the text of Genesis 2–3, but only in later Christian readings of it. This article also examines briefly Paul's appeal to Adam as a type of Christ. Although a historical Adam and Eve have been very important in the Christian tradition, they are not central to biblical theology as such. The doctrines of the Fall and original sin may be reaffirmed without a historical Adam and Eve, but invite reformulation given the overwhelming evidence for an evolving creation.[46]

In response to feedback the college has received about what this professor believes and teaches (and he is just one of many with compromising beliefs at this Christian college), the office of the president of Calvin College stated the following:

> What does Calvin College teach about evolutionary biology? Calvin affirms that the one true God is the creator and designer of the universe. The Calvin College Biology Department also clearly maintains that God, as the creator and designer of the universe, brought the world into being. With this as a firm foundation, the department also accepts the biological theory of evolution (descent with modification over time) to be the best explanation for understanding the commonality and diversity seen among all living creatures on earth.[47]

Dr. John Collins, Covenant Theological Seminary, St. Louis, Missouri

Basically, as long as you believe the human race started with Adam and Eve (whatever that means) and you believe there was a Fall (whatever that means) and believe sin entered the human race (whatever that means) and you believe God created (whatever that means) then you are being academic in the Christian world!

What you will find is what he means by "historical" is certainly not what many Christians mean by "historical" in regard to Adam and Eve. This is the typical "newspeak" discussed throughout this book as a result of the research results from the Christian institutions.

This, sadly, is an example of the typical type of "academia" being taught in most Christian colleges/seminaries across the nation.

Following are excerpts from a paper entitled "Adam and Eve as Historical People, and Why It Matters," by Dr. Jack Collins, professor of Old Testament at Covenant Theological Seminary in St. Louis, Missouri:

> Quite briefly, I take the biblical storyline to imply that Adam and Eve are historical persons at the headwaters of the distinctly human kind. To say that they are "historical," of course, lays on us no

requirement of "literalism" for reading Genesis, if the material itself does not invite it. I think, for example, that the account of Cain and Abel uses "anachronism," describing aspects of older times in terms of what the writer and his audience were familiar with. Therefore those who find that the farming and the crafts of Genesis 4 imply a Neolithic setting, are being unduly literalistic. Further, it is well established that the genealogies of Genesis 5 do not intend to list every generation; gaps are to be expected. There is no way to know what size gaps the literary conventions allow, or even if there are any limits at all; this is not the kind of information these genealogies aim to convey. Nothing in Genesis 2–4 tells us how long these events are supposed to have taken, which means the other people Cain fears could be his siblings, or their descendants. Of those who think of contemporary humans, collateral with Adam and Eve, the best are careful about what Genesis 4 does and does not imply.

From the paleontologists, we learn that Adam and Eve, if they are indeed at the headwaters of the human race, must come before such events as the arrival of modern humans in Australia, which means before about 40,000 BC. According to John Bloom's survey, there are two important gaps in the available record of human development. The first occurs with the appearance of anatomically modern humans around 130,000 BC. The second gap occurs when culture appears, around 40,000 BC. At this point, we find that art and "the complexity and variety of artifacts greatly increases." As Bloom observes, "At present either of these transitions seems sharp enough that we can propose that the special creation of man occurred in one of these gaps and that it was not bridged by purely natural means."

The geneticists give us two matters to account for. First, they conclude from the genetic similarities between humans and chimpanzees that humans and chimpanzees have some kind of "common ancestor." Second, some infer from features of the human genome that the human population needs to have been a thousand or more individuals, even at its beginning. I will not assess this DNA evidence; I do not know whether the evidence is only compatible with these conclusions, or strongly favors them. I cannot predict whether future geneticists will still think the same way about DNA as contemporary ones do. I do know that biologists' understanding of DNA (e.g., so-called "junk DNA" now appears to have a function) has changed over the years, but I cannot say what biologists might think in the future. Hence, rather than try to say whether these inferences are good or bad, I have sought ways to allow advocates of these conclusions to stay within the bounds of sound thinking. In other words, even if someone is persuaded that humans had "ancestors," and that the human population has always been more than two, he or she does not necessarily have to ditch all traditional views of Adam and Eve; I have tried to provide for these possibilities more than to contend for my particular preferences on these matters.

Young-earth creationists, and many old-earth creationists, commonly think of Adam and Eve as fresh creations, with no animal forebears. Others allow for God to have refurbished a preexisting hominid into Adam. While I am not making an issue of this, my first criterion (p. 159) shows why I think it is nevertheless crucial to affirm that, whatever the process, it was not a purely natural one. Regardless of where God got the raw material, we can say that humans are the result of "special creation."[48]

In his book *Science and Faith* Dr. Collins makes this statement:

Since I am not a cosmologist, I have no way of knowing whether the technical details of the Big Bang theory are sound or not. My own reading of Genesis means that I have no problem with the amount of time the theory calls for. The conclusion from these three lines of evidence seems to be fair, so far as I can tell. As long as we recognize that it's a theory in physics. I see no reason to reject it, I say this because this kind of theory can't tell us *why* we're here, only *how* we came to be here.[49]

It is interesting that he states he has "no way of knowing," but then goes on to basically accept it!

Further on, he states:

I conclude, then, that I have no reason to disbelieve the standard theories of the geologists, including their estimate for the age of the earth. They may be wrong, for all I know; but if they are wrong, it's not because they have improperly smuggled philosophical assumptions into their work.[50]

That's a sad statement illustrating he accepts man is neutral — instead of the biblical understanding that fallible man suppresses the truth in unrighteousness (Rom. 1).

Dr. Bruce Waltke, Knox Theological Seminary, Florida

Dr. Bruce Waltke, formerly a professor at Reformed Theological Seminary in Orlando, Florida, is now listed as distinguished professor of Old Testament for Knox Theological Seminary. The seminary website describes Dr. Waltke as one of the preeminent Old Testament scholars.

On the Biologos website, Dr. Waltke stated:

> I think that if the data is overwhelming in favor of evolution, [then] to deny that reality will make us a cult, some odd group that's not really interacting with the real world, and rightly so. We're not using our gifts nor trusting God's providence that brought us to this point of our awareness. Because I see all of history is in God's providence, and I think we're at a unique moment in history. So many strands are coming together. We're at almost, to my mind, the pinnacle of history. We're aware of these things, and to deny the reality would be to deny the truth of God in the world, and would be to deny truth. So I think it would be our spiritual death if we stopped loving God with all of our minds and thinking about it. I think it's our spiritual death.
>
> It's also our spiritual death in our witness to the world — that we're not credible, that we are bigoted, we have a blind faith, and this is what we are accused of. So I see this all as part of the growth of the church. We are much more mature by this dialogue that we're having, and I think this is how we come to the unity of the faith is that we wrestle with these issues.
>
> We're all in the body of Christ — one Lord, one faith, one baptism — and we may disagree with one other but we are really interacting in a very serious way, trusting God as truth and that we are testing what is true and holding fast to that which is good and we are the richer for it and if we don't do that we are going to die. And I think it's essential to us, or we'll end up like some small sect somewhere that retains a certain dress or certain language and then end up marginalized, totally marginalized, and I think that would be a great tragedy for the church, for us to become marginalized in that way.[51]

In his treatise on Old Testament theology Dr. Waltke also states:

> The best harmonious synthesis of the special revelation of the Bible, of the general revelation of human nature that distinguishes

between right and wrong and consciously or unconsciously craves God, and of science is the theory of theistic evolution.[52]

Of course, many more examples could be offered. The above I consider to be representative of where the majority of Christian academics at Christian institutions across the United States (and in fact, around the world) stand in regard to what they teach and write on the Book of Genesis and their approach to Scripture. This is generally the sad state of Christendom in the academic world. It is time for Christians to take a stand for biblical authority and go forth and demolish false unbiblical views.

Endnotes

1. Some of these were Comte de Buffon, James Hutton, Abraham Werner, and others, but it culminated with Charles Lyell in the 1830s. For more, see Ken Ham, editor, *The New Answers Book 2,* "How Old Is the Earth?" by Bodie Hodge (Green Forest, AR: Master Books, 2008).
2. www.answersingenesis.org.
3. William Dembski, *The End of Christianity: Finding a Good God in an Evil World* (Nashville, TN: Broadman & Holman Academic, 2009), p. 159.
4. Ibid., p. 154–155.
5. Ibid., p. 55.
6. Ibid., p. 77.
7. William A. Dembski, paper, "Christian Theodicy in Light of Genesis and Modern Science," p. 49.
8. The assumptions can be revealed in these questions: Initial amounts? Was any parent amount added? Was any daughter amount added? Was any parent amount removed? Was any daughter amount removed? How has the rate changed due to the environmental effects?
9. http://www.pointloma.edu/discover/about-plnu/history
10. http://biologos.org.
12. For a refutation of this, see Ken Ham, editor, *The New Answers Book 2,* "How Old Is the Earth?" by Bodie Hodge (Green Forest, AR: Master Books, 2008).
13. http://blogs.usatoday.com/oped/2009/08/we-believe-in-evolution-and-god-.html.
14. http://biologos.org.
15. G. Richard Bozarth, "The Meaning of Evolution," *American Atheist*, 20 Sept. 1979, p. 30.
16. http://atheists.org/atheism/Christmas.
17. www.nes.edu/NewsEvents/?NewsID=1610.
18. http://www.rfmedia.org/RF_audio_video/RF_podcast/What_is_Inerrancy_.mp3.
19. Transcription of William Lane Craig and Michael Coren on the Michael Coren Show. http://www.youtube.com/watch?v=_IQoLg7w-_4, accessed 4 Mar 2010 and again on 9 Aug 2010. The interview was on 6 Feb 2009 with Canadian TV host, Michael Coren (http://www.michaelcoren.com/bio.html).
20. John Walton, *The Lost World of Genesis One* (Downers Grove, IL: IVP Academic, 2009).
21. Ibid., proposition 6, p. 70.
22. Ibid., proposition 7, p. 77.
23. Ibid., proposition 8, p. 84.
24. Ibid., proposition 8, p. 82–83.

25. Ibid., proposition 9, p. 92.
26. Ibid., proposition 12, p. 108–109.
27. Ibid., proposition 9, p. 92.
28. Ibid., proposition 10, p. 95.
29. T. Desmond Alexander and David W. Baker, editors, *Dictionary of the Old Testament Pentateuch* (Downers Grove, IL: InterVarsity Press, 2003).
30. Ibid., p. 315.
31. Ibid., p. 322.
32. Ibid., p. 321.
33. Ibid., p. 321.
34. Ibid., p. 325.
35. Ibid., p. 320.
36. Howard J. Van Till, Robert E. Snow, John H. Stek, and Davis A. Young, *Portraits of Creation: Biblical and Scientific Perspectives on the World's Formation* (Grand Rapids, MI: W.B. Eerdmans Pub. Co., 1990), p. 6.
37. Ibid., p. 11.
38. Ibid., p. 80.
39. Ibid., p. 105–106.
40. Keith B. Miller, editor, *Perspectives on an Evolving Creation,* "Is the Universe Capable of Evolving?" by Howard J. Van Till (Grand Rapids, MI: Wm. B. Eerdmans Publ., 2003), p. 313–314.
41. Deborah B. Haarsma and Loren D. Haarsma, *Origins: A Reformed Look at Creation, Design, and Evolution* (Grand Rapids, MI: Faith Alive Christian Resources, 2007), p. 89.
42. Ibid., p. 111.
43. Ibid., p. 115.
44. Miller, *Perspectives on an Evolving Creation,* "Does Science Exclude God? Natural Law, Chance, Miracles, and Scientific Practice," by Loren Haarsma, p. 77.
45. Daniel C. Harlow, "Consensus in CRC: Bible Is Not Inerrant," *Chimes* (April 20, 2007): p. 17.
46. Daniel C. Harlow, "After Adam: Reading Genesis in an Age of Evolutionary Science," *Perspectives on Science and Christian Faith,* volume 62, number 3 (September 2010), p. 179.
47. http://www.calvin.edu/admin/provost/origins-discussion. The department's Statement on Evolution can be found at http://www.calvin.edu/academic/biology/why/evolution-statement10May2010.pdf.
48. Jack Collins, "Adam and Eve as Historical People, and Why It Matters," *Perspectives on Science and Christian Faith,* volume 62, number 3 (September 2010): p. 147–165.
49. C. John Collins, *Science and Faith: Friends or Foes?* (Wheaton, IL: Crossway Books, 2003), p. 233.
50. Ibid., p. 250.
51. Bruce Waltke, "Why Must the Church Come to Accept Evolution?" http://biologos.org/blog/why-must-the-church-come-to-accept-evolution/, posted March 24, 2010, and accessed and downloaded March 29, 2010. This was pulled from the website on about April 2, 2010.
52. Bruce K. Waltke, *An Old Testament Theology* (Grand Rapids, MI: Zondervan, 2007), p. 202–203.

Appendix B

Do You Really Understand "Worldview"?

Greg Hall

"Worldview" is not a uniquely Christian term. It is more of a philosophical term and was first used by German philosophers. In German, the word is *weltanshung*. Generally, it refers to how we view reality and life. In order for the concept of worldview to have significance for us, it pays to see what scholars have said about it, and how they define it. Dr. James W. Sire, in *The Universe Next Door* gives this definition:

> A worldview is a commitment, a fundamental orientation of the heart, that can be expressed as a story or in a set of presuppositions (assumptions which may be true, partially true or entirely false) which we hold (consciously or subconsciously, consistently or inconsistently) about the basic constitution of reality, and that provides the foundation on which we live and move and have our being.[1]

Though not originally a "Christian" word, Christian philosophers and theologians have used the word to help Christians understand that Christian faith is intended to be a framework (built upon the authority of the Word of God), by which we build the correct way of thinking about the reality and core view of life intended by our Creator. Being a Christian is not a matter of having a compartment of life that is religious and others that are secular — with the false idea that such a position is non-religious. In fact, there are ultimately only two religions in the world — you either start with God's Word or man's word.

The Scripture teaches us there is a God who expects us to live the whole of our lives, not part, in correspondence to His truth and purpose for all of life, based on the foundational propositional truths of God's Word.

For those interested in a very scholarly overview of the worldview discussion, you should have as a resource, *Worldview, the History of a Concept*, by Dr. David K. Naugle.[2] This book gives us a historical perspective on the various definitions offered by scholars including:

> "Worldview" in a Christian perspective implies the objective existence of the trinitarian God whose essential character establishes the moral order of the universe and whose word, wisdom, and law define and govern all aspects of created existence.[3]

I have had the fortune of being part of the Centurions Program, a ministry of *Prison Fellowship* devoted to helping believers understand the significance of worldview thinking. Even though there are some areas of concern regarding Genesis, nonetheless, I agree with Chuck Colson when he defines worldview like this:

> It is the sum total of our beliefs about the world, the "big picture" that directs our daily decisions and actions."[4]

The definition of "worldview" is the first step in understanding this important topic, but there is more to it than definition. It is important to understand the "content" of what goes into making a worldview.

In *The Universe Next Door*, Dr. Sire lists seven basic worldview questions. "If a worldview can be expressed in propositions, what might they be? Essentially, they are our essential, rock-bottom answers to the following seven questions:

1. *What is prime reality — the really real?* To this we might answer God, or the gods, or the material cosmos. Our answer here is the most fundamental. It sets the boundaries for the answers that can consistently be given to the other six questions.
2. *What is the nature of external reality, that is, the world around us?* Here our answers point to whether we see the world as created or autonomous, as chaotic or orderly, as matter or spirit; or whether we emphasize

our subjective, personal relationship to the world or its objectivity apart from us.

3. *What is a human being?* To this we might answer: a highly complex machine, a sleeping god, a person made in the image of God, a naked ape.

4. *What happens to a person at death?* Here we might reply: personal extinction, or transformation to a higher state, or reincarnation, or departure to a shadowy existence on "the other side."

5. *Why is it possible to know anything at all?* Sample answers include the idea that we are made in the image of an all-knowing God or that consciousness and rationality developed under the contingencies of survival in a long process of evolution.

6. *How do we know what is right and wrong?* Again, perhaps we are made in the image of a God whose character is good, or right and wrong are determined by human choice alone or what feels good, or the notions simply developed under an impetus toward cultural or physical survival.

7. *What is the meaning of human history?* To this we might answer: to realize the purposes of God or the gods, to make a paradise on earth, to prepare a people for a life in community with a loving and holy God, and so forth."[5]

So how does a worldview get developed? Where does it come from? As I stated earlier, in an ultimate sense (as exhibited in Genesis 3 concerning the temptation), there are only two worldviews. Either one bases one's thinking on the word of one who knows everything, who has always been there, who doesn't tell any lies, and has revealed to us what we need to know, or one has to build one's thinking on the fallible word of fallible man.

Now, we need to understand that there are many versions of these two ultimate worldviews. There are many that will compete for your attention. On what basis is one right? Aren't they all simply a matter of choosing (this would default to the religion of humanism, as humans would be the ultimate authority on the subject)? And further to this, who is to say one has merit, and others do not? Aren't they all equally valid (again, this would be more humanism)? But even so, these are questions with which we must contend. How will you answer?

According to Dr. Ronald Nash, three major tests should be applied when evaluating worldviews. They are: the test of reason, the test of experience, and the test of practice.[6]

The test of reason has to do with logic — and ultimately the only logical starting point is the infinite God of the Bible (who is the basis for the logic and its existence). In other words, if there is no God of the Bible, there is no basis for logic in the first place. Logic is predicated on the existence of the God of the Bible.

Regarding logic, students should know about the law of non-contradiction as fundamental to our ability to reason. It states: A cannot be B and non-B at the same time and in the same relationship. This is an important philosophic notion in the study of logic. Simply put, it means: two contradictory ideas cannot both be true. Where there is contradiction, one side or the other is in error. Not all ideas are equally valid. To employ the test of reason in worldview development is to determine, among competing ideas, which are reasonable and which might we believe to be true. Ultimately only one passes the test — the rest will exhibit logical fallacies. The only true worldview is that which begins with the infinite Creator God and His written revelation to man.

The test of reason alone is not enough upon which to build the content of a worldview. Dr. Nash says, "Worldviews must pass not only the test of reason; they must also satisfy the test of experience. Worldviews should be relevant to what we know about the world and ourselves."[7]

Here is a truth that many students need to connect with: *Your experience counts.* Sure it is considered subjective, but your experiences in life matter because the knowledge it represents is valuable and pertinent to your life. I am not suggesting that your personal observations are in any sense the exclusive test for developing worldview, but rather is *coherence* as a whole, where all aspects of reality work together. If your personal experience is your *only* criteria for developing worldview you are greatly mistaken. I am simply saying that your experience does matter.

The test of practice is how we evaluate our worldview in the circumstances of daily life (i.e., consistency). It is about how we actually live in a practical, down-to-earth way, with the ideas we profess to be true. For example, in an evolutionary worldview, people are merely animals that have no basis in wearing clothes. Yet inconsistently, these evolutionists betray their worldview by wearing clothes that come from a literal Genesis 3. The question is this: can the ideas and concepts stand up as a real explanation for the way you experience your life, and do they have application beyond your own life?

The content of a biblical Christian worldview must also be well developed and be solidly built on the authority of Scripture. You need to know the basic time-honored truths of the scriptural history and doctrine that serve as a basis for Christian theism — a biblical understanding of the nature and character of God and the true history of the universe as revealed by Him in His Word. Here is a short list of the many aspects of Scripture that provide a foundation for our worldview:

- He (through His Son, Jesus) created the universe *ex nihilo* (out of nothing) because He is the sovereign God.
- Though He is transcendent and other worldly, He is personal and immanent and longing to be involved in the lives of His creation.
- He has accomplished this through His Son Jesus who is God incarnate, Immanuel, God "with us."
- Jesus is the exact representation of God the Father.
- The Father has redeemed those who will believe in His Son as the atoning sacrifice for sin.
- God makes it possible to be connected with Him through His Holy Spirit who is God, "in us."
- His Spirit is our comforter and teacher and guide. He leads us into truth and is God's guarantee of His presence with us until the end of our lives.
- The Garden of Eden was real and our fore bearers made a decision of disobedience recorded in Genesis that affected the human family. Original sin is a reality.
- God gave the plan of redemption, the sacrifice of His Son, as the payment for the debt owed a Holy God for such an offense.

Beyond this, you need to have a command on why Christians believe the Bible to be God's Word to us. And you also need to know the evidence that confirms the fact His Word is trustworthy and true. You need to know how to answer the basic secular attacks of our day that cause people to doubt that God's Word is the true starting point for our worldview.

This is just an example to show you how your Christian worldview must start with the content we gain from the truths revealed in Scripture about God, His Son, Jesus, and the Holy Spirit. They are the building blocks upon which your worldview is built. To not understand them or to understand them wrongly is to build a faulty foundation. Christians must think clearly and scripturally about the basic tenets of theism if their worldview is to be biblical.

The Worldview of Naturalism

Contrary to the Christian worldview is the worldview of naturalism (which is an essential tenant in similar worldviews like humanism, materialism, and atheism). Keep in mind that when a person mixes naturalistic thinking with God's Word, their starting point really is man's word. Once fallibility is introduced to one's starting point — then that starting point is man's word, even if it is mixed with God's revelation. As was said earlier, there are ultimately only two worldviews.

The thinking behind naturalism goes something like this: the world and universe as you see it is all there is. There is no God, no Creator, no one to whom humans give an account of their lives. The naturalist believes death marks the end of life in this world with no prospect of life beyond in any form. For the naturalist, the universe is a closed system and therefore there is no need for humans to seek the involvement of a transcendent being.

Naturalism is a worldview that assumes it has succeeded at getting God out of the picture in every area of life. It is also intent in getting the biblical God and His written revelation out of our educational process. In large measure, it has been successful due to an often subtle influence as well as an overt and militant influence. The naturalistic worldview is the basis for the development of the public education curriculum of our schools. As Ben Stein so aptly put it in a movie,[8] God has been "expelled."

I think for the most part that this is a subtle fact among educators today. I don't think that most of them are even aware that they are part of the naturalist indoctrination. Try asking this question of your public school leadership: "What is the worldview or educational philosophy behind the curriculum of your school?" They will probably find it hard if not impossible to answer. If probed, they may think that Judeo-Christian principles are at the core of our public education system curriculum. Many are committed to the "Character Counts" movement, which borrows certain Christian values, but is completely mute on the source of those values.

I honestly think that many educators would be greatly concerned if they were aware of the naturalistic presuppositions beneath their work. One of the problems is they have been convinced that including God and His Word (the Bible) is religion, but eliminating them results in a neutral position. They don't understand there is no neutral position. One is either "for Christ or against." What they perceive wrongly as a neutral position is in reality an anti-God position — it is a religious position — the religion of naturalism/atheism. We have much work to be done in pointing this out to the Church, let alone the secular world.

The naturalistic worldview holds steadfastly to the idea of evolution and millions of years, as "the" explanation of the origin of life. The two are virtually inseparable in the Western mind. If there is no God, and if the physical reality is all there is, then life must have come into being by itself . . . somehow. That's where evolution (which needs millions of years to even be postulated) comes in. What is "evolution"? Dr. Michael Behe, who is basically a theistic evolutionist but is against pure naturalism, in *Darwin's Black Box*, defines it this way:

> Evolution is a flexible word. It can be used by one person to mean something as simple as change over time, or by another person to mean the descent of all life forms from a common ancestor, leaving the mechanism of change unspecified. In its full-throated, biological sense, however, evolution means a process whereby life arose from non-living matter and subsequently developed entirely by natural means. That is the sense that Darwin gave the word, and the meaning that it holds in the scientific community.[9]

Why Naturalism Survives

Despite massive amounts of scientific and philosophical arguments against it, the worldview of naturalism and the idea of evolution persist. Today there is a huge cloud of doubt hanging over the science of evolution. As Christians, we must pursue this information and honestly explore and openly criticize it when we see it for what it is.

It is all part of defending what we believe and know to be true. Disclosing such faulty ideas helps us make the case for the authenticity of the biblical account of the origin of life (2 Cor. 10:4–5). Evolution and naturalism as a belief about the origin and development of life is being shown by scientists to be no explanation for the origin of life at all. How then do we account for its persistence as the *only* explanation for the origin and diversification of life in the textbooks our students must read in our public schools?

The first reason is that those promoting evolution and naturalism are in control. They currently control the debate on the issues and they control what goes into textbooks. They do not include any other explanations for life because they don't want to. This intellectual dishonesty has been enabled by those of us who believe in God and creation, as we have abdicated our responsibility long ago for intellectual rigor on the major issues of our times. Basically, we walked away; they took over, and now we find it a stronghold in the educational process that is very hard to deal with. Also, many of us have succumbed to the false idea of neutrality, and thus backed off on defending the Christian position — only to allow these secularists to now be able to impose their religion on the education system and thus generations of our kids.

The second reason evolution persists is because it is absolutely necessary for the philosophical worldview of naturalism. The real battle about evolution is not one of operational science, but of philosophy. The belief in evolution as an explanation for the origin of all life on earth is religious — it is man's attempt to explain life without God. The religion of naturalism (or atheism) that is being taught to generations of students is the philosophy that attempts to totally remove God from the picture. For the naturalist, there is no God, no supernatural, and no life beyond death. That is their philosophical starting point — one, they are not prepared to question, regardless of the evidence that conflicts with it.

As Dr. Carl Sagan said, "The Cosmos is all there ever was or ever will be."[10] This is the naturalistic mantra. And it becomes very circular in its reasoning. People believe in evolution because of the naturalist worldview (naturalism is the focal point for their starting point but in reality, man being the ultimate authority is the underlying starting point). But the same people who believe in the naturalist worldview say they do so because of evolution. In reality, because they won't question their naturalistic starting point, they won't question evolution. See the problem? Why is this important? Why should anyone care?

1. The growing issues of concern in our culture have as their foundational cause the transition from a Christian worldview to principles now based on naturalism. The question about life's origin is used to justify this wrong foundation. Lose the battle here and you lost that battle in its entirety.

2. The philosophical assumptions of those who teach your children have the power, if left unchecked, to determine their destiny. This might scare you. It should. Those who control the textbooks and curriculum of our public education system have capitulated to naturalistic thinking and God has been removed, and we are paying the price.

Currently, we are losing the battle. By and large, we send our children away each morning to public schools, or have sent them to secular colleges or universities, to be inculcated with the subtle but pervasive ideas about naturalism and any other number of godless philosophies.

Lately, however, the subtlety of those who promote naturalism as the philosophy behind public education has been replaced by militancy — and our students and parents are increasingly feeling it. The goal of the current educational philosophy is certainly not neutral as is claimed (Matt. 12:30).

We can see that more clearly as this militancy emerges. The new goal is to convince students there is no such thing as transcendent or supernatural truths. The *only* source of truth is man, and God doesn't exist.

Of course, students are told that "science" confirms this naturalistic position. However, students are not being taught the distinction between historical science (beliefs about the past) and operational science (knowledge based on observation/repeatability/experimentation that builds technology). Students have been led to believe that if they don't believe in naturalism, they are giving up the science that built our technology. Sadly, this brainwashing in false ideas has had a devastating effect on these students. They, in essence, have been thoroughly indoctrinated in a secular worldview and convinced that this is a neutral position that is supported by unbiased scientists who are merely seeking the truth.

By systematically training our children from a biblical starting point, we can instill in them the necessary components of a biblical worldview. We must also consider that none of these arguments matter if our children are not followers of Christ. Preaching the gospel to them and helping them understand the true nature of repentance and faith in Christ is a crucial starting point. As we teach them apologetics and help them learn how to study the Bible to feed their own souls, we will be fostering a faith that will withstand the attacks from the world. We can help them understand the philosophies that have set themselves up against Christ and that through the empowering of the Holy Spirit they can fight these battles. Firmly grounding their worldview in Scripture offers them great hope and assurance that they can conquer the challenges from the world.

Endnotes
1. James W. Sire, *The Universe Next Door* (Downers Grove, IL: InterVarsity Press, 4th Edition, 2004), p. 17.
2. David K. Naugle, *Worldview* (Grand Rapids, MI: Wm. B. Eerdmans Publishing Co., 2002).
3. Ibid., p. 260.
4. Charles Colson, *How Now Shall We Live?* (Wheaton, IL: Tyndale House Publishers, Inc., 1999), p. 14.
5. Sire, *The Universe Next Door,* p. 20.
6. Ronald H. Nash, *Worldviews in Conflict* (Grand Rapids, MI: Zondervan Publishing House, 1992), p. 55.
7. Ibid., p. 57.
8. *Expelled: No Intelligence Allowed* is a 2008 documentary film, directed by Nathan Frankowski and hosted by Ben Stein.
9. Michael J. Behe, *Darwin's Black Box* (New York, NY: Free Press, 2006).
10. Carl Sagan, *Cosmos* (New York: Random House, 1980), p. 4.

Appendix C

The Documentary Hypothesis:
Moses, Genesis, and the JEDP?

Terry Mortenson and Bodie Hodge

In the past few hundred years, the Bible has been under severe attack by scientific and philosophical skeptics of all sorts. In this scientific age the most-attacked book of the Bible has arguably been Genesis, particularly the first 11 chapters. Long-age geology, big-bang cosmology, secular archaeology, liberal theology, and philosophical attacks on miracles in the Bible have deceived many people to believe that the Bible is not true and therefore cannot be trusted.

One of the major attacks on the Bible in the past three hundred years has been directed against Moses and his authorship of the Pentateuch, the first five books of the Old Testament (Genesis–Deuteronomy). Such attacks on these foundational books of the Bible come both from non-Christians as well as professing Christians.

Seminary courses, theology books, introductions to the Pentateuch in Bibles, and the secular media have promoted the man-made idea that Moses did not write the Pentateuch (also known as the Law or Torah). Instead, it is claimed that at least four different authors (or groups of authors) wrote various portions of these books over many centuries and then one or more redactors (editors) over many years combined and interwove everything together into its present form. For example, one translation of the Bible we surveyed said this in its introduction to the Pentateuch:

Despite its unity of plan and purpose, the book is a complex work, not to be attributed to a single original author. Several sources, or literary traditions, that the final redactor used in his composition are discernable. These are the Yahwist (J), Elohist (E), and Priestly (P) sources which in turn reflect older oral traditions.[1]

The introduction to the Old Testament in another Bible translation says that the J document was written by someone much later than Moses in the southern kingdom of Judah and the E document was written by someone in the northern kingdom of Israel.[2] Let's evaluate the arguments put forth in defense of this hypothesis.

The Documentary (or JEDP) Hypothesis

Various sections of the Pentateuch are assigned to various authors who are identified by the letters J, E, D, and P. Hence, it is called the *documentary hypothesis* (or the *JEDP model*[3]). As this hypothesis was developed by a number of Jewish and theologically liberal Christian scholars in the late 17th to the late 19th centuries, there were a number of different proposals of who wrote what and when. But by the end of the 19th century, liberal scholars had reached general agreement. The letters stand for:

J documents are the sections, verses, or in some cases parts of verses that were written by one or more authors who preferred to use the Hebrew name *Jahweh* (Jehovah) to refer to God. It is proposed that this author wrote about 900–850 B.C.

E documents are the texts that use the name *Elohim* for God and were supposedly written around 750–700 B.C.

D stands for Deuteronomy, most of which was written by a different author or group of authors, perhaps around the time of King Josiah's reforms in 621 B.C.

P stands for Priest and identifies the texts in Leviticus and elsewhere in the Pentateuch that were written by a priest or priests during the exile in Babylon after 586 B.C.

Then around 400 B.C. some redactors (i.e., editors) supposedly combined these four independently written texts to form the Pentateuch as it was known in the time of Jesus and modern times.

Development of the Documentary Hypothesis

Ibn Ezra was a very influential Jewish rabbi in the 12th century. While he believed in the Mosaic authorship of the Pentateuch, he noticed that a few verses (e.g., Genesis 12:6, Genesis 22:14) had some phrases that seemed mysteriously out of place.[4] But he never pursued these mysteries to resolve them.[5]

About five hundred years later, the famous Jewish philosopher Baruch (Benedict) Spinoza (1632–1677) picked up on what Ibn Ezra had stated and asserted that Ibn Ezra did not believe Moses wrote the Pentateuch. Others disagreed, pointing to other statements by Ibn Ezra that contradicted Spinoza's conclusion. In his book *Tractatus Theologico-Politicus* (1670), Spinoza, who was a pantheist and was subsequently excommunicated from the Jewish community and denounced by Christians, argued that Moses did not write the Pentateuch. Besides using the verses noted by Ibn Ezra, Spinoza offered a few other brief arguments against Mosaic authorship, which were easily answered by Christian writers in the following few decades.[6]

Nevertheless, further attacks on the Mosaic authorship of the Pentateuch began taking hold in France through Jean Astruc, whose book *Conjectures About the Original Memoirs Which It Appeared That Moses Used in Composing the Book of Genesis with Certain Remarks Which Help Clarify These Conjectures* was published in 1753. He believed Moses was the author of the Pentateuch, but he unlocked the door for the skepticism of later scholars.

Astruc basically questioned, as others had before him, how Moses knew what happened prior to his own life, (i.e., the history recorded in Genesis). In other words, where did Moses get information on the patriarchs? Of course, there are several ways Moses could have obtained this information: divine revelation, previously written texts passed down through the generations, and/or oral tradition from his ancestors.[7] Regardless, under the guidance of the Holy Spirit (2 Pet. 1:20–21), the books of Moses would be completely true and without error.

Astruc also noticed that *Elohim* (the Hebrew name for God in Genesis 1:1–2:3) was used in Genesis 1, but then the text switches to *Yahweh* (Jehovah) in chapter 2. Astruc claimed that these name changes indicated different sources that Moses used. Specifically, he thought that Genesis 1:1–2:3 was one creation account and Genesis 2:4–24 was a different creation account. Hence, we have the *Elohim* and *Jehovah* sections (or E and J documents).[8] Thus, the first assumption of the documentary hypothesis became established: The use of different divine names means different authors of the text.

The German scholar Johann Eichhorn took the next step by applying Astruc's idea to the whole of Genesis. Initially, in his 1780 *Introduction to the Old Testament*, Eichhorn said that Moses copied previous texts. But in later editions he apparently conceded the view of others that the J–E division could be applied to the whole of the Pentateuch, which was written after Moses.[9]

Following Eichhorn, other ideas were advanced in denial of the Mosaic authorship of the first five books of the Old Testament. In 1802, Johann Vater insisted that Genesis was made from at least 39 fragments. In 1805, Wilhelm De Wette contended that none of the Pentateuch was written before King David and that Deuteronomy was written at the time of King Josiah.

From here, the door flew open to profess that other portions of the Law were not written by Moses. Not only was there a J-document, E-document, and D-document, but then it was argued that Leviticus and some other portions of the Pentateuch were the work of Jewish priests, hence the P-documents.

And today, several variant views of documentary hypothesis exist, but perhaps the most popular is that of Dr. Julius Wellhausen proposed in 1895. Dr. Wellhausen put dates to the alleged four sources and none were earlier than around 900 B.C.[10] As noted Old Testament scholar Gleason Archer remarks, "Although Dr. Wellhausen contributed no innovations to speak of, he restated the documentary theory with great skill and persuasiveness, supporting the JEDP sequence upon an evolutionary basis."[11]

Even though a great many scholars and much of the public have accepted this view, is it really true? Did Moses have little or nothing to do with the writing of the Book of Genesis or the rest of the Pentateuch? Several lines of evidence should lead us to reject the documentary hypothesis as a fabrication of unbelievers.

Reasons to Reject the Documentary Hypothesis

There are many reasons to reject this skeptical attack on the Bible. First, consider what the Bible itself says about the authorship of the Pentateuch.

Biblical Witness to Mosaic Authorship

1. The chart below shows that the Pentateuch states that Moses wrote these books: Exod. 17:14; 24:4; 34:27; Num. 33:1–2; and Deut. 31:9–11. In his rejection of Mosaic authorship, Dr. Wellhausen nowhere discussed this biblical evidence. It is easy to deny Mosaic authorship if one ignores the evidence for it. But that is not honest scholarship.

2. We also have the witness of the rest of the Old Testament: Josh.1:8; 8:31–32; 1 Kings 2:3; 2 Kings 14:6; 21:8; Ezra 6:18; Neh. 13:1; Dan. 9:11–13; and Mal. 4:4.

3. The New Testament is also clear in its testimony: Matt. 19:8; John 5:45–47; 7:19; Acts 3:22; Rom. 10:5; and Mark 12:26. The divisions of the Old Testament were clearly in place in the Jewish mind long before

the time of Christ, namely, the Law of Moses (first five books of the Old Testament), the Prophets (the historical and prophetic books) and the Writings (the poetic books of Job, Psalms, Proverbs, etc.). So when Jesus referred to the Law of Moses, His Jewish listeners knew exactly to what He was referring.

Table 1: Selected Passages Confirming Mosaic Authorship

		Old Testament
1	Exodus 17:14	Then the Lord said to Moses, "Write this for a memorial in the book and recount it in the hearing of Joshua, that I will utterly blot out the remembrance of Amalek from under heaven" (NKJV).
2	Number 33:2	Now Moses wrote down the starting points of their journeys at the command of the Lord. And these are their journeys according to their starting points. . . .
3	Joshua 1:7–8	Only be strong and very courageous, that you may observe to do according to all the law which Moses My servant commanded you; do not turn from it to the right hand or to the left, that you may prosper wherever you go. This Book of the Law shall not depart from your mouth, but you shall meditate in it day and night, that you may observe to do according to all that is written in it. For then you will make your way prosperous, and then you will have good success.
4	Joshua 8:31	As Moses the servant of the Lord had commanded the children of Israel, as it is written in the Book of the Law of Moses: "an altar of whole stones over which no man has wielded an iron tool." And they offered on it burnt offerings to the Lord, and sacrificed peace offerings. (See Exodus 20:24–25.)
5	Joshua 23:6	Therefore be very courageous to keep and to do all that is written in the Book of the Law of Moses, lest you turn aside from it to the right hand or to the left.
6	1 Kings 2:3	And keep the charge of the Lord your God: to walk in His ways, to keep His statutes, His commandments, His judgments, and His testimonies, as it is written in the Law of Moses, that you may prosper in all that you do and wherever you turn.
7	2 Kings 14:6	But the children of the murderers he did not execute, according to what is written in the Book of the Law of Moses, in which the Lord commanded, saying, "Fathers shall not be put to death for their children, nor shall children be put to death for their fathers; but a person shall be put to death for his own sin." (See Deuteronomy 24:16.)

8	1 Chronicles 22:13	Then you will prosper, if you take care to fulfill the statutes and judgments with which the LORD charged Moses concerning Israel. Be strong and of good courage; do not fear nor be dismayed.
9	Ezra 6:18	They assigned the priests to their divisions and the Levites to their divisions, over the service of God in Jerusalem, as it is written in the Book of Moses. (This is taught in the Books of Exodus and Leviticus.)
10	Nehemiah 13:1	On that day they read from the Book of Moses in the hearing of the people, and in it was found written that no Ammonite or Moabite should ever come into the assembly of God. (See Deuteronomy 23:3-5.)
11	Daniel 9:11	Yes, all Israel has transgressed Your law, and has departed so as not to obey Your voice; therefore the curse and the oath written in the Law of Moses the servant of God have been poured out on us, because we have sinned against Him.
12	Malachi 4:4	Remember the Law of Moses, My servant, which I commanded him in Horeb for all Israel, with the statutes and judgments.
New Testament		
13	Matthew 8:4	And Jesus said to him, "See that you tell no one; but go your way, show yourself to the priest, and offer the gift that Moses commanded, as a testimony to them." (See Leviticus 14:1–32.)
14	Mark 12:26	But concerning the dead, that they rise, have you not read in the Book of Moses, in the burning bush passage, how God spoke to him, saying, "I am the God of Abraham, the God of Isaac, and the God of Jacob"? (See Exodus 3:6.)
15	Luke 16:29	Abraham said to him, "They have Moses and the prophets; let them hear them."
16	Luke 24:27	And beginning at Moses and all the Prophets, He expounded to them in all the Scriptures the things concerning Himself.
17	Luke 24:44	Then He said to them, "These are the words which I spoke to you while I was still with you, that all things must be fulfilled which were written in the Law of Moses and the Prophets and the Psalms concerning Me."
18	John 5:46	For if you believed Moses, you would believe Me; for he wrote about Me.
19	John 7:22	Moses therefore gave you circumcision (not that it is from Moses, but from the fathers), and you circumcise a man on the Sabbath.
20	Acts 3:22	For Moses truly said to the fathers, "The LORD your God will raise up for you a Prophet like me from your brethren. Him you shall hear in all things, whatever He says to you." (See Deuteronomy 18:15.)

21	Acts 15:1	And certain men came down from Judea and taught the brethren, "Unless you are circumcised according to the custom of Moses, you cannot be saved."
22	Acts 28:23	So when they had appointed him a day, many came to him at his lodging, to whom he explained and solemnly testified of the kingdom of God, persuading them concerning Jesus from both the Law of Moses and the Prophets, from morning till evening.
23	Romans 10:5	For Moses writes about the righteousness which is of the law, "The man who does those things shall live by them." (See Leviticus 18:1–5.)
24	Romans 10:19	But I say, did Israel not know? First Moses says: "I will provoke you to jealousy by those who are not a nation, I will move you to anger by a foolish nation." (See Deuteronomy 32:21.)
25	1 Corinthians 9:9	For it is written in the law of Moses, "You shall not muzzle an ox while it treads out the grain." Is it oxen God is concerned about? (See Deuteronomy 25:4.)
26	2 Corinthians 3:15	But even to this day, when Moses is read, a veil lies on their heart.

Take note of some the references back to Moses' work. For example, John 7:22 and Acts 15:1 refer to Moses giving the doctrine of circumcision. Yet John also reveals that this came earlier — in Genesis, with Abraham. Nevertheless, it is credited to Moses because it was recorded in his writings. The New Testament attributes all the books from Genesis through Deuteronomy as being the writings of Moses. So to attack the Mosaic authorship of the first five books of the Old Testament then is to attack the truthfulness of the rest of the biblical writers and Jesus Himself.

Moses' Qualifications to Write

Not only is there abundant biblical witness that Moses wrote the Pentateuch, Moses was fully qualified to write the Pentateuch. He received an Egyptian royal education (Acts 7:22) and was an eyewitness to the events recorded in Exodus to Deuteronomy, which contain many references or allusions to Egyptian names of places, people, and gods, as well as Egyptian words, idioms, and cultural factors. He also consistently demonstrated an outsider's view of Canaan (from the perspective of Egypt or Sinai).[12] And as a prophet of God he was the appropriate recipient of the written records or oral traditions of the patriarchs from Adam to his own day, which the Holy Spirit could use to guide Moses to write the inerrant text of Genesis. There is no other ancient Hebrew who was more qualified than Moses to write the Pentateuch.

Fallacious Reasoning of the Skeptics

A final reason for rejecting the documentary hypothesis and accepting the biblical testimony to the Mosaic authorship of the Pentateuch is the erroneous assumptions and reasoning of the liberal scholars and other skeptics.

1. They assumed their conclusion. They assumed that the Bible is not a supernatural revelation from God and then manipulated the biblical text to arrive at that conclusion. They were implicitly deistic or atheistic in their thinking.

2. They assumed that Israel's religion was simply the invention of man, a product of evolution, as all other religions are.

3. Based on evolutionary ideas, they assumed that "the art of writing was virtually unknown in Israel prior to the establishment of the Davidic monarchy; therefore there could have been no written records going back to the time of Moses."[13] This claim not only attacks the intelligence of the ancient Israelites, but also the Egyptians who trained Moses. Were the Egyptians incapable of teaching Moses how to read and write? Since the time the documentary hypothesis was first proposed, archaeologists have discovered scores of written records pre-dating the time of Moses. It is hard to believe that Israel's ancient neighbors knew how to write, but the Jews could not.

4. Liberal Bible scholars allegedly based their theories on evidence from the biblical text and yet they evaded the biblical evidence that refutes their theories. Theirs was a "pick and choose" approach to studying the Bible, which is hardly honest scholarship in pursuit of truth.

5. They arbitrarily assumed that the Hebrew authors were different from all other writers in history — that the Hebrews were incapable of using more than one name for God, or more than one writing style regardless of the subject matter, or more than one of several possible synonyms for a single idea.

6. Their subjective bias led them to illegitimately assume that any biblical statement was unreliable until proven reliable (though they would not do this with any other ancient or modern text) and when they found any disagreement between the Bible and ancient pagan literature, the latter was automatically given preference and trusted as a historical witness. The former violates the well-accepted concept known as Aristotle's dictum, which advises that the benefit of the doubt should be given to the document itself, rather than the critic. In other words, the Bible (or any other book) should be considered

innocent until proven guilty or considered reliable until its unreliability is compellingly demonstrated.

7. Although many examples have been found of an ancient Semitic author using repetition and duplication in his narrative technique, skeptical scholars assume that when Hebrew authors did this, it is compelling evidence of multiple authorship of the biblical text.

8. The skeptics erroneously assumed, without any other ancient Hebrew literature to compare with the biblical text, that they could, with scientific reliability, establish the date of the composition of each book of the Bible.[14]

9. To date, no manuscript evidence of the J-document, E-document, P-document, D-document, or any of the other supposed fragments have ever been discovered. And there are no ancient Jewish commentaries that mention any of these imaginary documents or their alleged unnamed authors. All the manuscript evidence we have is for the first five books of the Bible just as we have them today. This is confirmed by the singular Jewish testimony (until the last few centuries) that these books are the writings of Moses.

Is JEDP/Documentary Hypothesis the Same Thing as the Tablet Model of Genesis?

These two ways of dividing Genesis are not the same at all. The tablet model is based on the Hebrew word *toledoth*, which appears 11 times in Genesis (2:4; 5:1; 6:9; 10:1; 11:10; 11:27; 25:12; 25:19; 36:1; 36:9; 37:2) and helps to tie the whole book together as a single history. Our English Bibles translate *toledoth* variously as "this is the account" or "these are the generations" of Adam, Noah, Shem, etc. Scholars disagree about whether each *toledoth* follows or precedes the text with which it is associated, though we are inclined to agree with those scholars who conclude the former. In this case, the name associated with the *toledoth* is either the author or custodian of that section (see, for example, table 2 below). Regardless, the 11 uses of *toledoth* unite the book as a history of the key events and people from creation to the time of Moses.

Unlike the JEDP model, the tablet model shows a reverence for the text of Genesis and attention to these explicit divisions provided by the book itself. These divisions represent either oral tradition or written texts passed down by the Genesis patriarchs to their descendants,[15] which Moses then used to put Genesis into its final form under the inspiration of the Holy Spirit.

We think it very likely that Moses was working with written documents because the second *toledoth* (Gen. 5:1) reads "this is the book of the generations of Adam" where "book" is a translation of the normal Hebrew word meaning a written document. Also, the account of the Flood after the third *toledoth* (Gen. 6:9) reads like a ship's log. Only evolutionary thinking would lead us to conclude that Adam and his descendants could not write. Early man was very intelligent: Cain built a city (Gen. 4:17), six generations later people were making musical instruments and had figured out how to mine ores and make metals (Gen. 4:21–22), Noah built a huge boat for his family and thousands of animals to survive a year-long flood, etc.[16]

Table 2: Breakdown of the *Toledoth* Sections from Genesis 1–11

Beginning	End	Probable author of original work from which Moses drew
Genesis 1:1	Genesis 2:4a	Adam by direct divine revelation, so not connected with Adam's name
Genesis 2:4b	Genesis 5:1a	Adam
Genesis 5:1b	Genesis 6:9a	Noah
Genesis 6:9b	Genesis 10:1	Shem, Ham, and Japheth
Genesis 10:2	Genesis 11:10a	Shem
Genesis 11:10b	Genesis 11:27a	Terah
Genesis 11:27b	Genesis 25:12a	Abraham
Genesis 25:12b	Genesis 25:19a	Ishmael
Genesis 25:19b	Genesis 36:1a	Esau
Genesis 36:1b	Genesis 36:9a	Jacob?[17]
Genesis 36:9b	Genesis 37:2	Jacob
Genesis 37:2b	Genesis 50:26	Joseph

The biblical doctrine of the inspiration of Scripture does not require us to conclude that all the books of the Bible were written by God dictating to the human authors. Dictation was one means employed, very often in the prophetic books (e.g., the prophet says, "The Word of the Lord came to me saying …"). But much of the Bible was written from the eyewitness experience of the authors (e.g., 2 Pet. 1:16) or as a result of research by the author (e.g., Luke 1:1–4). And just as Christian authors today can quote truthful statements from non-Christian sources without thereby endorsing their wrong ideas, so the biblical authors could quote non-believers or non-biblical sources without introducing false statements into their divine writings (e.g., Josh. 10:13; 2 Sam. 1:18; Acts 17:28; Titus 1:12; Jude 14–15). So it is perfectly reasonable to think that Moses wrote Genesis from pre-existing, well-preserved oral tradition and/or written documents from the patriarchs.

Unlike those who affirm Mosaic authorship of Genesis and divide the text by the *toledoths*, JEDP adherents divide the text on the basis of the names of God that were used and say that, at best, Moses simply wove these texts together, often in contradictory ways. However, most JEDP advocates would say that Moses had nothing to do with writing Genesis or the rest of the Pentateuch, which were written much later by many authors and editors.

Answering a Few Objections

A number of objections have been raised by the proponents of the documentary hypothesis. Space allows us to respond to only a few of the most common ones, but the other objections are just as flawed in terms of logic and a failure to pay careful attention to the biblical text.

1. Moses couldn't have written about his own death, which shows that he didn't write Deuteronomy.

The death of Moses is recorded in Deuteronomy 34:5–12. These are the last few verses of the book. Like other literature, past and present, it is not uncommon for an obituary to be added at the end of someone's work after he dies, especially if he died very soon after writing the book. The obituary in no way nullifies the claim that the author wrote the book.

In the case of Deuteronomy, the author of the obituary of Moses was probably Joshua, a close associate of Moses who was chosen by God to lead the people of Israel into the Promised Land (for Moses was not allowed to because of his disobedience), and who was inspired by God to write the next book in the Old Testament. A similar obituary of Joshua was added by an inspired editor to the end of Joshua's book (Josh. 24:29–33).

2. The author of Genesis 12:6 seems to imply that the Canaanites were removed from the land, which took place well after Moses died.

Abram passed through the land to the place of Shechem, as far as the terebinth tree of Moreh. And the Canaanites were then in the land (Gen. 12:6; NKJV).

So another argument against Mosaic authorship of the Pentateuch is that an author, *after* Moses, had to have written this verse (Gen. 12:6). The very reason they argue this is due to the fact that Moses died prior to the Canaanites being removed, which occurred in the days of Joshua who began judging the Canaanites for their sin.

Two things can be said in response. First, Moses could have easily written this without knowing that the Canaanites would be removed after his death because, due to warring kingdoms or other factors, people groups did get removed from territories. So it was just a statement of fact about who was living in the land at the time of Abraham. But second, it could also be a comment added by a later editor working under divine inspiration. The editorial comment would in no way deny the Mosaic authorship of the Book of Genesis. Editors sometimes add to books by deceased authors and no one then denies that the deceased wrote the book.[18]

3. Genesis 14:14 mentions the Israelite region of Dan, which was assigned to that tribe during the conquest led by Joshua after Moses died. So Moses could not have written this verse.

> Now when Abram heard that his brother[19] was taken captive, he armed his three hundred and eighteen trained servants who were born in his own house, and went in pursuit as far as Dan. He divided his forces against them by night, and he and his servants attacked them and pursued them as far as Hobah, which is north of Damascus (Gen. 14:14–15; NKJV).

Genesis 14:14 mentions Dan. However, Dan in this context is not the region of Dan, that Israelite tribe's inheritance given when the Jews took the Promised Land, but a specific ancient town of Dan, north of the Sea of Galilee. It was in existence long before the Israelites entered the land. Jewish historian Josephus, just after the time of Christ, said:

> When Abram heard of their calamity, he was at once afraid for Lot his kinsman, and pitied the Sodomites, his friends and neighbours; and thinking it proper to afford them assistance, he did not delay it, but marched hastily, and the fifth night attacked the Assyrians, near Dan, for that is the name of the other spring of Jordan; and before they could arm themselves, he slew some as they were in their beds, before they could suspect any harm; and others, who were not yet gone to sleep, but were so drunk they could not fight, ran away.[20]

This specific place was known to Abraham as one of the springs of Jordan. It is possible that Rachel was already aware of that name, as it meant "judge," and used it for the son of her handmaiden (Gen. 30:6). It seems Rachel viewed this as the Lord finally turning the tide in judgment and permitting her a son. In the same way, this was where the Lord judged his enemies through Abraham.

But again, even if "near Dan" was added by a later inspired editor, this would not mean that it was inaccurate to say that Moses wrote Genesis.[21]

4. The author of Genesis 36:31 obviously knew about kingdoms in Israel which were only present well after Moses, so Moses could not have written this.

Such a claim is without warrant. Moses was clearly aware that this had been prophesied about the nation of Israel when the Lord told Abraham (Gen. 17:6) and Jacob (Gen. 35:11) that Israel would have kings. Also, Moses, himself, prophesied in Deuteronomy 17:14–20 that Israel would have kings. So knowing that kings were coming was already common knowledge to Moses.

Conclusion

There is abundant biblical and extra-biblical evidence that Moses wrote the Pentateuch during the wilderness wanderings after the Jews left their slavery in Egypt and before they entered the Promised Land (about 1445–1405 B.C). Contrary to the liberal theologians and other skeptics, it was not written after the Jews returned from exile in Babylon (c. 500 B.C.). Christians who believe Moses wrote the Pentateuch do not need to feel intellectually intimidated. It is the enemies of the truth of God that are failing to think carefully and face the facts honestly.

As a prophet of God, Moses wrote under divine inspiration, guaranteeing the complete accuracy and absolute authority of his writings. Those writings were endorsed by Jesus and the New Testament Apostles, who based their teaching and the truth of the gospel on the truths revealed in the books of Moses, including the truths about a literal six-day creation about 6,000 years ago, the Curse on the whole creation when Adam sinned, and the judgment of the global, catastrophic Flood at the time of Noah.

The attack on the Mosaic authorship of the Pentateuch is nothing less than an attack on the veracity, reliability, and authority of the Word of Almighty God. Christians should believe God, rather than the fallible, sinful skeptics inside and outside the Church who, in their intellectual arrogance, are consciously or unconsciously trying to undermine the Word so that they can justify in their own minds (but not before God) their rebellion against God. As Paul says in Romans 3:4, "Let God be true but every man a liar" (NKJV).

Endnotes

1. *The New American Bible* (Nashville, TN: Memorial Bible Publishers, 1976), p. 1.
2. *The Dartmouth Bible* (Boston, MA: Houghton Mifflin, 1961), p. 8–9.
3. Some scholars rearrange these letters as JEPD, based on the order they believe the sections were written.
4. "Now the Canaanite was then in the land" (Gen. 12:6) and "as it is said to this day" (Gen. 22:14) might suggest that those phrases were written later than the rest of the verses they are in. In other words, they look like editorial comments.
5. Allan MacRae, *JEDP: Lectures on the Higher Criticism of the Pentateuch* (Hatfield, PA: Interdisciplinary Biblical Research Institute, 1994), p. 63.
6. Ibid., p. 63-64. Spinoza's arguments included these: 1) Numbers 12:3 says that Moses was the most humble man of his day, but a humble man would not write that about himself; 2) Moses is spoken of in the third person in the Pentateuch, which he would not do if he was the author; and 3) Moses could not have written his own obituary (Deuteronomy 34:5–6). In reply, even if the few verses (Genesis 12:6; 22:14, Numbers 12:3; Deuteronomy 34:5–6) are comments added by an inspired editor many years after Moses, that does not undermine the accuracy of the biblical testimony that Moses is the author of the Pentateuch. Second, modern authors often write about themselves in the third person, so this is nothing unusual.
7. On this point, see Bodie Hodge, "How Was Moses Able to Read Pre-Tower of Babel Texts?" http://www.answersingenesis.org/home/area/feedback/2006/1027.asp, October 23, 2006.
8. MacRae, *JEDP,* p. 70–72.
9. MacRae, *JEDP,* p. 72–84.
10. Josh McDowell, *A Ready Defense* (Nashville, TN: Thomas Nelson, 1993), p. 137–139.
11. Gleason Archer, *A Survey of Old Testament Introduction* (Chicago, IL: Moody Press, 1985), p. 89 (p. 95 in the 1994 edition).
12. Archer, *A Survey of Old Testament Introduction,* p. 114–123.
13. Ibid., p. 175.
14. The points are explained in Archer, *A Survey of Old Testament Introduction,* p. 109–113.
15. All people need to know where they came from, where their place in history is, or they will be very confused people. Every culture, no matter how "primitive" (by our arrogant Western standards), teaches history to their children (how accurate that history may be is a separate question). It is therefore most unreasonable to think that the Genesis patriarchs would not record and pass on the history they had to the next generation. And studies of non-literate people groups have shown that they have much better memories for maintaining the accuracy of their oral traditions than people groups that rely primarily on written communication to learn and pass on information. See Kenneth E. Bailey, "Informal Controlled Oral Tradition and the Synoptic Gospels," Themelios 20.2 (January 1995): 4–11 (http://www.biblicalstudies.org.uk/article_tradition_bailey.html, accessed January 21, 2011), and "Oral Traditions — Oral Traditions as a Source and as a Method of Historical Construction," http://science.jrank.org/pages/10523/Oral-Traditions-Oral-Traditions-Source-Method-Historical-Construction.html, accessed January 21, 2011.
16. For more on this topic, see Henry Morris, *The Genesis Record* (Grand Rapids, MI: Baker Book House, 1976), p. 22–30; and Curt Sewell, "The Tablet Theory of Genesis Authorship," *Bible and Spade,* vol. 7:1 (Winter 1994), http://www.trueorigin.org/tablet.asp.
17. The record of Esau's descendants contains a toledoth before and after it, which is problematic for either view of the connection of the toledoth to the text. Perhaps it signifies

that the account of Esau (Gen. 36:1–9) was inserted into the account written by Jacob (Gen. 25:19–37:2), since Jacob (not Esau) was the son of promise in the Messianic line from Adam.

18. Though modern editors do this usually in a footnote, we cannot demand the same literary convention be applied to the ancient editors.

19. Just as "son of" in Hebrew doesn't always mean a literal father-son relationship, so the Hebrew word translated here as "brother" doesn't always mean a literal brother, but can refer more generally to a familial or tribal relative. In this case, Lot was Abraham's brother's son, i.e., Abraham's nephew.

20. "Revised Works of Josephus," Chapter 10: The Assyrian army pursued and defeated by Abram — Birth of Ishmael — Circumcision instituted, 1912–1910 B.C., taken from: The Online Bible, by Larry Pierce.

21. But let's assume for a moment that it was referring to the region Dan, where Israelites, who were from the tribe of Dan settled. Would this be a problem for Moses? No. It was Moses who wrote where the allotments would be! In Numbers 34:1–15, Moses described the general vicinity of the borders of the various tribes. So this would actually be further confirmation of Mosaic authorship, had this been referring to descendants of Israelite Dan's territory.

Appendix D

Institution Questionnaire

Bodie Hodge

n today's culture, where evolution and millions of years has infiltrated many schools (and churches), it is difficult to even begin looking for a college or university that stands on the authority of the Bible from the very first verse.

In an effort to help parents and students find a college or university (or even a Bible-believing church), *Answers in Genesis* put together a short "Institution Questionnaire."

This quick 15-question survey can be used to present to a pastor at a church or a Christian college to see if the institution really believes what the Scriptures say, whether they admit they adhere to biblical authority or not.

This questionnaire is written to carefully see what the institution believes. This should help you discern if the institution is truly biblical or not. Keep in mind none are perfect, but some are usually much better than others. What follows are merely 15 questions that could be helpful. Following that we have short answers, a couple of references, and brief explanations of what you can learn.

Name: _____

Name of Institution: _____

Date: _____

1. Is God triune (Father, Son, and Holy Spirit) or not?
2. When did death and suffering enter into the world (for man and for animals)?
3. Do you believe Jesus Christ is the Creator?
4. Do you believe the days in Genesis are literal approximate 24-hour days or not?
5. Is it proper to interpret Genesis to conform to what one already believes about the past, or should one change one's belief to conform to what Genesis says? In other words, should Genesis be interpreted in the style it is written (literal history) or should it be interpreted in some other fashion (i.e., in light of millions of years and evolution)?
6. Have human male and female been around since the beginning of creation, did they evolve from a lower life form, or did God create them millions of years after creation?
7. Do you believe there are intelligent alien life forms?
8. Did God use a big bang?
9. Was the Flood of Noah's day global or local (regional)?
10. Do you believe Satan/Lucifer rebelled before or after the end of day 6 of the creation week discussed in Genesis 1–Genesis 2:3?
11. Why don't people today believe the Gospel when we boldly preach it?
12. How many races of people did God create?
13. Was the fossil record primarily laid down by Noah's Flood and how does this relate to the age of the earth?
14. Is Genesis important when preaching the gospel in today's culture?
15. Are there any legitimate contradictions in the Bible?

College Questionnaire Answers with References
(similar to these are acceptable)

1. They better say yes!

Question 1 helps you realize if a school is mainstream or if it has been influenced by a cult that may deny the deity of Jesus Christ (John 1, Col. 1, and Heb. 1). Also, this should be an easy question to answer for most Christian institutions.

> References: "God Is Triune," by Bodie Hodge, *Answers in Genesis* website, AiG–U.S., February 20, 2008, http://www.answersingenesis. org/articles/2008/02/20/god-is-triune, and "The Trinity," by Dr. Mark Bird, Answers in Genesis website, God's Bible School and College, July 30, 2008, http://www.answersingenesis.org/articles/aid/ v3/n1/the-trinity.

2. When Adam and Eve rebelled, resulting in the Curse and the sentence to die from Genesis 2:17, Genesis 3:17, and Romans 5:12. If they believe death (of either mankind or animals) has been around prior to this, then they have a major problem. Also, animals were vegetarian in the beginning as was man (Gen. 1:29–30), so this points to no animal death prior to sin either.

Question 2 allows you to find out if the institution really believes in a literal curse in Genesis 3 and provides an answer for the common question "Why did God make the world like this?" Biblically, God made the world perfect (Gen. 1:31; Deut. 32:4) and due to man's sin, death and suffering came into the world. This is why we need a Savior to save us from sin and death and provide a new heaven and a new earth. Adam and Eve rebelled, resulting in the Curse and the sentence to die (Gen. 2:17; Gen. 3:17; Rom. 5:12). After sin, we find the first recorded death of an animal (Gen. 3:21) and from here, we find a relationship between human sin and animal death.

> References: Ken Ham, editor, *New Answers Book 1*, "How Did Defense/ Attack Structures Come About?" by Andy McIntosh and Bodie Hodge (Green Forest, AR: Master Books, 2006), http://www.answersingenesis. org/articles/nab/origin-of-attack-defense-structures, and "Biblically, Could Death Have Existed before Sin?" by Bodie Hodge, Answers in Genesis website, March 2, 2010, http://www.answersingenesis.org/arti- cles/2010/03/02/satan-the-fall-good-evil-could-death-exist-before-sin.

3. Yes!

Question 3 reiterates question one, but more directly. With these ques- tions up front, the institution should feel comfortable answering the survey questions. So at this point we can start getting into the meat of the subject.

> References: John 1; Col. 1; and Heb. 1. (See also the references from Question 1.)

4. Yes! This is confirmed by Exodus 20:11 and Exodus 31:17, also, Mark 10:6 (marriage came at the beginning of creation, thus only five days before, not millions of years, otherwise it would be the "end" of creation.

Question 4 allows you to really start testing to see if the institution believes the Bible as the authority, or if man's ideas about millions of years has begun to creep in. The Bible is clear that it was six days, not millions of years (Exod. 20:11 and 31:17). Otherwise, our basis for a "week" makes no sense.

References: Ham, *The New Answers Book 1*, "Could God Really Have Created Everything in Six Days?" *http://www.answersingenesis. org/Home/Area/answersbook/sixdays2.asp*, and the technical article, "The Days of Creation: A Semantic Approach," by James Stambaugh, first published in the *TJ* 5(1):70–78, April 1991, later revision published at the *Evangelical Theological Society*, *http://www. answersingenesis.org/docs/4204tj_v5n1.asp*.

5. No. Second Corinthians 4:2 and Proverbs 8:8–9 make it clear the Scriptures should be interpreted plainly/straightforwardly. This means metaphors are metaphors, literal history is literal history, poetry is poetry, parables are parables, etc. Thus, we should learn about history from a perfect, all-knowing God who has always been there, instead of trying to reinterpret what God says to conform to current imperfect and fallible beliefs about the past by those who weren't there.

Question 5 is important because you can determine how the institution thinks — whether biblically or "humanistically." Humanism is a religion that has humans as the ultimate authority. If the Bible is the authority, then we as fallible sinful human beings should change our views to conform to what God says in the Bible. But if one can simply reinterpret the Bible because of one's own thinking (e.g., the days in Genesis can't be ordinary because other humans say it was millions of years), then what is the real authority? It would be that person or humans in general. So humans would be sitting in authority over God and His Word in this case. This is one way to see if humanism, even if subtly, has crept into their thinking.

References: Ham, *The New Answers Book 1*, "Don't Creationists Believe Some 'Wacky' Things?" by Bodie Hodge, http://www.answers-ingenesis.org/articles/nab/creationists-believe-wacky-things.

6. Human male and female (Adam and Eve) have been around since the beginning of creation on day 6 specifically. This is confirmed by Mark 10:6 and Mathew 19:4. This means it cannot be billions of years after creation.

Question 6 reveals if the institution believes in long ages of some sort. If one answers that humans evolved, then they obviously don't believe the Bible in Genesis. But many say they believe Genesis literally but are really tacking on man's ideas about millions of years by reinterpreting Genesis. However, Jesus reveals the glitch from His own words in Mark 10:6. The context of Jesus' response is about divorce, which concerns marriage. Jesus referred back to Genesis 1 and 2 and even quoted them in the parallel passage in Matthew 19 and stated that at the *beginning* of creation God made them male and female. If Jesus was speaking about four thousand years [according to genealogies] after the creation week of six approximately 24-hour days, then day 6 and even soon after, would be the "beginning of creation." If one has long ages, then human male and female came about 13 to 15 billion years after the creation, which is the *end* of creation, thereby making Jesus out to be speaking a falsehood. So with this verse, Jesus is affirming a relatively young age of the earth.

> References: "But from the Beginning of . . . the Institution of Marriage? by Dr. Terry Mortenson, Answers in Genesis website, November 1, 2004, http://www.answersingenesis.org/docs2004/1101ankerberg_response. asp, and "Feedback: Are the Bible and Evolution Compatible?" by Bodie Hodge, Answers in Genesis website, AiG–U.S., June 13, 2008, http://www. answersingenesis.org/articles/2008/06/13/feedback-bible-evolution-incompatible.

7. No.

Question 7 reveals how much evolutionary thinking may have infiltrated.

> Reference: Ham, *The New Answers Book 1*, "Are ETs & UFOs Real?" by Dr. Jason Lisle, http://www.answersingenesis.org/articles/nab/are-ets-and-ufos-real.

8. No.

Question 8 exposes progressive creation, theistic evolution, and other compromised views. If an institution believes in the big bang, then they are holding to the atheistic view over God's view given in Scripture (astronomical evolution). In the big bang, it simply doesn't mesh with Scripture (i.e., see a few below in the chart). The big bang starts itself, it does not need God, so when Christians try to add the idea that God started the big bang, they basically say God didn't really do anything.

	Big Bang/Millions of Years	Genesis
1.	Sun before earth	Earth before sun
2.	Dry land before sea	Sea before dry land
3.	Atmosphere before sea	Sea before atmosphere
4.	Sun before light on earth	Light on earth before sun
5.	Stars before earth	Earth before stars
6.	Earth at same time as planets	Earth before all planets
7.	Death before man	Death after man
8.	Sun before plants	Plants before the sun

Reference: Ken Ham, editor, *The New Answers Book 2*, "Does the Big Bang Fit with the Bible?" by Dr. Jason Lisle (Green Forest, AR: Master Books, 2008), http://www.answersingenesis.org/articles/nab2/does-big-bang-fit-with-bible.

9. Global — it is clearly stating that it was a worldwide event in Genesis 6–8 (specifically Gen. 7:19–20).

Question 9 also reveals if one believes in long ages but from a different perspective. If the bulk of the fossil layers represent long ages, then a global Flood is impossible because it would have ripped up the layers and redeposited them. A local Flood also makes a mockery of the promise God made after the Flood to not send another Flood like this. It was clearly a global Flood as Genesis 6–8 teaches, because we have numerous local floods all the time.

Reference: Ham, *The New Answers Book 1*, "Was There Really a Noah's Ark & Flood?" http://www.answersingenesis.org/articles/nab/really-a-flood-and-ark, and Ken Ham, editor, *The New Answers Book 3*, "Was the Flood of Noah Global or Local?" by Ken Ham and Dr. Andrew Snelling (Green Forest, AR: Master Books, 2010).

10. Satan had to rebel after day 6 (probably not day 7 because God sanctified that day and made it holy). Otherwise, rebellion from God (sin) would have been declared "very good" in Genesis 1:31.

Question 10 reveals if the compromised view of gap theory is being held at the institution. Gap theorists have millions of years thrown in between Genesis 1:1 and 1:2. As the gap theory goes, the fossils layers are primarily from an alleged Luciferian Flood when Satan fell. This is strange since the bulk of the fossil layers would no longer be representative of atheism's long ages, which was what this alleged gap was trying to mix with Scripture in the first place! Also, if this were the case, then Lucifer's actions of rebellion would be very good because God declared all things very good at the end of day 6 (Gen. 1:31). So Satan had to have fallen after day 6, and likely not on day 7 which was holy, but soon after.

> References: Ham, *The New Answers Book 1*, "What About the Gap and Ruin-Reconstruction Theories?" http://www.answersingenesis. org/articles/nab/gap-ruin-reconstruction-theories, and "When Did Adam and Eve Rebel?" By Bodie Hodge, Answers in Genesis website, AiG–U.S., April 20, 2010, http://www.answersingenesis.org/arti-cles/2010/04/20/satan-the-fall-good-evil-adam-eve-rebel.

11. People today have the wrong foundational beliefs (an "evolutionary/millions of years" foundation) that teaches the Bible is wrong. We need to teach them the true history in the Bible so they will have a foundation for understanding why they need Jesus Christ as their Savior.

Question 11 reveals if the institution really understands *why* people are walking away from the Church at an alarming rate, or if they even realize the gravity of the problem. If people don't believe Genesis is true, then why would they believe the gospels (John 3:12)? Having generations of people brought up with teaching of long ages and evolution has seen nations like England have hardly any semblance of Christianity left. The same is now happening to the United States. Yet people toss out many ideas about why the Church is dying, but they rarely get to the root of the problem. Basically, the Church as a whole let the world train its children to believe humanism (evolution and millions of years are subsets of the religion of humanism). Thus, the next generation has been taught the Bible is not true and is walking away. See Proverbs 22:6.

> Reference: Ham, *The New Answers Book 1*, "How Can I Use This Information to Witness?" http://www.answersingenesis.org/articles/ nab/how-use-information-to-witness.

12. There is one race, the human race, where each person is a descendant of Noah and ultimately Adam and Eve.

Question 12 allows you to see if the institution really believes that all people came from Adam and Eve or if they have worldly racist ideas that have crept in. Evolutionary thinking has infiltrated the Church in many areas and on the issue of racism it has contributed significantly over the years. Christians should be leading the fight against racism.

> Reference: Ham, *The New Answers Book 1*, "Are There Really Different Races?" http://www.answersingenesis.org/Home/Area/ AnswersBook/races18.asp.

13. The global Flood of Noah would have laid down billions of dead things buried in sedimentary rock layers. Of course, there have been some changes since then that will add and remove some sediment (places affected by the post-Flood Ice Age, volcanoes, earthquakes, etc.)

Question 13 is a reiteration of Question 9 but focuses on the age of the earth, to see if they are consistent with a global Flood or not, so be sure to compare their answers to Question 9 with this answer.

According to the genealogies, from Adam to Christ is about four thousand years by most chronologists. This would give an age of the earth at about six thousand years. Any long age view, however, adopts man's ideas *over* God's Word in Genesis.

> Reference: Ham, *The New Answers Book 2*, "How Old Is the Earth?" by Bodie Hodge, http://www.answersingenesis.org/articles/ nab2/how-old-is-the-earth.

14. Yes. How can people fully understand the good news of being saved, if they don't understand the bad news in Genesis of why we are lost in the first place?

Question 14: Not everyone will get this correct, but if they do, then they've been listening to creation ministries — which is a good sign! In today's culture where basic Bible knowledge has severely suffered, how can people fully understand the good news of being saved, if they don't understand the bad news in Genesis of why we are lost in the first place? Don't be hard on a church or institution if they get this wrong. This is like a "bonus question" to see if they really get the message. But also note that this is not saying if one does not see the importance of Genesis, it does not mean they are not saved. It simply means they fail to realize the importance of the foundation of the gospel. One can believe in an old earth, for example, and be saved, but they are inconsistent in their treatment of the Word of God.

Reference: "What Does It Mean to Be 'Saved'?" by Bodie Hodge, Answers in Genesis website, April 21, 2009, http://www.answersingenesis.org/articles/2009/04/21/what-does-it-mean-to-be-saved.

15. No.

Question 15 gives you an understanding of how they view the Bible. Hopefully, they answer that the Bible is inerrant in the original autographs and that no legitimate contradictions exist, since God cannot contradict Himself (2 Tim. 2:13). But some Christians have a very low view of Scripture due to evolutionary influence, whether they realize it or not.

References: "Contradictions: Introduction," by Dr. Jason Lisle, Answers in Genesis website, September 29, 2008, http://www.answersingenesis.org/articles/2008/09/29/contradictions-introduction. See also Ken Ham, editor, *Demolishing Supposed Bible Contradictions* (Green Forest, AR: Master Books, 2010).

creationcolleges.org

In order to be mentioned on this site, the school's president (or an authority representing the college) has affirmed or endorsed the Answers in Genesis' statement of faith. In doing so, they are supporting the biblical-authority message of a young earth and literal six-day creation as described in Genesis. Each year, the college representative must reaffirm they are in agreement with this statement of faith. It should be noted that such affirmation by the college representative does not necessarily mean the entire college/university — including individual professors — will take the same stand.

AiG shares this college list with you in order to give you a good start in your search for a suitable Bible-upholding institution for your student. As we suggest in this book, parents and students need to conduct their own due diligence in their research, asking school representatives the right questions, with specific queries about Genesis. This will help them discern what is actually taught in the school's classrooms and how it lines up with Scripture.

1:1

answersingenesis

Appendix E

A Journey Toward Biblical Truth

Greg Hall

In this book we give examples of those who teach various concepts surrounding the debate of origins that are contrary to the Scripture. I wish I had been more transparent about my own personal compromises along this road in coming to the understanding I have today.

In my ministry, I have always believed in the inspiration, inerrancy, and infallibility of the Scripture. But I was also one for whom the evolution vs. creation debate seemed to be unnecessary. What did it matter how God created or in what time frame? I have reviewed sermons where I told my congregation that God is our Creator but also said that science has taught us that the universe is billions of years old and still in process of being created. I was a theistic evolutionist and so had no problem with that position just as so many academics do. I loved God and His Word, what was the big deal?

Then I began to be acquainted with some teaching that changed my ministry in a profound way. I would read R.C. Sproul, John MacArthur, Albert Mohler, Douglas Kelley, or Henry Morris and my mind began to change drastically. The origin of life debate was central to the authority of Scripture and our understanding of the nature and character of God. It all became acutely focused for me when attending the Centurions program with Chuck Colson and reading the work of he and Nancy Pearcy. Years later I became acquainted with Ken Ham of the Answers in Genesis ministry and all together began to realize that these men and women are right. The authority of the Scripture is at stake in this debate and, the truth is, the so-called "science" of evolution and long ages for the earth and universe is entirely incompatible with the biblical record. Naturalism is the religion of the age, and evolution is its dogma, and together they have devastated our culture. Biblical creationism is the only reasonable and true position for the believer.

Now while we are critical of compromised positions on these matters among Christian colleges, I can tell you about my experiences in the institution where I serve. I used to teach the senior capstone course. Several years ago, while I was formulating my thoughts on biblical creationism, I was teaching one day on the subject of the importance of the origins debate in our culture. I was trying the make the case for reading the Genesis account of creation in its literal, plain sense as God creating everything ex nihilo in six 24-hour days, just like the Scripture says. After I had been going on for a while a student raised her hand (a biology major I recall) and said, "You realize that the teaching of the biology department is evolution, right?" No, I didn't I had to admit.

I wonder how many times this account is repeated in Christian schools? I guess we just assume that the case for biblical creationism would at the very least be presented right alongside the teaching of the theory of evolution. In fact, you would think that the vast resources of those scientists who are helping the culture understand that the science behind evolution is very faulty would be brought into play in a helpful way to present the truth of biblical creationism to the Christian college student. At that time that was not the case. A compromise to be sure.

Since that time I have been meeting with members of our science faculty to discuss the origin issues. I have great conversations and find these academics are the ones very skeptical of the theory of evolution and very willing to get involved in understanding and presenting the biblical creation account. Among our religion faculty we have similar discussions. It is a very real issue for the leadership of our Christian schools to maintain this kind of interaction with faculty. Everyone is not always going to be on the same page, but I have found faculty very interested in talking about these important matters.

So when I join in the discussion of compromise in Christian schools do I intend to suggest that in my own personal journey or in the institution where I serve there is no such phenomena? Absolutely not. But there is in fact no more important issue for our times than whether or not we will accept biblical truth when it speaks about any matter. And it speaks clearly on the matter of the creation of all that exists by a sovereign God who spoke it into existence just like it says in Genesis 1 and 2. And I gladly join with those who believe in the literal truth of how God did it.

About the Authors

Ken Ham

Ken Ham is the president/CEO and founder of Answer in Genesis-U.S. and the highly acclaimed Creation Museum. He is also one of the most in-demand Christian speakers in North America. Ham, a native Australian, now resides near Cincinnati, Ohio, and is the author of numerous best-selling books. Ken hosts the daily radio program, "Answers . . . with Ken Ham," heard on more than 800 stations in America (and dozens more overseas) and is one of the editors and contributing authors for AiG's *Answers* magazine (a biblical worldview publication with over 70,000 worldwide subscribers).

Greg Hall

Greg Hall has served as president of Warner University since December of 1991. He earned his bachelor of arts in philosophy from the State University of New York, and his master of education and doctor of education in higher education administration from the University of Pittsburgh. Before coming to Warner University, Dr. Hall was the executive director of the Church of God in Western Pennsylvania for 7 years. He also served 14 years as a pastor in New York and Pennsylvania. He is a native of Jamestown, New York, and is an ordained minister.

Todd Hillard

Todd Hillard is a freelance writer from San Antonio, Texas, where he lives with his wife and five kids. A former youth pastor and missionary, he is passionate about taking the dreams and stories of others and bringing them to life on the written page. Todd was born and raised in the Black Hills of South Dakota. He received his BS in pre-med studies and psychology from the University of Utah and his MA in English from Arizona State University. He and his family lived in Turkey for two and a half years. He has 17 years of pastoral experience and has written more than 12 books.

Britt Beemer

Britt Beemer holds a BA from Northwest Missouri State University and has an MA from Indiana State University. In 1979, Beemer founded America's Research Group, a full-service consumer behavior research and strategic marketing firm. He currently serves as the director of research at America's Research Group, where he personally reviews all research and prepares and presents each strategic marketing plan. His work has been cited in the media, including the *Wall Street Journal*, the *New York Times*, Fox News, and many others.

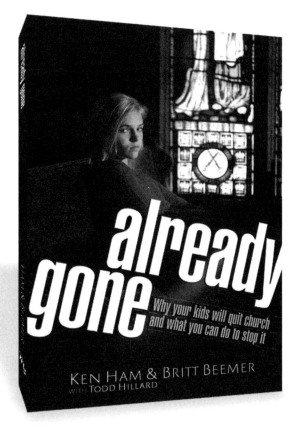

already gone

Why your kids will quit church and what you can do to stop it

Why your kids will quit church and what you can do to stop it

KEN HAM & BRITT BEEMER
WITH TODD HILLARD

Master
Books®

First printing: May 2009
Eleventh printing: August 2015

Master Books®, P.O. Box 726, Green Forest, AR 72638.
Master Books® is a division of the New Leaf Publishing Group, Inc.

ISBN-13: 978-0-89051-529-7
Library of Congress Number: 2009900148

Unless otherwise indicated, Scripture quotations are from the New American Standard Bible.

Cover Design: jdausa.com, photo provided by potthaststudios.com
Interior Design: Diana Bogardus

Photo credit, p. 162–164: Dan Clymer, Restoration House Ministries

Please consider requesting that a copy of this volume be purchased by your local library system.

Printed in the United States of America

Please visit our website for other great titles:
www.masterbooks.com

For information regarding author interviews,
please contact the publicity department at (870) 438-5288.

Master
Books®
A Division of New Leaf Publishing Group
www.masterbooks.com

Dedications

My parents, Elvin and Margaret Beemer, always told me they would rather see a sermon than hear one. My good friend Harold Anderson endured many challenges in recent years, but as each obstacle arose, his faith soared. I want to acknowledge and dedicate this book to Harold and to his enduring faith.

— *Britt Beemer*

I praise the Lord for the godly legacy of my parents who trained me to stand uncompromisingly and unapologetically on the authority of the Word of God. This book is not only a challenge from the authors, but from godly parents concerning what each one of us are doing toward preserving that godly legacy for subsequent generations.

Special thanks to my dear friends Jon and Sue Jones for allowing me sanctuary in their home to write my section of this book. . . .

And for the AiG donor who provided the funds for this valuable research.

— *Ken Ham*

Contents

Introduction

The large wooden doors shut behind me with a creak and a heavy thud. Outside, the incessant river of life continues to flow as millions of people jam the sidewalks and rush toward red double-decker busses. Beneath the streets, the London Underground moves the masses by the hundreds of thousands — like blood pulsing through the arteries of this vibrant, thriving society.

But inside, I can hear each of my careful footsteps echoing in the dim quiet. I inhale deeply, taking in the aroma of ancient stones and old books. I see rows and rows of ornate pews — seating for more than 3,000 — yet I am ushered into the small foyer area where around 30 chairs are set up and where I join a handful of elderly people with their heads bowed. Humbly and faithfully, those beside me say their prayers and listen to a brief message by a man who speaks of hope — but whose tired eyes seem to feel none of it.

It is Sunday. For hundreds of years the faithful have been walking through the heavy wooden doors on this day, at this time, to gather together and share in the timeless rituals of worship, prayer, and proclamation *that made this country the bastion of Christendom for centuries. But this morning I realize that I'm part of a funeral. But it is not the funeral of an individual; it is the funeral of an institution. Within months, the older generation will likely disband and the doors of this church will be shut and locked. The candles will never again be lit. The resounding anthem of the great hymns of our spiritual forefathers will never again echo in its passages.*

* * *

Since 1969, 1,500 churches in England have heard that final *thud* as their doors were shut after their final service after hundreds of years of active life.[1]

Most of the great churches still stand — grand buildings that just 60 years ago were the hub of vital and vibrant activity. Before World War II (and certainly during those turbulent years), churches such as the one I visited that day were the center of community and spiritual life. But now, the communities' life, such as it is, takes place outside of those buildings. Inside, many of them have become musty, dusty, and dark. The Victorian Society of the UK summarizes the situation in a publication entitled *Redundant Churches: Who Cares?*

> Invariably, it seems, churches become redundant. The country changes around them and for one reason or another they find themselves bereft of the worshippers needed to keep them going. Many, if not most, of the buildings seem eventually to find new uses, but it is not easy to generalize about how often these uses preserve their architectural and historic interest.[2]

It's not a small concern. Not far from the famous Westminster Abbey in London I found a sign that read: "Advisory Board for Redundant Churches."

---

1. The Victorian Society, No. 26, November 2007, http://www.victoriansociety. org.uk/publications/redundant-churches-who-cares/.
2. Ibid.

"Redundancy." The dictionary defines that word as "exceeding what is necessary or natural . . . needlessly repetitive." That is a disturbing term to describe a former place of worship, don't you think? Who cares about "redundant churches"? It seems not many these days. There are not many left to really care — except for those who see them for their "architectural" and "historical" value. Now emptied of their intended function, many also see the real estate value of these "needlessly repetitive" buildings. A special government agency oversees the distribution and preservation of these buildings. What does that sound like in formal language?

> The Redundant Churches Fund has as its object the preservation, in the interests of the nation and the Church of England, of churches and parts of churches of historic and archaeological interest or architectural quality, together with their contents, which are vested in the Fund by Part III of the Pastoral Measure 1983 (1983 No.1).[3]

In other words, if what's left has some value physically, it is sold or it is preserved. The rest is abandoned or bulldozed. What has become of the buildings worth keeping?

Other former places of worship have been turned into museums, clothing shops, music stores, liquor stores, nightclubs, and tattoo and piercing studios. One is even now used as a Sikh temple, and some have been converted into mosques.

Hundreds of these churches have ended up in the hands of private owners who convert them into offices or renovate them for use as personal homes or cottages.

It would be something of a relief if these former churches simply represented a shift from traditional worship toward more contemporary worship facilities, but that's not the case. The decline of the Church has followed the plummeting spirituality of a nation that has lost its roots — its foundation. England, the country that was once a cornerstone

---

3. http://www.opsi.gov.uk/si/si1994/Uksi_19940962_en_1.htm.

of western Christianity, is now, by and large, a wasteland of lost souls where the word "God" has many different definitions, with so few these days who would even think of "God" as the Creator God of the Bible.

According to a recent English Church Census:

- Regular churchgoers (of all denominations) amount to 6.3% of the total population.

- The proportion of churches per individuals is now one church to 1,340 people; the size of the average Sunday congregation, however, is 84.

- Between 1998 and 2005, there was an overall decline in regular church attendance of 15% — and the trend continues.

- 40% of regular churchgoers attend evangelical churches, but even these groups are seeing their numbers decline.[4]

All in all, only 2.5 percent of the population is attending Bible-based churches.

One United Kingdom news source in 2003 stated:

Holy Week has begun with an expert prediction that the Christian church in this country will be dead and buried within 40 years. It will vanish from the mainstream of British life, with only 0.5 percent of the population attending the Sunday services of any denomination, according to the country's leading church analyst . . . only 7.5 percent of the population went to church on Sundays and that, in the past 10 years — billed by the churches as the "Decade of Evangelism" — church attendance dropped by an "alarming" 22 percent.[5]

4. 2005 Evangelical Alliance, http://www.eauk.org/resources/info/statistics/2005 englishchurchcensus.cfm.

5. Ibid.

A church in the United Kingdom turned into a rock climbing center

A church (in John Bunyan's home town of Bedford, England) turned into a night club

A church in the United Kingdom turned into a theater

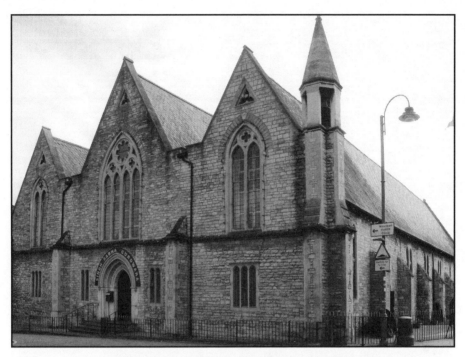

A church turned into a restaurant in the United Kingdom

*A church in the United Kingdom
turned into a Sikh Temple*

Another article in 2004 claimed: "Attendance at Britain's mosques has outstripped the number of regular worshippers in the Church of England for the first time. . . ."[6] I recently attended a church a couple hours north of London. It was a totally traditional Baptist service, but it was clear that it was a gathering of remnant believers from many backgrounds. It was a refreshing and unique sight to see excited people as the organ blasted out "The Old Rugged Cross"! Certainly, pockets of new life can be found, yet much of it is "imported." Since 2001, Africa has supplied the single largest pool of new British citizens, and many of the new arrivals bring with them the Pentecostal worship style that has drawn millions of Africans to Christian churches across the continent in the last several decades.[7] Other Bible-believing bodies of worshipers are holding their own and doing their best to reach out to the masses in this nation that now must be considered "post-Christian."

Empty churches now stand in the cities and the countryside as monuments to the triumph of the new religion of secular humanism. Hollow shells of buildings shadowing streets filled with hollow souls, the disease was the result of a predictable spread of ideas that seemed harmless enough to start with, and then mutated into a plague that killed the soul of an entire nation in two generations — and this same disease is being spread around the world. For instance, a news source in Australia quotes a university professor as saying, "Within the next 10–20 years, most of the main-line churches will be appropriately down on their knees praying for their own survival."[8]

Across the Atlantic, in the "One Nation Under God," the seeds of a free and God-fearing nation were planted only 250 years ago. Today, few people are aware of the spiritual epidemic that has wiped out the land of our Christian forefathers. England was the home of our great

6. "More Moslem Worshipers than Anglicans?" *British Church Newspaper*, February 20, 2004.

7. Associated Press, "Evangelicals Gain Strength in England, April 21, 2007."

8. Dr. David Tracy, associate professor, religion expert at Melbourne La Trobe University, quoted by Elissa Lawrence, "Losing Our Religion," *Sunday Mail*, Sunday Extra Section, Adelaide, Australia, December 29, 2002, p. 48.

spiritual ancestors — many of the greatest preachers, teachers, and evangelists of the last 200 years.

Few people are aware that the same epidemic has reached our own shores, spreading like an unstoppable virus.

When it comes to churches in America, our research shows that many are *Already Gone*.

A Heart for the Church

It is estimated that Ken Ham, president of Answers in Genesis and the new Creation Museum, has given more than 4,000 talks on the accuracy and authority of the Bible since 1973 (he started speaking full time in 1979) – plus has granted several hundred interviews with the world's media (NY Times, Washington Post, all the major US TV networks, the BBC several times, etc.).

Ken has given more biblical messages in various venues than an average pastor will give in a lifetime of sermons.

Among the many hundreds of churches in which he has spoken (in more than 20 countries), Ken has also spoken in some of America's largest and most influential churches – and thus has had his finger on the pulse of the church's health since moving to America in 1987:

- Calvary Chapel Costa Mesa, Calif. (Pastor Chuck Smith)—three times
- Harvest Christian Fellowship, Calif. (Pastor Greg Laurie)—three times
- Saddleback Comm. Church, Calif. (Pastor Rick Warren)
- Grace Community Church, Calif. (Pastor John MacArthur)—twice
- Thomas Road Baptist Church, VA (Pastor Jerry Falwell)—twice
- Bellevue Baptist Church, TN (Pastor Adrian Rogers)—twice
- First Baptist Church of Woodstock, GA (Pastor Johnny Hunt)—soon to be there a second time

Part 1:
An Epidemic on Our Hands

Epidemic (Ep-i-**dem**-ic)[1]

1. A disease or anything resembling a disease; attacking or affecting many individuals in a community or a population simultaneously.

2. Anything which takes possession of the minds of people as an epidemic does of their bodies; as, an epidemic of terror.

A majority of twenty-somethings — 61% of today's young adults — had been churched at one point during their teen years but they are now spiritually disengaged (i.e., not actively attending church, reading the Bible, or praying).

— George Barna[2]

1. Webster's Revised Unabridged Dictionary, © 1996, 1998 MICRA, Inc. , *Webster's Revised Unabridged Dictionary*. Retrieved December 09, 2008
2. http://www.barna.org/barna-update/article/16-teensnext-gen/147-most-twenty-somethings-put-christianity-on-the-shelf-following-spiritually-active-teen-years.

CHAPTER 1

Already Gone

> Guard what has been entrusted to you, avoiding worldly and empty chatter and the opposing arguments of what is falsely called "knowledge" — which some have professed and thus gone astray from the faith. Grace be with you (1 Tim. 6:20–21).

I dare you. I dare you to try it this Sunday. Look to the right, and look to the left. While the pastor delivers his message, while the worship team sings their songs, while the youth pastor gives his announcements, look to the right and look to the left. Look at the children and look at the teens around you. Many of them will be familiar faces. They are the faces of your friends' sons and daughters. They are the friends that your children bring home after youth group. They are *your* children . . . the ones who have been faithfully following you to church for years.

Now, imagine that two-thirds of them have just disappeared.

That's right, *two-thirds* of them — the boys and the girls, the kids who are leaders of the school's Bible club, the kids who sit in the back row with their baseball caps pulled low over their eyes — imagine that two-thirds of them have just disappeared from your church.

Yes, look to the left and look to the right this Sunday. Put down your church bulletin; look at those kids and imagine that two-thirds of them aren't even there. Why?

Because they are *already gone.*

It's time to wake up and see the tidal wave washing away the foundation of your church. The numbers are in — and they don't look good. From across Christendom the reports are the same: *A mass exodus is underway. Most youth of today will not be coming to church tomorrow.* Nationwide polls and denominational reports are showing that the next generation is calling it quits on the traditional church. And it's not just happening on the nominal fringe; it's happening at the core of the faith.

Is that just a grim prediction? Is that just the latest arm-twisting from reactionary conservatives who are trying to instill fear into the parents and the teachers of the next generation? No, it's not just a prediction. It's a reality — as we will document clearly from commissioned professional and statistically valid research later in this book. In fact, it's already happening . . . just like it did in England; it's happening here in North America. *Now.* Like the black plagues that nearly wiped out the general population of Europe, a spiritual black plague has almost killed the next generation of European believers. A few churches are surviving. Even fewer are thriving. The vast majority are slowly dying. It's a spiritual epidemic, *really.* A wave of spiritual decay and death has almost entirely stripped a continent of its godly heritage, and now the same disease is infecting North America.

Many of us saw it coming but didn't want to admit it. After all, our churches looked healthy on the surface. We saw bubbling Sunday schools and dynamic youth ministries. As parents and grandparents we appreciatively graced the doors of the church, faithfully dragging our kids with us, as our ages pushed into the 40s and 50s and beyond. But a vacuum was forming: there were the college students who no longer showed up for the Sunday worship service, the newly married couple that never came back after the honeymoon. . . . Sure, there were exceptions and we were grateful for their dedication. For the most part, however, we saw that the 20- and 30-somethings from our congregations were increasingly AWOL. To be honest, none of us really wanted to admit it, did we? And so we began to justify to ourselves that maybe it wasn't happening at all.

Recent and irrefutable statistics are forcing us to face the truth. Respected pollster George Barna was one of the first to put numbers to the epidemic. Based on interviews with 22,000 adults and over 2,000 teenagers in 25 separate surveys, Barna unquestionably quantified the seriousness of the situation: *six out of ten 20-somethings who were involved in a church during their teen years are already gone.*[1] Despite strong levels of spiritual activity during the teen years, most 20-somethings disengage from active participation in the Christian faith during their young adult years — and often beyond that. Consider these findings:

- Nearly 50% of teens in the United States regularly attend church-related services or activities.

- More than three-quarters talk about their faith with their friends.

- Three out of five teens attend at least one youth group meeting at a church during a typical three-month period.

- One-third of teenagers participate in Christian clubs at school.[2]

That's all well and good, but do these numbers stand the test of time? Is the involvement of churched children and teens continuing into young adulthood? Unfortunately not. Not even close. The Barna

---

1. Barna Research Online, "Teenagers Embrace Religion but Are Not Excited About Christianity," January 10, 2000, www.Barna.org.
2. http://www.lifeway.com/ArticleView?article=LifeWay-Research-finds-reasons-18-to-22-year-olds-drop-out-of-church.

research is showing that religious activity in the teen years does not translate into spiritual commitment as individuals move into their 20s and 30s (and our own research, you are about to discover, will illuminate you with reasons as to why this occurs).

Most of them are pulling *away* from church, are spending *less* time alone studying their Bibles, are giving *very little* financially to Christian causes, are *ceasing* to volunteer for church activities, and are *turning their backs* on Christian media such as magazines, radio, and television. What does this look like numerically for today's 20-somethings?

- 61% of today's young adults who were regular church attendees are now "spiritually disengaged." They are not actively attending church, praying, or reading their Bibles.

- 20% of those who were spiritually active during high school are maintaining a similar level of commitment.

- 19% of teens were never reached by the Christian community, and they are still disconnected from the Church or any other Christian activities.

Shortly after Barna blew the whistle on the problem, individual denominations and churches began to take an honest look at what was happening as their children and teens began disappearing into the young adult years. Their findings confirmed the trends that Barna had found. Dozens of groups have looked at the issue from slightly different angles. Each study yields slightly different results, but their conclusions are unanimously startling. For example, when the Southern Baptist Convention researched the problem, they discovered that *more* than two-thirds of young adults who attended a Protestant church for at least a year in high school stopped attending for *at least* a year between the ages of 18 and 22.[3]

---

3. http://www.lifeway.com/ArticleView?article=LifeWay-Research-finds-reasons-18-to-22-year-olds-drop-out-of-church.

Twenty somethings struggle to stay active in Christian faith.

20% churched as teen, spiritually active at age 29

61% churched as teen, disengaged during twenties

19% never churched as teen, still unconnected

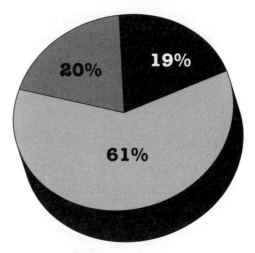

Source: The Barna Group, LTD 2006

There are exceptions, of course. Here and there we find a smattering of churches with vibrant participation from the 20-something age group. In some cities, we are seeing congregations develop that are made up almost exclusively of people from this age group. But unfortunately, these are the exceptions and not the rule. The trends that we are seeing can no longer be ignored. The epidemic is a reality. The abandoned church buildings of Europe are really just buildings, yet they are graphic symbols — warnings to those of us who are seeing the same trends in our local congregations: *we are one generation away from the evaporation of church as we know it.* Slowly but certainly the church of the future is headed toward the morgue and will continue to do so — unless we come to better understand what is happening and implement a clear, biblical plan to circumvent it.

The trends are known; more and more are finding out about them — but the vital question concerns what is the root problem of why this is happening. We need to know why if we are going to formulate possible solutions.

Who, Why, and What?

I began traveling and speaking in the United States in the 1980s. As an Australian, it didn't take long before I felt I had a good feeling for the pulse of American Christianity . . . and I saw some tremendous needs. At the time, America could rightly be labeled the greatest Christian nation on earth, the center of the economic world — and although the Church was equipped with nearly every conceivable tool and luxury for developing and expressing its faith — I could see that the Church was in great need.

Since moving to the United States in 1987, I have spoken in hundreds of different churches from many denominations, numerous Bible colleges, seminaries, and Christian conferences on American soil. I have talked with the pastors; I've listened to those in the congregations; I have experienced "worship" in almost every conceivable style and form. The ministry of Answers in Genesis is deeply committed to the American church. In fact, the faltering health of the Church in the greatest Christian nation on earth is what motivated my wife and me to move our family to this country in the first place. My wife and I testify that God called us as missionaries to America — particularly the American Church — to call it back to the authority of the Word of God beginning in Genesis.

The Bible calls the Church "the Body of Christ." Today, over 20 years after our move, the statistics prove that His body is bleeding profusely. The next generation of believers is draining from the churches, and it causes me great personal and professional concern. I've sat in the grand, but vacant, churches of Europe. I know where this is headed. Where Europe is today spiritually, America will be tomorrow — and for the same reasons, if the Church does not recognize where the foundational problem lies and address it.

When I began to seriously ponder Barna's numbers, naturally I wanted to find out more. For help, I called on a trusted and respected supporter of Answers in Genesis. As the chairman of America's Research Group, and as a leading marketing research and business analyst expert, Britt Beemer specializes in studying human behavior. Over the decades he has conducted dozens and dozens of surveys for leading corporations as well as small businesses. He analyzes the marketplace and the clientele, and makes recommendations that keep the companies excelling in a competitive world. When we were considering building the Creation Museum, we asked Britt if we could reasonably dream of 250,000 people visiting each year. Britt did his research and predicted that *400,000* people would visit the museum in the first year! He was wrong by two days. (The 400,000th visitor entered the museum 363 days after we opened.) Needless to say, when we had questions about the epidemic of people leaving church, we turned to him for answers.

Our goal was simple: We wanted to know *who* was leaving, *why* they were leaving, and *what* (if anything) could be done about it. To that end, Britt and his America's Research Group initiated a qualified study with probing questions to get powerful insight into the epidemic the Church is facing. To get to the core of the issues, his team studied *only* those whom we are most concerned about: every person in our sample said *they attended church every week or nearly every week when they were growing up, but never or seldom go today.*

We selected those between 20 and 30 who once attended conservative and "evangelical" churches. We wanted to look at the churches that claim to be Bible-believing congregations with Bible-preaching pastors. According to Barna, about 6 percent of people in their 20s and 30s can be considered "evangelical." This is about the same as the number of teenagers (5 percent).[4] The results from Britt's research would undoubtedly have been more drastic if we had considered more liberal congregations. We deliberately skewed the research toward conservatives so that we could all understand that whatever problems showed up would be much worse for the church population in general.

After 20,000 phone calls, with all the raw data in hand, Britt began to analyze the numbers. The things he discovered— as well as the things he *didn't* discover — began to shed light (in a quite astonishing way) on this monumental problem facing the future of Christianity.

---

4. www.barna.org.

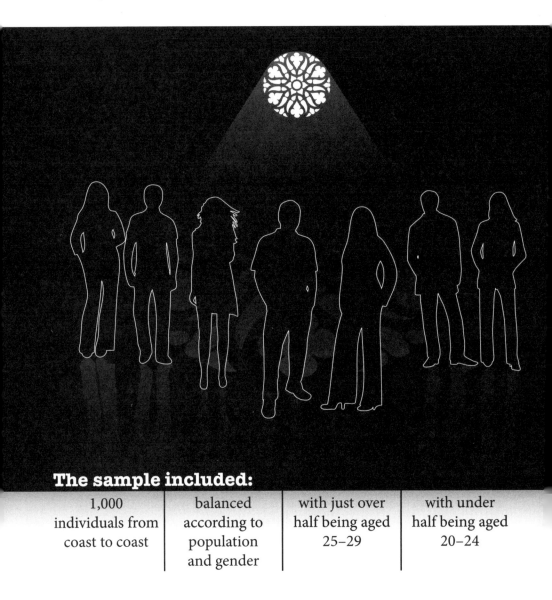

The sample included:

1,000 individuals from coast to coast	balanced according to population and gender	with just over half being aged 25–29	with under half being aged 20–24

First of all, he *didn't* discover anything abnormal about the group as a whole. There weren't an unusual number of homeschoolers, or secular school kids, who were leaving. There wasn't a significant number of females compared to males that had decided to leave. In other words, the 60 percent plus of the evangelical kids who choose to leave the church look pretty much like the 40 percent who decide to stay — at least on the outside. The breakdown of those who left really fits the profile of the evangelical population in general.

So at first, the *who* question didn't seem to give us many answers. So then, *why*? Why did they leave the church? When we asked them this open-ended question, we got an earful.

At first, we were surprised (and a little disappointed) that there wasn't a single reason. It would have been nice to find a single identifiable virus somewhere. How simple it would have been to stereotype the whole group and point out one germ that had been causing the sickness to spread. But the numbers didn't say that. *A single identifiable culprit didn't appear.*

Other researchers have come to similar conclusions. When LifeWay did their research for the Southern Baptist Convention, 97 percent of the "dropouts" listed one or more specific life-change issues as a reason they left church. The most frequent reason they gave for leaving church was almost an indifferent shrug of the shoulders: "I

The top 10 reasons were:

1.	12%	Boring service
2.	12%	Legalism
3.	11%	Hypocrisy of leaders
4.	10%	Too political
5.	9%	Self-righteous people
6.	7%	Distance from home
7.	6%	Not relevant to personal growth
8.	6%	God would not condemn to hell
9.	5%	Bible not relevant/not practical
10.	5%	Couldn't find my preferred denomination in the area

simply wanted a break from church" (27 percent). The transition into college and adulthood also affected many: "I moved to college and stopped attending church" (25 percent), and "work responsibilities prevented me from attending" (23 percent). Others simply "moved too far away from the church to continue attending" (22 percent).[5] In all honesty, these kinds of results just seemed too shallow for us at Answers in Genesis. And they seemed too superficial to Britt as well. We have a massive epidemic on our hands, and researchers seemed to be content with answers that sounded like "I just didn't feel very good," or "I wasn't there because I chose to be someplace else." Too many researchers accept simple, superficial answers. They acknowledge that there is a massive shift taking place in the spiritual lives of young adults, but when it comes to really figuring out what's going on, they kind of throw up their hands and sigh, "I guess that's just the way it is!"

End of story? Hardly. This is precisely why we teamed up with an expert like Britt Beemer who probes, and probes, and probes until he finds the right reasons. We found the real reasons, though some of them will shake many churches to their very core.

Never content with the easy answers that people give to justify their behavior, Britt is an expert in consumer behavior who taps into their minds as he finds out what people really believe in order to reveal what is driving their behavior. Until Answers in Genesis commissioned this study, never before had this type of research been conducted — and our research was formulated to not just deeply probe what people believe but answer the questions in regard to WHY people believe what they do. We can now identify the real answers as well as the causes affecting young people who leave the church.

As Britt studied his data, it was obvious that multiple issues are behind the exodus from church. The *why?* question would prove to be more complicated than many expected. But soon, as the numbers became more clear, patterns emerged, assumptions were destroyed,

---

5. http://www.lifeway.com/ArticleView?article=LifeWay-Research-finds-reasons-18-to-22-year-olds-drop-out-of-church.

and quirky findings surfaced. One of the most important and startling findings turned out not to answer the *why?* question, but rather the *when?* question.

Of these thousand 20 to 29-year-old evangelicals who attended church regularly but no longer do so:

95% of them attended church regularly during their elementary and middle school years	55% attended church regularly during high school	Of the thousand, only 11% were still going to church during their early college years

I think this is one of the most revealing and yet challenging statistics in the entire survey — and something we didn't expect. Most people assume that students are lost in college. We've always been trying to prepare our kids for college (and I still think that's a critical thing to do, of course), but it turns out that only 11 percent of those who have left the Church were still attending during the college years. Almost 90 percent of them were lost in middle school and high school. By the time they got to college they were already gone! About 40 percent are leaving the Church during elementary and middle school years! Most people assumed that elementary and middle school is a fairly neutral environment where children toe the line and follow in the footsteps of their parents' spirituality. Not so. I believe that over half of these kids were lost before we got them into high school! Whatever diseases are fueling the epidemic of losing our young people, they are infecting our students much, much earlier than most assumed. Let me say this again:

We are losing many more people by middle school and many more by high school than we will ever lose in college.

Many parents will fork out big bucks to send these students to Christian colleges, hoping to protect them in their faith. But the fact is, they're already gone. They were lost while still in the fold. They were disengaging while they were still sitting in the pews. They were preparing their exit while they were faithfully attending youth groups and Sunday schools.

What a reminder to parents (and Christian leaders) to do exactly what God's Word instructs us to do — to "train up a child in the way he should go . . ." (Prov. 22:6). And further, "These words which I command you today shall be in your heart. You shall teach them diligently to your children, and shall talk of them when you sit in your house, when you walk by the way, when you lie down, and when you rise up" (Deut. 6:6–7; NKJV). What a reminder to teach children from when they are born — and a reminder to be diligent in providing the right sort of training/curricula, etc., for children.

Sadly, I think many see children's programs as entertainment, teaching Bible stories, and so on, but when they get older we need to think about preparing them somehow for college — but as our research showed, by then they are already gone! For most, it was basically too late!

This topic regarding when we begin to lose our kids is where the study began to get very interesting and very illuminating. For example:

Those who no longer believe that all of the accounts and stories in the Bible are true:

39.8% first had doubts in middle school

43.7% first had their doubts in high school

10.6% had their first doubts during college

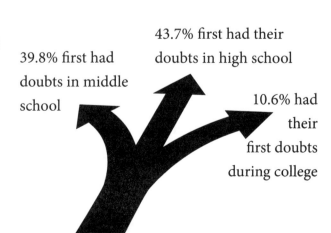

Clearly, there is a slightly delayed reaction going on. The doubts come first, followed shortly by departure. Students didn't begin doubting *in* college, they simply departed *by* college. Again, if you look around in your church today, two-thirds of those who are sitting among us have already left in their hearts, it will only take a couple years before their bodies are absent as well.

The Beemer study has a tremendous amount to offer the churches, the pastors, the parents, and the researchers who are sincerely looking into this problem. Britt's study didn't look just at behavior; he looked at belief. By making correlations between those beliefs and the behavior and intentions of those who have left the Church, the veil was lifted, powerful new insights were revealed, and very surprising results were illuminated. In the pages ahead we will give you the highlights of some of these numbers. But brace yourself, because in many instances the results are shocking, and they point a finger at many well-intentioned, firmly established programs and traditions of churches that are utterly failing the children who faithfully attend every Sunday morning.

You will need to swallow hard and be prepared to consider things very carefully; Be ready to give up long-held, cherished notions in regard to certain church programs of which perhaps you would never have considered the slightest possibility that there was such a serious problem as this research clearly showed.

First, we will investigate key aspects of the epidemic, including:

- the effects of Sunday school

- the two different kinds of kids who are leaving the Church and why it's so important to know the difference

- why the Church has lost its value and is now considered irrelevant

Second, we will investigate the solutions that are within our grasp:

- how to defend the Christian faith and uphold the authority of the Bible from the very first verse

- what it means (and doesn't mean) to live by the Bible

- the revolution that is reclaiming "church" in this culture

Along the way the investigation will be spiced up with a variety of fascinating findings regarding the following:

- music

- friends

- unbiblical church traditions

- teaching

- beliefs about Genesis

If you are a parent, a pastor, or a Christian educator, then this research is for you. Or maybe you are one of the millions of students who are thinking about leaving the Church or have already done so. If so, I challenge you to let the numbers speak for themselves and then be ready to allow God to use you in new ways to make a difference for the sake of the next generation and the Church. Even though the results were obtained in America, because it has had the greatest Christian influence in the world and has been an enormous influence on the world (Christian literature, missionaries, etc.), it is likely that such research would show similar (at best) or much worse results in other countries.

Yes, I challenge you. This Sunday, look to the left and then look to the right. According to our research, two-thirds of the children and teens you see will be gone in a matter of years. *What* can be done about it? Plenty, as you will soon see!

Britt's Bit: The AIG-ARG Connection

On behalf of Ken Ham, I want to thank you for picking up this book. I make my living generating numbers and statistics, and they are an important part of my personal ministry. When numbers and statistics are interpreted correctly they mean something. They aren't just arbitrary measurements for things that don't matter. Numbers do matter. They represent things that are real, that are measurable, that can be observed, and (in many cases) that can be changed with the right remedies. That's what America's Research Group is all about. At ARG we draw conclusions that are meaningful to our clients. We are behavioral scientists who study human behavior. ARG provides each client a foundation built on practical, useful information that ensures their ongoing success.

That's why I am such a firm believer in Answers in Genesis. Not only is their ministry important, but AIG is a reminder of what God can do through one person who steps out in faith and allows God to use them to defend and proclaim the truth. Ken moved his family to the United States more than 20 years ago, having started a ministry out of the trunk of his car and a few cardboard boxes in his house. I don't think anyone would have believed (particularly Ken) what God had in store for a ministry of such humble beginnings.

Today, the Answers in Genesis website gets *millions of visitors per year.* Tens of thousands of resources (books, DVDs, curricula, magazines, etc.) move through AIG's warehouse year after year. A small army of trained speakers are reaching tens of thousands of people face-to-face on every continent on the globe except Antarctica. (As far as I know, no one has volunteered to go there quite yet!)

I love keeping track of the AIG ministry and what people say about it. I've been tracking public opinion religiously (pun intended), and I have a deep desire to protect and to equip this ministry. When the Creation Museum opened, it created a national media tsunami, and at least one-third of the comments voiced about the ministry were clearly negative. The naysayers had their day, but they didn't last. Today, only 1/20th of the comments about the museum are negative. I think that is an amazing accomplishment. As I projected, 400,000 people came through those doors in the first year.

I make my living studying human behavior and attitudes statistically, which gives me a unique viewpoint of how and why people act the way they do. I sincerely invite you to come along with my friend and ministry cohort Ken Ham as he takes you on a personal tour through my numbers. I'll be throwing in my "bit" on a regular basis, giving you my take on the statistics and their importance. As you begin to understand the trends of the past, and see where the Church is at present, you will discover highly practical action points that will make a difference in the future. I believe that if you get a handle on a few of the numbers that describe what is happening in the Church today, you will see the potential for change that resides within you as a pastor, a parent, or a Christian educator. And that's important. The next generation is counting on us.

CHAPTER 2

Sunday School Syndrome

Everything I know I Learned in Kindergarten — title of a best-selling book for adults.

This Sunday morning a familiar scene will play itself out at churches from coast to coast. Minivans and SUVs will open like pop cans in the parking lots of various denominations, spewing forth their contents of kids. With Bibles in one hand and car-seats in the other, parents will herd their excited children toward the doors. In the hallways, the kids will split up by age and be welcomed into classrooms full of laughter and life and hope. Teachers will embrace these kids as if they are their own for about 45 minutes. They will pour their hearts and souls into the children and teens with the help of videos, various curricula resources, Bible stories, crayons, crackers, CD music, computer graphics, flannel graphs, white boards, cookies, cotton balls, popsicle sticks, prayers, and pipe cleaners. . . . It all looks so safe and so healthy — an inseparable part of the fabric of spiritual life in the western world.

"Did you often attend Sunday school?"

yes. 61%

no. 39%

In our survey of 1,000 20-somethings who regularly attended church as children and teens, we asked the question, "Did you often attend Sunday school?" In reply, 61 percent said yes; 39 percent said no. That's about what you would expect, isn't it? After all, not everyone is committed enough to make the effort to get to Sunday school, right? Only those who are more concerned about the spiritual and moral health of their kids, right? Because we all assume that Sunday school is good for them, correct? The ritual of Sunday school is so interwoven into American church life that it's hardly worth mentioning, right? Wrong. Our research uncovered something very disturbing:

> Sunday school is actually more likely to be detrimental to the spiritual and moral health of our children.

Now before you react to this, please hear us out and consider the research — real research that is statistically valid and gives us a true look at what is going on.

Compared to the 39 percent who do *not* go to Sunday school, contrary to what many of you may believe, the research showed that students who *regularly* attend Sunday school are actually:

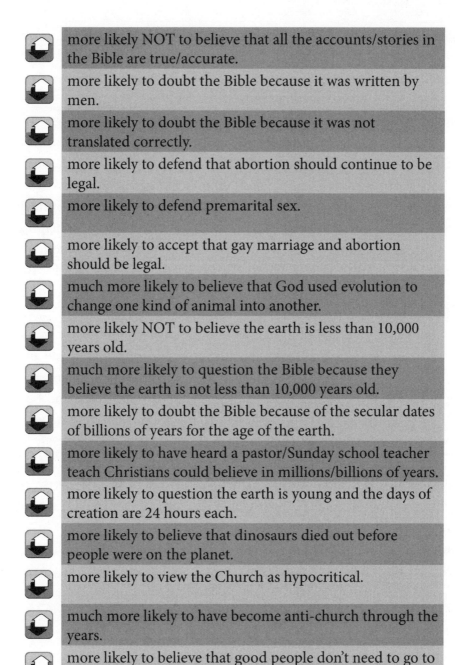

more likely NOT to believe that all the accounts/stories in the Bible are true/accurate.

more likely to doubt the Bible because it was written by men.

more likely to doubt the Bible because it was not translated correctly.

more likely to defend that abortion should continue to be legal.

more likely to defend premarital sex.

more likely to accept that gay marriage and abortion should be legal.

much more likely to believe that God used evolution to change one kind of animal into another.

more likely NOT to believe the earth is less than 10,000 years old.

much more likely to question the Bible because they believe the earth is not less than 10,000 years old.

more likely to doubt the Bible because of the secular dates of billions of years for the age of the earth.

more likely to have heard a pastor/Sunday school teacher teach Christians could believe in millions/billions of years.

more likely to question the earth is young and the days of creation are 24 hours each.

more likely to believe that dinosaurs died out before people were on the planet.

more likely to view the Church as hypocritical.

much more likely to have become anti-church through the years.

more likely to believe that good people don't need to go to church.

Read that list again. No, we don't have it backward. Yes, you're reading it correctly. These results are extremely alarming — in fact, quite shocking. (I had to look at it several times before I could believe it.) They are so contrary to what we would have assumed that they should feel like a rude slap in the face. And remember, these findings were the result of probing questions by a leading researcher who knows how to gather data and statistically analyze it to give us a true picture of the situation.

This was our most stunning and disconcerting result of the entire survey. First, we found out that we were losing our kids in elementary school, middle school, and high school rather than in college. Then we found out that Sunday school is one of the reasons why. The "Sunday school syndrome" is contributing to the epidemic, rather than helping alleviate it. These numbers are statistically significant and absolutely contrary to what we would expect. This is a brutal wake-up call for the Church, showing how our programs and our approaches to Christian education are failing dismally.

Before we investigate this further, however, I want to say a few words to those of you who are committed to Christian education inside and outside of the church. My hat goes off to you. I thank you. I sincerely commend you for taking action and giving your time, skills, and best efforts to invest in the future generation. We are not questioning your dedication, intentions, or passion. In fact, we believe that your efforts are far too often taken for granted and never thanked enough. We don't question your integrity and we certainly don't doubt your sincerity. In our survey, less than half of the students said they came to Sunday school to see their friends. That means that *you* were their contact point. *You* are the ones who are sincerely trying to build a bridge for them into a healthy spiritual adulthood. The problem is that, by and large, what you are doing isn't working. We need to ask some hard questions here. We need to be willing to swallow our pride, if necessary, as we find the answers. And we will offer solutions — real solutions — if the Church will take these findings to heart and be prepared to face the challenge head-on.

Disturbing Details

Three out of five individuals in our survey said they "often attended Sunday school." Of those who attended Sunday school, over seven in ten *said* Sunday school lessons were "helpful." Our results, however, disproved that perception.

In many situations, Sunday school didn't necessarily hurt, but it certainly didn't help. When asked, "Does the Bible contain errors?" sadly, Sunday school made no difference. (About 39 percent of each group said yes to this question.) When asked, "Do you believe you are saved and will go to heaven upon death?" there was almost no statistical difference — which really is very disconcerting. In most of the categories, there was such a slight difference between the "yes" or "no" answers of these two groups that the "I don't know" answers became a big factor. The results show that Sunday school is actually having an overall *negative* impact on beliefs, even though these differences were often quite slight in a number of instances. *The obvious conclusion is that Sunday school really had no impact on what children believed in these critical areas.*

For example, when asked if they believed in the creation of Adam in the Garden of Eden, Sunday school had no significant effect on the answers. The same can be said for the story of Sodom and Gomorrah and Lot's wife. The same can be said of Noah's ark and the global Flood. Belief in the Tower of Babel was nearly identical. In these areas Sunday school did nothing — it wasn't a help or a detriment. The numbers indicate that Sunday school actually didn't do *anything* to help them develop a Christian worldview. In several other areas, as shocking as this sounds, the reality we have to face is that Sunday school clearly harmed the spiritual growth of the kids. Consider these questions:

"Do you believe that God used evolution to create human beings?"

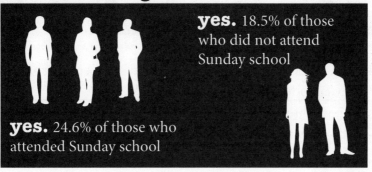

yes. 18.5% of those who did not attend Sunday school

yes. 24.6% of those who attended Sunday school

"Do you believe that God used evolution to change one kind of animal into another?"

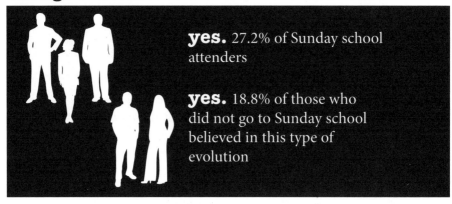

yes. 27.2% of Sunday school attenders

yes. 18.8% of those who did not go to Sunday school believed in this type of evolution

Toward the end of this chapter, we will give you an explanation as to why we believe such a situation exists.

It's safe to say that Sunday school attendance is tied to higher percentages of belief in evolution. The same can be said about important moral issues.

"Do you believe that premarital sex is wrong?"

47.7% of students who did not attend Sunday school believe that premarital sex is wrong

40.8% of Sunday school attenders believe that premarital sex is wrong

And what about the main issue we are concerned about in this book? Why are our kids leaving the Church?

These next three findings may shock you because you would naturally feel those who attended Sunday school would have deeper religious convictions. However, we found the exact opposite.

"Do you feel good people don't need to go to church?"

yes. 39.3% of Sunday school attenders

yes. interestingly, only 28.9% of non-attenders

"Do you feel the Church is relevant to your needs today?"

no. Only 39.6% of those who did not attend Sunday school felt like church is not relevant to their needs today.

no. 46.4% of Sunday school attenders

"Do you believe that you have become anti-church through the years?"

yes. 39.1% of those who attended Sunday school

yes. 26.9% of those who didn't go to Sunday school

This should cause us to gasp. When compared to those who never went to Sunday school, more Sunday school attenders believe that good people don't need to go to church, more feel like the church is less relevant, and more have become increasingly anti-church over the years.

The brutal conclusion is that, on the whole, the Sunday school programs of today are statistical failures.

Ouch!

I know that's going to hurt many of you who are devoted and dedicated to these programs — as well as those of you who are depending on these programs to properly influence your children. I'm sure various Sunday school curricula publishers will want to become defensive about their resources. But listen, if you are depending on these programs to properly teach and influence your children, it is just not happening.

Out of the 1,000 interviews, 606 were former Sunday school students, and the Church failed these people miserably. As children and teenagers they were there almost every Sunday; they were committed and they were present; they heard the lessons and they nodded their heads . . . and it had a nominal and even negative effect on their faith.

If I were a church leader, I would first sit down and cry and pour my heart out to the Lord. And rightly so. I would then find a new Sunday school curriculum that better prepares young people to maintain their faith. These numbers would be telling me that I need to earnestly look at some radical changes, and I would be working hard toward doing what is needed to reverse this situation.

Taught but Not Caught

All of these numbers would be a little bit easier to accept if we had surveyed a broader cross-section of Christian churches. If these numbers included all of the nominal, liberal churches (particularly those that don't even claim to stand on the Word of God), then these results would be a little bit more understandable. But they don't. Remember what we said at the beginning about the type of person we identified for this survey. These results have come from the Christian education programs of the most dedicated, Scripture-affirming churches out there — imagine what the situation must be in the Church as a whole!

Is it a problem of not being taught? Considering these people came from conservative church backgrounds, consider these numbers from our research:

- Of those who attended Sunday school, over 9 in 10 said that their Sunday school classes taught them that the Bible was true and accurate.

- Only 1 in 10 said their pastor/Sunday school teacher taught that Christians could believe in Darwinian evolution.

- One in 4 said their pastors and Sunday school teachers taught that Christians could believe in an earth that is millions or billions of years old.

- Over 4 in 5 said their pastor or Sunday school teacher taught that God created the earth in six 24-hour days.

- Only 1 in 16 said their pastors or Sunday school teachers taught that the Book of Genesis was a myth or legend and not real history.

Actually, as we will explain later on, there is a major problem with *how* they were taught. These people who went to conservative churches heard many of the right things for the most part (though the situation would be much less so on the whole), but did they "hear" in a way that

Further,

- 2/5 said the Bible contains errors.
- Less than 2/5 said they believe all the accounts and stories in the Bible are true and accurate.

equipped them to believe in their hearts what the Bible clearly stated, and were they equipped to be able to defend this teaching in the real world they live in?

Clearly, we do have a problem on our hands. The causes for the problems are many, but one thing is for sure: Sunday school isn't solving it. High school is when we lost nearly half of this group; a big group was lost even earlier in middle school due to doubt in the accounts and stories in the Bible being true. Of those who don't believe all the accounts and stories in the Bible are true and accurate, four in nine said they had their first doubts in high school.

As the astronaut exclaimed, "Houston, we have a problem!" We will look at our "problem" in great detail in the chapters ahead. Several major concerns will become evident: the concern over biblical authority, the history behind our descent into this abyss, and the great disconnect this has caused when people try to make a connection between their spirituality and reality. What are we going to do?

You will see later in the book that much can (and must!) be done. Great debate is raging right now about the future of Christian education programs. What are some of the ideas?

1. Should we eradicate?

This is a very extreme suggestion, but since we have an extreme epidemic on our hands, it needs to be at least discussed. A growing number of people within the evangelical church are suggesting that we do away with children's and youth ministries altogether. Consider these thoughts from the Reformed Baptist Church blog site *The World from My Window*[1]:

> It seems as if we are always trying to fix what is broken with youth ministry. Has it crossed anyone else's mind that maybe youth ministry shouldn't be fixed because youth ministry **IS** a major part of the problem?!

---

1. http://theworldfrommywindow.blogspot.com/2006/09/barna-confirms-teens-are-leaving.html.

. . . Just in case you were wondering. I am not anti-youth or anti-youth pastor. My two brothers function in the role of youth pastors (including the famous Ken Fields). I was a youth pastor for six years and I am greatly concerned with the future of our younger generations.

Is that idea too radical? Could it possibly be an improvement to get rid of Sunday school and youth ministries altogether? That almost sounds blasphemous. After all, aren't our concepts of "church" and "Sunday school" inseparable? Not necessarily. Just because our generation has always done it that way doesn't mean that we have to continue to do it that way. George Barna and Frank Viola note that Sunday school isn't even historical:

> The Sunday school is also a relatively recent invention, born some 1,700 years after Christ. A newspaper publisher named Robert Raikes (1736–1811) from Britain is credited with being its founder. In 1780, Raikes established a school in "Scout Alley" for poor children. Raikes did not begin the Sunday school for the purpose of religious instruction. Instead, he founded it to teach poor children the basics of education. . . . The Sunday school took off like wildfire, spreading to Baptist, Congregational, and Methodist churches throughout England.[2]

Part of the concern is that the mere existence of youth ministry and Sunday school allows parents to shrug off their responsibilities as the primary teachers, mentors, and pastors to their family. The other part of the concern is that, again, what we are doing just isn't working. If the existence of our Christian education programs in their current forms are certainly not helping — and in some situations even doing harm — why not dump them altogether?

---

2. George Barna and Frank Viola, *Pagan Christianity?* (Carol Stream, IL: Barna-Books, 2007), p. 212.

However, we are not advocating eradication! We want to be solution-oriented, as you will see, so that we can effectively reach these young people with the truth of God's Word.

2. Renovate

This recommendation isn't quite so extreme — and it is one we recommend. Our children need more training, more nurturing, more teaching than ever — but we need to turn things around so Sunday school isn't doing the opposite.

We believe it's possible that the current Christian education programs within the Church don't need to be eradicated, but they certainly need to be renovated. Churches need to appraise the teachers teaching Sunday School and ensure they know how to answer the skeptical questions and know how to teach apologetics — and know how to teach the age group being entrusted to them. It's one thing to tell students what to believe, it's another thing to teach and communicate that in a convincing and gripping way.

Churches need to totally reevaluate the curricula they use (including their VBS programs), and at the very least supplement at all age levels and all years with good apologetics curricula. And we are not just talking about creation apologetics — we mean general biblical apologetics as well. Most church-going adults cannot adequately defend the basics of their Christian faith or basic doctrines, let alone defend the faith against the skeptical questions of this scientific age. How many can really even properly answer questions such as: Where did the Bible come from? What does it mean to have faith? What does it mean that the Bible is inspired? Aren't there other books that some say should be in the Bible? How do you know Jesus is God? — just to name a few. More and more curricula (such as VBS programs and supplemental curricula for different ages) that is apologetic in nature is being produced to begin to fulfill the above need. Some resources are described in the bibliography.

When we talk of "renovating," we mean something much more aggressive than simply "redecorating." A little updating isn't going to do the job. The entire structure and focus of our programs need to be reconsidered; we need to be willing to make radical changes in the format and the style of these programs to determine how they can be most effective in teaching truth to our children and overcoming the issues that are undermining biblical authority in their thinking and driving them away from the Church.

Let's be honest. Our entire culture (including secular schools) is aggressively teaching the apologetics of evolution and secular human-ism. They teach our students how to defend a humanistic worldview, and they model that worldview. They show all the reasons that what they are teaching is supposedly true. The secularists are teaching our children how to defend the secular faith, and connecting it to the real world — and here we are in churches teaching wonderful Bible stories and reinforcing in their minds that they can believe the secularists and that the Bible is not really connected to the real world. No wonder we are losing them. (See the section for the Christian educator in chapter 7 which deals with solid curriculum for more details on the problems with Sunday school lessons.)

Unless the facts behind the Christian faith are clearly and convinc-ingly communicated in a way that students can learn and remember, their faith will not stand the assault of doubt from the world. It's not enough to just tell students, "Believe in Jesus!" Faith that is not founded on fact will ultimately falter in the storm of secularism that our stu-dents face every day.

In many cases, when we look at what is being taught in the Sun-day schools, we're just teaching on an inspirational or a moral level. The Sunday sermon usually dishes out more of the same. Neither one is providing the necessary support and education students need. In many cases, they are getting two lessons on a Sunday, and neither are really relevant to them. It's not just the Sunday school, it's the sermon, the VBS, it's most of the teaching programs — they are not helping them in this postmodern culture where it is becoming the norm to attack and marginalize Christians. They are not coping — they are not able to cope — they haven't been trained to cope.

Perhaps you agree with us that it's going too far to eradicate, but hopefully you will agree it's certainly time to renovate. Radical renovation is needed urgently. We are losing the next generation — we are losing the culture.

3. Don't delegate

Listen carefully. We're certainly not saying that Sunday school *can't* be effective in teaching the truth about God's Word. We're just saying that in its current form it *isn't*. If nothing else, a parent should look at these data and feel a rush of sober realization. If you, as a parent, have been putting the responsibility for the religious education of your child on your church's Sunday school, you need to realize that the statistics say the job isn't getting done. As we have seen, in many cases and for many different reasons, it's not helping, it's hurting. So this coming Sunday, don't feel like you have absolved yourself of responsibility when you drop your child at Sunday school. This is your job. Do not totally delegate it to someone else — as, sadly, many parents seem to do.

Deuteronomy 6:4–10 and Ephesians 6:1–4 clearly exhort parents to teach, disciple, and train their own children. Regardless of what's happening in the Sunday school youth groups, pulpit, and Bible studies of your church, the responsibility for ministry to our kids has never been removed from the parents. It's time to pick that ball up again and jump in the game. James H. Rutz, in his thought-provoking book *The Open Church: How to Bring Back the Exciting Life of the First Century Church,* has the heart and the courage to take an honest look at the Sunday school ritual and test its effectiveness:

> Take Sunday school for example. God's plan for religious education is Dad. It's a 4,000-year-old plan that's worked like a watch since the days of Abraham. But if your weekly gathering doesn't equip Dad to open his mouth at home and be a teacher of the Word — well, Sunday school is your next best bet. (Programming Dad would be easier.)[3]

---

3. James H. Rutz, *The Open Church: How to Bring Back the Exciting Life of the First Century Church* (Auburn, ME: SeedSowers, 1992), p. 19.

I understand what this author is saying, but we would say it is actually a 6,000-year-old plan, going back to the first dad, Adam.

If your parents shirked their responsibility for training you spiritually, you will need to break the chain of biblical illiteracy and spiritual irresponsibility in your family tree. If your church hasn't been stepping up to the plate to equip you, I would suggest a book I wrote with my brother Stephen, *Raising Godly Children in an Ungodly World — Leaving a Lasting Legacy*.[4] Steve and I had a great blessing of being raised by a father (and mother) who took creative and determined responsibility for teaching their kids from God's Word, and living a biblical life. Our father, as the spiritual head of the house, stood uncompromisingly on the Word of God, determined to be equipped to answer the skeptical questions of the age, setting an example for his children that prepared us for the ministries we are involved in today. We would gratefully pass on to you what he passed on to us so that you can pass it on to your kids. Again, don't delegate this. It's one of the most rewarding and important aspects of being a parent. And do it right now. There's no time to waste.

What is interesting to me is that a person who has not heard of the research being reported in this book, and who has never heard me speak on this topic, wrote to my brother Stephen after reading the book referred to above and said:

"I read your book *Raising Godly Children in an Ungodly World*. . . . I thoroughly enjoyed it and felt greatly challenged as a Sunday school teacher. I just realized how many people went through Sunday school in Australia and came out of it, and never come back to church again. It makes me reevaluate the role that I played at our Sunday school, whether I am playing my part right, drawing children to know God or pushing them away from God without even knowing it. Your book came in just as a wake up call!"

---

4. Ken Ham and Steve Ham, *Raising Godly Children in an Ungodly World* (Green Forest, AR: Master Books, 2008).

Not a Simple Epidemic

This Sunday, the ritual of Sunday school and teen ministry will again repeat itself. Through the data collected by Britt Beemer in this survey, we now know how typical Sunday school programs have affected our children. The Sunday school syndrome is a serious contributor to the overall problem of students exiting the Church. A true and urgent commitment to address the problem is probably more important than the specific solutions that are eventually implemented. Again, when 60 percent of our kids are leaving the Church, there will be no single solution to the overall problem — there is no single inoculation that will make us immune. The truth of the matter is that the epidemic affects each of us as individuals, because each of us is part of the greater Body of Christ. Together, working as a body, a multifaceted response to the disease can materialize. Lord willing, the mass exodus can be slowed, if not reversed, and be transformed into something new and more powerful than the typical, traditional forms we are now using.

Imagine if we started (in our homes and churches) raising generations of children who stood uncompromisingly on the Word of God, knew how to defend the Christian faith, could answer the skeptical questions of this age, and had a fervor to share the gospel from the authority of God's Word with whomever they met! This could change the world.

In the next chapter, we will look deeper into the lives of those who are leaving the Church. What the numbers taught us about them will be essential as you move into the future and discern what *you* can do to address this problem. Let there be no mistake, it's time to do something — it's time for *you* to do something. If not, you might as well sleep in this Sunday. The statistics show that not going won't hurt your kids one bit. In fact, they might be better for it.

Britt's Bit: Not by Chance

You have to be careful with numbers. People often say, "You can prove anything you want to with statistics," and they are partially right.

As a consumer researcher, I've seen people use every trick in the book to try to prove their point no matter whether the data supported it or not.

For example, what if a politician told you that "70 percent of students in the country scored above the national average"? Would you believe him? Could you believe him? No way. The law of averages says that half the country will be above average. (The other half, of course, will be below average.)

A news anchor recently said, "Over half of Americans approve of abortion." The truth is, only 38 percent approve of abortion, but 13 percent are still undecided. So by adding the undecideds with those who oppose it, they conclude that 50 percent accept it. A few years ago I was hired to conduct a study of 1,000 consumers across America. When we finished the survey we realized that we had omitted a question that the client really wanted. So, at our expense, we interviewed another 1,000 consumers with the original questions, plus the one new one. Amazingly, when I reviewed all the data from the two different surveys conducted within a week of each other, no answer varied more than 1.8 percent, well within the 3.8 plus or minus statistical error factor.

In this study, when we say that there is a difference between two numbers, we can prove that mathematically. When you hear statistics from other people, you'll just have to be careful and double check to make sure that they aren't twisting or fabricating what they are saying!

CHAPTER 3

Not What You'd Expect

God sees not as man sees, for man looks at the outward appearance, but the LORD looks at the heart (1 Sam. 16:7).

This Sunday, William and his family are going to sleep in. Across the street, Karen and her husband are going to do the same. The day will look much the same for each of them: breakfast in pajamas, the Sunday comics, a few chores around the house, an afternoon filled with some sort of an outing, movie, or a visit with family and friends.

On the outside, their lives look about the same — typical middle-class suburbanites, living out their days in the midst of the nine to five. Yes, Karen and William have a lot in common, but they also share something that isn't quite so obvious: Karen and William are former church kids. Two names out of the thousand that we surveyed. Perhaps they represent your neighbor next door, perhaps they are your siblings . . . perhaps they are *your* kids. Karen and William spent the better part of two decades in church on Sunday mornings. No more. They are already gone.

When dinnertime rolls around, however, we see something is drastically different about them. Before the meal is served, William and his family join hands and give sincere thanks for God's provision. Karen and her husband talk about current events in the news and the week ahead. When the dishes are done and the kids are tucked in, William will plop down on his bed and read the Bible he keeps on his nightstand. As the living words of Scripture resonate in his soul he senses the familiar and calming presence of the Holy Spirit in his heart. He dozes off in sincere prayer, asking for God's guidance and grace for the days ahead. "Maybe next Sunday . . . ," he thinks. "Yeah, maybe next week I'll go back." Karen and her husband, on the other hand, will catch a re-run on the television, make a few plans for the upcoming week, and turn off the light. If they think about God at all, the thoughts are skeptical. And going back to church never even crosses their mind.

Monday morning, William and Karen will wave to each other as they pull out of their driveways and head back to their jobs. Yes, on the surface they appear to be very similar people. But they're not . . . and that's not what we would expect.

The Dividing Line

When we commissioned Britt Beemer to study the kids who are leaving church, we knew that we could not be satisfied with superficial answers. We wanted to know *who, why,* and *what.* If there were simple answers to those questions, someone would have certainly found them by now (and would have become famous by applying the one-size-fits-all solution that would have solved the problem once and for all). Of course, that's not the case. Epidemics are never simple. There are root causes. There are things that cause them to accelerate. There are things that can be done to curb them from spreading. There are things that can be done to help those who are already sick get well.

Britt's data, as we expected, went deep. Rather than being satisfied with obvious observations that profile people like William and Karen, Britt went for the heart. And what he found proved to be profoundly descriptive and yet very simple and practical.

Central to this study was the issue of belief. You simply cannot explain the behavior without understanding the beliefs behind the behaviors. "Belief" is invisible. The only way to see it is through actions — yet the same actions might be the result of different beliefs. Remember that everyone in our sample of 1,000 grew up regularly going to church but seldom or never go today. Britt asked several questions to determine whether biblical belief was at the root of the exodus from the Church.

This was one of several "watershed questions" of the survey because those who accepted all the accounts and stories in the Bible had a much different viewpoint throughout all the questions in the survey. These questions and the results revealed in the survey helped us discern when these people's belief in the accuracy of Scripture began to be eroded in their thinking.

"Do you believe all the accounts/stories in the Bible are true/accurate?"

a full 38% of people who left the church answered yes

44% said no

18% didn't know

So it could also be said that a full 62 percent of the sample did not believe all the accounts and stories in the Bible. Affirming our earlier conclusions, most of those who do not believe in the full accuracy of the Bible began to doubt in elementary, middle, and high school (88 percent), while only 11 percent began to doubt in college.

You might think their belief systems were alike, but when Britt started asking further questions, it was clear that they were flowing in one of two different directions. We seemed to be dealing with two groups of people when it came to belief: those who believe the Bible and those who harbor serious doubts about the Scriptures.

We asked numerous questions about the Bible. Some of them related to evolution and the age of the earth, others questioned belief in specific historical biblical events. In our opinion, *88 percent of the people in the survey incorrectly answered at least one of these questions,* particularly questions dealing with the age of the earth.

But 12 percent of those surveyed answered all the questions correctly. So why did those 12 percent leave? They all went to church growing up. They still claim to believe the major tenets of the Christian faith . . . but there they are on our AWOL list. Clearly, factors other than their belief in the Bible and traditional Christian values have influenced their decision to leave. As we crunched the data from our survey, it became apparent that commonly held stereotypes of those who are leaving the Church are not altogether accurate. Church attendees tend to blame the epidemic on those who have left. We label them as apostate, insincere, uncommitted, lazy, or indifferent. You can believe that the Bible is true and intellectually accepted but still not feel called to go to church on Sunday. As we studied the research findings further, we soon found we were dealing with two different types of individuals who were no longer attending church: **those who come at least during Easter and/ or Christmas — and those who don't come at all.**

If you are a regular church attendee, these numbers will not be surprising to you. Christmas and Easter are definitely the big days at church. The irregular regular attendees almost always show up and you see this flood of new faces. They are not a regular part of the congregation yet have come to celebrate and remember the birth and Resurrection of Jesus Christ nonetheless — and they are probably parking in *your* spot and sitting in *your seats*. You might be surprised to be sitting next to one of those 20 year olds during a Christmas or Easter service.

"Do you attend church services at Easter or Christmas?"

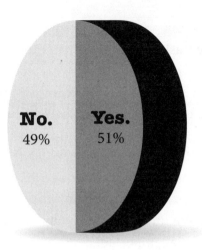

No.
49%

Yes.
51%

And then there were those who never come to church, not even at Easter or Christmas. Over 30 percent of those who never go to church also say that they "don't think of it at all." For them, church is out of sight and out of mind. (These guys are *really* already gone.)

What is one of the core issues that predict that someone will go to church to celebrate the Christian holidays as opposed to staying home? It appears that belief has a lot to do with it.

	Attend on holidays	**Never attend**
Do you believe all the books of the Bible are inspired by God?	72.8% said yes	50.2% said yes
Do you believe in creation as stated in the Bible?	87.2 % said yes	55.9% said yes
Do you believe in the creation of Adam and Eve in the Garden of Eden?	91.3% said yes	50.6% said yes
Do you believe all the accounts/ stories in the Bible are true/ accurate?	52.4% said yes	23.8% said yes
Do you believe you are saved and will go to heaven upon death?	72.2% said yes	58.7% said yes

In fact, when we asked them if secular science caused them to doubt the Bible, 56 percent of those who never attend said yes. A much smaller portion of those who worship on Christmas and Easter said yes (36.8 percent). Significantly, 44 percent of those who never attend church believe in evolution; while only 12 percent of those who visit on holidays believe the molecules to man theory.

Of those who don't ever come to church, 24 percent of those who believe that the Bible contains errors pointed to Genesis. Compare that to the group that still comes to worship at Christmas and Easter and we find out that a much smaller group falls in that category. Genesis issues are certainly an important contributing factor. Surprisingly, a full 50 percent of the people who do not go to church at all still believe in the creation of Adam and Eve, so there are obviously other issues that collectively are keeping them from church. Many of them believe in the Genesis accounts (though what many mean by this might not be a young-earth perspective), but they still don't go to church for other reasons.

The data support the idea that those who go at Christmas and Easter are still genuine believers who want to have a group worship experience and celebrate the most important events in Christianity. The non-attendees are much more prone to doubt.

Other questions gave more insight into the hearts of those who grew up in the church and yet do not regularly attend anymore. When we asked, "Is there any part of the church service that you miss today?" 72 percent of the holiday attendees said yes. (Only 27 percent of those who never attend said yes.) The Holy Spirit never gives up and will continue to challenge these 20 year olds due to this void in their spiritual lives. I believe the Holy Spirit is still speaking to these people. They feel the void. They know that something is missing. They know that the Church, for all its flaws, still has something to offer that they need.

Those who miss church gave a lot of different reasons. Some miss the teaching, some miss the special events. (Only about 7 percent said they missed the music, and nobody was missing Sunday school!) Most of them simply said, "I miss worshiping God." That's a powerful statement if you think about it — and it should remind us that we are dealing with souls and not statistics. In fact, it might be one of the most heart-breaking statements to come out of this entire survey: *"I miss worshiping God."* Of those who don't attend church anymore, half of them really do miss it. And of those who missed it, more missed "worshiping God" than anything else. Fifty Sundays of the year they choose to sleep in. But on Easter and Christmas, the pinnacles of Christian celebration, the lure is so strong that they can stand on the edge no longer, and they take their place in the corporate celebration of Jesus Christ.

Those Who Will Come Back When They Have Kids — and Those Who Won't

In our study, we wanted to probe another commonly held notion about those who leave the church. Most people believe that these young adults will be back when they have children of their own. According to the LifeWay survey,[1] 24 percent of those who return do so because "I had children and felt it was time for them to start attending." This reason was significantly more common for women than men (31 percent versus 13 percent). Also, 20 percent "got married and wanted to attend with my spouse." We wanted to find out much more, so we started with the following question:

"Do you expect to attend church regularly when you have children?"

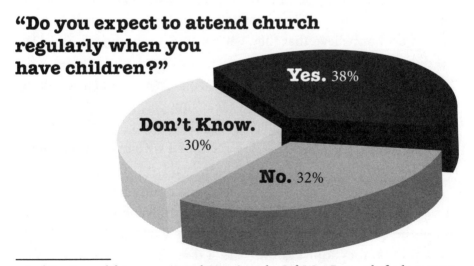

Yes. 38%

Don't Know. 30%

No. 32%

---

1. http://www.lifeway.com/ArticleView?article=LifeWay-Research-finds-reasons-18-to-22-year-olds-drop-out-of-church.

These are fairly standard results. Other people who have researched this come up with about the same numbers. About four in nine expected to go back to their same denomination, perhaps even the church that they grew up in. So there was almost an even split there as well. Let's read a little bit more into that: it would appear that about half want to go back to their roots — back to the same community in which they grew up. This is where they are comfortable; this is the experience that they want to pass on to their children. The other half are clearly looking for a change. They want something different. If they go back to church, they're going to break ties with their old ways, burn some bridges with their old denomination, and chart out into some new territory.

Things got interesting when we compared these results to their levels of belief. Take a look at these results! Notice there is a significant correlation between believing in the creation account and whether they will come back! There is a tie between what they believe about Genesis and their attitude toward Christianity — which is understandable. If the authority of God's Word is undermined in the first book (Genesis, as we outlined in the previous chapter), this leads to a slippery slide of unbelief about the whole of the Bible.

Amazingly, the research also showed that of those who expect to come back to church, 77.7 percent believe that they are saved. Only 8.4 percent do not believe that they will go to heaven upon death! (The rest didn't know.) That's a huge number. The correlation between what they believe, how they view Scripture, and what they plan on doing is huge. If we can do a better job of teaching proper belief, we will at least increase the possibility that these kids will return after they have children. It seems pretty obvious to me that if we had done this in the first place, many of them might not have ever left!

So about a third said they were never coming back and about a third are planning on it. What about the rest? When asked whether or not they would return to church after they have children, 30 percent said that they "don't know." The "I don't knows" from most surveys tend to get overlooked. We tend to think that these people are

	Planning on returning	**Never coming back**
Do you believe all the books of the Bible are inspired by God?	76.4% said yes	41.9% said yes
Do you believe in creation as stated in the Bible?	92.1% said yes	47.8% said yes
Do you believe in the creation of Adam and Eve in the Garden of Eden?	91.3% said yes	50.6% said yes
Do you believe all the accounts/stories in the Bible are true/accurate?	58.5% said yes	16.8% said yes

apathetic ("I don't know" = "I don't care"). I see something else here. I see an opportunity. Consider this seriously. A third said yes, they're coming back, a third said definitely no — but in between is an equally large segment who is hanging in the balance. They sincerely haven't been able to make up their minds as to whether they're going to return or not.

Half of those surveyed have friends that still go to church. More than half have been asked by their friends if they want to go to church with them. That's very encouraging, and that's probably why they're thinking of coming back. And what an opportunity for those who go to church.

This is what I see: I see a window of opportunity that any church-goer can take advantage of. Two-thirds of the people who have left the Church are either *planning* on coming back or they might be *considering* coming back. All it might take is a sincere invitation from a friend to encourage them to make the jump. But this window of opportunity is slowly closing. Consider this result from one of the Barna surveys:

> Even the traditional impulse of parenthood — when people's desire to supply spiritual guidance for their children pulls them back to church — is weakening. The new research pointed out that just one-third of twenty-somethings who are parents regularly take their children to church, compared with two-fifths of parents in their thirties and half of parents who are 40 years old or more.[2]

Two Questions, Two Groups

As you can see, we gained a lot of insightful information by asking the questions *Do you plan on returning to church after you have children?* and *Do you attend on Christmas or Easter?*

Because these questions are related, it's not surprising that respondents tended to answer them the same:

> 69 percent of those who plan on returning when they have kids also attend during the holidays
>
> 64 percent of those who do not plan on coming back never come on holidays

Based on these two questions, we can identify two groups that represent the extremes of those who have left the Church:

> Group 1: Those who never come to church at all and who never plan on returning (20.7 percent of all surveyed)

> Group 2: Those who come at Christmas and/or Easter and who plan on returning after they have children (26.4 percent of all surveyed)

---

2. Barna Research.

When we compare these two groups with their levels of belief discussed on the previous pages, very powerful correlations can be seen. Significantly, *belief in the Bible is a major predictor of behavior in both of these groups!*

Group 1 thinks that the service is boring, the agenda is too political, and that the Bible is not relevant. These people have a low level of belief in the Bible.

When reporting what they miss about church, those respondents in Group 1 said that they miss the music . . . but that's obviously not enough to persuade them to come back. They point to significant questions and scientific objections that they have with the Bible's reliability. They don't like the people and they don't believe the message, so there's really no reason for them to come back at all. *The Bible is irrelevant to them and the people are too*. They won't come back unless something changes on this level.

Group 2, on the other hand, has a much higher level of belief in the Bible. Three-quarters of them believe that they are saved and report relatively high levels of belief in biblical accuracy, authority, and history. The obvious point here is that *over half of the people who have left the Church are still solid believers in Jesus Christ*.

When asked what they miss about church, they report that they miss the pastor's teaching. What they object to, however, is hypocrisy, legalism, and self-righteousness. *The Bible is relevant to them, but the church is not.* This group needs to be convinced that Christians in the church are living by God's truth, and are living in a way that is relevant to their lives (such as being a positive influence on their children).

We could even create a separate subgroup from this group. Let's call it "Group 2+." This group represents a full 12 percent of all the people in the survey. *They answered every question about the Bible correctly and take a serious literal interpretation of the historical events in the Book of Genesis.* Many of them still come to church on Christmas and Easter, and many of them are planning on coming back after they have children. These are the ones who miss worshiping God the most. They were most turned off by the hypocrisy that they saw in the Church. It's likely that they have a growing disdain for this — or perhaps they have been personally hurt in some way because of it.

They see a great discrepancy between what the people are saying and the way that they are living; they may have been torn by what they heard a preacher preaching and what they saw him doing. I believe it very likely they have heard the pastor compromise in some way on Genesis — and they see this as hypocrisy when the Church claims to believe the Bible as the Word of God. These people want authenticity. They want grace, truth, and relevancy in the Body of Christ. They're not going to come back unless something changes on this level.

All of the people in this survey, to some extent, are having their hearts tugged on by the Holy Spirit. *Out of a thousand people, there was not a single person who gave us all the wrong answers all the time.* There were some items that everyone believed. They just couldn't suppress the truth that was in them. Even though they may not be walking in a spiritual Christian life, there might still be some light — a residual gleam — inside of them. They may have left the Church, but they still have a hope of the Church in them. If they find a church that is vibrant, authentic, defends the truth, stands solidly on biblical authority, and lives by the truth, they very well might come back.

There's one other interesting finding from this portion of the study that I want to bring up. In all honesty, I'm not exactly sure what to think about it, but the numbers are powerful enough — and the issue is so dominant in our culture — that it cannot be ignored. When asked this question, "Is premarital sex okay?" this is how many people answered yes:

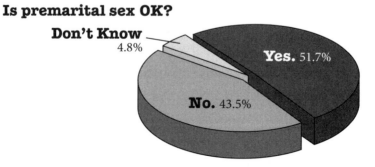

Is premarital sex OK?

Don't Know 4.8%

Yes. 51.7%

No. 43.5%

Wow. Those are huge numbers, but what do they mean?

- Is this group turned off by what the Bible has to say about premarital sex?

- Are they sexually active and feeling internal guilt and condemnation?

- Have they been shunned by the church because of their sexual activity?

- Have they been rejected by the church because of an unwanted pregnancy?

Without further study, we can only speculate. But this is certainly an area that deserves further research. The spread on these numbers is even greater than the spread regarding people's belief in the Book of Genesis (and yet, of course God's plan for male and female marriage is clearly founded in the Book of Genesis!). Clearly, something is going on here.

So we have Group 1 and Group 2, and their beliefs make all the difference. This key observation opens the door to powerful practical application. And that's what we're really trying to get to in the first place, isn't it? We know there's a problem out there; we now understand much better *who* is leaving the Church and *why* they're leaving the Church; but *what* do we do about it? Based on other questions that we asked in the survey, two general powerful application points can be made:

1. To defend and teach the Bible from the very first verse — the great need for practical and relevant apologetics teaching for all ages

2. To live an authentic, biblically based Christian life as individuals and as a church, so people will see Christ reflected in all that's done. Stop the hypocrisy!

In Part 2 we will expand on these two applications in great detail. *Be encouraged — there is much that can be done and there is much to do.* But before jumping in headfirst, we need to backtrack a little. In order to fully understand where it is that we need to go from here, we have to understand how we got here in the first place! Certainly, the decrease in the belief in the Bible and the embarrassing un-biblical atmosphere in many churches did not happen overnight. The spiraling descent can be described in one word: IRRELEVANCE. And by the time you finish the next chapter you will know exactly what that means and why it is so vital in the life of individuals and any church that wants to be relevant in the world and be a healthy, life-giving place to those who worship there.

Britt's Bit: Crunching Numbers

The fascinating and powerful thing about analyzing data and interpreting it correctly is that you can see things that are otherwise unseeable. If the research is done carefully and the numbers compared appropriately, the statistics allow us to describe behavior and also to understand the belief behind those behaviors.

One of the wonderful things about studying human behavior and the data collected from individuals is that you can sort and divide the data into subsets very quickly. The click of a mouse can instantly render visible data that was apparently invisible. Comparisons that took me days in 1979 can be accomplished almost instantaneously today. For example, in our survey we asked the question "Is there anything a teacher or professor did or said that caused you to doubt the contents of the Bible?" Depending upon their answers of either yes or no, we could separate the data to identify the true influences of those teachers or professors.

We interviewed 1,000 20 year olds and asked them 78 questions, which can give you an idea of how much information we could learn from these non-churched individuals. Their responses can be compared and contrasted *ad infinitum*. However, one should never become carried away with the amount of data they collect, but how it can be used to answer the questions facing Christian leaders like Ken Ham. Just because you can compare doesn't mean that there's always anything really important to discover. But if you are willing to dig around in the numbers, every once in a while you strike gold and discover some things that can change the course of your whole life (or, as in this case, two things that could change the course of the entire Church).

CHAPTER 4

The Short Road to Irrelevance

If I told you earthly things and you do not believe, how will you believe if I tell you heavenly things? (John 3:12).

Westminster Abbey will probably survive, at least for a while. While other churches in England are being converted and bulldozed by the dozens, this stunning and sprawling cathedral will continue to stand tall. It was first built to house a group of Benedictine monks in A.D. 1065. For the last 900-plus years it has been attacked, renovated, desecrated, and consecrated over and over, earning it a permanent place in history. Century after century, architects and craftsman have been adding to its grandeur. When I walk through the corridors beneath the breathtaking expanses of Gothic and Romanesque architecture, I get an entirely different feel than I did in the nearby church where only a few gray-haired parishioners sat in the dusty front rows. Westminster Abbey is alive with people and activity. Yes, it will survive — but not necessarily for the right reasons.

Westminster is part monastery. Its religious life revolves around a daily pattern of worship, prayer, song, and the Eucharist. Until the 19th century, Westminster was the third seat of learning in England, surpassed only by Oxford and Cambridge. It was here that the first third of the King James Old Testament and the last half of the New Testament were translated. But the thousands of people who come to visit every day rarely stop to pray, worship, or contemplate the Scriptures, because the Abbey is also part museum. The architecture, artwork, and icons are timeless and priceless; the architecture is unsurpassed. The cathedral is also part mausoleum. The throngs of camera-clad, backpack-toting tourists that flock here come to see the graves of leaders in the fields of religion, literature, and science. It is a pilgrimage of sorts — people coming from around the globe to pay homage before the graves of the likes of Geoffrey Chaucer, David Livingstone, Charles Dickens, Sir Isaac Newton, and Charles Darwin.

Charles Darwin? The founder of modern evolutionary theory? Buried in the floor of Westminster Abby? It's hard to believe, but I have stood there and looked at the grave myself. Isn't this the man who popularized the philosophy of evolution taking place over millions of years? What is he doing in here? He not only abandoned his church, but he strategically introduced ideas that were contrary to God's Word. Isn't it strange that the man credited with founding modern evolutionary theory should be buried in the same place that the King James Version of the Bible was translated?

No, that's more than strange; it's symbolic — a powerful example of the short road that the Church has followed into irrelevance. A man who popularized a philosophy that hit at the very foundation of the Church (the Word of God) is honored by the Church and buried in the foundation of the Church. It is symbolic indeed.

Darwin's popularity in the UK earned him a place of prominence on their most popular currency, the ten-pound note.

The Short Road[1]

The root of the word "relevance" comes from the word "relate." In order for something to be relevant, it has to connect (or relate) to something that is real and important. The problem we are studying, of course, is that 60 percent of the students who grow up in the Church have lost that connection. As we said in the last chapter, they fall into two groups: Group 1 believes that the Bible is irrelevant; Group 2 believes that the Church is irrelevant (unless it's a holiday or it's time to take the kids).

---

1. Most of the ideas in this chapter are covered in much greater detail in my book *Why Won't They Listen?* (Green Forest, AR: Master Books, 2002).

What happened? How did we get here? I believe it all started when the Church gave us "millions of reasons" to doubt the Bible. The Book of Genesis gives us a clear account of the creation of the universe, of the world, and of everything that lives, including humanity. A simple, literal interpretation of these passages makes it clear that this creation took place in six days, with God resting on the seventh, just a few thousand years ago. This history, as it is written concerning the creation of the universe and life, including the first two humans, Adam and Eve, and their fall into sin with the consequence of death — is foundational to all biblical doctrines. This is the foundational history for the gospel.

In the late 18th century and in the early 19th century, however, the idea that the earth is millions and billions of years old (rather than about 10,000) began to emerge in the scientific community of Europe. It wasn't a new idea, actually. Throughout human history, numerous cultures from different points of the globe have considered the universe to be old or even eternal. Dr. Terry Mortenson's excellent book, *The Great Turning Point*,[2] chronicles what happened next. At that time, many church leaders in England led their churches to adopt the millions of years and add them into the Scriptures. Some did this by reinterpreting the days of creation as long periods of time; others adopted ideas such as the "gap theory," attempting to fit millions of years into a supposed gap between the first two verses of Genesis. The shift was not arbitrary; it was calculated — particularly by deists who were looking for a so-called scientific justification for rejecting the Flood of Noah's day as an explanation for the fossil-bearing sediments, and for rejecting biblical authority in total, as advocates of this millions-of-years age for the earth. They saw this as devastating to the Bible's account of creation and the Flood and its connection to fossil layers.

Darwin, based on his own writings, was never a believer, and of course readily accepted the millions-of-years ideas. This actually

---

2. Terry Mortenson, *The Great Turning Point* (Green Forest, AR: Master Books, 2004).

paved the way for Darwin to present his ideas on biological evolution. After all, one needs an incomprehensible amount of time to postulate the idea that small changes observed in animals will somehow add up to the needed big changes for Darwinian evolution — for reptiles to change into birds, for ape-like creatures to change into human beings, etc. Not only did the old-earth idea contradict what the Bible says, but because it is ultimately an attack on biblical authority, it paved the way for the conclusion that the Bible cannot be trusted, and our existence is the result of natural processes.

As the Church compromised on the issue of millions of years, subsequent generations were put on a slippery slide of unbelief. The millions-of-years idea not only undermined the creation account, but it began to undermine the historical account of the Genesis Flood as well. Soon the idea of a local flood rather than a global flood was popularized.

In 1859, Darwin published his major influential work, *On the Origin of Species*, and 12 years later *The Descent of Man*, popularizing the idea of the evolution of animals and the evolution of ape-like creatures into humans. Much of the Church in England (and then across the United Kingdom and Europe) began to also adopt Darwin's ideas, reinterpreting the Genesis account of creation and proposing views such as "theistic evolution" (that God used evolution to bring the different life forms into being).

Such views also spread to America, where various church leaders also adopted such positions to add millions of years and evolutionary ideas to the Bible's account of origins, thus reinterpreting the days of creation, the creation account of Adam and Eve, and so on. Even many conservative churches adopted the gap theory — seeing this as a way of rejecting evolution but allowing for millions of years.

Many conservative churches, which did not know how to handle the millions of years and evolutionary teaching, basically sidestepped the issues. They would (as they do today) teach Genesis as true, not dealing with the teachings of the secular world that contradicted the account (such as millions of years, evolution, etc.) — but teaching the account of creation, the Flood, the Tower of Babel, and so on as a wonderful story. They may claim it to be true — but, nonetheless, it is just taught to the students as a story.

The Church began to make a disconnection at this point. It was the beginning of the road to irrelevancy: the Church gave up the *earthly* things (e.g., the biological, anthropological, astronomical, geological history as recorded in Genesis 1–11) and focused on *heavenly* things (spiritual matters, relationships, the gospel). When it came to science, the Church gave in to human notions. It was now acceptable to use man's ideas to re-interpret the Bible, rather than to use the Bible to judge man's ideas. At times, the Church has tried to introduce hybrid theories that accommodate both secular science's interpretations and biblical accounts. The day-age theory and the gap theory are two examples. Unfortunately, they hold true to neither the scientific evidence nor the Bible!

The real consequence of such compromise can be seen in this quote from Ron Numbers, a modern scholar who stated the following in answer to a question for the media:

> For creationists, history is based on the Bible and the belief that God created the world 6,000–10,000 ago. . . . We humans were perfect because we were created in the image of God. And then there was the fall. Death appears and the whole account [in the Bible] becomes one of deterioration and degeneration. So we then have Jesus in the New Testament, who promises redemption. Evolution completely flips that. With evolution, you don't start out with anything perfect, you start with primitive little wiggly things, which evolve into apes and, finally, humans. There's no perfect state from which to fall. This makes the whole plan of salvation silly because there never was a fall. What you have then is a theory of progress from single-celled animals to humans and a very, very different take on history, and not just human history.[3]

---

3. Gwen Evan, "Reason or Faith? Darwin Expert Reflects," *Wisconsin Week*, Feb. 3, 2009, www.news.wisc.edu/16176.

In the past, the most highly recognized and progressive scientists in the field were also highly trained theologians (including Pascal, Newton, and Galileo). They helped maintain the connection between the Bible and science, between the laboratory and the sanctuary. We still have progressive scientists who are strong believers, but when someone comes to church today, they expect to hear about theology (the study of God). Do they expect to hear about biology, geology, and anthropology? The answer is no, of course. This is a major problem. Certainly the Church would not see itself as a research institution teaching people how to use microscopes or develop new electronics and so on. But this is where people have been confused. Observational science, which builds our technology, is very different to historical or origins science, which is concerned with the origin of what we observe in the present. It was the historical or origins science that the Church gave up to the world — and thus disconnected the Bible from the real world.

In America today, where do you go to learn about the geological, biological, anthropological, or astronomical history of the universe? School. That's where our kids learn what they perceive is the real stuff, the *relevant* stuff. In Sunday school they learn "Bible stories." (By the way, if you look at the definition of "story," it means "fairy tale." The Bible has become so irrelevant in our culture today that that's what most people think it is — just a spiritual "fairy tale.") What has taken its place? Charles Darwin's evolutionary ideas and the belief in millions of years for the age of the earth and universe are now, by and large, both *welcomed* and *honored* in the European church. And the Bible? It is seen as irrelevant when it comes to issues in the real world. The great disconnect between the Bible and "real" life has taken place. The Bible, God, and the Church became irrelevant in less than three generations. Generations have gone down this slippery slide of unbelief, until they have now basically rejected the entire Bible and its message of salvation.

What happened in Europe is happening on this side of the Atlantic today. We are on the same road — the same slippery slide — and we have traveled down it a long, long way. We may not be as far along as they are, but understand this: the exact same trend that took place in Europe is happening today. Our spirituality has become compartmentalized. Yes, we go to church, but only to get our emotional and spiritual needs met. Then we walk out the doors and face a pagan world where we have to live by a whole different set of assumptions. We might say this doesn't matter, but let's be honest: in the back of everyone's mind is the question *"If I can't trust the Bible in the earthly things, why should I trust it in the spiritual things?"* This was the same challenge Jesus Christ, our Creator and Savior, put to Nicodemus in John 3:12.

What really happened to the Church in the United Kingdom and Europe, and America — in fact, across the Western world — was that the Church basically disconnected the Bible from the real world.

Churches today in America are not a place where one talks about geology, dinosaurs, fossils, or the age of the earth — that is left up to the schools and colleges. Effectively, the Church basically hands over the history of the universe to the secular educational institutions, and concentrates on the spiritual and moral aspects of Christianity. The Church actually disconnects the Bible from the real world. The children (and everyone else, through Sunday school lessons, youth studies, etc.) in the churches are really taught that in church, one doesn't deal with geology, biology, and so on — that is for school. In church, we talk about Jesus — we deal with doctrines and we study moral and spiritual matters — but anything pertaining to understanding geology, biology, astronomy, anthropology, and so forth is left for school.

If I asked you where students go to learn about geology, astronomy, biology, and anthropology, what would you say? The answer is always "school." Please understand this! Ninety percent of children from church homes attend public/government schools.[4] There, by and large, they are taught a biological, anthropological, geological, and astronomical history of the universe that totally contradicts the Bible's account of creation, the Flood, and the Tower of Babel.

---

4. http://nces.ed.gov/fastfacts/display.asp?id=65

Yes, the epidemic has spread to our shores. Our current generation of children is leaving the church in droves. We are less than one generation away from being a nation of hollow, empty churches. It is more than possible that we will be the few, remnant gray-haired believers who sit in nearly vacant pews on Sunday.

President Obama summed it up in his autobiography, published just before his election as president of the United States of America:

> Whatever we once were, we are no longer just a Christian nation; we are also a Jewish nation, a Muslim nation, a Buddhist nation, a Hindu nation, and a nation of nonbelievers.[5]

Millions of Reasons to Doubt

A progression is taking place — a slow and steady decay of belief. I firmly believe that in this era of history the decay begins with the belief that the world is millions and billions of years old — because this is really where the major attack on biblical authority in this age began. Our survey reflects this trend in America.

- 77% believe in Noah's ark and the global Flood

- 75% believe in Adam and Eve in the Garden

- 62% believe that Abraham fathered Isaac when he was a hundred years old

- 60% believe in the Tower of Babel

- yet *only* 20% believe *that the earth is less than 10,000 years old*

The number-one area of disbelief is the age of the earth. Because of the five major issues we studied, four of the five have strong majorities, but very few believe the earth is truly less than 10,000 years old.

---

5. Barack Obama, *The Audacity of Hope: Thoughts on Reclaiming the American Dream* (New York: Crown Publishers, 2006).

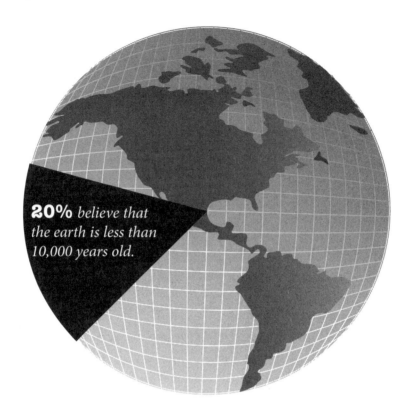

20% *believe that the earth is less than 10,000 years old.*

The age of the earth is the single most misunderstood issue among those who have left the Church. (It is also the most misunderstood issue among those who are still there!)

We live in an era where science has *supposedly* disproven the Bible in Genesis 1. What is the Church doing? Just like it did in Europe, it is sticking its head in the sand, compromising with the world.

Highly respected church leaders and theologians have given in. Many well-known Christian scholars, professors, evangelists, and the like have compromised the Bible with an old (millions-of-years) earth. You would probably be shocked if we placed a list of names here. Some of these Christian leaders have led many to Christ and have done a tremendous work in the spread of the gospel. Unquestionably, the ministry of these men has had a profound positive effect on multitudes of individual lives. Eternity has been changed because of their commitment and devotion to the gospel.

However, wittingly or unwittingly, they have been part of a vicious attack on biblical authority. Many would say that believing in millions of years is not important — as long as one accepts the gospel message about Jesus and His death and Resurrection. But as stated in chapter 2, the gospel message comes from the same book (the Bible) that records the Genesis account of history.

Recently a person was giving me an obvious dig at the ministry of AIG. He said, "The gospel doesn't rise or fall on the days of creation." My answer was, "That's true — it doesn't. But does the gospel rise or fall on the authority of Scripture? And does the authority of Scripture rise or fall on the days of creation?"

Faith in Christ alone saves — not whether a person believes in a young or old earth, or whether the days of creation are long periods of time. Romans 10:9 makes it very clear that salvation is tied to faith in Christ, *not the days of creation or the age of the earth.* There are many Christians (including many Christian leaders) who are truly saved, yet believe in millions of years and reinterpret the days of creation, or believe that God used evolution, or even that Noah's Flood was just a local event.

However, when a person believes in millions of years (or Darwinian evolution), and then reinterprets the days of creation to be long periods of time, they are undermining the very authority from which they get the message of the gospel. They are undermining the authority of the Word of God by taking man's fallible ideas on the age of the earth and using those ideas to change the clear meaning of the Word of God. It is an authority issue. Compromising Genesis has contributed to the loss of biblical authority in our nation and helped open the door to the secularization of the culture.

Here is a warning to any of us: if we teach such a compromised position to our children, be prepared for the great possibility they will open the door of compromise wider and get on that all-too-familiar slippery slide of unbelief. Believing in millions of years doesn't affect one's salvation, but it does affect how the next generation or those you influence view Scripture itself — and putting them on a slippery slide of unbelief has been the devastating consequence of such compromise.

It is interesting to note that many of these scholars who do compromise with millions of years agree that the obvious literal interpretation of Genesis shows that God created the earth in six approximately 24-hour days. Yet they adopt the interpretation of secular scientists regarding the age of the earth, rather than understanding that all dating methods are based on fallible assumptions and that it is God's Word that should be used to judge man's interpretation of the past — not the other way around. Whether we like to admit it or not, many of our contemporary champions of the faith are actually *undermining* the authority of the Bible (and thus the foundations of the Church) when they fail to defend what the Bible says about the age of the earth and the universe.

Our study showed that the majority of the people leaving the Church do not believe in evolution. This is actually the norm in our society as a whole. The universities and high schools are proclaiming evolution as an absolute fact. But after all their efforts, most people intuitively see it as false. Common sense tells them that something just doesn't "appear" by itself. Instinctively, human beings know that any complex organisms or mechanism must have an outside designer and creator to put them together. Those who take the time to study biochemistry, geology, physics, anthropology, paleontology, and genetics find even deeper problems within the idea of evolution. Many, many scientists have concluded that evolution couldn't have taken place, *no matter how much time was available.*

But the issue of the earth being millions of years old? This is the big stumbling block. When you go to zoos or museums, you see the issue of millions of years discussed (on signs, in videos, etc.) much more than you see the topic of evolution itself. History books, television programs, movie makers . . . everybody *assumes* that the earth and the universe are millions and billions of years old, so they *interpret* all the facts through that preconceived mindset. Then, when the Bible says that it happened in six days, they assume that the Bible is inaccurate, and that causes them to disbelieve the Bible more than any other single factor.

As I stated above, millions of years is really an incomprehensible amount of time — and you need an incomprehensible amount of time to even consider that evolution might have happened. When it comes to a major factor that has caused people to reject biblical authority, millions of years *is* the issue; it's not really evolution. If you can't believe in millions of years, you can't believe in evolution. In the 18th century, it was the age of the earth that caused the Church to begin to compromise the Word of God. This is why you have the day age theory, why you have the gap theory, why you have progressive creation. Each of these compromise positions on Genesis (as well as others) that are widely held in the Church, have one factor in common — supposedly fitting the millions of years in some way into the Bible's account of origins.

That's why Answers in Genesis is so passionate about defending the biblical account of creation in six days. People really can't believe, and don't want to believe, that their ancestors were apes. They look at the complexity of life forms and rhetorically ask, "How could we have come from a lifeless pile of slime . . . and where did the slime come from?!" But the issue of millions of years? That is so abstract and so incomprehensible that it's easier to accept. And since we've been told that it takes millions of years for something to evolve, then, in people's minds, it makes evolution plausible. Secular scientists need millions of years to make evolution happen. If they don't have millions of years, then the only alternative to explain our existence is to admit that there is an intelligent, personal force that created it in a relatively shorter period of time. Because most secular scientists believe in materialism (that only matter exists), they cannot accept the idea of "God." So, therefore, they must believe in millions of years — even though a proper interpretation of the evidence confirms that the earth is young, and that matter and life as we know it was created. Please visit our website if you haven't already! At www.answersingenesis.org you will find a tremendous amount of information and resources about this topic.

A belief that the earth is millions of years old, therefore, has two profoundly negative effects on people's beliefs:

1. It undermines the authority of the Book of Genesis and therefore the Bible as a whole.

2. It leaves open an excuse to justify that evolution could have occurred: given enough time, anything can happen.

Millions of years is the beginning of a slippery slope that slides down a predictable hill. When this happens, the authority of Scripture is compromised, and the authenticity of the Church is degraded. All across England — and now spreading from shore to shore in America — is an epidemic of unbelief with two major symptoms:

1. The Bible is no longer relevant to the skeptic because he/she has not been taught convincing apologetics for its historical accuracy beginning at Genesis 1:1.

2. The believer has found the Church to be irrelevant because of hypocrisy, a watering down of God's Word, and an unwillingness to be flexible with cultural forms in order to stay true to the principles of God's inerrant Word.

A major shift has already taken place in our culture. If we don't recognize it, we will forever be wasting our time, energy, and resources as we try to maintain our churches and reach the world for Jesus Christ. The Church and the Bible are no longer the places we go to learn historical science. The Church gave up that responsibility and relegated it to the world. We kept the spiritual things, the moral things, and the relationships things. This is what most preachers will preach about, but is it relevant? Do young people today make a connection if it isn't connected to physical reality? I don't think so. We need to go back and rebuild the foundation of truth in God's Word. We need to be willing to shift our strategies in order to meet the needs in this new era. By understanding the times in which we live, we will have much clearer wisdom as we work toward a plan to be effective in this new world.

To the Jews and to the Greeks

On the first Easter morning, Jesus showed the world that He had victory over sin, Satan, and death. During the 40 days after the Resurrection, He appeared to the Apostles from time to time to affirm them, encourage them, and to prove that He really was alive. During one of those meetings, He told them that the Holy Spirit would come upon them and that they would receive power to tell people about Him "in Jerusalem, and in all Judea and Samaria, and to the ends of the earth" (Acts 1:8; NIV). Within hours of the Holy Spirit coming upon Peter and the Apostles, they were on the streets of Jerusalem witnessing to the Jews by explaining how the Old Testament prophecies about the Messiah had come true — and *3,000* of the Jews believed what Peter said. They were baptized and joined the Church (Acts 2).

After Paul was converted, he began to take the message of Christ beyond Jerusalem and the Jewish community. As he took the gospel toward the "ends of earth" and into the Greek world, it was a different story:

> A group of Epicurean and Stoic philosophers began to dispute with him. Some of them asked, "What is this babbler trying to say?" Others remarked, "He seems to be advocating foreign gods." They said this because Paul was preaching the good news about Jesus and the resurrection. . . . "You are bringing some strange ideas to our ears . . ." (Acts 17:18–20; NIV).

Life in Athens was different than it was in Jerusalem. Peter's approach for sharing the gospel with the Jews didn't work for Paul with the Greeks. So did Paul give up? Did he say, "There must be something wrong with these people. They are pagan unbelievers. They are resistant to the gospel. Their hearts are hardened and they are resistant to coming to church"? So he washed his hands and went back to Jerusalem. Right?

Wrong.

Paul must have realized that there was something wrong with his approach. We can see how he completely changed his strategy. He started out by actually complimenting these men for their religious fervor. He acknowledged their idols and then began to teach them about their own "unknown God" who was part of their culture. Where did he start teaching? He started at the beginning — first of all by defining God:

> The God who made the world and everything in it is the Lord of heaven and earth and does not live in temples built by hands. And he is not served by human hands, as if he needed anything, because he himself gives all men life and breath and everything else (Acts 17:24–25; NIV).

The Greeks believed in many gods. Paul had to back up and explain to them that there was only one true God. He had to show that this one true God created all things and gave life to all things. Then, building from that foundation, Paul could finally explain the gospel, telling them about repentance, about judgment, and about the resurrection of the dead. How did they respond? Some of them sneered; others wanted to hear more; and a few men became followers of Jesus Christ. Yes, life was different in Athens compared to life in Jerusalem. But Paul was willing to recognize this and change his entire approach to ministry because of it. When Paul wrote to the Corinthians about his experience, he noted this important distinction:

> But we preach Christ crucified: a stumbling block to Jews and foolishness to Gentiles (1 Cor. 1:23; NIV).

In Jerusalem, the Jews had a firm foundation belief built on the Old Testament. They knew about the one true God and about sin; they knew about the Law and about blood sacrifices for sin . . . and they already knew about the coming Messiah. Although many refused to believe, thousands accepted the message about Jesus on the spot and joined the Church. "Christ crucified" was a stumbling block that momentarily tripped them up, but many of them quickly got over it and made it to the other side. To the Greek, however, all this talk about Jesus and the Resurrection was considered utter foolishness. They had no previous knowledge about the one true God, about sin, or about the Law. Paul had to go back and start at the very beginning.

It's time to wake up and realize that a significant portion of the Western culture must now be considered "post-Christian." The godly foundation that once existed in England is now almost totally gone. That same foundation is faltering in America. Basic Christian concepts can no longer be taken for granted. Our culture *used* to be like Jerusalem. People used to have a basic understanding of biblical concepts and terminology. Someone like Billy Graham is well known for his basic presentation of the gospel. Some might take issue with his theology or methods, but there is no doubt that he could come into town, gather the masses in stadiums, and share about the death and Resurrection of Jesus Christ. Thousands would repent and receive Christ as their savior. Even Australia, my homeland, used to be this way. Students could recite the Lord's Prayer; they knew the Ten Commandments; they had respect for the Bible. When evangelists came through town, people were converted en masse.

In the Western world of today, the crusade approach just doesn't shake a city like it used to. Our culture today is much more like Athens. Yes, there is a remnant of understanding and respect for the Bible throughout this country, but in many ways, when you share the gospel with someone today you need to know that you're sharing with someone who is more like the "Greeks" and a lot less like the "Jews." The basic foundation of the Judeo-Christian heritage in this country *no longer exists*. It's *already gone*. If you take someone to a crusade or you give them a typical Christian tract, they are bound to say, "What is this babbler trying to say? . . . You are bringing some strange ideas to our ears."

Not so long ago, people used to say, "The Bible says it. I believe it. That settles it." That's not the case anymore. Today, the average guy on the street is more apt to say, "Who cares what the Bible says! I doubt it. That settles it!" Many Christians want to get the Ten Commandments back in school. But why should we expect the educators to post the Ten Commandments when they don't believe the book that it came from! Or if you give them a tract that says, "God loves you and has a plan for your life," they are likely to retort by asking, "Who is god anyway?" A generation or two ago there was at least a basic belief in the Christian God. Now you are likely to hear a slew of questions like this:

- How do you know God exists?
- Where did God come from?
- What about ape-men?
- How did Noah get all the animals on the ark?
- What about carbon dating?

The Bible is not taken seriously by those outside of the Christian Church today. Most courts have given up asking someone to place their hand on a Bible while taking an oath of truthfulness. Now we just swear by ourselves. Due to the lack of Christian training and strong Sunday school programs, many young people come out of high school untrained and unequipped to face the challenges presented by other teachers and professors. Due to their lack of training in apologetics and defending their personal faith, we now see these types of answers:

Nearly four out of five said they had instructors in school who taught them that the earth was obviously millions of years old.

Three out of five said their school instructors taught that life definitely evolved from lower forms of life to more complex forms.

About three in ten said they left high school believing that the Bible is less true.

Four out of five felt like their college professors had an ungodly influence on the students and imposed their philosophy and moral agenda.

One in three admitted that something that they were taught at an academic institution caused them to doubt the Bible. (We suspect this number is much higher — 20-somethings like to think that they make their choices independently, but this is almost never the case!)

When you consider all of the cultural influences that affect our thinking (including television, movies, museums, magazines, textbooks, and teachers and professors), it becomes pretty obvious that we are living in Athens and not Jerusalem.

When Billy Graham retired, I saw that as symbolic. It was the end of the era of the "Jews" and the beginning of the era of the "Greeks." We will not have another Billy Graham type of response in today's present culture. His message can't be heard the same way in this culture. *If they won't believe what the Bible teaches about earthly things, how will they believe about the heavenly things?*

I believe that this is one of the core problems behind the epidemic and the exodus of young adults from the Church. We've really been teaching only half of the truth — and the other half we gave up. We preach the gospel of the Crucifixion and the Resurrection. We preach about "trusting Jesus" and we preach about morality — but all the while, the attack on Genesis is raging, causing doubt, fueling unbelief, and *undermining every single thing that we say.*

In the wake, we are dealing with all sorts of peripheral issues, including homosexual behavior, abortion, relativism, school violence, and pornography. We are preaching about these things, but the truth is that the next generation doesn't believe when these things are preached against and biblical morality is taught, because they don't believe in the authority of Scripture. The Scriptures have become irrelevant to them; they don't make the connection between the spiritual, scriptural things and real, practical things.

The authority of the Scriptures is the foundation. If that is not protected, everything will eventually crumble. In honesty, isn't that where we already are? If we look at our schools, our churches, and our families we have to admit that the relevance of Scripture is already gone in this culture.

That's the bad news. When it comes to the Bible and the Church, we've taken the short road to irrelevance. The good news is that we can do something about it. Answers in Genesis exists to deflect these incoming attacks on God's Word so that when the life-changing messages of the Bible are proclaimed, they can be communicated with authority. When people believe what we say about the earthly things, they will be able to believe the things that we speak about the heavenly things. How do we do that? *By defending the Word, living by the Word, and standing on the Word uncompromisingly.* If we commit to doing these three things, relevance can be regained.

Britt's Bit: The College Fix?

Christian colleges are woven into the fabric of western Christianity. Parents often send their kids to a Bible-believing college for a lot of different reasons. Sometimes it is the desire of the students themselves — they want to grow in their faith and receive a faith-based education. More often than not, though, I find that it is the parents who want to send their children to a safe Christian environment. Many of these parents are desperately hoping that the experience and the teaching will increase their children's faith and make them align their lives along biblical principles. In some situations, parents insist that a Christian education is the only one that they will pay for. The kids don't want to go, but the parents say they have no choice.

Do Christian colleges help? If parents knew the truth, they would, in most instances, probably put their money somewhere else. In the last ten years, I have read 35 to 40 studies done for Christian educators. The results were so deplorable that they never allowed them to be published in the marketplace. In one such study, a Christian college wanted to compare itself with a nearby secular school to show that the moral atmosphere on their campus was superior to their secular neighbors. There was just one problem: after all the data was accumulated, they found only a very small, marginal difference in the morality of the students during and after college.

If we are going to stop the epidemic, it needs to happen in the Church and in the home during the elementary, middle school, and high school years. A Christian college experience can be a very positive thing for a growing Christian's faith. But the numbers indicate that parents must look at their children's early years in elementary and middle school to make sure they are prepared to defend their faith. Because if they don't, before they even get to college, they are already gone.

Part 2:
Solutions within Our Grasp

As the English philosopher Edmund Burke is purported to have said, "All that is necessary for the triumph of evil is for good men to do nothing."[1]

What a reminder from Simon Peter to "Always be prepared to give an answer to everyone who asks you to give the reason for the hope that you have."

> Preach the word; be ready in season and out of season; reprove, rebuke, exhort, with great patience and instruction. For the time will come when they will not endure sound doctrine . . . they will turn away their ears from the truth and will turn aside to myths (2 Tim. 4:2–4).

---

1. thinkexist.com/quotation/all_that_is_necessary_for_the_triumph_of_evil_is/205479.html.

CHAPTER 5

The Ready Defense

But in your hearts set apart Christ as Lord. Always be prepared to give an answer to everyone who asks you to give the reason for the hope that you have. Do this with gentleness and respect (1 Pet. 3:15; NIV).

Susan is in fifth grade and she loves it. Typical of children her age, her learning curve seems to be going straight up. She loves making friends; she loves reading books; she loves her mom and dad (though she's not sure about her big brothers that pick on her); and she loves Jesus . . . sort of. In all honesty, she's not too sure about Jesus right now. Yes, Susan grew up in the Church and faithfully attended with her family on a regular basis. For the last several years she has enjoyed the bliss of faith as a child. Now, however, on the verge of adolescence, she is beginning to make her faith her own . . . or not. Her spiritual life is hanging in the balance and no one even knows that's the case.

On Monday morning, with a ponytail sticking out from the side of her head and her favorite cartoon character embossed on her backpack, Susan will go to school.

At school, Susan learns many things. She learns about history, mathematics, language, and science — both observational and historical science. She learns the science from men and women who wear white coats and safety glasses. They use test tubes and Bunsen burners. They dissect animals and use microscopes to look at cells, and they carry clipboards under their arms to record all of their scientific findings. To Susan, they look smart. They do research. They test hypotheses. They prove them with their experiments. Susan knows that these people deal with real things — things that you can touch and feel — the kinds of things that matter. She spends many hours a week learning from these people. And she sees that *they are dealing with fact.* Because of this, when the same people talk about the history of the universe, dinosaurs, fossils, the origin of life, and the like, and interpret them in a particular way (e.g., millions of years and evolution) — Susan thinks they are speaking with the same authority as when they discuss their observational science that involves what you can observe and experiment with directly. Susan can't discern the difference between observational and historical (origins) science; to her, it is all science. And, that is how it is usually presented anyway.

On Sunday morning Susan's mom and dad will dress her up and take her to church. For two hours or so, she will enjoy the company of friends under the care of committed Christian volunteers. To Susan, they look nice. They read stories to her. She is not sure if they are true or not — but they are nice stories. They don't really connect to reality and they come from an old book anyway. They help her with her crafts. They sing songs together. Susan knows that these are good people and that they are teaching her about things that can't be seen. They tell her what to believe about many things. She actually has a 90 percent chance that her pastor and teachers will tell her that God created everything. (Only 10 percent of all the people in our survey, which again, attended conservative churches, said that their pastor said it was okay to believe in Darwinism.)

However, there is a very strong likelihood she will get the idea she can believe in millions of years. Yes, this is a Bible-believing church after all. Or they will tell her *what* the Bible says, but they don't tell her *why* to believe. No charts, no time-lines, no experiments. She's learning about things that she can't touch or feel, and she's not entirely sure anymore that these things really matter. All in all, Susan will get about ten minutes of focused, spiritual input from adults this week at church, and none of it will include science. And she knows that *they are dealing with faith*.

Over the next few years, Susan's "worldview" (her philosophy of life) will be formed. She doesn't even know this is happening, but connections and assumptions are being made in her mind that will determine how she interprets everything that goes on around her for the rest of her life. By ninth grade or so, she will be able to articulate her worldview to herself and others. She will even think she came up with her worldview herself, but that's not true. Her belief has mostly been shaped by all of the input that she has been getting throughout her childhood. What has she learned? She has learned about the facts that supposedly govern the world, and she has learned about the faith that supposedly governs the heavens. The problem is that many of the "facts" that she has learned seem to contradict her faith — but no one talks about those things at church.

In her mind, there are obvious questions that no one seems to be asking:

- Why is there death and suffering if God is a good God?

- Why can't people of the same sex who love each other get married?

- Isn't it better to get divorced than live unhappily?

- How can the earth be only a few thousand years old when it "looks" so old?

- Why is Jesus the "only way"?

- How come dinosaurs have nothing to do with the Bible or church?

Because no one asks these questions, she assumes that no one has the answers to these questions. She realizes that church people seem to have faith *in spite of* the "facts" that she has been told. That didn't matter so much as a child, but now on the edge of adulthood, she begins to feel the disconnect: *The facts are relevant; faith is not. If you want to learn something that's real, important, and meaningful, you do that at school. If you want to learn something that is lofty and emotional, you do that at church. At school, they teach about everything — fossils, dinosaurs, marriage (different views, gay marriage, etc.), sex, the origin of life, what is "right" and "wrong," different religions — they learn about everything!*

Yes, she's still in elementary school, but she is on her way to being one of the 20-somethings who will leave the church and never come back — not even during the holidays; not even when she has children of her own. She's not cynical, she's just skeptical. She's not uncommitted, she's just indifferent. She will become what George Barna calls "the Invisible Generation" that brashly challenges us to respond to her honest questions:

> All I want is reality. Show me God. Tell me what he is really like. Help me to understand why life is the way it is and how I can experience it more fully and with greater joy. I don't want empty promises. I want the real thing. And I'll go wherever I find that truth system. — Lisa Baker, age 20[1]

Susan is already sliding down the slope of unbelief. She's *willing* to believe in something that is real, but no one offers her anything like that on Sunday morning. They tell her *what* to believe, but they do not tell her *why.*

---

1. George Barna, *The Invisible Generation: Baby Busters* (Barna research group, 1992).

No one talks about it at home either. By and large, what she is taught at secular school is not dealt with. She is given no answers. Even at Christian school, the textbooks don't really teach answers to the skeptical questions of the day. And even in most homeschools, kids may be taught the Bible is true, but many don't understand how a non-Christian thinks, nor are they prepared to answer the questions of the day. In many instances, the same compromises with or indifference about millions of years and evolution are no different than the compromising churches. In the vacuum of answers, her doubts begin to solidify.

When did Susan's problems start? Did they start with television? Did they start with secular school? Did they start in Sunday school? Actually, her problems started a long, long time ago . . . a long time ago in a garden.

Defenseless

Adam and Eve had it made. In fact, I don't even think we can imagine the beauty, the harmony, and the intimacy that they shared with each other, with the world, and with God. It was all "very good," as God proclaimed. In unhindered exploration of God's creation, they walked freely in the Garden of Eden, "naked and unashamed," without fear, without condemnation, without threat. Yes, it was very good, but it didn't last. God placed only one parameter on Adam and Eve: "of the tree of the knowledge of good and evil you shall not eat, for in the day that you eat of it you shall surely die." (Gen. 2:17).

The serpent in the garden was more sly than anything else that God had made. Having rebelled against God and having been thrown down from heaven, Satan laid down the doubt that would lead to the sin that would distort, decay, and bring death to the perfection that God had created. It was a simple and subtle scheme. It wasn't a direct accusation at first — just a hint of a suggestion. It was the beginning of doubt — the same doubt that plagues the generation that is now exiting the Church. Satan simply brought up a slight possibility:

Did God *really* say, "You must not eat from any tree in the garden? . . . You will not surely die" (Gen. 3:1–4; NIV, emphasis added).

Did God really say . . . ? It was the first attack on the Word of God. Since then, the attack has always been on the Word of God. The attack manifests itself in different ways during different areas of history. But the question is really always the same. *Did God really say . . . ?* Throughout the centuries, Satan has attacked the Word of God and attacked the human soul by casting doubt into the truthfulness of what God has said and the relevance of God's words in practical everyday life. In the last 100 years, the attacks have begun to sound more and more scientific:

- Did God really say that He created everything? Surely science has proven that the big bang happened spontaneously, without any outside force.

- Did God really say that He created the earth in six days? Surely science has proven that life evolved over millions and billions of years.

- Did God really say that He created life? Surely science has proven that the right chemicals in the right place over a long enough period of time will spontaneously generate living forms.

- Did God really say that He created humanity? Surely science has proven that the human race is really just a highly evolved life form that is the product of time and random chance.

- Did God really send a worldwide Flood in the time of Noah? Surely science has shown there never was a global Flood, and that the fossil layers were laid down over millions of years — not by a Flood.

The youth of today are wrestling with such questions. Fact seems to disprove faith. As we saw in the last chapter, how did the Church respond to this attack in England? By doing almost nothing. Actually, they did do something — they basically agreed one could accept the teachings of the world concerning the past, and reinterpret the Bible's account in Genesis. It focused on issues of faith and left its people defenseless against the so-called facts. To a certain extent, evangelical Christianity has done the same thing in America. Oh, yes, there are a few people in every congregation who seem to specialize in "apologetics." They are the brainiacs who read and study and seem to have a quick answer for everything. But they are few and far between. The rest of us try to ignore our doubts, leave the intellectual battles to someone else, and just focus on Jesus and the gospel.

But in this day and age, we must see that an attack on the Word of God *is* an attack on the gospel. Without the Word of God, we have no gospel. Without the Word of God, we have no morality. Without the Word of God, we have no record of our past and no prophecy for our future. Without the Word of God, Christianity cannot stand.

Biblical Authority Issues

Those of us who are born-again Christians believe that Jesus Christ bodily rose from the dead. After all, as Paul states in 1 Corinthians 15:14: "And if Christ has not been raised, then our preaching is vain, your faith also is vain." We believe, as real historical fact, that Jesus Christ bodily rose from the dead.

But let me ask you a question: how do you *know* Jesus Christ rose from the dead? You were not there, and you don't have a movie re-run, so how do you know? Because the Bible says, that's how. We accept that the Bible is the revealed Word of God — it is inerrant, inspired, the "God-breathed" revelation from our Creator. And as such, we let God's word speak to us through this written Word. If it is history, we take it as history. We don't try to force our ideas onto God's Word; we let it speak to us in the language and context in which it is written. How about Jesus actually walking on water? Or that Jesus fed thousands of people from just a few loaves and fishes? Or that Jonah was swallowed by a great fish? We know, because it's in the Bible.

But if I go to many churches in America and ask if God created everything in six ordinary days, that death of animals and man came after sin, that there was a worldwide Flood in the time of Noah and so on, I suddenly get responses like, "Well, we wouldn't say that. The days could be millions of years. God could have used evolution. Noah's Flood might have been a local event or really didn't make much impact on the earth," and all sorts of similar statements.

Now I want you to understand what has happened — this is key to understanding what has happened to our culture, and key to understanding why our kids are leaving the Church. This is the crux of the issue. It is an issue of authority — biblical authority.

It is true that the literal events of Genesis are foundational to all doctrine — to the gospel. In Matthew 19:4–7, when Jesus was explaining the doctrine of marriage, He quoted from the creation account of Adam and Eve to teach the doctrine of one man for one woman. The whole meaning of the gospel is dependent upon the account of the Fall of man, and thus original sin, as given in Genesis. Ultimately, every single biblical doctrine of theology, directly or indirectly, is founded in the historical account given in Genesis 1–11. And Genesis is written as typical historical narrative (not like the Psalms that are written as typical Hebrew poetry). If one undermines this history, or reinterprets it, or tries to claim it is myth or symbolic, then one undermines the foundation of the rest of the Bible, including the gospel.

But even given this, there is something far more crucial — it is the very WORD itself, the authority of the book we call the Bible.

The reason we know Jesus rose from the dead is that we take God's Word as written. The reason we know a fish swallowed a man is that we take God's Word as written. And if you take God's Word as written in Genesis (and it is written as history and quoted from as history throughout the Bible as did Jesus Himself in His earthly ministry), it is very clear that God created in six ordinary days, that man and animals were vegetarian before sin, there was a global Flood, and there was an event after the Flood called the Tower of Babel that formed the different people groups.

Thus, one can't have a fossil record of supposed millions of years before man containing evidence of animals eating each other, bones with diseases like cancer, and thorns said to be hundreds of millions of years old, when everything was described by God as "very good" and animals and man were vegetarian and there was no sin and thus no death and disease or thorns before Adam's rebellion. The ultimate reason so many in the Church (including professors at Bible colleges, seminaries, and Christian colleges) reinterpret the Genesis account of creation, or say it is not important, is because of the influence of the idea of millions of years and evolutionary teaching.

Here is the point. Stand back and consider the big picture. If we teach our children (or anyone) to take God's Word as written concerning the Resurrection, the miracles of Jesus, and the account of Jonah and the great fish that swallowed him but then tell them we don't need to take Genesis as written but can reinterpret it on the basis of the world's teaching about millions of years and evolution — we have unlocked a door.

The door we've unlocked is the door to undermine biblical authority. We are really saying, "We want you to take God's Word as written according to literature and language in certain places — but not here at the beginning in Genesis." What we have actually done is made man the authority over God's Word. We have taught our children that they can take what they learn at school and can reinterpret the Bible's clear teaching in Genesis to supposedly fit this into the Bible. By staying silent and not defending Genesis, we are "teaching" our children that we don't have to take God's Word as written, and man can reinterpret God's Word according to what the majority in the culture might believe.

Scripture teaches that if there is sin or compromise in one generation and it is not dealt with, it is usually observed to occur to a much greater extent in the next generation, and so on. When we unlock that door in Genesis, the next generation usually pushes that door open farther — and then the next generation farther again, and then the next farther again — until eventually all of the Bible is rejected. There is a loss of biblical authority each generation until it becomes an epidemic throughout the Church and nation. The structure of Christianity (its morality, its Christian worldview) collapses, to be replaced by a man-centered structure where moral relativism would pervade the culture. That is what we have seen across Europe, and before our very eyes in America.

An Open Door

So why do we tolerate ideas that undermine the authority of God's Word? We think that simply because a secular humanist or an atheist is not directly attacking Jesus or the Cross that he's not attacking them at all. If the mass media and education systems directly targeted Jesus and the Resurrection, most in the Church would be up in arms. But if the foundation of those beliefs is attacked and weakened first (the attack on the Word itself), then unbelief creeps across the country and through the Church slowly and surely, while we have to fight more and more for the things we value in our faith.

Many Christian organizations are spending millions of dollars and countless hours trying to change the culture. We are trying to get nativity scenes back on public grounds. We are trying to get the Ten Commandments back in the courtrooms. We're trying to get the Bible back in the classroom. (Actually, I don't think that's true. I don't think anyone even *hopes* that the Bible might someday be read and respected in the secular schools anymore.) But why in the world would the Bible (and its Ten Commandments, nativity scenes, and so on) be allowed in the classroom if the educators don't believe it's true. And the gospel? The message of Jesus comes from the same book that records the Genesis history of creation and the Flood. If they don't believe in the first part (which is written as history and quoted as history throughout the Bible), why would they believe in the rest?

The world, the devil, and even our sinful human tendencies have caused a deep, dark shadow of doubt to fall across God's Word. *Did God really say . . . ?* In regard to the events in Genesis — six literal days, and so on — most people would say no, because the Word of God has been under successful attack. In Europe the attack began when scientists threw doubt on the age of the earth. In America today, those same attacks are shattering the foundation upon which the Church and the gospel depend. Actually, the Bible itself warns us that such attacks will happen and we need to be ready for them. In 2 Corinthians 11:3, Paul warns us that Satan will use the same attack on us that he did on Eve:

> But I am afraid that, as the serpent deceived Eve by his craftiness, your minds will be led astray from the simplicity and purity of devotion to Christ.

And what was the method used on Eve? *"Did God really say . . . ?"* He got Adam and Eve to doubt and thus disbelieve the Word of God. This attack was meant to cause Adam and Eve to reinterpret God's Word based on their own appraisal of things. They looked at the evidence — the beautiful fruit — and decided that God's Word couldn't mean what they thought it meant. It was okay to reinterpret it and determine truth for themselves. I call this "the Genesis 3 Attack"! Genesis 3 Attacks have occurred over and over again throughout history. And in this era (particularly since the late 18th century), the Genesis 3 Attack has manifested itself as science attempting to disprove the account of creation, the Flood, and the Tower of Babel in Genesis. Our culture today is in great danger — the Genesis 3 Attack has hit the Church and the culture!

While I have very strong feelings about the direction that our culture is going, I do not believe that culture can be changed from the top down. Sure, you might get the laws changed for the next four years, but the next guy who gets voted in can erase everything. You might be able to win a few legal battles regarding freedom of speech, but before we know it, the next group will be telling us to sit down and shut up.

Why? Because they don't believe the book from which we speak. You see, the culture has changed from the foundation up, as reflected in the predominant secular worldview and relative morality. The culture went from being built on the foundation of God's Word to being built on the foundation of man's word. And this has also happened in the Church. When the Church adopted millions of years and evolutionary ideas into the Bible, they put man in authority over God's Word, making man the ultimate authority, not God! No wonder the kids are walking away from the Church!

At its heart, Answers in Genesis is not a creation-versus-evolution ministry, and we're not out to change the culture. The Bible doesn't say to go into all the world and change the culture, but to go into all the world and preach the gospel. The culture changed because hearts and minds changed in regard to the Word of God. To change the culture back, hearts and minds need to be changed toward God and His Word. When such changed hearts and minds, committed to the Word of God, shine light and distribute "salt" in the culture — then the culture will change.

We see it as our job to defend the Christian faith, stand on the authority of God's Word without compromise, and proclaim the gospel of Jesus Christ. And when the relevancy of the Word of God is restored, lives will be changed as the power and authority of the living Word of God empowers their lives. Then, we believe, these individuals will permeate the culture by living truthfully and honestly in harmony with godly principles . . . and *then* culture will be changed from the bottom up. That's what this ministry is all about. We strive to get information out there to change the foundation and worldview of individuals so the culture will naturally be changed from the heart.

We forget that the first attack by Satan was to cast doubt on the Word of God. How does that relate to the gospel today? Paul shared his concerns in the verse quoted previously from 2 Corinthians 11:3:

> But I am afraid that, as the serpent deceived Eve by his craftiness, your minds will be led astray from the simplicity and purity of devotion to Christ.

Satan deceived by his craftiness, the Word of God was compromised, and people's minds were corrupted from the simplicity of the gospel and Jesus.

But why should we be surprised? Psalm 11:3 says, "If the foundations are destroyed, what can the righteous do?" Our foundation is the Word of God. We need to defend the Word of God as one of our top priorities as Christians. If we are to give a strategic and effective response to the wave of souls who are leaving the Church, these issues must be addressed.

The Attack Today

In our survey, we asked the thousand young adults who have left the Church if they believed that all the accounts and stories in the Bible are true and accurate. Of those, 44 percent said no, 38 percent said yes, and 18 percent didn't know. We asked those who said no this follow-up question: If you don't believe all the accounts and stories in the Bible are true and accurate, what made you begin to doubt the Bible?

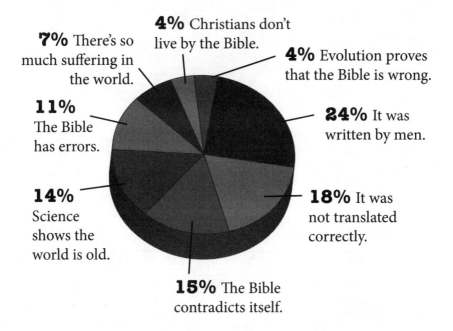

4% Christians don't live by the Bible.

7% There's so much suffering in the world.

4% Evolution proves that the Bible is wrong.

11% The Bible has errors.

24% It was written by men.

14% Science shows the world is old.

18% It was not translated correctly.

15% The Bible contradicts itself.

Look at those results again. If you add up all of the responses related to biblical authority, you'll see that 82 percent of those who said they did not believe all the accounts and stories in the Bible are true and accurate did so because of doubts about the authority of the Bible. Then we asked this other question: Does the Bible contain errors?

Forty percent said yes and another 30 percent didn't know. Only 30 percent said that the Bible does not contain errors. Of those who said that the Bible does contain errors, these were the supposed errors that they pointed out:

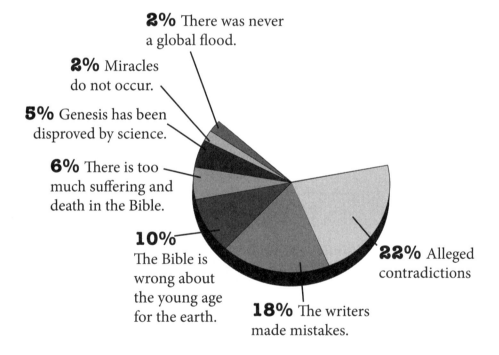

2% There was never a global flood.

2% Miracles do not occur.

5% Genesis has been disproved by science.

6% There is too much suffering and death in the Bible.

10% The Bible is wrong about the young age for the earth.

18% The writers made mistakes.

22% Alleged contradictions

These are the doubts that students like Susan are facing. These are the doubts that are plaguing the hearts of the next generation. For the group that will never come back to church and never comes on holidays, these issues are even more pronounced. It would seem logical, then, that if we are to strategically respond to the devastating epidemic of young adults who are leaving the evangelical Church, we should be addressing these issues. Responding to these attacks on our Bible should be at the forefront of our attempts to restore relevancy to the Word of God and make our churches relevant to this generation. It is so obvious we need to be teaching apologetics in our churches — creation apologetics and general Bible apologetics! The fact that this is not happening in the majority of our churches, nor in the majority of Bible and Christian colleges and seminaries, is one of the great travesties of this age in regard to the Church.

What is really happening?

A False Relevancy

Medical researchers often talk about a phenomenon called "the placebo effect." When trying to determine the effectiveness of a drug or treatment, sometimes researchers will intentionally give a group of people a pill that looks like the new medicine but really isn't. Amazingly, the people taking the false medicine sometimes *feel* better even though the pill is not actually helping them at all.

A similar thing is happening in the Church. In our efforts to slow the flood of young adults who are leaving, we often give the Church a placebo. We try to restore *cultural* relevancy without restoring *biblical* relevancy. As you'll see in the next chapter, I'm all about adopting religious forms that are appropriate to the culture of the upcoming generation. Becoming "culturally cool" can feel like it helps for a while, but it's really just a placebo, a Band-Aid for a much deeper disease. By simply making our services more attractive to the younger generation, we might feel better and they might feel better, but it's doing nothing to solve the core issue of the epidemic. All it does is sacrifice eternal truth for short-term attractiveness, and it turns a church into an organization that is driven by the felt needs of its young consumers.

Tell them what they want. Make them feel good. That's not what the doctor ordered. Yes, we need a good bedside manner, but the Church is sick and it needs to be told the truth — and they need to know that the truth hurts sometimes. (Okay, *a lot* of the time.)

One of my big frustrations with this "placebo effect" comes down to music. I have visited hundreds and hundreds of churches. Everywhere I go, music seems to be the central issue. Even in conservative churches everyone tries to make a big deal out of praise and worship. We think that if we can make it dynamic, energetic, and fit the style of the generation we're trying to reach, the epidemic will be stopped and young people will start flooding back into the Church. That's simply not the case. Our research showed that music is *not* a fundamental factor in young adults choosing to leave or stay at a church — but the preaching of God's Word is.

Now don't get me wrong. David used music to praise the Lord. God has created us to love music. We can use music to worship the Lord. But what I'm talking about is the fact that music is seen by many in the church as the most important part of the service — that it is the music that will draw people in. This is not what our research showed. Yes, people love music, but they want good teaching!

However, to try to restore relevancy to Scripture, what do we usually do these days? We add guitars and drums to the service. We think that the Church needs to follow the culture in order to be relevant. But cultural forms do not make you relevant, they just make you cool. Truth makes you relevant. It doesn't mean we can't make such reforms to be more contemporary — but the motive and priority are what is so important.

I watched an argument one time between the worship pastor and an associate pastor over how much time I would have to speak in the service. I was trying to get my computer set up, but I guess I was interfering with the rehearsal. The worship pastor got a little bent out of shape and told the other pastor, "Hey! Music is the most important part of this service!" Eventually the other pastor backed down. That day we had 20 minutes of praise and worship, 20 minutes of message, and 25 minutes of worship at the end. The Word of God was put in second place. The placebo was given precedent; the real medicine was given a token amount of time. I see that everywhere, by the way — in liberal churches, conservative churches, across all denominations. And besides, many times the music worship time is more of a stage production and entertainment time than it really is a worship time.

There is a war going on over the Word of God. This is not the time to focus on making people feel good. Through our survey, we can now better pinpoint the areas where they are struggling with doubt.

Resources for Reclaiming Biblical Relevance

Let's take another look at the situation that the first-century Apostles were facing and draw another parallel between their situation and ours today. Is a child like Susan growing up in Athens or is she growing up in Jerusalem? In other words, is she growing up as a "Jew" in a society where biblical belief is assumed, or is she growing up in a "Greek" society that is secular and skeptical?

The answer is that Susan is actually doing a little of *both*. Part of her is growing up in a church that believes. Christianity is the accepted norm on Sunday morning. The problem is that the moment she steps out the door, she enters a world that is more like Athens. Because of that, Susan's church should be "equipping the saints for the work of the ministry" in an unbelieving world by teaching her and her church to defend the Word of God from the very first verse against the skeptical attacks of this age. Not only would this help protect Susan's faith from the attacks she gets in the world, but it would also arm her and the rest of her congregation to take the offensive. In both situations, the foundation of the authority of the Word of God both inside and outside the Church needs to be rebuilt.

The Church needs to be reminded over and over why the majority of students begin to doubt the Bible in middle and high school — and then *diligently* deal with the issues by introducing relevant apologetics courses (teaching a logical, reasoned defense of the faith) by at least middle school (even before).

As I travel around the world teaching on biblical apologetics, I find that whether my audience is primarily secular or Christian, regardless of what country I'm in, I get asked the same basic questions — such as (to name only some of them):

- How do you know the Bible is true?

- Hasn't science disproved the Bible?

- Isn't the world millions of years old?

- What about carbon dating?

- How did Noah get all the animals on the ark?

- But don't we observe evolution because we see animals change — we see bacteria become resistant to antibiotics?

- If God created Adam and Eve, only two people to start with, where did all the people come from?

- How come there are so many different "races" of people?

- But dinosaurs don't fit with the Bible; how do you explain them?

- Where is the evidence for a global Flood?

- How can you believe in a loving God when there is so much death and suffering around us?

Most Sunday school lessons, sermons, Bible studies, etc., are not teaching people how to answer the questions of the day. They are not connecting the Bible to the real world. They are not teaching people how to defend their faith — and we wonder why we are losing them. Not only is apologetics (a logical defense of the faith) not taught in most churches and Sunday schools, it is not taught at most Bible colleges or seminaries — or is actually taught against! Church leaders today seem to think that programs, entertainment, music, and many other things are what is needed to reach people and keep them in church.

However, our research also showed something very different — that people want good Bible teaching. It is the preaching of the Word and making it relevant to them in today's world that they need and want. But this is not happening even in Sunday school in the majority of instances, let alone the rest of the church programs.

The Bible is not some "pie in the sky" philosophical book. It's a real book that is really connected to the real world. It is a history book that connects to dirt, fossils, stones, bones, tsunamis, earthquakes, oceans, mountains, death, and so on. It has *everything* to do with geography, biology, anthropology, and sociology. The Word of God has never changed, but the Church's perception of the Word of God changed when it failed to engage the scientific community on matters of fact as well as faith. It's time to change that and be true to the challenge that Peter left for each of us to follow:

> But in your hearts set apart Christ as Lord. Always be prepared to give an answer to everyone who asks you to give the reason for the hope that you have. Do this with gentleness and respect (1 Pet. 3:15; NIV).

Typical churches use materials that are more geared for "the Jew in Jerusalem" who has a developed religious background and lives in a religiously friendly society. That's just not the case anymore. Our society is now immersed in secularism. It's absolutely essential that we learn to defend the Bible and the Christian faith for the sake of our faith and our children's faith, and to evangelize a society that has a highly diminished understanding of biblical truth. I firmly believe that we are now in the era of the "Greeks" . . . yet our churches and Sunday schools are still teaching us like "Jews." See the problem?

We do not have a ready defense in most of our churches — *yet*. But, thankfully, God has supplied us with all the weapons and shields we need to defend ourselves and to take the offensive in reclaiming the relevance of God's Word in our churches and in this society. Our defense must be strategic. As families and as a Church, we need to think through the threats that lurk around us and be willing to protect our families and our churches from the onslaught of ideas that continually cause us to question if God really said what He says He did.

I'm advocating a completely new approach to how we educate ourselves as Christians! God's Word and the Christian faith *are* supported/confirmed by the facts. The disconnect between faith and fact is nothing but an illusion created by an overwhelming misinterpretation of the facts. Good observational science *supports* faith. It always has and it always will. It's time to bring the facts back into our faith. Training yourself, your family, and your church to be defenders of the faith is an exciting and empowering adventure. It can change the Church — it can change the world. It's time to attack doubt with courses and preaching and teaching that defend God's Word against the attacks of this age!

That sounds like a huge endeavor, and in some ways it is — in fact, it will take a *lifetime!*

But thanks to this survey, we now know where we need to focus our efforts *today.* We now know which lies are causing elementary, middle school, and high school kids to doubt the most:

- The Bible was written by men.

- The writers made mistakes.

- It was not translated correctly.

- The Bible contradicts itself.

- The Bible has errors.

- Evolution proves that the Bible is wrong.

- The Bible is wrong about the young age for the earth.

- Genesis has been disproved by science.

- There is too much suffering and death in the Bible.

When we interpreted all the data, questions arising about the Book of Genesis represented about 40 percent of all the concerns. Ultimately, if we are unable to defend Genesis, we have allowed the enemy to attack our Christian faith and undermine the very first book of the Bible. We need to be able to defend our faith from general attacks *and* defend against the specific attacks on the Book of Genesis. The number of resources now available is wonderful. To get you started, however, let me give you a manageable, balanced arsenal of shields and swords that you can use to arm yourself and your family and your church.

God's Word stands by itself and doesn't need defending — that is true — but, practically, in this culture we are talking about answering the skeptical questions to *uphold* the Word and proclaim why we can believe in the Bible's life-giving historical and scientific authority. That means we need to not only know the Bible, but we need to know *about* the Bible and why it is worthy of our complete faith. Do you see why that's so important now? Some great resources to get you started are listed in appendix 3.

This Sunday, take a second look at the kids coming through the door of your church. Like Susan, most will appear to be excited, enthusiastic, and engaged. The fact is, about 30 percent of them are kids who are beginning to wrestle with significant doubts about the relevancy of the Word of God. What can we do to help children like her? What can we do to protect our own kids as well as our own hearts from the attacks on God's Word? By defending and teaching the Bible from the very first verse and then depending on God to keep us faithful to our call!

CHAPTER 6

The Real Deal

And He said to them, "Rightly did Isaiah prophesy of you hypocrites, as it is written: 'THIS PEOPLE HONORS ME WITH THEIR LIPS, BUT THEIR HEART IS FAR AWAY FROM ME. BUT IN VAIN DO THEY WORSHIP ME, TEACHING AS DOCTRINES THE PRECEPTS OF MEN.' Neglecting the commandment of God, you hold to the tradition of men" (Mark 7:6–8).

In the last chapter, we addressed the absolutely essential need to defend the Christian faith/Word of God in order to restore relevancy to Group 1, the young adults who have left the church, never come on holidays, and never plan on returning. But that leaves the other half, Group 2: those who come at Christmas and/or Easter and who plan on returning after they have children. Compared to Group 1, this group has a much higher level of belief in the Bible. Three-quarters of them believe that they are saved, and the vast majority of them report relatively high levels of belief in biblical accuracy, authority, and history. The obvious point here is that *over half of the people who have left the Church are still solid believers in Jesus Christ.* What they object to, however, is hypocrisy, legalism, and self-righteousness. *The Bible is relevant to them, but the Church is not.*

Researcher George Barna highlights this problem:

> Loyalty to congregations is one of the casualties of young adulthood: twentysomethings were nearly 70% more likely than older adults to strongly assert that if they "cannot find a local church that will help them become more like Christ, then they will find people and groups that will, and connect with them instead of a local church." They are also significantly less likely to believe that "a person's faith in God is meant to be developed by involvement in a local church."[1]

We have to be honest: at least half of those who are leaving the Church haven't left the faith; they have left the fellowship. They wouldn't see it as a Bible problem (even though they obviously have issues that need addressing), but a church problem. As a result of all this number-crunching and data analysis, we strongly advocate that Christians and the Church everywhere begin to *defend the Word.* Yet defending the Bible is *not* our end goal. It's really just the beginning. When someone is convinced of the relevance of God's Word, they must then make a commitment to *live the Word.* Our concerns are twofold:

1. The "Church" has become an institution that no longer reflects the characteristics and priorities described in the Word of God.

---

1. "Most Twentysomethings Put Christianity on the Shelf Following Spiritually Active Teen Years," Barna Group, September 11, 2006, http://www.barna.org/barna-update/article/16-teensnext-gen/147-most-twentysomethings-put-christianity-on-the-shelf-following-spiritually-active-teen-years.

1,000 young adults . . . believe that the Church is relevant?

yes. 47% | **no.** 53%

When we asked the entire 1,000 young adults whether or not they believe that the Church is relevant, only 47 percent said yes, and a full 53 percent said no/don't know. And quite frankly, it's not just the 20-somethings who feel this way. In the book *Why Men Hate Going to Church,*[2] David Murrow addresses another major concern in church demographics: the Church is losing men as well as it is young adults.

2. David Murrow, *Why Men Hate Going to Church* (Nashville, TN: Nelson Books, 2005).

Men think church is irrelevant, too. The questions that young adults and men ask on Sunday mornings are *So what? Why should I go? If church doesn't work for me, what difference does it make?*

2. People within the Church are not living authentically Christian lives based on the Word of God.

About two-thirds of the people in Group 2 actually think that the Church *is* relevant. But they still don't go. Why is that? It seems to be more a matter of *heart* issues than *head* issues. Relationships with people (rather than relationships with God) seem to be the stumbling block.

"Do you feel the Church is relevant to your needs today?"

	Yes	No & Don't Know
All surveyed	47%	53%
Easter and/or Christmas attenders	60%	40%
Those coming back with kids	74%	26%

Notice that those who feel the Church is most relevant to their needs are those who intend to come back when they have kids. Not only do they see the value of the church experience for their children, but it's quite possible that they also know that the people they're having difficulty with will have moved on by then! Just to verify the results of that question, we asked this question:

"Do you feel good people don't need to go to church?"

	Yes	No & Don't Know
Easter and/or Christmas attenders	33%	67%
Those coming back with kids	27%	73%

Isn't this interesting! At least two-thirds of those who go to church on holidays and plan on coming back feel like good people *do* need to go to church . . . and yet they don't go regularly themselves! Why is that? I believe it's because the Church, and oftentimes the individuals in it, are not living by the Word in at least three critical areas: hypocrisy, teaching, and tradition. Each of these concerns can be remedied by a firm commitment by the Church and by the individuals in the Church to *live the Word.*

The Hypocrisy Infection

What is the number-one perception of the Christian church today? No matter how you slice it, it always comes down to one word — hypocrisy. Hypocrisy has far more to do with honesty (including one's approach to the Bible itself) and transparency than it does being perfect. It insinuates that people say one thing (for example, we believe the Bible is God's Word), and live another way (for example, don't really believe all the Bible). It implies that people force their own legalism on others but are blind to their own faults and sins — even as they are very judgmental toward those who struggle with their own temptations.

In our study, hypocrisy is more important than the church being too political, irrelevant, or boring. Not coincidentally, 20-somethings who have never been to church at all voice the same criticism. David Kinnaman notes this in his book *Unchristian: What a New Generation*

Really Thinks about Christianity . . . and Why It Matters.[3] In part, he discovered these perceptions:

1. Christians say one thing but live something entirely different.

2. Christians are insincere and concerned only with converting others.

3. Christians show contempt for gays and lesbians.

4. Christians are boring, unintelligent, old-fashioned, and out of touch with reality.

5. Christians are primarily motivated by a political agenda and promote right-wing politics.

6. Christians are prideful and quick to find fault in others.

We have to admit that there is an element of truth in many of these critical perceptions. Certainly, the Church is often falsely judged for things that it does not do and does not believe. If you look through that list, however, isn't part of the problem that individual Christians and the Church as a whole do not live (or really believe) what the Bible says? The LifeWay study discovered similar concerns. Fifty-eight percent of Church dropouts in their study selected at least one church- or pastor-related reason for leaving church. Most common was, "church members seemed judgmental or hypocritical" (26 percent). Another 20 percent "didn't feel connected to the people in my church." The final category of reasons, "religious, ethical, or political beliefs," contributed to the departure of 52 percent of church dropouts.[4]

I greatly suspect (as I have observed this myself) that part of the problem is that many see those in the Church who are against

---

3. David Kinnaman, *Unchristian: What a New Generation Really Thinks about Christianity* (Grand Rapids, MI: Baker Books, 2007).

4. http://www.lifeway.com/ArticleView?article=LifeWay-Research-finds-reasons-18-to-22-year-olds-drop-out-of-church.

gay marriage and other aberrant lifestyles coming across as hating homosexuals. Most Christians don't teach that marriage is founded in Genesis, and it is God's Word that speaks against gay marriage. It is not our opinion we are imposing on people. People need to see Christians building their thinking consistently on God's Word, beginning in Genesis, to understand where our worldview comes from. Sadly, many Christians just impose their Christian morality from the top down, and this causes major problems.

Irrelevant Messages

I will get into this more in the next chapter, but I firmly believe that one of the reasons people aren't living by the Word is that they aren't being taught the Word. And certainly, because there is currently so much compromise of history in Genesis, church people by and large just do not understand that the Bible has to be the foundation for all of our thinking. When church people (remember the Sunday school problem) are brought up to allow millions of years and evolutionary ideas to be added into Scripture, many consciously or unconsciously take fallible ideas to Scripture — instead of using Scripture as a foundation for their thinking. Thus their worldview becomes a mixture of biblical morality and human opinion.

Remember, these kids in our sample were in church almost every Sunday. But they heard the same old stuff — shallow, relational, and sentimental stuff that doesn't have meat and substance and doesn't really connect them to reality. Many pastors strive to give entertaining messages that leave the congregation feeling inspired. But unless these messages are based on the inspired Word of God, those feelings will quickly fade away. Christianity without the Bible is a nebulous, lofty religion that doesn't connect to anything in the real world.

After speaking in a church about connecting the Bible to the real world — teaching clearly that the history in Genesis is true and why the gospel based in Genesis is true — a mother and her teenage daughter came up to me. (I have had many similar encounters over the years.) The mother said, "I can't thank you enough. I have been struggling to get my teenage daughter to church. She keeps telling me it is a waste of time and it's not relevant. We've had major problems. But this morning, she sat on the edge of her seat listening to every word you spoke, and after you finished she told me that for the first time she now understands what church is all about — for the first time she understands why Christianity is relevant. You really connected the dots for her this morning."

I spoke to the woman's daughter at length to glean why she reacted in such a way, and I believe she represents the feelings of the majority of church kids. She didn't see the Bible as real — it didn't connect to the real world. She thought church was just about spiritual stuff — but school was about real stuff. She was tired of the same old stories she had heard since Sunday school. She thought what she was taught at school showed the Bible couldn't be true — and no one at home or church could give her answers to her questions. Her mum told me she didn't have a clue what to say about dinosaurs and science issues, and she had just told her daughter it didn't matter, but come to church and trust Jesus anyway! But such a situation is repeated over and over and over again in the Church, and it is not being dealt with.

Why aren't the believers coming to church? When the Church no longer speaks to them, it becomes less relevant; the Church becomes like a clanging gong — making noise but offering nothing of practical value for their lives in the real world.

I believe that those in the pulpit are also missing the opportunity to preach about the relevancy of the Church itself. What does the Bible say about how we are to function together as a Body? Why is it important that we do not forsake our gathering together? The average person sitting in the pew probably doesn't know these things . . . and those who are already gone certainly don't understand that enough to reconnect themselves with a vibrant body of Bible-believing people.

The Tradition Trap

Conservative evangelical churches pride themselves on doing things "by the Book." But is that really the case? When we consider what "church" is from a *biblical* perspective, we must seriously and honestly ask the question, *Are our churches built on the Word of God or the wisdom of man?* In the Western world, when you say "church," at least four things immediately come to mind: a building, an order of service, sermons/Sunday school, and musical worship. That's biblical "church," right? You tell me! How many of these "church" things are found in Scripture? How many of them are man-made traditions?[5]

A Building?

There is not a single place in the New Testament where the term "church" refers to a building — not one! It wasn't until A.D. 190 that Clement of Alexandria referred to a meeting place as a "church." He was also the first person to use the phrase "go to church."[6] Every single one of the appearances of the word *ecclesia* in the New Testament refers to *a gathering or network of believers in Christ, not a physical structure or place.*

An "Order of Service"?

Virtually every evangelical Christian service follows the same basic format for "church" every time we meet. In its most basic form, we have *opening prayer and music, the sermon, and the closing song and/or prayer.* Beyond that, most local churches have a very distinct format that also includes announcements, an offering, and (at predetermined times) "communion." Strange, but you can look through the entire New Testament and find no such order, nor any suggestion that Christian gatherings should follow such an order. That doesn't mean that the order of worship we use is wrong; we just have to be honest and say that there's nothing biblical about it at all . . . and yet it's one of the most important aspects of our modern definition of "church."

---

5. We are indebted to the research of Frank Viola and George Barna presented in the book *Pagan Christianity? Exploring the Roots of Our Church Practices* (Carol Stream, IL: BarnaBooks, 2007). While we don't necessarily affirm their applications, their exploration of the roots of our modern church practices is illuminating and very thought provoking.
6. Clement of Alexandria, *The Instructor,* Book 3, chapter 11.

Sermons and Sunday School?

In the Bible, the good news was obviously preached to the unbelieving masses (Acts 2; Matthew 6–7). Doctrine was shared through letters and taught in interactive small groups. By the fourth century, the "Church" had adopted a format for teaching where a single man stood in front of a passive audience and lectured.[7] This *can* still be a very useful format for teaching and preaching today, but it doesn't appear to be the format that was used in the first-century Church where teaching believers was done in an interactive small group setting. (Again, that doesn't mean that sermons are wrong; you just have to admit that they're part of our man-made tradition, and not biblical history.)

The same goes for Sunday school. Sunday school didn't appear on the scene until 1700 years after Christ. Robert Raikes of England gets the credit for starting the first Sunday school in 1780.[8] Again, I'm not saying that there's anything wrong with the idea of Sunday school (even though it's really not working right now), but you're not going to find it in the Bible; it's not a biblical element of "church." So then, if your Sunday school isn't working like it should, why not do something different!? I'm not saying you *should* do away with it (as we have stated earlier, we advocate major radical changes), but I am saying that you definitely *could* cancel your Sunday school program and not violate any specific example in Scripture.

Worship Music?

I have spoken in hundreds of different churches, and some sort of music is almost always included. I know that music can be a valid form of worship, and I love great God-honoring, worshipful music. Some claim church choirs were borrowed from Greek dramas and were used to accommodate pagan worship.[9] But choirs are men-

---

7. Edwin Hatch, *Influence of Greek Ideas and Usages* (London, Edinburgh: Williams and Norgate, 1891), p. 119.
8. Iris V. Cully and Kendig Brubaker Cully, *Harper's Encyclopedia of Religious Education* (New York: HarperCollins Publishers, 1990), p. 625.
9. H.W. Parke, *The Oracles of Apollo in Asia Minor*, (London; Dover, NH: Croom Helm, 1985), p. 102–103.

tioned in the Bible and were in existence before, during and after the Temple in the Old Testament. However, the point is Scripture does not mandate we have choirs.

In many evangelical churches, the choir has been replaced by a worship team who leads concert-style music and takes a considerable amount of the service time. Yes, music has a rich history in the Bible, but the *type* of worship that dominates and controls so much of "church" cannot be found in the New Testament . . . at all. I am only saying this to make a point that we don't have to do things just because it is tradition. As someone once said to me, "Do you know the seven last words of the Church? — we've never done it this way before!" And just because a church does something a different way doesn't mean everyone else has to follow!

If people want to make music the focal point of their service, they can — and many do. But the music is not really feeding the souls and protecting the minds of the congregation. Our statistics certainly show that music isn't the reason our young adults are leaving, and it's not the reason that they will come back. And again, we are not saying music is wrong — it is all a matter of what the focus and priority really should be.

Are we doing church "by the Book"? Just because we might be "conservative" or "traditional" doesn't mean that we are "biblical." It's safe to conclude that if one of the original Apostles visited one of our churches today, he wouldn't have any sort of clue that he was in a Christian gathering (unless he could understand our language). "Church" today is mostly driven by man-made traditions and not by the biblical mandates to defend the Word of God and live by the Word of God.

Many churches are waking up to this fact. Willow Creek (well-known for its seeker-sensitive approach to bring in people) recently had a look at what they were doing. Through a scientific survey like the one we conducted, they wanted to see if their church was really helping people grow. The findings shocked them:

We discovered that high levels of church activity *did not* predict increasing love for God or increasing love for other people. Now don't misread this! This does not mean that people highly involved in church activities don't love God. It simply means that they did not express a greater love for God than people who are less involved in church activities. In other words, an increasing level of activities did not *predict* an increase in love for God. Church activity alone made no direct impact on growing the heart . . . it was a flat line — and a stunning discovery for us.[10]

That is a tough pill to swallow. But at least they were willing to evaluate the effectiveness of what they are doing and consider making adjustments. Whether or not they make the right adjustments is another matter, of course.

When it comes to the modern-day church, I think one of the most piercing passages of Scripture is this:

They worship me in vain; their teachings are but rules taught by men. You have let go of the commands of God and are holding on to the traditions of men (Mark 7:6–8; NIV).

May we never hold to man-made religious traditions at the expense of defending God's Word and living God's Word. When it comes to "doing church," are we relying on man's wisdom or God's Word? If the forms and traditions that we use are working, then fine. But if they aren't working, we have a responsibility as well as the freedom to change what we are doing, provided that as a Church we do not neglect the commandments of God and worship God in vain.

---

10. Greg L. Hawkins and Cally Parkinson, *Reveal: Where Are You?* (South Barrington, IL: Willow, 2006), p. 35–36.

Rediscovering "Church"

Church can be defined many ways. It could be simply defined as *a group of individuals that prioritize the sharing of the Word of God and live by the principles of the Word of God.*

In order to stay true to such a definition, however, we must study God's Word to find out what the basic principles of "church" are! My challenge to you at this point is to *study for yourself* the principles and priorities of church in the New Testament.

Can I ask how you would define "church"? Is your definition based on man's thinking and tradition or God's Word? This is a critical, fundamental question. Yes, we are concerned about the exodus of young adults from the Church. But unless we know what the Bible means by "church," all of our efforts and concerns might be misguided. We need to be willing to question *all* assumptions that we have about "church" and let the Bible speak for itself when it talks about the Body of Christ.

The Greek word for "church" in the New Testament is *ecclesia*. It is used:

- 103 times in the New Testament;

- 20 times to refer to the universal Church;

- 34 times to refer to a group of churches;

- 49 times to refer to a specific local church.

I challenge you to take God at His Word and study both what the Bible says about Church *and* what it doesn't say. In order to see a glimpse of the Church in the first century, we must look at passages like Acts 2:42–47:

> They were continually devoting themselves to the apostles' teaching and to fellowship, to the breaking of bread and to prayer. Everyone kept feeling a sense of awe; and many

wonders and signs were taking place through the apostles. And all those who had believed were together and had all things in common; and they began selling their property and possessions and were sharing them with all, as anyone might have need. Day by day continuing with one mind in the temple, and breaking bread from house to house, they were taking their meals together with gladness and sincerity of heart, praising God and having favor with all the people. And the Lord was adding to their number day by day those who were being saved.

Descriptions like these give us a picture of what church is supposed to be all about: a community of people whose lives are empowered, directed, and energized by personal interaction with the Word of God and with each other. While some of the descriptions of the early Church are clearly cultural, many of them are universal as we discover the role of teachers, elders, deacons, and pastors — which also means there is structure as well as rules to abide by (for example, for disciplining when necessary). By connecting with what the Bible says about the Church, our churches connect with reality and regain the relevance that has been lost because we have focused only on our man-made traditions.

A very interesting New Testament study begins with a search of the words "one another." If you don't have a Bible study program on your computer, go to any of the online Bible search engines and type in those two words. You'll discover an amazing assortment of verses that describe what God really intended for lives to be like together as part of the Church.

A similar search can be made for the word "church." Read these passages and ask yourself, *Is this what "church" means to me? Do our traditions help us to be more like this kind of church or do they distract from the principles of the New Testament?* When you find clear principles and examples, pursue them with all your heart. If you don't find support for an aspect of "church" that you are used to or that you feel is being treated like a doctrine, know that it's only tradition. That doesn't mean that the tradition is necessarily bad. *Some traditions need to be kept, others are optional, and some need changing!*

One of the foundational biblical concepts for church is that we are to be a "body." Christianity is not a solo journey. How can you be a solid Christian in isolation? If you're in isolation, it means you're susceptible to the devil, evil, and you're not being held up by fellow believers. It's a rough world out there. We were not designed to go it alone. You might attend large worship services, but if you don't have those personal connections with the other members of the body, you're probably going to fall apart, because there's no one else there to help hold you together.

Unfortunately, the typical church does not provide these types of relationships or relevant teaching to their young adults. The Barna research indicates this trend:

> Much of the activity of young adults, such as it is, takes place outside congregations. Young adults were just as likely as older Americans to attend special worship events not sponsored by a local church, to participate in a spiritually oriented small group at work, to have a conversation with someone else who holds them accountable for living faith principles, and to attend a house church not associated with a conventional church. Interestingly, there was one area in which the spiritual activities of twentysomethings outpaced their predecessors: visiting faith-related websites.[11]

Because much of the conventional Church is neither defending the Word of God nor living by the Word of God, the young people who have left the Church — particularly those who still have strong levels of biblical belief — are trying to find it elsewhere. Very few are searching the Scriptures to discover what "church" is really supposed to be all about. All they know is that they're not finding it within the buildings

---

11. www.barna.org.

they grew up in, and they are willing to break with tradition to find it — even when it looks nothing like the church of their parents. Right or wrong, they are redefining what "church" means to their generation. I personally believe this is part of the reason why movements are arising in the Church that are not biblical in their beliefs but seem somewhat attractive on the outside and seem to be more "loving" and "gentle" and "caring." But in the long run, these churches have no real foundation — no real substance.

A Virtual Church?

Walt Wilson was a sales manager at Fairchild Semiconductor, a start-up executive at Apple Computer, and a Silicon Valley businessman. Now he is the chairman of Global Media Outreach, a ministry that is trying to help the Church enter the digital age:

> The business term to describe the shift from atoms to bits is called *radical discontinuity*. Basically, it is change that happens so fast that we don't know how to describe it or even forecast it. It would be a huge mistake to think the Church is immune to this development. It is not. Many seekers across the world have shifted to information on the Internet instead of going to a place called church. People are looking for God in the world of bits, not atoms.[12] The Internet is now becoming the funnel *into* the church. If you are not using the Internet to conduct real ministry, then you don't exist to the current generation of seekers — two million daily![13]

Home Churches?

Sensing that the conventional church has dropped the ball when it comes to defending God's Word and living God's Word, scores of believers are leaving the pews and heading for the couches of living

---

12. If you'd like to be a part of reaching the millions of people who are searching the Internet to find Christ, contact Global Media Outreach and become one of their virtual missionaries.
13. http://www.lausanneworldpulse.com/perspectives.php/1043?pg=all.

rooms across the country. The resurgence in the "home church movement" has been significant. The home church has its advantages and disadvantages, just like every other form of church. Many people feel that this movement is a step backward and that home churches lack accountability, order, resources, and authority. Those who attend them argue that the Church survived and thrived for 300 years in homes before they started to meet in official church buildings. Home churches can also lack the biblical structure (as given clearly in Scripture) that includes elders, deacons, etc. Many of the young adults who go to them, however, feel like they have been "burned" by a traditional church that does not understand them. They argue that the environment is informal, with less liturgy, and highly interactive. They try to make it known that home churches are not just a place where a bunch of renegade lone rangers go to tie up their horses once in a while.

The Para-church as a Church?

For hundreds of years, concerned individuals have formed organizations that take up the slack where the traditional churches have been dropping the ball. Some print and distribute Bibles, some are mission organizations, and others target high school or college campuses. They refer to themselves as the "para-church" — but in many ways many of them become churches unto themselves. Many of these organizations excel at defending God's Word and living by God's Word. They often have "staff" people who are highly trained and serve as mature "pastors" to their flocks. Most members of the para-church are encouraged to also participate in a local church. Many of them do so, but to be honest, relevant "church" is taking place for them somewhere else.

Answers in Genesis is a para-church organization, but we believe it is very important to ensure people understand that we are not a church as such, just a specialist organization raised up to assist the Church in carrying out the Great Commission and building up the body of believers.

Healthy debate will undoubtedly continue about "alternative churches." Around the country, many conventional churches are beginning to realize they need to use the Bible as their primary "operator's manual" for church. Many of the committed believers who are leaving Church as we know it are honestly wrestling with all these new definitions. Many have concluded that Church is not something you go to; it's something you are. Many who are seeking to "live the Word" are even finding themselves back in traditional evangelical or liturgical churches. Things might even look the same on the outside, but with the Bible at the heart of all they do, everything feels different on the inside.

Not an Option

Hopefully, you have already seen that being part of a church is not optional for a committed believer in Jesus Christ (Heb. 10:25). Britt and I are praying that one of the consequences of this book is that churches will be changed from the inside out by the Word of God. We also pray that committed believers will have the freedom to leave, if necessary, to find *a group of individuals that prioritizes the sharing of the Word of God, teaching how to defend the Christian faith and uphold the authority of the Word in today's world, and lives by the principles of the Word of God.* And we are also praying that those who have left the Church will find their way back into this type of fellowship. Because of that, we asked those who are planning on returning to Church after they have kids a couple of important questions:

1. Do your closest friends attend church regularly right now? A full 50 percent said yes.

2. Have any of your friends invited you to go back to church with them? Sixty-one percent had been asked!

These numbers are actually encouraging (somewhat). At least half of the people who have left still have a tight connection with someone who is involved in a church. Hopefully these are good churches, too! Many of them have already been asked if they want to come home.

Only 27 percent of those who never go to church, however, have friends that attend church now. Yes, there is something to be said about positive peer pressure . . . even for adults. It still gives them a natural connection to the Church. Of those young people who expect to come back in the future, 61 percent of their friends invited them to church. And you might be that someone! Waggoner, who headed up the Life-Way survey, had this to say:

> Church leaders should passionately and consistently challenge church members to maximize their influence with youth and young adults. Frequent and intentional contact can either prevent or counteract the tendency of some to drop out of church. . . . This return to church after being gone for at least a year is primarily the result of encouragement from others. The most common reason for returning is "My parents or family members encouraged me to attend" (39 percent). Twenty-one percent attribute their return to "My friends or acquaintances encouraged me to attend." Combined, 50 percent of those who return were influenced by the encouragement of either family or friends. Young adults also return to church when they feel the desire personally or sense God calling them back: "I simply felt the desire to return" (34 percent) and "I felt that God was calling me to return to the church" (28 percent).[14]

And please, please remember that 30 percent of *all* the people who've left the Church "don't know" if they will be coming back or not. That's not just a statement of indecision; we should read that as a statement of *possibility*. In their hearts, they're still wondering. Perhaps all they need is someone to reach out to them in a real way, with real

---

14. http://www.lifeway.com/ArticleView?article=LifeWay-Research-finds-reasons-18-to-22-year-olds-drop-out-of-church.

information, living a real Christian life. When it comes to church, they are looking for the real deal. Perhaps you need only let them know that the door is still open and that they're still always welcome to come back and be a part of the Body.

The Most Important Thing

Churches that defend God's Word and live by God's Word can once again become "the real deal" to the generation of young adults that has left and the next generation that is teetering on the edge. But I strongly encourage you to always remember that a church is a group of individuals . . . and you are an individual. We hope that you might actually be an agent of change within the group, but in all honesty, the *only* thing you can really control is yourself — and, in fact, the *most important* thing you can control is *yourself*. It's so easy to point a judgmental (and hypocritical) finger at the Church and think, *Oh, if only they would live by the Word.* But what about you: are you living by the Word? It turns out that this is a vital question for you personally — far more important than whether or not you are attending church. After Willow Creek realized that what they were doing as a church was not helping people grow spiritually, they set out to find out what does help. Four years, 200 churches, and 80,000 surveys later, they found this:

> Everywhere we turned the data revealed the same truth: spending time in the Bible is hands down the highest impact personal spiritual practice. More specifically, "I reflect on the meaning of Scripture in my life" is the spiritual practice that is most predictive of growth. . . . Reflecting on Scripture implies a contemplative process, one of thoughtful and careful deliberation. This practice of "reflecting on the meaning of Scripture in my life" is about using God's Word as a mirror that reflects back the truth of Scripture on the actions, decisions, and defense of one's daily life. This is not about skimming through a Bible passage or devotional in a mechanical

way. This is a powerful experience of personal meditation that catalyzes spiritual growth, starting at the very beginning of the spiritual journey.[15]

Now how such a church responds to this, of course, is another matter. If they don't understand the issues as Britt's research has discovered, and if they don't take an uncompromising stand on Genesis, then we would say it would all be to no avail in the long run.

We do have to defend the word in this post-Christian culture, as we have outlined in previous chapters; we must make the connection between fact and faith so that the Scriptures again become authoritative and relevant in the Church and in the culture. The Willow Creek research shows that it wasn't their progressive musical worship, it wasn't their dynamic small groups, and it wasn't their seeker-sensitive (watered down) Sunday sermons. True spiritual growth and a healthy church all start with an individual — with you — accepting the Word of God for what it is — the absolute authority — and treating it accordingly. The Bible from Genesis to Revelation is the living Word of God. The written, uncompromised Word of God in your mind and the presence of the Holy Spirit of Christ in your heart is the pure essence of Christianity. When you gather together a group of people with that, "church happens." Jesus said:

> I am the vine, you are the branches; he who abides in Me and I in him, he bears much fruit, for apart from Me you can do nothing (John 15:5).

When writing about the profound and powerful mystery of being a Christian, Paul wrote:

> I can do all things through Him who strengthens me (Phil. 4:13).

---

15. Greg L. Hawkins and Cally Parkinson, *Follow Me: What's Next for You?* (South Barrington, IL: Willow, 2007), p. 114.

Are you specifically willing to commit to live an authentic Christian life, to "live the Word" as God empowers you through His Holy Spirit so that you can be "the real deal" with Christ, with yourself, with your family, with the Church, and with the world? Brit and I pray so.

> Long for the pure milk of the word, so that by it you might grow in respect to salvation (1 Pet. 2:2).

Britt's Bit: It's Hard to Explain Sometimes

Every once in a while, some numbers just don't make sense. It makes you wonder how much people have really thought through their Christian teachings and their Christian faith. Sometimes I have to push myself back from my desk, scratch my head a little bit, look up at the ceiling, and wonder *what in the world are these people thinking?*

Do you believe that dinosaurs died out before people were on the planet?

60% of those who attend church on Easter and Christmas said yes.

32% of those who don't attend church at all said yes.

This is exactly backward of what we would expect. In every other area of belief, those who attend church at the holidays gave more accurate biblical answers to our questions . . . except this one! It's sad but true that many Christians have not logically thought through the earlier teachings in their lives. I believe those who attend church only on Christmas or Easter and those who don't attend at all are answering the question about dinosaurs based more upon movies they've seen than scriptural teachings. Sometimes you just have to accept that people are not always logical and therefore are never predictable.

But this was the one that really got me wondering: *Do you believe that God used evolution to change one kind of animal to another?*

- 24% said yes.

When we asked the same group this question: *Do you believe that humans evolved from apelike ancestors?*

- 30% said yes.

You would expect to have the same identical answer to both of these questions. However, we don't. And the reason we don't have the same answer is that these young people were not adequately equipped when they were younger to understand and defend the Scriptures.

CHAPTER 7

Welcome to the Revolution

"Insanity" is doing the same thing over and over and expecting a different result. — Anonymous

Desperate times call for desperate measures — and these are desperate times. We *do* have an epidemic on our hands. Survey after survey has revealed that over 60 percent of the children who grow up in our churches will leave them as they reach the threshold of young adulthood. The empty and obsolete churches of England foreshadow the future in America. Where England is today, we will be tomorrow[1] — unless we take strategic action now. We don't need a remodel; we need a complete renovation. We don't need a Band-Aid; we need radical surgery. It's time for a revolution; it's time for a new Reformation in the Church — to call the Church back to the authority of the Word of God, beginning in Genesis.

---

1. It is true that recent surveys show certain churches such as Evangelical and Pentecostal are growing, but overall church attendance across all denominations is way down.

No, the numbers are not good. By surveying a thousand young adults who have left solid Bible-believing churches, we have gotten a much clearer profile of the lost generation. More sobering is the fact that the current Sunday school is doing very little (at best) and can even be significantly detrimental to the beliefs and the faith of the children we send there.

We have shown that those who leave the Church can be broken into two categories: Group 1, which never comes to church during the holidays and has no plans on returning to church after they have children. This group has serious doubts about the relevancy of Scripture. Group 2, on the other hand, comes to church on Easter or Christmas or both, and will likely return to the Church after they have children. They have a relatively high level of belief in biblical truth, but they find the Church to be irrelevant.

So what is to be done? We have already established that we need to *defend the Word* and we need to *live the Word*. What does this mean for the young adults who are already gone? David Kinnaman points out a sobering challenge:

> There is considerable debate about whether the disengagement of twentysomethings is a lifestage issue — that is, a predictable element in the progression of people's development as they go through various family, occupational, and chronological stages — or whether it is unique to this generation. While there is some truth to both explanations, this debate misses the point, which is that the current state of ministry to twentysomethings is woefully inadequate to address the spiritual needs of millions of young adults. These individuals are making significant life choices and determining the patterns and preferences of their spiritual reality while churches wait, generally in vain, for them to return after college or when the kids come. When and if young adults do return to churches, it is difficult to convince them that a passionate pursuit of

Christ is anything more than a nice add-on to their cluttered lifestyle.[2]

Strategic search and rescue efforts need to continue helping those who have wandered from the flock find their way back. Many times a sincere invitation from a friend is all it takes. But even if they agree to come back, unless the Church is standing on the authority of the Word of God in an uncompromising way, teaching them how to answer the skeptical questions of the age, and challenging them to build their thinking in every area on God's Word — they will probably not stay.

The obvious remaining question, however, is this: *How do we curb the epidemic in the flock that is still under our care — the high school, middle school, and elementary students who are still coming in almost every Sunday?*

We believe that a four-pronged approach is in order. Parents, Christian educators, youth pastors, and pastors all have a role to play in the solution. All of us in the Body are called to defend the Word and live the Word. Our specific mandates, however, are unique, and our strategic action points vary depending upon where God has placed us. And teaching creation and biblical apologetics is a necessary part for all!

To Parents

Your Call

Defend the Word.
Live the Word.

Your Mandate

Be diligent to present yourselves approved to God as a workman who does not need to be ashamed, accurately handling the word of truth (2 Tim. 2:15).

Southern Baptist Convention researcher Ed Stetzer noted:

---

2. David Kinneman, *Unchristian: What a New Generation Really Thinks about Christianity — and Why It Matters* (Grand Rapids, MI: Baker Books, 2007).

There is no easy way to say it, but it must be said. Parents and churches are not passing on a robust Christian faith and an accompanying commitment to the church. We can take some solace in the fact that many do eventually return. But, Christian parents and churches need to ask the hard question, "What is it about our faith commitment that does not find root in the lives of our children?"[3]

That's not a rhetorical question. Why isn't our faith taking root in our children? First, it's possible that the parents themselves do not have a "robust Christian faith" to start with. Christianity is contagious, but children won't catch it unless the parents are infected. If your children aren't following Christ, you must first check to see if they're following your lead! Your first priority as a parent is to live the Word of God in a natural, sincere way. If you try to preach it to your kids without living it, you'll only add to the hypocrisy that turned so many of them away. Consider this challenge:

Hear, O Israel! The LORD is our God, the LORD is one! You shall love the LORD your God with all your heart and with all your soul and with all your might. These words, which I am commanding you today, shall be on your heart. You shall teach them diligently to your sons and shall talk of them when you sit in your house and when you walk by the way and when you lie down and when you rise up. You shall bind them as a sign on your hand and they shall be as frontals on your forehead. You shall write them on the doorposts of your house and on your gates (Deut. 6:4–9).

Parent, it's time to search your own heart and know your own ways and see if there is any hurtful way within you (Ps. 139:24). Do you love the Lord our God with all your heart and with all your soul and with

---

3. http://www.lifeway.com/ArticleView?article=LifeWay-Research-finds-reasons-18-to-22-year-olds-drop-out-of-church.

all your might? Do you take the words of God and treasure them in your heart and teach them to your kids by talking to them about God's Word as if it's a normal part of your life? *Is* it your life? The faith of your family starts with you. The Barna Group explained it this way:

> It's not entirely surprising that deep, lasting spiritual transformation rarely happens among teenagers — it's hard work at any age, let alone with the distractions of youth. And, since teenagers' faith often mirrors the intensity of their parents', youth workers face steep challenges because they are trying to impart something of spiritual significance that teenagers generally do not receive from home.[4]

Second, you need to realize that our society is no longer "Christian." Our kids are living in a culture that is saturated with counter-Christian messages built on a foundation of evolutionary secular humanism. It's your job to protect your kids and prepare them for life in this post-Christian society. You need to teach them how to answer the skeptical questions of this age. Show them that you do not compromise God's Word with man's fallible word (for example, by allowing millions of years or evolutionary ideas to invade Scripture and thus undermine biblical authority).

It's not just an issue of homeschooling; it is an issue of true biblical home education. If our survey should teach you anything, it's that you can no longer depend on the Sunday school and youth ministries in your church to educate your kids in the things of God. In all honesty, this was never their responsibility in the first place. This is your job; this is your responsibility; you need to step up to the plate and take charge.

Action Points

- **Humble yourself before God: submit yourself to Him to be used as a tool in His hand for ministry in your own home**. The strength and power of your ministry

---

4. www.barnagroup.org.

must come from the presence of the Holy Spirit working through you according to the Word of God. Trying to do this by yourself, rather than allowing God to work through you as He chooses, will eventually lead to failure.

If you now realize you have compromised God's Word (for example, in Genesis), then ask the Lord to forgive you, and admit to your children you were wrong and then diligently teach them how to answer skeptical questions and not compromise God's Word. Let your children see you have a high view of Scripture as you should.

- **Make the Word of God a natural presence in your home.** Follow the command in Deuteronomy chapter 6 to talk about the Word with your kids and spouse. Write them down and post them in prominent places in your home. Ask God to create inside of you a love for Him that flows from your whole heart, mind, soul, and spirit. If you need to study up on how creation relates to the gospel and the rest of Scripture, then read Genesis 1–11, the Gospel of John, the Book of Romans, and the last two chapters of Revelation. This will give you a good overview to start with.

- **Evaluate your church.** Is your church defending the Word and living by the Word? Chances are you're going to have to make a decision to either stay as a committed agent of change, or leave and join a church that already shares your stand in these areas.

Whatever you do, don't punt your responsibilities to somebody else. God has placed you in your family for a reason. He will give you the strength and wisdom that you need to carry out your mandate — if you humble yourself before Him and allow Him to work through you.

For a list of recommended resources, see appendix 4.

To the Christian Educator

Your Call

Defend the Word.
Live the Word.

Your Mandate

Let not many of you become teachers, my brethren, knowing that as such we will incur a stricter judgment (James 3:1).

Christian educators — those of you who serve in Sunday schools
and elementary Christian schools — our hats go off to you for your
sincere devotion to this next generation. At the same time, we have to
make an honest evaluation of the effectiveness of your efforts. What
you are doing is not working as it should. It's not getting through and
it's not doing the job. We know you are in a key position to make major
changes in the lives of your students. You are the M*A*S*H unit on
the front lines of this disease. You are the nurses and the doctors that
are positioned to counter the epidemic, and you *must* begin to defend
the Word with your pupils at a very young age. You must teach them
how to defend themselves and the Word of God in a secular world and
show them how the Bible connects to the real world.

Students are not being taught how to defend their faith, how to
answer skeptical questions, how to answer the questions of this age
concerning the age of the earth/evolution, etc. We know that many of
you are handed pre-made lesson plans. We know that you probably
haven't been trained in how to teach apologetics yourselves. We know
that many of you may even be harboring doubts of your own. It doesn't
have to be that way.

Action Points

- **Humble yourself before God**. Ask for His guidance and
  place your dependence fully on Him to lead you and empower you for the ministry that He entrusted to you. Shine

the light of God's Word into your heart and test whether you have stood on the Bible as the absolute authority, or whether you have compromised. The Lord forgives. Pray for the courage to take the stand you need to, always remembering:

> But whoever causes one of these little ones who believe in Me to stumble, it would be better for him to have a heavy millstone hung around his neck, and to be drowned in the depth of the sea (Matt. 18:6).

- **Make your own spiritual life a priority.** Far too often, faithful Christian educators are trying to feed their students when their own plate is empty. Take the time to pamper yourself spiritually. Read the Word for yourself. Prioritize nurturing times of prayer and meditation with the Lord. Study carefully the Word of God and allow the Holy Spirit to minister to your soul. Relevant books dealing with how to understand apologetics arguments for today's world, and how to logically argue the Christian faith against the skeptical questions of this era, are now available. Diligently prepare yourself for the task. Take care of yourself first and then God will work through you to take care of your students.

- **Take responsibility.** Your pastor is probably burned out and distracted with other things. Your Christian education director is probably relieved just to have you filling a spot in the program. But it's really God who's put you in this position, and you need to take full responsibility for what you're teaching and how you are teaching it. With sensitivity and determination you can also become a change agent in your program.

- **Get trained.** I know that most of you are volunteers, but you need to become pros. A tremendous amount of dynamic and encouraging training materials are available to you, no matter what your specific responsibility is in the Christian education system. Find a book; watch a DVD; go to a conference . . . your ministry will be the better because of it. Learn how to communicate to the age group you are dealing with.

- **Get armed to the hilt with solid curriculum.** With good materials, the devoted Christian educator becomes a very powerful influencer for truth. A lady who worked for a Christian publishing company that published Sunday school curricula once said to me, "You would love our Sunday school curricula. We teach the children that Genesis is true, and that there really was a global Flood. The students learn that Noah and the animals went on board the ark and came off the ark after the Flood. We make sure we tell the students this was a real event. Isn't that great?"

My response shocked her. I asked, "Tell me, did the curriculum actually teach the account of the Flood as real history — or just a story? Do you know one of the most asked questions concerning Noah and the ark? Did you explain how Noah could fit all the animals on the ark? [That is one of the skeptical comments of our day by which people claim the account of the Noah's ark cannot be true.] Tell me, did you connect the ark/Flood account to biology? Did you explain to them that Noah only took representative kinds of land animals on board the ark? [He would only need two of the dog kind, not all the dog varieties we see today; only two of the elephant kind; only two of the horse kind; two of the camel kind; and so on.] Did you teach them answers to the skeptical questions of the day to show them that they can defend the Christian faith against the skeptics of this age? Did you teach them from a perspective of apologetics, preparing them for the age they live in, for what they will be taught at school, for the skeptical questions about the Bible they will be confronted with — or did you just teach it to them as a *story*? Did you connect the Flood to the fossils? Did you prepare them for what they will hear on TV and at school concerning millions of years? Did you teach them that the fossils could not have been laid down millions of years before Adam sinned? Did you explain that the Flood makes sense of most of the fossil record? Did you connect the Flood to geology . . . or did you just teach the account as a *story*?"

These are just some of the questions in relation to the topic of the Flood and Noah's ark — but one would have to do much the same sort of thing with every topic. In other words, for each subject:

1. Define the skeptical questions of this age that are leveled against this particular account from the Bible.

2. Teach students how to answer these questions.

3. Find ways we can connect this account with the real world; for example, archaeology, biology, anthropology, astronomy, and geology.

4. Explore the practical application that can be made.

5. Ensure students understand historical events as real history, doctrine, etc., from this passage.

6. Explain to students how it all relates to biblical authority and the gospel.

7. Where possible, connect the topic back to Genesis — you may be surprised at how easy this will come to you once you begin to do it.

- **Teach Bible history, not Bible stories**. The point is, most Sunday school material just teaches stories! Most Sunday school teachers don't know how to answer the skeptical questions of the day. Sunday school is not preparing the children for what they will be taught at school; it is not preparing them to be able to defend the Christian faith. Most curricula ignores apologetics and just teaches (maybe in a more contemporary way perhaps) basic Bible stories — spiritual and moral matters. Most such teaching does not connect the Bible to the real world. And sadly, in most instances, children are either actively told to believe what they are taught at school, or by default, they are led to believe that this is what they must do.

Often those kids who attend Sunday school will ask their Sunday school teachers (or pastors and/or parents) about millions of years, or dinosaurs and associated topics, wanting an answer from an authority figure who represents, in their eyes, Christianity and the Bible. And what do they hear?

Sadly, in the majority of instances, the Sunday school teachers will tell them that that is not a topic for Sunday school/church — and/or just believe the Bible regardless — and/or they can believe in millions of years and evolution as long as they trust in Jesus. The most important thing as far as the teacher is concerned is that the students trust in Jesus — those questions the students asked about origins issues aren't that important. It doesn't matter what one believes about Genesis.

Not only do I know this from years of experience in the biblical creation apologetics ministry, but it is obvious from the plethora of Sunday school curricula, Bible study and youth curricula, and children's books. Most such resources either allow for millions of years of evolution, or just teach the Genesis account as Bible stories, not dealing with issues of the fossils, the age of the earth, and associated topics. Or they teach that there are different views on Genesis and it doesn't matter what one believes, or they ignore Genesis altogether.

And by the way, the word "story" actually means "fairy tale" — and in today's world, most people really do think "fairy tale" when they hear the word "story." We have got to stop telling kids today we are going to read them or teach them a "Bible story." We have to use different terms like "this *account* of . . ." or something similar to help them understand this is *real* history.

Remember, one of your major objectives is to help students make a link between their faith and fact. That's going to require that you bring historical (and observational) science back into the Church and back into your Sunday schools. You *can* help your students make a connection between the Bible and reality. Whatever you do, don't teach Bible "stories." Teach Bible *history*. Use real maps, real artifacts, and real illustrations of what really happened. Most of the pictures we present to our children look like cartoon fairy tales. Even the pictures that we present of Noah's ark make it look like an overgrown bathtub with animals' heads sticking out of the windows. We are not presenting Noah's ark as it really might have looked. We aren't making it look like a real boat. Make it as real as it really was.

For a list of recommended resources, see appendix 5.

To the Youth Pastor

Your Call

Defend the Word.
Live the Word.

Your Mandate

Train up a child in the way he should go, even when he is old he will not depart from it (Prov. 22:6).

Still, one of the most striking findings from the research is the broad base of opportunities that Christian churches in America have to work with teenagers. Overall, more than four out of five teens say they have attended a church for a period of at least two months during their teenage years (81%). This represents substantial penetration and significant prospects for influencing the nation's 24 million teens. —Barna Research.[5]

---

5. www.barna.org/...teensnext.../147-most-twentysomethings-put-christianity-on-the-shelf-following-spiritually-active-teen-years.

Those of you who work with teenagers are standing at the threshold of adulthood for teenagers who have grown up in the Church. Think about that for a moment. They are about to step out that door of the church, and approximately 60 percent of them will not come back after they leave your ministry. Are your students already gone? Kinnaman suggests a new test for a "successful" teen ministry:

> Much of the ministry to teenagers in America needs an over-haul — not because churches fail to attract significant numbers of young people, but because so much of those efforts are not creating a sustainable faith beyond high school. There are certainly effective youth ministries across the country, but the levels of disengagement among twentysomethings suggest that youth ministry fails too often at discipleship and faith formation. A new standard for viable youth ministry should be — not the number of attendees, the sophistication of the events, or the "cool" factor of the youth group — but whether teens have the commitment, passion, and resources to pursue Christ intentionally and whole-heartedly after they leave the youth ministry nest.[6]

That's probably something you don't get a chance to think about much. Many of you are fresh out of college and are thrust into churches that expect you to implement a "get them to come no matter what" approach. You're being paid to bring kids in and to keep them occupied. Fun, music, and entertainment can quickly become the focus of your creativity. (Defending the Word and living the Word become secondary priorities.) You have more to offer than that. You're strategically placed during a strategic time of life, and you can make a powerful difference that lasts a lifetime if you're willing to look past your attendance figures on a Wednesday night.

Action Points

- **Get on your knees and recommit yourself to effective ministry.** You may have to repent for trying to seek the approval

---

6. Ibid.

of other people rather than doing what you know God has called you to do. You may have to ask for forgiveness for compromising the Word of God in order to make your ministry attractive and fun for your students. Repent of all that, and ask God to lead you in a new and everlasting way.

- **Equip your parents.** This might be the most important thing you can do. Make "parental training" part of your job description and then go for it. I know this isn't a new thought, but how many youth pastors actually prioritize this type of strategic ministry? Work in conjunction with your Christian educators so that you can raise up an army of parents who can disciple and train their own kids from the cradle to graduation.

- **Develop teenagers' abilities to contemplate and develop their own personal worldview.** Most likely, your students are already being bombarded with secular influences. You can teach them how to defend the Word, and how to live the Word in an antagonistic, anti-Christian world.

For a list of recommended resources, see appendix 6.

To the Pastor

Your Call

Defend the Word.
Live the Word.

Your Mandate

I solemnly charge you in the presence of God and of Christ Jesus, who is to judge the living and the dead, and by His appearing and His Kingdom: preach the word; be ready in season and out of season; reprove, rebuke, exhort, with great patience and instruction. For the time will come when they will not endure sound doctrine; but wanting to have their ears tickled, they will accumulate for themselves teachers in accordance to their own desires, and will turn away their ears from the truth and will turn aside to myths (2 Tim. 4:1–4).

For the equipping of the saints for the work of service, to the building up of the body of Christ; until we all attain to the unity of the faith, and of the knowledge of the Son of God (Eph. 4:12–13).

Okay, pastors, now it's your turn. Its inventory time; it's honesty time. It's time to look inside your heart and inside your church and let God do a surprise inspection so you can face the statistical facts that came out of this study. Perhaps your church is one of the rare exceptions, but if it's not, you need to wake up and smell the coffee. You must be willing to suck up your pride and take some responsibility. *Two out of three of the teenagers who grew up in your church are already gone.* Is that "just the way it is," or is there something you can, should, and must be doing? Ask yourself these important questions:

1. Am I preaching the Word of God?

2. Am I defending the Word of God?

3. Am I and my church living the Word of God or am I perpetuating a religious institution that is trapped in tradition?

4. Have I compromised the Word, particularly in Genesis, and unwittingly undermined biblical authority to those who are already gone and those who will go?

5. Have I ensured that all the teaching curricula in the various church programs really is reaching the kids and parents where they are today? Is it just reaching the "Jew" or is it reaching the "Greeks"?

6. Have I allowed a philosophy to make the church look more like the world to try to attract people, instead of teaching relevant answers the world needs?

7. Is music the priority in the church or is teaching the Word the priority?

The answer to the first question might surprise you. After all the churches that he has surveyed, Britt believes that, if you're lucky, 20 percent of your congregation walks away feeling spiritually uplifted on a given Sunday morning. Let's face it: most people are tired of milk-toast messages. They want the real thing; they want to hear from the Scriptures that are living and active and sharper than any two-edged sword. The temptation is to back off the meat and potatoes and feed them sugar and spice — something that is exciting, dynamic, and entertaining. That might hold them for the moment, but in the long run it sacrifices your relevancy. People get bored; they wish for something that connects to the real world . . . and they fade away even more. When they come to your church hungry on a Sunday morning, do you give them a healthy dose of meat? Or do they only walk away with a temporary sweet taste on their tongue that will not last past noon?

All week long, those who attend your church are bombarded in their workplace and in the media by messages that undermine the authority of God's Word, particularly the Genesis accounts. Do you regularly defend God's Word from the pulpit? Have you equipped those sitting in the pews to give an answer for the hope that is in them? This is something that must be done. You may need to get out of your little Christian bubble for a while to understand what we are really talking about. Sit in a fast-food restaurant at lunchtime and listen to the high school students talking. Go stand by the water cooler in the break room of a major corporation and listen to the talk of the secretaries during break. It's a rough world out there. The people who come to find some rest and relief on Sunday are fighting a major battle against ungodly influences the other six days of the week. Are you giving them what they need to survive and thrive in the world? Have you ever really sat down with the young people and asked them questions to see at what point they are, what they really believe, and what the stumbling blocks are to their faith? You will find (if you ask the right questions) that millions of years and questions about science and Genesis are major issues with them.

And, have you become a slave to man-made religious traditions that are imprisoning your congregation and dictating your ministry? I think there's a good chance that you have . . . and I am so, so sorry about that. Countless pastors begin their ministry with the hope and the expectation that they will be a part of an authentic body of believers who experience the simplicity and purity of devotion to Christ. But usually the pastors themselves become casualties of burnout from man-made religious institutions that place huge burdens and expectations on their leaders. That's reality, but thankfully there are things that you can do about it.

Action Points

- **Reevaluate your call.** The demands on you as a pastor can quickly destroy your vision and purpose in ministry. I would challenge you to back off a little bit and rethink who you are, what you are doing, and why you are doing it. It might be time to dust off those distant dreams you had for vibrant ministry back in seminary. It might be time for a sabbatical. It is definitely time to make some radical changes in the way you do church.

- **Simplify and clarify your objectives.** Your primary call is to defend God's Word and live by God's Word. Your mandate is to preach the Word and to equip others to minister and live by the Word. It might be time to take a day or two and get away with a blank legal pad and your Bible and rethink what that means for you and your church. Are you just teaching about heavenly things — relationships, spiritual, and moral things? Have you ignored the "earthly things"?

- **Draw some lines in the sand.** If your ministry is driven by denominational and congregational expectations rather than Scripture, any changes that you make will expose you to pressure and complaint from those who feel safe with the status quo. It's likely that a certain faction within your church will think it's time for you to leave. You will likely need to draw some lines in the sand and say, "God's taking us in a new direction here. If you don't like it, it might be time for *you* to leave." Only you can decide whether or not it's worth the fight, but let me tell you that I've visited thousands of churches and I know that there *are* some things worth fighting for, and a vibrant new vision for unleashing God's Word in the local church is always preferable to a slow, draining, inevitable death of a congregation that is stuck in its old ways. You're likely to lose some people. But don't worry; chances are there is another irrelevant, anemic church building with plenty of empty pews just down the block. Give them the freedom to take the hike.

And if you do take a strong stand on Genesis, and accept no compromise, and begin teaching creation and general biblical apologetics, you will most likely receive complaints. Certain people who have compromised on these issues themselves (maybe a scientist, or teacher, or doctor) will say they will leave if you continue with such things. There will be pressure regarding financial support for the church — but what is more important? Isn't the priority the authority of Scripture and the teaching of the Word? God wants us to be faithful to the Word.

- **Defend the Word.** If you haven't taught good apologetics to your church, if you haven't equipped your Christian educators to do the same, you're in for a wonderful surprise: people love this stuff! It affirms their faith; it emboldens their witness; it helps them make a tangible connection between faith and fact. As many have said to us, "This makes the Bible so real!" Apologetics is one of the most life-giving things that you can inject into the veins of your church. A regular injection of Bible-defending, faith-affirming scientific and historical evidence will add new life to both you and your congregation. Don't hold back. They really want to have answers to the questions that cause them to doubt.

- **Teach the Word**. People want meat; they want something that is relevant; they want the Word of God. You need to understand that, and you are responsible for that. Period. Sure, you might lose some people who don't really believe the Bible in the first place, but you know what? You might as well speed up the process, because they are already gone.

- **Teach about the Word**. People want to know that "Jesus loves me." But quite frankly, because "the Bible tells me so" isn't going to be enough anymore. Before people will see the Bible as relevant, you need to teach them that it is authoritative and accurate. For example, does your congregation know what it means that the Bible is "inspired by God"? Some of our survey results would indicate that many people weren't even sure what that means. Many seem to think that that meant that the Bible was "inspirational," because many of them indicated that they believe the words of the Bible came from the wisdom of men and not from the declaration of God. You need to communicate to them what it means when we say that the Bible is "God breathed." They need general Bible apologetics as well as sound exegetical teaching.

- **Teach about the Church.** Our survey showed that 38 percent of the people who have left the Church still believe that the Bible is true, and yet the Church is not relevant enough to them to get them out of bed on Sunday morning. This reflects the failure of the Church to excite their young people by breathing life into the Scriptures. Christians need fellowship of other Christians in order to be able to grow spiritually and to be taught about Christian life. Too often, these young people view the Church through the hypocrisy of the Church leaders, and thus ignore those leaders' teachings.

- **Back off on the entertainment factor.** I recognize that you pastors are dealing with a number of different pressures. Fiscal responsibilities can place tremendous expectations upon you to bring in new people quickly and keep the ones that you have. The temptation is to go for the easy fix and focus on creating a church experience that is exciting, dynamic, and entertaining. Far too often this is done at the expense of legitimate community and the preaching of God's Word. What is the long-term result of a short-term fix? You sacrifice your relevancy. Because you're only feeding them sweet things that tickle their tongues, their hunger is rarely satisfied. They quickly come back expecting another bigger and better sugar fix. Deep inside, however, they really want some meat. And yet what do you do to keep their attention? You make your message even shorter and even more entertaining. Usually the emphasis turns more toward music, but that's a mistake. (Only 1 percent of the 1,000 young adults that we surveyed left the Church because of the music. A significant portion of those who left reported that they really did miss the preaching of God's Word.) Pretty soon this starts to spiral downward until you really are communicating nothing of substance and the Bible takes the back shelf in the church service.

- **Pass the torch.** Rather than just hoping the teenagers are going to come back after they graduate, why not put them in charge? Let's be honest, there are many things that we can do to make our churches more culturally relevant to the 20-something generation. Nobody knows how to do this more intuitively than they do. I would highly recommend commissioning a group of trusted elders who will walk alongside teens and mentor, disciple, and equip them to be unleashed in ministry to their own generation. While never compromising Scripture, they just might totally reinvent what "church" looks like for the upcoming generation. They will no doubt need training in apologetics so they can pass that information on.

Yes, desperate times require desperate actions. And the situation in the Church today, as we have shown, is critical and its future impact is at great risk. The exciting thing is that the decisions and commitment of a few can begin the healing process that stops the epidemic and infuses new life and vitality into the lives of 20-somethings and those who will follow in their footsteps. Parents, Christian educators, youth pastors, and pastors hold in their hands the medicine that can bring the cure to this spreading epidemic of apathy and disengagement.

One thousand 20-somethings have revealed the answer. They have shared why they have walked away. We now know what we can do. There is a solution. The question is now one of commitment to the "cure."

Are you willing to administer the "medicine" to those who need it so desperately?

For a list of recommended resources, see appendix 7.

Final Thoughts

Britain has lost its Christian soul. In this post-Christendom Britain, we cannot afford to neglect prayerful and spirit-led strategies for long-term change, for there is much work to be done.
— The Rev. Joel Edwards,
head of the Evangelical Alliance in England[7]

Recently I was made aware of another collection of photos of churches that had become "redundant" — useless leftovers that were not needed to fulfill their intended purpose.

---

7. 2005 Evangelical Alliance, http://www.eauk.org/resources/info/statistics/2005 englishchurchcensus.cfm.

A former Methodist church built in 1839 now houses the Historical Society of Amherst, New Hampshire.

A church building now serving as a business, Cabinet Press, located in Milford, New Hampshire.

A church facility in Milford, New Hampshire, that is now the home of Musical Instrument String Superstore.

Master An's Martial Arts College in Bedford, New Hampshire.

Repurposed church building which is the Town Hall of Auburn, New Hampshire

There's just one major difference between these churches and the ones we contemplated at the beginning of this book: these churches are not in England. They are in New England. As England is, so we will be if we don't take strategic action now. American Christianity could be on the edge of obsolescence in less than two generations. The epidemic is continuing to spread and will do so unless something is done.

But may I leave you with a different kind of vision? Consider the possibilities of a revolution, a reformation, and a renovation of church as we know it in America today. What if our churches were to truly become gatherings of individuals who defend God's Word and live by God's Word? Imagine the potential as millions of Bible-believing Christians in this country evaluate their own lives, their own families, their own churches, and their own country, and begin to strategically do their part by allowing God to use them in any way that He sees fit to protect the vital Body of Christ and to reach out to those who have left her and those who meet her.

Throughout human history, the course of human events has been turned many, many times by those who see what is, who see what is coming, and who lay down their lives to alter the course of the future for the betterment of all. Our country has forsaken its Christian soul. We need to see that for what it is and take action in prayerful and biblically based strategies.

Again, we call for a new reformation. In a sense (symbolically), we need to be nailing Genesis 1–11 on the doors of churches (akin to what Martin Luther did), seminaries, and Christian and Bible colleges, to call the Church back to the authority of the Word of God. In this era of history, we really "lost" that authority beginning in Genesis; that is where we need to reestablish it. When the Church gets back to the authority of the Word of God, then it can be the salt and light to influence the culture with God's Word to change hearts and minds — and consequently change the culture.

Martin Luther is purported to have stated:

If I profess with the loudest voice and clearest exposition every portion of the Word of God except precisely that little point which the world and the devil are at that moment attacking, I am not confessing Christ, however boldly I may be professing Him. Where the battle rages there the loyalty of the soldier is proved; and to be steady on all the battle front besides, is mere flight and disgrace if he flinches at that point.[8]

May the Lord bless you and keep you, may He cause His face to shine upon you and give you strength. Regardless of what the future holds for us, our families, our church, and our world, may we have the joy of knowing that we defended His Word and lived His Word for His glory and the sake of those He has chosen.

---

8. *Luther's Works.* Weimar Edition. Briefwechsel [Correspondence], vol. 3, p 81f., as translated by Dr. Werner Gitt from the German.

Appendix 1 — The Survey

Aggregate Answers

(Note: This is a sampling of the questions and answers from the study. It is not comprehensive because of space limitations, and is taken from an 18-page summary compiled at the conclusion of the study. For clarity, the definition of these numerical columns and the methodology of their calculation is given below.)

Frequency is the actual number of people who gave a specific response to the question. Cumulative Frequency (CF) is equal to the total number of people who gave that response plus all prior responses to the question which adds up to the total number of interviews conducted. Percent represents the percentage of people who gave that specific response to a question. Cumulative Percent (CP) is equal to the total percentage of people who gave that response plus all prior responses to the question which adds up to 100 percent.

Age?	FREQUENCY	CF	PERCENT	CP
25–29	528	528	52.8	52.8
20–24	472	1000	47.2	100

Regularly attend church when growing up — but never/seldom go today?	FREQUENCY	CF	PERCENT	CP
Yes	1000	1000	100	100

IF REGULARLY ATTENDED — Which church denomination did you attend?	FREQUENCY	CF	PERCENT	CP
Baptist Church	260	260	26	26
Lutheran	136	396	13.6	39.6
Church of God	84	480	8.4	48
Christian Church	72	552	7.2	55.2
Pentecostal	69	621	6.9	62.1
Church of Christ	69	690	6.9	69
Assembly of God	66	756	6.6	75.6
Non-denominational	61	817	6.1	81.7
Presbyterian	44	861	4.4	86.1
Community Church	38	899	3.8	89.9
Calvary Chapel	32	931	3.2	93.1
Bible Church	29	960	2.9	96
Christian and Missionary Alliance	17	977	1.7	97.7
Evangelical Free Church	15	992	1.5	99.2
Brethren	8	1000	0.8	100

Did you attend church regularly during elementary/middle school years?

	FREQUENCY	CF	PERCENT	CP
Yes	946	946	94.6	94.6
No	54	1000	5.4	100

Did you attend church regularly during high school?

	FREQUENCY	CF	PERCENT	CP
Yes	561	561	56.1	56.1
No	439	1000	43.9	100

Did you attend church regularly throughout your college days?

	FREQUENCY	CF	PERCENT	CP
No	530	530	53	53
Did not attend college	356	886	35.6	88.6
Yes	114	1000	11.4	100

Why have you stopped attending church?	FREQUENCY	CF	PERCENT	CP
Boring service	119	119	11.9	11.9
Legalism	117	236	11.7	23.6
Hypocrisy — leaders	111	347	11.1	34.7
Too political	98	445	9.8	44.5
Self-righteous people	92	537	9.2	53.7
Distance from home	75	612	7.5	61.2
Not relevant personally	63	675	6.3	67.5
God would not condemn to hell	57	732	5.7	73.2
Bible not relevant	50	782	5	78.2
Not find preferred denomination in area	50	832	5	83.2
Not feel worthy	42	874	4.2	87.4
No time	29	903	2.9	90.3
Don't know	24	927	2.4	92.7
Hypocrisy — parents	20	947	2	94.7
Bible not true	16	963	1.6	96.3
Unfriendly people	11	974	1.1	97.4
Music is poor	10	984	1	98.4
Misc	6	990	0.6	99
Unsure my belief	5	995	0.5	99.5
Just quit going	3	998	0.3	99.8
Always ask for money	2	1000	0.2	100

Did you often attend Sunday school?	FREQUENCY	CF	PERCENT	CP
Yes	606	606	60.6	60.6
No	394	1000	39.4	100

IF OFTEN ATTENDED SUNDAY SCHOOL — Feel Sunday school lessons were helpful?	FREQUENCY	CF	PERCENT	CP
Yes	436	436	71.95	71.95
No answer	394	436	0	71.95
No	114	550	18.81	90.76
Don't know	56	606	9.24	100

IF OFTEN ATTENDED SUNDAY SCHOOL — Did you attend to see friends?	FREQUENCY	CF	PERCENT	CP
No answer	394	0	0	0
No	336	336	55.45	55.45
Yes	261	597	43.07	98.51
Don't know	9	606	1.49	100

IF OFTEN ATTENDED SUNDAY SCHOOL — Feel lessons close to/different from school?	FREQUENCY	CF	PERCENT	CP
Very different	430	430	70.96	70.96
No answer	394	430	0	70.96
Close to what taught	176	606	29.04	100

IF OFTEN ATTENDED SUNDAY SCHOOL — Did classes teach that Bible was true?	FREQUENCY	CF	PERCENT	CP
Yes	569	569	93.89	93.89
No answer	394	569	0	93.89
Don't know	32	601	5.28	99.17
No	5	606	0.83	100

IF OFTEN ATTENDED SUNDAY SCHOOL — Did classes teach Bible could be defended?	FREQUENCY	CF	PERCENT	CP
No answer	394	0	0	0
Yes	344	344	56.77	56.77
No	167	511	27.56	84.32
Don't know	95	606	15.68	100

In high school, attend public/Christian/charter/home/Catholic?

	FREQUENCY	CF	PERCENT	CP
Public school	859	859	85.9	85.9
Christian school	69	928	6.9	92.8
Home school	34	962	3.4	96.2
Charter school	32	994	3.2	99.4
Catholic school	6	1000	0.6	100

Have instructors who taught that earth was millions of years old?

	FREQUENCY	CF	PERCENT	CP
Yes	785	785	78.5	78.5
No	192	977	19.2	97.7
Don't know	23	1000	2.3	100

Have instructors who taught that life evolved from lower forms?

	FREQUENCY	CF	PERCENT	CP
Yes	591	591	59.1	59.1
No	335	926	33.5	92.6
Don't know	74	1000	7.4	100

Because of school experience, leave high school believing Bible less true?

	FREQUENCY	CF	PERCENT	CP
No	670	670	67	67
Yes	278	948	27.8	94.8
Don't know	52	1000	5.2	100

Does the Bible contain errors?	FREQUENCY	CF	PERCENT	CP
Yes	397	397	39.7	39.7
Don't know	304	701	30.4	70.1
No	299	1000	29.9	100

IF CONTAINS ERRORS — Can you identify one of those errors for me?

	FREQUENCY	CF	PERCENT	CP
No answer	603	0	0	0
Alleged contradictions	88	88	22.17	22.17
Writers made mistake	73	161	18.39	40.55
Unsaved go to hell	64	225	16.12	56.68
No	51	276	12.85	69.52
Wrong about earth's age	40	316	10.08	79.6
Too much suffering and death	23	339	5.79	85.39

Genesis disproved by science	21	360	5.29	90.68
Miracles do not occur	10	370	2.52	93.2
Never was a global flood	8	378	2.02	95.21
Christ not really God	7	385	1.76	96.98
Trinity does not make sense	6	391	1.51	98.49
There is a hell	5	396	1.26	99.75
Misc	1	397	0.25	100

Do your parents still attend church regularly?	FREQUENCY	CF	PERCENT	CP
Yes	717	717	71.7	71.7
No	273	990	27.3	99
Don't know	10	1000	1	100

When you were younger, did your parents force you to go to church?	FREQUENCY	CF	PERCENT	CP
Yes	610	610	61	61
No	385	995	38.5	99.5
Don't know	5	1000	0.5	100

Do your closest friends attend church regularly right now?	FREQUENCY	CF	PERCENT	CP
No	649	649	64.9	64.9
Yes	337	986	33.7	98.6
Don't know	14	1000	1.4	100

Have any of your friends invited you to go back to church w/them?	FREQUENCY	CF	PERCENT	CP
No	505	505	50.5	50.5
Yes	479	984	47.9	98.4
Don't know	16	1000	1.6	100

Do you feel good people don't need to go to church?	FREQUENCY	CF	PERCENT	CP
No	562	562	56.2	56.2
Yes	352	914	35.2	91.4
Don't know	86	1000	8.6	100

Do you feel people w/college education less likely attend church?

	FREQUENCY	CF	PERCENT	CP
No	700	700	70	70
Yes	181	881	18.1	88.1
Don't know	119	1000	11.9	100

IF LESS LIKELY — Feel those w/college education influenced by professors?

	FREQUENCY	CF	PERCENT	CP
No answer	819	0	0	0
Yes	142	142	78.45	78.45
No	25	167	13.81	92.27
Don't know	14	181	7.73	100

Believe all the accounts/stories in the Bible are true/accurate?

	FREQUENCY	CF	PERCENT	CP
No	435	435	43.5	43.5
Yes	383	818	38.3	81.8
Don't know	182	1000	18.2	100

IF DON'T BELIEVE — What made you begin to doubt the Bible?

	FREQUENCY	CF	PERCENT	CP
No answer	565	0	0	0
Written by men	106	106	24.37	24.37
Not translated correctly	80	186	18.39	42.76
Contradicts itself	64	250	14.71	57.47
Science shows earth old	60	310	13.79	71.26
Bible has errors	48	358	11.03	82.3
Can't be a God with so much suffering	30	388	6.9	89.2
Christians don't live according to Bible	24	412	5.52	94.71
Evolution shows Bible cannot be trusted	19	431	4.37	99.08
Don't know	2	433	0.46	99.54
Misc	2	435	0.46	100

IF DON'T BELIEVE — When did you first have doubts?

	FREQUENCY	CF	PERCENT	CP
No answer	565	0	0	0
High school	190	190	43.68	43.68
Middle school	173	363	39.77	83.45
College	46	409	10.57	94.02
Elementary school	19	428	4.37	98.39
Don't know	7	435	1.61	100

Do you believe all the books of the Bible are inspired by God?

	FREQUENCY	CF	PERCENT	CP
Yes	617	617	61.7	61.7
No	211	828	21.1	82.8
Don't know	172	1000	17.2	100

Believe other holy books like the Koran are inspired by God?

	FREQUENCY	CF	PERCENT	CP
No	564	564	56.4	56.4
Don't know	291	855	29.1	85.5
Yes	145	1000	14.5	100

Believe in creation as stated in the Bible or in evolution?

	FREQUENCY	CF	PERCENT	CP
Biblical creation	718	718	71.8	71.8
Evolution	282	1000	28.2	100

Do you feel the Church is relevant to your needs today?

	FREQUENCY	CF	PERCENT	CP
Yes	469	469	46.9	46.9
No	437	906	43.7	90.6
Don't know	94	1000	9.4	100

IF NOT RELEVANT — In what way do you feel church is not fulfilling your needs?

	FREQUENCY	CF	PERCENT	CP
No answer	563	0	0	0
Not feeling closer to God there	143	143	32.72	32.72
Not practical	102	245	23.34	56.06
Not meeting emotional needs	95	340	21.74	77.8
Don't learn about more God	55	395	12.59	90.39
Not establishing friendships at church	18	413	4.12	94.51
Bible not true	10	423	2.29	96.8
Don't know	6	429	1.37	98.17
Misc	6	435	1.37	99.54
Not telling truth there	2	437	0.46	100

Do you believe in the creation of Adam & Eve and Garden of Eden?

	FREQUENCY	CF	PERCENT	CP
Yes	749	749	74.9	74.9
No	186	935	18.6	93.5
Don't know	65	1000	6.5	100

Believe Adam & Eve sinned and were expelled from the Garden?

	FREQUENCY	CF	PERCENT	CP
YES	748	748	74.8	74.8
No	165	913	16.5	91.3
Don't know	87	1000	8.7	100

Believe in story of Sodom & Gomorrah — Lot's wife turned to salt?

	FREQUENCY	CF	PERCENT	CP
Yes	618	618	61.8	61.8
No	256	874	25.6	87.4
Don't know	126	1000	12.6	100

Do you believe in Noah's ark and the global Flood?

	FREQUENCY	CF	PERCENT	CP
Yes	773	773	77.3	77.3
No	153	926	15.3	92.6
Don't know	74	1000	7.4	100

Do you believe there was a Tower of Babel as recorded in Genesis?

	FREQUENCY	CF	PERCENT	CP
Yes	631	631	63.1	63.1
No	196	827	19.6	82.7
Don't know	173	1000	17.3	100

Do you believe the earth is less than 10,000 years old?

	FREQUENCY	CF	PERCENT	CP
No	571	571	57.1	57.1
Don't know	224	795	22.4	79.5
Yes	205	1000	20.5	100

Has secular science dating the earth 6 billion years caused you to doubt Bible?

	FREQUENCY	CF	PERCENT	CP
Yes	464	464	46.4	46.4
No	424	888	42.4	88.8
Don't know	112	1000	11.2	100

Believe that God used evolution to change one kind of animal to another?

	FREQUENCY	CF	PERCENT	CP
No	562	562	56.2	56.2
Yes	239	801	23.9	80.1
Don't know	199	1000	19.9	100

Do you believe that humans evolved from an ape-like ancestor?

	FREQUENCY	CF	PERCENT	CP
No	543	543	54.3	54.3
Yes	301	844	30.1	84.4
Don't know	156	1000	15.6	100

Do you believe God used evolution to create human beings?

	FREQUENCY	CF	PERCENT	CP
No	608	608	60.8	60.8
Yes	222	830	22.2	83
Don't know	170	1000	17	100

Did pastor/Sunday school teacher teach Christians could believe Darwin?

	FREQUENCY	CF	PERCENT	CP
No	789	789	78.9	78.9
Don't know	116	905	11.6	90.5
Yes	95	1000	9.5	100

Ever teach that Christians could believe earth millions/billions years old?

	FREQUENCY	CF	PERCENT	CP
No	592	592	59.2	59.2
Yes	266	858	26.6	85.8
Don't know	142	1000	14.2	100

Ever teach that God created earth in six days, each 24 hours long?

	FREQUENCY	CF	PERCENT	CP
Yes	826	826	82.6	82.6
No	110	936	11	93.6
Don't know	64	1000	6.4	100

Ever teach that the Book of Genesis was a myth or legend?

	FREQUENCY	CF	PERCENT	CP
No	857	857	85.7	85.7
Don't know	76	933	7.6	93.3
Yes	67	1000	6.7	100

Believe Joseph was sold into slavery & became Pharaoh's closest advisor?

	FREQUENCY	CF	PERCENT	CP
Yes	534	534	53.4	53.4
Don't know	264	798	26.4	79.8
No	202	1000	20.2	100

Is there one idea you question more than the rest?

	FREQUENCY	CF	PERCENT	CP
No	415	415	41.5	41.5
Earth is young not old	298	713	29.8	71.3
Days of creation were 24-hour days	134	847	13.4	84.7
Really was Adam/Eve	116	963	11.6	96.3
Really was Noah's Flood	37	1000	3.7	100

Would you say questioning was beginning of your doubt in the Bible?

	FREQUENCY	CF	PERCENT	CP
No answer	412	0	0	0
Yes	327	327	55.61	55.61
No	183	510	31.12	86.73
Don't know	78	588	13.27	100

At what age did you begin to really question contents in Bible?

	FREQUENCY	CF	PERCENT	CP
High school years	457	457	45.7	45.7
Grades 7–9	293	750	29.3	75
Grades 4–6	128	878	12.8	87.8
Early college	112	990	11.2	99
Grades K–3	10	1000	1	100

Anything a teacher did/said that caused you to doubt the Bible?

	FREQUENCY	CF	PERCENT	CP
No	728	728	72.8	72.8
Evolution was true	119	847	11.9	84.7
Bible was attacked	60	907	6	90.7
Christians are hypocrites	38	945	3.8	94.5
Don't know	31	976	3.1	97.6
Atheism was true	9	985	0.9	98.5
Christians want to take over society	8	993	0.8	99.3
God described as unloving	7	1000	0.7	100

Did your parents' behavior influence you not to attend church?

	FREQUENCY	CF	PERCENT	CP
No	774	774	77.4	77.4
Yes	201	975	20.1	97.5
Don't know	25	1000	2.5	100

Do you expect to attend church regularly after you have children?

	FREQUENCY	CF	PERCENT	CP
Yes	381	381	38.1	38.1
No	322	703	32.2	70.3
Don't know	297	1000	29.7	100

IF ANY DENOMINATION — Why do you expect to attend this denomination?

	FREQUENCY	CF	PERCENT	CP
No answer	627	0	0	0
One I grew up with	170	170	45.58	45.58
Closest to my beliefs	116	286	31.1	76.68
Heard good things	30	316	8.04	84.72
Large denomination in area	29	345	7.77	92.49
Friend/relative is part of denomination	28	373	7.51	100

Do you attend any church services at Easter or Christmas?

	FREQUENCY	CF	PERCENT	CP
No	492	492	49.2	49.2
Both	235	727	23.5	72.7
Easter	163	890	16.3	89
Christmas	110	1000	11	100

IF DO NOT ATTEND — In what way do you view church today?

	FREQUENCY	CF	PERCENT	CP
No answer	508	0	0	0
Don't think of it at all	182	182	36.99	36.99
Hypocritical	89	271	18.09	55.08
Too political	69	340	14.02	69.11
Irrelevant	52	392	10.57	79.67
Boring	40	432	8.13	87.8
Caring	28	460	5.69	93.5
Social club	16	476	3.25	96.75
Loving environment	15	491	3.05	99.8
Misc	1	492	0.2	100

Is there any part of the church service that you miss today?

	FREQUENCY	CF	PERCENT	CP
Yes	500	500	50	50
No	454	954	45.4	95.4
Don't know	46	1000	4.6	100

IF MISS ANY PART - Which part do you still miss?	FREQUENCY	CF	PERCENT	CP
No answer	500	0	0	0
Worshiping God	103	103	20.6	20.6
Special events	96	199	19.2	39.8
Pastor's teaching	93	292	18.6	58.4
Outreach to community	77	369	15.4	73.8
Friends	68	437	13.6	87.4
Music	35	472	7	94.4
Sunday school class	27	499	5.4	99.8
Misc	1	500	0.2	100

Do you believe you are saved and will go to heaven upon death?	FREQUENCY	CF	PERCENT	CP
Yes	656	656	65.6	65.6
Don't know	208	864	20.8	86.4
No	136	1000	13.6	100

Do you believe you have become anti-church through the years?	FREQUENCY	CF	PERCENT	CP
No	608	608	60.8	60.8
Yes	343	951	34.3	95.1
Don't know	49	1000	4.9	100

Which of these make you question the Bible most?	FREQUENCY	CF	PERCENT	CP
None	326	326	32.6	32.6
Earth not less than10,000 years old	250	576	25	57.6
Too many rules	128	704	12.8	70.4
Creation account	121	825	12.1	82.5
Bible does not make sense of suffering/death	111	936	11.1	93.6
Miracles not true	29	965	2.9	96.5
Flood of Noah	24	989	2.4	98.9
Christ's divinity	11	1000	1.1	100

Is gay marriage morally acceptable?	FREQUENCY	CF	PERCENT	CP
No	741	741	74.1	74.1
Yes	164	905	16.4	90.5
Don't know	95	1000	9.5	100

Should abortion continue to be legal in most instances?

	FREQUENCY	CF	PERCENT	CP
No	488	488	48.8	48.8
Yes	380	868	38	86.8
Don't know	132	1000	13.2	100

Should science instructors be allowed to teach problems w/evolution?

	FREQUENCY	CF	PERCENT	CP
Yes	517	517	51.7	51.7
No	312	829	31.2	82.9
Don't know	171	1000	17.1	100

Should prayer be allowed in public schools?	FREQUENCY	CF	PERCENT	CP
Yes	718	718	71.8	71.8
No	178	896	17.8	89.6
Don't know	104	1000	10.4	100

Is premarital sex okay?	FREQUENCY	CF	PERCENT	CP
Yes	517	517	51.7	51.7
No	435	952	43.5	95.2
Don't know	48	1000	4.8	100

What is your family status?	FREQUENCY	CF	PERCENT	CP
Married/children	387	387	38.7	38.7
Single	296	683	29.6	68.3
Married	262	945	26.2	94.5
Single/children	55	1000	5.5	100

IF MARRIED — Were you married in a church?	FREQUENCY	CF	PERCENT	CP
Yes	454	454	69.95	69.95
No Answer	351	454	0	69.95
No	195	649	30.05	100

What is the last grade of school you have completed?	FREQUENCY	CF	PERCENT	CP
HS graduate	362	362	36.2	36.2
College graduate	328	690	32.8	69
Some college	256	946	25.6	94.6
Graduate school	44	990	4.4	99
Less than HS	10	1000	1	100

Combined income?	FREQUENCY	CF	PERCENT	CP
$50,000–$74,999	303	303	30.3	30.3
$36,000–$49,999	267	570	26.7	57
$24,000–$35,999	265	835	26.5	83.5
$15,000–$23,999	119	954	11.9	95.4
$75,000 and up	28	982	2.8	98.2
$6,000–$14,999	13	995	1.3	99.5
Under $6,000	5	1000	0.5	100

What is the occupation of the head of the household?	FREQUENCY	CF	PERCENT	CP
Blue collar	454	454	45.4	45.4
White collar	442	896	44.2	89.6
Government/military	52	948	5.2	94.8
Self-employed	41	989	4.1	98.9
Student/homemaker	9	998	0.9	99.8
Unemployed	2	1000	0.2	100

Location?	FREQUENCY	CF	PERCENT	CP
South Atlantic	180	180	18	18
E. North Central	170	350	17	35
Pacific	160	510	16	51
Middle	150	660	15	66
W. South Central	100	760	10	76
W. North Central	70	830	7	83
E. South Central	60	890	6	89
Mountain	60	950	6	95
New England	50	1000	5	100

Appendix 2 — The 15 Questions of Life

Can your child, your student or your church family answer the following questions?

In 1 Peter 3:15, God reveals the importance of being able to defend our belief in Christ, and as believers we do not need to fear engaging the culture of disbelief with the truth of God's purpose and vision for our lives.

Discover vital answers and starting points for these issues at:
www.answersingenesis.org/go/questionsoflife

1. Why am I here?
2. Who is God?
3. Who is Jesus and why is He the only path to salvation?
4. Why the Bible and not other holy books?
5. Why should the Bible be the authority in my life when making decisions and moral choices?
6. Why set boundaries on sexuality and marriage?
7. If we are descendents of one man and one woman where did all the different races come from?
8. How does one determine the value of a human life?
9. Dinosaurs and the Bible – how does that work?
10. What is wrong with the world (suffering and death) when God supposedly made everything perfect?
11. How can "what is wrong with the world" be made right?
12. Does "science" disprove or confirm history in the Bible?
13. Why does the age of the earth really matter to me and my life today?
14. Why is it important that I believe in a literal 6-day, 24-hour creation?
15. Did we evolve from apes-like creatures?

Appendix 3 — Resources for Upholding the Word

Books

- *More Than a Carpenter*, by Josh McDowell (Wheaton, IL: Tyndale House Publishers, 1977)
- *Always Ready*, by Greg Bahnsen (Powder Springs, GA: American Vision, 1996)
- *The Ultimate Proof of Creation*, by Jason Lisle (Green Forest, AR: Master Books, 2009)
- *The New Answers Book*, Vol. 1 and 2, Ken Ham, general editor (Green Forest, AR: Master Books, 2007 & 2008)
- *Ask Them Why*, by Jay Lucas (Schaumburg, IL: Regular Baptist Press, 2007)
- *Nothing but the Truth*, by Brian Edwards (Darlington, England: Evangelical Press, 2006)
- *The Young Earth*, by John Morris (Green Forest, AR: Master Books, 2007)
- *How Could a Loving God . . . ?* by Ken Ham (Green Forest, AR: Master Books, 2007)
- *The Answers Book for Kids*, Vols. 1, 2, 3, and 4, Ken Ham, editor (Green Forest, AR: Master Books, 2008)
- *The Long War Against God*, by Henry M. Morris (Green Forest, AR: Master Books, 2000)

Online Education

- Answers Education Online through Answers in Genesis website: answersingenesis.org/cec/courses/

Websites

- Answersingenesis.org
- ICR.org
- Creationresearch.org
- Christiananswers.net
- Masterbooks.net

DVDs

- Creation mini-series, Ken Ham (Answers in Genesis)
- How Do We Know the Bible Is True? Brian Edwards
- Creation: Science Confirms the Bible Is True, Jason Lisle (Answers in Genesis)
- God of Suffering, Tommy Mitchell (Answers in Genesis)
- Noah's Flood: Washing Away Millions of Years, Terry Mortenson (Answers in Genesis)
- Demolishing Strongholds DVD Curriculum (Answers in Genesis)

Appendix 4 — Resources for Parents

- *Raising Godly Children*, Ken Ham (Green Forest, AR: Master Books, 2008)
- *History Revealed Curriculum*, Diana Waring (Answers in Genesis)
- *Answers* Magazine: answersingenesis.org/articles/am
- God's Design Science Curriculum Set (Answers in Genesis)
- Bring your family to the Creation Museum.
- Answers in Genesis website: answersingenesis.org
- Genesis: Key to Reclaiming the Culture DVD, Ken Ham
- *The New Answers Book*, Vol. 1 and 2, Ken Ham, general editor (Green Forest, AR: Master Books)
- *The Lie: Evolution,* Ken Ham (Green Forest, AR: Master Books, 1987)
- Master Books website: masterbooks.net

Appendix 5 — Resources for Christian Educators

- Genesis: Key to Reclaiming the Culture DVD, Ken Ham (Answers in Genesis)
- History Revealed Curriculum (Answers in Genesis)
- *Noah's Ark, Thinking Outside the Box,* Tim Lovett (Green Forest, AR: Master Books, 2008)
- *Taking Back Astronomy,* Jason Lisle (Green Forest, AR: Master Books, 2006)
- *Answers* Magazine: answersingenesis.org/articles/am
- God's Design Science Curriculum Set (Answers in Genesis)
- Answers in Genesis website: answersingenesis.org (For the technical minded, see the Answers In-Depth section, Answers Research Journal at answersingenesis.org/arj, and the many technical books available through the website.)
- Demolishing Strongholds Curriculum Set (Answers in Genesis)
- *New Answers Book,* Vol. 1 and 2, Ken Ham, general editor (Green Forest, AR: Master Books, 2007 & 2008)
- *Adam's Wall Chart of World History* (Green Forest, AR: Master Books, 2007)
- *Annals of the World,* James Ussher (Green Forest, AR: Master Books, 2003)
- *Chronology of the Old Testament,* Floyd Jones (Green Forest, AR: Master Books, 2005)
- *Evolution Exposed,* Vol. 1 and 2 (essential for high school students and extremely helpful for educators), Roger Patterson (Answers in Genesis, 2007)
- *Old Earth Creationism on Trial,* Jason Lisle and Tim Chaffey (Green Forest, AR: Master Books, 2008)
- Master Books website: masterbooks.net

Appendix 6 — Resources for Youth Pastors

- *The Long War Against God*, by Henry M. Morris (Green Forest, AR: Master Books, 2000)
- Demolishing Strongholds DVD Curriculum (Answers in Genesis)
- *The Great Dinosaur Mystery Solved*, Ken Ham (Green Forest, AR: Master Books, 1998)
- The Bible Explains Dinosaurs DVD, Ken Ham (Answers in Genesis)
- Best Evidence DVD (Answers in Genesis)
- Bring youth groups to the Creation Museum.
- God of Suffering DVD, Tommy Mitchell (Answers in Genesis)
- Only One Race DVD, Ken Ham (Answers in Genesis)
- *Answers Books for Kids* series (for younger kids) (Green Forest, AR: Master Books, 2008)
- It All Begins with Genesis Curriculum (Jr high and up) (Answers in Genesis)
- Answers for Kids website: answersingenesis.org/kids
- Genesis: Key to Reclaiming the Culture DVD, Ken Ham (Answers in Genesis)
- *New Answers Book*, Vol. 1 and 2, Ken Ham, general editor (great for teens and up)(Green Forest, AR: Master Books, 2007 & 2008)
- *Adam's Wall Chart of World History* (Green Forest, AR: Master Books, 2007)
- *Creation: Facts of Life*, Gary Parker (great for teens and up) (Green Forest, AR: Master Books, 1980)
- *Evolution Exposed, Vol. 1 and 2* (essential for high school students) (Answers in Genesis)
- Created Cosmos DVD (Junior level and up) (Answers in Genesis)

Appendix 7 — Resources for Pastors

- *New Answers Book* Vol. 1 and 2, Ken Ham, general editor (Green Forest, AR: Master Books)

- *Coming to Grips with Genesis*, Terry Mortenson, Ph.D., Thane H. Ury, Ph.D, editors (Green Forest, AR: Master Books, 2008)

- *The Genesis Record*, Dr. Henry Morris (commentary on Genesis) (Grand Rapids, MI: Baker Book House, 1976)

- *Creation and Change*, Doug Kelly (Scotland, UK: Christian Focus Publications, 2003)

- *Old Earth Creationism on Trial*, Jason Lisle and Tim Chaffey (Green Forest, AR: Master Books, 2008)

- *Why Won't They Listen?* Ken Ham (Green Forest, AR: Master Books, 2002)

- Genesis: Key to Reclaiming the Culture DVD, Ken Ham

- Why Won't They Listen? DVD, Ken Ham (Answers in Genesis)

- Creation Mini-series, Ken Ham (DVD set includes Why Won't They Listen? and Genesis: Key to Reclaiming the Culture) (Answers in Genesis)

- *The Annals of the World*, James Ussher — for reference (Green Forest, AR: Master Books, 2003)

- *The Complete Works of Flavius Josephus* — for reference (Green Forest, AR: Master Books, 2008)

- *The Ultimate Proof of Creation* Jason Lisle (Green Forest, AR: Master Books, 2009)

- Organize a church trip to the Creation Museum.

- Answers Vacation Bible School sets (available on the Answers in Genesis website)

- Answers in Genesis website: answersingenesis.org

Ken Ham

The president/CEO and founder of Answers in Genesis-U.S. and the highly acclaimed Creation Museum, Ken Ham is one of the most in-demand Christian speakers in North America. Ham, a native Australian now residing near Cincinnati, Ohio, is the author of numerous books on the Book of Genesis, the accuracy and authority of the Bible, dinosaurs, and the destructive fruits of evolutionary thinking (including his co-authored book on the "races" and racism, *Darwin's Plantation*, and the bestseller, *The Lie: Evolution*). He appears frequently on American TV (in one year alone: Fox's The O'Reilly Factor and Fox and Friends in the Morning, CNN's The Situation Room with Wolf Blitzer, ABC's Good Morning America, the BBC radio/TV, and others).

Ken hosts the daily radio program "Answers . . . with Ken Ham," heard on more than 800 stations in America (and dozens more overseas) and is one of the editors and contributing authors for AIG's *Answers* magazine (a biblical worldview publication with over 70,000 worldwide subscribers). The new high-tech Creation Museum near the Cincinnati Airport — which attracted over 700,000 visitors (and several of the world's major media) in its first two and a half years of operation — was Ken's brainchild.

C. Britt Beemer

Britt Beemer holds a BA from Northwest Missouri State University and has an MA from Indiana State University. He worked for Congressman Bill Scherle (R-IA) from 1966–1974. After his work with Congressman Scherle, he was a senior research analyst for the Heritage Foundation. He then began to manage and conduct 14 senatorial campaigns, which included exacting research and demanding strategic planning.

In 1979, Beemer founded America's Research Group, a full-service consumer behavior research and strategic marketing firm. Recognized nationally as a premier marketing strategist, he has gained wide acclaim for his work on how, when, and why consumers select their products and services. His client list represents America's top retailers, leading brands, and smaller entrepreneurial companies. His knowledge of consumer preferences increases monthly as ARG conducts thousands of new interviews.

His work has been cited in the media, including the *Wall Street Journal*, the *New York Times, Investor's Business Daily, CNN, Fox News, Fox Business News*, and many others.

He is the author of *Predatory Marketing*, a book on strategic marketing. His second book, *It Takes a Prophet to Make a Profit*, is about emerging trends of the millennium. *The Customer Rules*, released in 2008, details how customer-focused businesses win.

Britt Beemer's expertise covers each phase of survey research, including questionnaire design, sample construction, and data analysis, but especially interpretation. He serves as the senior director of research at America's Research Group, where he personally reviews all research and prepares and presents each strategic marketing plan.

Todd Hillard

Todd Hillard is a freelance writer from San Antonio, Texas, where he lives with his wife and five kids. A former youth pastor and missionary, he is passionate about taking the dreams and stories of others and bringing them to life on the written page.

Todd was born and raised in the Black Hills of South Dakota. He received his BS in pre-med studies and psychology from the University of Utah and his MA in English from Arizona State University. He and his family lived in Turkey for two and a half years. He has 17 years of pastoral experience and has written more than 12 books.

IT'S TIME!

Return to the Church's Fundamental Mission & Bring Back the Lost Generation!

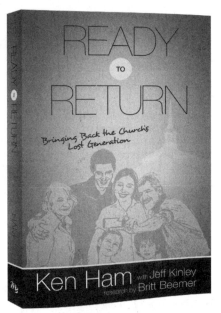

$13.99 | 978-0-89051-836-6

A large percentage of people have traded their beliefs for a more modern, secular worldview of compromise and "anything goes." Scripture fits together seamlessly without flaw, and what we are facing today is a generation that cannot link theological "cause and effect" together. In fact, they approach God's Word as if it were a dinner buffet where they can pick and choose what they do or do not want to follow in Scripture according to what is accepted or rejected by society. *Ready to Return* explores:

- Why this is happening, and more importantly, what can be done to bring back a godly generation

- New persuasive research that clearly reveals shocking details about views on the Church and faith by people in their 20s known as millennials

- Conclusive evidence we cannot ignore, showing lack of effective biblical apologetics in homes and churches, compromise with secular beliefs, secular education, and failures on the part of previous generations contributing greatly to this dilemma.

This book is a powerful call for the Church to renew its approach in reaching out to this generation. We need to become spiritual soldiers with a solid biblical battle plan, a proven strategy, and a willingness to present the truth. Much is at stake and the time is now! Are you ready to join the fight and help lost souls return to God?